University of Michigan Publications

LANGUAGE AND LITERATURE

VOLUME XXIV

THE LANGUAGE OF NATURAL DESCRIPTION
IN EIGHTEENTH–CENTURY POETRY

THE LANGUAGE OF NATURAL DESCRIPTION IN EIGHTEENTH-CENTURY POETRY

JOHN ARTHOS

ANN ARBOR · THE UNIVERSITY OF MICHIGAN PRESS
LONDON · GEOFFREY CUMBERLEGE, OXFORD UNIVERSITY PRESS
1949

PRINTED IN THE UNITED STATES OF AMERICA
BY THE CAYUGA PRESS · ITHACA · NEW YORK

To

<small>PROFESSOR</small> H. T. <small>PRICE</small>

> il mio veder s'avviva
> sì nel tuo lume, ch'io discerno chiaro
> quanto la tua ragion porti o descriva.

Preface

THE present study has been written in order to help establish a better understanding of the "stock diction" of eighteenth-century English poetry, and, in particular, of the diction commonly used in the description of nature. The language characteristic of so much of the poetry of this period has been severely criticized for a long time. But in the last twenty or thirty years some effort has been made to review the subject and the problem. Among the most notable studies are those by Myra Reynolds, Thomas Quayle, F. W. Bateson, and Geoffrey Tillotson. But several questions still remain to be answered, and more exhaustive analysis needs to be undertaken. This volume is an effort to provide answers for some of these questions and to begin the analysis that is required.

I think that earlier criticism generally neglected to assess the relationship of the language of eighteenth-century poetry to that of earlier periods, in English and in other literatures. And I think that most critics have overlooked the fact that much of the stock vocabulary of verse was widely used in the writings of naturalists and that it was part and parcel of old and now half-forgotten philosophies of nature. In the present study there is an effort to take account of such considerations for whatever they may signify in helping to answer certain questions: what does this poetic language consist of? what are its most characteristic terms and forms? what was it used most frequently to describe and name? and why did a century of poets value a stabilized diction as such?

The answers supplied here are not complete, but certain conclusions are reached, obvious enough in themselves, perhaps, though with a special emphasis: A large number of poets formed and exploited a stable language because they believed that the design of the world was stable. They knew something of the workings of the universe, the harmonious balance of its elements, the composition of the stars, and the principles of vegetation, and

their increasing knowledge pleased them for the proof it gave
of a well-ordered world.   The sure constancy of things was the
charm of nature; it was part of the pleasure of poetry to re-create
that charm.   For such a purpose the poets had come into a fortunate inheritance.   They had only to select an accurate, graceful vocabulary from the common store of poetry and philosophy,
one that was justified by the honor of its descent from the Augustans and by its truthfulness in the description of nature.   And
the store at their disposal had still another charm.   Many of its
terms belonged to philosophies of nature that were now being
constantly "reformed and improved," so that the old terms were
the fresher for their use by Boyle and Newton.

These, briefly, are the answers this study tries to justify.   To
support such conclusions it has been necessary to devise a book
something like a lexicon, and it may be useful here to describe
the plan of the work.   The argument of the study is contained
in the introductory chapters.   In the beginning chapter the
problem is defined by presenting a formal classification of the
elements of the stock diction of eighteenth-century English
poetry, which is immediately tested by an examination of the
language of Dryden's verse.   In the succeeding chapters the
study endeavors to establish the relationship of these formal
elements in their employment in the description of nature to the
language of earlier poetry and scientific literature.   There then
follow three appendixes that assemble the material evidence
upon which the argument depends.

In the first appendix there is presented an alphabetical list of
terms and phrases which are used over and over again in neoclassic poetry and which generally deserve to be considered
among its staple articles.   Under each term are first given verse
citations which illustrate the use of the term or which present
concepts pertinent to its use in earlier poetry.   These citations
are arranged chronologically and are meant to indicate the
variety and continuity of the use.   In general I have thought
it necessary to quote only a few examples from the poets of antiquity and the early Christian period, and it did not seem necessary to provide more than token evidence from the literature of
the Continent in the sixteenth and seventeenth centuries (but
for reasons discussed in the text I have been careful to cite Du

Bartas more fully). In illustrating the use of these terms in English poetry, however, I have attempted to supply enough examples of the occurrence of each term in the seventeenth century to establish clearly the wide employment of this vocabulary before the period which bears the chief notoriety for its development. But from the eighteenth century itself I have ordinarily drawn only one or two examples, knowing that the reader of the poetry of that period may supply innumerable instances for himself.

Immediately following the examples of the poetic use of these words comes a list of passages demonstrating the use of the same terms in scientific writing. These, also, are given in chronological order, and again I have thought it necessary to quote only a few passages from the literature of antiquity and of the sixteenth century. I have attempted, however, to illustrate the use of the seventeenth century by decades, quoting most fully from English writings, but for obvious reasons quoting liberally, also, from Latin works of the period. Here and there I have taken passages from the scientific literature of France and Italy in order to keep before the reader's mind the scope of the development of a common language for science and poetry. (I ought to explain that I have considered "scientific literature" to be any serious prose writing about the natural universe. I have not confined the citations to those writers who are important in the history of science, but have drawn almost equally on some other kinds of writers—alchemists, almanac makers, Rosicrucians, deist theologians—all of whom in their own ways were as much concerned as Hooke or Boyle with problems of language.)

Through the juxtaposition of the prose and poetic uses of these terms the evidence is arranged to bring out whatever relationship there may be between the uses of various terms in prose and poetry. Generally this relationship is self-evident, but when it has appeared that special comment would be helpful a brief note, or essay, has been supplied. Moreover, the significance of the use of several terms is made more apparent by the knowledge of the use of cognate terms, and cross reference is provided to such terms.

The second appendix is a collection of two-word periphrases assembled in an alphabetical order according to the words or concepts they represent. Under each term the citations are arranged by author in a roughly chronological order. Here I have also employed principles of selection that my reading seems to justify. I have quoted more fully from Lucretius and Virgil, for example, than from Lucan, because their influence was more important. I have cited Du Bartas very fully, though not exhaustively, in order to certify the scope of his practice. The citations from English poets are also not exhaustive, since this is not primarily a study of individual poets: in general, however, the number of citations offers a means of estimating the frequency of this form in the various poets.

The third appendix illustrates the use of adjectives formed with the suffix -y in English scientific writings chiefly prior to the eighteenth century, but with a few examples from that period itself. It seemed to me that a list of the poetic uses of this form was not necessary, since the reader may easily supply his own illustrations by opening almost any volume of eighteenth-century poetry. Nor did the list of prose uses need to be very long. It was necessary only to establish the variety of the scientific use of this form, and to indicate the theories and problems that led to its use.

These appendixes follow each other logically, not merely in support of the text but in relation to each other. The list of significant words raises questions concerned with the problem of making phrases, phrases in which many of these terms were used and used according to a scheme of definition which involved periphrasis. The use of periphrases, ordinarily composed of a generic noun and a qualifying adjective, raises questions concerned with the formation of appropriate adjectives as well as with the meaning of the noun. It was apparently necessary to develop a form amenable to the structure of the English language, adaptable on the one hand to the metrical requirements of verse and on the other to the requirements of scientific description. The appendix illustrating the use of adjectives formed with the -y suffix in scientific prose accordingly follows the appendix on periphrases, and in this appendix there is included a discussion of some of the linguistic problems involved in adapting this form to the needs of science.

There are several other elements that seem to me to be characteristic of the diction of eighteenth-century poetry. Though these are mentioned in the first chapter I do not believe that a fuller discussion of them is required in order to support the argument of the present work.   In view of the limitation of this study to the language of natural description, it should be remarked that the study could be extended to include other subjects and the diction used in their expression.   In order to indicate some of these subjects, the appendixes include a few illustrations not immediately relevant to the language of natural description.

Finally, the evidence assembled in the appendixes is bulky, but it has been selected according to whatever principles of economy I could manage.   It was necessary, I think, on the one hand, to supply enough evidence to support the general thesis of the study, and, on the other, to provide the kind of evidence, in sufficient quantity, necessary to justify and clarify the status of individual terms in their relationship to the general thesis.   I have omitted many relevant matters from consideration because I thought them dispensable and because it seemed proper to make this only one volume.   Economy has so far prevailed, in fact, that the Bibliography includes only a few items not cited in the text.   There are many other books that have been helpful in making this study, chiefly, perhaps, dictionaries, and of these chiefly the *New English Dictionary;* to all of them I must acknowledge my great debt obscurely.   And despite the bulk of the work I understand rather well that there are omissions due to ignorance.

*

*   *

A work like the present one, which wanders in so many fields of knowledge, could only have been made with the willing help of many people.   It was begun as a dissertation at Harvard under Professor Chester Noyes Greenough, and in that form was chiefly confined to a study of the language of Du Bartas, Sylvester, and Milton.   Professor Greenough suggested the subject of the study and guided me in a way I must always deeply appreciate; the present work owes immeasurably to his interest and example.

Studying abroad on a Sheldon Travelling Fellowship from Harvard, I was especially helped by Professor Mario Casella, of the University of Florence, and Mr. W. H. Robinson, the Libra-

rian of the Royal Society.   And I must merely list the names of
several who have helped me in many ways—Professor Campbell
Bonner, Professor L. I. Bredvold, Professor Morris Greenhut,
Professor N. E. Nelson, Professor H. T. Price, and Professor W.
G. Rice, of the University of Michigan; and at other times and
places, Professor G. N. Clarke, Professor C.-A. Fusil, Mr. W. G.
Hiscock, Miss Mary Marks, Professor Daniel Mornet, Professor
C. T. Onions, Mr. C. H. Parker, Professor H. E. Rollins, Dr.
George Sarton, Sir Charles Sherrington, and Mrs. K. M.
Wygant.

I am greatly indebted to the staffs of many libraries—of the
Harvard College Library, the library of the University of North
Carolina, the library of Northwestern University, the British
Museum, the Library of the Royal Society, the Bodleian, the
Bibliothèque Nationale, the Biblioteca Nazionale in Florence,
the library of the Vatican, and the library of the University of
Michigan.

Finally, I owe many thanks to Miss Grace E. Potter, who has
been thoughtful, patient, and most extraordinarily helpful in
preparing the manuscript for the press.

J. A.

Table of Contents

CHAPTER   PAGE

       PREFACE vii

       NOTE ON THE CITATIONS xiv

  I.   THE ELEMENTS OF STOCK DICTION I

  II.   THE APPLICATION OF NATURAL HISTORY TO POETRY   8

 III.   THE FORMATION OF A SCIENTIFIC LANGUAGE FOR NATURAL DESCRIPTION 30

 IV.   STABILITY AND CHANGE IN THE LANGUAGE OF NATURAL PHILOSOPHY 49

  V.   THE INTERCHANGE OF SCIENTIFIC LANGUAGE AND POETIC DICTION 67

       APPENDIXES

         Appendix A. Certain Words Significant in Eighteenth-Century Poetry, with Illustrations from Earlier Poetry and Scientific Literature 89

         Appendix B. Periphrases 356

         Appendix C. Epithets with the Suffix -y in English Scientific Literature 393

       BIBLIOGRAPHY 405

       INDEX 447

NOTE ON THE CITATIONS

BECAUSE of the number and varying nature of the citations in the present study, particularly in the appendixes, it has been necessary to set up a more or less arbitrary system of notations both for the titles of works and for their parts.

In the text itself titles are cited in the usual fashion, being given in full on their first occurrence in each chapter, and thereafter in such shorter form as was practicable. In the appendixes, however, the sources of the quotations are cited in the briefest significant form in relation to the Bibliography.

It seemed proper, in a study of language, to cite translations by the translator, and therefore the translated work is usually signified by the name of the original author in italics (Ex.: Pinnell *Croll*). Certain works whose titles are generally understood by mere reference to the author are cited by author and book and line number only (Ex.: Manilius IV. 81). The abbreviations used for the titles of individual poems should explain themselves without much difficulty. It was necessary to refer to Sylvester's poems in several editions, and though it was not too awkward to indicate the titles of the poems and the date of the edition in various places, in the appendix on periphrases the date of the edition itself seemed the most manageable reference (Ex.: *1605* 233). Dryden's poems are quoted from the Noyes edition, unless otherwise stated, and Pope's poems are quoted from Boynton's edition except as noted in the Bibliography.

Poems quoted from modern texts are cited by line number when that is possible (Ex.: Pope *Spring* 103); if the poem is divided into books, cantos, and stanzas, these divisions are indicated (Ex.: Spenser *F. Q.* III. xi. 3). There are certain exceptions to this practice, however. The works of Carew, Cowley, Drummond, Du Bellay, Góngora, Herbert of Cherbury, Herrick, Jodelle, Mure, Norris, Ronsard, Scarron, Scève, Traherne, and Vaughan are cited merely by volume (when there is more than one volume) and page number (Ex.: Ronsard IV. 363). The reasons for this procedure vary. Drummond and Ronsard are so treated because it would be tedious for the reader to run down a table of contents listing several hundred poems. As for Cowley, Waller's edition gives no line numbers, and while some of the poems might have been cited by stanza number, others could not; here it seemed simplest merely to put the page number after the author's name (Ex.: Cowley 236). The notations *Works*, *Carmina*, and the like, appear for various authors only when it is necessary to distinguish among several titles in the Bibliography.

Poems in early editions are cited by page numbers, except in those rather infrequent instances when it was practicable to give stanza or line numbers.

The long poems quoted from Saintsbury's *Minor Poets of the Caroline Period* are referred to by abbreviated title and book and line number. But the briefer poems are referred to by author, with the volume and page number following the notation *CP* (Ex.: Ayres, in *CP* II. 309).

The prose works are cited by volume and page number (Ex.: Boyle *Useful. Nat. Phil.* I. 97). It has been necessary, however, to cite signatures for some volumes, and to refer to certain lexicons by the pertinent headings.

CHAPTER I

The Elements of Stock Diction

ENGLISH poetry of the eighteenth century has long been criticized for its stereotyped language. The poets of that period seem to have been constantly misled by false notions of propriety and elegance, and particularly when they were describing nature. In some way, it appears, they came to agree upon a pretty well defined store of terms and figures as not merely the proper but the indispensable instrument of poetic expression. Succeeding poets took up this vocabulary decade after decade, and to modern readers it does not seem that they were aware of burdening themselves with a hackneyed language. Finally, however, Wordsworth and Coleridge with their new theories of diction undermined the idea that poetry had a special language reserved for it, and in time the diction they rebelled against fell into disuse. But neither the Romantic critics nor modern scholars have fully explained the prevalence and vitality of the diction they discarded. The large questions still remain—what did this stock language consist of, and why was it valued?

The present study is an attempt to answer these questions more fully than has been done before, at least with respect to that part of the language devoted to the description of nature. The primary assumption of the study is that eighteenth-century poets used their stock diction in good faith, fully convinced of its value. Their chief fault, I think, was in their failure to subordinate this conventional language to the purpose of the individual poem—which is perhaps to say that too often they misconceived the purpose of poetry. They must have been led to do this by mistaking the value of a stable vocabulary and a set style of phrase formation. And in order to understand their preoccupation with a stock language, the study of this poetry might begin with an analysis of certain terms which seem to

I

be a fixed part of their vocabulary and certain rhetorical and
grammatical forms.

*

*   *

Most of the English poetry written from Dryden's time to
the time of the Romantics is called neoclassic. Sometimes it is
known merely as eighteenth-century poetry, and the phrase is
useful, since a certain style and diction seem to have been characteristic of the whole period. Mr. Thomas Quayle has done
most to distinguish the chief features of the language of this
poetry, and he has determined that the important categories
are: a vocabulary and a style of phrase formation which together he calls "stock diction"; compound epithets; Latinisms;
personifications of abstract ideas; archaisms; and technical
terms.[1] These categories are reasonably comprehensive, and
their value may be tested by applying them to a considerable
body of verse, preferably by one author. Dryden's work provides sufficient material for such an examination, and as a
founder of the neoclassic school his language has a special
interest.

"Stock diction," in Quayle's sense, means, first, those words
and phrases which have a stereotyped character. These may
be words which are used over and over again; or they may be
words which, though infrequently used, share somehow a quality
that belongs to hackneyed words. This quality seems partly
dependent on irrelevance of meaning. For example, when the
phrase *shining sword* was first used, there was probably some com-
pelling reason for the epithet. But the phrase belongs to stock
diction, not merely because it is frequently used, but because it
is sometimes employed in a sentence where the epithet is either
of no value to the sense of the context or is contrary to the interest of it. These latter considerations seem to be applicable
to Dryden's lines:

> He rais'd his arm aloft, and, at the word,
> Deep in his bosom drove the shining sword.[2]

A second characteristic of stock diction is the use of adjec-

---

[1] *Poetic Diction, A Study of Eighteenth Century Verse* (London: Methuen, 1924).
[2] *Aeneid* XII. 1374–5, in *The Poetical Works of John Dryden*, ed. George R. Noyes
(Boston, 1909).

tives formed by adding the suffix -*y* to nouns.   Dryden, for example, used such words as *beamy*,[3] *bloomy*,[4] *moony*,[5] *roofy*,[6] *sluicy*,[7] and *snary*.[8]   This is evidently a conventional method of forming epithets, and *snary*, though it occurs only once, belongs to stock diction by virtue of the method of its formation.

Similarly, the use of the present participle as an epithet, although more limited than the use of adjectives with the -*y* ending, is a stock practice.   A peculiarity of the eighteenth-century use is that the active force of the participle is frequently irrelevant, and modern readers need to keep in mind a distinction between that and the common modern use.   For example, the phrase *rising ground* was a regular expression in the eighteenth century, in the most informal and unpolished writing and presumably in conversation.   Modern speakers, in America at least, are more comfortable saying, *a rise in the ground*, possibly because they feel that the present participle indicates an activity not perceived in a hill.   Many times, too, the present participle implies a degree of personification, as in the phrase *pleasing grove*,[9] and the modern speaker or writer would prefer to say *pleasant grove*.   The eighteenth-century use may be defined to be one where the participle indicates the nature of a thing rather than any phase of its activity.   It is the nature of a grove to please, but it is not making an effort to.   At any rate, the present participle is often used in this manner in verse, so much so that it may be said to be characteristic of the diction of eighteenth-century poetry.

A third element of stock diction is the periphrasis.   Some particular characteristic of a thing is referred to by an adjective, and the adjective modifies a general term to form a phrase whereby a substitute is supplied for the name of the thing. Dryden has many periphrases of this sort: *bearded product* (corn),[10] *loquacious race* (frogs),[11] *scaly flocks* (fish),[12] and *leafy nation* (leaves)[13] are typical examples.

A fourth characteristic of what Quayle calls stock diction is the use of certain favorite words.   For example, Dryden and

[3]*Aen.* VIII. 825.
[4]*Ibid.* IX. 276.
[5]*Ovid's Iphis and Ianthe* 33.
[6]*Georgics* III. 634.
[7]*Ibid.* I. 437.
[8]*Ibid.* IV. 361.
[9]*Ovid's Helen to Paris* 87.
[10]*Geo.* I. 113.
[11]*Ibid.* I. 521.
[12]*Ibid.* IV. 568.
[13]*Aen.* X. 571.

many another poet relied constantly on such words as *care* (*museful care*),[14] *genial* (*genial bed*),[15] *kind* (*leaky kind*),[16] and *store* (*fleecy store*).[17] But these words, too, are "stock" not merely through frequent use, but by the manner of their use, and are in fact most clearly part of a stock diction when they can be referred to certain habits of phrase formation. Nevertheless, their repeated occurrence is an important factor in the very concept of stock diction.

Quayle's second category in his analysis of the elements of the language of eighteenth-century verse includes the various methods of forming compound epithets. He has determined that there are seven main types: noun plus noun; noun plus adjective; noun plus present participle; noun plus past participle; adjective, or adjective used adverbially, plus another part of speech, usually a participle; true adverb plus a participle; and adjective plus a noun plus -*ed*.[18]

One or two from each of the types most used by Dryden may be given here by way of illustration: *Pension-Purse*,[19] *Comet-Eyes*,[20] *Nut-brown*,[21] *Tongue-valiant*,[22] *Sleep-compelling*,[23] *Sin-polluted*,[24] *hoarse-resounding*,[25] *slimy-born*,[26] *well mouth'd*,[27] *Sick-feathered*.[28]

There are, of course, other combinations of the parts of speech, but these just illustrated are in Quayle's judgment the most common forms to be found in the eighteenth century. The significance of their use as part of a stock diction is hardly to be comprehended in a single generalization, but that they form a characteristic part of this diction is evident.

---

[14]*Aen.* III. 572.   [16]*Lucretius* IV. 20.
[15]*Juvenal* VI. 76.   [17]*Geo.* III. 837.
[18]*Poetic Diction* 102. Another scheme of classifying compound epithets in English is used in Bernard Groom's study, *The Formation and Use of Compound Epithets in English Poetry from 1579* (S. P. E. Tract No. XLIX) (Oxford: Clarendon Press, 1937). Here the various formations are given names: "objective" (typified by *spirit-stirring*), "instrumental" (*foam-girt*), and so on. Categories of this sort are especially useful in literary criticism.
[19]*Absalom and Achitophel*. II. 321. Compound epithets are quoted from *The Poems of John Dryden*, ed. John Sargeaunt (London: Oxford University Press, 1929), because this edition preserves the hyphenation of the original printings.
[20]*Juvenal* X. 514.   [24]*Iliad* I. 437.
[21]*Ovid's Acis* 131.   [25]*Ibid.* I. 54.
[22]*Iliad* I. 336.   [26]*The Hind and the Panther* I. 311.
[23]*Palamon and Arcite* I. 550.   [27]*Horace's Second Epode* 49.
          [28]*Hind and Panther* III. 614.

Quayle's next category includes the various kinds of Latinisms.[29] Two types are particularly frequent in Dryden: words taken bodily from Latin and given an English spelling or form; and words already in good standing in English, but occurring in a construction that is Latin or in a sense that properly belongs to the Latin original rather than to the naturalized English use. Of the first class are *irremeable*,[30] *obtend*,[31] *diffide*,[32] *præscious*,[33] and *stridor*.[34] The second class includes most of Dryden's Latinisms, which may be illustrated by such usages as these: *with steel invades his brother's life*,[35] *in a round error*,[36] *inspire a pleasing gale*,[37] *horrid with fern*,[38] *his sinister hand*,[39] *the morning dew prevents the sun*.[40] In this class are also Latinisms of sentence or phrase order: *And open let thy stacks all winter stand*[41] and *white offer'd milk*.[42]

Most of Dryden's Latinisms occur in his translations, and it is clear that this is due to the very nature of the work. But a few of his terms—*inspire, invade*, and *horrid*—are also used by many other poets in original work, and as Latinisms are among the common ones.

The personification of abstract ideas and of material things is a notorious characteristic of neoclassic poetry. In Dryden the personification is chiefly accomplished by reference to pagan gods. Love is Cupid or Venus. Hardly more original are the references to nature and fortune as personalized forces—for example, such a one as "Nature is ever various in her frame."[43] Dryden, in fact, found it exceedingly difficult to keep an abstraction abstract, and his tendency to personify at the least opportunity may be observed in a description where a personal pronoun finally gives away his habitual interest:

> The pow'r that ministers to God's decrees,
> And executes on earth what Heav'n foresees,
> Call'd Providence, or Chance, or Fatal Sway,
> Comes with resistless force, and finds or makes her way.[44]

---

[29]His treatment of these is severely censured in the unsigned review in the London *Times Literary Supplement*, Dec. 25, 1924. My own very brief discussion of this form in Dryden, accordingly, is meant to avoid some of the difficulties of Quayle's analysis, although much of the review seems to me unfair.

[30]*Aen.* VI. 575.   [35]*Ibid.* I. 481.   [40]*Geo.* I. 384.
[31]*Ibid.* X. 126.   [36]*Ibid.* V. 772.   [41]*Ibid.* III. 499.
[32]*Ibid.* XI. 636.   [37]*Ibid.* V. 1098.   [42]*Aen.* IV. 660.
[33]*Ibid.* XI. 242.   [38]*Ibid.* IX. 519.   [43]*Persius* V. 67.
[34]*Ibid.* XII. 1258.   [39]*Mac Flecknoe* 120.   [44]*Pal. and Arc.* II. 210–13.

Comparatively rare is the intense and significant personification:

> Horror in all his pomp was there,
> Mute and magnificent without a tear.[45]

For personifications of material things the following may serve as examples: *tears, the dumb petitioners of grief,*[46] *th'innumerable crowd of armed prayers,*[47] *weighty Water, as her nature guides.*[48]

Archaisms are more frequently used by the imitators of Spenser than by Dryden, but even he to some extent justifies Quayle's inclusion of this element of style as one of the characteristics of eighteenth-century diction. Forced by the meter, Dryden makes a possibly archaic use of the prefix *be-*: *bewail'd,*[49] *benumbs,*[50] *bemoans.*[51] But he also uses such words as *hatter'd,*[52] *rathe,*[53] *bedight,*[54] and *whilom.*[55] Ordinarily his archaisms are satiric; the picturesque ones are more frequently found in such a poet as Thomson.[56]

Dryden made somewhat fuller use of technical terms from various fields, such as: *calking-iron,*[57] *linstocks,*[58] *geniture,*[59] *quartil,*[60] *cerrial,*[61] *snaffle.*[62] In general, he was of the opinion that terms of art were not properly directed to "men and ladies of the first quality," and thought their use more often than not a sign of affectation in a poet.[63]

*

*   *

These, then, are the important language forms which are characteristic of eighteenth-century poetry. Such a classification is valuable since this stereotyped language is distinguished not merely by certain words constantly repeated, but by certain methods of word and phrase formation as well. The enumeration and analysis of the forms, however, provides only the means

---

[45]*Threnodia Augustalis* 51–2.
[46]*Theocritus* XXIII. 28.
[47]*Thren. Aug.* 97–8.
[48]*Ovid's Pythagorean Philosophy* 372.
[49]*Aen.* VI. 318.
[50]*Ibid.* IX. 632.
[51]*Ovid's Ajax and Ulysses* 66.
[52]*Hind and Panther* 371.
[53]*Geo.* II. 134.
[54]*Juvenal* VI. 188.
[55]*Mac Flecknoe* 35.
[56]In *A Discourse Concerning the Original and Progress of Satire* Dryden expressed his view of the value of archaisms (*Essays*, ed. W. P. Ker [Oxford: Clarendon Press, 1926], II. 29).
[57]*Annus Mirabilis* 583.
[58]*Ibid.* 750.
[59]*To Sir Robert Howard* 104.
[60]*Pal. and Arc.* I. 500.
[61]*The Flower and the Leaf* 230.
[62]*Geo.* III. 296.
[63]See the "Dedication of the *Æneis*," in *Essays* II. 236.

of beginning a study of poetic diction. For it becomes immediately necessary to know the meaning of the words that are constantly repeated and the subjects that are treated in the various word and phrase forms. It is important to observe that periphrases are widely used in this period, but it is quite as important to know what they were used to describe and name. For the subject of poetry controls diction quite as much as do the grammatical and rhetorical forms that are available.

Since it is those passages in poetry concerned with natural description which seem to contain some of the most characteristic features of the stereotyped style, it is proper that a study of this diction continue with a consideration of nature as the subject of this poetry. Certain of the forms marked off by Quayle are perhaps more frequently found in poetry concerned with manners. But it is the adaptability of some of these forms to natural description that many readers particularly question. The frigidity and exaggeration of periphrasis, the cold and stilted use of personification, the squandering of compound epithets, the superabundance of epithets formed with the -y suffix— all these are faults long since observed in the poetry of natural description. It is important that these faults should be understood in order that the criticism of this diction may be properly informed. And one of the most satisfactory ways of undertaking such study is by reading what some earlier critics thought was wrong in all this.

CHAPTER II

The Application of Natural History to Poetry

HERE and there in the eighteenth century itself one finds a criticism of the standardized vocabulary of verse, and before the Romantic critics several sharp and significant observations had been made. There is, I think, a particular value in going back to two or three early critics to see what they thought caused the failure of so much of this poetry. Warton, Aikin, and Trapp were not obliged to justify a new method of poetry, as Wordsworth and Coleridge were, for they were less blinded by new interests, and they might be expected to understand the purposes of their contemporaries better than many later critics. It is possible, in fact, by assembling some of their criticism to comprehend most of the points of discussion that have seemed important to later writers. There appears to be no chronological development in the critical positions taken by these men, and what they had to say may be studied best by arranging their arguments according to the demands of the problem.

*

*   *

Joseph Warton thought Thomson's descriptions of nature much more pleasing than those of almost any other poet. The freshness of Thomson and the staleness of others were due to reasons clearly apparent to him:

Theocritus is indeed the great store-house of pastoral description; and every succeeding painter of rural beauty (except *Thomson* in his Seasons,) hath copied his images from him, without ever looking abroad into the face of nature themselves.[1]

However exaggerated, there are two points in this statement

---

[1]Prefatory Dedication to *The Works of Virgil, in Latin and English*, ed. Christopher Pitt and Joseph Warton (3d ed.; London, 1778), I. ii.

that are worth considering. Warton meant to say, first, that a large part of descriptive poetry contains images that have been handed down through the centuries, coming ultimately from antiquity. His other point is that the best poetical effect depends upon original perception. In this matter Warton took the position that poetic description cannot be interesting unless it is freed from hackneyed phrases and the tarnished associations of outworn mythology.[2] He failed to explain, however, by what principles a poet may form a language to express what he has seen by looking into the face of nature.[3]

John Aikin attacked the problem more directly. He began by quoting the foregoing passage from Warton with approval, saying:

If this be not strictly just, it is at least certain that supineness and servile imitation have prevailed to a greater degree in the description of nature, than in any other part of poetry. The effect of this has been, that descriptive poetry has degenerated into a kind of phraseology, consisting of combinations of words which have been so long coupled together, that, like the hero and his epithet in Homer, they are become inseparable companions. It is amusing, under some of the most common heads of description, in a poetical dictionary, to observe the wonderful sameness of thoughts and expressions in passages culled from a dozen different authors. An ordinary versifier seems no more able to conceive of the Morn without rosy fingers and dewy locks, or Spring without flowers and showers, loves and groves, than of any of the heathen deities without their usual attributes.[4]

---

[2]It is proper to recall here that Wordsworth, by overthrowing "poetic diction," hoped to establish a fit language for direct observation: "There will also be found in these volumes little of what is usually called poetic diction; as much pains has been taken to avoid it as is ordinarily taken to produce it; this has been done for the reason already alleged, to bring my language near to the language of men; and further, because the pleasure which I have proposed to myself to impart, is of a kind very different from that which is supposed by many persons to be the proper object of poetry. Without being culpably particular, I do not know how to give my Reader a more exact notion of the style in which it was my wish and intention to write, than by informing him that I have at all times endeavoured to look steadily at my subject; consequently, there is I hope in these Poems little falsehood of description, and my ideas are expressed in language fitted to their respective importance."—Preface to *Lyrical Ballads*, as printed in *The Poetical Works*, ed. Thomas Hutchinson, revised by Ernest de Selincourt (London: Oxford University Press, 1939), 936.

[3]There is a highly informative discussion of this question with regard to the criticism of Warton, Aikin, and others in Elizabeth L. Mann's "The Problem of Originality in English Literary Criticism, 1750–1800," *Philological Quarterly*, XVIII (1939), 97–118.

[4]*An Essay on the Application of Natural History to Poetry* (Warrington, 1777), 5–6.

Aikin was bored by this language because it was stereotyped, while its inaccuracy offended him.   In his view it was the duty of poets to observe nature closely and to describe it accurately. In this way their work would become interesting and even noble:

Still more narrow and unreasonable is that critical precept, which, in conformity to the received notion that fiction is the soul of poetry, obliges the poet to adopt antient errors in preference to modern truths; and this even where truth has the advantage in point of poetical effect.   In fact, modern philosophy is as much superior to the antient in sublimity as in solidity; and the most vivid imagination cannot paint to itself scenes of grandeur equal to those which cool science and demonstration offer to the enlightened mind.   Objects so vast and magnificent as planets rolling with even pace through their orbits, comets rushing along their devious track, light springing from its unexhausted source, mighty rivers formed in their subterranean beds, do not require, or even admit, a heightening from the fancy.   The most faithful pencil here produces the noblest pictures; and Thomson, by strictly adhering to the character of the *poet of nature*, has treated all these topics with a true sublimity, which a writer of less knowledge and accuracy could never have attained.[5]

Description is interesting and sublime when it is true, and the language which expresses the truth in matters of natural description is the language of natural philosophy—this is the way his argument runs.   The probability is, however, that Aikin meant to emphasize accuracy in matters of fact more than truth in philosophic conception.[6]

It is Aikin's opinion, then, that the stock language of poetry is generally bad because it is monotonous or hackneyed, and inaccurate or untruthful.   Nowadays, I think, "hackneyed" is usually applied to language whose more effective use is already generally known.   The constant repetition of anything is, of course, tedious, and to this extent modern readers will agree with Aikin's reasoning.   But it is not at all clear that inaccuracy should be regarded as the basic fault of this stereotyped phraseology, nor is it evident that this is the factor making words capable of hackneyed use.   The figure of the chariot of Phoebus was once, certainly, delightful.   It became dull through too frequent use, and not merely because people considered the

[5] "An Essay on the Plan and Character of the Poem," prefixed to *The Seasons*, by James Thomson (London, 1778), xv–xvi.

[6] He criticizes Pope, for example, for saying that the rose blossoms along with the crocus and violet, "though, in reality, some months intervene betwixt their flowering."—*Application of Natural History to Poetry* 20.

figure untruthful or inaccurate according to the advances of astronomy. For even now the figure is capable of use which is not hackneyed if it is supplied with a context of thought and imagination sufficient to allow for the development of poetic feeling. The truths of scientific observation are also unpoetic if they are deprived of such a context. *The solar orb* is perhaps a more accurate phrase than *the chariot of Phoebus*, but it is quite as capable of hackneyed use. The mere acceptance of the Copernican astronomy does not insure the freshness and power of a poem on the stars.

Aikin settled too easily the question of the relation of truth to poetry by accepting the claim of natural philosophy to represent truth. Most modern critics agree with him in preferring Thomson as a poet of nature to Pope, but not because Thomson's knowledge of nature was more accurate. They will agree that some of Pope's language is hackneyed, but they will not agree that words and phrases become hackneyed merely because they are inaccurate.

Furthermore, in emphasizing the excessive use of mythology Aikin neglected to take account of the innumerable terms of natural description which did not depend on mythological reference but quite obviously came from a poetical storehouse. Thomson drew from this source as frequently as Pope, but Aikin ignored this. The fact is that he and most of the critics who followed him failed to explain why the eighteenth century valued a stable diction simply because it was stable, a particularly serious omission when they were criticizing that diction for its staleness.

Warton and Aikin seem to me to anticipate much modern criticism of eighteenth-century poetry. These men were discontented with that poetry, and their criticism, in general terms, is what one is still likely to hear. But however acute and perceptive their statements, neither of them offered an adequate explanation of this special diction because they failed to question the concept of a fixed vocabulary for poetry. Coleridge later examined the idea rather carefully,[7] in what seems to me an unsuccessful effort to modify Wordsworth's explicit statement that there is no essential difference between the language of prose

[7]*Biographia Literaria*, ed. J. Shawcross (Oxford, 1907), II. 45–9 especially.

and verse.[8]   But the failure of Romantic criticism to answer all
the questions still raised about this diction is most apparent in
Wordsworth's own poetry, which contains so many of the stereotyped phrases he and Coleridge apparently condemned.[9]

It appears reasonable, therefore, to suppose that Warton,
Aikin, and Wordsworth were talking about different things.
They all complained of stereotyped and gaudy language, yet
Warton and Aikin failed to find that language in Thomson,
though to modern readers it is too obviously present.   And
Wordsworth used language it is part of his creed to disown.
The explanation must be that there are certain forms or groups
of words these critics had in mind, and that there are other ele-
ments of the eighteenth-century poetic vocabulary they approved
of which the modern reader assumes they disapproved.

It is therefore necessary to re-examine this stock diction, to
re-examine the very words of the vocabulary.   If we limit our
study to a certain number of words, we must recognize what the
principles of that limitation are, and not take it for granted that
Wordsworth or Aikin, or whoever, objects to the same things
that we do.   The order of our study must go something like
this: We must take up each stereotyped term individually, establish its claim to be part of the stock diction, and discover its

[8]Preface to *Lyrical Ballads*, in *Poetical Works* 937.   Mr. F. W. Bateson distinguishes various aspects of critical theory in the eighteenth century that I find it difficult to make use of in the present study in view of the fact that many of the stock
terms treated here seem to make up a fixed diction for the whole century.   But I
feel obliged at this point to quote a passage from his book to acquaint the reader
with the nature of his criticism: "The baroque theory of language, the theory of
'poetic diction', was that poetry should possess, in Gray's words, 'a language peculiar to itself'.   The functions of poetry and prose, it was maintained, are different, are even antithetical, and the further their words and word-order diverge the
better each was likely to be.   The Augustan position, on the other hand, was the
opposite of this.   Poetry, the Augustan would admit, is different from prose, it
does not require *all* the words and idioms of prose, but the condition of its health
and intelligibility is that those words that it does use—briefly, anything except
archaisms, vulgarisms, and technical terms—shall derive from that common fund
of language which it shares with prose.   The two theories were therefore mutually
contradictory.   But, as it happens, though the baroque theory was often attacked
by the later Augustans, especially by Johnson and Cowper, it was actually Wordsworth, a poet of quite another school, who finally discredited it."—*English Poetry
and the English Language* (Oxford: Clarendon Press, 1934), 86.

[9]See Marjorie L. Barstow, *Wordsworth's Theory of Poetic Diction* ("Yale Studies
in English," LVII) (New Haven, 1917).   The use of stock diction by Keats, Shelley, and Wordsworth is briefly but interestingly discussed by Ann Winslow, "Re-
evaluation of Pope's Treatment of Nature," *University of Wyoming Publications*, IV
(1938), 21–43.

meaning.   We must test the opinion that this diction as a whole and in its parts is derived from ancient poetry, and we must evaluate carefully the results of that test.   And we must return, finally, to a consideration of all those circumstances which might help to explain why a stable poetic diction should be desirable.

*

*   *

What needs first to be recalled is the extent of the use of many of these stock terms in earlier periods.   It is not desirable to list at this place very many of the passages that are accessible in the appendixes, but it is necessary to give a few examples of phrases and terms used over long periods in order to maintain the continuity of argument.

The phrase *liquid air*, for example, occurs in Empedocles,[10] Virgil,[11] Avitus,[12] Pontano,[13] Du Bellay,[14] Du Bartas,[15] Spenser,[16] Phineas Fletcher,[17] Sandys,[18] Chapelain,[19] Milton,[20] and Dryden.[21] A typical enough use is Blackmore's:

> The fluctuating Fields of liquid Air,
> With all the curious Meteors hov'ring there.[22]

Periphrases for fish are common in eighteenth-century poetry, but that such phrasing was a habit of long standing will be evident from the following list of similar phrases in the works

---

[10]Fr. 38, in *Die Fragmente der Vorsokratiker*, ed. Hermann Diels (2d ed.; Berlin 1906), I. 187.

[11]*Georgics* I. 404.

[12]*De Origine Mundi* (Basel, 1545), 54.

[13]*Urania* I. 247, in *Carmina*, Vol. I, ed. Benedetto Soldati (Florence, 1902).

[14]*Œuvres Poétiques*, ed. Henri Chamard (Paris: Société des Textes Français Modernes, 1908–31), III. 112.

[15]*La Première Sepmaine* II. 238, in *The Works*, ed. Urban T. Holmes, Jr., John C. Lyons, and Robert W. Linker (Chapel Hill: University of North Carolina Press, 1935–40).

[16]*Faerie Queene* V. iii. 25, in *The Poetical Works*, ed. J. C. Smith and E. de Selincourt (London: Oxford University Press, 1926).

[17]*The Purple Island* XI. xxiii, in *Poetical Works of Giles and Phineas Fletcher*, ed. Frederick S. Boas (Cambridge, 1908–9).

[18]*Ovid's Metamorphosis* (London, 1640), 205.

[19]*La Pucelle ou La France Delivree* (Paris, 1656), 187.

[20]*Comus* 979, in *The Student's Milton*, ed. Frank A. Patterson (New York: F. S. Crofts, 1934).

[21]*Aeneid* III. 571, in *The Poetical Works of John Dryden*, ed. George R. Noyes (Boston, 1909).

[22]*Creation* (London, 1712), I. 44–5.

of earlier writers: *squamoso pecu* (Plautus),[23] *squamigerum genus* (Lucretius),[24] *squamigeri gregis* (Ausonius),[25] *grex Squamigerûm* (Pontano),[26] *la troupe escaillée* (Ronsard),[27] *Squamiferos ciues* (Du Monin),[28] *animai squamosi* (Tasso),[29] *skalie Legions* (Sylvester),[30] *skalie Flockes* (Drummond),[31] *Scaly Kind* (Creech),[32] *scaly nations* (Dryden);[33] in the eighteenth century there is Pope's phrase *scaly breed*.[34]

One further epithet may be listed in illustration. Statius' use of *vocalis* is typical:

> Stupet omine tanto
> defixus senior, divina oracula Phoebi
> agnoscens monitusque datos vocalibus antris.[35]

The term was used in English verse in a similar way. Directly preceding the noun, it modified *sounds* (Drayton),[36] *reeds* (Milton),[37] *Muse* (Sherburne),[38] *Air* (Milton),[39] and *grove* (Dryden).[40]

These examples may serve as token evidence of the earlier use of many of the terms which are so often judged to be characteristic of eighteenth-century verse. One of the first observations to be made from an examination of the rather full lists in the appendixes is that the vast majority of the terms which belong to eighteenth-century diction belong also to the diction of

[23]*Rudens* 942.

[24]*De Rerum Natura* I. 162.

[25]*Mosella* 83, in *Poetæ Latini Minores*, Vol. I, ed. N. E. Lemaire (Paris, 1824).

[26]*Meteora* 1498–9, in *Carmina*.

[27]*Œuvres Complètes*, ed. Hugues Vaganay (Paris: Librairie Garnier, 1923–4), III. 79.

[28]*Manipulus Poëticus* (Paris, 1579), 6, appended to *Burgundionis Gyani Beresithias*.

[29]*Il Mondo Creato* III. 478, in *Poemi Minori*, ed. Angelo Solerti (Bologna, 1891).

[30]*Bartas, His Deuine Weekes & Works Translated* ([London, 1605]), 334.

[31]*The Poetical Works*, ed. L. E. Kastner (Manchester, 1913), I. 69.

[32]*The Five Books of M. Manilius, Containing a System of the Ancient Astronomy and Astrology* (London, 1697), (Bk. V, p. 81).

[33]*Georgics* III. 806.

[34]*Windsor Forest* 139, in *The Complete Poetical Works*, ed. Henry W. Boynton (Boston and New York, 1903). All the citations of Pope are from this edition except for poems which occur in Vols. II and IV of the Twickenham edition. For the poems cited from those volumes see the Bibliography.

[35]*Thebaid* I. 490–2.

[36]*Poly-Olbion* XIII. 61, in *The Works of Michael Drayton*, Vol. IV, ed. J. William Hebel (Oxford: Shakespeare Head Press, 1933).

[37]*Lycidas* 86.

[38]*Medea: A Tragedie* (London, 1648), 36.

[39]*Paradise Lost* IX. 530.

[40]*Eclogues* VIII. 31.

Lucretius and Virgil. Phrases like *humid kingdoms* and *painted birds* are almost indubitably to be traced to those writers. Accordingly, the first important fact gained from studying the extensive and ancient use of many elements of stock diction is that most of them are to be found in classic Roman poetry—commonly among the Augustan writers, and rather fully among earlier Roman poets.

The immediate conclusion that these writers provided models for the English Augustans is both obvious and important. It is necessary, however, to insist that their example was offered not merely in the texts of these writers, read for pleasure or studied in school, but indirectly also, through the work of all the poets who came under the influence of Lucretius and Virgil —almost everybody, perhaps, but particularly men like Prudentius, Buchanan, and Spenser.

Furthermore, this tradition was available not merely to poets who read widely, but to those who used handbooks, for these were produced in considerable number, especially after the middle of the seventeenth century. Here there were presented for the use of every schoolboy and every versifier the correct models of elegant composition. And the particular elegance to be striven for was Augustan.[41]

[41]One rather good means of estimating the influence of the Romans on English poetry is by the comparison of Latin and English phrase books. A few citations may serve to illustrate the nature of the ancient models that were offered for use and imitation, and the extent to which those models had already been assimilated in English in the seventeenth century.

Here, for example, are the phrases Johann Buchler gives under *Avis* in his *Flores sive Phrasium Poeticarum Thesaurus Absolutissimus* (Cologne, 1631), 57: "*Volucris. Ales. Omne genus auium . . . . Genus altiuolantum. Turba sonans agminis aliger. . . . greges volatiles.*" And here are phrases from Josua Poole's *The English Parnassus: Or, A Helpe to English Poesie* (London, 1657), 260–1: "The feathered people of the skie; airy people; Winged crew, train, troope; winged songsters."

The famous *Gradus ad Parnassum* has an obscure bibliographical history since in its later forms and under the name of the editor (Paul Aler) to whom it is usually attributed it is obviously a compilation of earlier works. One of its original editions may be from 1654 (Nicolas Chastillon, editor?), but the first (?) edition with Aler's name bears the date 1709. This collection gradually included terms and phrases from modern as well as classical Latin, and accordingly I shall quote from an edition in which the phrases have been winnowed to represent the best Augustan use (*Gradus ad Parnassum*, edited by the late Dr. Carey, revised by a member of the University of Cambridge, London, 1876).

Under *Astra* in this collection (p. 68) are given these phrases: "Æthereæ faces, tædæ. Sidereæ flammæ. Astrorum ignes. Æterni ignes. Signorum flammeus ordo. Ignes ætherei, siderei. Igneus astrorum chorus. Cœlivagæ flammæ." And

Evidence of this sort thus reinforces Warton's remark that the stock diction of his century was derived from ancient poetry, although it does not justify his naming Theocritus as the source of the language of natural description. [42]

A second fact learned from observing the occurrence of many elements of this diction in various periods is that its fullest use is in poems in which the description of nature is chiefly governed by didactic purposes. These are poems like the *De Rerum Natura*, the *Georgics*, and the *Astronomicon*, Avitus' *De Origine Mundi*, Pontano's *Urania*, Buchanan's *Sphaera*, Du Bartas's *Semaines*, Tasso's *Il Mondo Creato*, Fletcher's *Purple Island*, Henry More's *Psychozoia*, Blackmore's *Creation*, and Henry Brooke's *Universal Beauty*.

It will be observed also that this vocabulary is very seldom made use of in the Middle Ages, even in so comprehensive a work as the *Divine Comedy*. It was much employed by various Greek and Latin poets in the first eight centuries of the Christian era, but after that it came into distinct use again only with the Renaissance.

It is also to be noted that before Dryden poets did not make much use of this language in poems of character, like *The Testament of Cressid*, and even Shakespeare and Corneille employed

---

here are some of the phrases Poole (*English Parnassus* 499–500) culled from English poetry: "Heavens sparkling fires; Heavens bright torches; The starry senate of the night; Nights spangled host; The glittering sparkes."

The *Gradus* (p. 398) gives these epithets for sheep: "Imbellis, mollis, placida, lanigera, mansueta, mitis, blanda." Poole (*English Parnassus* 182) gives these: "Harmless, fleecy, silly, wealthy, wandering, straying, rambling, stragling, nibling, browsing, flocking, curled, bleating, grazing, gamesome, sportive, woolly, fruitful, gainful, fleece-bearing, fearful, weak-headed, seduced, rambling, broad-taild."

It should be apparent from such citations that a study of these phrase books would be very valuable. My own purpose in referring to them here, however, is merely to point them out as one of the media through which the influence of the Augustans was maintained.

[42]There are only a few traces in Theocritus of the diction that is much used by Latin poets. What stock terms there are have been imitated by later writers, but at best the direct influence of the Alexandrian poet upon the vocabulary of the English could not have been great. Besides, it is always dangerous to ascribe to Greek influence what might just as well be assigned to the Romans, since most writers in the seventeenth and eighteenth centuries, we may believe, found Latin much more manageable than Greek. That there were innumerable Greek sources for the Roman diction will be suggested by citations on later pages, but it is not to be assumed generally that these sources were directly drawn upon by English poets. Even Henri Estienne's great Greek *Thesaurus* could not very well outserve the *Gradus* of terms from a more familiar language.

it only sparely in their plays. Nor is it found much in pastoral poetry written in the style of Theocritus. This is partly explained, I think, by the form of such poems, made up of many short speeches, many of them concerned with personal affairs, and by the fact that this vocabulary is properly descriptive and didactic and not very well suited to most lyric or dramatic purposes. On the other hand, in such a play as *Don Sebastian* (1690) Dryden made a rather wide use of this diction, aided partly by the nature of his own rhetoric and partly by the vogue.

Another fact to be learned from observing the varied use of this stock language is that a single principle is apparently operating in the formation of any number of phrases. It is to be perceived in phrases like *liquid air* and *scaly kind*, in all the two-word periphrases, and in many compound epithets. It is the principle of definition, and various terms of natural description, controlled by this principle, are used to form phrases of definition. Such phrases make definitions by referring an object to its place in a philosophic or mythological scheme.

To illustrate the operation of this principle we may observe Cowley's phrase, *the liquid Sky*, in the light of his own note:

> Where never *Foot* of *Man*, or *Hoof* of *Beast*,
> The passage prest,
> Where never *Fish* did *fly*,
> And with short silver *wings* cut the low liquid *Sky*.

For *Fins* do the same Office to *Fish*, that *Wings* do to *Birds*; and the *Scripture* it self gives authority to my calling the *Sea* the *Low Sky*; where it says, *Gen*. I. 6. *Let there be a firmament in the midst of the waters, and let it divide the waters from the waters*.[43]

The same principle is apparent in the periphrasis where Dryden names stars by implying their function in the universe (candles for men to see by):

> Dim as the borrow'd beams of moon and stars
> To lonely, weary, wand'ring travelers,
> Is Reason to the soul; and, as on high
> Those rolling fires discover but the sky,
> Not light us here, so Reason's glimmering ray
> Was lent, not to assure our doubtful way,
> But guide us upward to a better day.
> And as those nightly tapers disappear,

---

[43] *The Muse*, st. 2, in *Poems*, ed. A. R. Waller (Cambridge, 1905), p. 185, and footnote 2, p. 187.

> When day's bright lord ascends our hemisphere;
> So pale grows Reason at Religion's sight;
> So dies, and so dissolves in supernatural light.[44]

The device of personification is likewise exploited to illustrate the nature of a thing in such a way that the personification becomes definition on another level of reference. This may be judged true of Dryden's lines:

> Time seems not now beneath his years to stoop,
> Nor do his wings with sickly feathers droop.[45]

But it is in the personification of material things that the use of the figure as a means of definition is more direct. In these lines of Thomson's, for example, personification is used to emphasize the nature of certain substances, the fluid nature of aether and the power of vapor to absorb light. Rephrased without the element of personification, such lines would need to contain explicit definitions:

> Meantime, light shadowing all, a sober calm
> Fleeces unbounded ether; whose least wave

---

[44]*Religio Laici* 1-11. In writing of French classicism M. Émile Krantz seems to me to give an acute analysis of the nature of periphrasis, and some of his remarks at least may be extended to apply to English poetry: "Quand un écrivain se propose, pour la perfection de son art, de donner à ses pensées un tour noble et d'exprimer les choses qu'il dit d'une façon qui ne soit pas commune, il faut bien qu'il cherche aux termes ordinaires des équivalents distingués et qu'il atteigne à l'originalité du style par d'ingénieuses ou de hardies alliances de mots. Sans doute chacun de ses mots, pris en particulier, est le mot propre qui désigne exactement une qualité de la chose; mais la chose elle-même n'est pas désignée par l'expression synthétique qui la représente tout entière d'un seul terme, et qu'on appelle son nom; elle l'est au contraire par une sorte de définition analytique qui renferme plusieurs termes, dont chacun exprime une qualité, et dont la somme exprime le tout. L'esprit classique étant, comme nous l'avons vu, essentiellement analytique, imprime au style son caractère et se crée sa langue à son image. Il tend alors à nommer les choses plutôt par leur définition que par leur nom. De là l'usage de la périphrase qui, lorsqu'elle est exacte, n'est pas autre chose qu'une sorte de définition. La définition n'est-elle pas elle-même une périphrase puisqu'elle substitue à la seule désignation de l'espèce l'énonciation du genre prochain unie à celle de la différence spécifique? Loin donc que la périphrase soit un abus de mots inutiles pour désigner, par une formule longue et complexe, une chose simple, elle est, dans l'esprit des vrais classiques, une expression analytique qui s'efforce de comprendre les attributs essentiels ou actuellement intéressants de la chose exprimée, afin d'en donner une notion plus nette et plus instructive. Elle joue donc, en littérature, le rôle considérable que Descartes attribue, en philosophie, à la définition. Elle n'est point une figure verbeuse, mais au contraire un développement d'idées ou un éclaircissement par images."—*Essai sur l'Esthétique de Descartes, Étudiée dans les Rapports de la Doctrine Cartésienne avec la Littérature Classique Française au XVIIᵉ Siècle* (Paris, 1882), 132-3.   [45]*To His Sacred Majesty* 27-8.

> Stands tremulous, uncertain where to turn
> The gentle current; while, illumined wide,
> The dewy-skirted clouds imbibe the sun,
> And through their lucid veil his softened force
> Shed o'er the peaceful world.[46]

The personification of objects through mythological reference is, of course, an obvious means of indicating the nature of a thing in terms of a personalized narrative. Figures of the sun as the father of things and the earth as the mother are but developments of thought around the facts of growth as we know them. The mixture of mythological and scientific reference in personification uses the terms of one scheme to describe and define the other:

> Comets, with swiftness, far, at distance, fly,
> To seek remoter Regions in the Sky;
> But tho' from *Sol*, with rapid haste, they roll'd,
> They move more slowly as they feel the Cold;
> Languid, forlorn, and dark, their State they moan,
> Despairing when in their *Aphelion*.
> But *Phœbus*, soften'd by their Penitence,
> On them benignly sheds his Influence,
> Recalls the Wanderers, who slowly move
> At first, but hasten as they feel his Love:
> To him for Mercy bend, sue, and prevail;
> Then Atoms crowd to furnish out their Tail.[47]

Compound epithets are often the means of more precise qualification and description than single epithets. They are, accordingly, of special value in descriptions where it is necessary to distinguish among several objects within a scheme of classification. They thus may become the precise and indispensable terms to qualify a generic term and so become the means of describing a subdivision. This, I think, may be seen in some lines of Milton's (the absence of a hyphen is not, I believe, significant):

> fruit of all kindes, in coate,
> Rough, or smooth rin'd, or bearded husk, or shell

---

[46]*Autumn* 957–63, in *The Complete Poetical Works*, ed. J. Logie Robertson (London, 1908).

[47]J. T. Desaguliers, *The Newtonian System of the World, The Best Model of Government: An Allegorical Poem* (Westminster, 1728), 28–30.

> She gathers, Tribute large, and on the board
> Heaps with unsparing hand.[48]

Such are the considerations that become significant, then, after we observe in detail the occurrence of this stock language in many periods of poetry—the authority of the Augustan example, the Renaissance revival of the diction, the preponderant use of this language in works where nature is described for didactic reasons, and the importance of many of the combinations of words as phrases of definition.   These observations may be taken to reinforce Aikin's criticism pretty well in its general outline, though they throw little light on what he meant by inaccuracy.   But by the nature of the evidence it becomes apparent that there are certain factors accounting for the growth of this stable diction not to be explained as the perverse desire of a century to propagate hackneyed language.   Aikin's criticism of inaccurate expression lacks force as soon as it is recognized that the Augustans, and especially Virgil, provide so many of the terms of this diction to later poets,[49] and if we substitute Virgil for Theocritus, we shall hardly be able to say that he looked into the face of nature and others after him did not, since Virgil's language, insofar as it is identical with that of later poets of nature, is equally "inaccurate."   Accepting Aikin's criticism fully, we might arrive at the paradox that this language was hackneyed to begin with.

It follows, then, in justice to Virgil and in the effort to correct Aikin's criticism, that some further examination of Virgil's language must be made.   For the principles governing his choice of language, if we knew them, might go far toward ex-

[48]*P. L.* V. 341-4.   In Greek and Latin the compound itself is often a phrase of definition and a periphrasis (for example, *quadrupedes*).   For further comment on this see below, p. 68, note 1.

[49]Mr. Geoffrey Tillotson goes this far: "He furnishes them with many actual words: *liquid, involve, purple, irriguous, refulgent, conscious, gelid, crown* (verb), *invade, painted* (used adjectivally).   *Care* comes straight from the *Georgics: cura* is Virgil's constant word for the job of the shepherd and farmer.   *Fleecy care* itself, in an age of poets who liked adjectives ending in -y and invented them by the hundred, springs readily from the juxtaposition: 'superat pars altera *curae, Lanigeros* agitare greges.' [*Geo.* III. 286-7.]   The phrase *sylvan scene* comes from another juxtaposition, this time in the *Aeneid:* 'silvis scena coruscis'.   [I. 164.]   Dryden spoke for many of these poets when he praised 'the *dictio Virgiliana*', adding 'in that I have always endeavoured to copy him.' [*Essays*, ed. W. P. Ker (Oxford: Clarendon Press, 1926), II. 148.]"—"Eighteenth-Century Poetic Diction," *Essays and Studies by Members of the English Association*, XXV (1939), 70-1.

plaining what made it desirable to imitate him, and so enable us to replace the charge of inaccuracy with more helpful criticism.

*

* *

Much earlier than either Warton or Aikin, Joseph Trapp undertook to formulate certain principles governing the use of epithets in verse. As a translator of Virgil and a student of natural philosophy he was particularly interested in problems concerning the choice of epithets for natural description. For him Virgil exemplified the proper application of the principles he was trying to define.

Trapp started with the proposition that if epithets contribute nothing to the sense of a description, in logic or in noteworthy detail, they had better not be used.[50] Such epithets make a style sterile and jejune; this was the common fault of ancients as well as moderns, and he cited Ovid and Buchanan. His quotation from the latter is illuminating:

> Dum procul à patria mœsti Babylonis in oris
> Fluminis ad liquidas forte sedemus aquas;
> Flevimus, & gemitus luctantia verba repressit,
> Inque sinus liquidæ decidit imber aquæ.

His comment is that we did not need to be admonished, even once, that water is liquid, much less twice in the space of three little verses.[51] There is no value in calling water liquid since everyone knows that, and the epithet neither modifies our understanding of the nature of water nor presents a more vivid image of it to us.

But with Virgil it was different. He called deer "timid" and tempests "sounding," and the epithets contributed necessary sense to the context. But he does not bore us by calling fire "hot" and cold "frigid."[52] The epithets he chose were

[50]"Hæ sunt in Epithetis deligendis observandæ leges, & raro, aut nunquam violandæ. Ea vero inserere, ut carminis solummodo hiatum adimpleant, quando prorsus inutilia sunt & supervacanea, & res, de qua agitur, per istas voces nec permovetur, nec augetur, nec illustratur, vitium est in scribendo fere maximum, & fieri vix potest, ut quis in gravius incidat."—*Prælectiones Poeticæ: In Schola Naturalis Philosophiæ Oxon. Habitæ* (Oxford, 1711), I. 90.

[51]*Ibid.* I. 90–1. The quotation is from Buchanan's version of Psalm CXXXVII, in *George Buchanan: A Memorial,* ed. D. A. Millar (St. Andrews, 1907), 365.

[52]"Istæ enim voces *timidi damæ,* & *tempestates sonoræ* non sunt ejusdem generis ac *ignis calidus,* vel *frigidum gelu;* (quæ quidem pene idem sonant ac *calidus calor,* vel

relevant to his purpose, suitable to the matter he was discussing, and not in mere repetition but in extension of meaning. Such a phrase as *tempestates sonoræ* is the proper Virgilian example, and modern poets ought strictly to observe the principles of that use. They should put out of their heads any notion that "beauties" may be culled indiscriminately from the *Gradus*, the *Flores Poetarum*, the *Elegantiæ Poeticæ*. Such collections, indeed, ought to be abolished for eternity.[53]

Trapp's criticism is interesting and valuable, coming as it does from a contemporary of Pope. He seems to be quite aware of the vicious habit of sticking in a line any epithet that fills out the meter and that has been used elegantly by some ancient poet. And he would agree with Warton and Aikin that poetry so fitted together is not written as a result of looking into the face of nature. But the emphasis of his criticism is rather different from Aikin's, and more searching. He criticizes poets for failing to make their language subservient to the purpose of the poem. Through this defect the integrity of a poem is destroyed. Ronsard had made the same point, again with reference to Virgil. Epithets, he had said, should be chosen to relate objects to the relevant circumstances of their existence. A boat is properly described as moving upon *flowing* water, because it is the flowing of the water that determines the motion of the boat.[54]

---

frigidum frigus, atque admodum absurdæ sunt, ut posthac ostendetur) sed adjuncta exprimunt *specialora*, & *minus essentialia;* ideoque in *quovis argumento* non sunt *ex æquo* temere usurpanda, sed in iis solummodo, quibus conveniunt pro *natura materiæ, quam tractamus.*"—*Prælectiones Poeticæ* (Oxford, 1711) I. 86–7.

[53]*Ibid.* I. 88. Some remarks of Coleridge may well be brought forward here: "I was, at that early period, led to a conjecture . . . that this style of poetry, which I have characterised above, as translations of prose thoughts into poetic language, had been kept up by, if it did not wholly arise from, the custom of writing Latin verses, and the great importance attached to these exercises, in our public schools. Whatever might have been the case in the fifteenth century, when the use of the Latin tongue was so general among learned men, that Erasmus is said to have forgotten his native language; yet in the present day it is not to be supposed, that a youth can *think* in Latin, or that he can have any other reliance on the force or fitness of his phrases, but the authority of the writer from whence he has adopted them. Consequently he must first prepare his thoughts, and then pick out, from Virgil, Horace, Ovid, or perhaps more compendiously from his Gradus, halves and quarters of lines, in which to embody them."—*Biographia Literaria* I. 12–13.

[54]"Je te veux advertir de fuir les epithetes naturelz qu'ilz ne servent de rien à la sentence de ce que tu veux dire, comme *la riviere coulante, la verde ramée,* et infinis autres. Tes epithetes seront recherchez pour signifier, et non pour remplir ton

This principle would be most thoroughly accepted, I suppose, by poets who intend that the epithets of natural description should illustrate the order of nature. According to this notion, epithets chosen to describe natural phenomena are relevant not merely to the sense of the immediate context, but also to the scheme of things in which these phenomena have existence outside the poem. This must be particularly true of the epithets in didactic poems like the *Astronomicon* or the *Creation*, but it is true to varying degree of all poems that have the natural world for subject. The scheme of nature may not be the plot or argument of the poem, but the names and descriptive epithets of natural objects in that poem must not merely carry forward the thought of the containing verse but must also establish identity of reference with some understood scheme of the universe. *The wandering moon* is a phrase whose epithet is presumably relevant in the context of any poem in which it occurs, following Ronsard's formula, but *wandering* is acceptable because the reader knows that the moon is a planet and, unlike the fixed stars, moves in courses which appear to vary.

Trapp's position is that the language of poetry should be true to the principles of philosophy, and in matters of natural description, to those of natural philosophy. He gave greater importance to philosophic truth than Aikin, and less to considerations of accuracy. For according to his writings mythology would provide acceptable figures if mythology were believed in. In Trapp's opinion natural philosophy offered a superior truth, and for that reason the poet might more properly take his figures from "physics."[55]

If this is the proper interpretation of Trapp's criticism, it is easy to see that he goes much beyond Aikin and most modern

---

carme, ou pour estre oyseux en ton vers: exemple, *Le ciel vouté encerne tout le monde,* J'ay dit *vouté,* et non *ardant, clair,* ny *haut,* ny *azuré.* d'autant qu'une voute est propre pour embrasser et encerner quelque chose. Tu pourras bien dire, *Le bateau va desur l'onde coulante,* pour ce que le cours de l'eau faict couler le bateau."—*Abbregé de l'Art Poetique Françoys,* in *Œuvres* IV. 478–9.

[55] "Rerum vero *Naturalium* indagatione nihil magis *nitet in carmine:* Hoc argumentum versibus adornantes, politissime ratiocinantur; & canunt, quæ explicant. Optime conveniunt Poesis & Philosophia, ea nimirum, quæ Physica appellatur; cum hæc illi tam abunde præbeat materiam descriptionibus, & ingenii flexibus accommodam, & idearum, vocumque, vatibus propriarum, fœcundissimam. Quid magis Poeticum, quam *canere—errantem Lunam, Solisque labores* . . . ."—*Prælectiones Poeticæ* (3d ed.; London, 1736), II. 61.

critics in showing what eighteenth-century diction might have
been expected to do.   And this with a contempt for the *Gradus*
which quite equals that of Coleridge.   At the same time, his
interest in natural science as the subject of poetry led him toward the understanding acceptance of at least one kind of stable
terminology.   Coleridge, on the other hand, condemned the use
of any language in poetry which was designed to serve the purposes of truth more than those of pleasure,[56] and he was, in
effect, pointing out the chief fault of Trapp's criticism.   Trapp
is generally arguing for poetry of the kind written by Aratus,
Lucretius, and Manilius, and he is led to admire Virgil too much
for what most modern readers would consider his minor virtues.
Trapp's belief that the primary value of epithets depends upon
the adequacy of their reference to the nature of the physical
universe as understood by philosophy ignores considerations of
emotion and decorum.   These he might neglect with less danger
in writing of some of his contemporaries, but he could do so only
fatally in discussing Virgil.   But even with respect to the eighteenth century he fails to appreciate fully the faults of its language, and, of course, he fails seriously to understand the principles of good diction.   Ignoring Virgil's use of epithets which
appear quite as irrelevant as Buchanan's *liquid*, he ignores those
factors which explain the stabilized characteristics of Virgil's
diction.

We ourselves might recall, for example, what he seems to
overlook, Virgil's use of such a word as *aeria:*

> illum surgentem vallibus imis
> aëriae fugere grues.[57]

It would be difficult to select any one of the senses of this epithet
as the particularly necessary one.   It might mean that these
birds fly in the air, that they are high-flying, that air is their
native element, or that the element of air is their primary constituent.   But considering that this word also modifies *elm*,[58]
doves,[59] *cloud*,[60] and *mountain*,[61] the reader might ordinarily be

[56]See *Biographia Literaria* II. 104, and the criticism of Erasmus Darwin, *ibid.*
I. 11–12.

[57]*Geo.* I. 374–5.   This epithet is listed by Buchler as one of four that might
be elegantly applied to *grus:* "*Aëria, querula, sæua, hyberna.*"—*Flores* 238.

[58]*Eclogues* I. 58.   [60]*Aeneid* VII. 705.
[59]*Ibid.* III. 69.   [61]*Ibid.* VI. 234.

content to allow it the least precise meaning, and for the rest accept it as merely a formal adjective, a conventional epithet of the sort found in Homer. That author used the phrase *wet sea* seven times, and the value of *wet* seems to consist merely in some incantational effect the word had acquired through traditional use. Virgil's use of *aeria* might be interpreted in the same way. As for *liquid*, Virgil used that word to modify *fountains*,[62] *clouds*,[63] *lakes*,[64] and *waves*,[65] and again it appears that the epithet was chiefly valued for its traditional associations. Such usage is, of course, comparable to that which attaches certain adjectives to persons and gods—*pious* Aeneas, *silver-footed* Thetis, *wily* Odysseus.

Trapp thus ignored the fact that Virgil had a kind of equivalent for the *Gradus* (as Homer had before him), and he therefore overlooked certain factors—the reverence for the past, for Homer and Ennius, the sense of fitness and of charm in taking over the sanctified language of the fathers of poetry, all such considerations that at times must have seemed to Virgil more important than thoughts of immediate contextual relevance.[66] Not that Trapp failed to perceive the value of a tradition; it is merely that the strength of his interest in natural philosophy led him to carry a fundamental part of his critical theory to an extreme. He disregarded whatever was not important to a certain kind of didactic poetry. And while he came closer than most critics I have found in providing an explanation of eighteenth-century diction, his criticism is ultimately misleading.

The late Milman Parry, in his study of the conventional Homeric epithet, paid careful attention to those very factors Trapp ignored, and it will be profitable to recall certain of his remarks, transferring such as we may to our consideration of Virgil's language:

As the fixed diction of the Augustan age can only be understood as the expression of a whole way of life which we may call the proper, so Homer's traditional diction is the work of a way of life which we may call the heroic, if one will give that word all the meaning it had for the men of Homer's time. It is a term which can only be understood in the measure that one can think

---

[62]*Geo.* II. 200.

[63]*Aen.* V. 525.

[64]*Ibid.* VII. 760.

[65]*Ibid.* V. 859.

[66]For an excellent study of Virgil's language see André Cordier, *Études sur le Vocabulaire Épique dans l' "Énéide"* (Paris: Société d'Édition "Les Belles Lettres," 1939).

and feel as they did, for the heroic was to them no more or less than the statement of all that they would be or would do if they could. To give form to
this heroic cast of thought they had the old tales that had come down in time,
and they had a rhythm in which to tell them, and words and phrases with
which to tell them. The making of this diction was due to countless poets
and to many generations who in time had found the heroic word and phrase
for every thought, and every word in it was holy and sweet and wondrous,
and no one would think of changing it wilfully. The Muses it was truly who
gave those poets voices sweeter than honey. And those parts of the diction
which did not carry the story itself, since their meaning was not needed for
understanding, lost that meaning, but became, as it were, a familiar music of
which the mind is pleasantly aware, but which it knows so well that it makes
no effort to follow it. Indeed, poetry thus approaches music most closely
when the words have rather a mood than a meaning. Nor should one think
that since the meaning is largely lost it ceases to matter if the meaning is good.
Though the meaning be felt rather than understood it is there, as it matters
whether music idly heard be bad or good. Of such a kind is the charm of
the fixed metaphor in Homer. It is an incantation of the heroic.[67]

This approach helps greatly to explain why a special diction
should be set aside for poetry, but it is not completely satisfactory in accounting for the eighteenth-century style, nor does it
answer all the questions that arise with respect to Virgil's diction. After all, the conventions of the literary epic cannot be
the same as those carried down by word of mouth through many
centuries. The very nature of imitation introduces different
factors and involves different purposes. One might suppose
that Roman epic writers modeled themselves on Homer or even
Empedocles, but allowing this does not solve our problem, since
we should still need to know why imitation was desirable. To
discover this we should undoubtedly be required to familiarize
ourselves with the whole character of Roman civilization, as
Parry said, but our knowledge of that character must arise out
of our understanding of many details, and an imitated, conventional language for poetic use is one of those details. Modeling
themselves on the Augustans, eighteenth-century writers were
imitating imitators. The question, of course, is why? And what
were they imitating?

Part of the answer for Virgil and Pope, if not for Homer, is
in the admiration of the proper, the decorous. Society always
builds up means of restricting crudeness and vulgarity, and sets

[67]"The Traditional Metaphor in Homer," *Classical Philology*, XXVIII (1933),
41–2.

store by elegant and graceful and witty manners.   Yet, when all this is allowed for, the fact remains that some of Virgil's diction and a lot of Pope's seems mere nonsense.

Aikin found the English diction weak because untruthful; Trapp found it unphilosophic.   To Wordsworth it was gaudy and to Coleridge frigid.   To Aikin and Trapp it would have been good if it had been accurate in describing nature and at the same time illustrative of the great philosophic truths which explain the order of things.   And if it had filled these qualifications, Wordsworth and Coleridge might have found it less gaudy and less frigid. [68]

The one factor which earlier criticism failed to take up in any detail has to do with the meaning of the individual terms of this diction.   It is quite possible that much of the failure to account for the pretty consistent use of a stock vocabulary during a whole century is due to the assumption that these terms meant what they seemed to mean, and nothing else.   In the eighteenth century their associations were taken for granted, and so there was no need for comment.   And in later periods it was quite forgotten that they might have had originally many important associations since completely lost.   It is possible that certain factors have been overlooked in this connection which may help considerably to explain what were regarded as the virtues of a stock language for poetry.   This at any rate seems to be a hypothesis worth entertaining.

For one of the conditions necessary to the acceptance of a stock poetic language would be that its terms have some significant association not immediately relevant to the context of its use.   That association would be brought to mind by the knowledge that the word did belong to a special vocabulary, and with this realization would come some recollection of the original purpose of the vocabulary.   That vocabulary need not be constructed primarily for poetic use.   Its elements would be employed in verse in two orders of meaning—primarily, of course, satisfying the sense of the containing lines, and secondarily

[68]Macaulay's criticism of Dryden's use of stock epithets is extremely suggestive, and it is only to be regretted that he did not explain himself more fully.   One sentence in particular bears quoting, and for Dryden's name we might substitute many others: "But Dryden was . . . one of those writers in whom the period of imagination does not precede, but follow, the period of observation and reflection."—*Critical, Historical and Miscellaneous Essays* (New York, 1860), I. 355.

drawing on associations to some degree foreign to the explicit statements of the verse.   The way in which this might be done may be illustrated by a theoretical example.   If someone were to write an epic of modern city life, and quite gratuitously one of the characters were mentioned in a certain line as *homo sapiens*, a modern reader would hardly be unduly distracted, and might be pleased to be reminded of man's place in the animal kingdom, pleased to be reminded of a fact by which he sets some store.   Such a use might give an especially flattering pleasure to someone interested in biology.   For others it might provide a kind of relief from the tension of the narrative, and possibly appear ornamental.   But however irrelevant at first sight, it is not likely that the term would cause the reader to remind himself of the whole scheme of classification of animal life.   For the most part it would excite merely the vague idea that the rational faculty somehow distinguished men from other animals.   While he would not be, supposedly, too much diverted, his pleasure would consist of being reminded of aspects of this civilization he was not immediately concerned with in the progress of the poem, but which at other times were of considerable importance and interest to him.   For such pleasure only reasonably familiar terms could be used.

A future student of such an epic might need to work over the classic texts of biology to establish the meaning of the reference in *homo sapiens*.   And according to the hypothesis of the present work, the modern reader must carry out that same process in examining the language of eighteenth-century verse. For if it should turn out that a considerable number of the terms used in natural description were of special importance to the investigations of natural philosophy, our examination would not merely contribute to a more exact understanding of the terms, but would confirm the further hypothesis that certain poets were interested in establishing a stock diction for poetry because natural philosophy had convinced them of the value of a stock language for all thought.   And in describing nature, they could do no better than adopt the language of natural description already fairly well worked out by scientists. [69]

[69]F. W. Bateson has made some acute observations along these lines, and he says: "The vocabulary of poetic diction can be paralleled in the numerous technical terms of science, philosophy and politics that were coined in the eighteenth

This, in fact, is pretty much true of the poetic diction of the eighteenth century. A considerable part of the terminology utilized in natural description had also an ancient and specific use in scientific writing. But to test the truth of this statement it is necessary to observe the number and nature of the significant terms that are common to poetic and scientific writing, and the extent and manner of their use. When this has been done with some thoroughness, progress will have been made in the attempt to understand why so many poets set a high value upon a stable and conventional language.

---

century. The motives that led the chemists to create a word like 'phlogiston' (first used in 1733) were ultimately identical with those that induced Thomson and the rest to call fishes a 'finny tribe'. Both words could have been replaced by others already in use, but they were not mere synonyms. [Up to this point I agree, but I disagree with what follows for reasons that will be apparent in the succeeding pages.] By restricting a general notion to a particular field they represented a gain in precision. 'Phlogiston' did not just mean the principle of inflammability, but that principle as used in the science of chemistry; and the 'finny tribe' was fishes considered solely as the subject of poetry. The tendency was therefore a natural development of the doctrine of 'perspicuity'."—*English Poetry and the English Language* 69–70.

CHAPTER III

The Formation of a Scientific Language for Natural Description

SOME of the common words of poetry—*aether*, *humor*, and *element*, for example—are clearly not to be separated from their scientific meanings. But a considerable number of poetical terms have scientific associations that are frequently overlooked. By reconstructing some of these associations, it may prove possible to clarify the relationship between the basic terminologies of science and the stock diction of poetry.

It may be observed first that some of the terms met frequently in poetry have had a really extensive and significant use in scientific writing. *Ambient*, for example, is one of the stock words of neoclassic poetry, especially as an epithet for air. Akenside's usage is typical:

> He spoke; when instant through the sable glooms
> With which that furious presence had involv'd
> The ambient air, a flood of radiance came
> Swift as the lightning flash.[1]

This phrase also occurs in a scientific context in the prose of William Gilbert,[2] Bacon,[3] Harvey,[4] Boyle,[5] Hooke,[6] and Halley.[7]

---

[1] *The Pleasures of Imagination* (1744), II. 636–9, in *The Poetical Works*, ed. Alexander Dyce (Boston, 1865).

[2] *De Magnete* (1600), facsimile published by Mayer and Müller (Berlin, 1892), 55.

[3] *Historia Vitæ et Mortis*, in *The Works*, ed. James Spedding, Robert L. Ellis, and Douglas D. Heath (New York, 1864), III. 361.

[4] *Exercitatio Anatomica de Motu Cordis et Sanguinis in Animalibus* (1628), facsimile in *Monumenta Medica*, Vol. V, ed. Henry Sigerist (Florence, 1928), 13.

[5] *An Examen of Mr. T. Hobbes his Dialogus Physicus De Naturâ Aëris* (London, 1662), 32.

[6] *Cometa*, in R. T. Gunther, *Early Science in Oxford* (London and Oxford, 1920–35), VIII. 230.

[7] In *Philosophical Transactions*, XVII (1693), 469. The eighteenth-century Italian definition of this term is interesting in this connection: "*Ambiente*. Quella

Crystal humor is another phrase common in seventeenth- and eighteenth-century poetry, usually describing tears, although it sometimes refers to the ordinarily liquid appearance of eyes. Here is the way Dryden used it:

> Fly back, ye films, that cloud her sight;
> And you, ye crystal humours bright,
> Your noxious vapours purged away,
> Recover, and admit the day.[8]

This phrase had been most notably used for many centuries, however, by writers on optics to describe one of the three liquid substances in the eye (the other two were the watery and the glassy humors). The concept and the phrase are found in the writings of Pollux,[9] Celsus,[10] Alhazen,[11] Hieronymus Fabricius,[12] Descartes,[13] Boyle,[14] William Briggs,[15] and John Harris.[16]

Congeal, to signify a process of hardening, not necessarily by freezing, is a common enough word in neoclassic poetry, and quite possibly more frequent in conversation than the other words that have been mentioned. A knowledge of the way this term was used in scientific writing is helpful in reading certain poetical passages, for example these lines of Thomson's:

> Thick clouds ascend, in whose capacious womb
> A vapoury deluge lies, to snow congealed.[17]

References to the process of hardening ("congealing") by which snow, dew, salt, ice, and stalactites are formed may be found in

---

materia liquida, che curconda alcuna cosa, e si dice comunemente dell'aria."—*Nuovo Dizionario Italiano-Francese*, ed. Francesco d'E. Alberti (2d ed.; [Venice] 1796).

[8]*King Arthur*, III. ii, in *The Works*, ed. Sir Walter Scott, revised by George Saintsbury (Edinburgh, 1882–93), VIII. 170.

[9]*Onomasticon*, ed. Eric Bethe (Leipzig, 1900), § II. Par. 71.

[10]*De Medicina* VII. vii. 13, ed. W. G. Spencer (LCL) (1935–8).

[11]As described by William Whewell, *History of the Inductive Sciences* (New York, 1866), II. 54.

[12]*De Visione, Voce, Auditu* (Venice, 1600) (*De Oculo Visus Organo Liber* 50).

[13]*La Dioptrique*, in *Œuvres*, ed. Charles Adam and Paul Tannery (Paris, 1879–1909), VI. 106.

[14]*Some Considerations Touching the Usefulnesse of Experimental Natural Philosophy* (Oxford, 1664–71), I. 97.

[15]*Ophthalmo-graphia, sive Oculi ejusq; partium descriptio Anatomica* (2d ed.; London, 1685), 33.

[16]*Lexicon Technicum: Or, An Universal English Dictionary of Arts and Sciences*, Vol. I (London, 1704), under "Humours."

[17]*Winter* 225–6, in *The Complete Poetical Works*, ed. J. Logie Robertson (London, 1908).

the writings of Jean Bodin,[18] Philemon Holland,[19] Bacon,[20] Comenius,[21] Dampier,[22] and John Morton.[23]

It is not practicable to repeat here very many of the words that occur in both verse and scientific prose, since the lists in the appendixes will make much of this evidence available, but these examples have been given merely to indicate the fact of common employment. In the lists it is important to observe not merely that poetry made use of certain words with special scientific meanings, but that it made emphatic use of them. A considerable number of these terms are among those most characteristic of neoclassic poetry, from both the peculiarity and the frequence of their use. Some we might judge were indispensable.

But it is not merely individual words that are common to the stock diction of verse and the special vocabulary of scientific writing. Several of the same methods of word and phrase formation are employed in both. Periphrases, for example, of the two-word sort much used by classic and neoclassic poets, belonged also to the conventional language of naturalists. Aristotle used the phrase τὸ πτερωτὸν γένος ("the feathered kind");[24] Pliny, *generis squamosi;*[25] Edward Wotton, *gallinaceo genere;*[26] Bishop Wilkins, *the ruminant kind;*[27] and Derham, *the feathered Tribe.*[28] A particularly interesting periphrasis is *briny ambient,* which Boyle used to denote the sea water of a certain experiment:

I wish'd several times that he had had with him a seal'd Weather-glass (for *ordinary* Thermometers would on that occasion have been unserviceable) to prevent some little doubt, that might be made, whether the intense Cold he

---

[18]*Universæ Naturæ Theatrum* (Lyon, 1596), 204.

[19]*The Historie of the World. Commonly called, The Naturall Historie of C. Plinius Secundus* (London, 1601), II. 414 (Bk. XXXI, chap. vii).

[20]*Natural History,* § 843, in *Works* V. 84.

[21]*Naturall Philosophie Reformed by Divine Light: or, A Synopsis of Physicks* (London, 1651), 131. I have been unable to learn the name of the translator of this work.

[22]*A New Voyage Round the World,* ed. Sir Albert Gray (London: Argonaut Press, 1927), 56.

[23]*The Natural History of Northampton-shire* (London, 1712), 144.

[24]*De Animalibus Historiæ* 490a12, in *Opera,* ed. U. C. Bussemaker, Fred Dübner, and Emil Heitz (Paris, 1848–74), III. 6.

[25]*Natural History* IX. xxiii. 56, ed. H. Rackham (LCL) (1938–40).

[26]*De Differentiis Animalium Libri Decem* (Paris, 1552), 109b.

[27]*An Essay Towards a Real Character, And a Philosophical Language* (London, 1668), 165.

[28]*Physico-Theology: or, A Demonstration of the Being and Attributes of God* (3d ed.; London, 1714), 27.

felt might not be only and chiefly in reference to his Body, which might be so alter'd, and dispos'd by this new briny Ambient, as to make such a disturbance in the course or texture of his Blood, as that which makes Aguish persons so cold at the beginning of the fit, though the temperature of the Ambient Body continue the same.[29]

Adjectives with a -*y* suffix, so noticeable a feature of English neoclassic poetry, are also common in scientific writing. Their most frequent use is to describe the appearance of the material of things. They also often indicate the nature of a substance, and so provide a specific reference to a scheme of classification. Many of these forms are listed in Appendix C, but several must be illustrated at this point.

The adjectives derived from the names of the four elements were regularly formed with the -*y* ending, and a quotation from an almanac of 1653, with its single inconsistent use, may serve to illustrate a typical application of these terms: "[The Celestial Signs] are divided into four Triplicities, *viz.* Fiery, Ayery, Watery and Earthly Triplicity."[30] In 1665 a writer in the *Philosophical Transactions* asked for certain information about soils in these terms:

The several kinds of the soyls of *England*, being supposed to be, either Sandy, Gravelly, Stony, Clayie, Chalky, Light-mould, Heathy, Marish, Boggy, Fenny, or Cold weeping Ground; information is desired, what kind of soyls your Country doth most abound with, and how each of them is prepared, when employed for *Arable*?[31]

Three other examples may be permitted to illustrate the constant reliance upon this form in describing objects of widely different nature:

Leaves; whether as to their *Superficies;* being Smooth, Unctuous, Shining, Rough, Prickly, Hairy, Wolly, &c.[32]

. . . *Liquors* [of plants], or other *Contained Parts*, are of such different *Kinds;* one being Watry, another Winy, a third *Oily*, a fourth *Milky*, and the like.[33]

I shall now proceed to the more observable Occurrences in the Kingdom of *Meteors*, to First, those of the *Watery* Kind.[34]

---

[29]*New Experiments and Observations Touching Cold* (London, 1683), 172.

[30]Claudius Dariott, *Dariotus Redivivus: Or a briefe Introduction Conducing to the Judgement of the Stars, enlarged by N. S.* (London, 1653), 3.

[31]I. 92.

[32]Wilkins, *Real Character* 68.

[33]Nehemiah Grew, *An Idea of a Philosophical History of Plants* (2d ed.; London, 1682), 4.

[34]Morton, *Natural History of Northampton-shire* 336.

Compound epithets are of occasional use to scientific description, particularly in botany, but they occur ordinarily in Greek or Latin forms—as *parthogenetic* and *terraqueous*. Native English forms are almost the exception, and it hardly seems worth while to list very many native terms since they may be matched by similar compounds in numerous fields of writing. Some illustration, however, may be called for.

Many names of plants, of course, are compound words: *Penny-royall*,[35] *Toad-flax*,[36] *Kidney-Wort*,[37] *Bird's-foot Trefoil*.[38] Now and then an occasional color term is made use of: *muske-colour*[39] and *Purple-floured*[40] illustrate the kind. *Wind-Engines*,[41] *Trade-wind*,[42] and *Land-Floods*[43] are examples of the way certain things were named by joining nouns together. Occasionally a term turns up which makes use of the present participle. The *remora* of the ancients was renamed the *Sucking-fish*.[44] Thomas Martyn rejected *Stem-clasping* as a botanical term in favor of *Amplexicaulis*.[45] It is of considerable significance that scientists so easily drifted into a use of Greek and Latin forms for words which were necessarily compound, finding those languages more resourceful than English.

There are many adjectival forms besides those with the *-y* suffix which are fairly common in scientific description, quite a few formed with the suffixes *-ish* and *-ive*, rather more with the suffixes *-ous*, *-ious*, and *-eous*. Several color terms make use of *-ish*—*blackish*,[46] *bluish*,[47] *Darkish*[48]—but other kinds of terms do also—*flattish* describing thistle seed,[49] *glewish* describing a liquid,[50]

[35]William Coles, *Adam in Eden: Or, Natures Paradise* (London, 1657), Hhhh₂. It is necessary to cite by the bulky signatures because the pagination is confused.
[36]*Ibid*. Ddd₃.
[37]*Ibid*. Mmm.
[38]Morton, *Natural History of Northampton-shire* 374.
[39]*Phil. Trans.* II (1668), 613.
[40]Coles, *Adam in Eden* Aaa₄b.
[41]*Phil. Trans.* I (1665), 112.
[42]Dampier, *New Voyage* 201.
[43]Morton, *Natural History of Northampton-shire* 87.
[44]Dampier, *New Voyage* 53.
[45]*The Language of Botany: Being a Dictionary of the Terms Made Use of in that Science, Principally by Linneus* (2d ed.; London, 1796), xv.
[46]Dampier, *New Voyage* 265.
[47]Morton, *Natural History of Northampton-shire* 65.
[48]John Pointer, *A Rational Account of the Weather* (2d ed.; London, 1738), 107.
[49]Coles, *Adam in Eden* Ll₂.
[50]Joannes Renodæus, *A Medicinal Dispensatory*, trans. Richard Tomlinson (London, 1657), 30.

roundish describing the shape of certain leaves.[51] A few *-ive* words are *attractive*,[52] *refractive*,[53] and *tersive*.[54] The *-ous* suffix is used in the very common words *bulbous*,[55] *Globous*,[56] *nitrous*,[57] *unctuous*,[58] and *vaporous*.[59] There are of course many others, and several of these are experiments designed to naturalize the Latin forms. These various *-ous* suffixes and spellings may be observed in a list of words printed by Robert Lovell in 1661: *saxeous, marmoreous, lapideous, glareous, sabulous, calculous, gemmose, succous, sulphureous.*[60]

The present participle is used distinctively in scientific prose as an epithet to point out some quality native to the thing described. Very often, more than indicating the appearance of a thing, it defines the nature of a thing. The present participle is employed in this way in many other fields, but I think its use in the writing of natural history is particularly noteworthy. Newton's use of *flaming* illustrates this application plainly: "All flaming Bodies, as Oil, Tallow, Wax, Wood, fossil Coals, Pitch, Sulphur, by flaming waste and vanish into burning Smoke . . . ."[61] *Burning-glass*, the old phrase for magnifying glass, illustrates a similar use, as do the epithets in the phrases *falling sickness, purging medicine, flying insects, freezing air, swimming creatures,* and *spreading branches.* Epithets of this sort are common in the prose of the seventeenth and eighteenth centuries, and it is not necessary to give more examples here.

*
*   *

It is such words and phrases, and word and phrase formations, that are common to verse and scientific prose. Of these the two-word periphrastic phrase of definition and epithets

[51]Coles, *Adam in Eden* Hhhh₂.

[52]Sir Isaac Newton, *Opticks*, reprinted from the 4th ed. (1730), ed. E. T. Whittaker (London: G. Bell, 1931), 383.

[53]*Ibid.* 274.

[54]Robert Plot, *The Natural History of Oxford-shire, Being an Essay toward the Natural History of England* (Oxford, 1677), 49.

[55]John Parkinson, *Paradisi in Sole Paradisus Terrestris* (London, 1629), 153.

[56]*Phil. Trans.* II (1667), 527.

[57]Newton, *Opticks* (1730), 380.

[58]Robert Boyle, *The Sceptical Chymist* (Oxford, 1680), 50.

[59]Alexander Rosse, *The New Planet no Planet* (London, 1646), 90.

[60]*Panzoologicomineralogia. Or a Compleat History of Animals and Minerals* (Oxford, 1661), f₂.

[61]*Opticks* (1730), 342.

formed with the suffixes -*y* and -*ing* are of particular value in providing means for the explanation of certain basic principles in the formation of a special language for science. And an understanding of the method and purpose of constructing these forms can be of considerable help in understanding the use of comparable forms in verse.

A study of scientific usage must begin with certain obvious considerations. It is to be remembered, first, that two fundamental activities of scientific investigation, observation and classification, need to have their results recorded in order that knowledge may be communicated and then improved. That which is observed must be named, and the name must represent the thing observed. Those things which share common qualities or properties must be classified—that is, arranged in groups, since in nature, it is the postulate of science, things exist in relation to each other. Terms must be found to name classes of things in such a way that the distinctive characteristics of those classes are exactly indicated, and so that the members of each class and the classes themselves may be known in their various relationships. Which is to say that the language used to record the results of nature study must make an accurate diagram of nature, and in its formation that language will, as far as possible, observe the same methods of logic that are used in the study of the natural objects themselves.

These are obvious enough considerations, and it is still more obvious that the need for accuracy in the use of terms increases with the extension of knowledge. When a class of plants, for example, is divided into an indefinite number of subclasses, it becomes increasingly necessary that the terms used to describe or name those subclasses be adequate to distinguish them clearly from each other. It would accordingly be very helpful if the terms of classification themselves indicated the recognition of similarities and differences—several terms, for instance, using the same root but different suffixes. Or if no such simple arrangement could be devised and it were necessary to use phrases of more than one word, it would be desirable to have certain known and stable rules governing the relations of those terms. Consequently, it is best if a single language is agreed upon to serve for the recording of scientific investigation. It must be a language with certain capacities to indicate relationships, through cases or prepositions or suffixes or compounds. A single language with this kind of scope and flexibility is also desirable in order to avoid difficulties that would arise from compounding terms of different languages. This becomes a necessity as knowledge increases and the difficulties of transferring terms from one language to another also increase.

To satisfy these demands one might suppose scientists would use Latin and never give the vernacular another thought. But this would have implied a failure of national feeling, and in the Renaissance that was unlikely. There were, of course, the two conflicting interests, the enthusiasm for classical learning and languages and that for the native speech. The conflict was long, and the result was, finally, a kind of compromise whereby the syntax of the vernacular and the terminology of the classic languages became the accepted means of expression for scientific workers. Something of the nature and progress of this conflict must be studied here, for a great deal depends upon our understanding certain reasons for the fluctuation of thought and practice in these matters.

Latin, of course, had long been accepted as the language of learned endeavor in the Western world, and continued to be of great importance to scientific investigators and philosophers throughout the seventeenth century. It is to be expected that with so long a history it would have contributed any number of special terms to naturalists, but it is also important to remember that inasmuch as men of the Renaissance were returning to the classics, as naturalists they were at first quite as intent upon the works of ancient writers as they were in looking at nature itself. [62] This, of course, was a circumstance favorable to Latin writing. The great scientists and naturalists were much read, and translated, but for obvious reasons Greek was not taken up as a language for scientific expression.

And yet though Latin was popular by the very nature of the Renaissance and as a language was adaptable to the "advancement of experience," it was nevertheless in time largely superseded by the various vernaculars. But it is important to note here that though by the seventeenth century a majority of sci-

[62]A very interesting discussion of the hold of antiquity upon medical science appears in Sir William Osler's *The Evolution of Modern Medicine* (New Haven, 1921), 126–31.

entific texts were written in modern languages, many important works were still being composed in Latin. One need only recall some of the writings of William Gilbert, Bacon, Descartes, Huyghens, Newton, and, in the eighteenth century, Linnaeus.[63]

It thus came about that the increasing popularity of the various vernaculars did not in all instances lead to the abandonment of the terminology developed in the classical languages and especially in Latin. It was not merely that modern investigators were obliged to study ancient texts in order to advance their own work, and so were obliged to accept the original terminology before they could modify or replace it, but they were constantly confronted with writings of their own era written in Latin, which could hardly do less than strengthen the usefulness of the oldest established terminology. Nor had science advanced so far that it proved necessary to introduce into the Latin of the *Principia*, for example, any considerable number of terms unknown to antiquity.

The power of ancient thought as well as the survival of the Greek and Latin languages created special difficulties hindering the establishment of vernacular terminologies, but there were others also. There was, first, the problem created by the use of vernacular words which are commonly known in nontechnical use. If these words are sufficiently well known, the common reader will often fail to regard them as technical terms, and the primary purpose of a specialized language will have been defeated—precise and unmistakable reference. This difficulty is very clearly observed in Hooke's efforts to fix the terms for describing the appearance of the sky in weather reports:

As let *Cleer* signifie a very cleer Sky without any Clouds or Exhalations . . . *Overcast*, when the Vapours so whiten and thicken the Air, that the *Sun* cannot break through . . . . *Cloudy*, when the Sky has many thick dark Clouds. *Lowring*, when the Sky is not very much overcast, but hath also underneath many thick dark Clouds which threaten rain.[64]

---

[63]Mr. Francis R. Johnson has estimated that ninety per cent of the scientific works published in England in the Elizabethan period were written in the vernacular, though on the continent the proportion was rather less (*Astronomical Thought in Renaissance England* [Baltimore: Johns Hopkins Press, 1937], p. 3, note 2). This very high estimate depends upon the definition of "scientific," and, of course, does not signify that Latin was unimportant.

[64]Quoted by Thomas Sprat, *The History of the Royal-Society of London* (2d ed.; London, 1702), 177.

A distinctly different problem arises with the use of coined terms, likely to be understood only by the specially trained student. Such words are of precise enough meaning, but they work against the establishment of a vernacular language because they are not adaptable to graceful use. For the interest in the vernacular involves the intention of writing in such a way that modern scientific works may compete with the ancient in literary excellence. This is the point of Brunot's remarks on certain seventeenth-century French writers, and it is equally applicable to Galileo and Boyle:

A d'autres occasions, les sciences parlèrent français, c'est vrai, et même bon français, témoin l'espèce d'encyclopédie qui porte le nom de *Physique de Rohault*. La chimie abandonna aussi son langage cryptographique, elle cessa d'être une Kabbale, à l'usage des seuls initiés, et le cours de Lémery, qui rompait si heureusement avec la tradition, se vendit, au dire des contemporains, "comme un ouvrage de galanterie ou de satire."[65]

The final factor leading to the general use of terms from the classical languages was, of course, the advancement of science itself. As formerly undreamed-of fields of knowledge were opened up it was necessary to invent terminology, and for the sake of specialized students, not merely for a polite audience. When this became the primary consideration, Greek and Latin were immediately made use of, eventually to the exclusion of most vernacular terms. Thomas Martyn, writing a botanical glossary in the late eighteenth century, made every effort to find English terms for the whole science, but found it impossible to insist upon their use. He recognized that the cause of his

[65]*Histoire de la Langue Française des Origines à 1900*, t. IV, Ière Partie (Paris, 1913), p. 418. Though not directly relevant here, the following remarks of Brunot's may serve to inform us of the nature of those terms which probably seemed foreign and cabalistic to the English as well as to the French: "Les théoriciens, arbitres du goût, Bouhours en particulier, nous ont dit aussi et répété leur horreur du mot pédant ou d'apparence pédante: *calvitie* ou *aptitude, atrabile* ou *système*. 'Il ne faut pas que, par des termes qui sont rudes pour leur bouche, les dames affectent de paraître un peu trop géographes. Je leur abandonne *climat, zone, détroit* et quelques autres; mais je ne veux point qu'elles me vient effrayer par des *longitudes* et des *latitudes*' (Vaumorière, *Art de plaire*, 320)."—*Ibid.* 421.
  With this may be compared a speech from Shadwell's *Virtuoso*, where he made fun of some of the scientific vocabulary being affected in his time: "O yes; there was a lucid Surloin of Beef in the *Strand*, foolish people thought it burnt, when it only became lucid and chrystalline by the coagulation of the aqueous juice of the Beef, by the corruption that invaded it."—*Complete Works*, ed. Montague Summers (London: Fortune Press, 1927), III. 164.

failure was the necessity to remain faithful to the language of
the best specialist study:

> Laying it down therefore as a first principle, that we ought to adhere as
> closely as possible to the Linnean language, it will be found that the number
> of terms, purely English, occurring in the Botanical Glossary, which is now
> offered to the public, is comparatively small.[66]

He then listed three pages of English terms with their Linnaean
equivalents, "that persons may judge for themselves how far
they would choose to depart from the original terms,"[67] implying, of course, that they would not choose to go far.   Here are
a few of the pairings: Beaked, *Rostratus;* Bellying, *Ventricosus;*
Eared, *Auritus;* Funnel-shaped, *Infundibuliformis;* Latticed, *Can-
cellatus;* Punched, *Pertusus;* Twining, *Volubilis.*[68]   For one thing,
the English terms were awkward, having no systematic structural
formation, but the chief objection to their use, I should think,
would be that they were too familiar, and not unmistakably
attached to some specialized meaning.   Martyn, therefore, preferred *fascicle* to *bundle, viscid* to *clammy, coriaceous* to *leathery,* and
crenate to *notched.*[69]
    Problems like these faced scientists in all fields of study, and
particularly when they were interested in writing for a wide
audience and in the periods when the investigations of science
could be followed by anyone with a moderate amount of learning.   For the use of vernacular or Latin terms was closely involved with considerations of style.   But the style of scientific
prose was affected not merely by the nature of individual terms,
the names of things and the epithets used to describe them.   It
was also qualified by the use of phrases, particularly phrases of
definition, and these play an especially important part in deter-
mining the scientific way of writing.   Accordingly, before more
general considerations of style may be taken up, it is proper to
study the methods by which many of these phrases were formed.
    There are, as we have seen, various processes by which the
meaning of a common term is fixed so that it becomes a technical
term.   Old words are earmarked for special use and new words

[66]*Language of Botany* xv.
[67]*Ibid.* xv.
[68]*Ibid.* xv–xvii.
[69]*Ibid.* xviii.   Martyn further advised against the use of similar English terms
on pp. xx–xxi.

are constructed. These processes are important to all science, but they were first developed systematically by Linnaeus in botany. He, it seems, was the first to apply thoroughly the idea that the principles underlying the formation of a terminology are exactly those which belong to science itself. The nature of the problem and the way it was solved may be clearly observed in Whewell's description:

The stalks, leaves, flowers, and fruits of vegetables, with their appendages, may vary in so many ways, that common language is quite insufficient to express clearly and precisely their resemblances and differences. Hence botany required not only a fixed system of *names* of plants, but also an artificial system of phrases fitted to *describe* their parts: not only a *Nomenclature*, but also a *Terminology*. The Terminology was, in fact, an Instrument indispensably requisite in giving fixity to the Nomenclature. The recognition of the kinds of plants must depend upon the exact comparison of their resemblances and differences; and to become a part of permanent science, this comparison must be recorded in words.[70]

Once the details of observation have been collected, they must be classified in a systematic way, and the basis of the system is a comparison of resemblances and differences. Linnaeus discovered the simplest method of reference to this large body of knowledge, "designating each kind of plant by a *binary* term consisting of the name of the *genus* combined with that of the *species*."[71] Furthermore, as Whewell observed:

The formation of a good descriptive language is, in fact, an inductive process of the same kind as those which we have already noticed in the progress of natural history. It requires the *discovery of fixed characters*, which discovery is to be marked and fixed, like other inductive steps, by appropriate *technical terms*. The characters must be so far fixed, that the things which they connect must have a more permanent and real association than the things which they leave unconnected.[72]

By such methods a nomenclature may be constructed which is both accurate and perfectly indicative of a scheme of classification which has previously been formed. But the result may be a phrase of many more than two terms, if it is to distinguish each species from all others in all respects. Even were this allowable, and not too bulky, such a phrase should be a complete and exact definition, which is in many instances not to be looked for. Descriptive phrases ought rather to represent types than be ex-

[70]*The Philosophy of the Inductive Sciences* (London, 1840), I. lxi.
[71]*Ibid*. I. lxii.
[72]*History of the Inductive Sciences* II. 391.

haustive definitions.   When this becomes the aim, it is possible
to construct a phrase with only two terms.   For example, until
Linnaeus what we call *Rosa alpina* was known as *rosa campestris,
spinis carens, biflora.*[73]   Linnaeus discovered the value of a trivial
name to comprehend all distinctive qualities and so indicate
the species.

Though Aristotle and Theophrastus had not worked out
schemes of classification in ways completely acceptable to modern scientists or created terminologies as satisfactory as the Linnaean, they nevertheless did apply the principle of classification
to the animal and the vegetable worlds.   And in Aristotle, for
example, there are many classes of animals singled out and
classified by a two-word phrase such as τὸ πτερωτὸν γένος
("the feathered kind"),[74] which, as a phrase, distinguishes the
class quite adequately because, "while other animals are some
hairy, some scaly, some covered with scaly plates, birds alone
are feathered."[75]   The process of forming such phrases was well
understood in the sixteenth and seventeenth centuries, though
not in the context of thought supplied by Linnaeus.   Here is a
group of similar terms occurring under the chapter heading "*De
Divisionibus animalium irrationalium*":

> Quædam dicuntur *animalia volatilia*, ut aves: quædam *natatilia*, ut pisces
> . . . . Quædam sunt *aërea*, quæ degunt in aêre, ut aves: quædam *aquea*, ut
> pisces . . . . Quædam animalia *diligunt societatem*, & gregatim incedunt, ut
> cervi, cameli & quædam verò *fugiunt societatem*, ut aves uncis unguibus . . . .
> Quædam sunt *animalia domestica*, ut mulus, capra, vacca, canis, &c. quædam
> vero *sylvestria*, ut Elephas, Lepus, Camelius, &c.[76]

Terminology of this sort, however unstable, bears reference to
various schemes of classification, and the terms are comparable
to those general use has appropriated for certain animals,
whereby we easily understand that the *timid* beast is a rabbit,
the *roaring* one a lion, the *hairy* one a goat.[77]   A more comprehensive scheme of classification may be observed in the work of

[73]Whewell, *History of the Inductive Sciences* I. 392.
[74]See above, p. 32.
[75]*On the Parts of Animals*, ed. W. Ogle (London, 1882), 130 (Bk. IV, chap. 12).
[76]Wolfgang Franzius, *Historia Animalium Sacra* (Leyden, 1624), 28.
[77]Comenius' picture book of 1658 gives any number of these standard epithets
as they were applied to animals and other objects.   His phrasing was Latin, but
it should also be instructive to quote from the English translation (from the edition

a French botanist of the eighteenth century who used terms of particular interest to readers of poetry:

Plus une Métode a de Classes, moins elle a d'Ordres, de Sections ou de sub-divisions; elle n'en a comunément que de 3 sortes, savoir des Classes, des Genres & des Espèces; & moins elle en a, plus elle est parfaite & facile. Moins au contraire une Métode a de Classes, plus elle a d'Ordres de divisions sub-alternes, qui vont quelquefois jusqu'au nombre de 8, savoir 1° Classes ou Parties, 2° Légions, 3° Falanjes, 4° Centuries, 5° Cohortes, 6° Ordres ou Sec-tions, 7° Genres, 8° Espèces.[78]

The final factor to be considered in the study of the growth of a scientific terminology is the importance given to the style of their writing by the scientists, for the acceptability of many

---

of 1727). The Arabic numbers refer to the features of the picture which are singled out for description.

"In the *Earth* are	"In *Terra* sunt
high *Mountains*, 1.	Alti *Montes*, 1.
Deep *Vallies*, 2.	Profundæ *valles*, 2.
Hills rising, 3.	Elevati Colles, 3.
Hollow Caves, 4.	cavæ Speluncæ, 4.
Plain *Fields*, 5.	Plani *campi*, 5.
Shady *Woods*, 6.	Opacæ Sylvæ, 6."

—*The Orbis Pictus*, ed. C. W. Bardeen (Syracuse, 1887), 13.

"The spotted *Panther*, 2.	"Maculosus, *Pardo* (Panthera) 2.
The *Tyger*, 3.	*Tygris*, 3.
the cruellest of all.	immanissima omnium.
The Shaggy *Bear*, 4.	Villosus *Ursus*, 4.
The ravenous *Wolf*, 5.	Rapax *Lupus*, 5.
The quick sighted *Ounce*,	*Lynx*, 6. visu pollens,
6. The tayled *fox*, 7.	Caudata *Vulpes*, 7.
the craftiest of all	astutissima *omnium*.
The *Hedge-hog*, 8.	*Erinaceus*, 8.
is prickly.	est aculeatus." —*Ibid.* 36–7.

[78]Michel Adanson, *Famille des Plantes* (Paris, 1763), I. cvi. This author re-marked a little earlier, "Les Genres sont . . . un Ouvraje des modernes, &, par ainsi dire, de notre siécle."—*Ibid.* I. civ. Whewell commented on this terminology: "But the most received series is *Classes, Orders, Genera,* and *Species;* in which, how-ever, we often have other terms interpolated, as *Sub-genera,* or Sections of genera. The expressions *Family* and *Tribe,* are commonly appropriated to natural groups; and we speak of the Vegetable, Animal, Mineral *Kingdom;* but the other meta-phors of Provinces, Districts, &c., which this suggests, have not been commonly used."—*Philosophy of the Inductive Sciences* I. 486.

It should be observed that some of these military terms were applied to fish in ancient scientific writing. Aelian mentioned fishes traveling in ἴλας, φάλαγγας, λόχους ("squadrons, phalanxes, legions") (*De Natura Animalium Libri XVII,* ed. Abraham Gronovius [Basel, 1774], ix. 53). A. W. Mair used this reference in commenting on Oppian's similar terminology—see *Halieutica* I. 438–45, in *Oppian, Colluthus, Tryphiodorus* (LCL) (1928).

terms depends upon stylistic considerations of a more general
nature than those hitherto considered. And the existence of
ancient models exerts still another kind of influence in these
matters.

The success of this or that terminology depends upon the
adequacy of the scheme of classification it expresses. The fact
that John Ray and Linnaeus used terms also found in Aristotle
means that Aristotle's scheme of classification was good in many
respects, that his terminology was adequate, and that there was
no reason why it should not be used with reference to improved
schemes of classification. The methods of forming certain
phrases in antiquity and in the modern period were inductive,
and when the phrases were not identical they nevertheless were
of a similar nature grammatically, and so similarly influenced
the style of scientific prose.

There are unquestionably many other factors affecting the
methods of writing scientific description, and they vary, of course,
with the subject matter and with individual writers. Those
which have been pointed out are of general importance. There
remains to discuss briefly one further consideration of use in
studying the relationship of scientific and poetic language in the
seventeenth and eighteenth centuries, particularly. This has to
do with the desire of scientists to write pleasingly and gracefully.

It is first of all to be remarked that at this time the investigations of science were not recorded in highly technical periodi-
cals of the modern sort. Even the advanced publications were
in many respects amateurish, and there were besides all sorts of
books and pamphlets—almanacs, herbals, medical handbooks—
written for the "popular" audience. Most of the writings on
mathematical subjects and some of those on optics and anatomy
were quite beyond the grasp of the layman, and some of the
alchemical writings were highly complex. But almost everything else of a scientific nature might have been read under-
standingly by any interested person. Some of the reasons for
this may be seen in observing the conditions under which essays
were printed in the *Philosophical Transactions* of the Royal Society
for some years after its founding in the middle seventeenth
century.

The Society began in the association of a few gentlemen of
similar tastes at Gresham College. As its activities increased,

members or friends began sending in communications concerning some recent experiments they had been making, or other matters of interest, very often in the form of letters. A gentleman in one county would write to another of a certain strange meteor, shall we say. Then, for one reason or another, whether the friend thought the communication interesting or whether the writer himself thought it important, the description of the event would be sent on to Oldenburg, or whoever was acting as the secretary of the Society. If the letter interested him, it would be printed in the *Transactions*, with its style unchanged and only the personal greetings omitted. The style of these letters was not recondite. Occasionally it had a kind of easy formality, at other times it was homely. The writers were primarily educated men, by their own lights, and only secondarily what we nowadays should call scientists.[79] At their best they wrote like Galileo, in dialogues of considerable polish and charm, or like Boyle, who presented the argument of *The Sceptical Chymist* as the discussion of a group of friends sitting in a garden. Many might have expressed their aims as Harvey did, hoping that by their industry "profit... might... accrew to the republick of literature."[80] Walter Charleton, however, apparently meant to express his opinions less ambitiously or else despaired of attaining any rhetorical excellence:

I put them into a dress of *Language* so plain and familiar, as may alone evince, my design was to write of this Argument, neither as an Orator, nor as a Moral Philosopher; but only as a *Natural* one, conversant in *Pathology* and that too, more for his own private satisfaction, than the instruction of others.[81]

Familiarity and simplicity were important to many naturalists as they considered the problems of writing. A sixteenth-century editor of Seneca advised students of natural science who were to write in Latin to choose terms that were not merely intelligible, but that could be easily spoken.[82] Robert Plot thought a familiar language might be trusted to explain the very nature of things by virtue of its simplicity:

[79]The word *scientist* was coined in 1840 by Whewell (*New English Dictionary*).

[80]*The Anatomical Exercises*, translator unknown, ed. Geoffrey Keynes (London: Nonesuch Press, 1928), 18.

[81]*Natural History of the Passions* (London, 1674), A₅.

[82]J. L. Strebaeus, in the preface to *Naturalium Quæstionum ad Lucilium libri septem*, ed. Matthew Fortunatus, Erasmus, and Strebaeus (Paris, 1540), Aᵢib.

And these [descriptions] I intend to deliver as succinctly as may be, in a plain, easie, unartificial Stile, studiously avoiding all ornaments of Language, it being my purpose to treat of Things, and therefore would have the Reader expect nothing less then Words . . . .[83]

The scientists of these centuries were, after all, men educated in the humanist tradition, and even as "plain speakers" they were in a manner compelled to model themselves upon ancient writers. Much of their work was in the assimilation of ancient thought, and much of their writing could only be in borrowed language.[84] Whether their field of investigation was medicine or natural history, it might be expected that they paid particular attention to Galen or Pliny, but in the establishment of their language and their style, writing in Latin or the vernacular, it is probable that they did not think of themselves as scientists writing. They may have considered themselves philosophers or essayists or even naturalists, but as such they were men of letters.[85] Accordingly, however pressing the necessity to establish scientific terminologies, there was probably no desire to establish a purely scientific language or a scientific style. Plainness and simplicity may have been judged desirable, and Sprat's manifesto is clear enough,[86] but it must be emphasized that the tendency was away from the esoteric. This had been true of ancient science, and it remained true of modern as long as the state of knowledge permitted. And modern writers might have been very content to study Pliny, or model their vernacular style after his, assured that he provided a safe guide for the needs

[83]*Natural History of Oxford-shire* 2.

[84]See, for illuminating examples, Léon-Henri-Marie Carleer, *Examen des Principales Classifications Adoptées par les Zoologistes* (Brussels, 1861).

[85]The curriculum of the schools would also have been important in the establishment of literary style, and Mr. Foster Watson's comment on the teaching of natural history in the middle seventeenth century is of interest here: ". . . the religiously-minded schoolmasters, and they were a much more important element than is ordinarily supposed, would draw their notions of animals, not from the progressive zoological writers, such as they were, nor from the old mediaeval sources, but from Du Bartas's *Première Semaine ou Creation du Monde*, or John Swan's *Speculum Mundi*, 1635."—*The Beginnings of the Teaching of Modern Subjects in England* (London, 1909), 192–3. (Swan's work has been shown to be more than half a compilation from Du Bartas—see W. R. Abbot, *Studies in the Influence of Du Bartas in England, 1548–1641*, MS thesis [1931] in the library of the University of North Carolina, pp. 105–19.) This of course should be compared with the sort of reading Milton set his pupils, which included Columella, Manilius, Aratus, and Lucretius (see *The Student's Milton*, ed. Frank A. Patterson [New York: F. S. Crofts, 1934], xxiii).

[86]*History of the Royal-Society* (1702) 41–2.

of communication. Even a translator of poetry, Christopher Wase, recognized the value of that source:

The advancement of experience do's necessarily propagate new words; therefore *Pliny*, who hath written the History of Nature, must needs contain a lucid catalogue of words, and is undoubtedly the best Dictionary, or to speak more modernely, the best *Janua linguæ Latinæ*.[87]

As for those who preferred the vernacular, their theories often demanded that all imported words be abolished from writing, since they weakened the native style.[88] Furetière's doctrine was the counsel of idealism:

Les termes des Arts et des Sciences sont tellement engagés avec les mots communs de la Langue, qu'il n'est pas plus aisé de les séparer que les eaux de deux rivières à quelque distance de leur confluent.[89]

So far have modern writers deserted the idea of excellent writing in technical treatises, that now we are likely to accept only those technical terms which do not appear English, and what is easy to read is suspect.

*
* *

It is in these various ways, then, that it is possible to provide

---

[87]*Grati Falisci Cynegeticon. Or, A Poem of Hunting . . . . Englished and Illustrated* by Christopher Wase (London, 1654), b₃.

[88]See, for example, Nathaniel Fairfax, *A Treatise of the Bulk and Selvedge of the World* (London, 1674), b₆–b₇b: "And in earnest, if the knack of borrowing, or robbing and pilfering rather, gets but a little further ground amongst us, at the scantling it has done hitherto, it will in time to come be harder for an Englishman to speak his own tongue without mingling others with it, than to speak a medly of sundry others without bringing in his own . . . . And inasmuch as that *Fellowship* of *Worthies* in *London*, who are now embodied under the name of *Royal*, have given us already so many new things, and are daily starting more, neither named nor known by those before us; and for the enriching of the *English* tongue, as well as fulfilling of *Englands* stores, have thought fit their discoveries should almost wholly come abroad in our own Speech, as they are happily made in our own Land: I think it will well become those of us, who have a more hearty love for what is our own than wanton longings after what is others, to take light and life from such happy beginnings, and either to fetch back some of our own words, that have been justled out in wrong that worse from elsewhere might be hoisted in, or else to call in from the fields and waters, shops and work-housen, from the inbred stock of more homely women and less filching Thorpsmen, that well-fraught world of words that answers works, by which all Learners are taught to do, and not to make a Clatter . . . ." I am indebted for this reference to F. W. Bateson, *English Poetry and the English Language* (Oxford: Clarendon Press, 1934), 53.

[89]Antoine Furetière ("*Fact.* I, 20") as quoted by Brunot, *Histoire de la Langue Française*, t. IV, Ière partie, p. 430.

some explanation for the use in poetry of the vocabulàry of science. When we understand something of the method by which words and phrases are formed for the purposes of scientific description, we become able to determine that similar purposes in poetic description may be fulfilled similarly. And the continuity of scientific language is still another fact of immediate relevance to any consideration of a stable poetic language in matters of natural description. For the language of science was relatively stable over so many centuries because the increase of knowledge had not in that time caused the overthrow of many basic concepts. Though immense gains in both knowledge and theory were made in the sixteenth and seventeenth centuries, many ideas remained as significant to the members of the Royal Society as they had been to Greek scientists. These were concepts of great philosophic interest, important to theologians and poets as well as physicists, ideas concerning the nature of creation and the laws of matter. It was the relative stability of many of these concepts that accounts for the stability of the language used to express them, and for the use of common elements of that language in both poetry and prose.

And so, before much can be made of the use of identical terms and similar phrases in verse and scientific prose, some study must be given to a few concepts important to any philosophy of nature. In this way it will become possible to understand more clearly the value of a stable language for science and poetry.

CHAPTER IV

Stability and Change in the Language
of Natural Philosophy

SINCE scientific knowledge is carried from one generation to another largely by means of written records, the terminology employed should be as nearly fixed as possible. Yet, as new theories are constructed and others modified or done away with, and as knowledge is increased, many of the terms that survive suffer important changes of meaning. Some of the stability of a fixed terminology, we may judge, is illusory, yet it has often been thought better that the same term be used in a different sense than that an entirely new term be adopted.

Epicurus, for example, used the word στοιχεῖον to signify one of the four material elements of the universe, and the word *element* was taken by Lucretius as the synonym. That word came over into English, and in 1600 we may find William Gilbert using it in the same sense. Seventeenth-century alchemists, however, made it signify something quite distinct from the material substance of earth, air, fire, and water; for them it referred to the four "principles" of the universe. And at present, of course, it is used with reference to the ninety-odd forms of matter. *Aether* is another word that has remained in constant use with many different meanings—the Homeric one of a lofty region of the sky, the Cartesian one of an aerial fluid, and the modern one of a drug, to mention only a few. These two words are enough to show how the same terms bear witness by their very use to profound changes of meaning. They continue to be employed because they provide a reminder of variations of meaning as well as continuity.

It is obvious that changes of meaning of this sort arose from the development of new and different schemes of thought. By the very nature of change, new meanings are but variations of old ones, and wide difference of meaning came about in most

49

instances, I should think, only gradually. Moreover, we may generally assume that whenever an important term was first used in a new sense it was provided with an explanatory context to distinguish it. Descartes, for example, using the word *aether* in speculating on the nature of sound, is obliged to make clear how the meaning he attaches to the term is different from that of others. His use of the word, in fact, must take account of all the important meanings attached to it by earlier philosophy, but particularly those that were relevant to acoustical theory. The scientist, then, according to the nature of his work, uses old words in authorized meanings, or makes old words new, or coins new ones. But when he uses an old word in a sense which is different from that of its established use, he must indicate the circumstances under which he changes its meaning.

The reader's problem is often difficult. If he happens upon the word *aether* in reading Descartes he may discover from the immediate context that it names a tenuous, fluid, pervasive substance, but he may not know if aether has still other qualities. He may not know if it is a kind of air or fire or even a liquid. He may not know whether or not it is an element, or how it is distinguished from the four elements. Nor may he know why this Greek word rather than some other was chosen. All these things can be made known to him only by a systematic reading of Descartes, and by the study of theories Descartes made use of. Ultimately, in order to understand fully the significance of this concept in Descartes's thought, it will be necessary for the reader to review theories in which *aether* represents a kind of fire, the life-giving breath, a rarefied part of the atmosphere, and so on. A modern reader might also find it useful to define Descartes's notion in the light of subsequent speculation on magnetism and interstellar space. Which is to say that any one meaning of an important term may be clarified by reference to its other meanings, and by reference to the theories which establish those meanings.

Terms of a scientific sort are accordingly meaningful in reference to a system of concepts which have been formed to explain the nature of the physical universe. And since changes of meaning come with changes of systems and philosophies, the ideal scientific term would supply an exact reference to the particular

scheme of thought and ultimately the philosophy which authorized its use in a particular context.   And unless it represents a
completely new concept, it should be a word whose latest sense
is controlled by its former senses, and it should be used in such
a way that it will be adaptable to still other variations of meaning.   That is, whatever *aether* may mean to Anaxagoras or
Descartes, in its special connotations, to them and to all others
it must signify a tenuous substance something like air only
thinner.[1]

Thus, in considering the growth of scientific language we are
not merely studying changes in the meanings of individual words,
but we are also studying systems of the universe.   It thus comes
about that we study *groups* of words, collections of terms relating
to each other by virtue of the conceived relationship between
the things they name.   *Aether* must be defined in terms of *elements*.   The *elements* of the physical universe are related to the
humors of the body.   The *microcosm* is thus compared with the
macrocosm, and *aether* is compared with the *vital* breath of man.
When the idea is accepted of a world broken into component
parts, or *elements*, there is formed the idea of the *attraction* and
repulsion of bodies, or of love and strife in chaos.   Then it becomes necessary to entertain notions of harmony and discord,
of motion and of a prime mover, and so of purpose.   Thus,
Thales and Boyle, once they have undertaken to study the nature of elements, are soon involved in questions concerning the
purpose of the world.   And the modern reader, observing their
uses of the word *element*, understands those uses properly only
when he is acquainted with the writers' philosophies.

This might mean that a student of the past needs to examine
the philosophies of all important thinkers with great thoroughness
if he is to master a special terminology through all its history.

[1]The problem for the modern reader of ancient science is a little more difficult
when he comes across terms that seem perfectly familiar.   The phrase, *the middle
region of the air*, for example, might ordinarily be taken to mean some part of the
atmosphere halfway between here and the stars.   This it might signify to both
seventeenth-century and modern readers.   But to many in the earlier period it also
stood for a thick air full of vapors which engendered rain and snow and lightning.
It is easy to see how that phrase might survive several centuries, losing its special
meaning and retaining its general one.   And the modern reader might be ignorantly
satisfied with attaching only the general meaning to a seventeenth-century use
which actually included much more.

That task need not be undertaken at this place, for the present problem of the relation of scientific and poetic language may be sufficiently illuminated by a brief review of a few important and rather stable concepts. When it is recalled that, until the present mathematical explanation of the universe by physical science, the basic concepts of the origin and nature of the universe were comparatively stable, a brief paraphrase of these concepts may prove acceptable. For all that is needed is to show how this stability of theory explains the survival and valid use of so many scientific terms for more than twenty centuries.

*

* *

One of the most familiar concepts of all speculation is that bodies are made up of constituent parts. Both the Egyptians and the Greeks reasoned that all natural bodies were composed of some combination among the four primary elements, earth, air, fire, and water. These four elements were judged primary through observation of the basic qualities of matter. The moisture of a liquid was due to the presence of water as one of its constituents. Fire was an element of any compound in which heat was determined to reside. And so on. "For every body is either hot or cold, moist or dry; and by combining these qualities in all possible ways, men devised four elementary substances."[2] Aristotle used this reasoning, borrowing it from the Pythagoreans.[3] Some philosophers made one of the elements the original form of the others—for Thales the primary element was water, for Anaximenes air, for Heracleitus fire. From such speculation arose theories concerning the single nature of all things, as opposed to the more widespread doctrine of the contrarieties of elements.

But whether matter was considered reducible to one or four fundamental forms, it was always necessary to account for the existence of the universe in some even temporarily stable condition. This was done, of course, by means of the theory that the antagonisms and affinities of bodies were resolved in balance or harmony, or by the theory that all things were part of an

[2]William Whewell, *The Philosophy of the Inductive Sciences* (London, 1840), I. 363.

[3]W. C. D. Dampier-Whetham, *A History of Science and Its Relations with Philosophy and Religion* (New York: Macmillan, 1931), 37.

ever-changing flux. Pliny's description of the activities of the elements adequately represents the reasoning of those who held the first theory:

I neither see any doubt made as touching the elements, That they bee foure in number. The highest, Fire: from whence are those bright eies of so many shining starres. The next, Spirit, which the Greekes and our countrimen by one name called Aire: Vitall this element is, and as it giveth life to all things, so it soone passeth through all, and is intermedled in the whole: by the power whereof, the Earth hangeth poised and ballanced just in the middest, together with the fourth element, of the Waters. Thus by a mutuall intertainement one of another, diverse natures are linked and knit together: so as the light elements are kept in and restrained by certaine weights of the heavier, that they flie not out: and contrariwise, the massier bee held up, that they fall not downe, by meanes of the lighter which covet to be aloft. So, through an equall endevor to the contrarie, each of them hold their owne, bound as it were by the restlesse circuit of the very world . . . .[4]

The most famous conception of the flux was that developed by Heracleitus, according to whom:

Nothing is either this or that, but everything is becoming. This perpetual becoming has its source in the vital fire, which is transformed into all things and which is perpetually one and many at the same time . . . . It was on the ground of experience that he based his affirmation of the union of contraries. The changes which transform fire into water, then into earth, form the up-road. The changes which inversely transform earth into water, then into fire, are called the down-road. Thus between the earth and the sky there is a perpetual exchange of effluxes following a double way, ascending and descending. From the earth and sea arise effluxes, some dry, others moist. The former are of an igneous nature, they are collected in the hollow basins which constitute the heavenly bodies, at the moment when these rise on the horizon; they then ignite to become extinguished when setting, giving a residuum of water. The damp effluxes, by their mixture with the dry ones, form an atmospheric air, which extends to the moon, whence the water falls back either as rain, or frozen in the form of snow. The various proportions of the dry and moist effluxes determine the vicissitude of days and nights, months and seasons. In winter, for example, the sun in its course is lower on the horizon, and it causes a greater evaporation of the damp layers near the earth, hence the aqueous element threatens to predominate and to completely extinguish the sun, and this is why the sun must return to the north to find there new sustenance.[5]

Pervading most theories of elemental composition, struggle, and harmony was the notion that the activity of the elements

[4]Philemon Holland, *The Historie of the World. Commonly called, The Naturall Historie of C. Plinius Secundus* (London, 1601), I. 2 (Bk. II, chap. v).

[5]Arnold Reymond, *History of the Sciences in Greco-Roman Antiquity*, trans. Ruth Gheury de Bray (New York: E. P. Dutton, n.d.), 30–1.

was directed by some informing purpose. This purpose could be perceived in even the most objective analyses, and it is important for us to observe several of the various ways in which philosophers supposed it to be operating. Here, for example, is the Empedoclean notion:

These elements have natural attractions or repulsions for each other which cause them to combine or to separate. They float in two surrounding media, which are love and hatred. These media, although invisible to the senses, are material forces just like the ether of the physicists. They act indifferently on all bodies. Love, for example, has the effect of uniting elements whose natural affinities do not impel them to unite; hatred, on the contrary, separates the bodies which are naturally inclined to combine . . . . In the beginning the four elements formed a harmonious spherical whole, entirely enveloped by love; around the universe thus constituted extended the finite medium of hatred.[6]

Seneca's version is important and interesting:

The Egyptians made foure elements, and then of euery one of them two male and female. They suppose the aire to bee the male because it is winde, female because it is obscure and still. [They call the sea manly water, every other kind of water they call womanly.] They call fire masculine, because it burneth with a flame; feminine, because it shineth without hurting by touching. The stronger earth they call male, as for example, stones, and rocks: they assigne the name of female to that which is manuable and fit to be employed.[7]

The emphasis of most ancient writers was inevitably teleological, and though this was in part superstitious it was also the result of a reasonable effort to account for the vital force in things.[8] For it was natural to suppose that, since the elements

---

[6]Reymond, *History of the Sciences in Greco-Roman Antiquity* 40–1.

[7]*The Workes* . . . , *Both Morrall and Natural*, trans. Thomas Lodge (London, 1614), 813 (Bk. III, chap. xiv). The part in brackets is supplied from *Physical Science in the Time of Nero, Being a Translation of the Quaestiones Naturales*, John Clarke (London, 1910), 125.

[8]See Clara Camenzind, *Die antike und moderne Auffassung vom Naturgeschehen mit besonderer Berücksichtigung der mittelalterlichen Impetustheorie* (Langensalza: Hermann Beyer, 1926), 9: "Wollen wir das Wirken in der Natur im Sinne der antiken Auffassung uns verständlich machen, so müssen wir von der Voraussetzung ausgehen, dass jeder Körper mit einer besonderen, nach Zielen strebenden Lebenskraft begabt sei. Es ist daher mehr oder weniger alles, was in der Natur geschieht, ein vernunftiges Geschehen. Nicht nur die Handlungen der Menschen, auch jeder Vorgang in der Natur—selbst das Fallen eines Steines—scheint auf ein bestimmtes Ziel gerichtet zu sein. Ist das Ziel erreicht, so strebt der Körper nicht mehr weiter; er verharrt ruhig da, wo er seiner Schwere oder Leichtigkeit entsprechend ruhen kann. Diesem Prinzip gemäss sucht jeder schwere Körper die im Mittelpunkt der Welt ruhende Erde zu erreichen, das Leichte dagegen die äussersten Grenzen der Peripherie."

were the basis of matter, they were also the basis of life. They were the substance from which all things were created, and from which they were thereafter fed (*Elementa quasi Alimenta*).[9] They were accordingly conceived as spiritual principles or as material seeds or atoms. For Aristotle each element was πανσπερμία.[10] Henry Power, writing in 1664, had a similar conception:

... we doe believe that they [spirits] are universally diffused throughout all Bodies in the World, and that Nature at first created this ætherial substance or subtle particles, and diffused them through-out the Universe, to give fermentation and concretion to Minerals; vegetation and maturation to Plants; life, sense, and motion to Animals; And indeed, to be the main (though invisible) Agent in all Natures three Kingdoms Mineral, Vegetal, and Animal.[11]

The atomic elements of Epicurus and Lucretius were called σπέρματα and *semina*.[12] For certain alchemists they were the "wombs" in which the seeds of things come to fruition.[13] Paracelsus knew them as "souls."[14]

It was with the help of conceptions like these that the doctrine of "native elements" was developed. This might have been summarized in the propositions that the earth is the matrix of minerals, stones, and animals; the air of meteors; the water of fish; the fire of igneous meteors.[15] There was not always agreement, of course, upon the matrix of this or that creature, there were often fundamental disagreements, but the conception itself was almost universal. It is accordingly necessary to show something of the extraordinary detail with which this idea was worked out. Lambert Daneau, as one example, may be quoted for the opinion of certain church fathers on the composition of fish:

Concretio aquæ in producendis Piscibus statim ad Dei vocem, & iussum facta est. Ergo aqua ita constricta, incrassata, vel potius firmiter coagulata est,

---

[9]Johann Amos Comenius, *Naturall Philosophie Reformed by Divine Light: or, A Synopsis of Physicks* (London, 1651), 85.

[10]*De Generatione et Corruptione* 314a29, in *Opera*, ed. U. C. Bussemaker, Fred Dübner, and Emil Heitz (Paris, 1848–74), II. 432.

[11]*Experimental Philosophy* (London, 1664), 61.

[12]See Katharine C. Reiley, *Studies in the Philosophical Terminology of Lucretius and Cicero* (New York, 1909), 39–40.

[13]Oswald Croll, *Philosophy Reformed & Improved in Four Profound Tractates. The I. Discovering the Great and Deep Mysteries of Nature*, trans. H. Pinnell (London, 1657), 96.

[14]*Three Books of Philosophy Written to the Athenians*, trans. H. Pinnell(London, 1657), 33, paginated separately in the volume *Philosophy Reformed & Improved in Four Profound Tractates*—see footnote 13, above.

[15]See Johannes-Henricus Alsted, *Encyclopædia* (Hessen-Nassau, 1630), 677; and Comenius, *Naturall Philosophie Reformed* 71–2.

vt corpus piscium solidum, ac tenax ex aquis fieret humidum illud quidem, & frigidum vi, effectu, qualitate: sedtamen consistentia, & ὑποστάσει sua firmum, & bene compactum. Quod Dominus postea ita temperauit, vt & calor naturalis in iis Animalibus inesset: & sensus quoque, & motus: adeò vt & respiratione, id est, refrigeratione, ac ventilatione egeant. Ergo vt rectè scripsit Ambrosius, Aqua, & Pisces sunt eiusdem inter se generis, & materiæ. Id quod & Medici docent, & ipsa Piscium natura, qui extra aquas, statim putrescunt, ac moriuntur, velut à propria natura, & matrice auulsi, vt est Is. 50. vers. 2. Denique cibus ipse & victus ex piscium esu frequens nostram sententiam confirmat. Itaque frigidi pisces in loco frigido, nempe Aquis, sunt à Deo collocati propter naturæ similitudinem, & cognationem: & vt esset quædam proportio inter locum, & locatum.[16]

William Gilbert described the origin of metals in a similar way, and in language which is quite significant to the present study:

Latent enim in tellure metallorum & lapidum abdita primordia, vt in peripheria, herbarum & stirpium. Terra enim ex profundo puteo eruta, vbi nulla suspicio concepti seminis esse videatur, si in altissima turri posita fuerit, herbam producit virentem, & iniussa gramina, Sole & cœlo terræ incubantibus; atque illa quidem quæ in illa regione sunt spontanea; suas enim vnaquæque regio herbas producit, & stirpes, sua etiam metalla.[17]

It is the theory of native elements that accounts for the use of certain epithets:

All that is comprehended of flesh and of spirit of life and so of body and soul is called animal—a beast—whether it be airy as fowls that fly, or watery as fish that swim, or earthy as beasts that go on the ground and in fields, as men and beasts, wild and tame, or other that creep and glide on the ground.[18]

The doctrine of native elements was also used to oppose the idea of spontaneous generation:

That God almighty did at first create the Seeds of all Animals, (that is, the Animals themselves in little) and dispers'd them over the superficial Part of the Land and Water, giving Power to those Elements to hatch and bring them forth; which when they had done, and all the Animals of these created Seeds were produced and perfected, there remained no more Ability in them to bring forth any more; but all the succeeding owe their Original to Generation.[19]

---

[16]Lambert Daneau, *Physices Christianæ Pars Altera; Sive De Rervm Creatarvm Natvra* (4th ed.; Geneva, 1606), 202–3.

[17]*De Magnete* (1600), facsimile published by Mayer and Müller (Berlin, 1892), 21.

[18]Bartholomeus Anglicus, *De Proprietatibus Rerum*, trans. J. Trevisa (London, 1535), Bk. XVIII, chap. i. Quoted from H. W. Seager's *Natural History in Shakespeare's Time* (London, 1896), 8. For a fuller exposition of this idea see below, pp. 149–56.

[19]John Ray, *Three Physico-Theological Discourses* (4th ed.; London, 1721), 45.

We may thus see coming into focus the picture of a world of elements, attaining some kind of balance from time to time in accordance with the teleological forces which control their activities, and it is to these primary elements that living creatures owe their existence. What needs yet to be explained, however, is the presence of a vital force in this scheme of things, its origin, and the method of its operation. If we can get an adequate idea of this, we shall be able to understand the nature of the relationship which was thought to exist between living creatures and the four elements, between the microcosm and the macrocosm.

Perhaps the most ancient notion explaining the vital force is that in which all natural processes are considered to be the result of the marriage of the elements. Aristotle gave Anaxagoras credit for the belief that the earth was the mother of plants and the sun the father.[20] But the basic idea (originally Oriental) had been worked out much more fully by the Egyptians, and the etiological discussion of Isis and Osiris which we find in Diodorus of Sicily is well worth studying:

These two gods, they hold, regulate the entire universe, giving both nourishment and increase to all things by means of a system of three seasons which complete the full cycle through an unobservable movement, these being spring and summer and winter; and these seasons, though in nature most opposed to one another, complete the cycle of the year in the fullest harmony. Moreover, practically all the physical matter which is essential to the generation of all things is furnished by these gods, the sun contributing the fiery element and the spirit, the moon the wet and the dry, and both together the air; and it is through these elements that all things are engendered and nourished. And so it is out of the sun and moon that the whole physical body of the universe is made complete; and as for the five parts just named of these bodies— the spirit, the fire, the dry, as well as the wet, and lastly, the air-like—just as in the case of a man we enumerate head and hands and feet and the other parts, so in the same way the body of the universe is composed in its entirety of these parts.

Each of these parts they regard as a god and to each of them the first men in Egypt to use articulate speech gave a distinct name appropriate to its nature. Now the spirit they called, as we translate their expression, Zeus, and since he was the source of the spirit of life in animals they considered him to be in a sense the father of all things. And they say that the most renowned of the Greek poets also agrees with this when he speaks of this god as

The father of men and of gods.

---

[20]*De Planctis* 817a27, in *Opera* IV. 21.

The fire they called Hephaestus, as it is translated, holding him to be a great god and one who contributes much both to the birth and full development of all things. The earth, again, they looked upon as a kind of vessel which holds all growing things and so gave it the name "mother"; and in like manner the Greeks also call it Demeter, the word having been slightly changed in the course of time; for in olden times they called her Ge Meter (Earth Mother), to which Orpheus bears witness when he speaks of

> Earth the Mother of all, Demeter giver of wealth.

And the wet according to them, was called by the men of old Oceanê, which, when translated, means Fostering-mother, though some of the Greeks have taken it to be Oceanus . . . .

The air, they say, they called Athena, as the name is translated, and they considered her to be the daughter of Zeus and conceived of her as a virgin, because of the fact that the air is by its nature uncorrupted and occupies the highest part of the universe; for the latter reason also the myth arose that she was born from the head of Zeus.[21]

Many of the resources of mythology were used in the development of the idea of the amorous heaven impregnating the earth, from whom are brought forth all the great gifts of sustenance.[22] Lucretius developed the idea magnificently, but the pedantic notions of the Stoics were of perhaps even greater influence. These philosophers handed down to the Middle Ages and later periods the notion of Jove as the life-giving fiery aether, Juno as the air, Neptune as the sea, Pan as nature, and so on.[23] Then there was the extraordinary conception of Kepler that the sun is God the Father, the sphere of the fixed stars is God the Son, and the aether, which is the medium of the sun's influence upon the planets, is the Holy Ghost.[24]

Another variation upon ideas of divine marriage as the explanation of the origin of things is the important conception found in Genesis of the bird of God brooding upon the waters. This notion was developed by St. Basil on the authority of a Syrian philosopher's reading of the text.[25] It was taken up

---

[21]*Diodorus of Sicily*, trans. C. H. Oldfather (LCL) (1933–5), I. 39–43.

[22]See Ernest Renan, "Paganism," in *The Greek Genius and Its Influence*, ed. Lane Cooper (New Haven, 1917), 263.

[23]Charles W. Lemmi, *The Classic Deities in Bacon, A Study in Mythological Symbolism* (Baltimore: Johns Hopkins Press, 1933), 10.

[24]See E. A. Burtt, *The Metaphysical Foundations of Modern Physical Science* (New York: Harcourt, Brace, 1927), 48.

[25]Jerome's reading of Genesis I. 2 is *ferebatur*. Basil took over the reading of the Syrian: "Aiebat igitur ille Syrorum linguam indicatiorem esse: & ob affinitatem quam habet cum hebraica lingua: sententias aliquo modo scripturarum magis attingere: Itaque talem huiusce dicti sententiam esse dicebat: Verbum hoc:

many times in the succeeding centuries,[26] most famously perhaps
in *Paradise Lost*, and it had a kind of correspondence with the
idea of a world soul as postulated by Aristotle.[27]
But however this vital force was thought to be infused, its
presence in nature was for many centuries one of the prime facts
to be faced by natural philosophy.   The frame of elements, in
flux or harmony, was the substance from which living things
were created, and the elements themselves were formed to support life, and were guided by the original creating force.   Such
reasoning was ultimately tested by the analogy of man as the

---

ferebatur: profouebat / uitalemque [ʒωτικήν] fecunditatem: aquarum nature
prebebat / sumunt / atque interpretantur incubantis auis effigie uimque uitalem
quandam imprimentis in ea quæ ab ipsa fouentur: Talem hanc uocem asserimus
sententiam indicare super aquas inquem spiritum dei ferre / idest ad fecunditatem uitalem aquæ naturam sanctum spem preparare."—*Hexameron*, trans.
Johannes Argyropolus (Rome, 1515), p. Xₐ₋ᵦ.

[26]See Lambert Daneau, *Physique Françoise* (Geneva, 1581), 122; Maury
Thibaut de Maisières, *Les Poèmes Inspirés du Début de la Genèse à l'Époque de la Renaissance* (Louvain: Librairie Universitaire, 1931), 20. A most interesting philosophical or scientific application of this figure or theory was made by Comenius
(*Naturall Philosophie Reformed* 45–6):

|"Motion
therefore
is of | Spirit }
Light } which is called the motion of | agitation.
diffusion. |

| | Matter
which is
caused
by | the fire and is called
the motion of | expansion.
contraction. |

| | | some
body | draw-
ing by | connaturalitie, as of aggregation.
a secret virtue, as of sympathie.
connexion, as of continuitie. |

thrusting or inforcing, *as of impulsion*

it self, (that it may be   *libration.*
well with it self)
as the motion of   *libertie.*

First, the spirit moved it self upon the waters with the motion of *Agitation.* then
the light being sent into the matter, penetrated it every way with the motion of
Diffusion. by and by the matter above, where the light pressed through, being
heated and rarified, dilated it self with the motion of *Dispansion;* but below, it
coagulated it self with the motion of *Contraction.*   And all the more subtle parts
gathered themselves upwards, the grosser downwards, with the motio[n]s of *Ag-
gregation* and *Sympathy* . . . . and whither soever one part of the matter went, others
followed by the motion of *Continuity:* or if one rushed against others, they gave way
by the motion of *Impulsion*, but the grosser parts did poise themselves, (flying from
the heat which came upon them from above) about the Center, to an exact Glo-
bosity, with the motion of *Libration.* there was no motion of Liberty, because there
was no externall violence, to put any thing out of order."

[27]Daneau, however, argued against Aristotle on this point, *Physice Christiana, Sive,
Christiana de Rerum Creatarum Origine, & vsu disputatio* (4th ed.; Geneva, 1602), 77–8.

microcosm with the universe as the macrocosm.   For man, in
the doctrine traceable to the *Timaeus*, was in all features of his
composition intimately related to the natural world.   To begin
with, the four humors of the body derived their qualities from
the elements; according to Plato blood was related to fire,
phlegm to water, yellow bile to air, and black bile to earth.[28]
Flesh was believed to be "a kind of ferment made with fire and
water and earth, containing an acid and saline admixture."[29]
In Cicero's terms the theory went:

> If anyone should ask the source from which we have moisture and heat which
> is diffused throughout the body, and even the earthy firmness of the flesh, and
> lastly the air we breathe, it is clear that we have taken one from the earth,
> another from liquid, another from fire, and another from the air which we
> inhale by breathing.[30]

With the basic relationship established it was easy to work
out the details, and it is interesting to see how this might be
done to the last particular.   There is, for example, the passage
in Raleigh's *History of the World:*

> Man, thus compounded and formed by God, was an abstract or model,
> or brief story of the universal. . . . *Deus igitur hominem factum, velut alterum
> quendam mundum, in brevi magnum, atque exiguo totum, in terris statuit;* "God there-
> fore placed in the earth the man whom he had made, as it were another
> world, the great and large world in the small and little world;" for out of
> earth and dust was formed the flesh of man, and therefore heavy and lumpish;
> the bones of his body we may compare to the hard rocks and stones, and
> therefore strong and durable; of which Ovid:
>
> > Inde genus durum sumus, experiensque laborum,
> > Et documenta damus qua simus origine nati.
>
> > From thence our kind hard-hearted is,
> > Enduring pain and care,
> > Approving, that our bodies of
> > A stony nature are.

His blood, which disperseth itself by the branches of veins through all the
body, may be resembled to those waters which are carried by brooks and
rivers over all the earth; his breath to the air; his natural heat to the enclosed
warmth which the earth hath in itself, which, stirred up by the heat of the

---

[28]See Dampier-Whetham, *History of Science* 37.

[29]*Timaeus* 72D, translated by P. Ansell Robin in *The Old Physiology in English
Literature* (London, 1911), 26.

[30]*De Natura Deorum* II. xviii, translated by Robin in *Old Physiology* 26–7.   See
also Thomas Fortescue's translation of Pedro Mexia, *The Forest, or Collection of
Historyes* (London, 1576), 94.

sun, assisteth nature in the speedier procreation of those varieties which the earth bringeth forth; our radical moisture, oil, or balsamum, (whereon the natural heat feedeth and is maintained,) is resembled to the fat and fertility of the earth; the hairs of man's body, which adorns, or overshadows it, to the grass, which covereth the upper face and skin of the earth; our generative power, to nature, which produceth all things; our determinations, to the light, wandering, and unstable clouds, carried every where with uncertain winds; our eyes, to the light of the sun and moon; and the beauty of our youth, to the flowers of the spring, which, either in a very short time, or with the sun's heat, dry up and wither away, or the fierce puffs of wind blow them from the stalks; the thoughts of our mind, to the motion of angels; and our pure understanding, (formerly called *mens*, and that which always looketh upwards,) to those intellectual natures which are always present with God; and, lastly, our immortal souls (while they are righteous) are by God himself beautified with the title of his own image and similitude.[31]

Such notions are directly related to certain astrological beliefs, as when various parts of the body, the liver, the brain, and so on, are thought to be dominated by this or that planet. The most significant of these ideas is that which considers the sun to be the heart of the universe. According to this notion the sun is properly the source and perpetual renewer of life, just as in man the heart is the fountain of the vital spirit.[32] There was ancient as well as modern authority for considering the sun in such terms:

Unde ab Heraclito Fons Luminis Cœlestis, ab Orpheo Lux Vitæ & Oculus Mundi, seu vivificus Cœli Oculus, qui omnibus rebus calorem, lucem, vitamque inspirat dicitur . . . . A Paracelso Sol vocatur Spiraculum Vitæ Elementorum: à Platone & Zoroastro Cœlestis & Invincibilis Ignis vocatus est . . . .[33]

Clemens Alexandrinus eloquently explained the sun's power:

The Sun is infused in all things, intimate in all things, by him so many glorious Lamps of Heaven do shine, by him the Elements stand, the Winds blow, the Plants florish, living Creatures have sense; and what is wonderfull, at the same moment of time he produces the Day here and the Night there . . . . He passeth into Waters, then into Hayle; being ever one and the same Artifect of six hundred Arts; he paints the Clouds with Azure colour, cloathes the tops of Mountains with Gold.[34]

But the special reference which explains the comparison of the sun with the heart is that which makes it the source of the vital

[31]*The Works*, ed. William Oldys and Thomas Birch (Oxford, 1829), II. 58–9.
[32]See Oswald Croll, *Basilica Chymica* (Frankfurt, 1609), 208.
[33]*Ibid*. 209.
[34]Translated by William Lilly, *Annus Tenebrosus, or The Dark Year (1652)* (London, 1652), 21.

heat present in every living creature.[35]   William Harvey developed this notion further, considering aether the medium through which vital heat was transferred from the sun to the heart and blood of animals.[36]   Comenius on the other hand merely thought that the light from the sun was the primary vivifying force.[37]   And all these ideas were not much more than sophisticated developments of the conception of the sun as the father of things, the great fertilizing power of the universe.

But there was still another explanation of the intimate union of man and the physical universe, the assumption of a world soul whose source was not the sun, but upon which the sun as well as all other things depended for continuing existence.   This soul was breathed in by living creatures, and it nourished the sun and stars as well.   Such, for example, was the theory of Democritus, that the soul was made of fire atoms which are breathed in from the atmosphere.[38]   This fitted very well with the Aristotelian notion that the soul is identical with the heat of the body, and when breathing once stops, the soul escapes.[39] It was likewise one of Galen's basic principles that life was spirit drawn from the general world spirit by breathing.[40]   All such speculation may be seen to pertain to the idea of the relation of the great and little worlds as that is supported by various theories of the material composition of the soul.   While not exhaustive, Walter Charleton's discussion of such theories is full enough to indicate the extent of their influence.   He has been discussing Willis's *De Anima Brutorum:*

> You are not therefore to look upon the Description of the nature and affections of a Sensitive Soul therein delivered, as a supposition newly excogitated, and unheard of by former ages.   For to Men conversant in the Theories of Physiologists concerning that Subject, it is well known, that all the Ancients

---

[35]See Daneau, *Physice Christiana* 155; Daniel Widdowes, *Naturall Philosophy: Or A Description of the World* (London, 1621), 11; Plutarch, *Libellus De Facie, Quæ in Orbe Lunæ Apparet*, in Johann Kepler's *Mathematici Olim Imperatorii Somnium* (Frankfurt, 1634), 117–18; Nicholas Culpeper, *Mr. Culpepper's Treatise of Aurum Potabile* (London, 1656), 86.

[36]See Dampier-Whetham, *History of Science* 161.

[37]*Naturall Philosophie Reformed* 79.

[38]Burtt, *Metaphysical Foundations of Modern Physical Science* 79.

[39]*On Respiration* 472a5, in *Opera* III. 539.   Compare the similar idea in Pliny (Holland, *Pliny* I. 346 [Bk. XI, chap. xxxviii]).

[40]Charles Singer, *A Short History of Medicine* (New York: Oxford University Press, 1928), 56–8.

were so far from holding the Soul of a Brute to be other than *Corporeal*, that they for the most part taught their Disciples, that the Soul of *Man* was so too: except a few of them, namely *Pythagoras*, *Plato*, and in some favorable sense *Aristotle* (when he defined the Soul by that enigmatical term ἐντελέχεια) and his Sectators, *Aristoxenus* and *Dicæarchus*, when they called it a *Harmony*. True it is indeed, they were much divided in their opinions about the *Substance* or *Matter* of a Soul; some imagining it to be of Fire, as *Heraclitus*, *Democritus*, *Hipparchus*, and the *Stoicks;* some conceiving it to be on the contrary of a Watery nature, as *Hippon*, and *Thales;* others fancying it to be composed of Water and Earth, as *Xenophanes;* others, of Earth and Fire, as *Parmenides;* others again, of all the four Elements, as *Empedocles:* and yet notwithstanding they unanimously consented in these points, that this Corporeal Soul is divisible; composed of particles extremely small, subtil and active; diffused through or coextens to the whole body wherein it is contained; produced at first by generation out of the seed of the parents; perpetualy recruited or regenerated out of the purest and most spirituous part of the nourishment; subject to Contraction and Expansion in passions; and finally dissolved or extinguished by death.[41]

*

* *

In this brief account we may see some of the ways by which the teleological view of the universe was supported. The world was composed of elements, and the activities of those elements were directed by innate purpose; the elements being the stuff of the human body, that body likewise partook of purposive existence. Life itself was due to various productive qualities in the elements, which were both the seedbeds and the seed, but it was nourished and maintained also by special essences in the atmosphere, themselves possibly of an elementary constitution.

The analogies derived from such reasoning were often no more than that—for little serious weight could be put upon the supposed likeness of grass upon the earth with the hair upon a man's head. But if the analogies were not in all terms satisfactory, they were nevertheless inescapable. For it was a principle that could by no means be denied, that the universe was a living body. Stones and minerals grew, plants were sensitive,[42] love and hatred ruled the world.

[41]*Natural History of the Passions* (London, 1674), bb$_6$–bb$_7$. According to the *Dictionary of National Biography* this is a translation of the work of a well-known French preacher, Senault, but I have not been able to find the original.

[42]In this connection an Elizabethan discussion of the nature of plants is illuminating: "Anaxagoras being moued (I know not wherewith) affirmed that there was not onely a desire in them to tarie and continue in their state, but also that they had and felt both sorrow and pleasure: and his reason he gathered of the

These then are some of the concepts that remained fairly stable in the philosophic thinking of many centuries—down to, say, the Newtonian period. It is not important to claim that any one of them was the dominant theory of any period; it is merely necessary to recognize that they were important doctrines or conceptions. As such it is to be expected that there should go hand in hand with them a reasonably constant terminology. That constancy we may judge from the lists at the end of this book.

But before referring the reader to them, it may serve a useful purpose to describe the appearance of the world and its nature in a kind of epitome, as it was before the mathematical and mechanistic views prevailed (some of the significant words are italicized, for most of them will be treated later as terms of particular significance in poetry and scientific prose):

The world is made of four *elements* in perpetual struggle, or flux. Earth, air, fire, and water mingle with each other to form every object and living creature in the universe, and whatever is compounded is in time broken up. That which is solid becomes *fluid* or *liquid*, and *liquids* become solid. The great *globe* of the earth, suspended in the *ambient air*, is made of these four *elements*. The very rivers were once solid *crystal*, but by the process of time have become a *crystal humor*. As for the sea, the sun's heat causes that to send forth *exhalations* which become *humid* clouds in the middle *regions* of the air, containing the *seeds* of rain and snow. When they have matured, they descend to the earth again, congealed as solids or *humors*. The earth also *exhales vapors*, and these eventually become dry and fiery me-

distillation of humor in the Plant his Leaues, and of the Leaues increase. Plato saith that they be moued and led by appetite for the necessitie of their prouision in nourishing. Both of these Aristotle in his first booke de Plantis, refelleth and reproueth by argument: whereupon we entende not to stande. Yet may it be doubted forasmuch as with Theophrast and such others, rather yea, than nay is aunswered. And they bid vs looke in eche their appearance. Doth not the Cucumber hate the Oliue, and where the one is, the other through a certaine malice, prospereth not: Contrariewise, doth not the Vine loue and embrace the Elme, and prospereth the better, the nigher one is set by another: And as of these questions is had, so may there also doubtes be made of the other. But let euerie man iudge of these as they list. I had rather be still then haue a doe herein." John Maplet, *A Greene Forest, or a naturall Historie*, reprinted from the edition of 1567, ed. W. H. Davies (London: Hesperides Press, 1930), 50–1.

teors, lightning, thunder, comets, and many other portentous phenomena. Some of these *vapors* find their matrices also in the clouds.

These elements as they change from *fluid* to solid or back again make of the universe a vast *distilling* apparatus, or limbec, a great *frame* of circulation, a *machine*. This process is guided by the demands of all things for compensation and nourishment since it is in their nature to desire continuing existence and to be perpetually a part of the *fabric* of nature. The sea nourishes the clouds, which in turn nourish the sea. Fiery *vapors* from the earth feed the sun, and its *rays* fertilize the earth so that things may grow and breathe forth other *vapors*. The sun and stars drink in the fiery *aether* as if it were *liquid light*. The *crystal sky* itself is *congealed* water. The processes of elemental *distillation*, the compounding of hot and cold and moist and dry, are evidence that all things are male or female, and that it is by marriage of the *elements* that all natural objects are created.

For the *elements* are *living matter*, infused with *vital* warmth, containing the *seeds* of all living creatures. Beasts are variously earthy, airy, fiery, or watery in their nature, according to the predominating *element* in their composition and according to their *native element*, in which they were born and from which they are chiefly nourished. Plants also take their nature from the *genial elements*, and are produced from *seeds* resting in the *kindly* earth or water. Minerals also grow from *seeds* in the womb of the earth. The elements are the *generous* parents of all nature, and all things which grow from *seed* are distinguished lastingly as families, generations, and *kinds*. They make up *tribes* and *nations* of plants, fish, beasts, meteors, all the three *kingdoms*, animal, vegetable, and mineral. For all things are related, born of the same *elements*.

The surface of the earth is divided into *zones* and *climes*, marking off the areas between the *poles*. The universe surrounding the earth is likewise divided into *zones*, of air, *aether*, and fire, and in the various *regions* set aside for them the winds, the sun, the stars and planets rule. The *aether* is by some thought to be a *thinner* and purer air than the atmosphere of the middle *region*, which is thick with *vapors*, but according to others it is the *region* of elemental fire, from which all fiery bodies are born, the stars and all flaming things on earth. It is said by some to be the *native element* of salamanders, and by others to be the *vital* breath of all living things. It is in its composition, like air and fire, *liquid*, and the sun and moon and planets *swim* in it, just as birds *swim* in the *liquid air* and fish in the sea. It is the *liquid sky* that the sun drinks and it is the food of the sun's fire. Some believe that stars are burning *orbs* or cups of *aether*, though others think they are metal studs fastened in a *crystal* ceiling. But whatever its form, *aether* is the vital air both of heavenly fires and living creatures, the breath of the universe.

For the universe is indeed a living body, the macrocosm. It has a heart, the sun, which is the source of the natural warmth in the earth, as the heart's blood is the source of warmth in the microcosm of man. It sees by the light of the sun and stars and moon, as man sees by the *visual rays* which come forth from his eyes. The *humors* of the body are linked indissolubly with the *elements*, and the world's body is the living universe. And in it as in man, in the actions of its constituent *elements* and the creatures of the *elements*, is revealed the fulfillment of divine purpose, which governs fire in its rising, air in its *yielding*, the sea in its buoyancy, stars in their shining. The warring *elements* and the conflicting *humors* make order out of chaos because they are controlled by the purpose of the maker of the universe. For the *elements* in their mingling nourish each other, and so provide for the continuance of life and the eventual completion of the design.

CHAPTER V

The Interchange of Scientific Language
and Poetic Diction

THE names science and poetry find for things will coincide when science and poetry share a common view of nature. To a scientist who thought the world comparable to the human body, even mythological terms would be available. If natural philosophers believed the world instinct with purpose, there could be no pathetic fallacy for poetry. But it is one thing to say that for many centuries all thinkers were agreed that the universe was the living creature of God's will, and quite another to say that in each period of history down to the time of Newton men accepted the teleological view in exactly the same way. It is of the first importance to recognize the long survival of certain concepts, but it is equally important to recognize the different forms these concepts took. For ultimately most of them were destroyed by the mechanistic or the mathematical view of the universe, and that destruction was made possible by virtue of these variations. Plato's macrocosm is not the same as Basil's, the aether of Anaxagoras differs greatly from Kepler's, and yet the words are the same.

The study of the diction of poetry, accordingly, becomes a study of many relationships. Dryden read both Descartes and Lucretius, and the terms he used to describe nature at certain times were influenced by the different meanings he found in those writers. Boyle also read Lucretius and Descartes, and his language was formed by both the poet and the philosopher. Poets and scientists of necessity borrowed from each other, and ultimately questions of priority are not important although the obligations are. Knowledge of the state of such obligations in certain periods of history may accordingly be helpful to anyone studying the significance of a language common to both science and poetry.

67

It is unfortunately not possible to undertake here any useful discussion of the Greek didactic poems of the fifth and fourth centuries, and we may merely remember that the full text of Empedocles is lost. It is important to recall the existence of such poems, however, particularly whenever questions arise of the debt of Latin poetic diction to Greek. For not even the language of the dramatists provides more than a hint of sources which are almost certainly Greek.[1]

The situation with respect to the Alexandrians is not much

[1] In the appendixes citations from Ennius and some others of the early Latin writers will suggest still earlier Greek sources for a considerable part of their diction. Compound words like *caelicola, quadrupes,* and *frugifer* are equivalent to Greek forms found in Homer and the dramatists, and in Latin verse the use of such words was certainly encouraged by the establishment of the hexameter after the Greek model (see Cornelia C. Coulter, "Compound Adjectives in Early Latin Poetry," *Trans. and Proc. Amer. Philol. Assn.,* XLVII [1916], 165). The linguistic problems concerning the transmission of these forms have been pretty well settled, but the loss of many texts makes speculation on stylistic relationship very insecure.

It may be observed here that compound words of this sort used singly are the equivalent of two-word periphrases. *Squamigeri, lanigerae, cornigeri* must be translated in English by an adjective and a collective term (*scale-bearers, woolly ones, horned kind*). Writers in French are generally compelled to follow a similar procedure despite the efforts of Ronsard and Du Bartas to imitate *coelifer, pinifer,* and similar Greek forms. (For an interesting discussion of this subject see le Sieur Des-Marests, *La Comparaison de la Langue et de la Poësie Françoise, Avec la Grecque & la Latine, Et des Poëtes Grecs, Latins & François* [Paris, 1670], 16.) And it is the absence of many of these compounds and periphrases in the surviving Greek poetry that makes speculation difficult. Moreover, the problem is complicated not merely by the loss of certain epics, but also by the destruction of much of the work of the Alexandrians, particularly poems like the one on *Causes* by Callimachus.

The influence of the hexameter upon the use of the Greek and Latin compound has an interesting parallel in English neoclassic verse. The heroic couplet demanded phrases of a certain accentual pattern, and in the lack of compounds like *squamigeri* writers made use of phrases like *scaly kind, feathered troops,* and *finny race.* I do not know whether these poets discovered that this kind of periphrasis in a naturally iambic rhythm corresponded to the dactylic compound in a hexameter line. If this parallel was not consciously exploited, it may nevertheless be claimed that prosodically the two-word periphrasis was the native form proper to the English imitation of the classic style.

The frequent use of such phrases in the rhyme position reinforces the use of the periphrasis in a way comparable to the use of the compound in hexameters. For in such a position the generic word tended to become less important in itself and was important chiefly for its rhyme. This accounts for some of the casualness of such phrases, since no importance is attached to differences of meaning in any number of words of collective meaning. This, of course, is in part the point of Pope's remarks in the *Essay on Criticism.* The monosyllabic terms were of special use in rhyming, but dissyllables like *nation* and *people* were equally serviceable at other parts of the line and quite as indistinct in meaning.

clearer, but Professor Mackail has offered some illuminating theories. His conception is that these poets were interested in art for its own sake. In the pastoral they were developing a form whose value was to be judged by its capacity to explain a new feeling for nature arising from weariness with city life. In the didactic poem they were trying to express the value of systematized knowledge as that was known to science, but in a form which might still be called poetry. And in the romantic epic they were combining these various motives, hoping to create an art form which was satisfactory in that it solved its own problems. This effort toward "a new synthesis of poetry," Professor Mackail believes, was completed by Virgil.[2]

If it is true that they were unable to accomplish what they set out to do, their preoccupation with detail becomes understandable. In a scientific period they might be expected to be more sympathetic to Empedocles than to Homer, but it is important to understand that for their age science lacked the completeness of vision it once had. As has been well said, "In the beginning science was a great poem; now it is merely a prosaic inventory."[3] And since the scientific view was fragmentary and disjointed, poems on scientific subjects—Aratus on weather signs and Nicander on drugs—suffered from the same faults. The only pattern perceptible in the arrangement of the details is that of an inventory.

This criticism must be modified in one important respect. For if philosophic understanding provided no unity for such poems, an intense didactic interest did give unity of a sort, and it was this which appealed to Lucretius, Virgil, and Oppian. For the didactic interest was part of the fabric of science itself, and this attracted verse writers to the subject, as Joseph Warton ably showed in his *Reflections on Didactic Poetry*. Something of the way in which science and poetry were brought together in this respect may be learned in reminding ourselves of the condition of science in a more primitive state than we are accustomed to think of it. As Couat pointed out, in the time of Aratus' *Phaenomena* (around 260 B.C.):

[2] J. W. Mackail, *Lectures on Greek Poetry* (London, 1911), 188–9.
[3] Auguste Couat, *Alexandrian Poetry under the First Three Ptolemies, 324–222 B.C.*, trans. James Loeb (London: Heinemann, 1931), 473.

. . . astronomical science was nothing more than simple empiricism set off by a few attempts at scientific explanation. The science of astronomy arose in Greece from the need which farmers and sailors felt to know the divisions of time and to foresee the changes of season. This is what was in the minds of the peasants of Boeotia and of the sailors on the Aegean when they observed the rising and setting of the stars. In this wise, a popular astronomy, that of Homer and Hesiod, was developed. Scientists made use of it without controlling the results scientifically, while adding to it far-reaching hypotheses. Nor did they neglect the practical forecasts that are meant for peasant and mariner. We meet with them in most of the ancient astronomical documents that have come down to us, and consequently in the poems of Aratus as well. From Hesiod down to the Alexandrian poet, we can follow the track of this tradition. Democritus added a calendar to his treatise on astronomy, of which Geminus or some copyist has preserved fragments; among other things, we learn from them that there are heavy rains at the rising of Arcturus, that the Eagle usually announces thunder, that the weather grows stormy with the rising of the Lyre . . . .[4]

Supporting that sort of interest in scientific knowledge was curiosity about natural history, and an activity which increased tremendously after Alexander's expeditions. It became fashionable to paint pictures of wild animals upon the walls of houses, and it is supposed that the same kind of interest led Nicander to write the *Theriaca*.[5] A like curiosity led Theocritus to describe scenery in the greatest detail, distinguishing the features of plants and animals with an exactness which often seems pedantic.[6]

And again, the failure of this poetry to become anything more is partly explained by the nature of the contemporary science. The desire for universal knowledge had given way before the interest of the specialist. Men like Eudoxus, Nicias, and Euclid were astronomers, physicians, and geometricians, with little claim to be natural philosophers. They collected their knowledge, and when they had finished, it could still be said, ". . . the material of each science goes on accumulating; as yet no science has been born."[7] Others worked over this material

---

[4]Couat, *Alexandrian Poetry* 475–6.

[5]W. Y. Sellar, *The Roman Poets of the Augustan Age: Virgil* (Oxford, 1877), 48.

[6]"Il appelle les choses par leur nom: il désigne avec précision les plantes, les arbres, les animaux; il sait quels sont les fruits dont les parfums se confondent dans la senteur de l'été; il nomme les arbres qui se penchent sur la fontaine de Bourina; il désigne avec précision le taureau qui ménace, le bouc entier, la vache amaigrie et malade, l'odeur de la présure; il n'a pas de vains scrupules de noblesse et de fausse élégance. Il imite le sifflement des bergers rappelant leur troupeau (σίττα), et le cri moqueur de la jeune fille qui s'enfuit (πυππυλιάζει)."—Alfred and Maurice Croiset, *Histoire de la Littérature Grecque* (Paris, 1887–99), V. 204–5.

[7]Couat, *Alexandrian Poetry* 472–3.

in the great tasks of enumeration and classification, substantiating the investigations of Aristotle. They were satisfied if they could catalogue the kinds of things adequately,[8] a preoccupation they shared with the eighteenth century. Failing in great ideas, they were unable to hand on to poetry more than their own limited visions.

But finally Lucretius, following Democritus and Epicurus, undertook full and significant treatment of some of the great concepts of natural philosophy, attempting a synthesis. Although his materialism was explicitly opposed to the great teleological philosophies, it is nevertheless true that "the world, as Lucretius conceives it, is at all events as much an organism as a tree, perhaps not much less so than an animal."[9] Virgil also conceived of the world as a living thing, in less passionate terms than those of Lucretius, but with the help of almost as much scientific information. He understood clearly that there was a spirit breathing through the universe, governing its life. And the body of the universe he thought of in the terms of the texts of science:

> Principio caelum ac terram camposque liquentis
> lucentemque globum lunae Titaniaque astra
> spiritus intus alit, totamque infusa per artus
> mens agitat molem et magno se corpore miscet.
> inde hominum pecudumque genus vitaeque volantum
> et quae marmoreo fert monstra sub aequore pontus.
> igneus est ollis vigor et caelestis origo
> seminibus, quantum non corpora noxia tardant
> terrenique hebetant artus moribundaque membra.[10]

In poems like the *Georgics* and the *Astronomicon*, however, the practical didactic interest created an important kind of unity. Yet, whether written for the farmer or the mariner or the amateur, such poems were meant to be instructive in more than a knowledge of detail. Edward Sherburne's preface to his translation of Manilius (1675) seems to me to describe extremely well what must have been part of the purpose of writing such poems, and much of the reason they were read, in Roman times and later:

[8]Mackail, *Lectures on Greek Poetry* 194.
[9]John Masson, *The Atomic Theory of Lucretius* (London, 1884), 147.
[10]*Aeneid* VI. 724–32.

The High Esteem, which the Antient *Romans* had for Astronomical Learning; appears even by their Publick Games in the *Circus Maximus;* whose Order and Disposition represented that of the Heavens. The *Circus* being of an *Elliptical* or *Oval* Figure; having twelve Gates or Entries resembling the twelve Signs of the Zodiack. In the Midst *an Obelisque,* as the *Sun:* On each side thereof three *Metæ,* denoting the other Six Planets, which in their respective Courses mark out the several Intervals or Spaces, into which the Mundane System is divided. So that the *Circensian Games* seem not to have been so much, an Exercise of Charioting and Racing, as an *Astronomical Cursus;* wherein the People were not only delighted by the Exhibition of corporal Games, but had their Minds also instructed to apprehend the Course and Order of the Celestial Bodies, which in the Great *Circus* of the World are continually moving.

This Method of inculcating Knowledge with Delight (though in a different way) *Manilius* hath likewise pursued; who intending to exhibit to the Age wherein he lived the Rudiments of Astronomy, chose to represent the same in a Poetical Dress, that so his Readers might be allured to relish with the greater *Gusto* the initiating Principles of a Science not easily acquired; and he thereby gain to himself the Repute which good Poets chiefly affect, of being able at once both to instruct and please.[11]

The terminology of Lucretius and Manilius was scientific, and a considerable number of Virgil's descriptive terms were used as accurately as scientists would desire. The point is that many of the important Roman poets, following the example of the Alexandrians, were prepared to search out a language authorized in other contexts for the description of nature. This they could do with some confidence since their own philosophies agreed rather well with those of the investigators whose special business it was to develop such scientific terminology. The coincidence of terms in Aristotle, Virgil, and Pliny is possible because these men shared various attitudes toward nature, and agreed in many matters of natural philosophy. That this is a proper conclusion may be affirmed here briefly by mere reference to the terms Seneca used to describe the maker of the universe, matching them with whatever examples from poetry come to mind—*artifex operum; rectorem custodemque uniuersi, animum ac spiritum mundi* (νοῦς *et* πνεῦμα); *operis huius dominum et artificem.*[12] As long as the interests of science and poetry were identical, the literature of each was open to the other's exploitation, and in certain important respects this continued to be true till, in build-

[11] *The Sphere of Marcus Manilius Made An English Poem* (London, 1675), a.
[12] Commented on by Armand Pittet, *Vocabulaire Philosophique de Sénèque, Ire Livraison* (Paris: Société d'Édition "Les Belles Lettres," 1937), 113.

ing upon the work of Copernicus, it became the obligation of science to "read man out of nature."

The effort of the early Christian period as well as of the contemporary pagan schools was to reinforce all those aspects of ancient philosophy which affirmed divine purpose guiding all the processes of nature. Christian poets—Lactantius, Prudentius, Victor, Avitus—and pagan writers of many schools—Oppian, Claudian, Nonnos, and Pisidas—apparently united in the imitation of Virgil to this effect. The emphasis Christian poets gave to the older philosophy has been well described by a French scholar:

C'est surtout dans la façon dont nos poètes ont envisagé la création et compris la nature qu' éclate cette influence de l'idée religieuse et du christianisme sincère dont toute leur œuvre est animée. Ainsi que nous l'avons déjà indiqué, pour eux, comme pour tous les fidèles, la nature est avec l'homme en relations constantes et nécessaires; . . . et, tandis que le paganisme n'y voyait que des lignes et des formes plus ou moins harmonieuses et une fête perpétuelle pour les sens, nos écrivains bibliques la regardaient avec raison comme un voile qui nous cache le Créateur et un reflet de ses grandeurs infinies . . . .[13]

And pagan writers were in these matters more Christian than they knew.

St. Basil in his prose sermons on the creation of the universe in six days set the pattern for the considerable number of hexaemeral poems written between the fourth and eighth centuries.[14] It was his purpose to describe the creation and to show how the universe in all its extent was the work of God. It was necessary to know the works of God in detail in order to understand His greatness, and to understand how life continued in praising Him. Accordingly, Basil read Aristotle, Aelian, Strabo, Ptolomy, Archimedes, Eratosthenes, Galen, and Euclid for the detailed knowledge and the speculation he needed in order to fill out the account of creation written in Genesis.[15] The material he assembled was available to the poets who followed him, if they themselves were not disposed to search out the original sources.

[13]L'Abbé Stanislas Gamber, *Le Livre de la "Genèse" dans la Poésie Latine au Vme Siècle* (Paris, 1899), 178.

[14]See Frank E. Robbins, *The Hexaemeral Literature, A Study of the Greek and Latin Commentaries on Genesis* (Chicago, 1912), 42.

[15]See Leo V. Jacks, *St. Basil and Greek Literature* (Washington: Catholic University of America Press, 1922).

But in any case, Victor, Dracontius, Ennodius, and the others described the creation in much the same manner, using whatever scientific material was available, and employing techniques closely related to those of Lucretius, Virgil, and Manilius.   M. Gamber's generalizations on the use of science by these poets seem to me amply justified:

> On voit facilement par là que, si la science de nos poètes est en défaut, elle n'est pas moins imparfaite que celle des écrivains de leur époque, qui eux-mêmes ont ajouté foi aux enseignements des naturalistes anciens. Il y aurait lieu de faire la même observation, si nous voulions rapporter ici toutes les opinions scientifiques qu'ils ont émises en décrivant l'œuvre des six jours. Lorsque, par exemple, Dracontius indique certains signes précurseurs de la pluie ou du beau temps, et qu'il énumère les phénomènes de la nature qui peuvent être considérés comme d'heureux ou tristes présages; lorsque Marius Victor explique comment la voûte azurée du ciel consiste en une substance ferme et solide, qui "protège la terre contre les ardeurs excessives des flammes éthérées," ou bien quand il nous parle de ce concert suave qu' exécutent les sphères célestes en roulant sur leur axe, l'un et l'autre ne font que reproduire ce qu'ils ont lu dans Aristote, Cicéron, Pline ou Elien, comme aussi saint Epiphane, saint Ambroise, saint Basile et Théodoret.[16]

Moreover, writing in verse, often in hexameters, these writers were evidently following the example of the Augustans, directly imitating them, but also making use of such works as the *Cynegetica* of Nemesianus and the *De Re Rustica* of Palladius.[17]   And there were at the same time poets outside the Christian tradition who were themselves adding to the literature of the didactic description of natural phenomena, and who quite conceivably were made use of by the writers whose effort was to describe the Christian basis of creation.   Writers like Oppian (or the two authors who go by that name), Manethon, and Pisidas in Greek, Gratius, Ausonius, and Claudian in Latin were interested in the poetic use of scientific material in ways quite comparable to those followed by the Christian hexaemeral poets.   But throughout all the works of pagan and Christian is apparent the bright and persistent influence of Virgil.   He was a storehouse of language and imagery, and in nothing more so than in matters concerning nature.   It even seems that Nonnos was frequently translating Virgil's epic diction into Greek.   There were times when for philosophic reasons, among others, the Lucretian in-

---

[16]*Le Livre de la "Genèse"* 76.

[17]See Pierre de Labriolle, *History and Literature of Christianity from Tertullian to Boethius*, trans. Herbert Wilson (London: Kegan Paul, 1924), 317–18.

fluence was stronger, but for the most part it is of course not safe to ascribe to Lucretius' direct influence what was handed on by that poet to Virgil. However that may be, Alexandrianism in poetry as well as in science, mingled with the first Christian poetry, was thus to perpetuate its influence for later centuries.

For the great source of English poetic diction in the description of nature is Sylvester's translation of Du Bartas,[18] and Du Bartas's poems were the culmination of a revival of interest in the early hexaemeral literature. Basil's homilies were printed in 1532 with a preface by Erasmus. Latin translations were published in 1515, 1520, 1523, 1525, 1531, and several times later in the century. Of some of the poems on the creation there were editions in 1498 (Juvencus Hispanus), 1508 (Avitus), 1510 (Hilary of Poitiers), 1536 (Marius Victor), 1558 (Justinus). The poems of Dracontius, Hilary, Victor, Avitus, and Cyprianus Gallus were published in one volume in 1560. Pisidas was printed for the first time in 1584, the Greek text being accompanied by a Latin translation. And each of these poets was reprinted several times during the century.[19]

There has been little agreement in the past about the relation of the earlier and the later hexaemeral literatures, but De Maisières has clearly demonstrated the obligation of Du Bartas to St. Basil, at least. More important than influence, however, is the similarity of the two bodies of poems, not merely in the large subject but in the details and the phraseology. The fact is that both groups of writers drew upon pretty much the same sources for their scientific knowledge, and shared, to one degree or another, the didactic method that had been developed by Lucretius and Virgil. Du Bartas's *La Semaine* (1578), Tasso's *Le Sette Giornate del Mondo Creato* (1592), Murtola's *Della Creazione del Mondo* (1608), Passero's *L'Essamerone* (1609), Acevedo's *Crea-*

---

[18] I should like to call attention to a remark of George Saintsbury's which I am quite certain deserves the reader's full subscription: "The man of pure science may regret that generations should have busied themselves about anything so unscientific; but with that point of view we are unconcerned. The important thing is that the generations in question [the seventeenth century] learnt from Sylvester to take a poetical interest in the natural world."—*A History of Elizabethan Literature* (New York, 1912), 290–1. For a rather detailed study of Sylvester, see also John Arthos, "Studies in the Diction of Neo-Classic Poetry," MS thesis (1937) in the Harvard College Library.

[19] I owe most of this information to Maury Thibaut de Maisières, *Les Poèmes Inspirés du Début de la Genèse à l'Époque de la Renaissance* (Louvain: Librairie Universitaire, 1931), a brief but sound and valuable study.

cion del Mundo (1615)—all these followed the same pattern, and many, of course, took advantage of Du Bartas's example. It is, in any event, that poet whose influence was most significant, and a study of certain aspects of his poetry can be of the greatest help in analyzing the nature of the characteristic poetic diction of the eighteenth century.

*

*　　*

The chief effect of Du Bartas's poetry depends upon the strange and unfortunate interaction between the two worlds that held conviction for him. Part of his mind was absorbed with the idea of man alone in the presence of God. And yet he continually revealed a passionate preoccupation with the sensual nature of things. The world attracted him, and he could justify this because, like himself, everything in it—stones, birds, stars—was the witness of God's power, and was, like him, praising God by the fact of its existence. The universe and all its parts demanded personification. And mythological figures were acceptable because they could be used to show purpose operating in the universe. They did not seem to compromise the poet's Protestantism, and they made considerable contributions to his sensual imagery. An example of the way in which he combined these various resources may be seen in an apostrophe to the sun:

> Je veux tout sur-le-champ trompeter qu'en la sorte
> Qu'au milieu de son corps le Microcosme porte
> Le cœur, source de vie, et qui de toutes parts
> Fournit le corps d'esprits par symmetrie espars,
> Que de mesme, o soleil, chevelu d'or, tu marches
> Au milieu des six feux des six plus basses arches
> Qui voutent l'univers, à fin d'esgalement,
> Riche, leur departir clarté, force, ornement.
> En louant ton ardeur qui penetre, subtile,
> La solide espaisseur de la terre fertile,
> Qui va dans ses roignons le mercure cuisant,
> Qui change un palle souffre en un metal luisant,
> Je sors de la carriere et, peu constant, desire
> Chanter que, si ton œil cessoit un jour de luire,
> L'air non purgé par toy en eau se resoudroit,
> Et sur les monts plus hauts Neptun refloteroit.[20]

[20]*La Premiere Sepmaine* IV. 531–46, in *The Works*, ed. Urban T. Holmes, Jr., John C. Lyons, and Robert W. Linker (Chapel Hill: University of North Carolina Press, 1935–40).

He was also able to personify the material elements of nature without using mythological terms, although obviously profiting by mythological conceptions:

> Mais craignant que le feu, qui ses freres enserre,
> Pour estre trop voisin, ne cendroye la terre,
> Comme arbitres nommez, Dieu commence estaler
> Entre si grans haineux et l'Amphitrite et l'air.
> L'un d'eux ne suffisoit pour esteindre leur guerre:
> Le flot, comme parent, favoroisoit la terre,
> L'air du feu son cousin soustenoit le parti;
> Mais tous deux, unissant leur amour departi,
> Peuvent facilement apointir la querelle
> Qui sans doute eust deffait la machine nouvelle.[21]

And yet, as is the common result when the senses are the standards of certainty by which we judge the reality of the universe, nature is taken to be a machine:

> Dieu est l'ame, le nerf, la vie, l'efficace,
> Qui anime, qui meut, qui soustient ceste masse.
> Dieu est le grand ressort, qui fit de ce grand corps
> Jouer diversement tous les petits ressorts.[22]

The fact is that Du Bartas's purposes were confused, and he could find no other resolution for them than in making an encyclopedia:

> Sans maistre et sans travail, en suçant le laict dous,
> Nous apprenions la langue entendue de tous;
> Et les sept ans passez, sur la poudre de verre
> Nous commencions tirer la rondeur de la terre,
> Partir, multiplier, et montant d'art en art,
> Nous parvenions bientost au sommet du rempart,
> Où l'encyclopedie en signe de victoire
> Couronne ses mignons d'une eternelle gloire.[23]

---

[21]*Ibid.* II. 285–94.

[22]*Ibid.* VII. 143–6.

[23]*Babylone* 243–50, in *Works.* Marcel Raymond's description of the cause of Du Bartas's failure is worth quoting: "Toutes choses sont contenues dans la Création, et sollicitent le regard de Dieu; toutes choses, en conséquence, méritent de figurer dans l'œuvre du poète, qui a le droit, dans ses métaphores, de rapprocher les plus éloignées. Libre à lui 'd'écheler les cieux' et de s'attarder, sitôt après, dans des descriptions qui nous paraissent triviales. Et sans doute, on peut blâmer Du Bartas de tout ramener à la terre, ou du moins de charger de matière les corps célestes eux-mêmes. On s'en prend alors au tour propre de son imagination, qui lui montre partout, et jusque dans l'Éden, des biens réels et saisissables."—*L'Influence de Ronsard sur la Poésie Française (1550–1585)* (Paris: Librairie Champion, 1927), II. 290.

There has come down an anecdote which explains a great deal
about the manner in which the forces of nature were to be conceived, and which also provides an interesting comment on what
was earlier said about parts of the language of Theocritus:

> . . . ce qu'en raconte Gabriel Naude, que Du Bartas s'enfermait quelquefois
> dans une chambre, se mettait, dit-on, à quatre pattes, et soufflait, gambadait,
> galopait, pour être plus plein de son sujet; en un mot, il ne récitait pas sa
> description, il la *jouait*. Si l'anecdote n'est pas vraie, elle mérite de l'être.
> Dont ce procédé ou ce manège part d'une fausse vue de l'imitation poétique,
> qui ne doit être ni une singerie, ni un langage de perroquet. C'est encore ce
> malheureux travers de poésie imitative qui a fait dire à Du Bartas, en parlant
> de l'alouette et de son gazouillement:

> > La gentille Alouette avec son tire-lire
> > Tire l'ire aux fâchés; et d'une tire tire
> > Vers le pôle brillant . . . .[24]

This identification of the worlds of science and religion and
sensual experience was Du Bartas's means of assimilating the
poetry of the past that appealed to him; for the cultivation of a
personal style he depended largely on the extension of practices
already well known. More immediate than the influence of the
early hexaemeral literature was that of the Pléiade, whose critical principles and poetic practices he followed closely, sometimes to the point of absurdity. *Les Semaines* has been called an
attempt to complete what Ronsard's *Hymnes* failed to carry
through.[25] Ronsard's explicit advice was for poets to make the
fullest use of technical terms, acquainting themselves with the
language of falconry, hunting, mining, foundry work, and other
such pursuits.[26] Nor is there any doubt of the great debt Du
Bartas owed to the poets of the Jeux floraux, with whom he
may be said to have begun his career. His interest in various
sciences and in natural philosophy can be clearly traced to his
apprenticeship in this school of writing.[27] And it is clear that
he likewise made use of Lucretius, Virgil, and Ovid, though

---

[24]Sainte-Beuve, *Les Grands Écrivains Français du XVIᵉ Siècle: Les Poètes*, ed.
Maurice Allem (Paris: Librairie Garnier, 1926), 241.

[25]Raymond, *L'Influence de Ronsard* II. 289. Du Bartas also followed faithfully
the doctrine of Ronsard mentioned above, pp. 22–3, note 54.

[26]*Abbregé de l'Art Poetique Françoys*, in *Œuvres Complètes*, ed. Hugues Vaganay
(Paris: Librairie Garnier, 1923–4), IV. 474.

[27]See J. C. Dawson, *Toulouse in the Renaissance* (New York: Columbia University Press, 1923), 55–6 especially.

there are only a few traces of his direct obligation to them.[28] The fact is that, for the most part, it is impossible to distinguish between his direct and indirect obligations to the Roman poets.[29]

The point is that Du Bartas, in expressing a philosophy of nature, brought together the vocabularies of the ancients in poetry and science to solve the same problems the early hexaemeral writers once faced. He took up the task in the somewhat different light of his Calvinism, and he was able to draw upon Solinus, Rondelet, and Gesner as well as Aelian and Pliny for his scientific knowledge.[30] With their help he brought together certain poetical interests and methods that were important to his age, and he was especially successful in developing a kind of strident imagery to express his materialism. More the result of a sensual bias than a philosophic attitude, this approach accorded very well with the increasingly materialistic emphasis of contemporary science. It is not possible to exaggerate the detailed thoroughness with which Du Bartas devised a concrete language to express conceptions well enough described in more general terms. His description of what happened when the spirit of God moved over the face of the waters may be quoted as a final example of this characteristic:

> Ainsi qu'un bon esprit, qui grave sur l'autel
> De la docte memoire un ouvrage immortel,
> En troupe, en table, au lict, tout jour pour tout jour vivre,
> Discourt sur son discours, et nage sur son livre;

[28]See, for example, Georges Pellissier, *La Vie et les Œuvres de Du Bartas* (Paris, 1883), 130–49.

[29]On the other hand, it is Professor C.-A. Fusil's opinion that the French scientific poetry written between 1700 and 1750 was modeled directly upon the Augustans, and upon Renaissance Latin writers like Pontano and Buchanan. It is his belief that Du Bartas was ignored by the "scientific poets" of the eighteenth century (*La Poésie Scientifique de 1750 à nos jours* [Paris, 1917], 42–3). But it is clearly evident that in the seventeenth century Chapelain and La Fontaine imitated Du Bartas directly, and a case might be made out for Genest's knowledge of that author, despite M. Fusil's statement excluding eighteenth-century writers. Nevertheless, the point is a good one and may be made similarly of many English poets. For though the diction of eighteenth-century English poetry owed immeasurably to Sylvester, many of the individual poets may have been quite ignorant of his work. They may have modeled themselves upon Lucretius and Virgil, and have been unaware that their English vocabulary came from Sylvester at second or third hand.

[30]See L. Delaruelle, "Recherches sur les sources de Du Bartas dans la 'Première Semaine,'" *Revue d'Histoire littéraire de la France*, XL (1933), 321–54; and *The Works of Du Bartas*, ed. Holmes, I. 128.

> Ainsi l'Esprit de Dieu sembloit, en s'esbatant,
> Nager par le dessus de cest amas flottant . . . .
> Ou bien comme l'oiseau qui tasche rendre vifs
> Et ses œufs naturels et ses œufs adoptifs,
> Se tient couché sur eux, et d'une chaleur vive,
> Fait qu'un rond jaune-blanc en un poulet s'avive;
> D'une mesme façon l'Esprit de l'Eternel
> Sembloit couver ce goufre, et d'un soin paternel
> Verser en chasque part une vertu feconde,
> Pour d'un si lourd amas extraire un si beau monde. [31]

Du Bartas's influence in England came largely through Sylvester's translation, [32] and Sylvester's poetic method was as closely imitative of Du Bartas's as it very well could be, modified, of course, by the nature of the English language, and some of its peculiarities exaggerated by Sylvester's rather more boisterous temperament. His translation is not literal, but one might say that his imagination was. For there are very few images or conceits in Sylvester which are not also to be found in Du Bartas, though not always in the passage being translated. His exuberance gave his poetry a quality Du Bartas's lacked, even while it doubled the excesses of the original. But he thereby provided a much ampler storehouse of diction for the poets of natural description who followed.

*
*   *

As we observe the extent to which succeeding generations owed their poetic language to Du Bartas, and the extent to which their language and his and that of the Augustans and of the first hexaemeral writers were the same, there arise several questions concerning the continuity of natural philosophy. For, allowing for differences in the meaning of individual words, it is apparent that a considerable number of the important terms of natural description were used in the poetry of all these periods, and they must have referred to similar schemes of thought. They must have referred to comparable notions about the creation, about the kinds of phenomena to be observed in the natural world, and about the continuance of life. Some of these funda-

[31] *I Sem.* I. 289–304.
[32] See W. R. Abbot, *Studies in the Influence of Du Bartas in England, 1584–1641,* MS thesis (1931) in the library of the University of North Carolina.

mental and rather stable concepts have been pointed out. We know that even in the eighteenth century the conception of God as a spirit moving upon the face of the waters to create the universe was to many a mandatory idea. But there are differences in the way an idea may be accepted, and one of the striking features of eighteenth-century poetry is that the same language used to express the same ideas is somehow stamped with a style that distinguishes it from the Augustan, or the hexaemeral, or Sylvester's. There is, for the bare reminder, Blackmore's description:

> Thou on the Deep's dark face, Immortal Dove,
> Thou, with almighty Energy didst move
> On the wild Waves, Incumbent didst display
> Thy genial Wings, and hatch primæval Day.
> Order from Thee, from Thee Distinction came,
> And all the Beauties of the wondrous Frame:
> Hence stampt on Nature we Perfection find,
> Fair as th' Idea in th' Eternal Mind.[33]

Two factors, I think, go far to explain the special tone of eighteenth-century verse—the nature of the changes in natural philosophy and the general acceptance of the idea that poetry requires a stock language for certain purposes as much as science. It has been said that the change from the synthetic philosophies of Athens to the analytic sciences of the Alexandrians is parallel to the change from Scholasticism to the science of Galileo and Newton.[34] It appears that as the Alexandrian period was characterized by the growth of special sciences, so the sixteenth and seventeenth centuries were primarily engaged in the collection of material and in speculation on special subjects. They provided the means of later synthesis, without accomplishing so much themselves. More specifically, following the lead of Aristotle, his successors were drawn to speculate on the vast new world the conquests of Alexander gave them, but instead of using their knowledge to form philosophies of the universe they felt a greater necessity to catalogue and systematize their new information. Similarly, the discovery of America was followed by the work of Gesner, Gilbert, Kepler, and Harvey, some of them making new and important hypotheses,

---

[33]*Creation* (London, 1712), I. 26–33.
[34]W. C. D. Dampier-Whetham, *A History of Science and Its Relations with Philosophy and Religion* (New York: Macmillan, 1931), 37.

although mostly within limited fields, but spending much of their time merely in improving ancient catalogues. In both periods this kind of specialization signified more than a disinclination to work in the interests of philosophic synthesis; it also meant that such effort was to some degree impossible. For both periods in history the orthodox synthesis had broken down, and there was a failure of belief in an innate purpose governing the processes of nature. It is not so much that skepticism was complete, but understanding was deficient. Virgil was able to perceive some unity in the intellectual efforts of the preceding age, yet in some respects the hexaemeral writers were more convincing. And the deists of the eighteenth century managed to tie a good many loose ends together.

It has already been remarked that in the Alexandrian period and in Virgil's time gardens became popular, and in the late seventeenth and eighteenth centuries botanic and "physic" gardens were established in England for purposes of study.[35] But there were no sermons in these gardens, and flowers as such no longer "solicited the regard of their Creator." In the eighteenth century men and the things of nature were not bound together in a common life of praise:

> Contrast . . . Newtonian teleology with that of the scholastic system. For the latter, God was the final cause of all things just as truly and more significantly than their original former. Ends in nature did not head up in the astronomical harmony; that harmony was itself a means to further ends, such as knowledge, enjoyment, and use on the part of living beings of a higher order, who in turn were made for a still nobler end which completed the divine circuit, to know God and enjoy him forever. God had no purpose; he was the ultimate object of purpose. In the Newtonian world, following Galileo's earlier suggestion, all this further teleology is unceremoniously dropped. The cosmic order of masses in motion according to law, is itself the final good. Man exists to know and applaud it. All the manifold divergent zeals and hopes of men are implicitly denied scope and fulfilment; if they cannot be subjected to the aim of theoretical mechanics, their possessors are left no proper God, for them there is no entrance into the kingdom of heaven. We are to become devotees of mathematical science; God, now the chief mechanic of the universe, has become the cosmic conservative. His aim is to maintain the *status quo*.[36]

---

[35] Foster Watson, *The Beginnings of the Teaching of Modern Subjects in England* (London, 1909), 171.

[36] E. A. Burtt, *The Metaphysical Foundations of Modern Physical Science* (New York: Harcourt, Brace, 1927), 293–4.

This, at any rate, is a direction that philosophy took, and in understanding that fact we are helped to "place" many a poetical reference and figure. It is the philosophical attitude which accounts to a considerable extent for the tone of the language of poetry. Take, for example, Dryden's lines in the *Song for St. Cecilia's Day* (1687), where he has modified the Pythagorean concept according to the needs of his own philosophy or taste:

> From harmony, from heav'nly harmony
> This universal frame began:
> When Nature underneath a heap
> Of jarring atoms lay,
> And could not heave her head,
> The tuneful voice was heard from high:
> "Arise, ye more than dead."
> Then cold, and hot, and moist, and dry,
> In order to their stations leap,
> And Music's pow'r obey.
> From harmony, from heav'nly harmony
> This universal frame began:
> From harmony to harmony
> Thro' all the compass of the notes it ran,
> The diapason closing full in Man.[37]

Dryden says explicitly that the inspiring soul of Music compels the elements in their combining and struggling; for the contrast of philosophy, one need only remember Lucretius' *natura daedala rerum*, the deep voluptuousness of the life-giving force in his world. One may contrast, also, Du Bartas's view of elemental combination with the imitative mythology of Milton to see how new attitudes seriously affect the sense of old ideas. Compare Du Bartas's description of creation out of chaos[38] with these lines of Milton's:

> Exuit invisam Tellus rediviva senectam,
>   Et cupit amplexus, Phœbe, subire tuos;
> Et cupit, & digna est, quid enim formosius illâ,
>   Pandit ut omniferos luxuriosa sinus,
> Atque Arabum spirat messes, & ab ore venusto
>   Mitia cum Paphiis fundit amoma rosis.[39]

---

[37]Lines 1–15, in *The Poetical Works of John Dryden*, ed. George R. Noyes (Boston, 1909).

[38]See above, p. 77.

[39]*Elegia Quinta* 57–60, in *The Student's Milton*, ed. Frank A. Patterson (New York: F. S. Crofts, 1934).

Either description is fanciful enough. But an important part of the difference is in the critical awareness of Milton that his description is fanciful and Du Bartas's strained conviction that he is describing the truth.

One may similarly contrast the flux of Heracleitus with Newton's idea of a compensatory principle governing the workings of the universe:

> . . . for as the seas are absolutely necessary to the constitution of our earth, that from them, the sun, by its heat, may exhale a sufficient quantity of vapors, which, being gathered together into clouds, may drop down in rain, for watering of the earth, and for the production and nourishment of vegetables; or being condensed with cold on the tops of mountains (as some philosophers with reason judge), may run down in springs and rivers; so for the conservation of the seas, and fluids of the planets, comets seem to be required, that, from their exhalations and vapors condensed, the wastes of the planetary fluids spent upon vegetation and putrefaction, and converted into dry earth, may be continually supplied and made up; for all vegetables entirely derive their growth from fluids, and afterwards, in great measure, are turned into dry earth by putrefaction . . . .[40]

What is important is the change of attitude toward processes which in other respects are pretty much agreed upon. Lucretius was able to identify Venus and Nature by means of a sensual imagery which appears in no way to be forced. But for Du Bartas the same imagery involved an important contradiction between his religion and his native materialism. This was a common problem in the sixteenth century, and some later generations found a solution for it in the acceptance of various mechanistic philosophies. They still used the same imagery, but under these new conditions it had lost much of its strength. Dryden's description of the harmonious elements, for instance, gives them no sensual or emotional interest. He can no longer conceive of them as male and female, acting in accordance with some innate and divine purpose. Instead, their activity creates a pattern which is imposed by an external force, and the only purpose of the pattern is that it please the observer, man or God. The imagery is no longer confused, nor is it any longer warm. At its best it is serene, but it is often cold and uninteresting. Pope described rather well the fundamental attitude:

[40]*Sir Isaac Newton's Mathematical Principles of Natural Philosophy and His System of the World, Translated into English by Andrew Motte in 1729*, ed. Florian Cajori (Berkeley: University of California Press, 1934), 529–30. For the passage from Heracleitus see above, p. 53.

Ask for what end the heav'nly bodies shine,
Earth for whose use,—Pride answers, "'Tis for mine:
For me kind Nature wakes her genial power,
Suckles each herb, and spreads out ev'ry flower;
Annual for me the grape, the rose, renew
The juice nectareous and the balmy dew;
For me the mine a thousand treasures brings;
For me health gushes from a thousand springs;
Seas roll to waft me, suns to light me rise;
My footstool earth, my canopy the skies!'[41]

God's function is primarily to observe, and so is the poet's and the philosopher's. Thomson wrote of Newton:

All intellectual eye, our solar round
First gazing through, he, by the blended power
Of gravitation and projection, saw
The whole in silent harmony revolve.
From unassisted vision hid, the moons
To cheer remoter planets numerous formed,
By him in all their mingled tracts were seen.
He also fixed our wandering Queen of Night,
Whether she wanes into a scanty orb,
Or, waxing broad, with her pale shadowy light,
In a soft deluge overflows the sky.
Her every motion clear-discerning, he
Adjusted to the mutual main and taught
Why now the mighty mass of waters swells
Resistless, heaving on the broken rocks,
And the full river turning—till again
The tide revertive, unattracted, leaves
A yellow waste of idle sands behind.[42]

The *anima mundi*, or however the central life of the universe might be conceived, had disappeared, the teleological view of things was destroyed. And the marriage of the elements, the impregnation of the earth with the sun's rays, and all the other figures which explained the universe were deprived of their personalized nature. When poets decided that the figures of mythology were worn out, that a knowledge of Copernicus would provide more valid images, they were in fact also subscribing to the new mathematical emphasis of philosophy. Personification in the description of nature became pretty much an ornamental

[41]*Essay on Man* I. 131-40, in *The Complete Poetical Works*, ed. Henry W. Boynton (Boston and New York, 1903).
[42]*To the Memory of Sir Isaac Newton* 39-56, in *The Complete Poetical Works*, ed. J. Logie Robertson (London, 1908).

device.   John Jones's theorizing in his preface to the *Halieuticks*
described the attitude of many contemporary poets:

'Tis one of the most admirable Secrets in Poetry to heighten small things
by a noble manner of Expression; the meaner therefore any Subject is, the
more capable it is of being adorned.   As there is a regular Gradation of
created Beings from Man down to the lowest Vegetable, the *Naturalist* seems
to have the advantage in a Subject which is capable of being improved by
borrowing it's Metaphors and Allusions from Objects of a superiour Nature.
His Trees and Plants are influenced with the passions of Desire and Aversion,
Joy and Grief; and his Animals seem to rival Mankind in their Virtues and
Perfections.   The *Naturalist* and *Epic* Poet borrow mutually from each other:
the one, in magnifying the Character of his Hero, finds himself obliged to fetch
his Comparisons from the most remarkable Qualities of inferiour Creatures,
the other, after a more easy and natural manner, adds a dignity to his Subject
by alluding to the Hero . . . .   Those Faculties in the Souls of Brutes, which
bear an Analogy to the Will and Passions, and enable them to act with a resemblance of the Virtues and Vices of Mankind, furnish the Poet with frequent
occasions of insinuating the Precepts of Morality after the most easy and per-
swasive manner.   While he represents in the most lively colours their natural
Affection and Piety, their generous Friendship, Courage, and Contempt of
death, he seems to upbraid Mankind either with the want of those Virtues, or
not possessing them in a far superiour degree.[43]

So much for general speculation upon the shifting philosophies of an age.   Professor Lovejoy's *The Great Chain of Being*
supplies us with as much information as we need on this score.
For the rest, our understanding of the philosophy of each poet
depends upon individual study.   The degree to which his diction reflects the deist rather than the Scholastic philosophy is
determined only by a study of his work.   Whether the classic,
Augustan diction was used with eighteenth-century scientific
connotations can be learned only from a study of a poet and a
poem; such use cannot be postulated for all eighteenth-century
poets in equal degree.   Much depends upon the scientific knowledge possessed by a writer, and this we discover as we may.

Nevertheless, "the scientific vocabulary" of verse, however
Macaulay may have meant it,[44] is a good phrase to describe the
language of description in neoclassic poetry.   It is not to be supposed that all English poets took up Sprat's cry to do away with
hackneyed figures and draw upon the great resources of scientific

[43]Preface to *Oppian's Halieuticks, Of the Nature of Fishes and Fishing of the Ancients*,
trans. William Diaper and John Jones (Oxford, 1722), 8–9.
[44]*Critical, Historical and Miscellaneous Essays* (New York, 1860), I. 367.

knowledge, or that all French poets agreed with Chênedollé to create "la poésie scientifique" and to discard the figures of mythology whose charm had long since faded.[45] But an eighteenth-century French poet, writing under the influence of Thomson, uttered a phrase that may be applied to a great number of contemporary English poets: ". . . les anciens aimaient et chantaient la campagne, nous admirons et chantons la nature."[46] For "nature" was properly the subject of poetry in quite the same sense that it was the subject of science.[47] The function of poetry and science was often the same, and in the tradition of humane learning no hard and fast distinctions were made. The naturalist and the poet borrowed from each other, shared common interests and attitudes, and constructed a common language to fulfill their common functions. In time much of the special vocabulary shared by the two lost its original associations and became identified chiefly as "poetic diction," partly, probably, through a defect of memory. The "nature" of Thomson and Saint-Lambert differed so much from the "nature" of

[45]Fusil, *La Poésie Scientifique* 56.

[46]Jean François Saint-Lambert, *Les Saisons, Poëme*, ed. le Comte de Boissy-D'Anglas (Paris, 1828), xxvii. First printed in 1769.

[47]As Sherburne remarked, Manilius was to be read not merely for the elegance of his verse, but also for his foresight in anticipating many of the truths of modern astronomy:

"First, The Opinion of the Fluidity of the Heavens, against the *Aristotelian Hypothesis* of Solid Orbs, appears in this Work to have been expressly delivered by *Manilius* near 1700 years since; which, by the Noble *Tycho, Galilæo, Scheinerus*, and others, have of late Dayes with all the *Acumen* of convincing Reason been defended, and demonstrated.

"Secondly, That the Fixed Stars are not all in the same Concave Superficies of the Heavens, equally distant from the Center of the World, but that they are placed at unequal Distances in the Æthereal Region, some higher, some lower, (whence the Difference of their apparent Magnitudes and Splendor) is by the famous *Kepler* (*Epitom. Astron.* l. I,) and other Modern Astronomers lately asserted; and seems by many to be taken for a Novel Opinion; which yet in this Piece we find to have been many Ages since, declared by our Author.

"Thirdly, The Assertion, which by the most knowing Astronomers of these Times is embraced, affirming the Fixed Stars to be of a fiery Nature and Substance, and consequently endued with native and propper Lustre, and that they are (as *Galilæo* terms them) so many Suns, conform, and like unto this Sun of ours, appears in this very Poem to have been long since maintained by our *Manilius*.

"Fourthly, What by help of the Telescope hath been lately detected and demonstrated by *Galilæo, Kepler*, and others, *that the Galaxie is a Congeries of Numberless small Stars*, was by the sole Perspicil of Reason, discovered by the Ancients, and is here by our Author proposed as the most probable Solution of that *Phænomenon*."—*Sphere* a_1b.

the romantics that even the claims of the scientific terminology to accuracy were misunderstood. Later writers, ignorant of the vocabulary of an outdated natural philosophy, were cut off from the knowledge of associations that belong to so much of the language of natural description in poetry. Some such explanation must account for the failure of many later critics to give the poetry of that period its due.

It may very well be that many poets accepted the idea of a conventional language for poetry because they considered the interests of poetry and natural philosophy to be the same in many important respects. Scientific writing required a set vocabulary formed according to set principles, and it must therefore follow that poetry's needs were similar. This is the extreme conclusion. It is, of course, truer of some poets than of others. But its general validity seems proved by the fact that so many of the same terms are found in scientific prose and in the poetry of the eighteenth century. The evidence in the appendixes is assembled in support of that thesis.

Certain Words Significant in Eighteenth-Century Poetry, with Illustrations from Earlier Poetry and Scientific Literature

APPENDIX A is an alphabetical list of certain words found frequently in the English poetry of the eighteenth century. Under each word are given examples of its use, proceeding from antiquity to the beginning of the eighteenth century. These quotations are followed, when desirable and possible, by passages from scientific prose, also chronologically arranged. Occasionally a word occurs so frequently in a number of fixed applications that it was practicable to distinguish among its uses by grouping the quotations; there are, consequently, the separate entries "Crystal humor," "Crystal sky," and "Crystal water." Occasionally, too, an idea denoted by the key word was so precisely expressed in synonymous terms that passages containing such synonyms are also given. Other passages, moreover, are included in order to explain theories underlying the use of certain significant terms.

The words I have selected for illustration are only a small portion of what might be considered the stock vocabulary of natural description in the poetry of the eighteenth century. According to my reckoning there are at least four hundred additional terms that might profitably be considered and that have been omitted for lack of space, and because the words that have been treated provide enough information for a general study.

Various principles have guided the selection of the terms illustrated in this appendix. Some words stood in special need of clarification as having scientific meaning and application. Others are included for the primary purpose of indicating the frequency or scantiness of earlier use. Still others were selected as representatives of many cognate terms, and some of these, for this reason, are provided with extensive commentaries.

The quotations from antiquity and the Renaissance are chosen in order to point out those writers who, in themselves or as members of a school, were particularly important in the establishment of various conventional elements as part of this poetic language. The French, Italian, Spanish, and Portugese writers of the seventeenth and eighteenth centuries, however, are cited merely as token evidence of the continued occurrence of these terms in languages other than English.

I have endeavored in quoting from the scientific literature of the seventeenth century to give examples by decades, in an effort to establish the frequency as well as the fact of the scientific use of terms important in poetical description. This has been done in order to indicate their continuous use, since that is an important factor in suppositions concerning the associations of meaning available to poetic description.

I have almost always given the earliest occurrences I have found of the various terms in poetry, but in some instances significance rather than priority of use has determined the selection. It is hoped that enough passages are quoted to indicate the variety and scope of traditional uses. I have quoted most fully from the writings of the seventeenth century, and examples are given from each decade when my reading allows it. This has been done to overcome the rather common belief that the traditional diction of the eighteenth century was not widely employed before Dryden. On the other hand, one or two quotations from Dryden or Pope or Thomson seem sufficient to illustrate eighteenth-century practice, for any reader of the poetry of that period may easily supply numerous examples of these significant words.

The dates preceding the quotations are those of the editions followed. Modern editions have been used when it has been especially desirable or convenient, and then the dates given are those of the basic texts followed by the modern editors. Otherwise, first editions are generally cited. There are a few exceptions—Sandys, Sprat, Derham, and some others—and these I have quoted from later printings because the first editions were not immediately accessible when I consulted these authors. It may be remarked, however, that the purpose of the listing is generally served as well by citations from later editions.

A translation is provided for all passages quoted in Greek;

I am responsible for the English if no other translator is indicated.
For an explanation of the system of abbreviations see page xiv.

Adust

Ara dabat fumos herbis contenta Sabinis
Et non exiguo laurus adusta sono.
—Ovid *Fasti* I. 343–4.

Praeparat innumeras puppes Acherontis adusti
Portitor.
—Lucan III. 16–17.

1585 Hoc [mare], sæpius feruore adustum frigido,
Ac turbulentis fluctuum concursibus,
Quasi Mænas insanas & furens.
—Morellus *Pisidas* 370–1.

1593 But so his humor I frame, in a mould of choller
adusted,
That the delights of life shall be to him dolorouse.
—Sidney II. 208.

1617 La adusta Libia sorda aun mas lo sienta
Que los aspides frios que alimenta.
—Góngora II. 262.

1618 Arso il polmone, & il ceruel fumante
Di piu adusto vapor intorno sparso.
—Murtola *Creat. Mondo* VI. xvi. 30.

1638 He could not quiet his impatient lust
Till he had shown the ensigns of his habit;
His parèd crown, with Venus' rays adust.
—Whiting, in *CP* III. 530.

circa In exoletâ nascitur iam infans casâ;
1648 Hospes jumentis; brumæ adustus frigore.
—Wren *Parentalia* 193.

1655 We leave adust Massilias barren Coast.
—Fanshawe *Lus*. V. vi.

1656 Th' adust
And penetrable poison of hot Lust.
—T. Harvey *Mantuan* 39.

1667 The brandisht Sword of God before them blaz'd
Fierce as a Comet; which with torrid heat,
And vapour as the Libyan Air adust,
Began to parch that temperate Clime.
—Milton *P. L.* XII. 633–6.

1675 Or seems that old Opinion of more sway
That the Sun's Horses here once ran astray,

Adust—*continued*

And a new Path mark'd in their straggling flight
Of scorched Skies, and Stars adusted Light?
—Sherburne *Sphere* 49.

1700   Choler adust congeals our blood with fear.
—Dryden *Cock and Fox* 156.

1728   No meagre, Muse-rid Mope, adust and thin,
In a dun nightgown of his own loose skin.
—Pope *Dunc.* II. 37–8.

1744   And hence in climes adust
So sudden tumults seize the trembling nerves.
—Armstrong *Health* I. 182–3.

Leonis adipes cum rosaceo cutem in facie custodiunt a vitiis candorem-
que; sanant et adusta nivibus articulorumque tumores.—Pliny *Nat.
Hist.* XXVIII. xxv.

1504   Unde est quod aqua pluuialis nonnunquam rubea videtur?   Ex adusta
& sicca terrestreitate.—Reisch *Margar. Phil.* dd₆b.

1558   Itaque si terra salsa & adusta sit, exhalatus ex ea humor eiusmodi erit,
atque etiam pluuia.—Foxius *Aqua. Gener.* 123.

1560   Adustos humores expurgat fumus terræ, epithymus, aqua lactis, lapis
stellatus, lapis armenius.—Pictorius *Med. Simpl.* 11–12.

1594   A Copper body, or brasse pot, with a pewter Limbecke, and a glasse
receyuer, are all the necessarie Instruments for the extracting of these
oiles, and the greater the potte, or bodie is, and the more you distil at
once, you shal make both the lesse waste, and the oyles will be in lesse
daunger of adustion.—Plat *Chim. Concl.* 3.

1620   Those . . . are atrabiliary, which abound with choler adust, because
their stomacks are very dry.—Venner *Via Recta* 43 (wrongly numbered
34).

1627   Therefore softer bodies must be put into bottles; and the bottles hung
into water seething, with the mouths open, above the water, that no
water may get in: for by this means the virtual heat of the water will
enter; and such a heat as will not make the body adust or fragile.—
Bacon *Works* IV. 213.

1640   Thus the Elaianian Satyr did rave, and rend the very ayre with his
loud clamors, but in regard they are but the fruits of adusted choler,
and the evaporations of a vindicative spirit.—Howell *Dodon. Grove* 27.

1651   Temperate Sulphur giveth Sweetnesse.   Adust Sulphur giveth Bitter-
nesse.—Comenius *Nat. Phil. Ref.* 63.

1657   The Indies, or black Myrabolanes, do purge Melancholy, and black or
adust Choler.—Coles *Adam in Eden* Nn₂.

1677   There lies another [ocher] of a much redder hue, which first receiving
the steams of the earth, is now in the way of becoming a ruddle, and

Adust—*continued*

in process of time when it grows adust, may at last change into a black chalk.—Plot *Oxford*. 57.

1686 That which is most subtile is Adustive, is proved by most evident Arguments. For Fire converts to its own Nature, every of those things, which is of affinity to it; because it is of affinity to every adustible Thing, and to the subtile adustible, it is of greater affinity.—Russell *Geber* 90.

Aether[1]

ὡς τῶν ἐρχομένων ἀπὸ χαλκοῦ θεσπεσίοιο
αἴγλη παμφανόωσα δι' αἰθέρος οὐρανὸν ἷκε.

—Homer *Il*. II. 457–8. (Even so from their innumerable bronze, as they marched forth, went the dazzling gleam up through the sky unto the heavens.—Tr. A. T. Murray.)

ὧδε δ' ἀναπνεῖ πάντα καὶ ἐκπνεῖ· πᾶσι λίφαιμοι
σαρκῶν σύριγγες πύματον κατὰ σῶμα τέτανται,
καί σφιν ἐπὶ στομίοις πυκιναῖς τέτρηνται ἄλοξιν
ῥινῶν ἔσχατα τέρθρα διαμπερές, ὥστε φόνον μέν
κεύθειν, αἰθέρι δ' εὐπορίην διόδοισι τετμῆσθαι.
ἔνθεν ἔπειθ' ὁπόταν μὲν ἀπαΐξηι τέρεν αἷμα,
αἰθὴρ παφλάζων καταΐσσεται οἴδματι μάργωι.

—Empedocles (Diels, Fr. 100). (And thus does all breathe in and out. In all, Over the body's surface, bloodless tubes Of flesh are stretched, and at their outlets, rifts Innumerable along the outmost rind Are bored; and so the blood remains within; For [aether], however, is cut a passage free. And when from here the thin blood backward streams, The [aether] comes rushing in with roaring swell.—Tr. Leonard.)

χρόνον τάδ' ἦν τοσοῦτον, ἔστ' ἐν αἰθέρι
μέσῳ κατέστη λαμπρὸς ἡλίου κύκλος
καὶ καῦμ' ἔθαλπε.

—Sophocles *Antig*. 415–17. (So went it, until the sun's bright orb stood in mid heaven, and the heat began to burn.—Tr. Jebb.)

οὔτε γὰρ ὄρος σκιερὸν οὔτε νέφος αἰθέριον
οὔτε πολιὸν πέλαγος ἔστιν ὅ τι δέξεται
τώδ' ἀποφυγόντε με.

—Aristophanes *Birds* 349–51. (For

---

[1]See also ELEMENT, LIQUID LIGHT, THIN AND THINNER, VITAL, and see under the periphrases for SKY, pp. 381–4.

Aether—*continued*

never shall be found any distant spot of
ground, Or shadowy mountain covert, or
foamy Ocean wave, Or cloud in Ether
floating, which these reprobates shall
save From the doom that upon them I
will wreak.—Tr. Rogers.)

Ἄλλοι δέ, σποράδην ὑποκείμενοι ' Ὑδρογοῆϊ,
Κήτεος αἰθερίοιο κὰι 'Ιχθύος ἠερέθονται
μέσσοι νωχελέες καὶ ἀνώνυμοι.

—Aratus *Phaen.* 389–91. (Other stars,
sparsely set beneath Hydrochoüs, hang on
high between Cetus in the heavens and the
Fish, dim and nameless.—Tr. G. R. Mair.)

Principio tonitru quatiuntur caerula caeli
Propterea quia concurrunt sublime volantes
Aetheriae nubes contra pugnantibu' ventis.
—Lucretius VI. 96–8.

Namque volans rubra fulvus Iovis ales in
    aethra
Litoreas agitabat aves turbamque sonantem
Agminis aligeri.
—Virgil *Aen.* XII. 247–9.

Ignis in aetherias uolucer se sustulit oras.
—Manilius I. 149.

Haec super inposuit liquidum et gravitate
    carentem
Aethera nec quicquam terrenae faecis ha-
    bentem.
—Ovid *Met.* I. 67–8.

Ecce uenit noua progenies,
Aethere proditus alter homo.
—Prudentius *Cath.* III. 136–7.

Ignibus aethereis caelesti sede locatis.
—Dracontius *Laud. Dei* (*Praefatio* 141).

Tum Pater omnipotens æterno lumine lætum
Contulit ad terras sublimi ex æthere vultum,
Illustrans quodcumque videt.
—Avitus *Initio Mundi* 46–8.

1572   Ves aqui a grande machina do mundo,
Eterea, & elemental, que fabricada
Assi soy do saber alto, & profundo.
—Camoens *Lus.* 174.

Aether—*continued*

1578   Ah, digne n'est telle gent parjurée
De voir long temps la lumiere aitherée.
—Ronsard VI. 406.

1585   Et fingere æthereos [οὐρανοὺς] globos de stercore.
—Morellus *Pisidas* 38b.

1585   La lance, le chevron, le javelot bruslant
S'esclattent en rayons, et la chevre, paree
De grands houpes de feu, sous la voute etheree
Bondit par-cy par-là.
—Du Bartas *I Sem.* II. 632–5.

1596   How-euer these, that Gods themselues do call,
Of them doe claime the rule and souerainty:
As, Vesta, of the fire æthereall.
—Spenser *F. Q.* VII. vii. 26.

1605   Th' ætheriall Aire, whereby wee breath and liue.
—Sylvester *Div. Wks. (6th Day)* 215.

1614   With incense dim the bright ethereal fires.
—W. Browne *Inner Temple Masque* 110.

1622   A hill that thrusts his head into th'etheriall fire.
—Drayton *Poly-Olb.* V. 284.

1627   Perchance that spirit, that all the world maintaines,
And the poiz'd earth in empty aire susteines,
Through these Cirrhæan caues dooes passage gett,
Striuing with his æthereall part to meete.
—May *Lucan* H₃b.

1647   She Uranora hight, because the fire
Of Æthers essence she with bright attire,
And inward unseen golden hew doth dight,
And life of sense and phansie doth inspire.
—More *Psychozoia* I. xv.

1659   As if to outrun desire,
Each nimble stroke, quick as aethereal fire
When winged by motion, fell.
—W. Chamberlayne *Phar.* V. v. 699–701.

1667   Let ther be Light, said God, and forthwith Light
Ethereal, first of things, quintessence pure
Sprung from the Deep.
—Milton *P. L.* VII. 243–5.

1675   Fire up to the Æthereal Confines flew,
And a round Wall of Flame 'bout Nature drew,
The subtle Air possest the second Place
Diffus'd throughout the vast Globes middle space,

Aether—*continued*

Whence its hot Neighbour draws cool Nourishment:
The third Lot level'd the wide Seas Extent,
And in a liquid Plain the Waters spread,
Whence hungry Air is by thin Vapours fed;
Prest down b' its Sediment, Earth lowest fell.
  —Sherburne *Sphere* 13.

[Cancer, Capricorn, and so on]
Which (Parallels) One Course with Heaven partake,
And equal Rise with that and Setting make,
Since in th' Æthereal Texture they observe
Their stated Distance, and thence never swerve.
  —*Ibid.* 45.

1690   The god of love stands ready to revive it,
With his ethereal breath.
  —Dryden *Don S.* II. i, in *Works* VII. 365.

1698   Red meteors ran across th' ethereal space.
  —Dryden *Geo.* I. 657.

1712   [The sun] should ne'er advance to either Pole,
Nor farther yet in liquid Ether roll.
  —Blackmore *Creation* II. 309–10.

1716   Comment de tous les points d'une Circonférence
L'Ether dans sa Fluidité
Vers un Centre certain pousse avec violence
Des Corps où nous voyons tant d'inégalité.
  —Genest *Prin. Phil.* 80.

1734   Whate'er of life all-quick'ning ether keeps,
Or breathes thro' air, or shoots beneath the deeps,
Or pours profuse on earth, one Nature feeds
The vital flame, and swells the genial seeds.
  —Pope *Man* III. 115–18.

1746   By the touch ethereal roused,
The dash of clouds, or irritating war
Of fighting winds, while all is calm below,
They [nitre and sulphur] furious spring.
  —Thomson *Summer* 1113–16.

So likewise of air, there is the most translucent kind which is called by the name of aether [αἰθήρ], and the most opaque which is mist and darkness.—Plato *Timaeus* 58D (LCL 145).

Thus [the ancients], believing that the primary body was something different from earth and fire and air and water, gave the name *aither* to the uppermost region, choosing its title from the fact it "runs always" (ἀεὶ θεῖν) and eternally. (Anaxagoras badly misapplies the word when he uses *aither* for fire.)—Aristotle *De Caelo* 270b21 (LCL 25).

Aether—*continued*

Cœli porro siderumque substantiam appellamus ætherem [αἰθέρα] . . . quum sit elementum a quatuor illis diversum, incorruptum atque divinum.—Pseudo-Aristotle *De Mundo* 392a9, in *Opera* III. 628.

1515 Estque qui apud eos ipsum ætheris corpus quod nec ignis est ut inquiunt nec aer nec terra nec aqua nec omnino quid unum ipsorum simplicium corporum propterea quod simplicibus quidem rectus modus accommodatur.—Argyropolus *Basil* VIb.

1581 Quant au Ciel & aux Estoilles ou Astres qui y sont, nous disons que leur substance est etheree.—Daneau *Phys. Fran.* 25.

1588 Nullatenus igitur ductum certi alicuius orbis, tanquam illi affixus, sequebatur hic Cometa, sed potiùs liberè, propria sibi ingenita & naturali motus Scientia, in liquidissimo Æthere ferebatur.—Brahe *Mundi Æth.* 268.

1602 Ætheream regionem & cœlestem, quidam à summo cœlo ad lunæ orbem definiunt, quem ipsum esse illius quoque regionis partem censent. Elementarem autem ab eo loco, qui huic orbi & spheræ subiicitur ad imum vsque terræ centrum. Alij tamen lunam ipsam ad terrenam & elementarem mundi regionem potiùs putant pertinere, de qua varia hominum opinione videndus est Plutarch.—Daneau *Phys. Christ.* 128.

1614 Anaxagoras maintaineth that [lightning] distilleth from the etheriall region, and that from this so great heate of the heauens many doe fall, which were long time kept and enclosed in the clouds.—Lodge *Seneca* 783.

1621 The firmament is the orbe of the moueable heauen: contayning the world, which consisteth of Ethereall and elementall parts. The Ethereall part compasseth the Elemental: and is not variable: it containeth, 10. spheres, and is in continuall motion being moued from the East to the West in 24. houres and maketh the naturall day.—Widdowes *Nat. Phil.* 5–6.

1634 Dicunt autem, partes Ætheris splendidas quidem & subtiles ob raritatem, cœlum; condensatas verò & coactas in angustum, Astra factas esse: Ex hisce verò inbecillimum maximèque turbulentum esse Lunam. Atqui non tamen ideò segregatam ab æthere videre licet Lunam, sed adhuc multò interiorem illam circumire, profundamque & spaciosam sub se habere ventorum [regionem; atque in illa, cum universali cœli vertigine] torqueri etiam Comata sidera. Adeò non coacta, & quasi obvallata sunt momentis gravitatis & levitatis corpora singula, sed ratione longè diversa sunt concinnata.—Kepler *Plutarch* 118.

1640 The terme (World) may be taken in a double sense, more generally for the whole Vniuerse, as it implies in it the elementarie and æthereall bodies, the starres and the earth. Secondly, more particularly for an inferiour World consisting of elements.—Wilkins *New World* 37.

Aether—*continued*

1644   Ethereall substance being extreme rare, must perforce be eyther extreme liquid, or extreme brittle.—Digby *Two Treat.* 281.

1651   And so on the third day, there came the foure greatest bodies of the World out of the matter already produced, Æther, (that is, the Firmament or Heaven) Aire, Water and Earth.—Comenius *Nat. Phil. Ref.* 13.

1655   Præterea, quoniam globus telluris ætheri, a solis motu pulso, innatat, partes ætheris telluri impingentes undequaque per ipsius telluris superficiem expandentur.—Hobbes I. 383.

1656   *Possidonius* defineth a Star, a divine body, consisting of æthericall fire, splendid and fiery, never resting, but alwaies moving circularly.—Stanley *Hist. Phil. 8th Part* 105.

1660   Vt semel finiam, non possunt globuli ætherei Soli propriores moveri, premi, vel impelli, quin vno, & eodem tempore, cæteri secundùm lineas rectas dispositi propellantur.—Du Hamel *Astr. Phys.* 9.

1661   Now then, when any part of the Brain is strongly agitated; that, which is next and most capable to receive the motive Impress, must in like manner be moved. Now we cannot conceive any thing more capable of motion, then the fluid matter, that's interspers'd among all bodies, and contiguous to them. So then, the agitated parts of the Brain begetting a motion in the proxime Æther; it is propagated through the liquid medium, as we see the motion is which is caus'd by a stone thrown into the water . . . . And thus the motion being convey'd, from the Brain of one man to the Phancy of another.—Glanvill *Van. Dogm.* 200–201.

1662   Whereas I deny not but that the Atmosphere or fluid Body that surrounds the terraqueous Globe, may, besides the grosser and more solid Corpuscles wherewith it abounds, consist of a thinner Matter, which for distinction sake I also now and then call Ethereal.—Boyle *Examen of Hobbes* 14.

1674   He believes the Sensitive Soul to consist in a Congeries of Animal Spirits, since he conceives that Soul to be a thing different from them, and to consist of a matter yet more subtile and æthereal.—*Phil. Trans.* IX. 112.

1678   Through what parts of the universe [the comet] moved, and how far distant it was at several times? Whether in the lower Regions near the Earth in the Atmosphere, or near it, or in the Heavens, or fluid Æther, with which the space of the Heavens is filled?—Hooke *Cometa*, in Gunther *Early Science in Oxford* VIII. 224.

1683   But this is not harder to conceive than in that of a Spiders-Web, whose Mucous substance and Expansion very well answers to that of the Retina (whilst in its due position or Expansion in the Eye;) and as the least breath of Wind moves the one, so the least gale of the Etherial or lucid matter causes a vibration in the other.—*Phil. Trans.* XIII. 175–6.

Aether—*continued*

1690 Et je ne crois pas que ce mouvement se puisse mieux expliquer, qu'en supposant ceux d'entre les corps lumineux qui sont liquides, comme la flame, & apparemment le soleil, & les étoilles, composez de particules qui nagent dans une matiere beaucoup plus subtile, qui les agite avec une grande rapidité, & les fait frapper contre les particules de l'ether, qui les environnent, & qui sont beaucoup moindres qu'elles.—Huyghens XIX. 469.

1698 The Matter of Minerals is a dead passive thing, in which there is included a Light which is cloathed (*vitali aura ætheria*) as I may speak. —Hortolanus *Golden Age* 152.

1704 It appears also that the unequal refractions of difform rays proceed not from any contingent irregularities; such as are veins, an uneven polish, or fortuitous position of the pores of Glass; unequal and casual motions in the Air or Æther.—Newton *Opt.* (Bk. II) 46.

Ambient

κορυφῇ δὲ θεῶν ὁ πέριξ χθόν' ἔχων
φαεννὸς αἰθήρ.
—Euripides, Fr. 911. (The highest of the gods is the shining aether, surrounding the earth.)

Nec circumfuso pendebat in aere tellus
Ponderibus librata suis.
—Ovid *Met.* I. 12–13.

1614 The point of time wrought out by ambient yeares.
—Chapman *Odys.* 2.

1640 Her porous bosom doth rich odours sweat;
Whose perfumes through the ambient air diffuse
Such native aromatics, as we use.
—Carew 125.

1651 Neæra's Lips, (to which adds Grace
The ambient Whiteness of her Face).
—Stanley *Anacreon* 66.

1667 This which yeelds or fills
All space, the ambient Aire wide interfus'd
Imbracing round this florid Earth.
—Milton *P. L.* VII. 88–90.

1675 The watry Girdle of the Ambient Main,
Does either Hemisphere divide, and chain.
—Sherburne *Sphere* 18.

1685 Must England still the scene of changes be,
Toss'd and tempestuous, like our ambient sea?
—Dryden *Prol. to The Unhappy Favorite* 18–19.

Ambient—*continued*

1698   Rais'd in his mind the Trojan hero stood,
And long'd to break from out his ambient cloud.
—Dryden *Aen.* I. 812–13.

1714   Then gazing up, a glorious Pile beheld,
Whose tow'ring summit ambient clouds conceal'd.
—Pope *Temple of Fame* 25–6.

Phœnix autem aerem circumfusum [τὸν μὲν ἀέρα τὸν περιέχοντα] quærit calidum, ut fructum queat maturare.—Theophrastus *De Causis Plant.* III. xvii. 4.

Pars nostra terrarum, de qua memoro, ambienti (ut dictum est) oceano velut innatans longissime ab ortu ad occasum patet.—Pliny *Nat. Hist.* II. cxii. § 242.

Terra quidem stat, aqua uero circumposita circa terram: haec autem continet aeris amictus terram et superpositam aquam ambiens, et circa aeris sphaeram ea quae dicitur ignis.—Priscian 82.

1560   Vita in calore consistit: qui in uiuentibus omnibus nisi temperaretur ac refrigeraretur mediocriter, non duraret. Refrigeratio autem hæc contingit alijs forinsecus tantùm ambiente elemento refrigerante: ut plantis, partim ab aere, partim à terra: & insuper alimento. nam alimentum quoque primum refrigerat.—Gesner *Icones Animal.* 9.

1600   Effluuia illa non sunt flatus, nam emissa non impellunt quicquam; sed absque vllâ sensibili renitentiâ effluunt, & attingunt corpora. Humores sunt summè attenuati, aëre ambiente multò subtiliores.—W. Gilbert *Magnete* 55.

1606   Aristotelis à refrigerationis, seu respirationis modo distinguit omnia Animalia in hoc ipso penè Hebræorum .i. Scripturæ sententiæ assentiens, qui Animalia à respiratione definiunt. Nam, ait ille, alimentum primùm omnium refrigerat Animalia: deinde eadem refrigerat ambiens elementum, velut Aer, aut Aqua.—Daneau *Phys. Christ.* 200b.

1620   Water bee the most ancient drinke, and to those that inhabit hot countries, profitable and familiar, by reason of the parching heat of the ambient aire.—Venner *Via Recta* 24.

1630   Vous la verrez plus blanchastre qu'elle n'estoit auant qu'on la rougit au feu; comme si l'air espessi & adherant luy donnoit cette couleur, qui, avec le tems, se ternit & s'efface, mesmement en lieu humide; d'autant que l'air ambient destrempant cil qui adhere au boulet, le r'appelle à son premier estre.—Rey *Essais* 46.

1632   Cosa, che a me pare, che habbia molto del difficile, nè saprei intender come la Terra corpo pensile, e librato sopra'l suo centro; indifferente al moto, & alla quiete, posto, e circondato da vn' ambiente liquido, non douesse cedere ella ancora, & esser portata in volta.—Galileo *Dial.* 113.

Ambient—*continued*

1655 The ambient æther being of a fiery nature by the swiftnesse of its motion, snatcheth up stones from the earth, which being set on fire, become starres, all carried from East to West.—Stanley *Hist. Phil. 2d Part* 11.

1658 *Ambient*, (Lat.) encircling, compassing round, an Epithete properly belonging to the aire.—Phillips *World of Words*.

1662 And even if our Receiver be unstopt, not under water, but in the open Air, the ambient Air will violently press in with a noise great and lasting enough to argue that the Glass was far from being full of such Air before.—Boyle *Examen of Hobbes* 32.

1665 De Aquis sive Oceano Geocosmum ambiente, mariumque per occultos meatus communicatione.—Kircher *Mundus Subt.* I. 85.

1678 The light parts of the ambient Cloud seemed to spread gradually towards that side of it, which was opposite to the Sun.—Hooke *Cometa*, in Gunther *Early Science in Oxford* VIII. 219.

1694 Warmth does seperate the particles of Water and emit them with a greater and greater Velocity as the heat is more and more intense, as is evident in the steam of a boyling Cauldron, wherein likewise the Velocity of the Ascent of the Vapours does visibly decrease till they disappear, being dispersed into and assimulated with the Ambient Air. —*Phil. Trans.* XVII. 469.

1704 So then the thickness of a plate [of glass] requisite to produce any Colour, depends only on the density of the plate, and not on that of the ambient medium.—Newton *Opt.* (Bk. II) 27.

Attrite

1667 　　　Ere this diurnal Starr
　　　Leave cold the Night, how we his gather'd beams
　　　Reflected, may with matter sere foment,
　　　Or by collision of two bodies grinde
　　　The Air attrite to Fire, as late the Clouds
　　　Justling or pusht with Winds rude in thir shock
　　　Tine the slant Lightning, whose thwart flame driv'n down
　　　Kindles the gummie bark of Firr or Pine.
　　　　　—Milton *P. L.* X. 1069–76.

Posse et attritu, dum in praeceps feratur, illum quisquis est spiritum accendi; posse et conflictu nubium elidi, ut duorum lapidum, scintillantibus fulgetris.—Pliny *Nat. Hist.* II. xliii. 113.

Non miraris, puto, si aëra aut motus extenuat aut extenuatio incendit: sic liquescit excussa glans funda et attritu aëris velut igne destillat. ideo plurima aestate sunt fulmina, qua plurimum calidi est: facilius autem attritu calidorum ignis existit.—Seneca *Nat. Quæst.* II. lvii. 2.

1615 It remaineth therefore that a sound is made when as two bodyes offending or iustling one against another, the medium wherein they are

Attrite—*continued*

mouued endureth betwixt them a compression, that compression endeth in attrition, that attrition in fraction, and that fraction kindleth as it were at resonance.—Crooke *Body of Man* 692.

1655 Præterea ex attritu duorum corporum, ut ligni contra lignum, non modo caloris gradum aliquem generari experimur, sed et ignem. Est enim motus ille, pressionis modo in hanc, modo in illam partem reciprocatio; ex quo motu necessario fit, ut quod in utroque ligno includitur fluidi, modo huc, modo illuc distrahatur; et, per consequens, conetur erumpere; et aliquanto post erumpens fiat ignis.—Hobbes I. 373–4.

1656 Multæ quoque sunt ejus & propè violentæ procreationes, cùm & solidorum ictu gignatur, ut lapidum: & attritu pressuque, ut igniariorum, quæque impetu incitata feruntur, velut eorum, quæ inflammantur liquanturque.—Turnebus *Theophrastus* 1.

1657 Attrition is by Sylvius taken for a certaine manner of preparation, whereby some certaine Medicaments were grated or rubbed on a stone, such as are brought to us from Naxia, an Isle of Cyprus.—Tomlinson *Renodaeus* 62.

1677 Flints, Pebbles, Sand, and whatever else by any quick and sudden attrition may have its parts kindled into sparks.—Plot *Oxford*. 71.

1700 There are others that make the Stomach it self to be the great Instrument of Digestion, but in a different manner: And they suppose it to be perform'd by an Attrition, as if the Stomack, by those repeated Motions, which are the necessary Effects of Respiration, when it is distended by the Aliment, did both rub or grind off some minuter Particles from the grosser Parts, and by continually agitating the Mass of Food, make those Parts, which are not contiguous to the Stomack, strike one against another, and break one another in pieces, until they are all attenuated.—*Phil. Trans.* XXI. 234.

1712 The Mineral Springs become thus impregnated by Attrition, as they speak, that is, by the Water's wearing and rubbing off that Mineral and other Matter from the Sides of its Subterranean Chanels, as it passes along in them.—Morton *Northampton*. 324.

1718 Moreover, in case the Particles of Water were any ⸱wise Angular or Oval, why are they not become quite round, by a perpetual Attrition against each other for so long a time? That being the last Figure assumed by most Bodies after the attrition of their Angles.—J. Chamberlayne *Nieuwentyt* II. 544.

Augment

1567 Moreover, Springs and mighty Meeres and Lakes he did augment.
—Golding *Ovid's Met*. I. 41.

Augment—*continued*

1578   Et de mes pleurs le Loir s'est augmenté.
        —Ronsard I. 225.

1579   Thou pleasaunt spring hast luld me oft a sleepe,
        Whose streames my tricklinge teares did ofte augment.
        —Spenser *S. C.: Aug.* 155–6.

1605   And with sad murmurs she lamenteth so
        That her strange moane augments the Parents woe.
        —Sylvester *Div. Wks.* (*5th Day*) 188.

1613   Fain would they tell their griefs, but know not where;
        All are so full, nought can augment their store.
        —W. Browne *Brit. Past.* I. v. 203–4.

1622   Wharfe, which by thy fall
        Dost much augment my Ouze.
        —Drayton *Poly-Olb.* XXVIII. 453–4.

1640   Her face with fervor flashes.
        And as a dying cinder, rak't in ashes,
        Fed by reviving windes, augmenting, glowes.
        —Sandys *Ovid's Met.* 124.

1656   Meats augment the body, and
        Do nourish it.
        —Evelyn *Lucretius* 63.

1656   L'ombre, au silence jointe, augmente son soucy.
        —Chapelain *Pucelle* 388.

1667   Hither as to thir Fountain other Starrs
        Repairing, in thir gold'n Urns draw Light,
        And hence the Morning Planet guilds his horns;
        By tincture or reflection they augment
        Thir small peculiar.
        —Milton *P. L.* VII. 364–8.

1682   Le cœur le [le fièvre] fomentoit, c'est au cœur qu'
            s'augmente,
        Et qu'enfin parvenant jusqu'à certain excés
        Il acquiert un degré qui forme les accés.
        —La Fontaine *Quin.* 18.

1698   And froth and foam augment the murm'ring tides.
        —Dryden *Aen.* X. 305.

1713   In her chaste current oft the Goddess laves,
        And with celestial tears augments the waves.
        —Pope *Win. For.* 209–10.

1612 Augmentum non est motus localis, ut vult Cardanus: neque fit secundùm
      materiam, neque secundùm formam, ut putat Alexander: sed est muta-

Augment—*continued*

tio magnitudinis, quæ fit per extensionem: extensio autem per additionem.—Alsted *Syst. Phys.* 115.

1622   In the beginning or augmentation of Opthalmia, or any flux of the Eye, it is good to vse diuertiues, defensatiues, and fictions before.— Banister *Guillemeau* b₆.

1634   [Blood-letting] augmenteth the strength, for thereby the body is discharged of griefe. Wherefore the vertue is augmented.—Arnoldus de Villanova *Regiment of Health* 180.

1644   Now referring the particular motions of liuing creatures, to an other time: we may obserue that both kindes of them, as well vegetables as animals do agree in the nature of sustaining themselues in the three common actions of generation, nutrition, and augmentation; which are the beginning, the progresse, and the conseruing of life.—Digby *Two Treat.* 213.

1651   An accidentall mutation of a thing is, when it increases or decreases, or is changed in its qualities: the first is called augmentation, the next diminution, the last alteration.—Comenius *Nat. Phil. Ref.* 70.

1657   And that is called Aliment, which internally assumed, doth nourish and augment the body, as Bread, Wine, the flesh of all flying and four footed Creatures, except ravenous and rapacious.—Tomlinson *Renodaeus* 6.

1664   Le mesme eau courante va changeant la mesure, suiuant qu'elle change de vistesse, c'est à dire qu'elle diminuë de mesure lors qu'elle augmente en vistesse, & que lors qu'elle augmente en mesure, elle diminuuë en vistesse.—Saporta *Castelli* 7.

1670   Ordinarily, at the end of two or three dayes, the half-filled Vessel begins to heat, and this heat augments for several dayes successively.— *Phil. Trans.* V. 2003.

1696   All Generation is with us nothing, as far as we can find, but Nutrition or Augmentation of Parts.—Whiston *New Theory* 224.

Ball[1]

1567   Then first bicause in every part, the earth should
         equall bee,
     He made it like a mighty ball, in compasse as we see.
     —Golding *Ovid's Met.* I. 35–6.

1584   Mais çà, tournons un peu l'estincellante bale,
     Et subtils jettons l'œil dessus la vouste australe.
     —Du Bartas *Colom.* 529–30.

1597   From under this terrestrial ball
     He [the sun] fires the proud tops of the eastern pines.
     —Shakespeare *Rich. II* III. ii. 41–2.

---

[1]See also GLOBE, ORB, SPHERE.

Ball—*continued*

1605 Tigurines, Lombards, Vandals, Visigothes,
Haue swarm'd (like Locusts) round about this Ball.
—Sylvester *Div. Wks.* (*Colon.*) 456.

1616 Thou wondrest Earth to see hang like a Ball,
Clos'd in the gastly Cloyster of this All.
—Drummond I. 80.

1622 Thou whose eye surveys this earthly ball,
And sees our actions ere they be begun.
—Hannay *Son.* XIX.

1633 So of three parts fair Europe is the least,
In which this earthly Ball was first divided.
—P. Fletcher *Purple Isl.* V. v.

ante Great Jove, who rules and fills the spacious all,
1642 The ever-moving spheres, the fixèd ball.
—Godolphin, in *CP* II. 255.

1652 Tell, tell how pond'rous Earth's huge propless ball
Hangs poisèd in the fluent hall
Of fleeting air.
—Benlowes *Theoph.* V. xix.

1675 Round is the Moon to sight,
And with a swelling Body barrs the Light;
Hence never wholly Lucid is her Ball,
Whence the Sun's Beams on it obliquely fall.
—Sherburne *Sphere* 16.

1685 As if great Atlas from his height
Should sink beneath his heavenly weight,
And with a mighty flaw, the flaming wall
(As once it shall)
Should gape immense, and rushing down, o'erwhelm
this nether ball.
—Dryden *Thren. Aug.* 29–33.

1697 But since Earth did not to a Bottom fall,
But hangs, and yielding Air surrounds the Ball.
—Creech *Manilius* (Bk. I) 9.

1712 The Fire, that dwells beneath the Lunar Ball,
To meet ascending Earth, must downward fall.
—Blackmore *Creation* V. 633–4.

1713 O Cyrus! Alexander! Julius! all
Ye mighty Lords that ever rul'd this Ball!
—J. Hughes *Ode to Creator* 5.

Band[1]

1558   Regarde, ô Ceres la grande,
Danser la rustique bande
Des laboureurs assemblez
A la semence des bledz.
   —Du Bellay V. 14.

1578   Et du pere Ocean les bandes escaillées.
   —Ronsard VI. 69.

1591   And the rebellious bands,
That rush out through the woods.
   —James I *Furies* 349–50.

1605   Sathan assisted with th' infernall band.
   —Sylvester *Div. Wks.* (*7th Day*) 238.

1610   The Band, that now in Tryumph shines,
And that (before they wear invested thus)
In earthly bodies carried heavenly mindes.
   —G. Fletcher *Christs Triumph after Death* xxxi.

1631   Soone was I loosed from my slavish band,
And straight preferd to have a large command.
   —P. Fletcher *Sicelides*, in *Works* I. 252.

1656   Pour accomplir son Oeuure, aussi-tost il commande
A l'vn des Messagers de l'Angelique bande.
   —Chapelain *Pucelle* 18.

1656   Grant I amongst thy Sheep may stand,
Sequestred from the Goatish Band.
   —Drummond II. 191.

1667   He err'd not, for by this the heav'nly Bands
Down from a Skie of Jasper lighted now.
   —Milton *P. L.* XI. 208–9.

1685   Take, of a thousand souls at thy command,
The basest, blackest of the Stygian band.
   —Dryden *Alb. and Alban.* II. i, in *Works*, VII. 260.

1700   The fright was general; but the female band
(A helpless train) in more confusion stand.
   —Dryden *Theo. and Hon.* 310–11.

Beam[2]

1563   Now rageth Titan fyerce aboue
His Beames on earth do beate.
   —Googe 62.

---

[1]See also BREED, BROOD, CHOIR, CITIZEN, CREW, FLOCK, FRY, HERD, HOST, INHABITANT, KIND, LEGION, NATION, PEOPLE, RACE, SEED, SHOAL, SQUADRON, TRAIN, TRIBE, TROOP.
[2]See also RAY (*of light*), RAY (VISUAL RAY).

Beam—*continued*

1599   This true Prometheus first made man of earth,
          And shed in him a beame of heauenly Fire.
              —Sir John Davies *Nosce Teipsum* 26.

1605   As the Earths grosse body doth Eclipse
          Bright Cynthias beames.
              —Sylvester *Div. Wks.* (*Eden*) 272.

1614   As Phœbus beames do banish
          A sable cloud, so did the god evanish.
              —Mure I. 112.

1633   The Lightning-flash from swords, casks, courtilaces,
          Wth quiv'ring beams begilds the neighbour grasses.
              —Sylvester *Div. Wks.* (*Yvry*) 552.

1633   Men force the Sunne with much more force to passe,
          By gathering his beames with a christall glasse.
              —Donne *Woodward* 20–1.

1645   Mark what radiant state she spreds,
          In circle round her shining throne,
          Shooting her beams like silver threds,
          This this is she alone.
              —Milton *Arcades* 14–17.

1667   The Sun, my father, bears my soul on high:
          He lets me down a beam, and mounted there,
          He draws it back, and pulls me through the air.
              —Dryden *Ind. Emp.* V. ii, in *Works* II. 397.

1667   The mounted Sun
          Shot down direct his fervid Raies to warme
          Earths inmost womb.
              —Milton *P. L.* V. 300–302.

1668   No pale-fac'd Moon does in stoln beams appear.
              —Cowley 251.

1671   For inward light alas
          Puts forth no visual beam.
              —Milton *S. A.* 162–3.

1682   Dim as the borrow'd beams of moon and stars.
              —Dryden *Rel. Laici* 1.

1727   The lip pale-quivering, and the beamless eye
          No more with ardour bright.
              —Thomson *Summer* 1045–6.

1555   The Raynbowe is the shyning, and rebounding of beamys of light, that
       tourne to the contrarie vapour agayne, in the cloude.—Dygges *Prognost.* 27.

Beam—*continued*

1627 The beams of light, when they are multiplied and conglomerate, generate heat.—Bacon *Works* IV. 290.

1651 A flying dragon, is a long, thick, fat fume, elevated in all its parts: for which cause being kindled, it doth not dart it selfe downward, but sidewayes like a dragon, or sparkling beam.—Comenius *Nat. Phil. Ref.* 132.

1653 The Application happeneth, when as the Circles or Beams of the Planets come to joyn together by a corporall Conjunction, or by aspect of the one half of their Diameters, or when one Planet is distant six deg. from a true aspect, or that he do joyn unto another by the half of his Beams. —Dariott *Redivivus* 45.

1659 Dyals are of two sorts, Pendent, and Fixed. Pendent are such as are hung by the hand, and turned towards the Sun; that by its Beams darting through smal Pin-holes made for that purpose, the hour of the Day may be found.—Moxon *Tutor Astr.* 136.

1662 For, not onely the learned Gassendus, but I know not how many other Atomists (besides other Naturalists) Ancient and Modern, expressly teach the Sun-beams to consist of fiery Corpuscles, trajected through the Air, and capable of passing through Glass.—Boyle *Examen of Hobbes* 55.

1675 This Comet or Meteor is called in English a Beam or Post; in Latine, *Trabs;* in Greek, πυρίκη Δοκίς, i.e. *Ignita Trabs.*—Sherburne *Sphere* 61.

1683 Rain-Water is not only exhaled by the Beams of Heavens from the most clear and subtel Fountains, and impregnated with the Cœlestial Influences, but also is, as it were, strained with the Airy Motions and Winds, which fill it with a Saline and Balsamick Vertue.—Tryon *Way to Health* 146.

1704 In the Sun's beam which was propagated into the Room through the hole in the Window-shut, at the distance of some Feet from the hole, I held the Prism in such a Posture, that its Axis might be perpendicular to that Beam.—Newton *Opt.* (Bk. I) 22.

Belt[1]

1544   Le Dieu Imberbe au giron de Thetys
            Nous fait des montz les grandz umbres descendre.
                —Scève 37.

1578   Et celle qui entr'ouvre
            Les flots à l'environ,
            Et riche se descouvre
            Dans l'humide giron.
                —Ronsard III. 222.

1584   Un rayon mesureur, mille ailez arpenteurs,
            Pour partager la terre en climats et ceintures.
                —Du Bartas *Colom.* 224–5.

---

[1]See also CLIMATE AND CLIME, ZONE.

Belt—*continued*

1605   Include not all within this Close confind,
        That labouring Neptunes liquid Belt doth bind.
          —Sylvester *Div. Wks.* (*Eden*) 277.

1634   Look up, and mark where the broad Zodiac
        Hangs like a Belt about the breast of heaven.
          —Carew 140.

1655   See with how rich a Belt this Orb is crost!
        How broad, how glitt'ring with Embroyderies!
        Where the twelve Starry Animals do make
        The Sun's twelve Houses in the Zodiake.
          —Fanshawe *Lus.* X. lxxxvii.

1675   [The milky way] shines a glittering Belt with bright
          Stars grac'd,
        And girdles with its golden Fires Heavens Waste.
          —Sherburne *Sphere* 48.

        The watry Girdle of the Ambient Main,
        Does either Hemisphere divide and chain.
          —*Ibid.* 18.

1700   An hundred times the rolling sun
        Around the radiant belt has run.
          —Dryden *Sec. Masque* 2–3.

Breed[1]

1597   This happy breed of men, this little world.
          —Shakespeare *Rich. II* II. i. 45.

1605   Beare mighty Forrests full of Timber Trees, . . .
        Spew spacious Riuers, full of fruitfull breed.
          —Sylvester *Div. Wks.* (*Colon.*) 461.

1609   Some would haue gelt him, but that same would spill
        The Wood-gods breed, which must for euer liue.
          —Spenser *F. Q.* VII. vi. 50.

1627   Mounted high
        Upon thy Pegasus of heavenly breed.
          —P. Fletcher *Locusts* V. xxxiv.

1637   That this your husband is of serpent breed,
        Either of Cadmus' or of Hydra's seed.
          —Marmion *Cup. and Psy.* I. iii. 109–10.

1640   But I, great Nereus and blue Doris Seede,
        Great in so many sisters of that breede.
          —Sandys *Ovid's Met.* 242.

---

[1]See also BAND, BROOD, CHOIR, CITIZEN, CREW, FLOCK, FRY, HERD, HOST, INHABITANT, KIND, LEGION, NATION, PEOPLE, RACE, SEED, SHOAL, SQUADRON, TRAIN, TRIBE, TROOP.

Breed—*continued*

1655   Neither of Turkish-blood nor breed, am I.
     —Fanshawe *Lus.* I. lxiv.

1713   With looks unmov'd, he hopes the scaly breed,
     And eyes the dancing cork and bending reed.
     —Pope *Win. For.* 139–40.

1722   Kinds yet unsung, of the Testaceous Breed,
     On Sea-beat Rocks, or sandy Hillocks feed.
     —Diaper *Oppian's Hal.* I. 480–1.

Brine and **Briny**

     εὐθὺς δὲ κώπης ῥοθιάδος ξυνεμβολῇ
     ἔπαισαν ἅλμην βρύχιον ἐκ κελεύματος.
     —Aeschylus *Pers.* 396–7. (Instantly,
     at the word of command, with the even
     stroke of foaming oars they smote the
     briny deep.—Tr. Smyth.)

     Verrunt extemplo placide mare: marmore flavo
     Caeruleum spumat sale conferta rate pulsum.
     —Ennius *Ann.* 384–5.

     Unde sibi exortam semper florentis Homeri
     Commemorat speciem lacrimas effundere salsas
     Coepisse.
     —Lucretius I. 124–6.

     Tot lecti proceres ter denis navibus ibant
     Subsidio Troiae et campos salis aere secabant.
     —Virgil *Aen.* X. 213–14.

1505   Et cursu certant ventis, perque æquora currunt
     Navibus, et curva sulcant vada salsa carina.
     —Pontano *Urania* III. 1303–4.

1572   Pera que estes meus versos vossos sejano
     E vereis ir cortando o salso argento.
     —Camoens *Lus.* 4.

1578   Penchant bas la teste et les yeux
     Dans le sein des plaines salées.
     —Ronsard III. 38.

1585   Il saute au poil retords, et sa dent affilee
     Le trenche finement dessous l'onde salee.
     —Du Bartas *I Sem.* V. 299–300.

1592   Le cose che la terra in sen produce,
     O nutre 'l mar nel salso umido grembo.
     —Tasso *Mondo Creato* IV. 461–2.

Brine and **Briny**—*continued*

1596   And the light bubbles daunced all along,
Whiles the salt brine out of the billowes sprong.
—Spenser *F. Q.* II. xii. 10.

1605   Such th' Indian Gulfe, and such th' Arabian Brine.
—Sylvester *Div. Wks.* (*3d Day*) 78.

1616   Mine Eyes, dissolue your Globes in brinie Streames.
—Drummond I. 53.

1622   As all the watry brood, which haunt the German deepes,
Upon whose briny Curles, the dewy morning weepes.
—Drayton *Poly-Olb.* XX. 79–80.

1645   The Ayr was calm, and on the level brine,
Sleek Panope with all her sisters play'd.
—Milton *Lyc.* 98–9.

1651   Not yet in Womans shape, but like a Cow,
Who seem'd to swim, and force (enraged) through
The briny Sea her way.
—Stanley *Anacreon* 40.

1656   Like to that
Which he of Homer doth commemorate,
Whose Ghost dissolv'd in briny tears came in.
—Evelyn *Lucretius* 21.

1698   His son Cupavo brush'd the briny flood.
—Dryden *Aen.* X. 279.

1746   And the briny deep,
Seen from some pointed promontory's top
Far to the blue horizon's utmost verge,
Restless reflects a floating gleam.
—Thomson *Summer* 167–70.

Brood[1]

1596   But wholy wast, and void of peoples trode,
Saue an huge nation of the Geaunts broode.
—Spenser *F. Q.* III. ix. 49.

1605   The earthly Bands and all the ayrie broods.
—Sylvester *Div. Wks.* (*Arke*) 396.

1613   For verily since old Deucalion's flood,
Earth's slime did ne'er produce a viler brood.
—W. Browne *Brit. Past.* I. iv. 69–70.

---

[1]See also BAND, BREED, CHOIR, CITIZEN, CREW, FLOCK, FRY, HERD, HOST,
INHABITANT, KIND, LEGION, NATION, PEOPLE, RACE, SEED, SHOAL, SQUADRON,
TRAIN, TRIBE, TROOP.

Brood—*continued*

1630   And with my Draughtnet then, I sweepe the streaming
          Flood,
          And to my Tramell next, and Cast-net from the Mud,
          I beate the Scaly brood.
          —Drayton *Nimph.* VI. 145–7.

1640   The Serpents brood by you selfe slaughtred lyes.
          —Sandys *Ovid's Met.* 125.

1645   Hence vain deluding joyes,
          The brood of folly without father bred.
          —Milton *Il P.* 1–2.

1655   They are of that inhumane Brood,
          Which, from their mountains neer the Caspian Sea,
          The fruitful Lands of Asia overflow'd.
          —Fanshawe *Lus.* I. lx.

1667   Though all the Giant brood
          Of Phlegra with th' Heroic Race were joyn'd.
          —Milton *P. L.* I. 576–7.

1682   The fly-blown text creates a crawling brood,
          And turns to maggots what was meant for food.
          —Dryden *Rel. Laici* 419–20.

1697   The titmouse, and the peckers' hungry brood.
          —Dryden *Geo.* IV. 18.

1713   From the' Ægle, Sov'reign of the Sky,
          To each inferior Feather'd Brood.
          —J. Hughes *Ode to Creator* 4.

Buxom[1]

1596   Then gan he tosse aloft his stretched traine,
          And therewith scourge the buxome aire so sore.
          —Spenser *F. Q.* I. xi. 37.

1600   Some spread their sails, and some with strong oars sweep
          The waters smooth, and brush the buxom wave.
          —E. Fairfax *Tasso* XV. xii.

1605   Faire fall thee buxome Aire that yet dost hold
          The sent of her late presence.
          —John Davies of Hereford *Wit. Pilgr.* E₄b.

1613   A sacrifice transcends the buxom air.
          —W. Browne *Brit. Past.* I. v. 802.

1667   Thou and Death
          Shall dwell at ease, and up and down unseen
          Wing silently the buxom Air.
          —Milton *P. L.* II. 840–2.

---

[1]See also YIELDING.

Buxom—*continued*

1700   The crew with merry shouts their anchors weigh,
Then ply their oars, and brush the buxom sea.
—Dryden *Cym. and Iph.* 612–13.

Choir[1]

ὅπου πεντήκοντα κορᾶν
Νηρήιδων ποσὶ χοροὶ
μέλπουσι ἐγκύκλιοι.
—Euripides *Ipheg. Taur.* 427–9. (Where in
dance-rings sweeping The fifty Nereids sing.
—Tr. Way.)

ὡς δ᾽ ὅτ᾽ ἀπ᾽ Αἰθιόπων τε καὶ Αἰγύπτοιο ῥοάων
ὑψιπετὴς γεράνων χορὸς ἔρχεται ἠεροφώνων.
—Oppian *Hal.* I. 620–1. (As when from
the Ethiopians and the streams of Egypt there
comes the high-flying choir of clanging Cranes.
—Tr. A. W. Mair.)

Mischiate sono a quel cattivo coro
De li angeli che non furon ribelli,
Nè pur fedeli a Dio, ma per sè fuoro.
—Dante *Inf.* III. 37–9.

1572   Ou que os celestes Coros inuocados
Decerano a ajudallo, & lhe darano
Esforço, força, ardil, & coraçano.
—Camoens *Lus.* 164.

1585   Afin que le sainct chœur des deitez marines,
Admirant la douceur de mes chansons divines,
Traine mon corps à bord.
—Du Bartas *I Sem.* V. 471–3.

1596   The trees did bud, and earely blossomes bore,
And all the quire of birds did sweetly sing.
—Spenser *F. Q.* II. vi. 24.

1605   And so I say of all the winged quiars,
Which mornly warble, on greene trembling briars
Eare-tickling tunes.
—Sylvester *Div. Wks.* (*Bab.*) 422.

1615   Grullas no siguen su coro
Con mas orden que esta grei.
—Góngora II. 233.

1622   The mirthfull Quires, with their cleere open throats,
Unto the joyfull Morne so straine their warbling notes.
—Drayton *Poly-Olb.* XIII. 51–2.

---

[1]See also BAND, BREED, BROOD, CITIZEN, CREW, FLOCK, FRY, HERD, HOST,
INHABITANT, KIND, LEGION, NATION, PEOPLE, RACE, SEED, SHOAL, SQUADRON,
TRAIN, TRIBE, TROOP.

Choir—*continued*

1640   I might have lustfull thoughts to her, of all
              Earths heav'nly Quire the most Angelicall.
                  —Randolph *Poems* 47.

1651   The voluntary Quire of Birds she feeds.
                  —Davenant *Gond*. III. v. 23.

1667   And joynd thir vocal Worship to the Quire
              Of Creatures wanting voice.
                  —Milton *P. L.* IX. 198-9.

1679   Last night I dreamt Jove sat on Ida's top,
              And, beckoning with his hand divine from far,
              He pointed to a choir of demi-gods.
                  —Dryden *Tro. and Cres.* V. i, in *Works* VI. 373.

1686   See (worthy friend) what I would do
              (Whom neither Muse nor Art inspire),
              That have no friend in all the sacred quire.
                  —Flatman, in *CP* III. 306.

1709   For her, the feather'd quires neglect their song.
                  —Pope *Autumn* 24.

Citizen[1]

1578   Soit les oiseaux vagues hostes de l'air,
              Soit les poissons citoyens de la mer.
                  —Ronsard IV. 335.

1585   Les nageurs citoyens de la venteuse mer.
                  —Du Bartas *I Sem.* V. 30.

1592   I cittadini del celeste regno.
                  —Tasso *Mondo Creato* IV. 674.

1605   The Formes of all things in the Waters found:
              The various manners of Sea-Citizens.
                  —Sylvester *Div. Wks.* (*5th Day*) 145.

1613   Where all this forest's citizens for shade
              At noon-time come.
                  —W. Browne *Brit. Past.* I. i. 510-11.

1614   The savage citizens, which life did leed
              In wods and waters.
                  —Mure I. 132.

1630   If this be Death our best Part to vntie
              (By ruining the Iaile) from Lust and Wrath,

---

[1]See also BAND, BREED, BROOD, CHOIR, CREW, FLOCK, FRY, HERD, HOST, IN-
HABITANT, KIND, LEGION, NATION, PEOPLE, RACE, SEED, SHOAL, SQUADRON,
TRAIN, TRIBE, TROOP.

Citizen—*continued*

    And euery drowsie languor heere beneath,
    It turning deniz'd Citizen of Skie?
       —Drummond II. 32.

1656   Les volans Citoyens, pour soustenir l'orage,
    De leurs toits creuassés reparent le dommage.
       —Chapelain *Pucelle* 448.

1687   His wild disorder'd walk, his haggard eyes,
    Did all the bestial citizens surprise.
       —Dryden *Hind and Panth.* 166–7.

Cleave[1]

1578   Lors à terre vola le guide:
    Et elles, d'ordre le suivant,
    Fendoient le grand vague liquide,
    Hautes sur les ailes du vent.
       —Ronsard III. 55.

1596   [A dove] And with her pineons cleaues the liquid firmament.
       —Spenser *F. Q.* III. iv. 49.

1603   Le garrot empenné siffle dans l'air fendu
    Ainsi qu'une fusee.
       —Du Bartas *Decad.* 64–5.

1605   The nimble winged traine
    That cleaue the Aire.
       —Sylvester *Div. Wks.* (*Tri. Faith*) 573.

1613   Auxilíâr taladra el aire luego
    Vn duro Sacre, en globos no de fuego.
       —Góngora II. 117.

1622   Crying Salsbury, S. George, with such a horrid shout,
    That cleft the wandring clowds.
       —Drayton *Poly-Olb.* XVIII. 548–9.

1637   Then with angelic speed, when he had left
    The Air's high tracts, and the three regions cleft,
    Before her face he on the meadow sate.
       —Marmion *Cup. and Psy.* II. ii. 161–3.

1645   The ruddy waves he cleft in twain,
    Of the Erythræan main.
       —Milton *Ps. cxxxvi* 45–6.

1654   With painted oars the youths begin to sweep
    Neptune's smooth face, and cleave the yielding deep.
       —E. Waller *His Maj. Escaped* 41–2.

---

[1]See also CUT, PASSAGE, PLOUGH, YIELDING.

Cleave—*continued*

1655   Thither through sliced Seas their way they wrought
          Where a calm Bay the crooking shore includes.
          —Fanshawe *Lus.* IX. liii.

1698   All sail at once, and cleave the briny floods.
          —Dryden *Aen.* III. 18.

1713   Not half so swift the trembling doves can fly,
          When the fierce eagle cleaves the liquid sky.
          —Pope *Win. For.* 185–6.

1716   Ceux qui soutenoient que le Monde,
          Comme nous l'assurons, est plein,
          Faisoient voir qu'un Poisson, d'un mouvement soudain,
          Sans laisser après lui de Vuide,
          Fend de Thetis le Sein humide.
          —Genest *Prin. Phil.* 47–8.

1555   There be thre kyndes of lightninges, drye, moyst and clere. Drye do not burne, but cleaue, depart, or diuide.—Dygges *Prognost.* 31.

1581   Car comme les poissons fendent l'eau par le mouuement de leurs ælerons allans tousiours deuant eux: & par le mouuement de leur queue ils guident leur chemin ou pour tourner, ou pour aller droit: ainsi voyons nous que les oiseaux vont & nagent par l'air, en le fendant de leurs æles, comme les poissons font l'eau, & guident leur chemin de leur queue comme font les poissons.—Daneau *Phys. Fran.* 284.

1621   Ampelite is a pitchie Earth, cleauing and blacke.—Widdowes *Nat. Phil.* 31.

1651   The audible quality is called sound; which is a cleaving of the air sharply stricken, flowing every way.—Comenius *Nat. Phil. Ref.* 64.

1685   A worthy Gentleman . . . was pleas'd to acquaint me that the Miners [of Mendip], within these twelve months, had gotten a new way of Cleaving Rocks with Gunpowder.—*Phil. Trans.* XV. 854.

Climate and Clime[1]

         ὃν οὐ μία πατρὶς ἀοιδὸν
         κοσμεῖται, γαίης δ' ἀμφοτέρης κλίματα.
         —*Greek Anthology* IX. xcvii. (The poet
         whom not one country honours as its own,
         but all the climes of two continents.)

         εἰς ῥαχίην Ζεφύροιο παρ' Ἑσπέριον κλίμα γαίης,
         αἱ δὲ Νότου παρὰ πέζαν ἀλήμονες.
         —Nonnos *Dionys.* XXXIV. 350–1. (These
         to the uplands of Zephyros in the western clime
         of the world, others travelling along the plain of
         Notos.—Tr. Rouse.)

---

[1]See also BELT, EMPIRE, KINGDOM, REGION, ZONE.

Climate and Clime—*continued*

1563   Alas that here were Ptholome,
With Compasse Globe in hande,
Whose Arte shuld showe me true the place,
And Clymate where I stande.
    —Googe 113–14.

1585   Car si tost que Titan, renovellant sa peine,
Sur les gelez climats le beau printemps rameine.
    —Du Bartas *I Sem.* III. 137–8.

1592   Altri volar da lunge
Sogliono in terra estrana, e 'n altro clima
Cercar più caldi Soli innanzi al verno.
    —Tasso *Mondo Creato* V. 830–2.

1600   At last we 'gan approach that woful clime
Where fire and brimstone down from heav'n was sent.
    —E. Fairfax *Tasso* X. lxi.

1605   His Loue, which visites earthly Climes
In plumie Shape.
    —Sylvester *Div. Wks.* (*Colum.*) 486.

1613   Qual tigre, la mas fiera
Que clima infamò Hircano.
    —Góngora II. 65.

1617   Eye of our westerne World, Mars-daunting King,
With whose Renowne the Earths seuen Climats ring.
    —Drummond I. 149.

1622   To see those Northerne Climes, with great desire possest,
Himselfe he thither ship'd.
    —Drayton *Poly-Olb.* XIX. 200–1.

1633   And I should be in the hott parching clyme,
To dust and ashes turn'd before my time.
    —Donne *Eleg.* XX. 19–20.

1648   Since they sometime,
Forsake ne're more to see't, their Native Clime.
    —Sherburne *Seneca's Answer* 28.

1656   Nor ought imports it on what clime one stands.
    —Evelyn *Lucretius* 69.

1667   Is this the Region, this the Soil, the Clime,
Said then the lost Arch Angel, this the seat
That we must change for Heav'n?
    —Milton *P. L.* I. 242–4.

1675   Th' uncertain Times
Of Day and Night, differing in different Climes.
    —Sherburne *Sphere* 5.

Climate and **Clime**—*continued*

1690   Here the warm planet ripens and sublimes
        The well-baked beauties of the southern climes.
        —Dryden *Don S.* II. ii, in *Works* VII. 372.

1713   At one wide View His Eye surveys
        His Works, in every distant Clime.
        —J. Hughes *Ode to Creator* 4.

1716   Aussi quand il [le soleil] paroît au plus lointain Tropique,
        Et qu'il nous semble fuir vers le Cercle Antarctique,
        A chaque pas qu'il marque en ces autres Climats,
        Nous voyons dans nos Champs avancer les Frimats.
        —Genest *Prin. Phil.* 123.

        In the frigid climes [κλίμασι] the cold shatters many brass and clay
        vases.—Plutarch *De Primo Frigido* 952a5.

1567   The like dissent is in porcions of ground with diuers Inhabitants of
        opposite quarters and Climates.—Maplet *Greene Forest* 3–4.

1609   Gemmas etiam aliquas in quouis cœli climate produci posse, docet
        noua Zemla sub arctico circulo posita, in qua totum littus.—Boodt
        Gem. Hist. 13.

1612   Therefore England should be in the ninth Clime, because the distance
        of paralleles from the Equator is after Orontius in the ninth Clime, all
        one in our eleuation.—Cogan *Haven of Health* vi.

1627   Plants brought out of hot countries will endeavour to put forth at the
        same time that they usually do in their own climate.—Bacon *Works*
        IV. 416.

1651   *Clima* Gręcè κλίμα, idest scala, vel gradus scalarum; est Zonula in
        superficie Sphæræ, præsertim terrestris, comprehensa à duobus circulis
        Æquatori parallelis, vel ab Æquatore, & vno eius Parallelo.—Ricciolus
        Almagest. Nov. t. I. 24.

1659   The Ancients have yet otherwise divided the Earth into four and
        twenty Northern Climates, and four and twenty Southern Climates:
        so that in all there is eight and forty Climates. The Climates are altered
        according to the half hourly increasing of the longest daies; for in the
        Latitude where the longest daies are increased half an hour longer then
        they are at the Equator (viz. longer then 12 hours) the first Climate
        begins; and in the Latitude where they are increased an whole hour
        longer then in the Equator, the second Climate begins.—Moxon *Tutor
        Astr.* 28.

1671   Those that live in those warmer Regions where it never freezes . . . have
        divers of them derided the Relations of what happens in gelid Climates
        as ridiculous.—Boyle *Useful Nat. Phil.* II (*Ignorance* 6).

1672   D'où il suit qu'il y a en tout soixante climats.—Rohault *Phys.* II. 39.

Climate and Clime—*continued*

1675 They are call'd *Climata, quasi Inclinamenta*, as it were deflexions from a right Position of Sphere, or so many steps and degrees, mounting from the Æquator towards the Pole. The Antients reckon'd only seven . . . . But Modern Astronomers and Geographers reckon 48.—Sherburne *Sphere* 45.

1686 That Air too much heated either by the reflex beams of the Sun, or by Mineral fumes (above the heat of the ambient Air of the Clime) must be none of the healthiest.—Plot *Stafford.* 33.

1697 The Air of these Islands is temperate enough considering the Clime. —Dampier *New Voyage* 81.

Conduit[1]

1574 Mais à si saint propos Pharon clost le conduit
De sa profane oreille.
    —Du Bartas *Judit* II. 151–2.

1598 Dumbe sorrow spake alowd in teares, and blood
That from her griefe-burst vaines in piteous flood,
From the sweet conduits of her sauor fell.
    —Chapman *Hero and Leander* IV. 262–4, in *Poems.*

1599 [Eyes and ears] These Conduit pipes of knowledge, feed
    the mind.
    —Sir John Davies *Nosce Teipsum* 44.

1616 In Waues of Woe thy Sighes my Soule doe tosse,
And doe burst vp the Conduits of my Teares.
    —William Alexander, in Drummond I. 74.

1623 Though now this grained face of mine be hid
In sap-consuming winter's drizzled snow,
And all the conduits of my blood froze up.
    —Shakespeare *Com. of Errors* V. i. 311–13.

1633 Just in that instant when the serpents gripe,
Broke the slight veines, and tender conduit-pipe,
Through which this soule from the trees root did draw
Life.
    —Donne *Progr. of the Soule* 121–4.

1648 The while the conduits of my Kine
Run Creame, (for Wine.)
    —Herrick 350.

1652 Saints the wall,
True Pastors conduits, Grace the font, Love cements all.
    —Benlowes *Theoph.* III. lxxxiv.

---

[1]See also SLUICE.

Conduit—*continued*

1660   Man's architect distinctly did ordain
          The charge of muscles, nerves, and of the brain,
          Thro' viewless conduits spirits to dispense.
              —Dryden *Astræa* 165–7.

1668   Where the old Mother Night does grow,
          Substantial Night, that does disclaime,
          Privation's empty Name,
          Through secret conduits monstrous shapes arose.
              —Cowley 226.

1716   Dans les Conduits secrets des Arteres, des Veines,
          Les flots de notre Sang incessamment poussez.
              —Genest *Prin. Phil.* 151.

1622   The eyes are indued with two sorts of nerues or sinews, whereof the
       first are called *optici* in Greeke, and *visuales* in Latine, which is in Eng-
       lish, sinewes pertaining to sight, whereof either eye hath one proper
       vnto it, which differ from other sinewes, because they are neither of so
       sound and firme substance, but soft, and within full of little holes
       (albeit this hollownesse is not so euident in them that are dead) which
       are as small Conduit pipes and little gutters [comme de petits aque-
       ductz & petits canaux[1]].—Banister *Guillemeau* A₁₀.

1650   Then is it established, beyond the question of any the most Pyrrhonian
       Incredulity, that the Sanation of Wounds; at distance, is not rightly
       adscriptive to the single power of Nature, converting the blood suc-
       cessively distilling from its intersected Conduits, into a genial Balsam.
       —Charleton *Van Helmont* D₂b.

1653   All the scruples which were antiently motioned concerning the distribu-
       tion of the Chylus, and of the blood throughout the same conduit, do
       cease, for the Venæ Lacteæ carry the Chylus to the Liver, and there-
       fore these conduits are apart, and can be obstructed apart.—W. Harvey
       Anat. Exer. 129.

1695   The Water, which some suppose to pass continually from the bottom
       of the Sea, to the Heads of Springs and Rivers, through certain sub-
       terranean Conduits or Chanels.—J. Woodward *Nat. Hist. Earth* 41.

Congeal

          Victa racemifero lyncas dedit India Baccho:
          E quibus, ut memorant, quicquid vesica remisit,
          Vertitur in lapides et congelat aere tacto.
              —Ovid *Met.* XV. 413–15.

1596   The hore
          Congealed litle drops, which doe the morne adore.
              —Spenser *F. Q.* IV. xi. 46.

---

[1]Guillemeau *Traité des Maladies* 8b.

Congeal—*continued*

1600   A chilling frost congealed every vein.
         —E. Fairfax *Tasso* IX. lxxviii.

1611   As the rigor of long Cold congeals
         To harsh hard Wooll the running Water-Rils.
         —Sylvester *Div. Wks.* (*Troph.*) 534.

1622   Like thunder when it speaks most horribly and lowd,
         Tearing the ful-stuft panch of some congealed clowd.
         —Drayton *Poly-Olb.* XII. 483-4.

1627   All lands within those Westerne climates are
         Hardened by Winters dry coniealing aire.
         —May *Lucan* F_4.

1638   And if sharp frosts did, in her absence, steal
         Into this place, and glaz'd the tattling streams,
         Then into crystal would the springs congeal.
         —Whiting, in *CP* III. 463.

1645   That snaky-headed Gorgon sheild
         That wise Minerva wore, unconquer'd Virgin,
         Wherwith she freez'd her foes to congeal'd stone.
         —Milton *Comus* 446-8.

1647   Consuming into tears, shall feel
         Each tear into a pearl congeal.
         —Hall, in *CP* II. 222.

1659   Her bright eyes,
         Those stars whose best of influence scarce had power
         To thaw what grief congealed into a shower
         Of heart-disburthening tears.
         —W. Chamberlayne *Phar.* III. ii. 12-15.

1676   My tears are all congealed, and will not flow.
         —Dryden *Aureng-Zebe* V. i, in *Works* V. 285.

1712   Ferment the Glebe, and genial Spirits loose,
         Which lay imprison'd in the stiffen'd Ground,
         Congeal'd with Cold, in frosty Fetters bound.
         —Blackmore *Creation* II. 193-5.

1746   Thick clouds ascend, in whose capacious womb
         A vapoury deluge lies, to snow congealed.
         —Thomson *Winter* 225-6.

1555   A cloude resolued into water, in the fall congelated, maketh Hayle.
     —Dygges *Prognost.* 28.

1596   Quid est nix? Spumosus imber leuissimè congelatus.—Bodin *Theat.* 204.

1601   Salt commeth either of an humor congealed, or els dried.—Holland *Pliny* II. 414 (Bk. XXXI, chap. vii).

Congeal—*continued*

1627   The concretion of bodies is (commonly) solved by the contrary; as ice, which is congealed by cold, is dissolved by heat.—Bacon *Works* V. 84.

1634   Dans la neige, où il y a quantité d'air, estant appellée pour cette raison du Philosophe Escume, le froid resserrant dans la vapeur ou nuë congelée, l'air qui estoit meslé auec elle, & faisant par ce moyen dans la neige ce que l'agitation de l'eau faict dans l'escume.—La Chambre *Nouv. Pens.* (*Lumière* 21).

1646   Ice is only water congealed by the frigidity of the air.—T. Browne II. 89.[1]

1651   Frost is congealed dew.—Comenius *Nat. Phil. Ref.* 131.

1659   Thousands can witness that their bloods are not so greasie as to be melted in the Scortching heat of the one [zone], or so watry as to be congealed in the Icy frosts of the other.—Moxon *Tutor Astr.* 28.

1677   To Congele, is to suffer those Bodies to grow hard by cold, which fire before had melted and liquefied.—Glaser *Compl. Chym.* 12.

1684   Water issuing out at a crack . . . by the Cold of the external Air, was congealed to an hard Ice.—R. Waller *Acad. Cimen.* 98.

1697   [Sall, an island] hath its Name from the abundance of Salt that is naturally congealed there.—Dampier *New Voyage* 56.

1712   [Stalactites are] produc'd . . . by a gradual Descent and Congelation of watery Drops.—Morton *Northampton.* 144.

Conscious

     Tam pudor incendit viris et conscia virtus.
       —Virgil *Aen.* V. 455.
     Sua narret Ulixes,
     Quae sine teste gerit, quorum nox conscia sola est.
       —Ovid *Met.* XIII. 14–15.

1602   Però che dentro al sen materno regna
     Conscia virtù.
       —Valvasone *Caccia* I. cxlix.

1628   The fyre-brands of a conscious brest,
     Shall of thy terrours not be least.
       —Mure I. 167.

1638   Whilst conscious she her looks with red would dress,
     Fearing her pulse was traitor to her mind.
       —Whiting, in *CP* III. 463.

1640   When I but frown'd in my Lucilius brow,
     Each conscious cheek grew red.
       —Randolph *Looking Glasse* 11.

---

[1]Quoted from the 1672 edition.

Conscious—*continued*

1648   Three-formed Hecate! that dost display
        On nightly mysteries thy conscious Ray.
            —Sherburne *Medea* 1.

1667   Grosser sleep
        Bred of unkindly fumes, with conscious dreams
        Encumberd, now had left them.
            —Milton *P. L.* IX. 1049–51.

1676   Age has not yet
        So shrunk my sinews, or so chilled my veins,
        But conscious virtue in my breast remains.
            —Dryden *Aureng-Zebe* II. i, in *Works* V. 232.

1700   And, panting, in each other's arms embrac'd,
        Rush to the conscious bed, a mutual freight.
            —Dryden *Sig. and Guis.* 230–1.

1713   When long provok'd, thy Wrath awakes,
        And conscious Nature to her Center shakes.
            —J. Hughes *Ode to Creator* 5.

Convey

1595   Those little streames so broken
        He vnder ground so closely did conuay,
        That of their passage doth appeare no token.
            —Spenser *Colin* 141–3.

1605   Ha' ye seene a Towne expos'd to spoile & slaughter,
        (At victors pleasure) where laments and laughter
        Mixtly resound; some carrie, some conuay,
        Some lugge, some loade.
            —Sylvester *Div. Wks.* (*Bab.*) 416.

1616   [Dolphins] As ready to convey the Muses' brood
        Into the brackish lake.
            —W. Browne *Brit. Past.* II. ii. 244–5.

1622   Their fountaines that derive, from those unpittied Woods,
        And so much grace thy Downes, as through their Dales
            they creep,
        Their glories to convay unto the Celtick deep.
            —Drayton *Poly-Olb.* XVII. 418–20.

1637   Her soul within his body stay'd,
        Till he therein his virtues had convey'd.
            —Marmion *Cup. and Psy.* I. iii. 261–2.

1640   Heaven doth conveigh
        Those first from the darke prison of their clay
        Who are most fit for heaven.
            —Habington *Castara* 88.

Convey—*continued*

1651   When from the fatal Forrest Hubert rode,
         To Brescia he and Borgio bent their way;
         That their, though dead, yet much important load,
         They might with horrour to the Camp convay.
         —Davenant *Gond.* II. iii. 1.

1668   As Rivers lost in Seas some secret vein
         Thence reconveighs, there to be lost again.
         —Denham *Cooper's Hill* 35–6.

1676   My brother's body see conveyed with care,
         Where we may royal sepulture prepare.
         —Dryden *Aureng-Zebe* V. i, in *Works* V. 294.

1697   United God the World's Almighty Soul
         By secret methods rules and guides the Whole;
         By unseen passes He himself conveys
         Through all the Mass, and every part obeys.
         —Creech *Manilius* (Bk. I) 12.

1709   Go, gentle gales, and bear my sighs away!
         To Delia's ear the tender notes convey.
         —Pope *Autumn* 17–18.

1722   The Bloodless Crusty Race, who crawling play,
         Tho' no swoln Veins the purple Life convey.
         —Diaper *Oppian's Hal.* I. 1075–6.

1615   It remaineth that wee proceede vnto the second cause of this consent which is by a gristly Canale like a water-pipe which is conueighed from the second hole of the Eare vnto the Mouth & Pallate.—Crooke *Body of Man* 701.

1627   Impression of the air with sounds asketh a time to be conveyed to the sense.—Bacon *Works* IV. 237.

1640   Dame Nature, in framing humane bodies did . . . discover . . . providence in the distribution of veines and arteries for the easie conveyance of bloud into each part.—Howell *Dodon. Grove* 31.

1651   [A dream] carries the vitall spirit along with it, when at the sense of something, either pleasing or displeasing, it conveyes it self to and fro through the body.—Comenius *Nat. Phil. Ref.* 192.

1666   For the Dogs necks cannot be brought so near, but that you must put two or three several Quills more into the first two, to convey the bloud from one to another.—*Phil. Trans.* I. 354.

1674   Which Salt . . . being once dissolved in Rain, and Dews, and thereby insinuated into the Earth, or otherwise caught and conveyed into Vegetables, they are soon speciated.—*Phil. Trans.* IX. 173.

1684   The Conveying and Propagating (which is a kind of Conserving) of Sounds, is much help'd by duly placing the Sonorous Body, and also by the Medium.—*Phil. Trans.* XIV. 477.

Convey—*continued*

1697 Therefore we did immediately cut Bamboes, and made Spouts, through which we conveyed the Water down to the Sea-side.—Dampier *New Voyage* 270–1.

1704 And consequently that whiteness must be allowed a mixture of all Colours, and the Light which conveys it to the Eye must be a mixture of Rays indued with all those Colours.—Newton *Opt.* (Bk. II) 47.

For because dense Bodies conserve their heat a long time, and the densest Bodies conserve their heat the longest, the vibrations of their parts are of a lasting nature, and therefore may be propagated along solid fibres of uniform dense matter to a great distance, for conveying into the Brain the impressions made upon all the Organs of sense.
—*Ibid.* (Bk. III) 135.

1712 The greatest Part of the Fluid Mass, which is conveyed into Plants, does not settle or abide there.—Morton *Northampton.* 400.

Crew[1]

1596   Another Damsell of that gentle crew.
                —Spenser *F. Q.* II. ix. 40.

1605   Or rather, teach me dyue, that I may view
            Deepe vnder water all the Scalie criew.
                —Sylvester *Div. Wks.* (*5th Day*) 146.

1616   A Crue of Virgins made a Ring about Her.
                —Drummond I. 14.

1627   The watry Moone, cold Vesper, and his crew
            Light up their tapers.
                —P. Fletcher *Locusts* I. v.

1640   Nor death, with all his terrors, could affright;
            Lowd Women, wine-bred rage, a lustfull crew
            Of Beasts, and Kettle-drums, should thus subdew?
                —Sandys *Ovid's Met.* 52.

1656   From all the villages a lusty Crew
            Of youthful Men and Maids.
                —T. Harvey *Mantuan* 13.

1667   Nor stood unmindful Abdiel to annoy
            The Atheist crew.
                —Milton *P. L.* VI. 369–70.

1668   There 'mong the Blest thou dost for ever shine,
            And wheresoere thou casts thy view
            Upon that white and radiant crew,
            See'st not a Soul cloath'd with more Light then Thine.
                —Cowley 37.

---

[1]See also BAND, BREED, BROOD, CHOIR, CITIZEN, FLOCK, FRY, HERD, HOST, INHABITANT, KIND, LEGION, NATION, PEOPLE, RACE, SEED, SHOAL, SQUADRON, TRAIN, TRIBE, TROOP.

Crew—*continued*

1698   The fatal jav'lin flew,
              Aim'd at the midmost of the friendly crew.
                  —Dryden *Aen.* XII. 410–11.

1709   Adieu, my flocks; farewell, ye sylvan crew.
                  —Pope *Winter* 91.

Crystal humor[1]

NOTE.—*Crystal humor* in verse is at times apparently a periphrasis for tears, whereas at other times it may merely describe the eyeball. The phrase clearly belongs to optics. According to a theory which seems to have come down from antiquity (although certain important ideas were contributed by Alhazen, an Arabian scientist of the eleventh century), there are three humors in the eye, the watery, the glassy, and the crystal.[2] This theory was constructed in opposition to the optics of Ptolemy, and those ancient views generally, where fire and water were considered to be the important elements of the eye.[3]

The prose quotations below will indicate the universal use of the phrase *crystal humor* in the seventeenth century, but it is to be observed that most of the writers on optics do not claim that tears themselves are made of the crystal humor of the eye. It would appear, then, that such a use in poetry was not necessarily meant to be exact. For passages that illustrate the nature of tears, see pages 388–9.

1550   Le beau cristal des sainctz yeulx de Madame
              Entre les lyz & roses degoutoit.
                  —Du Bellay I. 89.

1584   Et tout-joignant voici
              L'obscure Cataracte, et l'Amafrose aussi,
              Dont l'une par l'amas d'une humeur trop grossier
              Dedans l'optique nef clost l'huis de la lumiere,
              Et l'autre d'une toile emmantelee, envieux,
              La crystalline humeur qui reluit en ses yeux.
                  —Du Bartas *Furies* 331–6.

1596   In whose faire eyes, like lamps of quenched fire,
              The Christall humour stood congealed rownd.
                  —Spenser *F. Q.* III. v. 29.

1605   The Cristall humour shining in the ball.
                  —Sylvester *Div. Wks.* (*Fur.*) 340.

1613   Within this place (as woful as my verse)
              She with her crystal founts bedew'd his hearse.
                  —W. Browne *Brit. Past.* I. v. 159–60.

---

[1] See also HUMOR.
[2] William Whewell, *History of the Inductive Sciences* (New York, 1866) II. 54.
[3] John I. Beare, *Greek Theories of Elementary Cognition from Alcmaeon to Aristotle* (Oxford, 1906) 9–10, 14.

Crystal humor—*continued*

1622   Which eye-bred humour so hath chang'd thy [Thames']
         nature,
     Thy fishes think they live not in thy water.
         —Hannay *Eleg.* II. 29–30.

1638   Her rosies dewed with melting crystal reeked,
     And sorrow did her trembling heart inter.
         —Whiting, in *CP* III. 517.

1646   Fairest, when thy eyes did pour
     A crystal shower,
     I was persuaded that some stone
     Had liquid grown.
         —Hall, in *CP* II. 197.

1655   She spares
     Beams to her tears, as tapers lend their light;
     And should excess of tears rob her of sight,
     Two of these moist sparks might restore 't: our eyes
     And humour watery crystalline comprise:
     Why may not then two crystal drops restore
     That sight a crystal humour gave before?
         —Hammond, in *CP* II. 517.

1656   Idmon, who, whether Sun in East did rise
     Or dive in West, pour'd Torrents from his Eyes
     Of liquid Chrystall, under Hawthorne shade.
         —Drummond II. 141.

1659   The spring-tides fill
     Her eyes, those crystal seas of grief.
         —W. Chamberlayne *Phar.* II. v. 288–9.

1691   Fly back, ye films, that cloud her sight;
     And you, ye crystal humours bright,
     Your noxious vapours purged away,
     Recover, and admit the day.
         —Dryden *King Arthur* III. ii, in *Works* VIII. 170.

1767   Mark
     The curious Structure of these visual Orbs,
     The Windows of the Mind; Substance how clear,
     Aqueous, or chrystalline!
         —Jago *Edge-Hill* III. 28–31.

Super his [membranulis] gutta umoris est, ovi albo similis, a qua videndi
facultas proficiscitur: crystalloides a Graecis nominatur.—Celsus VII.
7. 13.

1600   [According to Galen] Atqui in oculo pars lucida, diaphanaque Crystallinus est humor. Ergo crystallinus pars ea est, in qua sola visile re-
cipitur.—H. Fabricius *De Visione* 50.

Crystal humor—*continued*

1615 From the braine, turne the eye of thy mind to the Gates of the Sun
and Windowes of the soule, I meane the eyes, and there behold the
brightnesse of the glittering Cristall, the purity and neate cleannesse
of the watery and glassy humors.—Crooke *Body of Man* 15.

1637 Et l'experience monstre que celle du milieu [de l'œil], L, qu'on nomme
l'humeur cristaline, cause a peu prés mesme refraction que le verre ou
le cristal.—Descartes *Œuvres* VI. 106.

1651 The fabrick of the eyes is admirable. For beneath the fore-head of
every living creature, God hath hollowed out in the skull two windows,
into which the outmost membrane of the brain, sends two things like
bags, filled with the humorus that come from the braine. In the midst
of which there is a pipe woven together of an opacous thin membrane,
yet full of a most pure chrystalline humour: they call it the apple of
the eye, in which vision is properly made, this is encompassed with a net-
work, full of a watery or glassie humour.—Comenius *Nat. Phil. Ref.* 188.

1664 Without some skill in Opticks, it will be hard for an Anatomist to shew
the Wisdom of God in making the Chrystalline humour of the Eyes
of Men onely of a somewhat convex or lenticular form, rather than as
those of Fishes of an almost perfectly Spherical one.—Boyle *Useful.
Nat. Phil.* I. 97.

1676 Speaking of the Crystallin humor, he observes, that the anterior part
thereof, in Man and Quadrupeds, resembles the segment of a greater
Ellipse.—*Phil. Trans.* XI. 747.

1685 Supponimus itaque quod in fœtu humor crystallinus primò sub forma
guttulæ roscidæ è Nervo Optico in oculi cavitatem . . . delabitur; quæ
à cambio nervi lentè distillanti aucta in formam humoris crystallini
facesset.—Briggs *Ophthalmo.* 33.

1704 The Chrystalline, or Icy Humour, which is contained in the Tunica
Uvea, and is thicker than the rest.—Harris *Lex. Tech.* (under *Humours*).

Crystal sky

NOTE.—The old notion that the sky was made of some crystalline substance
need not be described here at length, but we may note, in view of such a
phrase as Milton's "Crystallin Ocean," that this crystal was considered by
some to be long-frozen ice: "Hoc cœlum, quæ est extima huius expansionis
regio, tam pellucidum & tanquam Chrystallus (quæ nihil est aliud, quàm aqua
per diuturnum tempus congelata)."[1] It differed from rock crystal in that it
was frozen from air.[2] That the sky was also thought of as liquid is probably
due to the concept of the aether as liquid.

1572   Pera o Ceo cristalino aleuantando,
              Com lagrimas os olhos piedosos.
              —Camoens *Lus.* 58b.

[1]Daneau *Phys. Christ.* (1606) 39.
[2]See Plutarch's ascription of this idea to Empedocles, in *De Plac. Phil.* 888b2.

Crystal sky—*continued*

1590   Vp to the clowdes, and thence with pineons light,
        To mount aloft vnto the Christall skie.
        —Spenser *Muio.* 43–4.

1592   Di qual materia sian le stelle e 'l cielo,
        Dicalo quel che lui spiegò d'intorno,
        Qual picciol velo, o quasi leggier fumo
        Fermare 'l volle: e 'l fé costante e fermo
        Piu di cristallo assai ch'al gel s' induri.
        —Tasso *Mondo Creato* II. 169–73.

1603   Car de nostre Sauveur la chair faite divine
        S'en vola par dessus la voute cristaline.
        —Du Bartas *Schisme* 567–8.

1605   Mine Eye lookt ouer that Heau'ns Christall wall.
        —John Davies of Hereford *Wit. Pilgr.* B₂b.

1605   Lett's thinke that God those Waters doth digest
        In that steepe place: for, if that, Nature heere
        Can forme firme Pearle and shining Cristall cleere
        Of liquid substance; lett's beleeue it rather
        Much more in God, the Heau'ns and Natures Father.
        —Sylvester *Div. Wks.* (*2d Day*) 70–1.

1614   Heaven's cristall vaults she wearyes more to view.
        —Mure I. 128.

1622   Kind Nature's Quiristers increast,
        Mounting in crystal skies.
        —Hannay *Philo.* 471–2.

1634   Let not a Star of the luxurious race
        With his loose blaze stain the sky's crystal face.
        —Carew 142.

1646   Heaven the Christall Ocean is.
        —Crashaw *Weeper* iv.

1647   Great Palace of the Empiree,
        Of which the spheares are the foundation,
        The walls of glasse, a fluid sea,
        Eternity thy long duration.
        —Stanley *Ps. cxlviii* 5.

1655   Upon a Christal Throne, with stars imbost,
        Sublime The Father sate.
        —Fanshawe *Lus.* I. xxii.

1667   So hee the World
        Built on circumfluous Waters calme, in wide
        Crystallin Ocean.
        —Milton *P. L.* VII. 269–71.

Crystal sky—*continued*

1690   For were even paradise itself my prison
Still I should long to leap the crystal walls.
—Dryden *Don S.* II. i, in *Works* VII. 359.

1714   Late, as I rang'd the Crystal Wilds of Air,
In the clear Mirror of thy Ruling Star
I saw, alas! some dread Event impend.
—Pope *Rape of the Lock* I. 107–9.

Crystal water[1]

NOTE.—The word *crystal*, used with reference to water, may very often be taken to describe a shining, transparent appearance. But there are certain occurrences of this word in verse where it is clear that something more than the mere appearance of the water is of concern. In several of the passages quoted below it seems that the substance of water is identical with that of crystal. And the fact is that from antiquity to well into the eighteenth century theories were seriously propounded to prove just that identity and, particularly, to show that crystal was formed of water. As Sir Thomas Browne reported:

Hereof the common Opinion hath been, and still remaineth amongst us, that Crystal is nothing else but Ice or Snow concreted, and by duration of time, congealed beyond liquation . . . . Pliny is positive in this Opinion: *Crystallus fit gelu vehementius concreto:* the same is followed by Claudian, not denied by Scaliger, some way affirmed by Albertus, Brasavolus, and directly by many others. The venerable Fathers of the Church have also assented hereto; As Basil in his *Hexameron*, Isidore in his Etymologies, and not only Austin, a Latine Father, but Gregory the Great, and Jerome upon occasion of that term expressed in the first of Ezekiel.[2]

Here, for example, is part of Claudian's poem on a piece of crystal in which a drop of water may be seen:

Possedit glacies naturae signa prioris
Et fit parte lapis, frigora parte negat.
Sollers lusit hiems, imperfectoque rigore
Nobilior vivis gemma tumescit aquis.[3]

Some writers accounted for the nature of crystal by maintaining that there were two kinds of ice. Daneau's explanation was:

Nam quum aqua momentaneo quodam frigore, etsi magno, conglaciatur, est gelu leuius, statímque liquefieri potest. Ea igitur est glacies ordinaria. Quæ autem aquæ magno & diuturno frigore congelascunt, & indurantur, veluti per decem vel viginti annos continuos, appellantur Crystallus, qualis in Alpinis montibus nobísque vicinis reperiri solet, & quidem pretiosissima atque purissima. Illíc enim solet concrescere tam fortiter & robustè, vt lapidis sit dura, de quo glaciei genere est.[4]

---

[1]See also the periphrases for ICE, pp. 372–3.
[2]*Pseud. Epidem.*, in *Works* II. 87. See also: Aristotle *Meteor.* 385b7, in *Opera* III. 619; Pliny *Nat. Hist.* XXXVII. ii. 9; Seneca *Nat. Quaest.* III. xxv. 12; Argyropolus *Basil* XXVIIb.
[3]No. XXXIII.
[4]*Phys. Christ.* (1606) 50b. For other similar theories see Brunfels, *Onomast. Med.* (1534), under *Crystallus;* Bodin *Theat.* (1596) 227; W. Gilbert *Magnete* (1600)

Crystal water—*continued*

It is easy to understand how crystal and ice might from their appearance be thought to be of the same substance. And such an identification would be strengthened by the very word *crystal*, which in its Greek form means ice. But there were aspects of the theory which were much less naïve than this, and these developed from speculation about the difference between fluids and solids. Remembering that water was one of the four primary elements, we are prepared for Plato's notion that minerals are to be classed as waters. There are, then, two kinds of waters, the liquid and the fusible. The liquid kind is fluid by the nature of the particles which make it up. But the fusible kind is liquid only when mixed with fire; when it is isolated from fire it becomes solid. It is in this way that in the regions of the air hail is formed, and on the earth itself, ice (κρύσταλλος).[1] Newton's conception is quite in harmony with this:

Water, which is a very fluid tasteless Salt, she [Nature] changes by Heat into Vapour, which is a sort of Air, and by Cold into Ice, which is a hard, pellucid, brittle, fusible Stone; and this Stone returns into Water by Heat, and Vapour returns into Water by Cold.[2]

Kynaston apparently had some learning on this subject, to judge from the beginning of one of his love poems:

> Learn'd lapidaries say the diamond
> Bred in the mines and mountains of the East,
> Mixt with heaps of gold-ore is often found,
> In the half-bird's half-beast's, the Griphon's, nest,
> Is first pure water easy to be prest,
> Then ice, then crystal, which great length of time
> Doth to the hardest of all stones sublime.[3]

There remains to be mentioned but one other notion connected with such speculation, and that has to do with the natural or normal state of liquids and solids. In general, ice would be the "natural" form of water according to such theories. In more modern terms, the presence of heat was considered an external cause, and with such cause removed, water would naturally be found in a solid form: "L'Eau reçoit successivement les consistances differentes de dureté, & de liquidité: son estat naturel est d'estre glacée."[4]

It will not be necessary, I think, to provide a list of the occurrences of the epithet *crystal* in scientific writing, its use there being almost entirely restricted to describing external appearance. It may be observed, however, that the *New English Dictionary* notes the use of *crystal* to mean ice for the first time in the Anglo-Saxon translation of Psalm cxlvii. 6; its last instance of such a use is from Coverdale's translation of Ecclesiastes xliii. 20.

52; Swan *Spec. Mundi* (1643) 156, 290; W. Johnson *Lex. Chym.* (1657) 70; Goldsmith, *Hist. Earth and Animated Nature* (1774) I. 175.

[1]Plato *Timaeus* 58D–E, 59D–E (LCL 145, 149).

[2]*Opt.* (1730) 374–5.

[3]*To Cynthia*, in *CP* II. 166.

[4]Mariotte *Eaux* (1686) 3.

Crystal water—*continued*

Manibusque ministrat
Niliacas crystallos aquas, gemmaeque capaces
Excepere merum.
—Lucan X. 159–61.

Talis in argento non fulget gratia, tantam
Nec crystalla dabunt nitido de frigore lucem.
—Avitus *Orig. Mundi* 14.

1505   Ac primum ut gelido crescunt humore liquentes
Crystalli, quas post frigentia rupibus antra
In densum cogunt guttisque rigentibus anni
Et longo durant labentia secula cursu.
—Pontano *Meteor.* 288–91.

1578   Sous le crystal d'une argenteuse rive,
Au mois d'Avril une perle je vy.
—Ronsard I. 107.

1584   Qu'un ru traine-gueret, de son cours violant
Des fleuves ne souilloit le crystal doux-coulant.
—Du Bartas *Eden* 75–6.

1592   Onde l'aure odorate innanzi al giorno
Spirano mormorando: e piove intanto
Il rugiadoso e cristallino umore.
—Tasso *Mondo Creato* IV. 380–2.

1596   Or as the Cyprian goddesse, newly borne
Of th' Oceans fruitfull froth, did first appeare:
Such seemed they, and so their yellow heare
Christalline humour dropped downe apace.
—Spenser *F. Q.* II. xii. 65.

1600   I walkt along a streame for purenesse rare,
Brighter then sun-shine, for it did acquaint
The dullest sight with all the glorious pray,
That in the pibble paued channell lay.
No molten Christall, but a Richer mine,
Euen natures rarest alchumie ran there,
Diamonds resolud, and substance more diuine.
—Marlowe, in *Eng. Parnassus* 351.

1605   But, when the Winters keener breath began
To christallize the Baltike Ocean.
—Sylvester *Div. Wks.* (*H. C.*) 363.

1613   Estos arboles pues vee la mañana
Mentir florestas i emular viàles,
Quantos murò de liquidos crystales
Agricultura vrbana.
—Góngora II. 75.

Crystal water—*continued*

1613   The siluer skaled fish that softlie swimme,
Within the brookes and Christall watry brimme.
—Dennys *Secrets of Angling* B₇b.

1622   [Fountains] So crystalline and cold, as hardneth stick
to stone.
—Drayton *Poly-Olb*. XIV. 314.

1630   The Seas in tumbling Mountaines did not roare,
But like moist Christall whispered on the Shoare.
—Drummond II. 45.

1640   The Goddesse then above the Crystall Spring
Her head advanc't.
—Sandys *Ovid's Met*. 92.

1645   Nor wet Octobers torrent flood
Thy molten crystal fill with mudd.
—Milton *Comus* 929–30.

1655   The silver Moon's reverberated Ray
Trembled upon the Chrystal Element.
—Fanshawe *Lus*. I. lviii.

1656   Une Fontaine claire,
Qui, cauant par son cours vn naturel canal,
Roule sur le grauier son liquide crystal.
—Chapelain *Pucelle* 135.

1668   The beauteous Drop first into Ice does freez,
And into solid Chrystal next advance.
—Cowley 428.

1668   This shining piece of Ice
Which melts so soon away
With the Suns ray,
Thy verse does solidate and Chrystallize,
Till it a lasting Mirror be.
—Cowley 186.

1672   Like fishes gliding in a crystal brook.
—Dryden *I Conq. Gran*. IV. i, in *Works* IV. 79.

1709   As in the crystal stream I view my face,
Fresh rising blushes paint the wat'ry glass.
—Pope *Summer* 27–8.

1746   The loosened ice,
Let down the flood and half dissolved by day,
Rustles no more; but to the sedgy bank
Fast grows, or gathers round the pointed stone,
A crystal pavement, by the breath of heaven
Cemented firm.
—Thomson *Winter* 725–30.

Cut[1]

τοτὲ μὲν νοτίαν στείχων πρὸς ὁδόν,
τοτὲ δ' αὖ βορέᾳ σῶμα πελάζων,
ἀλίμενον αἰθέρος αὔλακα τέμνων.
—Aristophanes *Birds* 1398–
1400. (First do I stray on a
southerly way; Then to the north-
ward my body I bear, Cutting a
harbourless furrow of air.—
Tr. Rogers.)

Tot lecti proceres ter denis navibus ibant
Subsidio Troiae et campos salis aere secabant.
—Virgil *Aen.* X. 213–14.

Ac prius ignotum ferro quam scindimus aequor.
—Virgil *Geo.* I. 50.

ὡς τότε μυριόφυλοι ἁλὸς τέμνουσι φάλαγγες
Εὔξεινον μέγα κῦμα.
—Oppian *Hal.* I. 626–7. (Even so in
that season those myriad-tribed phalanxes
of the sea cut the great waves of the Euxine.)

Hæc fatus, leuibus liquidum secat aera pennis,
Mortalem fugiens aciem.
—Avitus *Orig. Mundi* 56.

1505   Et sinuosa means niveis secat æthera cygnis.
—Pontano *Urania* I. 225.

1585   Je sçay bien que tu tiens tel rang parmy la troupe
Qui de l'air orageux les plaines entrecoupe
Que fait le basilic.
—Du Bartas *I Sem.* V. 903–5.

1596   There they in their trinall triplicities
About him wait, and on his will depend,
Either with nimble wings to cut the skies.
—Spenser *Heav. Love* 64–6.

1605   The Phœnix, cutting th' vnfrequented Aire.
—Sylvester *Div. Wks.* (*5th Day*) 175.

1611   The ship her course did cut,
So swiftly, that the parted waues, against her ribs did rore.
—Chapman *Il.* 11.

1622   Choice Chelmer comes along, a Nymph most neatly cleere,
Which welneere through the midst doth cut the wealthy Sheere.
—Drayton *Poly-Olb.* XIX. 95–6.

[1]See also CLEAVE, PASSAGE, PLOUGH, YIELDING.

Cut—*continued*

1640   Borne by crosse windes, he cuts the ayrie Maine.
        —Sandys *Ovid's Met.* 71.

1656   The Waters yeeld to shoving fish (say they)
        When gliding through they cut the liquid way.
        —Evelyn *Lucretius* 35.

1668   As brighter Lightning cuts a way
        Clear, and distinguisht through the Day.
        —Cowley 228.

1684   Let my dear Agis, cut the angry Tide,
        And reach his Port, and there securely ride.
        —Creech *Theocritus* 45.

1698   Then ply their oars, and cut their liquid way
        In larger compass on the roomy sea.
        —Dryden *Aen.* V. 274–5.

1722   Swift as an Arrow cuts the liquid Skies.
        —J. Jones *Oppian's Hal.* V. 602.

        οὕτω καὶ τὰ πετεινα κατα τον αερα νηχομενα, τεμνουσι μεν τουτον.—
        Pollux *Hist. Phys.* 16.   (Thus birds, swimming in the air, cut it.)

1515   Nam uti pisces humorem secant [τέμνουσι[1]] agitatione quidem pen-
        narum ad loca priora quæ petunt proficiscentes / caude uero muta-
        tione flexiones sibi rectosque impetus gubernantes / Sic & in uolatilibus
        fieri conspicere licet / Aerem pennis aliisque fundentibus simili natan-
        tibus modo.—Argyropolus *Basil* XXXVIb.

1555   Etenim volatilia donec in altum aëra secant, non facile capiuntur.—
        J. Fabricius *Diff. Animal.* 223.

1627   The cause given of sound, that it should be an elision of the air (whereby,
        if they mean anything, they mean a cutting or dividing, or else an at-
        tenuating of the air) is but a term of ignorance.—Bacon *Works* IV. 237.

1644   [Certain atoms of fire] being more dense then the ayre in which they
        are carryed, must of necessity cutt their way through that liquide and
        rare medium.—Digby *Two Treat.* 80.

1651   For as a living creature will not be cut, so also water, air, yea the world
        it self; by reason of that universall spirit, uniting all things in it, which
        also when a separation is made (as in the wounds of living creatures,
        in the cutting of the water, in the parting of the air may be seen) makes
        the matter close again.—Comenius *Nat. Phil. Ref.* 33–4.

1665   He wishes above all things, that it might be very exactly observed, at
        what Angle the way of the Comet cuts the Æquator.—*Phil. Trans.* I. 6.

1677   Strings [of a viol] of the same cize move equally fast, because they cut
        the Air with the same facility.—Plot *Oxford.* 289.

---

[1]Migne *Patr. Gr.* XXIX. 169.

Cut—*continued*

1718   The wonderful Manner whereby a Bird cuts the Air with his Wings
       upwards and downwards.—J. Chamberlayne *Nieuwentyt* II. 643.

1733   Such a Structure [the bird's body] renders it more adapted to cut the
       Air, and make itself a Passage through that Element.—Humphreys
       Pluche II. 25.

Diffuse

1596   The charme and venim, which they druncke,
            Their bloud with secret filth infected hath,
            Being diffused through the senselesse truncke.
            —Spenser *F. Q.* II. ii. 4.

1611   When sleepe, doth through his powers diffuse
            His golden humor.
            —Chapman *Il.* 53.

1633   As of this all, though many parts decay,
            The pure which elemented them shall stay;
            And though diffus'd, and spread in infinite,
            Shall recollect, and in one All unite.
            —Donne *To the Lady Bedford* 23–6.

1640   At first she nourisheth her griefe with teares:
            Which weeping eyes diffuse.
            —Sandys *Ovid's Met.* 164.

1652   Thy valley cloth'd with Love will harvest joys diffuse.
            —Benlowes *Theoph.* II. lxxvi.

1671   My trust is in the living God who gave me
            At my Nativity this strength, diffus'd
            No less through all my sinews, joints and bones.
            —Milton *S. A.* 1140–2.

1675   Then since the arid Vapour is not us'd
            To be alike attracted, or diffus'd;
            Hence several Shapes to Meteors are assign'd.
            —Sherburne *Sphere* 60.

1698   Beneath the shade which beechen boughs diffuse.
            —Dryden *Ecl.* I. 1.

1713   From rip'ning Hay diffusive Odours rise.
            —Gay *Rural Sports* 10.

1722   Whatever verdant Plants the Rocks produce
            A noisome Poison from their Pores diffuse.
            —J. Jones *Oppian's Hal.* V. 830–1.

1606   Est enim, calor lucis huius cœlestis vis seu vigor sese per omnia hæc
       inferiora insinuans, per singula membra se diffundens, internè latens
       & corpora vegetans & viuificans.—Daneau *Phys. Christ.* 8b.

Diffuse—*continued*

1632 Vedete, come la reflession, che vien dal muro, si diffonde verso tutte le parti opposteli.—Galileo *Dial.* 65.

1651 Colours as well as light diffuse themselves through the aire, and are in the eyes of all beholders.—Comenius *Nat. Phil. Ref.* 65.

1662 A lump of common Salt being thrown into a pot of water is there dissolved into minute bodies, whereof many are carried to the very top of the water, and are so exquisitely diffused and mingled with the liquor, that each least drop of it contains numbers of Saline Corpuscles.—Boyle *Examen of Hobbes* 85.

1674 In Pleasure, the Soul dilateth herself as much as she can, that is, she diffuseth the spirits, as her Emissaries, to meet and receive the good represented to her.—Charleton *Nat. Hist. Passions* 83.

1680 Est mira quædam & hæc radiorum natura & proprietas, quod in actinobolismo radii radiis nullâ ratione permisceantur, neque frangantur, neque in diversa abeant, sed unusquisque recto sibi tramite fundatur. —Kircher *Physiol.* 80.

1690 If Luminous bodies act on our Eyes, not by a substantial diffusion of extreamly minute particles, as the Atomists would have it, but by a propagated Pulsion of some Subtile matter contiguous to the shining body, (as the Cartesians and many other Philosophers maintain).—Boyle *Languid Motion* 58–9.

Distil[1]

Hinc illaec primum Veneris dulcedinis in cor
Stillavit gutta et successit frigida cura.
—Lucretius IV. 1059–60.

Omne nemus misit uolucres omnisque cruenta
Alite sanguineis stillauit roribus arbor.
—Lucan VII. 836–7.

Iam mella de scopulis fluunt,
Iam stillat ilex arido
Sudans amomum stipite.
—Prudentius *Cath.* XI. 73–5.

μάγγανα φαρμακόεντα κατασταλάουσα κομάων.
—Nonnos *Dionys.* XIV. 174. (She distilled poisoned drugs over their hair.—Tr. Rouse.)

1505 Dona legens selecta manu ac redolentibus hortis
Errantis sequitur florum dea, coniugis auræ
Flant super, et liquidis distillat odoribus æther.
—Pontano *Urania* I. 208–10.

---

[1]See also EXHALATION, EXHALE, INFUSE.

Distil—*continued*

ante   Le Ciel pleure ung depart, le Ciel faict distiller
1573   Une pluye soudaine.
    —Jodelle 240.

1578   J'aime l'esponge aussi, d'autant qu'elle est utile
    A m'essuyer le pleur qui de mes yeux distile.
    —Ronsard V. 340.

1584   Le ciel embrasse-tout œilladoit ceste plaine,
    Que de ses rochers cambrez le doux miel distilloit.
    —Du Bartas *Eden* 58–9.

1596   And the dull drops that from his purpled bill
    As from a limbeck did adown distill.
    —Spenser *F. Q.* VII. vii. 31.

1605   The Night is she that with her sable wing
    In gloomie Darknes hushing euery thing,
    Through all the World dumb silence doth distill.
    —Sylvester *Div. Wks.* (*1st Day*) 19–20.

1613   The Meadowes greene are hoare with siluer dewes,
    That on the earth the sable night distills.
    —Dennys *Secrets of Angling* D₈b.

1613   Troncos me offrecen arboles maiores,
    Cuios enxambres, o el Abril los abra
    O las desate el Maio, ambar destilan,
    I en ruecas de oro raios de el Sol hilan.
    —Góngora II. 48.

1622   Cold Dewes, that over head from thy foule roofe distill.
    —Drayton *Poly-Olb.* XXVI. 417.

1630   His food was Blossomes, and what yong doth spring,
    With Honey that from virgine Hiues distil'd.
    —Drummond II. 12.

1640   As pitch distilleth from the barks black wound.
    —Sandys *Ovid's Met.* 168.

1645   Your fiery essence can distill no tear.
    —Milton *Circumcision* 7.

1656   Drops which do oft distill,
    Hollow hard stones.
    —Evelyn *Lucretius* 31.

1667   His dewie locks distill'd
    Ambrosia.
    —Milton *P. L.* V. 56–7.

1698   From juniper unwholesome dews distil.
    —Dryden *Ecl.* X. 112.

Distil—*continued*

1713   In vain kind seasons swell'd the teeming grain,
         Soft showers distill'd, and suns grew warm in vain.
         —Pope *Win. For.* 53–4.

1553 Voco autem distillationem hinc, transmutationem in substantiam
tenuiorem, manente qualitate.—Cardanus *Varietate* 656.

1601 In processe of time, as they grow bigger, the old Bees distil and drop
meat into their mouthes.—Holland *Pliny* I. 318 (Bk. XI, chap. xvi).

1615 These holes are called by Fallopius in his obseruations *Puncta Lachry-*
malia, as also by Platerus, because thorough them the teares doe distill.
—Crooke *Body of Man* 537.

1627 It is reported by some of the ancients, that there is a tree called occhus,
in the valleys of Hyrcania, that distilleth honey in the mornings.—
Bacon *Works* IV. 435.

1630 Les Chymistes, qui ne pouuans commodement faire leurs extraits
auecques l'eau commune, ont accoustumé de se seruir l'eau distillée,
ou bien de la rosée, qui n'est autre chose que de l'eau passée par le
grand alambic de la nature: car telle eau, comme plus subtile, penetre
mieux la substance des simples.—Rey *Essais* 40.

1633 Under the skinne, humors lightly resort out of the skull: which thence
distilling downe by pericranium into the adherent membran, doe at
length issue out into the eye.—Banester *Tumors* 74.

1644 La pluye se fait quand les nuës espaissies par la froidure de la moyenne
region de l'air distillent & se tournent en gouttes d'eau.—Du Moulin
Phys. 120.

1655 Lightning distills from the æther.—Stanley *Hist. Phil. 2d Part* 12.

1658 *Pluvia, et Imber, stillat e Nube, guttatim.*—Comenius *Orbis Pictus* 12.
(Rain, and a small Shower, distilleth out of a Cloud, drop by drop.
—Tr. Hoole [1659], reprinted in 1727.)

1678 There is not yet certainly (that I know or have heard of) any other
way of making salt water fresh, but by Distillation; which, had there
been such an Art, it would in all probability have been made use of,
and so there is little probability that the Springs at the top of a high Hill
should proceed from the Sea-water strained through the earth. But
were there such a filtration known I hinted in my Attempt, published
anno 1660 about Filtration, how somewhat of that kind might be explained. Fourthly, That this Operation is constantly and most certainly performed by Nature both in exhaling and drawing up fresh
steams and vapours from the Sea, and all moyst bodies, and in pre-
cipitating them down again in Rain, Snow, Hail, but of the other we
have no certainty.—Hooke *Spring*, in Gunther *Early Science in Oxford*
VIII. 369.

Distil—*continued*

1686   Vapors . . . are exhaled into the Air for Clouds and distill again in rains.—Plot *Stafford*. 63–4.

1693   *Ponna*, distilling a Substance like the *Gutta Gamba* . . . . *Perin-Toddali*, a sort of *Zyzyphus* or *Jujube* distilling our common *Lacca.—Phil. Trans.* XVII. 685.

1697   [Dragon trees] are about the bigness of our large Apple-trees, and about the same heighth; and the Rind is blackish, and somewhat rough. The Leaves are of a dark Colour; the Gum distils out of the Knots or Cracks that are in the Bodies of the Trees.—Dampier *New Voyage* 312.

1704   Distillation, is drawing off some of the Principles of a Mixture, as the Oyle, Spirit, Water, &. in proper Vessels, by the help of Fire.—Harris *Lex. Tech.* (under *Distillation*).

Diurnal[1]

Nam non longinquum spatium labere diurnum,
Non hiberna cito volvetur curriculo nox.
—Cicero *Aratus' Phaen.* 297–8.

Exiguam petit requiem, dum Lucifer ignes
Evocet Aurorae, currus Aurora diurnos.
—Ovid *Met.* IV. 629–30.

1593

Et con voi di qualunque altro non schiua
Stanco per l'astro di camin seluaggio
Posar su'l verde d'vna herbosa riua
Non men la notte, ch'al diurno raggio.
—Valvasone *Caccia* I. xxiv.

1604

But all doe shine
As well nocturnall, as diurnall fires,
To adde vnto the flame of our desires.
—Jonson *Kings Coronation* 725–7, in *Ben Jonson* VII. 108.

1622

Whose like the Sunne nere sawe in his diurnall way.
—Drayton *Poly-Olb.* XII. 80.

1623

Ere twice the horses of the sun shall bring
Their fiery torcher his diurnal ring.
—Shakespeare *All's Well* II. i. 164–5.

1651

So pleasant and delightful was the Place,
That Heavens great Eye in its Diurnall Race,
Yet ne'r beheld another like unto 't.
—Sherburne *Salmacis* 7.

---

[1]Not in Ennius, Lucretius, Virgil, Lucan, Spenser, Donne, or Pope.

Diurnal—*continued*

1655   The Sun in his diurnal ring
        From Thetis' lap delay.
              —Hammond, in *CP* II. 496.

1667   Ere this diurnal Starr
        Leave cold the Night.
              —Milton *P. L.* X. 1069–70.

1712   Next see, Lucretian Sages, see the Sun
        His Course Diurnal and his Annual run.
              —Blackmore *Creation* II. 155–6.

1728   The Earth a double Course did run,
        Diurnal round it self, and Annu'al round the Sun.
              —Desaguliers *Newt. Syst.* 3.

1589   Aequinoctialis, seu æquator, qui & cingulum primi mobilis dicitur, est
        circulus maximus per æquidistantiam ab vtroque polo mundi diurno
        motu descriptus.—Maginus *Coelest. Orb.* 1.

1600   De terrestris globi diurna reuolutione magnetica, aduersus primi
        mobilis inueteratam opinionem, probabilis assertio.—W. Gilbert
        Magnete 214.

1612   Mare sequitur motum Lunæ diurnum.—Alsted *Syst. Phys.* 136.

1626   Ros est vapor qui statu vernali & autumnali, virtute solari, tempore
        diurno, in altum attrahitur.—Fludd *Meteor. Cosmica* 77.

1632   Ma la conuersion diurna si dà per moto proprio, e naturale al globo
        terrestre, & in conseguenza a tutte le sue parti.—Galileo *Dial.* 135.

1646   The chiefe businesse of this Chapter (you say) is to defend the earths
        diurnall motion.—Rosse *New Planet* 74.

1657   But such things as are concreted with diurnall cold, are very hard to
        melt, as Gold, Brass, and Iron, the fusion whereof rather pertains to
        such as are exercised in Metals.—Tomlinson *Renodaeus* 74.

1666   But the first that I know of, who took in the consideration of the Earth's
        motion, (Diurnal and Annual) was Galilæo.—*Phil. Trans.* I. 265.

1672   En jettant les yeux sur la sphere artificielle, qui represente la sphere
        naturelle du monde, l'on s'apperçoit qu'entre les cercles diurnes que le
        Soleil décrit chaque jour, il n'y a que l'equateur qui soit coupé en deux
        également par nostre horison, & que ceux qui sont dans la partie sep-
        tentrionale du monde, ont l'arc diurne plus grand que le nocturne, au
        lieu que ceux qui sont dans la partie meridionale ont au contraire l'arc
        nocturne plus grand que le diurne.—Rohault *Traité de Physique* II. 27.

1678   There are then two ways, by which we may come to some certainty
        of what distance a Comet is; and those are, first the Parallax of its
        Diurnal motion, or its Parallax caused by the Diurnal motion of the
        Earth.—Hooke *Cometa*, in Gunther *Early Science in Oxford* VIII. 234.

Diurnal—*continued*

1687   Ut defectus Parallaxeos diurnæ extulit Cometas supra regiones sub-
lunares, sic ex parallaxi annua convincitur eorum descensus in regiones
Planetarum.—Newton *Principia* 474.

1694   Let us for a first supposition put, that the whole surface of the Globe
were all Water very deep, or rather that the whole Body of the Earth
were Water, and that the Sun had his Diurnal course about it.—*Phil.
Trans.* XVII. 469–70.

1700   Besides the Diurnal and Annual Revolutions, there must also be a
Third, to account for that slow Motion of the fixed Stars, upon the
Poles of the Ecliptick, in about 25000 Years.—*Phil. Trans.* XXI. 286.

Element[1]

NOTE.—*Element* in the past has been a word of such wide application that an
apparently casual use of it by any poet would with difficulty be assigned a
precise meaning in a philosophical context. (For example, certain limitations of meaning may be observed under *Element* [*native*].)   And yet, the very
ambiguity of the reference is occasionally a source of power.   The prose passages given below (pp. 146–9), coming as they do from men of many different
philosophies, may prove useful to an understanding of certain passages in
poetry.   The statements of various historians of science are also illuminating:

That bodies are composed or made up of certain parts, elements, or principles, is
a conception which has existed in men's minds from the beginning of the first
attempts at speculative knowledge.   The doctrine of the four elements, earth, air,
fire and water, of which all things in the universe were supposed to be constituted,
is one of the earliest forms in which this conception was systematized; and this
doctrine is stated by various authors to have existed as early as the times of the
ancient Egyptians.   The words usually employed by Greek writers to express these
elements are ἀρχή, a principle or beginning, and στοιχεῖον, which probably meant
a letter (of a word) before it meant an element of a compound . . . .   The mode in
which elements form the compound bodies and determine their properties was at
first, as might be expected, vaguely and variously conceived.   It will, I trust,
hereafter be made clear to the reader that the relations of the elements to the compound involves a peculiar and appropriate Fundamental Idea, not susceptible of
being correctly represented by any comparison or combination of other ideas, and
guiding us to clear and definite results only when it is illustrated and nourished by
an abundant supply of experimental facts . . . .   The first notion was that compounds derive their qualities from their elements by *resemblance:*—they are hot in
virtue of a hot element, heavy in virtue of a heavy element, and so on.   In this
way the doctrine of the *four elements* was framed; for every body is either hot or cold,
moist or dry; and by combining these qualities in all possible ways, men devised
four elementary substances.[2]

Elementa appears in literary Latin for the first time in Lucretius.   The meanings
in which it occurs are "beginnings", "letters of the alphabet" and finally "atoms"
. . . .   It is, on the whole, a reasonable view to hold that Lucretius took over the

---

[1]See also AETHER, ENGENDER, JAR, LIQUID AIR, LIQUID FIRE, LIQUID SKY, SEED,
VITAL.
[2]William Whewell *The Philosophy of the Inductive Sciences* (London, 1840) I. 362–3.

Element—*continued*

term στοιχεῖον through the Latin *elementum* from Democritus, possibly through Epicurus, in the original sense of the Greek, namely "letters".[1]

It may be helpful to present, as well, a brief summary by a modern scholar of the manner in which various ancient philosophers considered the four elements to be linked to the four humors of the human body:

The human body, as a form of matter, was said to be composed of the four elements. Plato in his account of the creation of man makes the Demiurgus assign the immortal souls to the created gods to be combined with particles derived from the four elements; and he describes flesh as "a kind of ferment made with fire and water and earth, containing an acid and saline admixture" [*Timaeus* 72D]. He seems to have owed this theory to Hippocrates. Cicero thus states [*Nat. Deorum* II. xviii] the doctrine:—"If anyone should ask the source from which we have moisture and heat which is diffused throughout the body, and even the earthy firmness of the flesh, and lastly the air we breathe, it is clear that we have taken one from the earth, another from liquid, another from fire, and another from the air which we inhale by breathing."[2]

And, finally, attention may be turned to the comment of another modern scholar on the use of this term in seventeenth-century writing:

The orthodox alchemist of the seventeenth century used the words *element* and *principle* in a loose and elusive manner, sometimes as exchangeable terms, sometimes with different, but undefined meanings; and he asserted that there exists one fundamental principle (or element) which can be separated from "imperfect bodies," in all of which it is hidden, and can "by art be brought to perfection." Boyle, on the other hand, used the two words *elements* and *principles* as synonymous; as meaning definite substances, each having properties that distinguish it from all others, which being themselves "perfectly unmingled," that is, not made of any other bodies, can "be brought to afford" (to use his own cautious phrase) substances different from themselves, by being "immediately compounded" with other elements, and into which all "mixt bodies are ultimately resolved."[3]

> Omnia enim magis haec e levibus atque rutundis
> Seminibus multoque minoribu' sunt elementis
> Quam tellus.
> —Lucretius V. 455–7.

> Proximus est aer illi levitate locoque;
> Densior his tellus elementaque grandia traxit
> Et pressa est gravitate sua.
> —Ovid *Met.* I. 28–30.

> Rupisse uidentur
> Concordes elementa moras rursusque redire
> Nox manes mixtura deis.
> —Lucan V. 634–6.

---

[1] Katharine C. Reiley, *Studies in the Philosophical Terminology of Lucretius and Cicero* (New York, 1909) 56–7.

[2] P. Ansell Robin, *The Old Physiology in English Literature* (London, 1911) 26–7.

[3] M. M. Pattison Muir, *A History of Chemical Theories and Laws* (New York, 1907) 18.

Element—*continued*

ὑψιφανὴς Αἰθέρ, κόσμου στοιχεῖον ἄριστον.
—*Orphica* (*Hymn* V. 4). (Lofty-shining
aether, most excellent element of the universe.)

Deus, ignee fons animarum,
Duo qui socians elementa,
Uiuum simul ac moribundum,
Hominem, pater, effigiasti.
——Prudentius *Cath.* X. 1–4.

1549 Sans luy, du ciel le haut temple,
Large & ample,
En ruyne tumberoit,
Avecq' chacun element,
Tellement
Discorde par tout seroit.
——Du Bellay III. 13.

1558 Tout cela qui depuis a remply ce grand vuyde,
L'air, la terre, & le feu, & l'element liquide.
——Du Bellay II. 152.

1572 Farâyr ver o frio & fundo assento,
Secreto leito do humido elemento.
——Camoens *Lus.* 166b.

1585 Où tous les elemens se logeoient pesle-mesle;
Où le liquide avoit avec le sec querelle.
——Du Bartas *I Sem.* I. 227–8.

Le ciel, masle, s'accouple au plus sec element,
Et d'un germe fecond, qui toute chose anime,
Engrosse à tous momens sa femme legitime.
——*Ibid.* II. 360–2.

1592 Così l'arte divina insieme avvinse,
Quasi catena inanellata e salda,
Gli elementi fra lor varî e discordi.
——Tasso *Mondo Creato* I. 381–3.

1594 And round about her tear-distained eye
Blue circles stream'd, like rainbows in the sky.
These water-galls in her dim element
Foretell new storms to those already spent.
——Shakespeare *Lucrece* 1586–9.

1596 And greedie gulfe does gape, as he would eat
His neighbour element in his reuenge.
——Spenser *F. Q.* I. xi. 21.

Element—*continued*

1605   Now the chiefe Motiue of these Accidents,
Is the dire discord of our Elements.
—Sylvester *Div. Wks. (2d Day)* 39.

1613   Del liquido elemento,
Laminas vno de viscoso azero.
—Góngora II. 103.

1616   Where Elementall Brethren nurse their Strife,
And by intestine Warres maintaine their Life.
—Drummond I. 68.

1620   Que donc l'air et la flamme et la pesante masse
Des plus bas Elements s'arment contre ma foy.
—Bertaut *Œuv. Poét.* 335.

1627   But nothing wrought so much destruction
At Sea as Seas opposed Element,
The fire.
—May *Lucan* E₈b.

1633   Why doe the prodigall elements supply
Life and food to mee, being more pure then I,
Simple, and further from corruption?
—Donne *Div. Poems: Son.* XII. 2–4.

1633   Shee [Cynthia] swaies the Floods, and shews (by Evidence)
Her Selfe sole Law of liquid Elements.
—Sylvester *Div. Wks. (Hymn of Almes)* 519.

1640   Three Elements, at lest, dispeopled be,
To satisfy judicious gluttony.
—Randolph *Poems* 3.

1655   To the low bottom of the Ocean sent,
Cold mattrice of the humid Element.
—Fanshawe *Lus.* X. xxxv.

Breaking the Element of molten Tyn,
Through horrid storms I lead to thee the Dance.
—*Ibid.* VIII. lxxiii.

1656   Dans le profond Abysme, où du Monde est le centre,
Le terrestre Element forme vn spacieux ventre.
—Chapelain *Pucelle* 374.

1667   Light shon, and order from disorder sprung:
Swift to thir several Quarters hasted then
The cumbrous Elements, Earth, Flood, Aire, Fire,
And this Ethereal quintessence of Heav'n
Flew upward.
—Milton *P. L.* III. 713–17.

Element—*continued*

1677   Aire, and ye Elements the eldest birth
        Of Natures Womb, that in quaternion run
        Perpetual Circle, multiform; and mix
        And nourish all things.
        —Milton *P. L.* V. 180–3.

1668   There Thou thy self do'st in full presence show,
        Not absent from these meaner Worlds below;
        No, if thou wert, the Elements League would cease,
        And all thy Creatures break thy Natures peace.
        —Cowley 251.

1676   Rich in itself, like elemental fire,
        Whose pureness does no aliment require.
        —Dryden *Aureng-Zebe* V. i, in *Works* V. 300.

1681   While Nature to his Birth presents
        This masque of quarrelling Elements.
        —Marvell *Unfortunate Lover* 25–6.

1692   Abstrusas rerum causas, quo semine litem,
        Quo pacem Natura paret, quis corpora motus
        Urgeat, indomitos undis quid misceat ignes,
        Qui nexus elementa ligent, fælicior ætas
        Conspexit tandem; cunctisque ignota priorum
        Abdita laxantur vasti penetralia mundi.
        —Fell, in *Mus. Angl. Anal.* (1st ed.) 48.

1698   Winds, rain, and storms, and elemental war.
        —Dryden *Geo.* I. 612.

1707   Avant les Siècles, la Matière
        Impuissante, & sans mouvement,
        N'étoit qu'une Masse grossière
        Où se perdoit chaque Elément.
        —La Motte *Odes* 77.

1722   And Storms their elemental War discharge.
        —J. Jones *Oppian's Hal.* IV. 512.

1730   By nature cast
        Naked and helpless out amid the woods
        And wilds to rude inclement elements.
        —Thomson *Autumn* 47–9.

For with the earthy in us we perceive the earth, with the watery the water, with the aethereal the divine aether, with the fiery the devouring fire.—Empedocles (Diels, Fr. 109).

Quoniam autem elementorum [στοιχείων] causæ quatuor sunt determinatæ, atque ex earum conjugationibus evenit, ut quatuor quoque exsisterent elementa [στοιχεῖα], quorum duo activa sunt, calor et frigus, duo vero passiva, siccitas et humiditas.—Aristotle *Meteor.* 378, in *Opera* III. 609.

Element—*continued*

1546   The bodye of man is compact of foure humours, y^t is to saye: Bloud,
        Phlegme, Choler, and Melancholye, whyche humours are called the
        sonnes of the Elementes, because they be complexioned lyke the foure
        elementes.   For lyke as the ayre is hote and moyste: so is the bloud
        hote and moyest.   And as fyer is hote and drye: so is choler hote & drye.
        And as water is colde and moyst: so is phlegme colde and moyste.
        And as the yearth is colde and dry: so melancholy is colde and drye.
        —Phayer *Reg. Life* A.

1555   A fyry cloude, appering in the element, like a litel pyllar, is a token of
        earthquakes to come.—Dygges *Prognost.* 29.

1560   His omnibus [piscibus], quoniam parum caloris habent, elementum
        ambiens sufficit.—Gesner *Icones Animal.* 9.

1569   L'element de la terre, encor' qu'il soit party en plusieurs Isles, n'est
        qu'vn corps, qui est rond en sa proportion, soit qu'il semble plat comme
        nous auons cy deuant dict.—Chastel *Gomara* 6.

1594   The outwarde part of the wood is brought both to such a hardnesse
        and likewise to such a drinesse . . . for want of moisture and sappinesse,
        neither the Element of earth, nor yet of water can make any penetra-
        tion into it.—Plat *Jewell House* 33.

1600   In maris verò, & aquarum profunditatibus, aut scopuli, ingentesque
        rupes, aut lapides minores, aut arenæ, aut terræ cœnosæ à nauiganti-
        bus, dùm profunditates metiuntur, inueniuntur.   Elementum terræ
        Aristotelicum nusquàm apparet, illudunturque Peripatetici vanis suis
        de elementis insomniis.—W. Gilbert *Magnete* 41.

1602   The Skie, skies, firmament, element, Heauens, heauens, of ye same
        signification.—Withals *Diction.* 1.

1614   The Egyptians made foure elements, and then of euery one of them
        two male and female.   They suppose the aire to bee the male because
        it is winde, female because it is obscure and still.   [They call the sea
        manly water, every other kind of water they call womanly.[1]]   They
        call fire masculine, because it burneth with a flame; feminine, because
        it shineth without hurting by touching.   The stronger earth they call
        male, as for example, stones, and rocks: they assigne the name of female
        to that which is manuable and fit to be employed.—Lodge *Seneca* 813.

1640   But for the elementary world, all things are in a kind of restlesse con-
        flict; The Elements themselves, which are the primitive ingredients of
        all bodies, are in perpetuall combat, they still encroach one upon an-
        other, and labour to repell each other, but amongst the rest the fire is
        most vigorous and ravenous, the earth hath frequent fits of the Palsie,
        the Sea is never still, the aire is agitated with winds, and new monsters
        and meteorological impressions are hourely engendred; so in humane
        bodies composd of this stuffe, there is an incessant warfare amongst

─────────────────

[1]This sentence is supplied from John Clarke's translation, p. 125.

Element—*continued*

the humours for predominancy, and while this naturall war lasteth, the earth cannot be without civill and politicall preliations, the mind following most commonly the temper of the body.—Howell *Dodon. Grove* 202.

1644   And this I haue tryed often; staying vnder water as long as the necessity of breathing would permitt me.   Which sheweth that the ayre being smartly moued, moueth the water also, by meanes of its continuity with it; and that liquid element, being fluide and getting into the eare, maketh the vibrations vpon the drumme of it like vnto those of ayre.—Digby *Two Treat.* 253.

1651   There are foure Elements, Skie, Air, Water, Earth.   That is, there are four faces of the matter of the world reduced into formes, (for at the first it was without form) differing especially in the degree of rarity and density.—Comenius *Nat. Phil. Ref.* 79.

For earth is nothing else but thickned and hardned water: water, nothing but thickned air: air, subtilized water: water, liquified earth.— *Ibid.* 81.

1652   The overflowing of the watery Element hath ever been reputed Prodigious unto the People where it happened.—W. Lilly *Annus Tenebr.* 4.

1656   They know that the Garden of Eden, as the Scripture calls it, in which Adam was created, and which he was set to till, was created also of pure Elements uncorrupted, equally and harmonically proportioned, even in the highest perfection, and that all the sustenance there whereupon man lived was pure, made of pure Elements, not Elements elementated, as the rest of the world was which the Lord made for beasts to live in.—Culpeper *Treat. Aurum Potab.* 8.

1657   The nourishments of Naturall things are the fruits of those seeds which spring up in the foure wombs or Elements.—Pinnell *Croll* 96.

1668   He can tell you fine things of the fiery Element under the Moon, and the Epicycles of the Stars.—Glanvill *Plus Ultra* 119.

1680   A Man may rationally enough retain some doubts concerning the very number of those materiall Ingredients of mixt bodies, which some would have us call Elements, and others Principles.   Indeed when I considered, that the Tenents concerning the Elements, are as considerable amongst the Doctrines of natural Philosophy, as the Elements themselves are among the bodies of the Universe, I expected to find those Opinions solidly establish'd, upon which so many others are superstructed.—Boyle *Scept. Chym.* 10.

1686   After Stones made out of waters and resembling inanimate figures, come we next to such as represent the formes of Animals, the Inhabitants of that Element.—Plot *Stafford.* 182.

1698   He considers those Alterations which befal the Superficial or Exteriour Parts of [the Earth]: shewing that the upper or outermost Stratum of

Element—*continued*

Earth, being the common Fund and Promptuary out of which the matter of all Animals and Vegetables is derived, and into which, that matter is at last all returned back again, is in a continual Flux and Revolution; and takes occasion here to Discourse of the first Particles or Elements of Natural Things.—*Phil. Trans.* XIX. 121.

1714   That the Center of Gravity of fish (of great Consideration in that fluid Element) is always placed in the fittest Part of the Body.—Derham *Physico-Theol.* 404.

1759   Elementa sunt corpora simplicissima, atmosphæram Planetarum constituentia, spatia inter Astra forte replentia:

TERRA opaca, fixa, frigida, quiescens, sterilis.
AQUA diaphana, fluida, humida, penetrans, concipiens.
AER pellucidus, elasticus, siccus, obvolitans, generans.
IGNIS lucidus, resiliens, calidus, evolans, vivificans.
—Linnaeus *Animal. Method. Dispos.* 2.

Element (native)[1]

NOTE.—In agreement with the theory that four elements—earth, air, fire, and water—composed the material universe, it became a settled practice to consider plant and animal life both according to the predominance of one of these elements in the particular plant or animal and according to the element most frequented, whether for shelter or nourishment. With the support of such reasoning, it became customary to name and describe many animals and plants by reference to the element of their habitat or to the primary element of their composition. Birds might be called airy, fish watery, and so on.

A great number of the periphrases for animals in poetry are properly referred to some such doctrine, though sometimes the identification is not at all easy, as in Milton's line, "Down from a Hill the Beast that reigns in Woods."[2]

Various of the passages of poetry that follow are chosen to illustrate the concept of native elements in language where the reference is unmistakable. But it has also seemed worthwhile to include a number of quotations in which the theory itself is not precisely indicated but to which some aspect of the theory is applicable. Occasionally, as in Virgil's lines, the reference to the theory exists only by analogy, but the analogy, I think, is given point by such reference.

ἐκ τούτων γὰρ πάνθ' ὅσα τ' ἦν ὅσα τ' ἔστι καὶ ἔσται,
δένδρεά τ' ἐβλάστησε καὶ ἀνέρες ἠδὲ γυναῖκες,
θῆρές τ' οἰωνοί τε καὶ ὑδατοθρέμμονες ἰχθῦς.
—Empedocles (Diels, Fr. 21). (For all things that are and have been and shall be are nourished from these [elements], trees and men and women and beasts and birds reared in the sea.)

---

[1]See also NATIVE (*adjective*), VITAL.
[2]*P. L.* XI. 187.

Element (native)—*continued*

Ante leves ergo pascentur in aethere cervi,
Et freta destituent nudos in litore piscis.
—Virgil *Ecl.* I. 59–60.

Hic segetes, illic veniunt felicius uvae,
Arborei fetus alibi, atque iniussa virescunt
Gramina. nonne vides, croceos ut Tmolus odores,
India mittit ebur, molles sua tura Sabaei,
At Chalybes nudi ferrum, virosaque Pontus
Castorea, Eliadum palmas Epirus equarum?
Continuo has leges aeternaque foedera certis
Imposuit natura locis, quo tempore primum
Deucalion vacuum lapides iactavit in orbem,
Unde homines nati, durum genus.
—Virgil *Geo.* I. 54–63.

οὐ μὲν γὰρ γαίης πολυμήτορος ἔλπομαι ἅλμην
παυροτέρας ἀγέλας οὔτ' ἔθνεα μείονα φέρβειν.
—Oppian *Hal.* I. 88–9. (The briny sea
feeds not, I ween, fewer herds nor lesser tribes
than earth, mother of many.—Tr. A. W.
Mair.)

1585   Car puis qu'il est ainsi que le sec element
Ses propres animaux ne nourrist seulement,
Ains, qui plus est, encor du laict de ses mammelles
Repaist du ciel flottant les escadres isnelles,
Et les ventres gloutons des troupeaux escaillez
Qui fendent les seillons des royaumes salez,
Tellement que la terre est ou mere ou nourrice
De ce qui court, qui vole, et qui nage, et qui glisse.
—Du Bartas *I Sem.* II. 315–22.

1595   Then needs another Element inquire
Whereof she mote be made; that is the skye.
—Spenser *Amor.* lv.

1604   When down the weedy trophies and herself
Fell in the weeping brook. Her clothes spread wide,
And, mermaid-like, awhile they bore her up;
Which time she chanted snatches of old tunes,
As one incapable of her own distress,
Or like a creature native and indued
Unto that element.
—Shakespeare *Hamlet* IV. vii. 175–81.

1608   Ciascun pesce del mare i proprij gorghi
Hebbe de la Natura, oue dimore;
Altri andò per le piaggie, altri, oue sgorghi
Di picciol riuo cristallino humore.
—Murtola *Creat. Mondo* V. xii. 4.

Element (native)—*continued*

1629?
Heere strayes
The Leviathan hudge,
By thee which form'd, heerin to play,
This element doth lodge.
—Mure II. 154.

1633
For, all, as Vassals, at thy beck are bent,
And breathe by Thee [tobacco], as their new Element.
—Sylvester *Div. Wks.* (*Tobacco Battered*) 575.

1645
I took it for a faëry vision
Of som gay creatures of the element
That in the colours of the Rainbow live.
—Milton *Comus* 297–9.

1646
But they that mov'd by confidence, and clos'd
In one refining flame, and never los'd
Their thoughts on earth, but bravely did aspire
Unto their proper element of fire.
—Hall, in *CP* II. 200.

1651
To Streets (the People's Region) early Fame
First brought this grief, which all more tragick make.
—Davenant *Gond.* II. ii. 1.

See there wet Divers from Fossone sent!
Who of the Seas deep Dwellers knowledge give;
Which (more unquiet then their Element)
By hungry war, upon each other live.
—*Ibid.* II. v. 12.

1667
Up led by thee
Into the Heav'n of Heav'ns I have presum'd,
An Earthlie Guest, and drawn Empyreal Aire,
Thy tempring; with like safetie guided down
Return me to my Native Element.
—Milton *P. L.* VII. 12–16.

Let th' Earth bring forth Fowle living in her kinde,
Cattel and Creeping things, and Beast of the Earth,
Each in their kinde. The Earth obey'd, and strait
Op'ning her fertil Woomb teem'd at a Birth
Innumerous living Creatures, perfet formes,
Limb'd and full grown: out of the ground up rose
As from his Laire the wilde Beast where he wonns
In Forrest wilde, in Thicket, Brake, or Den;
Among the Trees in Pairs they rose, they walk'd:
The Cattel in the Fields and Meddowes green:
Those rare and solitarie, these in flocks
Pasturing at once, and in broad Herds upsprung.
The grassie Clods now Calv'd, now half appeer'd

Element (native)—*continued*

> The Tawnie Lion, pawing to get free
> His hinder parts, then springs as broke from Bonds,
> And Rampant shakes his Brinded main; the Ounce,
> The Libbard, and the Tyger, as the Moale
> Rising, the crumbl'd Earth above them threw
> In Hillocks.
>   —*Ibid*. VII. 451–69.

1668   Lo the third Element does his Plagues prepare,
        And swarming Clouds of Insects fill the Air.
              —Cowley 223.

1674   Princes, Heavens antient Sons, Æthereal Thrones,
        Demonian Spirits now, from the Element
        Each of his reign allotted, rightlier call'd,
        Powers of Fire, Air, Water, and Earth beneath.
              —Milton *P. R.* II. 121–4.

1681   See how the Orient Dew,
        Shed from the Bosom of the Morn
        Into the blowing Roses,
        Yet careless of its Mansion new;
        For the clear Region where 'twas born
        Round in its self incloses:
        And in its little Globes Extent,
        Frames as it can its native Element.
              —Marvell *Drop of Dew* 1–8.

1682   In city clubs their venom let 'em vent,
        For there 't is safe, in its own element.
              —Dryden, *Epilogue to The Loyal Brother* 26–7.

1687   The birds to wanton in the air desire;
        The Salamander sports himself in fire;
        The fish in water plays; and of the earth,
        Man ever takes possession at his birth.
        Only unhappy I, who born to grieve,
        In all these Elements at once do live.
              —Ayres, in *CP* II. 294.

1692   Thus long I am content,
        And rest as in my element.
              —Norris 80.

1698   Nature seems t' ordain
        The rocky cliff for the wild ash's reign.
              —Dryden *Geo.* II. 156–7.

1722   With Fate his [a dying whale's] native Element conspires,
        Boils in his Veins, and darts contagious Fires.
              —J. Jones *Oppian's Hal.* V. 353–4.

Element (native)—*continued*

One is bound to suppose that it is by necessity, and for the sake of motion that [creatures with lungs] are so made, just as there are many that are not so made; for some are made from a larger proportion of earth, such as the genus of plants, and others from water, such as the water animals; but of the winged and land animals some are made from air and some from fire. Each has its system in its appropriate element.—Aristotle *On Respiration* 477a25, in *On the Soul* (LCL) 461–3.

Water animals [τὰ δ' ἔννδρα] are less long-lived than land animals, not merely because they are moist, but because they are watery [ὑδατώδη]; this kind of moisture is easily destroyed, because it is cold and easily congealed.—Aristotle *On Length of Life* 466b30, in *On the Soul* (LCL) 401.

Even in life, we may see the attraction of like to like operating in animals just as it did in the upward and downward growth of plants . . . . Those that have most fire in them fly up into the air; those in which earth preponderates take to the earth, as did the dog which always sat upon a tile. Aquatic animals are those in which water predominates. This does not, however, apply to fishes, which are very fiery, and take to the water to cool themselves.—Empedocles paraphrased, in J. Burnet *Early Greek Philosophy* 283.

1515   Singula namque genera piscium accomodata sibi loca natura distribuunt: in illisque uitam degunt nec aliena loca unquam expetunt: neque aggrediuntur / Sed intra suos se leta continent fines.—Argyropolus *Basil* XXXIII.

1555   Alia syluas frequentant, vt fera pleraque omnia, tarandus, tragelaphus, ceruorumque adeò genus omne, boum genus syluestre, armelini, sobellæ, nöerza et murium genera syluestria.—J. Fabricius *Diff. Animal.* 32.

1560   Animalium Divisio, Secundum Elementa, In Quibus Habitant. Animalium tria summa sunt genera: Aues, Pisces, & Terrestria. Piscium nomine nunc communiùs sumpto, Aquatilia omnia comprehendimus. Terrestria dicimus, quæ. Aristoteles πεζὰ: Theodorus malè pedata. nam Angues etiam πεζοὶ sunt, cum pedibus careant. Insecta ambigunt. plurima enim terrestria sunt: sed & aquis sua non desunt insecta: & quædam eorum in aëre uolitant. Singulorum autem multæ sunt uariæque differentiæ. A forma: unde sunt genera & species. A materia, ut à partibus. Ab accidentibus, ut à moribus, à uictu: ab usu, qui ad homines pertinet. Et aliæ quædam. Nos hîc de ijs præcipuè dicemus, quæ ab elementis in quibus degunt, sumuntur differentiæ, ex Scaligeri ferè commentarijs. Alia enim in uno: alia in duobus elementis uiuunt, quæ amphibia dixeris, multò latiùs patente hoc uocabulo, quàm uulgò accipiatur. Deinde etiam quomodo secundum refrigerationem caloris natiui differant, ex Aristotelis sententia. —Gesner *Icones Animal.* 9.

Element (native)—*continued*

1596   Triplex mundi regio, scilicet elementaris, ætherea cælestis, triplicem hominis naturam denotant: hominum viscera, & quæcunque subsunt præcordiis, regionem referunt elementarem, in qua sola fit generatio & corruptio: præcordia quæ vitali calore æstuant, diaphragmate à visceribus diuisa, ætheream regionem: cerebrum verò cælestem, quæ intelligibili natura constat.—Bodin *Theat.* 410.

1606   Et quoniam iussæ sunt volare supra terram, & versus superficiem expansionis cœlorum, eam naturam sunt sortitæ, quæ illi loco esset maximè apta & consentanea: ac iis præsertim aquis conueniens & consentiens, in quarum regione, seu expansione volant, nempe Aquis cœlestibus.   Sunt igitur Aues, vti illæ Aquæ, subtiles, & agiles: sunt tenues: sunt calidæ: sunt leues.   Sed tamen sunt Aues ex aquis istis inferioribus.   Nam si ex illis superioribus & cœlestibus nascebantur, nihil necesse erat eas volando eum locum quærere, in quo vti natæ essent: ita perpetuò habitassent . . . .   Ergo ex istis Aquis Aues ortas esse corporis earum Materia probat apertissimè, cùm Plumis, id est, multis aqueis, & humidis excrementis earum corpora constent: & domicilij ratio probat quoque, quia etsi in expansione cœli nonnunquam versantur, subsidunt tamen in hac inferiori parte mundi sidentes vel in Montibus, vel in Arboribus, vel in Aquis ipsis: dum quiescere volunt. Dominus autem vnicuique rei à se conditæ pro ratione suæ naturæ locum aptum, & idoneum dedit: itémque naturam quoque pro loci illis designati ratione congruentem.—Daneau *Phys. Christ.* 216–17.

1609   Differentiæ Lapidum & Gemmarum à loco natali & à modo ortus. —Boodt *Gem. Hist.* 4 (in chapter heading).

1612   Animalium aliqua unico tantùm in elemento habitant, atque ex eo vivunt: igni Pyrausta, aëre Manucodiata, aquâ Apua, terrâ Bufo.— Alsted *Syst. Phys.* 164.

1637   And [God] implanted in every one its nature, that is, a vertue to observe the place, manner, & kind assigned unto it.—Comenius *Gate of Tongues* 3.

1651   The elements are the four greatest bodies of the world, of which others are generated.   That the lesser bodies of the world, which are infinite in number, and in forms, are really compounded of the elements, resolution shewes.   For when they are corrupted, they return into the elements.   And sense teacheth.   For all things have some grosseness, from the earth; some liquor from the water; some spirituosity from the air: some heat from heaven; and because all things that live, are nourished by these, they are thence called *Elementa quasi Alimenta*, as if you should say nourishment.—Comenius *Nat. Phil. Ref.* 84–5.

1657   The body of the Element is a dead and dark thing; the Spirit is the life, and is divided into Astra's which out of themselves give their growth and fruit; And as the Soule seperateth its body from it selfe and (yet) dwells in it, so also these spirituall Elements in the seperation of all things have severed the visible bodies from themselves by sepera-

Element (native)—*continued*

tion . . . . From the Element of the Earth proceedeth an Earthy body, from the Element of Water floweth a watry body, from the Element of Aire an Aiery body breatheth forth, & is compact in its own Nature, from the Element of Fire a body of Fire shines out, *viz.* the visible Heaven, and is compact in its own substance. From these bodies of the Elements things that grow doe proceed and come forth, and out of these the fruit by the mediation and operation of the Astra's; for no visible body is of it selfe and from it selfe, but from its own invisible Element and Astrum. The visible Astra's or Stars in the Firmament flame forth from the Fiery Body; therefore fire is the food and preservation of the Starrs . . . . Mettalls, Salts, Mineralls grow out of the body of the Water. From the body of the Earth spring Trees and Hearbs.—Pinnell *Croll* 37–8.

1667   In hac opinione de orto & generatione brutorum plantarumque hoc rectè ac à sacra Scriptura non abhorrens, quod de terra materiam sui ortus habeant, uti & pisces de aqua. De piscibus ex qua productis asserit Moses. Gen. I. vv. 20, 21. quum ait, *Deum jussisse initio, producant aquæ reptilia animantia, atque ita aquas produxisse maximos cetos & omnia animalia repentia scilicet in aquis,* id est natantia. Nam de iis reptilibus quæ in terra repunt asserit Moses v. 24. *quod è terra sint producta.* De reliquis terrestribus animantibus incedentibus pedibus versu eodem 24 & 25. asserit, *quod de terra genus suum ducant.* De volatilibus verisimillimum videtur ex Mose, *quod tam ex aqua, quàm terra originem suam habeant:* id doctiores Judæi sentiunt: idque ideo, quod capit. Gen. versu 20 dicatur, *Producant aquæ reptile & volatile, quod volet supra terram:* versu vero 22. cap. 1. & cap. 2. v. 19. Moses jungat volatile cæli bestiis agri, dicatque *Deum formavisse tam aves è terra quàm istas.* Unde plerique doctiores Judæos sequuti volucribus ortum attribuunt de terra simul & aqua: alii verò ex sola terra, ob verba versus 22. cap. 1. & 19. cap. 2. alii autem de solâ aquâ, ob versum 20. & 21. cap. 1. Quid ni autem res ista juxta ipsissima Mosis verba ita se habere possit; ut dicatur quoddam genus avium esse ortum ex aqua & terra junctim; ut cygnos, anseres, anates, querquedulas, mergos & omnes illas quæ tam in terra incedunt, quam in aquis natant? Aves autem illas, quæ ab aquis abhorrent easque fugiunt, originem suam habere è sola terra? atque respectu utriusque generis, Mosen his solam terram pro origine tribuere, illis aquam & terram? Certè videntur habere aquatiles illæ aves plus aquei, quam in sola terra sedem suam habentes: carnes tum illarum humidiores & ponderosiores sunt: harum verò sicciores & leviores. Terra porrò per se sicca est, sed aqua aliqua mixta humida & gravior. Hactenus quidem de eo antiquis Philosophis cum Mose convenit, quod terra & aquæ genialisque cæli Solis præsertim calor, ipsaque limositas & putredo terræ inhærens sint origo piscibus, animalibus terrestribus & avibus. Sed in eo à Mose diffident quod cæcâ quadam opinione existimarint quod elementa illa sensum nullum habentia, à suâ naturâ hanc habeant fœtificandi vim atque energiam; cum Moses innuat, eam

Element (native)—*continued*

ipsis inditam à Deo ejusque potente & omnia efficiente verbo.—Milius *Orig. Animal.* 11–13.

1677   Which great fecundity [of the Isis], as it argues the goodness of the Element, so 'tis no whether to be referr'd, as to its original cause, but to the various Salts upon which depend the propagation of all sorts of Species's.—Plot *Oxford.* 27.

1683   Every Country and Climate does by Gods divine Appointment and good Providence, bring forth such Herbs, Fruits and Grains, as are proper and most agreeable to the Constitutions of the People born in that place, both for Food and Physick.—Tryon *Way to Health* 215.

1691   Again, though the Water being a cold Element, the most wise God hath so attempered the blood and bodies of Fishes in general, that a small degree of heat is sufficient to preserve their due consistency and motion and to maintain Life.—Ray *Wisdom of God* 10.

1714   As the Surface of the Terraqueous Globe is bespread with different Soils, with Hills and Vales, with Seas, Rivers, Lakes and Ponds, with divers Trees and Plants, in the several Places; so all these have their Animal Inhabitants, whose Organs of Life and Action are manifestly adapted to such Places and Things; whose Food and Physick, and every other Convenience of Life, is to be met with in that very Place appointed it. The Watery, the Amphibious, the Airy Inhabitants and those on the Dry Land Surface, and the Subterraneous under it, they all Live and Act with Pleasure, they are gay, and flourish in their proper Element, and allotted Place, they want neither for Food, Cloathing or Retreat; which would dwindle and die, destroy, or poison one another, if all coveted the same Element, Place, or Food.—Derham *Physico-Theol.* 168–9.

1738   For it is no wonder that Water-Fowl do delight most in that Air that is most like (their Natural Element) Water.—Pointer *Weather* 27.

Empire[1]

Non illi imperium pelagi saevumque tridentem,
Sed mihi sorte datum.
—Virgil *Aen.* I. 138–9.

1505   Agnoscant auræ imperium, maria alta tremiscant.
—Pontano *Urania* I. 242.

1590   The race of siluer-winged Flies
Which doo possesse the Empire of the aire.
—Spenser *Muio.* 17–18.

1591   Celuy qui fit la vageuse tumeur,
La terre bigarree, et le celeste empire.
—Du Bartas *Magnif.* 386–7.

----

[1]See also CLIMATE AND CLIME, KINGDOM, REGION, REIGN.

Empire—*continued*

1604 The moist star
Upon whose influence Neptune's empire stands
Was sick almost to doomsday with eclipse.
  —Shakespeare *Hamlet* I. i. 118–20.

1614 A rod he bears, by which he calls againe,
And sends downe soules to Plutoes dark empires.
  —Mure I. 110.

1640 The Goddesse now in either Empire swayes:
Six moneths with Ceres, six with Pluto stayes.
  —Sandys *Ovid's Met.* 92.

1651 That alternate tydes be found
The Seas ambitious waves to bound,
Lest o'r the wide Earth without End
Their fluid Empire should extend.
  —H. Vaughan 85.

1656 Il n'est point de vaisseau, qui, d'vn cours plus rapide,
Raze les vastes champs de l'Empire liquide.
  —Chapelain *Pucelle* 255.

1659 The day was on the glittering wings of light
Fled to the western world, and swarthy night
In her black empire throned.
  —W. Chamberlayne *Phar.* V. i. 201–3.

1673 So mounting up in ycie-pearled carr,
Through middle empire of the freezing aire.
  —Milton *Fair Inf.* 15–16.

1678 How many Dukes, and Earls, and Peers,
Are in the Planetary Spheres;
Their Airy Empire.
  —Butler *Hudibras* II. iii (p. 158).

1681 Then Musick, the Mosaique of the Air,
Did of all these a solemn noise prepare:
With which She gain'd the Empire of the Ear.
  —Marvell *Music's Empire* 17–19.

1713 The shady empire shall retain no trace
Of war or blood, but in the sylvan chase.
  —Pope *Win. For.* 371–2.

Enamel

1572 Olha estoutro debaxo, que esmaltado
De corpos lisos anda, & radiantes.
  —Camoens *Lus.* 175.

1578 Et à l'envy la terre où elle passe,
Un pré de fleurs émaille sous ses piez.
  —Ronsard I. 50.

Enamel—*continued*

1585   Le doux-flairant tapis des esmaillez rivages.
         —Du Bartas *I Sem.* V. 131.

1600   The golden sun rose from the silver wave,
         And with his beams enamel'd every green.
         —E. Fairfax *Tasso* I. xxxv.

1602   El tagarote Africano,
         Que la Hespañol garça vee,
         En su noble sangre piensa
         Esmaltar el cascauel.
         —Góngora I. 229.

1605   Th' inammell'd Valleys, where the liquid glasse
         Of siluer Brookes in curled streames doth passe.
         —Sylvester *Div. Wks.* (*Colon.*) 461.

1616   Gold-smith of all the Starres, with Siluer bright
         Who Moone enamells, Apelles of the Flowrs.
         —Drummond I. 8.

1622   Crown'd with embroidred banks, and gorgeously arraid
         With all th' enamild flowers of manie a goodly Mead.
         —Drayton *Poly-Olb.* III. 411–12.

1623   He makes sweet music with the enamell'd stones.
         —Shakespeare *T. G. of V.* II. vii. 28.

1633   Her amber hair, like to the sunnie ray,
         With gold enamels fair the silver white.
         —P. Fletcher *Purple Isl.* XII. lxxxv.

1640   Downe from the enamel'd skie
         She slides to earth.
         —Sandys *Ovid's Met.* 6.

1646   Take a full view of this enamelled ball,
         Both where it may be seen
         Clad in a constant green,
         And where it lies
         Crusted with ice.
         —Hall, in *CP* II. 208.

1656   Le Iour, d'vn jaune d'or, peint la crouppe des monts,
         Et de perles, sans nombre, emaille les vallons.
         —Chapelain *Pucelle* 448.

1667   Blossoms and Fruits at once of golden hue
         Appeerd, with gay enameld colours mixt.
         —Milton *P. L.* IV. 148–9.

1668   There Silver Rivers through enamell'd Meadows glide.
         —Cowley 161.

Enamel—*continued*

1681 He gave us this eternal Spring,
Which here enamells every thing.
—Marvell *Bermudas* 13–14.

1716 Si-tôt que l'Horison voit la riante Aurore,
Des Champs & des Forêts l'Email se recolore.
—Genest *Prin. Phil.* 184.

1743 Of all th' enamell'd race, whose silv'ry wing
Waves to the tepid zephyrs of the spring.
—Pope *Dunc.* IV. 421–2.

Engender[1]

15th For Gold that cometh from the Oare,
cent. Is nourished with fowle Sulphur:
And Engendred upon Mercury he ys,
And nouryshed by Erth and Sulphur I wys.
—Pearce the Black Monk, in Ashmole *Theat.*
Chem. (1652) 274.

1557 L'Acacia engendre ceste gumme,
Dont escriuains vsent & teinturiers.
De la cueillir Arabes sont ouuriers:
Et pour autant gumme Arabic se nomme.
—Belon *Portr. Oyseaux* 119.

1585 Dieu non content d'avoir infus en chaque espece
Une engendrante force, il fit par sa sagesse
Que sans nulle Venus des corps inanimez
Maints parfaits animaux ça bas fussent formez.
—Du Bartas *I Sem.* VI. 1035–8.

1591 Out of the earth engendred men of armes
Of Dragons teeth, sowne in the sacred sand.
—Spenser *Rome* X. 129–30.

1605 Or rather, as two fruitfull Elmes that spred
Amidst a Cloase with brookes enuironed,
Ingender other Elmes about their rootes.
—Sylvester *Div. Wks. (Colon.)* 445–6.

1611 Make fish with fowle, Camels with Whales engender.
—Chapman *Il. (To the Reader* A₁).

1613 Quantas produce Papho, engendra Gnido,
Negras violas, blancos alhelies.
—Góngora II. 46.

1620 Infiniz animaux que la poussiere engendre.
—Bertaut *Œuv. Poét.* 470.

---

[1]See also ELEMENT (NATIVE).

Engender—*continued*

1640   And with the Lightning, Winds ingendring Snow.
            —Sandys *Ovid's Met.* 1.

1656   So are Vapours bred,
            By what e're power, and how engendered.
            —Evelyn *Lucretius* 47.

1668   By repercussion Beams engender Fire,
            Shapes by reflexion shapes beget.
            —Cowley 108.

1682   Yet monsters from thy large increase we find,
            Engender'd on the slime thou [London] leav'st behind.
            —Dryden *Medal* 173–4.

1687   And me as little can moist Autumn please,
            Engend'ring fogs, that season's all disease.
            —Ayres, in *CP* II. 326.

1712   The scorching Sun would with a fatal Beam
            Make all the Void with Births malignant team,
            Engender Jaundice, spotted Torments breed.
            —Blackmore *Creation* II. 708–10.

1547   Niuosæ nubes spiritus aerii in se habent plurimum, unde uentos ali-
        quando generant, præsertìm in situ opposito.—Mizaldus *Meteor.* 15.

1567   [Crystal] groweth in Asia and Cyprus, and especially vpon the Alpes
        and highe Mountaines of the North Pole.   It engendreth not so much
        of the waters coldenesse, as of the earthinesse mixt withall.—Maplet
        Greene Forest 17.

1571   Iron the most necessary and profitable of all other metalls, & yet as
        ill used of many as any other, is generated of such substaunce as syluer
        is, but myxed with a redde minerall.—Fulke *Meteors* 68.

1601   Clouds are engendred by vapours which are gone up on high, or els
        of the aire gathered into a waterie liquor.—Holland *Pliny* I. 20 (Bk.
        II, chap. xlii).

1622   It may be called also by an Aposteme, being in the substance of the
        braine, or in the skins and coates which couer the same, and from too
        much fulnesse and windinesse, which is heaped together and ingendred
        in the eye.—Banister *Guillemeau* B₃.

1630   In mediâ aëris regione duo meteora ignita puriora generantur: Stella
        cadens, & Lancea ardens.—Alsted *Encyclo.* I. 705.

1651   For how could a thunder-bolt be generated in the clouds, if stony
        vapours did not ascend into the cloud?—Comenius *Nat. Phil. Ref.* 100.

1653   For we do see, that by motion, heat and spirit is ingender'd and pre-
        serv'd in all things, and by want of it vanishes.—W. Harvey *Anat. Exer.*
        92.

Engender—*continued*

1655　He [Anaximenes] held that the Air is the principle of the Universe, of which all things are engendred, and into which they resolve.—Stanley *Hist. Phil. 2d Part* 6.

1664　Ie ne puis trouuer estrange qu'on appelle mutation de forme cét extréme changement, qui fait qu'on ne reconnoist plus rien de ce qui paroissoit en une masse, a la difference de ces changements, qui étant moindres sont appelez simples alterations de qualité: Mais ie ne puis concevoir ce qui fait imaginer à plusieurs qu'une forme perisse, & qu'un autre s'engendre.—Descartes *Monde* (*Mouvement et Repos* 18–19).

1677　By Authors they are called Stalagmites, and seem . . . to be generated of pearls of dew, setled on the stones as they lie in the Fields.—Plot *Oxford*. 95.

1697　It is reported of these [turtles], that they are nine Days engendering, and in the Water; the Male on the Female's Back.—Dampier *New Voyage* 81.

1729　The Production of Something which before was not, we call Generation; thus we say Fire is generated, when we see Fire where the Wood was before; so likewise we say a Chicken is generated, when we see a Chicken in the room of an Egg.—Clarke *Rohault* I. 17.

1738　If the Moon blushes, and is redder than usual, Winds are engendering, and Storms will arise.—Pointer *Weather* 99.

Exhalation[1]

1583　　　Car quand Titan leué nos campagnes regarde,
　　　　Et ses trais enflammés sur nos demeures darde,
　　　　Il boit la freche humeur, & le nuage épais
　　　　De tant d'exhalaizons fuiant le pesant fais,
　　　　Distille son fardeau en pluie ruisselante.
　　　　　—Du Monin *Urano*. 15b.

1585　　　Mais quand l'exhalaison
　　　　Des engourdis hyvers surmonte la maison,
　　　　De mesme elle s'enflamme, et faite un nouvel astre.
　　　　　—Du Bartas *I Sem.* II. 611–13.

1590　　　As when a fiery exhalation
　　　　Wrapt in the bowels of a freezing cloude,
　　　　Fighting for passage, makes the Welkin cracke,
　　　　And casts a flash of lightning to the earth.
　　　　　—Marlowe *Tambur.* 1487–90.

1605　　　If th' Exhalation hot and oyly proue,
　　　　And yet, as feeble, giueth place aboue
　　　　To th' Aerie Regions euer-lasting Frost.
　　　　　—Sylvester *Div. Wks.* (*2d Day*) 53.

---

[1]The Latin form of this word is not found in Lucretius, Virgil, or Lucan.　For cross reference, see also DISTIL, EXHALE, VAPOR.

Exhalation—*continued*

1613   The sun,
Whose golden beams in exhalation,
Though drawn from fens, or other grounds impure,
Turn all to fructifying nouriture.
—W. Browne *Brit. Past.* I. iii. 171–4.

1627   As when from mores some firie constellation
Drawes up wet cloudes with strong attractive ray,
The captiv'd seas forc't from their seat and nation,
Begin to mutinie, put out the day,
And pris'ning close the hot drie exhalation,
Threat earth, and heaven, and steale the Sunne away.
—P. Fletcher *Locusts* II. xi.

1640   Sol, obscur'd in shrowds
Of exhalations, breaks through vanquisht clowds.
—Sandys *Ovid's Met.* 92.

1656   And Sols bright flame fresh nourishments invite
In azure Sphears, 'cause heat the Center flyes,
And joyns to exhalations which arise.
—Evelyn *Lucretius* 77.

1667   Whether they [comets] unctuous exhalations are,
Fir'd by the sun, or seeming so alone.
—Dryden *Ann. Mir.* xvii.

1667   Meanwhile the Southwind rose, & with black wings
Wide hovering, all the Clouds together drove
From under Heav'n; the Hills to their supplie
Vapour, and Exhalation dusk and moist,
Sent up amain.
—Milton *P. L.* XI. 738–42.

1695   L'adorable Flambeau du Monde,
Sortant du vaste sein de l'Onde,
Y paroist aux yeux ébahis.
Non tel que dans nos froids Païs,
Des obliques traits qu'il nous darde,
Eblöuissant qui la regarde,
Et dissipant sur l'Horizon
Quelque légere exhalaison.
—Scarron I. 32.

1712   The Balmy Spoils of Plants, and fragrant Flow'rs,
Of Aromatick Groves, and Mirtle Bow'rs,
Whose odoriferous Exhalations fan
The Flame of Life, and recreate Beast and Man.
—Blackmore *Creation* II. 131–4.

Exhalation—*continued*

1730   Now, by the cool declining year condensed,
       Descend the copious exhalations, checked
       As up the middle sky unseen they stole.
           —Thomson *Autumn* 707–9.

Exhalations [ἀναθυμιάσεις] arise from earth as well as from sea; those from sea are bright and pure, those from earth dark. Fire is fed by the bright exhalations, the moist element by the others.—*Diogenes Laertius* (quoting Heracleitus) IX. 9 (LCL II. 417).

1515   Vmbramque eam in qua nox ipsa consistit circa hanc nostram plagam copiosam adeo facit: ut refrigescat quidem aer inde telluri propinquus omnes aut exhalationes humide circa nos coacte imbrium glaciei niuisque copiosissime causam atque materiam prestent.—Argyropolus *Basil* XXIXb.

1547   Fumorum ex quibus meteorum omne exoritur, duæ sunt species. Vna calida perinde ac sicca, terrestris & inflammabilis: quæ ut Latinis exhalatio & expiramentum, ita Græcis ἀναθυμίασις καὶ θυμίαμα rite dici consueuit. Hanc terra ubique ferè porosa & foraminulenta, sua & cælestium corporum ui partit, & exhalat. Altera calida est & humida, ex aqua & madefactis terræ partibus, imperante cælo & insita natura in sublime exhausta: cui Græci ὁ ἄτμος Latini uaporis nomen dederunt.—Mizaldus *Meteor.* 7b.

1555   A comet is a flame, working in a drye, hote, slymye exhalation, drawen vp to the hyest part of the ayre.—Dygges *Prognost.* 31.

1571   The mater whereof the moste part of Meteores dooth consiste, is either water or earth, for out of yᵉ water, proceade vapors, and out of the earth come exhalations.—Fulke *Meteors* Fol. 2.

1581   Mais quant à l'euaporation & exhalation qui est seiche, quand telle exhalation est poussee par le froit, en telle façon qu'elle se pourmeine par l'air, elle s'appelle Vent.—Daneau *Phys. Fran.* 38.

1596   Quid est fulmen? Est inflammata exhalatio geniorum ope agitata, & à superioribus potestatibus deorsum disiecta, cum ingenti fragore, quem tonitru vocant, ac teterrimo sulphuris odore.—Bodin *Theat.* 208.

1621   A vapour is a moist smoake drawn from water and is easily resolued into water. Exhalation is a dry smoake drawne from the earth, easie to fire, from exhalation arise fiery impressions which burne like fire, as pillers, dartes, candles, goates, shooting starres, fiery Dragons, darke streames, fooles fire, and such like fiery meteors.—Widdowes *Nat. Phil.* 16.

1630   Vapor est exhalatio calida & humida, maximam partem aquea.—Alsted *Encyclo.* I. 704.

1644   Quantum ad exhalationes, longè plures qualitates admittunt quàm vapores, ob majorem quam habent partium differentiam. Hîc autem sufficit notasse, crassiores fere nihil esse præter terram, qualem in fundo

Exhalation—*continued*

vasis cernimus in quo pluvia vel nivalis aqua resedit; subtiliores verò nil aliud quàm spiritus aut aquas vitæ, quæ semper priores è corporibus destillatis surgunt.—Descartes *Œuvres* VI. 659.

1651   The olfactile quality is called odour; which is a most thin exhalation of the taste.—Comenius *Nat. Phil. Ref.* 64.

1667   [Le soleil] tire les Vapeurs de l'Eau, & les Exhalaisons de la Terre.— Pomey *Indic. Univer.* 13.

1678   The Aristotelian Philosophy for a long time prevailing, made the world believe [comets] to be nothing but Exhalations from the Earth, drawn up into the higher Regions of the Air.—Hooke *Cometa,* in Gunther *Early Science in Oxford* VIII. 234.

1683   Besides, the Earth being (according to those we reason with) the coldest, heaviest and solidest of Elements, it is not so probable, as to excuse them from need of proving it, that those excessively cold Agents, that freez the Clouds into Snow and Hail, should be terrene Exhalations carried up to the Middle Region of the Air, especially since it must be done by Agents, either hard to be guess'd at, or considerably hot.—Boyle *Exper. Cold* 164.

1694   For whilst Wood is burning, much Smoak and Exhalation flies away from it, by the force of the Heat.—Blome *Le Grand* II. 47.

1709   That Exhalations and Vapors are the matter of Rain, is not to be doubted.—*Phil. Trans.* XXVI. 342.

Exhale[1]

Terra exalat auram ad auroram humidam.
     —Pacuvius *Incert.* 56.

Exhalantque lacus nebulam fluviique perennes,
Ipsaque ut interdum tellus fumare videtur.
     —Lucretius V. 463–4.

Quae tenuem exhalat nebulam fumosque volucris,
Et bibit umorem et, cum vult, ex se ipsa remittit,
Quaeque suo semper viridi se gramine vestit.
     —Virgil *Geo.* II. 217–19.

Saltem mitificos incendia lenta uapores
Exhalent aestuque calor languente tepescat.
     —Prudentius *Hamart.* 963–4.

1585   De la façon qu'on void, lors que l'aube bigarre
Le plancher de Cathay d'une couleur bisarre,
Fumer les mornes lacs, et dans le frais de l'air
Par les pores des champs les vapeurs s'exhaler.
     —Du Bartas *I Sem.* II. 281–4.

---

[1]See also EXHALATION, VAPOR.

Exhale—*continued*

1598   And be no more an exhal'd meteor,
        A prodigy of fear and a portent.
        —Shakespeare *I Henry IV* V. i. 19–20.

1605   Two sorts of Vapours by his heat exhales
        From floating Deepes, and from the flowerie Dales.
        —Sylvester *Div. Wks.* (*2d Day*) 48.

1613   A la torre de luzes coronada
        Que el templo illustra i a los aires vanos
        Artificiosamente da exhalada
        Luminosas de poluora sáètas,
        Purpureos no cometas.
        —Góngora II. 73–4.

1616   Did here her Eyes exhale mine Eyes salt Showrs?
        —Drummond I. 41.

1622   Untill the mounting Sunne,
        Through thick exhaled fogs, his golden head hath runne.
        —Drayton *Poly-Olb.* XIII. 83–4.

1640   And now with pitchie fogs obscures the day,
        From earth exhal'd.
        —Sandys *Ovid's Met.* 256.

1651   Then into Rivers Brooks the Painter powres,
        And Rivers into Seas; which (rich before)
        Return their gifts, to both, exhal'd in Showrs.
        —Davenant *Gond.* II. vi. 58.

1656   Le grand corps de Norgale,
        Parmy son sang fumeux, sa dure vie exhale.
        —Chapelain *Pucelle* 64.

1667   When Orient Light
        Exhaling first from Darkness they beheld.
        —Milton *P. L.* VII. 254–5.

1686   With her the soul of Poesie is gone,
        Gone, while our expectations flew
        As high a pitch as she has done,
        Exhal'd to Heaven like early dew.
        —Flatman, in *CP* III. 300.

1698   Straight all his hopes exhal'd in empty smoke.
        —Dryden *Geo.* IV. 710.

1713   No noisome Vapour, or dark Cloud exhales,
        But gentle Drops, fresh Dews, and pleasing Gales.
        —Diaper *Dryades* 6.

Exhale—*continued*

1615 Fast and thight it [a membrane of the eye] is, not onely for resistance, but also for the better conseruation of the watery and glassie humours that they sweat not out, and that the thinne spirites might not penetrate through it and so exhale.—Crooke *Body of Man* 556.

1627 The sea-sands seldom bear plants. Whereof the cause is yielded by some of the ancients, for that the sun exhaleth the moisture before it can incorporate with the earth and yield a nourishment for the plant.—Bacon *Works* IV. 415.

1638 As that part of our aire which is neerest to the earth, is of a thicker substance than the other, by reason tis alwaies mixed with some vapours, which are continually exhaled into it. So is it equally requisite that if there be a world in the Moone, that the aire about that should be alike qualified with ours.—Wilkins *World in Moone* 138-9.

1651 Cold stops the pores of a body, that the spirituall parts cannot go out and exhale.—Comenius *Nat. Phil. Ref.* 76.

1653 [The sun] oft-times stirres up clouds by his heat, exhaling the vapours from the earth into the middle region of the aire, and there again by his heat dissolving them into rain.—Dariott *Redivivus* 259.

1667 The Sun did heat the Air, and exhale the Vapours, which after did settle on those hills.—*Phil. Trans.* II. 499.

1677 To Evaporate and to Exhale differ from one another in this, that dry bodies are exhal'd, and moist ones evaporated.—Glaser *Compl. Chym.* 14.

1684 The South Sea, where probably the Suns Influence being great, Exhales those moist Particles which afterwards incorporate themselves with the Winds.—R. Waller *Acad. Cimen.* 9.

1698 He has found Clods of Earth and Gravel which have been so put in, which as they have been more or less distant from the fountain of Allum, from whence these Vapours did exhale, were more or less impregnated with Alum.—*Phil. Trans.* XIX. 182.

1704 Which changes [of colors in plants] seem to be effected by the exhaling of the moisture which may leave the tinging corpuscles more dense, and something augmented by the accretion of the oyly and earthy part of that moisture.—Newton *Opt.* (Bk. II) 59.

1738 Likewise many Chops and Clefts in the Ground, shew that abundance of Nitrous and Sulphureous Vapours have been exhal'd from the Earth.—Pointer *Weather* 103.

Expire

1596   But that faire lampe, from whose celestiall ray
              That light proceedes, which kindleth louers fire,
              Shall neuer be extinguisht nor decay,
              But when the vitall spirits doe expyre,
              Vnto her natiue planet shall retyre.
                  —Spenser *Beauty* 99-103.

Expire—*continued*

1614   Her breath expiring, ane eternall sleep
        Did piece and piece vpon her senses creep.
           —Mure I. 144.

1622   Incouraging his men the adverse troupes among,
        With many a mortall wound, his wearied breath expir'd.
           —Drayton *Poly-Olb.* XXII. 1138–9.

1638   Some marrow-lancing eye perchance may quarrel,
        'Cause with the bridal torch my muse expires.
           —Whiting, in *CP* III. 539.

1640   Their rowling eyes together set in death;
        Together they expire their parting breath.
           —Sandys *Ovid's Met.* 107.

1648   What Ætna (under which Typhæus lies
        Expiring Flames) our rage shall equallize?
           —Sherburne *Medea* 23.

1655   'Twixt these expiring Rivers' Mouthez wide
        From the broad Countrey a long point extends.
           —Fanshawe *Lus.* VII. xix.

1671   [Antaeus] Throttl'd at length in the Air, expir'd and fell.
           —Milton *P. R.* IV. 568.

1698   What rocks did Ætna's bellowing mouth expire
        From her torn entrails!
           —Dryden *Geo.* I. 636–7.

1713   Heav'ns! what new wounds! and how her old have bled!
        She saw her sons with purple death expire.
           —Pope *Win. For.* 322–3.

Fabric[1]

        Saturnius me sic infixit Iuppiter,
        Iovisque numen Mulciberi ascivit manus.
        Hos ille cuneos fabrica crudeli inserens
        Perrupit artus.
           —Cicero *Aeschylus*, in *Scripta* IV. iii. 353.

        Inpune ne forsan sui
        Patris periret fabrica [*i.e.*, homo].
           —Prudentius *Cath.* XI. 43–4.

1618   Ne più di un Mondo già fabricar volse
        Il Rè dei Mondi e Prencipe increato.
           —Murtola *Creat. Mondo* I. i. 13.

1623   And, like the baseless fabric of this vision,
        The cloud-capp'd towers, the gorgeous palaces.
           —Shakespeare *Tempest* IV. i. 151–2.

---

[1]See also FRAME.

Fabric—*continued*

1628   Shaking the World, ev'n to the ground,
Razde from its center, laid profound,
Dissolving what earth's fabricke crownde
With greatest Arte, or fame.
—Mure I. 157.

1640   Assist, you Gods (from you these changes spring)
And, from the Worlds first fabrick to these times,
Deduce my never-discontinued Rymes.
—Sandys *Ovid's Met.* 1.

1667   He his Fabric of the Heav'ns
Hath left to thir disputes, perhaps to move
His laughter at thir quaint Opinions wide
Hereafter.
—Milton *P. L.* VIII. 76–9.

1668   How the Great Fabrick [of the heart] does proceed,
What time and what materials it does need.
—Cowley 417.

1676   The specious tower no ruin shall disclose,
Till down at once the mighty fabric goes.
—Dryden *Aureng-Zebe* V. i, in *Works* V. 293.

1686   She open'd her astonish'd eyes
To see the goodly fabric of the second Temple rise.
—Flatman, in *CP* III. 386.

1700   Nor breathing veins, nor cupping will prevail;
All outward remedies and inward fail.
The mold of Nature's fabric is destroy'd,
Her vessels discompos'd, her virtue void.
—Dryden *Pal. and Arc.* III. 755–8.

1716   Peut-on trop admirer la fabrique des Plantes?
—Genest *Prin. Phil.* 202.

Historia Naturalis de Mundi Fabrica ex Genesi . . . Ιστορια φυσικη εις την κοσμοπολαν εκ της Γενεσεως.—Pollux (1792) 6.

1543   De Humani Corporis Fabrica.—Vesalius (in title).

1596   Qua igitur ratione fabricam mundi huius opifex instituit?—Bodin *Theat.* 17.

1601   Inter omnia, quæ passim admiranda in hominis fabrica conspiciuntur, illud maximè videtur esse admirabile; quod, quæ tanquam superuacanea & noxia, extra corpus propelluntur, sæpenumero vtilia ad necessarias, & nobilissimas actiones Natura faciat.—H. Fabricius *Locutione* 1–2.

1606   But as in this fabrick of the world (which we may call the true image of a perfect and most absolute commonweale,) the Moone, as the soule

Fabric—*continued*

of the world, comming neerer vnto the Sunne, seemeth to forsake this perspirall and elementarie region.—Knolles *Bodin* 7.

1620　Sphaera Mundi, seu Cosmographia, Demonstratiua, ac facili Methodo tradita: In Qua Totius Mundi Fabrica, Una cum Novis, Tychonis, Kepleri, Galilæi, aliorumque Astronomorum continetur adiuuentis.—Blancanus (in title).

1637　Et en suite i'y avois monstré quelle doit estre la fabrique des nerfs & des muscles du cors humain, pour faire que les esprits animaux, estant dedans, ayent la force de mouuoir ses membres.—Descartes *Methode* 55.

1641　Mans body a curious Fabrick, but fallen much into decay, and by ill usage, more decayes every day.—H. Woodward *Gate to Sciences* 36.

1653　Therefore, in this place . . . I shall onely endeavour to refer those things to their proper uses and causes, which do appear in the administration of Anatomie, about the fabrick of the heart and arteries.—W. Harvey *Anat. Exer.* 101.

1664　This magnificent Fabrick of the Universe, furnished and adorned with such strange variety of curious and usefull Creatures.—Boyle *Useful. Nat. Phil.* I. 3.

1665　I have . . . busied myself in surveying the most esteem'd Fabricks of Paris, and the Country round; the Louvre for a while was my daily Object.—Wren *Parentalia* 261.

1668　Whereas men do now begin to doubt, whether those that are called the Four ELEMENTS be really the *Primordia rerum*, First Principles, of which all mixed Bodies are compounded; therefore may they here be taken notice of and enumerated, without particular restriction to that Notion of them, as being onely the great Masses of natural Bodies, which are of a more simple Fabric then the rest.—Wilkins *Real Character* 56.

1678　For if you view the fibres of a muscle encompassed only with the air, you cannot discover the small parts out of which it is made: but if the same be put into a liquor, as water, or very clear oyl, you may clearly see such a fabrick as is truly very admirable.—Hooke *Cometa*, in Gunther *Early Science in Oxford* VIII. 310.

1683　The Fabrick of the Teeth makes more for Senior Redi's opinion, they being thus hollow, and having that large slit towards the end.—*Phil. Trans.* XIII. 47–8.

1698　It was a surprising sight to see the sport of Nature in the Fabrick and hardening of these Bones.—*Phil. Trans.* XIX. 23.

1700　It would be too great a Depretiating of them [planets], and a too much Over-valuing of the Earth, to suppose them not to be likewise Adorned with the more admirable Productions and Fabricks of Plants, and Animals.—*Phil. Trans.* XXI. 340.

Face

Implenda est mundi facies, corpusque per omne
Quidquid ubique nitet uigeat quandoque notandum est.
—Manilius I. 811–12.

Et iam Plias hebet, flexi iam plaustra Bootae
In faciem puri redeunt languentia caeli.
—Lucan II. 722–3.

Passimque horrentibus umbris
Squalescit cœli facies.
—Pontano *Urania* III. 32–3.

1584   Toutesfois l'Immortel voulut que nostre race
De ce vaste univers couvrist toute la face.
—Du Bartas *Colon.* 613–14.

1596   When suddeinly a grosse fog ouer spred
With his dull vapour all that desert has,
And heauens chearefull face enueloped.
—Spenser *F. Q.* II. xii. 34.

1605   Yet would the Lord, that Noahs fruitfull Race
Should ouer-spread th' Earths vniuersall Face.
—Sylvester *Div. Wks.* (*Colon.*) 459.

1622   He saw bright Phœbus gaze upon her Christall face.
—Drayton *Poly-Olb.* XXI. 56.

1640   The furious Monster eagerly doth chace
His shadow, gliding on the Seas smooth face.
—Sandys *Ovid's Met.* 71.

1645   Ergóne marcescet sulcantibus obsita rugis
Naturæ facies, & rerum publica mater
Omniparum contracta uterum sterilescet ab ævo?
—Milton *Naturam Non Pati Senium* 8–10.

1656   Mais, auant que le jour sorte du sein de l'Onde,
Et rende la Couleur à la face du Monde.
—Chapelain *Pucelle* 198.

1667   The bare Earth, till then
Desert and bare, unsightly, unadorn'd,
Brought forth the tender Grass, whose verdure clad
Her Universal Face with pleasant green.
—Milton *P. L.* VII. 313–16.

1675   Changing to paler white Heavens azure Face.
—Sherburne *Sphere* 49.

1697   First let my Muse whole Nature's Face design,
It's Figure draw, and finish every Line.
—Creech *Manilius* (Bk. I) 7.

Field

Quid undas
Arguit et liquidam molem camposque natantis?
—Lucretius VI. 404-5.

Principio caelum ac terram camposque liquentis
Lucentemque globus lunae Titaniaque astra
Spiritus intus alit.
—Virgil *Aen.* VI. 724-6.

In mare perveniunt partim, campoque recepta
Liberioris aquae, pro ripis littora pulsant.
—Ovid *Met.* I. 41-2.[1]

1505   Me per apertos
Aeris immensi campos summoque vagantem
Æthere, mox toto numerantem sidera cœlo
Duxisti.
—Pontano *Hort. Hesp.* I. 30-3.

1574   Le Ciel pleure ung depart, le Ciel faict distiller
Une pluye soudaine ez campagnes de l'aer.
—Jodelle 240.

1585   [Le soleil] Attire incessament deux sortes de vapeurs,
Et des champs ondoyans, et des champs porte-fleurs.
—Du Bartas *I Sem.* II. 471-2.

1592   Signoreggiate in mar gli umidi pesci,
E ne i campi de l'aria i vaghi augelli.
—Tasso *Mondo Creato* VI. 1762-3.

1596   The lilly, Ladie of the flowring field.
—Spenser *F. Q.* II. vi. 16.

1605   Th' euer-trembling field
Of scaly folke.
—Sylvester *Div. Wks.* (*Handie Crafts*) 378.

1613   Sereno dissimula mas orejas
Que sembró dulces quexas
Canoro labrador, el forastero
En su vndosa campaña.
—Góngora II. 94.

1630   With Trumpets, which thrice-lowder Sounds doe yeeld
Than deafening Thunders in the airie Field.
—Drummond II. 62.

1645   Where day never shuts his eye,
Up in the broad fields of the sky.
—Milton *Comus* 977-8.

---

[1]Freind's note (1696): "*Campo:* Æquor dicit aut mare."

Field—*continued*

1656 Desja du Firmament les plus viues estoilles,
Des campagnes de l'air perçoient les sombres voiles.
—Chapelain *Pucelle* 41.

1685 Debarred of heaven your native right,
And from the glorious fields of light.
—Dryden *Alb. and Alban.* II. i, in *Works* VII. 257.

1698 Now seas and skies their prospect only bound;
An empty space above, a floating field around.
—Dryden *Aen.* V. 12–13.

1714 Ye know the Spheres and various Tasks assign'd,
By Laws Eternal, to th' Aerial Kind.
Some in the Fields of purest Æther play,
And bask and whiten in the Blaze of Day.
—Pope *Rape of the Lock* II. 75–8.

Flock[1]

1591 The silent flocks, that do,
All skalie, cleave the stormie fluds.
—James I *Furies* 345–6.

1596 As when two rams stird with ambitious pride,
Fight for the rule of the rich fleeced flocke.
—Spenser *F. Q.* I. ii. 16.

1605 For well I know, thou holdest worthily
That place among the Aerie flokes that fly.
—Sylvester *Div. Wks.* (*5th Day*) 185.

1622 The blissless briers the coat had torn
The fleecy flock had lately worn.
—Hannay *Philo.* 1409–10.

1630 Were all ignoble Sea, and marish vile
Where Proteus Flockes danc'd measures to the Tyde.
—Drummond II. 28.

ante
1640 By them the feathred flocks of heaven
Themselvs do place by payrs.
—Mure II. 153.

1655 The Waters of the Consecrated Deep,
Where Protheus's Flocks their Rendezvouses keep.
—Fanshawe *Lus.* I. xix.

---

[1]See also BAND, BREED, BROOD, CHOIR, CITIZEN, CREW, FRY, HERD, HOST, INHABITANT, KIND, LEGION, NATION, PEOPLE, RACE, SEED, SHOAL, SQUADRON, TRAIN, TRIBE, TROOP.

Flock—*continued*

1659   Seeing not far from hence
His flock, the emblems of his innocence.
    —W. Chamberlayne *Phar*. II. iv. 207–8.

1667   As a Heard
Of Goats or timerous flock together throngd.
    —Milton *P. L.* VI. 856–7.

1678   A Flock, whose fleeces were as smooth and white
As those, the wellkin shews in Moonshine night.
    —H. Vaughan 657.

1698   This Neptune gave him, when he gave to keep
His scaly flocks, that graze the wat'ry deep.
    —Dryden *Geo.* IV. 567–8.

1709   To closer shades the panting flocks remove.
    —Pope *Summer* 87.

Fluid[1]

Sed quod amara vides eadem quae fluvida constant,
Sudor uti maris est, minime mirabile habeto;
Nam quod fluvidus est, e levibus atque rutundis
Est, et squalida multa creant admixta doloris
Corpora.
    —Lucretius II. 464–8.

Rursus abundabat fluidus liquor omniaque in se
Ossa minutatim morbo conlapsa trahebat.
    —Virgil *Geo.* III. 484–5.

Quoque magis puras umor secessit in undas
Et saccata magis struxerunt aequora terram
Adiacuitque cauis fluuidum conuallibus aequor.
    —Manilius I. 162–4.

Traxit iners caelum fluuidae contagia pestis
Obscuram in nubem.
    —Lucan VI. 89–90.

οἵη σὺν φιλότητι διακρίνας ἐκέδασσας
αἰθέρα τ' αἰγλήεντα καὶ ἠέρα καὶ χυτὸν ὕδωρ
καὶ χθόνα παμμήτειραν, ἀπ' ἀλλήλων μὲν ἕκαστα.
    —Oppian *Hal.* I. 412–14. (With what loving-kindness
thou hast marked out and divided the bright sky and the
air and the fluid water and earth, mother of all, and established them apart from each other.—Tr. A. W. Mair.)

---

[1]See also Humid, Liquid air, Liquid fire, Liquid light, Liquid sky, Liquid
water.

Fluid—*continued*

Ipse super fluidas plantis nitentibus undas
Ambulat.
    —Prudentius *Apoth.* 655–6.

Et quot sunt fluctus, tot forsan in æquore pisces
Luserunt fluido per cærula vasta natatu.
    —Dracontius *Carm. Deo* I. 236–7.

ἢ τὴν ἄβυσσον τοῦ χυθέντος ἀέρος,
ψυχρουμένην νῦν καὶ πάλιν πυρουμένην.
    —Pisidas *Hex.* 374–5. (The abyss of
the fluid air, at one time congealed and
at another set afire.)

1505   Putres glebæ, quæque æquora rastris
Molle sonent fluidum facile admissura liquorem.
    —Pontano *Hort. Hesp.* I. 129–30.

1562   Les bras haut estendus, à haute, et pleine voix
De region si sainte invoque par trois fois
Son Ange tutelaire, et de fleuves fluides
La salue arrousee, et sage en ses Druides.
    —Scève 236.

1585   C'est la terre qui fait par ces membres solides
Et visibles leurs feux, et leurs corps non fluides.
    —Du Bartas *I Sem.* II. 921–2.

1645   Denique quicquid habet cælum, subjectaque cœlo
Terra parens, terræque & cœlo interfluus aer.
    —Milton *Ad Patrem* 86–7.

1647   But Neptune thou that rul'st the foaming maine
Be pleas'd to help me; sure I shall obtaine
A sight of this great God who is my guide,
Nor else could I these fluid paths have tride.
    —Stanley *Poems and Trans.* (*Trans.* 11).

1657   Or if we think, that fluid thought, like seed,
Rots there to propagate some fouler deed.
    —King, in *CP* III. 234.

1665   Fumidus it sursum vapor, & frigentis aheni
Hæsit vbi lateri incluso, algoremque recepit,
Paulatim rorem fluidus densatur in vdum.
    —Rapin *Hort.* 25.

1668   As water fluid is, till it do grow
Solid and fixt by Cold;
So in warm Seasons Love does loosely flow,
Frost only can it hold.
    —Cowley 113.

Fluid—*continued*

1682 Si l'humeur bilieuse a causé ces transports,
Le sang vehicule fluide
Des esprits ainsi corrumpus,
Par des accés de tierce a peine interrompus,
Va d'artere en artere attaquer le solide.
—La Fontaine *Quin.* 8.

1693 That pow'rful Juice [wine], with which no Cold dares mix,
Which still is fluid, and no Frost can fix.
—Congreve *Exam. Poet. 3d Part* 236.

1712 Nor would the Meads their blooming Plenty boast,
Did uncheck'd Rivers draw their fluid Train
In Lines direct, and rapid seek the Main.
—Blackmore *Creation* I. 606–8.

1716 Dans l'Espace fluide où la Terre est placée,
Toujours flottante & balancée,
Comme les autres Corps qui sont placez ainsi.
—Genest *Prin. Phil.* 92.

1741 Si fluidum aëreum nebulas sublime volantes
Sustentans justo libramine fortiùs undam
Mercurii sursum impellat.
—Anon., in *Mus. Angl.* (5th ed.) II. 243.

1757 Wide as the Atlantic and Pacific seas,
Or as air's vital fluid o'er the globe.
—Dyer *Fleece* IV. 695–6.

The kinds of water are, primarily, two, the one being the liquid [τὸ ὑγρόν], the other the fusible kind [τὸ χυτόν].—Plato *Timaeus* 58D (LCL 144, 145).

1600 Terrenam molem, siue potiùs telluris compaginem, & crustam, ex duplici materiâ consistere omnibus patet, omnes confitentur; ex fluidâ nempè & humidâ; & ex constanti magis & sicca.—W. Gilbert *Magnete* 51.

1606 [Parhelij] Sunt radij Solis, qui in fluida & iam penè in aquas conuersa nube illustrius propter illius liquefactionem fieri iam cœptam collucent. —Daneau *Phys. Christ.* 43.

1636 Il est aysé de conclure par ce que nous auons dit iusques à present, que le Son n'a point d'autre suiet que l'air exterieur, ou les autres corps fluides, qui enuironnent les corps sonnants, comme l'eau, le vin, ou l'air interieur qui fait partie desdits corps.—Mersenne *Harmonie Univer.* 9.

1644 Deinde cogitemus, cùm, consensu Philosophorum fere unanimi, vacuum in rerum naturâ non detur, & tamen omnia corpora, vel experientiâ teste, plurimis poris pervia hient, necessariò hos meatus materiâ quâdam repletos esse perquam subtili & fluidâ, quæ serie non interruptâ ab astris ad nos extensa sit.—Descartes *Œuvres* VI. 587.

Fluid—*continued*

1655   Et denique ex fluidissimo æthere, locum omnem, quicunque est in
        universo, reliquum ita occupante, ut locus nullus relinquatur vacuus.
        —Hobbes I. 348.

1662   There are many bodies that are now solid, which by Comminution,
        Motion, and other requisite alterations, may be parts of a fluid body:
        As hard Ice may be turned into fluid Water.—Boyle *Examen of Hobbes* 77.

1678   And as in the History of the Creation, we have an account of the pro-
        duction of light, immediately after the making of matter, which is a
        motion of recess from the center of the shining body.   Next that, a
        Firmament which divided between the waters or the fluids of the one,
        and the fluids of another part of the world.   And in the third place,
        the collections of the particular fluids to one center, as the center of the
        Earth: and lastly, out of that collection of fluids appeared the dry and
        solid land.   So I conceive the most proper way of speculating on these
        great productions of the omnipotent Creator, may be to begin with the
        consideration of light, or the motion of recess from the center of a body.
        Next, with the consideration of the cause of the separating of fluid from
        fluid, as Æther from Æther, as I may so call differing Æthers; because
        we have not distinct names in use, and the reason of their congloba-
        tion, the Æther from the Air, the Air from the Water, the Water from
        Quicksilver, Oyl, or other fluid.—Hooke *Cometa*, in Gunther *Early Sci-
        ence in Oxford* VIII. 230–1.

1686   Le plus leger, c'est à dire le moins pesant des corps fluides est la flame.
        —Mariotte *Eaux* 88.

1696   *Chaos, i. e.* a confused fluid mass or congeries of heterogeneous Bodies.
        —Whiston *New Theory* 51.

1714   And the Wings [of a bird] so nicely are set to the Center of Gravity, as even
        in that fluid Medium, the Air, the Body is as truly ballanced, as we could
        have ballanced it with the nicest Scales.—Derham *Physico-Theol.* 166.

1725   Quomodo autem in aere fluido, motus eiusmodi vehemens suscitetur,
        qui ventum efficiat, res certe implicita multis difficultatibus & sub-
        tilioris indaginis est.—Hoffmann *Opusc. Phys.* I. 11–12.

1730   If [the smallest particles of matter] slide upon one another, the Body
        is malleable or soft.   If they slip easily, and are of a fit Size to be agi-
        tated by Heat, and the Heat is big enough to keep them in Agitation,
        the Body is fluid; and if it be apt to stick to things, it is humid.—New-
        ton *Opt.* 394–5.

Frame[1]

        Una dies dabit exitio, multosque per annos
        Sustentata ruet moles et machina mundi.
            —Lucretius V. 95–6.

---

[1]The passages of poetry given here indicate that *machina* and *compages* were
used in verse as equivalents of the English word *frame*, and Du Bartas certainly
used *la machine* as Milton used *frame:*

Frame—*continued*

Haec loca praecipuas uires summosque per artem
Fatorum effectus referunt, quod totus in illis
Nititur aeternis ueluti compagibus orbis.
    —Manilius II. 801–3.

Quippe stimulo fluctuque furoris
Conpages humana labat, pulsusque deorum
Concutiunt fragiles animas.
    —Lucan V. 118–20.

Ille autem supera compage soluta
Nec solitus sentire metus expavit oborta
Sidera.
    —Statius *Theb.* VIII. 31–3.

Pone hoc caducum uasculum
Conpage textum terrea.
    —Prudentius *Peristep.* V. 301–2.

1505
Quæ tamen inter
Aeris immensos campos neptunniaque arva,
Quod sibi perpetui constaret machina mundi,
Congessi.
    —Pontano *Urania* I. 930–3.

1563
The Peacocks plume shal not me pas
That nature finely framde.
    —Googe 66.

1596
Before this worlds great frame, in which al things
Are now containd, found any being place.
    —Spenser *Heav. Love* 22–3.

1598
The frame and huge foundation of the earth
Shak'd like a coward.
    —Shakespeare *I Henry IV*. III. i. 16–17.

Le flot, comme parent, favorisoit la terre,
L'air du feu son cousin soustenoit le parti;
Mais tous deux, unissant leur amour departi,
Peuvent facilement apointir la querelle
Qui sans doute eust deffait la machine nouvelle.
    —Du Bartas *I Sem.* II. 290–4.

For as Earth, so hee the World
Built on circumfluous Waters calme, in wide
Crystallin Ocean, and the loud misrule
Of Chaos farr remov'd, least fierce extreames
Contiguous might distemper the whole frame.
    —Milton *P. L.* VII. 269–73.

It should also be remarked that A. H. Gilbert thought Milton's use of *frame* was similar to Galileo's use of *macchina* (see "Milton and Galileo," *Studies in Philology,* XIX [1922], 167).
For the use of a comparable term, see FABRIC.

Frame—*continued*

1605   Thear is no Theame more plentifull to scanne,
Then is the gloriously goodly frame of Man.
    —Sylvester *Div. Wks.* (*6th Day*) 205.

1610   The Sun it selfe outglitters, though he should
Climbe to the toppe of the celestiall frame.
    —G. Fletcher *Christs Triumph after Death* xi.

1627   The falling worlds now iarring frame no peace,
No league shall hold.
    —May *Lucan* A₂b.

1633   The world did in her cradle take a fall,
And turn'd her braines, and tooke a generall maime,
Wronging each joynt of th' universall frame.
    —Donne *Anat. of the World* 196–8.

1640   When, Sea, Earth, ravisht Heaven, the curious Frame
Of this World's masse, should shrink in purging flame.
    —Sandys *Ovid's Met.* 3.

1656   We in few lines will this assertion clear,
That of a solid, and eternal frame
Bodies there be which Principles we name,
And seeds of things, from whence the total sum
And mass of all created beings come.
    —Evelyn *Lucretius* 43.

1668   What art thou, Love, thou great mysterious thing?
From what hid stock does thy strange Nature spring?
'Tis thou that mov'st the world through every part
And holdst the vast frame close, that nothing start
From the due Place and Office first ordain'd.
    —Cowley 285.

1675   Made up of Atoms Nature's Frame
Exists, and shall resolve into the same.
    —Sherburne *Sphere* 12.

1698   Nor can my mind forget Eliza's name,
While vital breath inspires this mortal frame.
    —Dryden *Aen.* IV. 485–6.

1734   All are but parts of one stupendous Whole,
Whose body Nature is, and God the soul;
That changed thro' all, and yet in all the same,
Great in the earth, as in th' ethereal frame.
    —Pope *Man* I. 267–70.

1504   Prima autem omnium spherarum maxima mundi machina tota dicitur.
Ipsa enim in se omnia continet.—Reisch *Margar. Phil.* sb.

Frame—*continued*

1574   I am bould to offer unto your Lordship, hopinge, ere it bee longe, to ffinishe a columne sustayninge a regular body platonicall, garnished with solar dialls, sutche as I thinke hitherto in this land hath not beene seene, to bee placed in soome of your Lordshipps gardeyns, as aptly serving for uses diurnall as that other frame for conclusions doon by night.—T. Digges (*Progr. Science*, ed. Halliwell 7).

1600   Terrenam molem, siue potiùs telluris compaginem, & crustam, ex duplici materiâ consistere omnibus patet, omnesque confitentur; ex fluidâ nempè & humidâ; & ex constanti magis & sicca.—W. Gilbert *Magnete* 51.

1602   That faire, and beautifull frame of the world.   Elegans illa ornatequè totius vniuersi machina.—Withals *Diction.*[1] 16.

1627   In the frame of nature there is, in the producing of some species, a composition of matter which happeneth oft, and may be much diversified.—Bacon *Works* IV. 459.

1632   Ma quello sopra di che la parte fà in stanza, è l'hauere a concedere, che vna stella fissa habbia ad esser non pure eguale, ma tanto maggiore del Sole, che pure amendue sono corpi particolari situati dentro all' orbe stellato: E ben parmi, che molto a proposito interroghi quest' autore, e domandi.   A che fine, & a benefizio di chi sono macchine tanto vaste? prodotte forse per la terra, cioè per un piccolissimo punto? —Galileo *Dial.* 362–3.

1644   Quod nullo modo videbitur mirum iis, qui scientes quàm varii motus in automatis humanâ industriâ fabricatis edi possint; idque ope quarumdam rotularum aliorumve instrumentorum, quæ numero sunt paucissima, si conferantur cum multitudine ferè infinitâ ossium, musculorum, nervorum, arteriarum, venarum aliarumque partium organicarum, quæ in corpore cujuslibet animalis reperiuntur; considerabunt humani corporis machinamentum tanquam automatum quoddam manibus Dei factum, quod infinities meliùs fit ordinatum, motusque in se admirabiliores habeat, quàm ulla quæ arte humanâ fabricari possint.— Descartes *Œuvres* VI. 571.

1653   Moreover, from the constitution of the fibers and their motive frame, as likewise in the muscles, we may see the action and use of the heart. —W. Harvey *Anat. Exer.* 114.

1661   Thus we cannot know the cause of any one motion in a watch, unless we were acquainted with all its motive dependences, and had a distinctive comprehension of the whole Mechanical frame.—Glanvill *Van. Dogm.* 214.

1668   By WORLD, Universe, is meant the Compages or Frame of the whole Creation.—Wilkins *Real Character* 51.

---

[1]First edition 1554.

Frame—*continued*

1675   Where I say that the frame of nature may be nothing but ether condensed by a fermental principle, instead of these words write, that it may be nothing but various contextures of some certain ethereal spirits, or vapours, condensed as it were by precipitation.—Newton, in Rigaud II. 389.

1680   For the Fire does but Dissolve the Cement, or rather Shatter the Frame, or structure that kept the Heterogeneous Parts of Bodies together.—Boyle *Scept. Chym.* 86.

1687   Oftentimes also emancipated, pointed, and penetrating Atoms flow in the Air, which entring in at the Pores of the Body, disturb its whole Oeconomy or frame.—Midgley *Nat. Phil.* 193.

1696   That the words here [in Scripture] us'd of Creating, Making, or Framing of things, on which the main stress is laid; in the stile of Scripture are frequently of no larger importance than the Proposition we are upon does allow; and signifie no more than the ordering, disposing, changing, or new modelling those Creatures which existed already, into a different, and sometimes perhaps a better, and more useful state than they were in before.—Whiston *New Theory* (*Mosaick Creation* 7).

1730   A dense Fluid can be of no use for explaining the Phænomena of Nature, the Motions of the Planets and Comets being better explain'd without it.   It serves only to disturb and retard the Motions of those great Bodies, and make the Frame of Nature languish.—Newton *Opt.* 368.

Fry[1]

1579   The dapper ditties, that I wont deuise,
        To feede youthes fancie, and the flocking fry,[2]
        Delighten much.
            —Spenser *S. C.: Oct.* 13–15.

1605   That meeke man
        Who dry-shod guides through Seas Erythrean
        Old Iacobs Frye.
            —Sylvester *Div. Wks.* (*Colum.*) 486.

1610   Then will I sport me with the scaly frie.
            —Heath *Epigr.* B₃b.

1622   The Sea-meaw, Sea-pye, Gull, and Curlew heere doe keepe,
        As searching every Shole, and watching every deepe,
        To find the floating Fry.
            —Drayton *Poly-Olb.* XXV. 123–5.

---

[1]See also BAND, BREED, BROOD, CHOIR, CITIZEN, CREW, FLOCK, HERD, HOST, INHABITANT, KIND, LEGION, NATION, PEOPLE, RACE, SEED, SHOAL, SQUADRON, TRAIN, TRIBE, TROOP.

[2]Explained as fish by "E. K."

Fry—*continued*

1638   Don passed through these into an inner room,
Where was another rank of virgin-fry.
—Whiting, in *CP* III. 455.

1640   Through Christall streams you might descry
How vast and numberless a fry
The fish had spawn'd.
—Randolph *Poems* 98.

ante   Sitting one day beside the banks of Mole,
1650   Whose sleepy stream by passages unknown
Conveys the fry of all her finny shoal.
—W. Browne *Visions* I. 1–3.

1655   Now did Aurora, beautiful and cleer,
Out of the Welkin chase the golden Fry.
—Fanshawe *Lus*. III. xlv.

1667   Each Creek & Bay
With Frie innumerable swarme.
—Milton *P. L.* VII. 399–400.

1678   Ev'n from that distance thou the Sea do'st spie
And sporting in its deep, wide Lap the Frie.
—H. Vaughan 606.

1686   And still the same appear'dst to be
Among the beasts and scaly fry.
—Flatman, in *CP* III. 386.

1748   Along the brooks, the crimson-spotted fry
You may delude.
—Thomson *Castle of Ind*. I. xviii.

Generous

Omnes civili generosa a stirpe profectam
Vitare ingentem cladem pestemque monebant.
—Cicero, in *Scripta* IV. iii. 399–400.

Excipit haec iuuenis generosi sanguinis Argus
Qua iam non medius descendit in ilia uenter.
—Lucan III. 723–4.

Hoc uidit princeps generosi seminis Abram.
—Prudentius *Apoth*. 28.

1505   Hæc sedes, hæc est generosi regia Martis.
—Pontano *Urania* II. 162.

1578   Ayant pris des Saxons sa race genereuse.
—Ronsard V. 281.

Generous—*continued*

1613   Entre el confuso pues, zeloso estruendo
De los cauallos ruda haze armonia,
Quanto la generosa cetreria.
    —Góngora II. 112.

1614   My generous wine, consuming as they list.
    —Chapman *Odys*. 19.

1640   The generous Horse that from the Race of late
Return'd with honour, now degenerate.
    —Sandys *Ovid's Met*. 128.[1]

1655   For valiant spirits (which are still the same
With generous) [o generoso animo, & valente[2]].
    —Fanshawe *Lus*. I. lxviii.

1671   Force, which to a generous mind
So reigning can be no sincere delight.
    —Milton *P. R*. II. 479–80.

1676   Force never yet a generous heart did gain.
    —Dryden *Aureng-Zebe* II. i, in *Works* V. 225.

1698   Boil this restoring root in gen'rous wine.
    —Dryden *Geo*. IV. 399.

1711   The winged courser, like a gen'rous horse,
Shows most true mettle when you check his course.
    —Pope *Criticism* I. 86–7.

1734   Man, like the gen'rous vine, supported lives.
    —Pope *Man* III. 311.

Genial

        Lucent genialibus altis
Aurea fulcra toris, epulaeque ante ora paratae
Regifico luxu.
    —Virgil *Aen*. VI. 603–5.

        Carpite purpureas uiolas
Sanguineosque crocos metite!
Non caret his genialis hiems.[3]
    —Prudentius *Peristep*. III. 201–3.

1505   Spiret et e nitidis genialis amaracus aris.
    —Pontano *Hort. Hesp*. I. 588.

1578   Pere germeux, genial, et qui fais
Comme il te plaist les guerres et la paix,

---

[1]Compare Wotton's classification of three kinds of horses: "Equus generosus.
Equ mularis.   Equ uulgaris."—*Differ*. (1552) 86.
   [2]Camoens *Lus*. (1572) 12.
   [3]See also Virgil *Geo*. I. 302: "genialis hiems."

Genial—*continued*

Dæmon et Dieu nourricier de ce monde,
Qui du chaos le caverne profonde
Ouvris premier, et paroissant armé
De traits de feu, Phanete fus nommé.
—Ronsard VI. 428.

1595 And thou glad Genius, in whose gentle hand,
The bridale bowre and geniall bed remaine.
—Spenser *Epithal.* 398–9.

1617 Pallas en esto, laminas vestida,
Quinto de los Planetas, quiere al quarto
De los Philippos, duramente hecho
Geníàl cuna su pabes estrecho.
—Góngora II. 276.

1638 That this blest day may count more moments' flight
Than could the stout Alcides' genial night.
—Whiting, in *CP* III. 471.

1648 You nuptiall Powers! and thou Lucina, Head,
And carefull Guardian, of the Geniall Bed.
—Sherburne *Medea* 1.[1]

1656 For when the Springs return brings the clear day
And Genial West with kindely gales doth play.
—Evelyn *Lucretius* 15.

1668 So, nothing yet in Thee is seen,
But when a Genial heat warms thee within,
A new-born Wood of various Lines there grows.
—Cowley 73.

1692 Love did great Nothing's barren womb
Impregnate with his genial fire.
—Norris 136.

1698 Starve 'em, when barns beneath their burthen groan,
And winnow'd chaff by western winds is blown;
For fear the rankness of the swelling womb
Should scant the passage, and confine the room;
Lest the fat furrows should the sense destroy
Of genial lust, and dull the seat of joy.
—Dryden *Geo.* III. 216–21.

1713 In genial Spring, beneath the quiv'ring shade,
Where cooling vapours breathe along the mead,

---

[1]Sherburne's note (p. 56): "The Geniall bed was called as Scaliger supposes *à Generando*, or as others, *quia in honorem Genii sternebatur*, it was by the Greekes called παράβυσος in regard it was covered over with a vaile."

Genial—*continued*

> The patient fisher takes his silent stand,
> Intent, his angle trembling in his hand.
> —Pope *Win. For.* 135–8.

1722   Some [fish] spring spontaneous from the genial Slime.
—Diaper *Hal.* I. 1307.

1728   By thee disposed into congenial soils,
Stands each attractive plant.
—Thomson *Spring* 564–5.

1650   Then is it established, beyond the question of any the most Pyrrhonian Incredulity, that the Sanation of Wounds; at distance, is not rightly adscriptive to the single power of Nature, converting the blood successively distilling from its intersected Conduits, into a genial Balsam. —Charleton *Prol.* to Van Helmont *Paradoxes* D₂b.

1653   Postremo, si vim genialem et vivificantem in rebus consulas, quæ ad rerum principia manuducat eaque manifestet, etiam aëris potiores partes esse videntur; adeo ut aëris et spiritus et animæ vocabula usu nonnunquam confundantur.—Bacon *Works* V. 303–4.

1656   Nam & lumen ab eo [sole] proficiscitur, & genitalis in animantibus & stirpibus calor.—Turnebus *Theophrastus* 3.

1661   The Primogenial light, which at first was diffused over the face of the unfashion'd Chaos, was afterwards by Divine appointment gathered into the Sun and Stars, and other lucid bodies, which shine with an underived lustre.—Glanvill *Van. Dogm.* 2.

1667   Hactenus quidem de eo antiquis Philosophis cum Mose convenit, quod terra & aquæ genialisque cæli Solis præsertim calor, ipsaque limositas & putredo terræ inhærens sint origo piscibus, animalibus terrestribus & avibus.—Milius *Orig. Animal.* 13.

1677   The Spanish Potado requires diligent culture, much Sun, and a light and pregnant Garden-soyl.—*Phil. Trans.* XII. 852.

1694   [Serpents, scorpions, and the like] through the extremity of cold in the Winter, lie void of sense and motion; and for the time in all appearance, totally deprived of Life, that is, while the Blood ceases to be in agitation, and the generation of Spirits is for the present stopt; which Animals, when the Genial Spring, as Mantuan expresseth it, gives new primordia to things, the motion of the Blood being renewed by heat, are again raised to Life.—Blome *Le Grand* II. 228.

1702   [Edmund Dickenson] treats next of the primigenial Fire and Light, or of the first Heaven, and shews after what order it was made, upon a motion of the Particles.—*Phil. Trans.* XXIII. 1087.

1738   The kind Influence of the Sun, which by its Congenial Warmth both brings to Perefection the Eggs of Insects, and brings to Maturity the Fruits of the Ground.—Pointer *Weather* 120.

Glass and Glassy[1]

NOTE.—For the most part conceits and epithets which describe water as glass may be judged to derive legitimately from the appearance of water under various conditions. There can hardly be doubt, however, that the use of *glass* and *glassy* gained something by association with those ideas which made it seem reasonable to describe water as crystal. This is all but explicit in Milton, where at one time he calls the upper sphere of the air "the cleer Hyaline, the Glassie Sea,"[2] and at another, the "Crystallin Ocean."[3]

Apart from the long tradition of *glass* as an epithet in poetry it should also be remarked that the Coverdale translation of Revelations xv. 2 has the phrase "Glassye sea," which became in the Authorized Version "sea of glass."

I have not been able to find any considerable scientific theory that would justify the phrase *liquid glass* as a definition for water. There is one reported statement approximately to this effect,[4] and it would have been quite possible to make the identification in conjunction with those theories according to which water was in its natural state when it was frozen, and was indeed a kind of stone, the primary element of all minerals.[5] Boyle, it happens, once used the phrase *liquid glass*, but such use is very unusual:

Having put into one small Earthen Vessel an Ounce of the most pure Gold, and into another the like weight of pure Silver, he plac'd them both in that part of a Glass-house Furnace wherein the Workmen keep their Metal, (as our English Artificers call their Liquid Glass) continually melted.[6]

The theory that glass is the primary element of metals is explicitly stated in this way:

That dry and most precious Liquor, doth constitute the Radical Moisture of Metalls, wherefore of some of the Ancients it is called Glasse, for Glasse is extracted out of the Radical Moisture, closely lurken in Ashes which will not give place, unless it be to the Hottest Flame.[7]

Still another reason, however, to justify the use of *glass* in reference to water is a pun wherein the Latin word for ice, *glacies*, might exploit the same theories that are drawn on when water is called *crystal*, since the Greek word for crystal itself means ice. I cannot refrain from remarking that, however involved such a process of description may be, Sylvester once described a basin of water as *liquid Ice*.[8]

---

[1]See also CRYSTAL HUMOR, CRYSTAL SKY, CRYSTAL WATER.

[2]*P. L.* VII. 619.

[3]*Ibid.* 271.

[4]"'This Glass lay long in the earth, though Helmont affirms that Glass there dissolves, putrifies and turns to water, in few years. Which though true in our finer Crystal, as to the saline part, yet seems not so of Glass in general."—Merrett *Neri* (1662) (*Epistle* by Merrett) 224. See also Evelyn *Terra* 19 (quoted on p. 246 below).

[5]See above under CRYSTAL WATER, pp. 130–1.

[6]*Scept. Chym.* (1680) 56.

[7]Hortolanus *Golden Age* (1698) 24.

[8]*Div. Wks.* [1611] (*Troph.*) 543.

Glass and Glassy—*continued*

A final comment on the background of these words may be left to the English translator of an early work on the art of making glass:

Aristophanes seems to be the first that mentions this word ὕαλος, now rendered Glass . . . in Nubibus, Act. 2. Scen. 1 . . . .   Whereon the Scholiast thus, *Druggists sold precious stones as well as Medicaments.*   And that the Antients call'd κρίον, (the same with κρύσταλος) Crystal.   That Homer knew not the name, and that with him and the Antients, the word *Electrum* was used, the Scholiast there testifieth, though he himself clearly describes our Glass in these words.   *We properly call that Glass which being melted by fire from a certain herb burnt to prepare certain vessels.*   Hesichius hath not the word ὕαλος, in this sense, but Hyalen, Hyalon, Hyaloen, shining and Diaphanous.   The Etymologist hath it in this sense and fetcheth the Etymon from ὕειν, to rain, from the likeness it hath to ice (which is congeled rain or water) in consistence and Diaphaneity, and in this sense, as some glass from glacies ice.[1]

> Vitrea te Fucinus unda,
> Te liquidi flevere lacus.
> —Virgil *Aen.* VII. 759–60.

> Ceu mediis iterum nascatur ab undis
> Atque habitet vitreum tacitis radicibus amnem.
> —Statius *Silvae* II. iii. 4–5.

> Vitreoque lacus imitate profundo
> Et rivos trepido potis aequipare meatu,
> Et liquido gelidos fontes praecellere potu.
> —Ausonius *Mosella* 28–30.

> Praebent rupta locum stagna uiantibus,
> Riparum in faciem peruia sistitur
> Circumstans uitreis unda liquoribus,
> Dum plebs sub bifido permeat aequore.
> —Prudentius *Cath.* V. 65–9.

1579

> Car mes larmes n'aiant mon soleil darde-feu,
> Roidiront en glaçons l'onde Plutonienne,
> Et me feront chemin par la glaceuse plaine
> Du palus stygien.
> —Du Monin *Manip. Poet.* 49–50.

1590

> Qui, royne, va fendant le cristal de ceste onde,
> Blesme, pousse à ce bruit hors du verre flottant
> Son chef coiffé d'un jong à longs fils degoutant.
> —Du Bartas *Yvry* 324–6.

1596

> He built by art vpon the glassy See
> A bridge of bras.
> —Spenser *F. Q.* II. x. 73.

------

[1]Merrett *Neri* (1662) (*Epistle* by Merrett) 219–20.

Glass and Glassy—*continued*

1600   When winter's freezing cold
Congeals the streams to thick and harden'd glass.
—E. Fairfax *Tasso* XIV. xxxiv.

1605   Th' inammell'd Valleys, where the liquid glasse
Of siluer Brookes in curled streames doth passe.
—Sylvester *Div. Wks. (Colon.)* 461.

1617   The Tritons, Heards-men of the glassie Field,
Shall giue Thee what farre-distant Shores can yeeld.
—Drummond I. 152.

1622   Within my liquid glasse, when Phæbus lookes his face,
Oft swiftly as he swimmes, his silver belly showes.
—Drayton *Poly-Olb.* XXVI. 236–7.

1627   So when the golden Sun with sparkling ray
Imprints his stamp upon an adverse cloud,
The watry glasse so shines, that's hard to say
Which is the true, which is the falser proud.
—P. Fletcher *Locusts* II. xxv.

1633   Pace with her native streame, this fish doth keepe,
And journeyes with her, towards the glassie deepe.
—Donne *Progr. of the Soule* 251–2.

1640   Or when as Cippus in the liquid glasse
Beheld his hornes, which his beliefe surpasse.
—Sandys *Ovid's Met.* 276.

Her selfe oft by that liquid mirror drest.
—*Ibid.* 68.

1651   The Youth with pleasure on the Floud doth gaze,
And in that watery glasse his Face survaies.
—Sherburne *Salmacis* 13.

1651   These floating Mirrours, on whose Brow
Their various figures gently glide,
For love of her shall gently grow,
In faithful Icy fetters ty'd.
—Stanley *Sylvia's Park* 169.

1667   Another Heav'n
From Heaven Gate not farr, founded in view
On the cleer Hyaline, the Glassie Sea.
—Milton *P. L.* VII. 617–19.

1668   A pure, well-tasted, wholsome Fountain rose;
Which no vain cost of Marble did enclose;
Nor through carv'd shapes did the forc'ed waters pass,
Shapes gazing on themselves i' th' liquid glass.
—Cowley 259.

Glass and Glassy—*continued*

1698   One summer's night and one whole day they pass
        Betwixt the greenwood shades, and cut the liquid glass.
        —Dryden *Aen.* VIII. 127–8.

1709   As in the crystal spring I view my face,
        Fresh rising blushes paint the wat'ry glass.
        —Pope *Summer* 27–8.

1728   The uncurling floods, diffused
        In glassy breadth, seem through delusive lapse
        Forgetful of their course.
        —Thomson *Spring* 159–61.

Glide[1]

        Summissaque gens animantum
        Floreat et vivant labentes aetheris ignes.
        —Lucretius I. 1033–4.

1600   But when the gliding sun was mounted high,
        Jerusalem, behold, appear'd in sight.
        —E. Fairfax *Tasso* III. iii.

1605   Which, toward the Sea, the more he flies his source,
        With growing streames strengthens his gliding course.
        —Sylvester *Div. Wks.* (*Arke*) 386.

1614   When watchfull Dido from her palace spy'd
        The Trojane fleet alongst the coast to glyde.
        —Mure I. 135.

1627   Why doe the starres their course forsaking glide
        Obscurely through the ayre?
        —May *Lucan* B₃.

1633   Fishes glide, leaving no print where they passe.
        —Donne *Wotton* 56.

1640   As when a falling starre glides through the skie.
        —Sandys *Ovid's Met.* 28.

1656   Le ruisseau qui naguere en ses bords languissoit,
        Et, sur le moite sable, à peu de bruit, glissoit.
        —Chapelain *Pucelle* 226.

1656   Since through the Rocks and Caves moist humour slides,
        And in abundant drops the water glides.
        —Evelyn *Lucretius* 33.

1661   Where in new depths the wond'ring fishes glide.
        —Dryden *To His Maj.* 112.

---

[1]See also SLIDE.

Glide—*continued*

1667   As Ev'ning Mist
        Ris'n from a River o're the marish glides.
        —Milton *P. L.* XII. 629–30.

1675   This Worlds huge Mass fram'd into One Entire
        Of different Parts, as Earth, Air, Water, Fire,
        A Power Divine, whose sacred Influence glides
        Through all its Limbs, with tacit Reason guides.
        —Sherburne *Sphere* 18.

1698   A serpent from the tomb began to glide.
        —Dryden *Aen.* V. 112.

Globe[1]

        Quotiens Cyclopum effervere in agros
        Vidimus undantem ruptis fornacibus Aetnam,
        Flammarumque globos liquefactaque volvere saxa.
        —Virgil *Geo.* I. 471–3.

        Aut neque terra patrem nouit nec flamma nec aer
        Aut umor, faciuntque deum per quattuor artus
        Et mundi struxere globum prohibentque requiri
        Ultra se quicquam, cum per se cuncta crearint.
        —Manilius I. 137–40.

        Quaeque in his uigent sub alto solis et lunae globo.
        —Prudentius *Cath.* IX. 15.

1505   Interdum rapidos amnes est cernere passim
        Diffluere, et totum in pluvias descendere cœlum;
        Tantus in aerio sese globus orbe coegit.
        —Pontano *Meteor.* 206–8.

1562   Car du pondereux globe equalibrant au tiers
        Les cieux hauts elle voit plus grands de maints quartiers.
        —Scève 254.

1563   A God there is, that guyds the Globe,
        And framde the fyckle Sphere.
        —Googe 63.

1572   Mas antes pai, que em quanto o Sol rodea
        Este globo de Ceres & Neptuno,
        Sempre suspirarâ por tal aluno.
        —Camoens *Lus.* 133.

1578   Et de tes piedz la terre vas foulant
        Dessus un globe incessament roulant.
        —Ronsard VI. 233.

---

[1]See also BALL, ORB, SPHERE.

Globe—*continued*

1585   Siue hunc bipartitum globus [η σφαῖραν] instar fornicis
       Sursum eleuatum aut eminentem prædicet,
       Seu versus ipsum orbem infimum labi putet.
       —Morellus *Pisidas* 4b.

1585   Et les ondes oignant les bords dont s'entrebaisent
       Leurs globes tournoyans, d'une humeur froide apaisent
       La chaleur, qui, naissant, de leurs prompts mouvemens,
       Ne feroit qu'un brandon de tous les elemens.
       —Du Bartas *I Sem.* II. 925–8.

1596   Such was this Gyaunts fall, that seemd to shake
       The stedfast globe of earth, as it for feare did quake.
       —Spenser *F. Q.* I. viii. 23.

1605   I loue to looke on God; but in this Robe
       Of his great Works, this vniuersall Globe.
       —Sylvester *Div. Wks.* (*1st Day*) 6.

1614   Planets, which the rest in beauty scorne,
       And glist'ring bright, each in a golden robe,
       With gloriows lustre, grace heaven's azure globe.
       —Mure I. 110.

1616   By that time Night had newly spread her robe
       Over our half-part of this massy globe.
       —W. Browne *Brit. Past.* II. v. 901–2.

1622   As though the vast descent,
       Through this Terrestriall Globe directly poynting went
       Our Antipods to see.
       —Drayton *Poly-Olb.* XXVI. 445–7.

1638   Copernicus his tenet's verified,
       The massy globe does 'bout its centre ride.
       —Whiting, in *CP* III. 482.

1645   Seu sempiternus ille syderum comes
       Cæli pererrat ordines decemplicis,
       Citimúmve terris incolit Lunæ globum.
       —Milton *De Idea Platonica* 16–18.

1651   And Earth in half a Globe be pent no more.
       —Davenant *Gond.* II. vi. 40.

1667   From hence, no cloud, or, to obstruct his sight,
       Starr interpos'd, however small he sees,
       Not unconform to other shining Globes.
       —Milton *P. L.* V. 257–9.

1668   As Earths low Globe robs the High Moon of Light.
       —Cowley 249.

Globe—*continued*

1675   Or that the Heavenly Spheres and Globe of Earth,
       From Fire, not such blind Matter, drew their Birth.
       —Sherburne *Sphere* 12.

1691   Globes of hail poured down
       And armed winter, and inverted day.
       —Dryden *King Arthur* III. i, in *Works* VIII. 165.

1698   The liquid half of all the globe is lost.
       —Dryden *Aen.* IX. 160.

1712   If Planetary Orbs the Sun obey,
       Why should the Moon disown his Sov'raign Sway?
       Why in a whirling Eddy of her own
       Around the Globe Terrestrial should she run?
       —Blackmore *Creation* II. 473–6.

1713   When Nature shew'd her yet unfinish'd Face,
       And Motion took th' establish'd Law
       To roll the various Globes on high.
       —J. Hughes *Ode to Creator* 2.

1742   A part how small of the terraqueous globe
       Is tenanted by man!
       —Young *Night Thoughts* I. 285–6.

1515   Qui signifer appellat duodecim in partis diuiso cum in triginta dierum
       spacio partem sol eius globi transeat duodecimam quem in errantem
       appellant.—Argyropolus *Basil* XXVIII.

1543   Principio advertendum nobis est, globum est mundum.—Copernicus
       Revolut. Orb. Cælest. 1.

1581   Or ils dient que l'air est espandu tout à l'entour du globe de l'eau &
       de la terre, tout ainsi qu'vn habillement.—Daneau *Phys. Fran.* 402.

1600   Mouetur tellus primariâ suâ formâ & naturali desiderio, ad suarum
       partium conseruationem, perfectionem, & ornatum, versus præstan-
       tiora: quod magis verisimile est quàm vt fixi illi luminosi globi, tum
       errones, & præstantissimus & diuinus sol.—W. Gilbert *Magnete* 224.

1604   Thus, without doubt the Heaven is of a round and perfect figure; and
       the earth likewise imbracing and ioyning with the water, makes one
       globe or round bowle framed of these two elements, having their
       bounds & limits within their own roundnes & greatnes.—Grimestone
       Acosta 5–6.

1604   Mittamus igitur immania illa de Oceano, & inania: fines suos habet, &
       cum Terrâ vtiliter vno velut corpore, & orbe, Natura iunxit.   Hoc Stoici
       quoque nostri senserunt (in Laërtio) . . . . *Mediam esse Terram (totius
       Uniuersi:) post hanc, Aquam globosam, quæ idem centrum cum terrá habet, ita
       vt Terra sit in Aquá.* Vera hæc sunt, & examinemus. Ait, *aquam
       globosam.*]   Certum est, tumet & attolitur, & altitudine suâ vel montes

Globe—*continued*

terræ æquat. Cur non cadit? quia centrum cum terrâ idem habet, eoque vergit. Balbus Stoicus, apud Ciceronem: *Eademque ratione mare, cùm supra terram sit, medium tamen terræ locum expetens, conglobatur undique æqualiter, neque redundat unquam, neque effunditur.*—Lipsius *Physiol. Stoic.* 113.

1622   Globus flammæ, quem Castorem vocabant antiqui, qui cernitur navigantibus in mari, si fuerit unicus, atrocem tempestatem prænunciat. —Bacon *Works* III. 286.

1632   Io credo, che il globo lunare sia differente assai dal terrestre.—Galileo *Dial.* 54.

1634   Etenim offendit ipsos Empedocles eo, quod Lunam facit stiriam aëris grandineam, à globo [σφαίρας] ignis comprehensam & obsessam.— Kepler *Plutarch* 104–5.

1646   In the Hebrew text, the word [*holam*] which signifieth the whole universe of heaven and earth, is not used in any of these places; but the word [*Tebel*] which signifieth the round globe of the earth, or the habitable world, as Pagnine hath it.—Rosse *New Planet* 51.

1651   Stars are fiery globes, full of light and heat, with which the skie glitters on every side.—Comenius *Nat. Phil. Ref.* 116.

1659   A Globe according to the Mathematical Definition, is a perfect and exact round Body contained under one surface. Of this form (as hath been proved) consists the Heavens and the Earth.—Moxon *Tutor Astr.* 4.

1675   Le Soleil n'est qu'un globe de matiere subtile.—Gadroys *Syst.* 214.

1681   After y[e] chaos was separated from y[e] rest, by y[e] same principle w[ch] promoted its separation, (w[ch] might be gravitation towards a centre,) it shrunk closer together, and at length a great part of it condensing, subsided in y[e] form of a muddy water or limus, to compose this terraqueous globe.—Newton, in D. Brewster II. 452.

1697   And, generally speaking, of the Solids heavier than the Fluid, those which contain a greater Quantity of Matter, in respect of their Surface, will descend fastest; as a Globe of Gold sooner than the same Quantity in Leaf; and a Globe of Stone sooner than a lesser Globe of Gold. —Arbuthnot *Exam. Woodward* 22.

Herd[1]

1596   Proteus is Shepheard of the seas of yore,
             And hath the charge of Neptunes mightie heard.
                 —Spenser *F. Q.* III. viii. 30.

---

[1]See also BAND, BREED, BROOD, CHOIR, CITIZEN, CREW, FLOCK, FRY, HOST, INHABITANT, KIND, LEGION, NATION, PEOPLE, RACE, SEED, SHOAL, SQUADRON, TRAIN, TRIBE, TROOP.

Herd—*continued*

1605   The names of Birdes,
Of Water-guests, and Forrest-haunting Heards.
    —Sylvester *Div. Wks.* (*Bab.*) 425.

1616   So great Diana frays a herd of roes.
    —W. Browne *Brit. Past.* II. ii. 814.

1622   Old Proteus hath been knowne to leave his finny Heard,
And in their sight to spunge his foame-bespawled beard.
    —Drayton *Poly-Olb.* II. 439–40.

1640   Retaynes his Rod:
With which he drives his Goates (like one that feeds
The bearded Heard).
    —Sandys *Ovid's Met.* 7.

1659   Those meadows need
No shearing—where in untold droves did feed
His bellowing herds.
    —W. Chamberlayne *Phar.* I. iii. 3–5.

1667   So hear the scaly herd when Proteus blows.
    —Dryden *Ann. Mir.* xv.

1667   Down he alights among the sportful Herd
Of those fourfooted kindes.
    —Milton *P. L.* IV. 396–7.

1690   And I should break through laws divine and human,
And think them cobwebs spread for little man,
Which all the bulky herd of nature breaks.
    —Dryden *Don S.* V. i, in *Works* VII. 466.

1705   To the thick Woods the woolly Flocks retreat,
And mixt with bellowing Herds confus'dly bleat.
    —Addison *Campaign* 12.

1730   The vulgar stare: amazement is their joy
And mystic faith,—a fond sequacious herd!
    —Thomson *Summer* 1705–6.

Host[1]

1578   Soit les oiseaux vagues hostes de l'air,
Soit les poissons citoyens de la mer.
    —Ronsard IV. 335.

1585   De mesme l'Eternel ne bastist l'univers
Pour les hostes des bois, des ondes et des airs.
    —Du Bartas *I Sem.* VI. 419–20.

---

[1]See also BAND, BREED, BROOD, CHOIR, CITIZEN, CREW, FLOCK, FRY, HERD, INHABITANT, KIND, LEGION, NATION, PEOPLE, RACE, SEED, SHOAL, SQUADRON, TRAIN, TRIBE, TROOP.

Host—*continued*

1596   They saw an hideous hoast arrayd,
       Of huge Sea monsters, such as liuing sence dismayd.
       —Spenser *F. Q.* II. xii. 22.

1605   Fit sence-full Names vnto the Hoast that rowes
       In waterie Regions.
       —Sylvester *Div. Wks. (6th Day)* 224.

1622   The vast and queachy soyle, with Hosts of wallowing waves.
       —Drayton *Poly-Olb.* XXV. 15.

1630   Starres, Hoste of heauen, yee Firmaments bright Flowrs.
       —Drummond II. 43.

1652   Those happy mansions, glorious Saint, discover,
       Where the bright Host of Spirits hover!
       —Benlowes *Theoph.* VI. i.

1667   My self and all th' Angelic Host that stand
       In sight of God enthron'd.
       —Milton *P. L.* V. 535–6.

1690   I knew you both; and (durst I say) as heaven
       Foreknew, among the shining angel host,
       Who would stand firm, who fall.
       —Dryden *Don S.* IV. iii, in *Works* VII. 440.

1714   His warlike Amazon her Host invades,
       Th' Imperial Consort of the Crown of Spades.
       —Pope *Rape of the Lock* III. 67–8.

Humid[1]

Terra exalat auram atque auroram humidam.
    —Pacuvius *Incert.* 56.

Iamque domum mirans genetricis et umida regna
Speluncisque lacus clausos lucosque sonantis
Ibat.
    —Virgil *Geo.* IV. 363–5.

Vacat imbribus Arctos
Et Notos, in solam Calpen fluit umidus aer.
    —Lucan IV. 70–1.

Sed cum spiritibus tenebrosis nocte dieque
Congredimur, quorum dominatibus umidus iste
Et pigris densus nebulis obtemperat aër.
    —Prudentius *Hamart.* 514–16.

ὡς κείνων οἰστρηδὸν ἐπόψεαι ὑγρὸν ὅμιλον
εἱλομένων.
    —Oppian *Hal.* IV. 142–3. (Even

---

[1]See also FLUID.

Humid—*continued*

so shalt thou behold the humid crowd
of the Mullets passionately thronging.—
Tr. A. W. Mair.)

Idem aridi fœtus satorum vt sint facit,
Reddit liquorum idem vapores humidos [ὑγρὰς ἰκμάδας],
Hos namque miscet cursibus per aërem.
            —Morellus *Pisidas* 12.

Post etiam clausi uasto sub gurgite pisceis
Respirant lymphis, flatusque sub æquore ducunt:
Quæque negant nobis, illis dant humida uitam.
            —Avitus *Orig. Mundi* 7.

1549   Le Lesbien ses vers sonnoit
        Parmy les armes non timide,
        Ou quand à sa nef il donnoit
        Repos sur le rivaige humide.
            —Du Bellay III. 112.

1572   Mas ja as agudas proas apartando,
        Hiano as vias humidas de argento.
            —Camoens *Lus.* 30.

1578   Tout seul me suis perdu par les rives humides.
            —Ronsard VI. 339.

1584   Le pilote sçavant,
        Aydé par les souspirs d'un favorable vent,
        Avec moins de travail l'ailé vaisseau ne guide
        Sur le sel azuré de la campaigne humide.
            —Du Bartas *Furies* 155–8.

1591   The winged fleeting Ship,
        That softlie on the azure salt
        Of humide fielde doth slip.
            —James I *Furies* 333–5.

1591   A litle noursling of the humid ayre,
        A Gnat vnto the sleepie Shepheard went.
            —Spenser *Gnat* 282–3.

1603   For bloud is hot, and humid, like the aire.
            —John Davies of Hereford *Micro.* 64.

1627   So when the South (dipping his sable wings
        In humid seas) sweeps with his dropping beard
        The ayer, earth, and Ocean.
            —P. Fletcher *Locusts* II. xl.

1630   The humid Swimmers dye along the shoare.
            —Drummond II. 57.

Humid—*continued*

1640   But, while I speak, behold, the humid Night
             Beyond th' Hesperian Vales hath ta'ne her flight.
             —Sandys *Ovid's Met.* 26.

1651   As oft the humid Night had wrapt the Skies
             In her black Mantle, wrought with Stars like Eyes.
             —Sherburne *Salmacis* 3.

1656   When scorching Phœbus all inflam'd doth fly,
             To cool his heat in humid Aquary.
             —T. Harvey *Mantuan* 82.

1656   Ainsi, lors que le Sud, des Monts de Barbarie,
             Sur l'humide Element s'est lancé de furie.
             —Chapelain *Pucelle* 261.

1667   The Sun that light imparts to all, receives
             From all his alimental recompence
             In humid exhalations.
             —Milton *P. L.* V. 423-5.

             Where Rivers now
             Stream, and perpetual draw thir humid traine.
             —*Ibid.* VII. 305-6.

1675   Whither as Earth transpires its Native fumes,
             Those humid Spirits the hot Air consumes.
             —Sherburne *Sphere* 60.

1698   As often as the night obscures the skies
             With humid shades.
             —Dryden *Aen.* IV. 504-5.

1716   Quelques Sages pensoient qu'il [le soleil] seroit consumé
             En versant tant de feux dans sa vaste Carriere,
             Sans l'humide Aliment des Vapeurs exprimé,
             Qui l'entretient toujours dans sa force premiere.
             —Genest *Prin. Phil.* 91.

1727   Beside the dewy border let me sit,
             All in the freshness of the humid air.
             —Thomson *Summer* 622-3.

Terrenus vapor siccus est et fumo similis, qui ventos fulmina tonitrua facit; aquarum halitus umidus est et in imbres et nives cedit.—Seneca *Nat. Quaest.* II. xii. 4.

1555   Or comme les choses froides & humides sont conseruees en leur estre naturel par leur semblable, c'est à dire en lieu froid & humide, tout ainsi qui veult engarder les oeufs de se corrompre par le chaud, il les fault tenir en lieu frais.—Belon *Hist. Oyseaux* 31.

1581   Or en ce mesme monde l'eau ou la nature humide, est ce que nous auons accoustume d'appeller, les Riuieres, Mers, & marais.—Daneau *Phys. Fran.* 30.

Humid—*continued*

1620 [*Humidum*] Significat enim et quod circa aliud corpus facile se circum-
fundit; et quod in se est indeterminabile, nec consistere potest; et quod
facile cedit undique; et quod facile se dividit et dispergit; et quod facile
se unit et colligit; et quod facile fluit et in motu ponitur; et quod alteri
corpori facile adhæret, idque madefacit; et quod facile reducitur in
liquidum, sive colliquatur, cum antea consisteret. Itaque cum ad hujus
nominis prædicationem et impositionem ventum sit, si alia accipias,
flamma humida est; si alia accipias, aër humidus non est; si alia, pulvis
minutus humidus est; si alia, vitrum humidum est.—Bacon *Works* I. 263.

1646 Common fusion in Metals is also made by a violent heat, acting upon
the volatile and fixed, the dry and humid parts of those bodies.—T.
Browne II. 93.[1]

1651 Humidity (or humour) is the liquidnesse of the parts of the body, and
aptnesse to be penetrated by one another; siccity on the contrary is a
consistency, and an impenetrability of the parts of the body. So a
clot hardned together either with heat or cold, is dry earth, but mire
is moist earth, water is a humid liquour, but ice is dry water.—Comenius
Nat. Phil. Ref. 56.

1655 Quomodo a motu solis elevantur e mari et locis humidis particulæ
aqueæ, unde fiunt nubes, explicatum est.—Hobbes I. 391.

1674 Quandò autem rerum corruptio à calido, humidoque extraneis insti-
tuitur; motus intestinus à particulis nitro-aereis ab aere suggestis
præcipuè efficitur.—Mayow *Tract.* 61.

1684 Unde in cella vinaria, quam ferventi musti crassiores halitus implent,
& in cryptis subterraneis, in quibus humidus aer torpet, fax accensa
se tuetur.—Du Hamel *Phil. Vetus et Nova* II. 63.

1686 L'Eau est encore appellé humide par quelques Philosophes, mais c'est
proprement ce qui est moüillé d'eau qu'on doit appeller humide, & en
ce sens l'air est humide quand il est·beaucoup remply de vapeurs
acqueuses.—Mariotte *Eaux* 2.

1700 A more powerful and intense Heat must needs hurry up a larger
quantity of that Matter along with the humid Vapors that form rain,
than one more feeble and remiss ever possibly can.—*Phil. Trans.* XXI.
220.

Humor[2]

Frigori miscet calorem atque humori aritudinem.
—Ennius *Varia* 46.

Floridis velut enitens
Myrtus Asia ramulis,
Quos Hamadryades deae

---

[1]Quoted from the 1672 edition.
[2]See also CRYSTAL HUMOR, JUICE.

Humor—*continued*

Ludicrum sibi roscido
Nutriunt umore.
—Catullus LXI. 21–5.

Vere novo, gelidus canis cum montibus umor
Liquitur et Zephyro putris se glaeba resolvit.
—Virgil *Geo.* I. 43–4.

Nunc redit ad Syrtes et fluctus accipit ore,
Aequoreusque placet, sed non et sufficit, umor.
—Lucan IX. 756–7.

Circumfluus umor
Ultima possedit solidumque coercuit orbem.
—Ovid *Met.* I. 30–1.

1572   A clara forma ali estaua esculpida
Das agoas entre a terra desparzidas,
De pescados criando varios modos,
Come seu humor mantendo os corpos todos.
—Camoens *Lus.* 98b.

1578   Cest astre des cieux,
Qui bien nourry de l'humeur mariniere
Respand au ciel une rousse lumiere.
—Ronsard VI. 482.

1591   And all her Sisters rent their golden heares,
And their faire faces with salt humour steep.
—Spenser *Teares* 111–12.

1592   Onde l'aure odorate innanzi al giorno
Spirano mormorando: e piove intanto
Il rugiadoso e cristallino umore.
—Tasso *Mondo Creato* IV. 380–2.

1603   Jadis de Jerico la terre salpetreuse,
Pour ne s'aboissonner que d'une humeur nitreuse,
Avortoit de ses fruicts.
—Du Bartas *Schisme* 599–601.

1605   For the salt humour of his Element
Serues him (alone) for perfect nourishment.
—Sylvester *Div. Wks.* (*5th Day*) 150.

1613   El celestial humor recien quaxado
Que la almendra guardò, entre verde i seca.
—Góngora II. 41.

1620   [L'or] chassera du cœur toute contagion:
Empeschera le sang de putrefaction:
Augmentera le baume & l'humeur radicale.
—Hesteau *Poème Phil.* 24.

Humor—*continued*

1648   And with the Christal humour of the spring,
Purge hence the guilt, and kill this quarrelling.
      —Herrick 78.

1656   Cloaths become moist, wch we on shoars display;
Spread in the Sun, again, they dry appear:
But neither how that humour entred there
Can we perceive: nor by what means it flies
The heat so soon, and consequently dries.
Therefore that which is humid separates
By minute parts, which no eye penetrates.
      —Evelyn *Lucretius* 31.

1667   Th' Arch-chimic Sun so farr from us remote
Produces with Terrestrial Humor mixt
Here in the dark so many precious things.
      —Milton *P. L.* III. 609–11.

A stream of Nectarous humor issuing flow'd
Sanguin, such as Celestial Spirits may bleed.
      —*Ibid.* VI. 332–3.

Over all the face of Earth
Main Ocean flow'd, not idle, but with warme
Prolific humour soft'ning all her Globe.
      —*Ibid.* VII. 278–80.

1668   Here Davids joy [dreaming] unruly grows and bold;
Nor could Sleeps silken chain its vio'lence hold;
Had not the Angel to seal fast his eyes
The humors stirr'd, and bad more mists arise.
      —Cowley 301.

1681   For, as when raging fevers boil the blood,
The standing lake soon floats into a flood,
And ev'ry hostile humor, which before
Slept quiet in its channels, bubbles o'er.
      —Dryden *Abs. and Achit.* I. 136–9.

1682   Le bois verd, plein d'humeurs est long a s'alumer:
Quand il brûle l'ardeur en est plus vehemente.
      —La Fontaine *Quin.* 19.

1687   From him the wits their vital humour bring:
As brooks have their first currents from the Spring.
      —Ayres, in *CP* II. 338.

1698   When the contracted limbs were cramp'd, ev'n then
A wat'rish humor swell'd and ooz'd again.
      —Dryden *Geo.* III. 729–30.

Fortasse enim leves truncos frondesque in lacu sparsas pinguis umor
apprehendit ac vinxit.—Seneca *Nat. Quaest.* III. xxv. 9.

Humor—*continued*

1555 Rayn is a colde vapour, an erthy humour: or fumosities, out of waters
or earth drawen vp by the vertue of the Sunne, to the nether part of
the middle space of the ayre.—Dygges *Prognost.* 27.

1567 Galactites is a stone in colour ashie, in taste verie sweete and pleasant,
which being pressed or grouned, yeeldeth and giueth a certaine Milkie
and watrish humor.—Maplet *Greene Forest* 22.

1581 La rosee est vn humeur subtil consideré en sa substance.—Daneau
Phys. Fran. 36.

1600 Quæ verò ex aquâ & terrâ magis commixta, & vtriusque elementi
simili ruinâ conflata sunt, (in quibus terrena magnetica vis deformata,
& sepulta manet; aqueus verò humor inquinatus cum terrâ copiosori
coiuerit, in se non concreuerit, sed terreno immiscetur) nullo modo
ex se allicere quicquam quòd non contigerint, aut loco dimouere
possunt.—W. Gilbert *Magnete* 52.

1601 They may evidently perceive their clothes wet with a clammie humour
of honie.—Holland *Pliny* I. 315 (Bk. XI, chap. xii).

1602 Semen & materiam rerum omnium formabilem esse oportuit, & vt ita
loquar, ductilem & tractabilem, id quod sine humore esse non poterat
in terra. Itaque terra humorem admistum habuit, quæ natura sua
sicca & dura quædam res est, nec sibi cohærens nec in longum aut
latum tractabilis, nisi colligante, & emolliente humore talis fieret.—
Daneau *Phys. Christ.* 111–12.

1622 Concerning the humours whereof the eye is made: the first called
aqueus, that is, the waterish humor, because it is not vnlike water settled
in the formost part of it, betweene the hornie membrane and that
which is called *Uuea*, and some part of the crystaline humor.—Banister
Guillemeau A7–8.

1628 Fistulis potius opus esset Naturæ (& quidem quales Bronchia sunt an-
nularibus, ut semper pateant, & neque concidant, & ut omnino vacua
sanguine permaneant ne humor aeris transitum impediat, uti mani-
festum est, quando pulmones pituita Bronchiis vel infarcta, vel paululum
admissa laborant) sibilo, & strepitu oborto dum respiramus.—W. Harvey *Exer. Anat.* 18.

1637 Planta fibris radicum humorem imbibens alescit. A Plant sucking the
humour by the little haires of the roote takes nourishment.—Comenius
Gate of Tongues 17.

1644 Natura tamen, ut primo prospiceret, multa adhibuit. Etenim, pel-
lucidis & nullo colore imbutis humoribus oculum replens, effecit ut
actiones extrinsecus venientes sine ullâ mutatione ad fundum illius
pertingant.—Descartes *Œuvres* VI. 615.

1653 Not to trouble our selves here with any dispute concerning it, whether
the winde be a terrene humour or a collision of the air alone.—Dariott
[Spark] *Redivivus* 278.

Humor—*continued*

1655   Insunt in concluso aere corpuscula illa mota, ut supposuimus, motu simplice, motum suum habentia liberum, sed quæ descendente humore aqueo paulatim cohibentur, oppletisque aqua interstitiis, pars quidem ætherea penetrando aquam egreditur.—Hobbes I. 371.

1657   Some [medicines] are also called *Emphrastica*, which obstruct the pores with a glewish humour, and fill them with clammy matter.—Tomlinson *Renodaeus* 30.

1676   Humors are parts of the Body, fluid and moist; observable to the sight and touch.—Cooke *Marrow of Chirurgery* 4.

1684   Est enim aer spirabilis potius, quam liquidus: & licet in sensu Aristotelico sit humidissimus, humor tamen dici non potest.—Du Hamel *Phil. Vetus et Nova* 70.

1698   We broke this Bone also, and perceiv'd in this Sinus a ropy and clear humour, in the middle of which there was a body like in figure consistence and colour to a greater one, which we had before taken out. —*Phil. Trans.* XIX. 473.

1718   And to the End, that the Countenance should not always appear Weeping and cover'd with Tears, that there are Passages contrived, by which this Humour at the usual Times can be discharged into the Nostrils. And the same Humour in extraordinary Occasions, being changed into a flood of Tears, we are then much more sensible of the Course of them into the Nostrils.—J. Chamberlayne *Nieuwentyt* I. 216.

Image

Omne genus quoniam passim simulacra feruntur,
Partim sponte sua quae fiunt aere in ipso,
Partim quae variis ab rebus cumque recedunt
Et quae confiunt ex horum facta figuris.
Nam certe ex vivo Centauri non fit imago,
Nulla fuit quoniam talis natura animantis;
Verum ubi equi atque hominis casu convenit imago,
Haerescit facile extemplo, quod diximus ante,
Propter subtilem naturam et tenvia texta.
    —Lucretius IV. 735–43.[1]

Aut ubi odor caeni gravis aut ubi concava pulsu
Saxa sonant vocisque offensa resultat imago.
    —Virgil *Geo.* IV. 49–50.

Quam si fraterna prohiberet imagine tellus
Insereretque suas flammis caelestibus umbras.
    —Lucan VI. 503–4.

---

[1]Dryden comments thus on Lucretius' use of *image*: ". . . as Lucretius tells us, who has used this word of *image* oftener than any of the poets."—*Apology for Heroic Poetry*, in *Essays* I. 187.

Image—*continued*

Et deserta iacens domini cœlestis imago,
Omne decus mentis turpi deiecerat actu.
—Avitus *Orig. Mundi* 47.

1552   De la mort l'efroyable[1] image
Est tousjours peinte en leur visage.
—Du Bellay IV. 192.

1585   Qui pourra soustenir sur les cieux les plus clers
Du visage de Dieu les foudroyans esclers?
Qui le pourra trouver separé de l'ouvrage,
Qui porte sur le front peinte au vif son image?
—Du Bartas *I Sem.* I. 125–8.

1592   Perchè nascendo 'l Sole, imbruna e perde
De l'alma Luna la rotonda imago.
—Tasso *Mondo Creato* IV. 285–6.

1596   Ioyous, to see his ymage in mine eye,
And greeu'd, to thinke how foe did him destroy.
—Spenser *F. Q.* I. iv. 45.

1605   A man may finde a iuster Policie,
Or truer Image of a calme Estate.
—Sylvester *Div. Wks.* (*7th Day*) 255.

1614   And death his image in her face did paint.
—Mure I. 122.

1633   So hath grace
Chang'd onely Gods old Image by Creation,
To Christs new stampe, at this thy Coronation.
—Donne *Div. Poems: Tilman* 16–18.

1651   Thou do'st my Syres old Rangers Image beare.
—Davenant *Gond.* I. ii. 61.

Instinct, the inward Image, which is wrought
And given with Life, be like thaw'd wax defac'd!
—*Ibid.* I. iii. 69.

1667   Less winning soft, less amiablie milde,
Then that smooth watry image.
—Milton *P. L.* IV. 479–80.

In his own Image hee
Created thee, in the Image of God
Express.
—*Ibid.* VII. 526–8.

1668   And let the Hills around reflect the Image of thy Voice.
—Cowley 157.

---

[1]Translating Buchanan (*Mem.* 250), "mortis imago."

Image—*continued*

1686   Gaze up, some winter night, and you'll confess
Heaven's a large gallery of images.
    —Flatman, in *CP* III. 412.

1692   But kissed, and took her, trembling, in my arms;
And in that fury of my love, I stamped
This image of my soul.
    —Dryden *Cleom.* I. i, in *Works* VIII. 278–9.

1714   A heav'nly Image in the Glass appears.
    —Pope *Rape of the Lock* I. 125.

1746   A faint erroneous ray,
Glanced from the imperfect surfaces of things,
Flings half an image on the straining eye.
    —Thomson *Summer* 1687–9.

1571   Wherefore upon such a cloude, the sunne beames strykynge, as uppon a smoothe glasse, doe expresse the image of ye sunne unperfectly, for the great distance.—Fulke *Meteors* 36b.

1600   Qua ratione fit vt in templis & promptissimè sonus excipiatur, & exquisitissimè imago vocis, quam echo vocant, referatur reddaturque.—H. Fabricius *De Auditu* 13.

1627   Put a looking-glass into a bason of water; I suppose you shall not see the image in a right line, or at equal angles, but aside. I know not whether this experiment may not be extended so as you might see the image, and not the glass.—Bacon *Works* V. 39.

1644   Et quò majora & lucidiora hæc simulacra sunt, eò perfectius videntur; adeo quidem ut, si oculum admodum profundum struere possemus, cujus pupilla esset valde ampla, & in quo superficies refractionem efficientes figuram haberent quæ huic magnitudini responderet, eò ampliores objectorum corporum imagines in ejus fundo exprimerentur.—Descartes *Œuvres* VI. 605.

1651   Appearing Meteors, are the images of things in clouds, variously expressed by the incident light: of which sort there are observed seven: Chasma, Halo, Parelius, Paraselene, Rods, Colours, the Rainbow.—Comenius *Nat. Phil. Ref.* 134–5.

1663   Imago est similitudo materiæ radiantis, orta ex divergentiâ, vel convergentiâ radiorum, singulorum materiæ radiantis punctorum, à punctis singulis, vel ad puncta singula unius superficiei.—Gregory *Optica* (*Script. Opt.* 6).

1674   When the image of any new and strange object is presented to the Soul, and gives her hope of knowing somwhat that she knew not before; instantly she admireth it.—Charleton *Nat. Hist. Passions* 87–8.

1704   In a very dark Chamber at a round hole about one third part of an Inch broad made in the Shut of a Window I placed a Glass Prism,

Image—*continued*

whereby the beam of the Sun's Light which came in at that hole might
be refracted upwards toward the opposite Wall of the Chamber, and
there form a coloured Image of the Sun.—Newton *Opt.* (Bk. I) 18.

1709   Suppose two eyes A and B: A from some distance looking on the Pictures in B sees them inverted, and for that reason concludes they are
inverted in B.   But this is wrong.   There are projected in little on the
Bottom of A, the Images of the Pictures of, suppose, Man, Earth, &c.
which are Painted on B.—Berkeley *Vision* 132–3.

Incumbent

Ac velut Edoni Boreae cum spiritus alto
Insonat Aegaeo sequiturque ad litora fluctus;
Qua venti incubuere, fugam dant nubila caelo.
—Virgil *Aen.* XII. 365–7.

Tum super incumbens pallentia uolnera lambit
Ore uenena trahens et siccat dentibus artus.
—Lucan IX. 933–4.

1585   Tum pronus incumbens ad imum gurgitem,
Et conuolutus ad cauum voraginis,
Vortigine æstuo, palóque vagus, & denuo
Ad humum reflecto limus cursum meum.
—Morellus *Pisidas* 62b.

1652   Theophil, thy Love-Song can't assuage
The fate incumbent on this age.
—Benlowes *Theoph.* III. c.

1667   Then with expanded wings he stears his flight
Aloft, incumbent on the dusky Air
That felt unusual weight.
—Milton *P. L.* I. 225–7.

1674   With wings expanded wide, ourselves we'll rear,
And fly incumbent on the dusky air.
—Dryden *State of Inn.* I. i, in *Works* V. 127.

1698   As when loud Boreas, with his blust'ring train,
Stoops from above, incumbent on the main.
—Dryden *Aen.* XII. 542–3.

1703?   'Tis said, that thunder-struck Enceladus
Groveling beneath th' incumbent mountain's weight,
Lyes stretch'd supine, eternal prey of flames.
—Addison *Aen.* 3, in *Works* I. 46.

1722   The sable Plain
Looks gay, and whitens with th' incumbent Grain.
—J. Jones *Oppian's Hal.* IV. 616–17.

Incumbent—*continued*

1727　　What need I mention those inclement skies
　　　　Where frequent o'er the sickening city, plague,
　　　　The fiercest child of Nemesis divine,
　　　　Collects a close incumbent night of death.
　　　　　　—Thomson *Summer* 1052–5.

1741　　Dispersas & jam sublime volantes
　　　　Quòd si sustineat nebulas compressior Aër,
　　　　Continuò tubulo incumbens, vis præravat ingens
　　　　Mercurium, sursumque Metallum fortiùs urget.
　　　　　　—Anon., in *Mus. Angl.* (5th ed.) II. 187.

Sed ceterae quoque stellae non minus terrena quam incumbentem terris spiritum afficiunt et cursu suo occursuue contrario modo frigora, modo imbres aliasque terris turbide iniurias mouent.—Seneca *Nat. Quaest.* II. xi. 2.

1606　　Alij igitur putant id fieri propter incumbentes Mari nebulas & caliginem, quæ ita illud comprimunt, coercent, & vndiquaque cogunt, vt longiùs aqua effluere non possit.—Daneau *Phys. Christ.* 68.

1662　　And 'tis very unlikely that the Earthy Atomes, contiguous to the restagnant Mercury at the bottom of the Hill, should be able by their weight to keep suspended a Cylinder of Mercury of above three Inches, unless the contiguous Air were gravitated upon by the weight of other incumbent parts of the Atmosphere.—Boyle *Examen of Hobbes* 25.

1668　　The reason that this remainder of the Mercury doth not descend also, is, because such a Mercurial Cylinder is just equiponderant to one of the incumbent Atmosphere that leans upon the Quicksilver in the Vessel, and so hinders a further descent.—Glanvill *Plus Ultra* 61.

1675　　Now as the rest of incumbent and subjacent Earths approach this [surface mould] in virtue, so are they to be valued.—Evelyn *Terra* 5.

1679　　The particles of vapours, exhalations, and air do stand at a distance from one another, and endeavour to recede as far from one another as the pressure of the incumbent atmosphere will let them.—Newton, in D. Brewster I. 413.

1686　　The sea water being presst too with a vast weight of Air which is always incumbent upon its spacious superficies.—Plot *Stafford.* 79.[1]

---

[1]Hooke made an interesting attempt in the following passage to find a substitute for the word *incumbent;* he used *pressing* instead, the word which Plot and Newton employ along with *incumbent:* "I shall only insist upon this one Experiment of the Velocity of Fluids, vented or running at several depths below the Superficies of that Fluid. In which it is observable, that the quantity of water running within a certain space of time is always in a Subduple proportion to the height of the pressing Fluid above the hole."—*Lampas* (1677), in Gunther *Early Science in Oxford* VIII. 186.

Incumbent—*continued*

1687　Ex Hypothesi multis experimentis confirmata, quod compressio aeris
sit ut pondus Atmosphæræ incumbentis, quodque gravitas sit reciproce
ut quadratum distantiæ locorum à centro Terræ.—Newton *Principia* 503.

1712　[Fissures] were filled by the common Sand of that Stratum mouldering
down into them, which of a White became Black, being stained by a
Black Earth drain'd down upon it from amongst the Soil, and Clay,
of the Incumbent Strata.—Morton *Northampton*. 81.

Infuse[1]

Atlantis, cinctum adsidue cui nubibus atris
Piniferum caput et vento pulsatur et imbri,
Nix umeros infusa tegit.
　　　—Virgil *Aen*. IV. 248–50.

Multumque madenti
Infudere comae quod nondum euanuit aura
Cinnamon externa nec perdidit aera terrae.
　　　—Lucan X. 165–7.

Qui spiritus olim
Ore superfusus patrio uolitabat in undis.
　　　—Prudentius *Apoth*. 667–8.

1599　　　And why did God in man this Soule infuse?
　　　　　—Sir John Davies *Nosce Teipsum* 37.

1611　　　O you that haue infusde
　　　　　Soule to this Infant; now set downe, this blessing
　　　　　　on his starre.
　　　　　—Chapman *Il*. 94.

1613　　　Many spells then using,
　　　　　The water's nymph 'twixt Marine's lips infusing
　　　　　Part of this water.
　　　　　—W. Browne *Brit. Past*. I. ii. 307–9.

1622　　　I know he deem'd I willing did amiss,
　　　　　Which did more sorrow in my soul infuse.
　　　　　—Hannay *Sher. and Mar*. II. 537–8.

1633　　　Yet when new spring her gentle rayes infuse,
　　　　　All storms are laid.
　　　　　—P. Fletcher *Purple Isl*. I. xxii.

1638　　　But that the cunning matron did infuse
　　　　　Some atoms of the Quiris into cream.
　　　　　—Whiting, in *CP* III. 498.

1640　　　Two Adders from her crawling haire she drew;
　　　　　And those at Athamas and Ino threw:

---

[1]See also DISTIL.

Infuse—*continued*

These up and downe about their bosomes roule;
And with infus'd infection sad the Soule.
—Sandys *Ovid's Met.* 70.

1648   His griping hands let Ophiuchus loose,
And the squeez'd venome of his Snake infuse.
—Sherburne *Medea* 38.

1659   That engine of the world, mysterious love,
The way that fate predestinated, when
'Twas first infus'd i' the embryo.
—W. Chamberlayne *Phar.* I. iii. 226–8.

1667   Her looks, which from that time infus'd
Sweetness into my heart, unfelt before.
—Milton *P. L.* VIII. 474–5.

1668   If Heav'en to men such mighty thoughts would give,
What Breast but thine capacious to receive
The vast Infusion?
—Cowley 388.

1698   All soft'ning simples, known of sov'reign use,
He presses out, and pours their noble juice.
These first infus'd, to lenify the pain,
He tugs with pincers, but he tugs in vain.
—Dryden *Aen.* XII. 592–5.

1746   Still let my song a nobler note assume,
. And sing the infusive force of Spring on man.
—Thomson *Spring* 867–8.

1606 Alter autem lucis huius vsus est, vt per hunc ipsum calorem calor natiuus (qui dicitur rebus omnibus necessarius) infundatur, vt vires illis ad vitam, & proprias functiones perficiendas dentur.—Daneau *Phys. Christ.* 12.

1609 Quando Solis Peripheria in Cœlo volvitur & permeat vias seu plateas itineris Cœlestis . . . confortando illarum vim, & operationem, quam in Aëre habent, excitat (cum Marte videlicet Calorem, cum Saturno Frigus) & unicuique infundit Lumen, vitam, & motum usque ad infima & profundissima loca Terræ.—Croll *Basil. Chym.* 208–9.

1614 A warme ayre is infused thereunto, which serueth in steade of fire.—Lodge *Seneca* 819.

1630 Ores, si on demande la cause de cette augmentation: dira Cardan que ce soit l'esuanouïssement de la chaleur celeste? Ainçois elle est y infuse plus largement par le moyen des rayons solaires.—Rey *Essais* 67.

1651 Scripture . . . testifieth that a certain vertue was infused by God through the whole world, susteining and quickening all things.—Comenius *Nat. Phil. Ref.* 21.

Infuse—*continued*

1657 The faculties and vertue therefore wherewith mixt bodies are indued (like the soule in mans body from the beginning of the Creation) is not from without, nor infused into them by a momentaneous position of the Stars.—Pinnell *Croll* 77.

1670 This Earth is infus'd in water, and after 3 dayes the water is powr'd off.—*Phil. Trans.* V. G_1.

1676 The particles of any tincture may have their size or density altered by the infusion of another liquor.—Newton, in D. Brewster I. 414.

1687 Infusion, is the steeping in water: the same wth Maceration.—Evelyn *Gardiner* 17.

1700 The Bodies in the Cavities of the other Tubes that had their lower Ends immers'd in Water wherein Saffron, Cochinele, &c. had been infused, were tinged with Yellow, Purple, &c.—*Phil. Trans.* XXI. 210.

Inhabitant[1]

1585 Sunt Cochleæ terrenæ & æquoris incolæ
Ingentium causæ bonorum paruulæ.
—Pisidas *Mundi Opificium* 1553–4.

1592 E le gregge, e gli armenti, e i vaghi augelli,
E gli abitanti ancor del mare ondoso.
—Tasso *Mondo Creato* VI. 1872–3.

1600 O, thou wilt be a wilderness again,
Peopled with wolves, thy old inhabitants!
—Shakespeare *II Henry IV* IV. v. 137–8.

1633 The free inhabitants of the Plyant aire.
—Donne *Progr. of the Soule* 215.

1637 A numerous multitude of ants,
Her neighbours, the next field's inhabitants.
—Marmion *Cup. and Psy.* II. ii. 57–8.

1645 A wild inhabitant of the air.
—E. Waller *To the Mutable Fair* 54.

1668 The Heavens seem'd decently to bow,
With all their bright Inhabitants.
—Cowley 252.

1675 For though it had been furnish'd out so well,
Yet no Inhabitant on Earth did dwell.
—Traherne 242.

---

[1]See also BAND, BREED, BROOD, CHOIR, CITIZEN, CREW, FLOCK, FRY, HERD, HOST, KIND, LEGION, NATION, PEOPLE, RACE, SEED, SHOAL, SQUADRON, TRAIN, TRIBE, TROOP.

Inhabitant—*continued*

1687   Yet still the wing'd inhab'tants of the wood
          Sing, as my change they had not understood.
          —Ayres, in *CP* II. 288.

1697   Th' inhabitants of seas and skies shall change,
          And fish on shore and stags in air shall range.
          —Dryden *Ecl.* I. 79–80.

1697   Skill'd in the wing'd inhabitants of air,
          What auspices their notes and flights declare.
          —Dryden *Aen.* III. 463–4.

1651   So now the heaven of heavens had for inhabitants, the Angels; the visible heaven, the starres, the air birds, the water fishes, the earth beasts.—Comenius *Nat. Phil. Ref.* 15.

1657   The foure first are Inhabitants of the Garden, and require a loose ground which hath been long manured.—Coles *Adam in Eden* Nn₃b.

1658   Ita maxima Corpora mundi, quatuor Elementa, sunt plena Habitatoribus suis.—Comenius *Orbis Pictus* 7. (Thus the greatest Bodies of the World, the four Elements, are full of their own Inhabitants.—Tr. Hoole, 1727.)

1686   After Stones made out of waters and resembling inanimate figures, come we next to such as represent the formes of Animals, the Inhabitants of that Element.—Plot *Stafford.* 182.

1695   That not only Men, Quadrupeds, Birds, Serpents, and Insects; the Inhabitants of the Earth and Air: but the far greatest part of all kinds of Fish likewise, the Inhabitants of the Sea, of Lakes, and of Rivers, suffered under the Fury of the Deluge, and were killed and destroyed by it.—J. Woodward *Nat. Hist. Earth* 165.

1700   Among the Inhabitants of the Air, which are very numerous. The humbing Bird is the most curious.—*Phil. Trans.* XXI. 438.

1714   The Watery, the Amphibious, the Airy Inhabitants, and those on the Dry-land, they all Live and Act with Pleasure, they are gay, and flourish in their proper Element, and allotted Place.—Derham *Physico-Theol.* 168–9.

Invade

         Opturgescit enim subito pes, arripit acer
         Saepe dolor dentes, oculos invadit in ipsos.
          —Lucretius VI. 658–9.

         Velox currit per tela uenenum
         Inuaditque manum.
          —Lucan IX. 829–30.

1595   No toong can tell, nor any forth can set,
         But he whose heart like sorrow did inuade.
          —Spenser *Astro.* 171–2.

Invade—*continued*

1608   Let it fall rather, though the fork invade
        The region of my heart.
            —Shakespeare *Lear* I. i. 146–7.

1616   When the hot dog-star rains his maladies,
        And robs the high and air-invading Alps
        Of all their winter-suits and snowy scalps.
            —W. Browne *Brit. Past.* II. i. 928–30.

1627   Our axes first did that strange wood inuade.
            —May *Lucan* R₂.

1637   Each invade
        The other with embraces, and fulfil
        A tedious scene of counterfeit good will.
            —Marmion *Cup. and Psy.* I. iv. 100–2.

1640   What compel'd
        Those cruell hands t' invade your fathers life!
            —Sandys *Ovid's Met.* 126.

        The dire Pyreneus still invades my sight.
            —*Ibid.* 90.

1651   Least the sharp Ayr should his new health invade.
            —Davenant *Gond.* II. vii. 67.

        This gay unusual sight;
        Which Commet-like, their wondring Eies invades.
            —*Ibid.* III. iii. 33.

1656   Here near these Alders is a cooling shade,
        The milder aire here gently doth invade
        The trembling leaves with murmurs (pleasing prate.)
            —T. Harvey *Mantuan* 5.

1660   An horrid stillness first invades the ear,
        And in that silence we the tempest fear.
            —Dryden *Astraea* 7–8.

1675   Bold Seamen the blind Ocean did invade.
            —Sherburne *Sphere* 7.

1693   Diffusive Cold does the whole Earth invade,
        Like a Disease, through all its Veins 'tis spread.
            —Congreve *Exam. Poet. 3d Part* 235.

1700   From thence the noise, which now, approaching near,
        With more distinguish'd notes invades his ear.
            —Dryden *Theo. and Hon.* 105–6.

1633   If the matter begin to be white and soft, and mingled with tears, or
        have invaded both the eies at once, there is danger of ulcers.—Banester
        Tumors 68.

Invade—*continued*

1659   For Example, those great Heats, which so long ago usually came about the middle of July, at which time the Dog-star arose in those days, do now likewise invade us about the middle of July.—Gassendi *Van. Jud. Astr.* 18.

1674   From this arrest of the blood in the heart, by strong constriction of the nerves thereunto belonging; we may with reason derive that same anxious oppression, and chilling weight which men commonly feel in their breast, when they are invaded by violent Fear.—Charleton *Nat. Hist. Passions* 123 (wrongly numbered 132).

It is very rarely found, that from Grief either long and obstinate, or violent and suddainly invading, any man hath fallen into a swoon, or been suddenly extinguished.—*Ibid.* 152.

1684   When Wood is reduced to that thinness, that its closeness or Porosity may conveniently be examined, it will easily enough give passage, even unto visible, odorable, and tinging Corpuscles though they invade it not in the form of a Liquor, but of dry Exhalations, so they be not incommensurate to its Pores.—Boyle *Porosity* 88.

1690   We can so contrive it, that a flame does not come to invade onely the surface that invests a body, but comes to be intermingled with the smaller . . . parts it consists of.—Boyle *Languid Motion* 36.

1695   The said Mud being reposed along the Shores near the *Ostia* of those Rivers, and by that means making continual Additions to the Land, thereby excluding the Sea, daily invading and gaining upon it.—J. Woodward *Nat. Hist. Earth* 43.

Jar[1]

1596   The feeble Britons, broken with long warre,
              They shall vpreare, and mightily defend
              Against their forrein foe, that comes from farre,
              Till vniuersall peace compound all ciuill iarre.
                 —Spenser *F. Q.* III. iii. 23.

1609   Right and wrong,
              Between whose endless jar justice resides,
              Should lose their names.
                 —Shakespeare *Tro. and Cres.* I. iii. 116–18.

1613   And what's the reason else of thunder,
              Of lightning's flashes all about,
              That with such violence break out,
              Causing such troubles and such jars,
              As with itself the world had wars?
                 —W. Browne *Brit. Past.* I. ii. 82–6.

---

[1]See also ELEMENT.

Jar—*continued*

1633   For Him, the jarring Elements agree.
        —Sylvester *Div. Wks.* (*Little Bartas*) 395.

1640   One face had Nature, which they Chaos nam'd:
        An undigested lump; a barren load,
        Where jarring seeds of things ill-joyn'd aboad.
        —Sandys *Ovid's Met.* 1.

1659   The intestine jarr
        Of Elements, which on each other prey.
        —Sprat *Plague* Bb.

1667   If Natures concord broke,
        Among the Constellations warr were sprung,
        Two Planets rushing from aspect maligne
        Of fiercest opposition in mid Skie,
        Should combat, and thir jarring Sphears confound.
        —Milton *P. L.* VI. 311–15.

1685   What help, when jarring elements conspire,
        To punish our audacious crimes?
        —Dryden *Alb. and Alban.* III. i, in *Works* VII. 278.

1740   Where Bile, and wind, and phlegm, and acid jar,
        And all the Man is one intestine war.
        —Pope *Horace's Sat.* II. ii. 71–2.

Juice[1]

        Hic alienus ovis custos bis mulget in hora,
        Et sucus pecori et lac subducitur agnis.
        —Virgil *Ecl.* III. 5–6.

        Pollutos cantu dirisque uenefica sucis
        Conspersos uetuit transmittere bella Philippos.
        —Lucan VI. 581–2.

        κερασσάμενος δὲ κυπέλλῳ
        ἰκμάδα λυσιμέριμνον ἀλεξικάκου πόρεν οἴνου
        παιδὶ νέῳ καὶ μητρὶ κατηφέι.
        —Nonnos *Dionys.* XIX. 17–19. (He
        mixed, and in a cup gave the young man
        and the downcast mother that winejuice
        which resolves all cares and drives away
        all trouble.—Tr. Rouse.)

        Perpetuo uiret omne solum, terræque tepentis
        Blandæ inter facies stant semper collibus herbæ,
        Arboribusque comæ: quo cum se flore frequenti
        Diffundunt, celeri confortant germina succo.
        —Avitus *Orig. Mundi* 14.

---

[1]See also HUMOR.

Juice—*continued*

1596   For though like withered tree, that wanteth iuyce,
        She old and crooked were.
          —Spenser *F. Q.* IV. i. 31.

1600   The archers shot their arrows sharp and keen,
        Dipp'd in the bitter juice of poison strong.
          —E. Fairfax *Tasso* XVIII. lxviii.

1611   So let the bloods and braines of them, and all they shall
          produce,
        Flow on the staind face of the earth; as now, this sacred
          iuice.
          —Chapman *Il.* 44.

1638   Allowed her pulse, and juice of clouds to sup.
          —Whiting, in *CP* III. 495.

1640   [Creation of men and women from stones]
        The Earthy parts, and what had any juyce,
        Were both converted to the body's use.
          —Sandys *Ovid's Met.* 4.

1648   Those Herbes which bloome with a pestiferous flow'r,
        She culls; the Iuice indu'd with banefull pow'r
        From roots distorted wrings.
          —Sherburne *Medea* 39.

1656   Through each thing living alimental juyce
        Extends, shrubs grow, and fruit in time produce.
          —Evelyn *Lucretius* 33.

1665   How poor are they then, whom if we but greet,
        Think that raw juyce, which in their lips we meet,
        Enough, to make us hold their Kisses sweet!
          —Herbert of Cherbury 70.

1671   Where ever fountain or fresh current flow'd
        Against the Eastern ray, translucent, pure.
        With touch ætherial of Heav'ns fiery rod
        I drank, from the clear milkie juice allaying
        Thirst, and refresht.
          —Milton *S. A.* 547–51.

1687   Ye herbs, that richest med'cines can produce,
        Come quickly and afford such sov'reign juice,
        As from her heart may all the pains remove.
          —Ayres, in *CP* II. 320.

1698   Strange death! for, when the thirsty fire had drunk
        Their vital blood, and the dry nerves were shrunk,
        When the contracted limbs were cramp'd, ev'n then
        A wat'rish humor swell'd and ooz'd again,

Juice—*continued*

Converting into bane the kindly juice
Ordain'd by nature for a better use.
—Dryden *Geo.* III. 727–32.

Not birdlime, or Idæan pitch, produce
A more tenacious mass of clammy juice.
—*Ibid.* IV. 57–8.

1698   Betwixt their horns the purple wine he sheds;
With the same gen'rous juice the flame he feeds.
—Dryden *Aen.* XII. 262–3.

1713   Refreshing Moisture cools the thirsty Mead,
Extends the Stalk, and swells th' unfolded Seed;
Restores the Verdure of the tarnish'd Leaves,
And ev'ry gladsome Herb the rip'ning Juice receives.
—Diaper *Dryades* 6.

1716   Et de son Sein humide agité doucement,
Des Plantes & des Fruits [la terre] fait sortir l'Aliment,
Ce Suc précieux qu'elle enferme.
—Genest *Prin. Phil.* 122.

1621   Succinum is Bitume, like a stone, exceeding hard, named, Ex succo, the Iuyce of the earth.—Widdowes *Nat. Phil.* 30.

The new and best Nut-meg is full of iuyce or oyle, smelling sweete.—*Ibid.* 33.

1622   This affect [night blindness] groweth from the weakenesse of the head, and grossenesse of the spirits of sight, as also from the humours and coates of the eyes, and principally of that *cornea* or horny coate, which are broken and stuffed with a thicke slimy iuice [vn suc gras & visqueux[1]].—Banister *Guillemeau* C₈₋₉.

1644   In plantis tria hæc [liquidi] distinguenda, χυμὸς, χυλὸς, καὶ ὀπὸς .... Alii ὀπὸν humorem vocant, qui ab aliquo expresso, inciso, vel etiam sponte manat; quod verò exprimitur χυλὸν & quod ab incisione, vel sponte defluit δάκρυον appellant, cum δάκρυον aliis lachryma sit, quæ sponte defluit, ac non raro etiam gummi instar concrescit, uti thus, & alia.   Sed has definitiones non exactè observarunt veteres.—Bodaeus *Theophrastus* 965.

1652   The Roots [of comfry] are great and long, spreading great thick Branches under ground, black on the outside and whitish within, short or easie to break, and ful of a glutinous or clammy Juyce of little or no tast at al.—Culpeper *Eng. Phys.* 37.

1656   Now the cause of this Petrifying property, is a stony-juice; for the water which contains the Seeds of so many things, that of stones doth especially coagulate therein.—Evelyn *Lucretius* 130.

---

[1]Guillemeau *Traité des Maladies* 27b.

Juice—*continued*

1657   In the first genus are contained all kinds of Plants, their several parts, and what is deduced from them, as roots, barks, stalks, woods, boughs, leaves, flowers, fruits, seeds, gums, rosins, juices, drops, liquors, misseldews, mosses, cottens, nuts.—Tomlinson *Renodaeus* 8.

Some hold that the name syrup is more probably derived from ὁπός juice and σύρω to draw, as it were a juice extracted.—*Ibid.* 98.

1664   The Juyce of Plants which is their nutriment, has the same analogy with Vegetables, as blood with Animals.—Le Febure *Body of Chym.* 1.

1665   It is a kind of Petrolium, and contains no other Mineral Juice, but that of Sulphur, which seems to be thus distilled by Nature under ground.—*Phil. Trans.* I. 136.

1667   We must rest in the Ancient Doctrine, which layeth the task of conveighing the *Succus nutritius*, to the Breasts and Womb, upon the Arteries; unless the Nerves be call'd in for aid, for conveighing some of the Spirituous Juyce, to be mixed with the Nutritious, to give life and vigour.—*Phil. Trans.* II. 510.

1670   His opinion therefore is, that Coral is form'd out of a glutinous Juyce, which being turn'd into Stone by a salt, abounding in it, riseth up in the form of a Shrub.—*Phil. Trans.* V. G₄b.

1683   The Yellow Juice as wel of a live Viper, and even a vext one, as of one that is either newly dead, or hath been so for several daies, contains in it no poyson at all.—*Phil. Trans.* XIII. 47.

1694   Il y a donc lieu de croire que les fleurs qui sont attachées aux jeunes fruits, sont comme autant de visceres particuliers destinez pour la préparation des sucs qui servent de premiere nourriture à ces fruits. Le suc nourricier circulant dans les feuilles des fleurs se prépare, & se filtre de telle maniere dans leurs vaisseaux, & dans leurs petits sacs, que les parties les plus propres pour la nourriture des jeunes fruits, se séparant d'avec les plus grossieres, sont portées dans ces fruits; tandis que ce qui n'est pas propre pour leur nourriture est receû dans les étamines ou filets.—Tournefort *Elem. Bot.* I. 47.

1696   In August I have observed the Clusters both Green and Ripe of *Perichymenum Ger.* very Leaky; which upon nearer and heedful Inspection, I found to be a thin clammy Juice, or Liquid Gum, which falls down upon the Leaves, and keeps its Liquid Form there.—*Phil. Trans.* XIX. 373.

Kind[1]

NOTE.—*Kind*, in the sense of *genus*, is perhaps the single most significant term of the stock diction of neoclassic poetry; accordingly, its uses in earlier poetry are cited here in more fullness than seemed necessary in the treatment of most other words. The word itself, of course, must be considered with other ge-

---

[1]See also BAND, BREED, BROOD, CHOIR, CITIZEN, CREW, FLOCK, FRY, HERD, HOST, INHABITANT, LEGION, NATION, PEOPLE, RACE, SEED, SCALY KIND, SHOAL, SQUADRON, TRAIN, TRIBE, TROOP.

Kind—*continued*

neric terms, particularly those indicated in the footnote at the bottom of page
215, but the list below contains passages from poetry in which *kind* and only
its most obvious foreign equivalents—*genus, genre,* and the like—are used.
Following this list, however, is another, presenting Greek and various additional Latin generic terms arranged alphabetically.   It seemed proper to assemble these terms and the examples of their use here rather than to inter-
sperse them throughout this appendix, particularly since many of them may
not be referred to a single English equivalent and since, assembled as a group,
they provide a useful illustration of the variety of generic nouns available for
periphrases in the classic writings.

> At Romulus pulcher in alto
> Quaerit Aventino, servat genus altivolantum.
> —Ennius *Ann.* (Lib. I) 80–1.

> Propter stagna ubi lanigerum genus piscibus pascit.
> —Ennius *Sat.* (Fr. VII) 66.

> E mare primum homines, e terra posset oriri
> Squamigerum genus et volucres.
> —Lucretius I. 161–2.

> Nox erat et terras animalia fessa per omnis
> Alituum pecudumque genus sopor altus habebat.
> —Virgil *Aen.* VIII. 26–7.

> Et genus omne avium mediis e partibus ovi,
> Ni sciret fieri, quis nasci posse putaret?
> —Ovid *Met.* XV. 387–8.

> Hic genus arboreum procero stipite surgens
> Non lapsura solo mitia poma gerit.
> —Lactantius *Phoen.* 29–30.

1505
> Nec rursus opes luxumque fluentem
> Non hominum, non alituum genus et pecus et grex
> Squamigerûm sensere, gravi et doluere ruina.
> —Pontano *Meteor.* 1497–9.

1557
> She may be well comparde
> Vnto the Phenix kinde:
> Whose like was neuer sene nor heard,
> That any man can finde.
> —*Tottel's Misc.* I. 156.

1562
> Animaux jà créés en genres, et especes
> Par chams, et prés herbus, bois, et forests espesses.
> —Scève 195.

1567
> I must destroy both man and beast and all the mortall
>   kinde.
> —Golding *Ovid's Met.* I. 215.

Kind—*continued*

1579   Terrificísque licèt ferueret fluctibus æquor,
Quod tremulo varians agitabat Cynthia cornu,
Et genus Astræum diuersa per æquora largas
Exereret fauces, scopulísque allideret undas.
      —Du Monin *Manip. Poet.* 5.

1585   Bastissant une nef, et par mille travaux
Conservans là dedans tous genres d'animaux.
      —Du Bartas *I Sem.* II. 1075–6.

1596   But all the Satyres scorne their woody kind.
      —Spenser *F. Q.* I. vi. 18.

1599   This doth she [the soul], when from things particular,
She doth abstract the vniuersall kinds,
Which bodilesse, and immateriall are,
And can be lodg'd but onely in our minds.
      —Sir John Davies *Nosce Teipsum* 24.

1603   Had we the prudence of the brutish kinde,
We would prevent these Passions Stormes with ease.
      —John Davies of Hereford *Micro.* 88.

1605   God, not contented, to each Kind to giue
And to infuse the Vertue Generatiue:
Made (by his wisedome) many Creatures breed
Of liue-lesse bodies, without Venus deed.
      —Sylvester *Div. Wks.* (*6th Day*) 228.

1613   Diez a diez se calaron, ciento a ciento,
Al oro intúitiuo, inuidíàdo
Deste genero alado.
      —Góngora II. 117.

1614   This said; away blue-eyd Minerua went
Vp to Olympus: the firme Continent,
That beares in endlesse being, the deified kind.
      —Chapman *Odys.* 87.

1616   The diuerse Shapes of Beasts which Kinds foorth bring.
      —Drummond I. 70.

1622   O let me yet the thought of those past times renew,
When as that woody kind, in our umbragious Wyld,
Whence every living thing save onely they exild,
In this their world of wast, the soveraigne Empire swayd.
      —Drayton *Poly-Olb.* XXII. 1618–21.

That there was not a Nymph to Jollity inclind,
Or of the wooddy brood, or of the watry kind,
But at their fingers ends, they Ribbels Song could say.
      —*Ibid.* XXVII. 143–5.

Kind—*continued*

1633   For may not hee
Bee so, if every severall Angell bee
A kind alone?
—Donne *Hymne to the Saints* 5–7.

1633   His snow-white steed was born of heav'nly kinde.
—P. Fletcher *Purple Isl.* XII. lxiii.

1638   Though't be i' the' nonsuch of the female kind.
—Whiting, in *CP* III. 442.

1647   I hate and highly scorn that Kestrell kind
Of bastard scholars.
—More *Cupids Conflict* 319–20.

1651   Then to those Woods the next quick *Fiat* brings
The Feather'd kinde.
—Davenant *Gond.* II. vi. 57.

1656   Since every thing
So slowly from it's proper seeds doth spring,
And rising do their kinds preserve to show
How of their matter nourished they grow.
—Evelyn *Lucretius* 25.

1663   But I deny they are the same,
More than a Maggot and I am.
That both are *Animalia*
I grant, but not *Rationalia:*
For though they do agree in kind,
Specifick difference we find.
And can no more make Bears of these,
Than prove my Horse is Socrates.
—Butler *Hudibras* 92.

1667   The dastard crow, that to the wood made wing,
And sees the groves no shelter can afford,
With her loud caws her craven kind does bring.
—Dryden *Ann. Mir.* lxxxvii.

1667   Down he alights among the sportful Herd
Of those fourfooted kindes, himself now one.
—Milton *P. L.* IV. 396–7.

Let th' Earth bring forth Fowle living in her kinde,
Cattel and Creeping things, and Beast of the Earth,
Each in their kinde.
—*Ibid.* VII. 451–3.

1668   And every Dust did an arm'ed Vermine prove,
Of an unknown and new-created kind.
—Cowley 222.

Kind—*continued*

1680   The scatter'd Lovers of the Feather'd kind,
Seeking when danger's past to meet again,
Make moan, and call, by such degrees approach.
—Otway *Orphan* V. i. 239–41.

1687   The Panther, sure the noblest, next the Hind,
And fairest creature of the spotted kind.
—Dryden *Hind and Panth.* 327–8.

1694   Virgins are like the silver finny race,
Of slippery kind, and fishes seem in part.
—Ayres, in *CP* II. 356.

1697   And He that then is born shall be inclin'd
To spoil the Sea, and kill the Scaly Kind.
—Creech *Manilius* (Bk. V) 81.

1698   These pois'nous plants, for magic use design'd,
(The noblest and the best of all the baneful kind).
—Dryden *Ecl.* VIII. 135–6.

1709   The Fowls, and Beasts, and ev'ry Sylvan Kind,
Down to the meanest Insects Heav'n design'd.
—Roscommon *Prayer of Jeremy* iv.

1712   And then advanc'd to Wonders yet behind,
Survey'd, and sung the Vegetable Kind.
—Blackmore *Creation* VII. 613–14.

1713   While weighty Seeds fall from their native Cells,
And near their Mother-Stem: Papescent Kinds
Far from their Homes are born by sweeping Winds.
—Diaper *Dryades* 10.

1730   A various sweetness swells the gentle race [of pears],
In species different, but in kind the same.
—Thomson *Autumn* 633–4.

1746   The mineral kinds confess thy mighty power.
—Thomson *Summer* 134.

Greek and Latin Generic Terms

ἀγέλη

φθίνουσα δ' ἀγέλαις βουνόμοις τόκοισί τε
ἀγόνοις γυναικῶν.
—Sophocles *Oed. Rex* 26–7. (A
blight is on the grazing herds of cattle,
and women fruitless in travail.)

παταγοῦσιν ἄπερ πτηνῶν ἀγέλαι.
—Sophocles *Ajax* 168. (Like
flocks of birds they clap their
wings.)

Kind—*continued*

ἄμφω δ᾽ αἱ μὲν ἔασι διάκριτοι ἐν νεπόδεσσιν,
οἱ δ᾽ ἐνὶ χερσαίῃσιν ἀριστεύουσ᾽ ἀγέλῃσιν.
—Oppian *Hal.* III. 441–2. (And the Red
Mullets have the same distinction among the
finny tribes as Swine have among the herds of
the land.—Tr. A. W. Mair.)

γενεά

οἵη περ φύλλων γενεή, τοίη δὲ καὶ ἀνδρῶν.
—Homer *Il.* VI. 146. (Even as the
generations of leaves are those of men.)

ἰλλομένων ἀρότρων ἔτος εἰς ἔτος
ἱππείῳ γένει πολεύων.
—Sophocles *Antig.* 339–40.
(Turning the soil with the offspring of horses [mules?], as the
ploughs go to and fro from year
to year.—Tr. Jebb.)

εἰσέρχεται μὲν ἰχθύων πλωτῷ γένει.
—Sophocles, Fr. 941 (678).
(She [Venus] gains an entrance into
the swimming generation of fishes.)

πτηνῶν τε γένη κατακοιμάσθω.
—Aristophanes *Thesmo.* 46.
(Sleep, generation of winged
creatures.)

Δή ποτε καὶ γενεαὶ κοράκων καὶ φῦλα κολοιῶν
ὕδατος ἐρχομένοιο Διὸς πάρα σῆμ᾽ ἐγένοντο.
—Aratus *Phaen.* 963–4. (Ere now, too,
the generations of crows and tribes of jack-
daws have been a sign of rain to come from
Zeus.—Tr. G. R. Mair.)

γενέθλη

ἥ δ᾽ ἄλκιμον ἦτορ ἔχουσα
πάντη ἐπιστρέφεται θηρῶν ὀλέκουσα γενέθλην.
—Homer *Hymn* XXVII. 9–10. (But the
goddess with a bold heart turns every way de-
stroying the race of wild beasts.—Tr. Evelyn-
White.)

ἀλλ᾽ εἰ τὰ θνητῶν μὴ καταισχύνεσθ᾽ ἔτι
γένεθλα, τὴν γοῦν πάντα βόσκουσαν φλόγα
αἰδεῖσθ᾽ ἄνακτος Ἡλίου.
—Sophocles *Oed. Rex* 1424–6. (But if

Kind—*continued*

you feel no shame before the generations of mortals, at least revere our lord the Sun whose fire nurtures all.)

κείνοις εὖ μὲν ἄρουρα φέρει στάχυν, εὖ δὲ γενέθλη
τετραπόδων.

—Callimachús *Hymn* III. 130–1. (For them the tilled land bears corn abundantly, and the four-footed breed prospers.)

εἶδε γάρ, εἶδεν ὄνειρον ὁμοίιον, ὡς παρὰ λόχμῃ
χαιτήεις κεκόρυστο λέων λυσσώδεϊ λαιμῷ
καὶ βαλλίων ἐλάφων κεραὴν ἐδίωκε γενέθλην.

—Nonnos *Dionys.* XX. 256–8. (For he had seen, he had seen another such dream, how a maned lion in the woods with ravening throat all ready gave chase to the horned generation of swift deer.—Tr. Rouse.)

γένος

Χρύσεον μὲν πρώτιστα γένος μερόπων ἀνθρώπων
ἀθάνατοι ποίησαν 'Ολύμπια δώματ' ἔχοντες.

—Hesiod *Works and Days* 109–10. (First of all the deathless gods who dwell on Olympus made a golden race of mortal men.—Tr. Evelyn-White.)

οἱ δ' ὅτε μὲν κατὰ φῶτα μιγέντ' εἰς αἰθέρ' ἵκωνται
ἢ κατὰ θηρῶν ἀγροτέρων γένος ἢ κατὰ θάμνων
ἠὲ κατ' οἰωνῶν, τότε μὲν τὸ λέγουσι γενέσθαι.

—Empedocles (Diels, Fr. 9). (But when these mingle in men and in the race of wild animals and of plants and birds and come out into the light, this is called birth.)

ὦ τρισμακάριον πτηνὸν ὀρνίθων γένος.

—Aristophanes *Birds* 1707. (O thrice-blessed winged race of birds!)

ἦ γὰρ ἀεὶ πλωτῶν σιφλὸν γένος ὑγρὰ θεόντων.

—Oppian *Hal.* III. 183. (Gluttonous verily always is the race of the swimming tribes that roam the water.—Tr. A. W. Mair.)

καὶ νεπόδων ὤδινε νόθον γένος, ἐκ λαγόνων δὲ
ὑγρὴν ἰχθυόεσσαν ἀνηκόντιζε γενέθλην.

—Nonnos *Dionys.* XXVI. 272–3. A bastard brood of marine creatures, a shoal of wet fish she shot out of her womb.—Tr. Rouse.)

Kind—*continued*

ἔθνος

ὥς εἰπὼν ζωστῆρι θοῶς συνέεργε χιτῶνα,
βῆ δ᾽ ἴμεν ἐς συφεούς, ὅθι ἔθνεα ἔρχατο χοίρων.
—Homer *Odys.* XIV. 72–3. (So saying,
he quickly bound up his tunic with his belt,
and went to the sties, where the tribes of swine
were penned.—Tr. A. T. Murray.)

ὦ πταναὶ θῆραι χαροπῶν τ᾽
ἔθνη θηρῶν, οὓς ὅδ᾽ ἔχει
χῶρος οὐρεσιβώτας.
—Sophocles *Philoct.* 1146–8. (Ye
feathered prey, and ye nations of
bright-eyed beasts who dwell in this
place, roaming the hills.)

ἀυτὰ γὰρ ἔστιν ταῦτα, δι᾽ ἀλλήλων δὲ θέοντα
γίγονται ἀνθρωποί τε καὶ ἄλλων ἔθνεα θηρῶν.
—Empedocles (Diels, Fr. 26). (For these
are all, and as they course through one another they become men and the nations of
other animals.)

ἔθνεά τοι πόντοιο πολυσπερέας τε φάλαγγας
παντοίων νεπόδων, πλωτὸν γένος Ἀμφιτρίτης.
—Oppian *Hal.* I. 1–2. (The nations of the
sea and the far-scattered phalanxes of all kinds
of finny creatures, the swimming race of Amphitrite.)

τίς ἐκστρατεύει παγκενὴ τὴν ἀκρίδα;
ἔθνος πτερωτὴν εἰς φθορὰν Αἰγυπτίων;
—Pisidas *Hex.* 1250–1. (Who drew
up in battle array the all-destroying
locusts, the winged nation to bring
ruin to the Egyptians?)

εἰληδά

καὶ ποτε καὶ κέπφοι, ὁπότ᾽ εὔδιοι ποτέονται,
ἀντία μελλόντων ἀνέμων εἰληδὰ φέρονται.
—Aratus *Phaen.* 916–17. (Anon, too,
the stormy petrels when they flit in calm,
move in companies to face the coming
winds.—Tr. G. R. Mair.)

σπέρμα

τὸ γὰρ βρότειον σπέρμ᾽ ἐφ᾽ ἡμέραν φρονεῖ,
καὶ πιστὸν οὐδὲν μᾶλλον ἢ καπνοῦ σκιά.
—Aeschylus, Fr. 227 (399). (For mor-

Kind—*continued*

tal kind taketh thought only for the day, and hath no more surety than the shadow of smoke.—Tr. Smyth.)

σπορά

γυναῖκες, Ἑκάβη ποῦ ποθ᾽ ἡ παναθλία,
ἡ πάντα νικῶσ᾽ ἄνδρα καὶ θῆλυν σποράν
κακοῖσιν;

—Euripides *Hecuba* 658–60. (O women, where is Hecuba, the all-wretched, who surpasses in grief all men, and all female seed?)

σπόρος

ἧς οἷα τυτθὸν ᾽Αμφίβαιος ἐκβράσας
τῆς κηρύλου δάμαρτος ἀπτῆνα σπόρον.

—Lycophron *Alex.* 749–50. (Wherefrom Amphibaeus shall toss him forth, as it were the tiny unfledged brood of the halcyon's bride.—Tr. A. W. Mair.)

στίχος

καὶ δρυσὶ καὶ ποταμοῖσι μίαν ξυνώσατο φωνήν
Νηιάδας καλέουσα καὶ ῾Αδρυάδας στίχας ὕλης.

—Nonnos *Dionys.* XIV. 8–9. (One all-comprehending summons was sounded for trees and for rivers, one call for Naiads and Hadryads, the troops of the forest.—Tr. Rouse.)

στόλος

χωρεῖ γὰρ εἰς πῦρ, εἰς ὕδωρ, εἰς ἀέρα,
εἰς γῆν, ἐν ἄστροις, ἐν φυτοῖς, ἐν ὀρνέοις,
εἰς πᾶν τὸ νηκτὸν, εἰς τὸν ἕρποντα στόλον.

—Pisidas *Hex.* 898–900. (For Thy power enters into fire and water and air, into the earth and stars and plants and birds, into every company of swimming and creeping creatures.)

στρατός

μύρμων τὸν ἐξάπεζον ἀνδρώσας στρατόν.

—Lycophron *Alex.* 176. (Turning into men the six-footed army of ants.)

χερσὶ δ᾽, ὅσον σθένος ἐστίν, ἐπειγομένοις τε πόδεσσι
σεύει ἀμυνόμενος διερὸν στρατόν.

—Oppian *Hal.* II. 444–5. (With hands

Kind—*continued*

and pushing feet he does all he can to shove
and drive away the watery army.)

τέκνον

λιμναῖα κρηνῶν τέκνα,
ξύναυλον ὕμνων βοὰν
φθεγξώμεθ'.

—Aristophanes *Frogs* 211–13.
(We children of the fountain and
the lake, let us wake our full choir-
shout.)

φῦλον

νῦν δὲ γυναικῶν φῦλον ἀείσατε, ἡδυέπειαι
Μοῦσαι Ὀλυμπιάδες, κοῦραι Διὸς αἰγιόχοιο.

—Hesiod *Theog.* 1021–2. (But now,
sweet-voiced Muses, dwellers upon Olympus,
daughters of aegis-bearing Zeus, sing of the
tribe of women.)

τηλουρὸν δὲ γῆν
ἥξεις, κελαινὸν φῦλον, οἳ πρὸς ἡλίου
ναίουσι πηγαῖς.

—Aeschylus *Prom.* 807–9. (Thou
shalt come to a distant land where a
dark race dwells, by the waters of
the sun.)

φῦλον ἄμουσον ἄγουσα πολυσπερέων καμασήνων.

—Empedocles (Diels, Fr. 74). Leading the
songless tribe of fish of many seed.)

ἕπεσθε νῦν γάμοισιν ὦ
φῦλα πάντα συννόμων
πτερυγοφόρ' ἐπὶ πέδον Διὸς.

—Aristophanes *Birds* 1755–7.
(O follow to our nuptial rites even
to the floor of Zeus, all winged
tribes who are related to us.)

ἀμφὶ δὲ σούβῳ
φῦλον ἅπαν νεπόδων τὸ πολύπλανον ἐπτοίηται.

—Oppian *Cyneg.* II. 433–4. (About the
Subus, indeed, the whole wandering tribe of
fishes is fluttered.—Tr. A. W. Mair.)

Kind—*continued*

φύσις

κουφονόων τε φῦλον ὀρνίθων ἀμφιβαλὼν ἄγει
καὶ θηρῶν ἀγρίων ἔθνη πόντου τ' εἰναλίαν φύσιν
σπείραισι δικτυοκλώστοις,
περιφραδὴς ἀνήρ.

—Sophocles *Antig.* 341–4. (The light-witted birds of the air, the beasts of the weald and the wood He traps with his woven snare, and the brood of the briny flood. Master of cunning he.—Tr. Storr.)

χορός

χορὸς δ' ἀναύδων ἰχθύων ἐπερρόθει
σαίνοντες οὐραίοισι τὴν κεκτημένην.

—Sophocles, Fr. 762 (700). (And a chorus of voiceless fish, wagging their tails, applauded their mistress [Amphitrite?].)

'Ἥλιον καὶ Ζῆνα καὶ αἰθέρα καὶ χορὸν ἄστρων.

—Nonnos *Dionys.* XXXII. 7. (Sun and Zeus and sky and the choir of stars.)

agmen

It nigrum campis agmen [*i.e.*, elephants].
—Ennius *Ann.* 474.

Ac velut ingentem formicae farris acervum
Cum populant hiemis memores tectoque reponunt,
It nigrum campis agmen praedamque per herbas
Convectant calle angusto.
—Virgil *Aen.* IV. 402–5.

Quis nam in aciem educit locustarum agmina
Aligera, collecta in neces Ægyptias?
—Morellus *Pisidas* 1223–4.

armentum

Tu cornifrontes pascere armentas soles.
—Pacuvius 2.

Quippe ita Neptuno visum est, immania cuius
Armenta et turpis pascit sub gurgite phocas.
—Virgil *Geo.* IV. 394–5.

chorus

Atque hanc conuexi molem sine fine patentis
Signorumque choros ac mundi flammea tecta.
—Manilius II. 117–18.

Kind—*continued*

coetus

Ut quondam exterrita amoris
Scylla novos avium sublimis in aere coetus
Viderit.
—Virgil *Ciris* 48–50.

cohors

Iam pectora ferro
Terribilesque innexa iubas ruit agmine nigro
Latratuque cohors.
—Valerius Flaccus VI. 110–12.

Innumerae comitantur aves stipatque volantem
Alituum suspensa cohors.
—Claudian *Phoenix* 76–7.

exercitus

Cum cerea reges
Castra movent fagique cava dimissus ab alvo
Mellifer electis exercitus obstrepit herbis.
—Claudian *Proserp.* II. 125–7.

gens

Eum vasti circum gens umida ponti
Exsultans rorem late dispergit amarum.
—Virgil *Geo.* IV. 430–1.

Hanc circum uariae gentes hominum atque ferarum
Aeriaeque colunt uolucres.
—Manilius I. 236–7.

Occidit aeriae celeberrima gloria gentis
Psittacus, ille plagae viridis regnator Eoae.
—Statius *Silvae* II. iv. 24–5.

Exilit inde volans gens plumea laeta per auras
Aera concutiens pennis crepitante volatu.
—Dracontius *Laud. Dei* I. 242–3.

grex

Superat pars altera curae,
Lanigeros agitare greges hirtasque capellas.
—Virgil *Geo.* III. 286–7.

Hoc trahit in pelagi caedes et uulnera natos
Squamigeri gregis.
—Manilius V. 658–9.

Conspirat uno foederatus spiritu
Grex christianus, agmen inperterritum
Matrum, uirorum, paruulorum, uirginum.
—Prudentius *Peristep.* X. 56–8.

Kind—*continued*

pecus, -oris

Visust in somnis pastor ad me adpellere
Pecus lanigerum eximia pulchritudine.
—Accius *Praetext.* 19–20.

Nec non et pecori est idem dilectus equino.
—Virgil *Geo.* III. 72.

O imitatores, servum pecus, ut mihi saepe
Bilem, saepe iocum vestri movere tumultus!
—Horace *Epist.* I. xix. 19–20.

Nunc pecus æquoreum celabrabere, magne Silure.
—Ausonius *Mosella* 135.

pecus, -udis

Praeter eat genus humanum mutaeque natantes
Squamigerum pecudes.
—Lucretius II. 342–3.

Nam qualis quantusque cavo Polyphemus in antro
Lanigeras claudit pecudes atque ubera pressat.
—Virgil *Aen.* III. 641–2.

plebs

Praebent rupta locum stagna uiantibus,
Riparum in faciem peruia sistitur
Circumstans uitreis unda liquoribus,
Dum plebs sub bifido permeat aequore.
—Prudentius *Cath.* V. 65–9.

Qui ponti facies, numerum novit arenae,
Femina quem jurans fallere nulla potest;
Astrorum plebem, qui calles spectat amantum,
Cynthia cui certis cornibus innotuit.
—Ennodius *Carm.* II. lxxxiv. 1–4.

Ut plebs pinnivola caeli concrescat in auris
Et squamosa sali fluidis concrescat in undis.
—Eugenius *Carm.* XX. 21–2.

saeclum

Interiectaque sunt terrarum milia multa
Quae variae retinent gentes et saecla ferarum.
—Lucretius IV. 412–13.

turba

An maior densa stellarum turba corona
Contexit flammas et crasso lumine candet,
Et fulgore nitet collato clarior orbis?
—Manilius I. 755–7.

Kind—*continued*

Tracta magicis cantibus
Squamifera latebris turba desertis adest.
—Seneca *Medea* 684–5.

vulgus

Praecipue, medio cum luna implebitur orbe,
Certa nitent mundo tum lumina; conditur omne
Stellarum uulgus, fugiunt nise nomine dignae.
—Manilius I. 469–71.

Effunde pontum, vulgus aequoreum cie
Fluctusque ab ipso tumidus Oceano voca.
—Seneca *Hippol.* 957–8.

The remaining animate creatures are divided into three great classes
[γένη], one of birds, one of fishes, and one of whales.—Aristotle *De Animal. Hist.* 490b9, in *Opera* III. 7.

Quibus cordi est educatio generis equini, maxime conuenit prouidere actorem industrium et pabuli copiam quae utraque uel mediocria possunt aliis pecoribus adhiberi.—Columella *Rust.* VI. xxvii.

Piscium feminae maiores quam mares. in quodam genere omnino non sunt mares, sicut erythinis et channis; omnes enim ovis gravidae capiuntur. vagantur gregatim fere cuiusque generis squamosi.—Pliny *Nat. Hist.* IX. xxiii. § 56.

1515 Educant aquæ reptilia uiuentium animarum per genus: Aliud genus est cetarium / aliud piscium tenuuium genus in piscibus item innumera discrimina sunt per genera sane distincta: Quorum: & nomina propria sunt: & pabulum uarium & figura / & magnitudo: & carnium qualitates / haud eedem / sed diuerse Maximis singula differentiis inter sese discrepant: Sub uariisque formis; atque diuersis specie collocantur.—Argyropolus *Basil* XXXIII.

1538 *Genus, generis,* is the begynnynge of euerye thynge, eyther of the persone that ingendred it, or of the place, where it was ingendred . . . . Also it signifieth kynde. *genus uitae,* a kynd of lyfe . . . . Also it signifieth that, whiche containeth many sondry kyndes, as Animal comprehendeth a man, a byrde, a fyshe, and euery of them is genus to that, whiche in theym is comprehended. As a brute beast is genus to a horse, a lyon, a bulle, a dogge, &.—Eliot *Diction.* I_{ii–iii}.

1552 Ciuilis generis est homo, apis, uespa, formica, grus.—Wotton *Differ.* 2b.

Et terrestre quod sanguinem habet & pedibus caret, genus serpentum est.—*Ibid.*

1596 Quot sunt genera plantarum? Duo quidem summa, scilicet arbor & herba: & vtraque frugifera aut ·infrugifera, vtriusque quamplurimè species . . . . Quotuplex est animal? Duplex, intelligens & brutum. Quotuplex est animal intelligens? Duplex, cœleste & sublunare.

Kind—*continued*

Quotuplex est animal cœleste? Duplex, visibile & inuisibile: huius generis sunt Angeli cœlestes ac cœli: illius stellæ errantes & inerrantes.—Bodin *Theat.* 134.

1596   Quotuplex est animantium generatio?   Sextuplex, quædam enim sine marium, ac fœminarum congressu prodeunt, vt Vermes . . . aut medio interiecto, puta ouis positis, vt omnia insectorum, serpentium, præter Viperam, & auium ac piscium crustaceorum, & squammeorum genera. —*Ibid.* 300.

1601   Of the shell fish kind are the Dactyli.—Holland *Pliny* I. 269 (Bk. IX, chap. lxi).

1621   There be sexes of Herbes, as of other liuing things, some of which more helpe, namely, the Male or Female according to their kindes.— Widdowes *Nat. Phil.* 48.

1629   There are two principall kindes of Peonie, that is to say, the Male and the Female.   Of the male kinde, I haue onely known one sort, but of the Female a great many.—Parkinson *Paradisus Terr.* 341.

1651   Cùm propter sensum necessariò efficitur, ut fiant membra similaria in animalibus; & cùm vis sentiendi, vis movendi, & vis nutriendi in eodem membro contineantur; (*scil. primogenito*) fit necessariò, ut membrum (quod primum principia ejusmodi tenet) & simplex existat, ut omnium sensibilium sit capax; & dissimilare, ut moveat & agat.   Quamobrem, *inquit* [Aristotle], in sanguineo genere, cor tale habetur membrum; in exsangui autem, proportionale.—W. Harvey *Gener. Animal.* 158–9.

1656   *Genus* is a comprehension of many Notions referred to one, as, a living creature, for this includes all living creatures . . . .   *Species* is that which is contained under the Genus: as, under living creature is contained man.—Stanley *Hist. Phil. 8th Part* 35.

1657   The most effectuall of all the Brooms is the Spanish kind.—Coles *Adam in Eden* Ccc₃.

1657   Animall, Vegetable, and Minerall principles are one and the same in all things, but have various Receptacles; for there is one of Vegetables, another of Mineralls, for all these proceed from one most principall and generall principall kind (which is the generall seed of all things or subject of the first matter, and to be distributed into three principall kinds, Animall, Vegetable, and Minerall) from which Nature hath the nature of Quick-silver to create every other Compound.—Pinnell *Croll* 103.

1664   Growing without any such Roots; as Willows, are all the Vimineous kinds, which are raised of Sets only.—Evelyn *Sylva* 3.

1664   Succus iste Nervosus à Cerebro & Cerebello in appendicem medullarem derivatus, exinde per Nervos in totum genus nervosum usque blando allapsu defertur, ac integrum ejus systema irrigat.—Willis *Cerebri Anat.* 243.

Kind—*continued*

1667 Nec libenter pisces, ut & reliqui greges animalium, ex nativis suis locis demigrant longinque, sed amant commorari, velut in patria & adhærere suæ agnatæ familiæ, in genitalibus suis aquis, gentilique salo. Unde fit ut in diversis aquis diversæ species generis squamati inveniantur, & piscatu educantur.—Milius *Orig. Animal.* 53.

1668 The ruminant kind are most usually the prey for the rapacious kind of beasts.—Wilkins *Real Character* 165.

1672 Panis, è vegetabilium genere confectus, simul ac famelico offertur ventriculo, famem extemplò abigit.—Wedel *Sal. Vol.* 31.

1677 I could not perceive any manifest ebullition, so as to judge whether the salt contained in this residence, were either of the acíd or lixiviate kind.—Plot *Oxford.* 41.

1684 Wonderful is the Force wherewith the Digestion of the Hen, and Duck-Kind is performed.—R. Waller *Acad. Cimen.* 160.

1694 J'espere que l'on connoîtra dans la suite, que l'auteur de la nature qui nous a laissé la liberté de donner les noms qu'il nous plairoit aux genres des plantes, a imprimé un caractere commun à chacun de leurs especes, qui doit nous servir de guide pour les ranger à leur place naturelle.—Tournefort *Elem. Bot.* I. 20.

1697 Here are great plenty of Potatoes, and Yams, which is the common Food for the Natives, for Bread-kind.—Dampier *New Voyage* 288.

1712 So having taken leave of them, we may now proceed to the Animals of the Feathered Kind.—Morton *Northampton.* 423.

1738 There are other more harmless Meteors of the Fiery Kind.—Pointer *Weather* 188.

1796 *Genuses* making an awkward plural, and *genera* not being English; I have often wished that we might be allowed to substitute *kind* for *genus*, and *sort* for *species.*—Martyn *Lang. Bot.* (under *Genus*).

Kindly

1563   And nature hath so planted in eche degrée,
        That Crabbes like Crabbes wil kindly cral and crepe.
           —*Mirr. Magistr.* (*Blacke Smyth* 38–9).

1595   And shortly after, euerie liuing wight
        Crept forth like wormes out of her slimie nature,
        Soone as on them the Suns life giuing light,
        Had powred kindly heat and formall feature.
           —Spenser *Colin* 859–62.

1605   [Wine] Cheeres the sad heart, increaseth kindly heat.
           —Sylvester *Div. Wks.* (*3d Day*) 94.

1622   Stung with the kindly rage of loves impatient fire.
           —Drayton *Poly-Olb.* III. 222.

Kindly—*continued*

1633   Great power of Love! with what commanding fire
Dost thou enflame the worlds wide Regiment,
And kindely heat in every heart inspire.
—P. Fletcher *Purple Isl.* X. 4.

1647   Where cold raw heavie mist
Sols kindly warmth and light resists.
—More *Resolution* 97–8.

1656   And that unless a proper season sends
Indulgent showres, and kindly moisture lends
Unto the shrubs.
—Evelyn *Lucretius* 61.

1667   Mean while the tepid Caves, and Fens and shoares
Thir Brood as numerous hatch, from the Egg that soon
Bursting with kindly rupture forth disclos'd
Thir callow young.
—Milton *P. L.* VII. 417–20.

1678   Mine was an age when love might be excused,
When kindly warmth, and when my springing youth
Made it a debt to nature.
—Dryden *All for Love* III. i, in *Works* V. 384.

1687   Never more closely does the tender vine
About the shady elm her lover twine,
Nor the green ivy more affection bring
When she about her pine does kindly cling.
—Ayrès, in *CP* II. 287.

1709   So may kind rains their vital moisture yield,
And swell the future harvest of the field.
—Pope *Winter* 15–16.

1713   A kindly Warmth th' approaching Sun bestows,
And o'er the Year a verdant Mantle throws.
—Gay *Rural Sports* 3.

1601   Of kindly Wines made of the best Grapes.—Holland *Pliny* I. 413 (Bk. XIV, chap. vi).

1629   The other tall kinde [of fig tree] is nothing so good, neither doth beare ripe Figges so kindly and well, and peraduenture may be the white ordinary kinde that commeth from Spaine.—Parkinson *Paradisus Terr.* 566.

1664   The Trees growing more kindly on the South side of an Hill, then those which are expos'd to the North, with an hard, dark, rougher, and more mossie Integument.—Evelyn *Sylva* 12.

1676   Here are likewise Apricocks, and some sorts of English Plums, but these do not ripen so kindly as they do in England.—*Phil. Trans.* XI. 628.

Kindly—*continued*

1682   And the Sap by the amplitude, and great porosity of the Pith, being herein more copious, its Fermentation also will be quicker; which we see in all Liquors, by standing in a greater quantity together, proceeds more kindly.—Grew *Anat. Plants* 24.

1697   [Branches] take up so much Sap, as not only hinders the Fruit in growth, but in kindly ripening.—Meager *Art Garden.* 4.

1697   The Grass which grows here is very kindly, thick and long.—Dampier *New Voyage* 84.

1712   But being sow'd in the Clayey Soil, it either ripens not at all, or not so kindly and well.—Morton *Northampton.* 55.

Kingdom[1]

Ipsae regem parvosque Quirites
Sufficiunt, aulasque et cerea regna refigunt.
—Virgil *Geo.* IV. 201–2.

Iamque domum mirans genetricis et umida regna
Speluncisque lacus clausos lucosque sonantis
Ibat.
—*Ibid.* IV. 363–5.

Uobis auctoribus umbrae
Non tacitas Erebi sedes Ditisque profundi
Pallida regna petunt.
—Lucan I. 454–6.

Non aliter iam regna poli, iam capta Typhoeus
Astra ferens Bacchum ante acies primamque deorum
Pallada et oppositos doluit sibi virginis angues.
—Valerius Flaccus *Argon.* IV. 236–8.

1505   Quandoquidem obiectas urens sol dum coquit undas
Et radiis infestat agens neptunnia regna.
—Pontano *Meteor.* 123–4.

1578   Mais forcez moy ses longues rides,
Et ne vous souffrez decevoir,
Que vostre pere n'alliez voir
Dessous ses royaumes humides.
—Ronsard III. 37.

1585   Et les ventres gloutons des troupeaux escaillez
Qui fendent les seillons des royaumes salez.
—Du Bartas *I Sem.* II. 319–20.

---

[1]See also CLIME AND CLIMATE, EMPIRE, REGION, REIGN.

Kingdom—*continued*

1591   The troubled kingdome of wilde beasts behelde,
Whom not their kindly Souereigne did welde,
But an vsurping Ape with guile suborn'd.
     —Spenser *Hubberd* 1231–3.

1592   Da l'altra parte de gli ondosi regni
L'errante abitator non solo è muto.
     —Tasso *Mondo Creato* VI. 187–8.

1599   Dismounted from the high-aspiring hills
Which the all-empty airy kingdom fills.
     —Middleton *Prologue to Micro-Cynicon,* in *Works* V. 483.

1605   Whether he suruey
The vast salt kingdomes, or th' Earth's fruitfull clay.
     —Sylvester *Div. Wks. (6th Day)* 206.

1613   De quanta surca el aire acompañada
Monarchia canora.
     —Góngora II. 83.

1622   The Sea-gods, which about the watry kingdome keepe,
Have often for their sakes abandoned the Deepe.
     —Drayton *Poly-Olb.* II. 441–2.

1640   What hath thy brother done (by equall Fate
Elected to the wavy Monarchie)
That Seas should sinke, and from thy presence flie?
     —Sandys *Ovid's Met.* 28.

1646   Tertia spumantis diffusa palatia Nerei
Adspicit, & vasti regna profunda maris.
     —Barlaeus *Poemata* II. 4.

1647   Tell me the People that do keep
Within the Kingdomes of the Deep.
     —Herrick 340.

1655   Those Chiefs, who, in the Kingdoms of the Morn,
Their name in Armes unto the starres did heave.
     —Fanshawe *Lus.* I. xiv.

1675   Doctors in Deed as well as Title; men
That natures Tripple Kingdome throughly Ken.
Know all that Animals, Plants, or Mines, can
Contribute to the use or Cure of Man.
     —Dryden(?).[1]

1692   Tertia debetur liquidi victoria regni.
     —Ford, in *Mus. Angl. Anal.* (1st ed.) 132.

---

[1]From a poem ascribed to Dryden by W. G. Hiscock in *Times Literary Supplement*, April 18, 1936, p. 340.

Kingdom—*continued*

1705   With winged Speed He [Churchill] rides
             Undaunted o'er the lab'ring Main, t' assert
             Thy [Anne's] liquid Kingdoms.
               —J. Philips *Blenheim* 429–31.

1746   How dead the vegetable kingdom lies!
             How dumb the tuneful!
               —Thomson *Winter* 1026–7.

1612   Omnia elementata in tria veluti regna sunt divisa.   Duo sunt regna,
       quorum quodlibet per se stare potest, etsi alia duo non essent.   Est
       regnum minerale, vegetabile, & animale.—Alsted *Syst. Phys.* 207.

1623   Aer est regnum ventorum.   Neque hoc beneficentiam aeris eleuat,
       quasi scil. venti sint turbulenti ciues, qui in mundi Rep. tumultus ac
       seditiones excitent.—Alsted *Theol. Nat.* 311.

1642   Gazophylacium Rerum Naturalium E Regno Vegetabili, Animali et
       Minerali Depromptarum, Nunquam Hactenus in Lucem Editarum.—
       Besler (in title).

1650   And first of all know, that Nature is divided into three Kingdoms;
       two of them are such that either of them can subsist of it self, if the
       other two were not; there is the Minerall, Vegetable, and Animall
       Kingdom.—French *Sandivogius* 22.

1661   Notitia Regni Mineralis, Seu Subterraneorum Catalogus.—Jonston
       (in title).

1677   Such formed stones as either in name, or thing, or both, relate to the
       Heavenly Bodies or Air; and next, such as belong to the Watery King-
       dom.—Plot *Oxford*. 80.

       Of Arts relating to Brutes, I have met with none extraordinary con-
       cerning the winged Kingdom, but the new sort of boxes, or Colony
       hives for Bees.—*Ibid.* 263.

1684   I for my part know no Subject in the whole Mineral kingdom so gen-
       erall and lasting for the fuel of these Mountains, as the Pyrites.—*Phil.
       Trans.* XIV. 517.

1695   The Opinion, that [fossils] are not what they seem to be; that they are
       no Shells, but meer Sportings of active Nature in this subterraneous
       Kingdom.—J. Woodward *Nat. Hist. Earth* 38.

1712   I shall now proceed to the more observable Occurrences in the King-
       dom of Meteors, to First, those of the Watery Kind.—Morton *North-
       ampton.* 336.

1735   Systema Naturæ per Regna Tria Naturæ.—Linnaeus (in title).

Lambent

             Tactuque innoxia mollis
             Lambere flamma comas et circum tempora pasci.
               —Virgil *Aen.* II. 683–4.

Lambent—*continued*

1668   As useless to despairing Lovers grown,
As Lambent flames, to men i'th' Frigid Zone.
      —Cowley 81.[1]

1693   Ev'n love (for love sometimes her Muse express'd)
Was but a lambent flame which play'd about her breast.
      —Dryden *Killigrew* 83–4.

1700   How lambent Flames from life's bright Lamp arise,
And dart in emanations through the eyes.
      —Garth *Dispensary* 3.

1712   Let Hail and Rain, let Meteors form'd of Fire
And lambent Flames, in this blest Work conspire.
      —Blackmore *Creation* VII. 756–7.

1746   The lambent lightnings shoot
Across the sky.
      —Thomson *Summer* 1700–1.

1651   *Ignis lambens*, is a fat exhalation coming from a living body, heated with motion, and kindled at its head, or near about.—Comenius *Nat. Phil. Ref.* 134.

1653   Oleum lampadum magnis frigoribus scintillat: nocte suda, circa equum sudantem, conspicitur nonnunquam lux quædam tenuis: circa capillos quorundam hominum accidit, sed raro, lux etiam tenuis, tanquam flammula lambens.—Bacon *Works* IV. 133.

1667   Ce Feu, qui s'appelle *Ignis Lambens*, paroit quelquefois sur la teste des Hommes & des animaux, & n'a du tout point d'ardeur.—Pomey *Indic. Univer.* 14.

1668   Lambent fire is, A thin unctuous exhalation made out of the Spirits of Animals, kindled by Motion, and burning without consuming any thing but it self. Called Lambent, from Licking over, as it were, the place it touches. It was counted a Good Omen.—Cowley, note in *Poems* 359.

1712   Those called Lambent Fires are more frequently seen upon Pork and Hog's Flesh, than upon any other Flesh whatsoever.—Morton *Northampton.* 454.

Legion[2]

1578   Comme les fils des oursaux Aquilons,
Qui vont soufflant à leurs fieres venues
Loin devant eux les legions des nues.
      —Ronsard VI. 354.

---

[1]From *The Mistress*, first printed in 1647.
[2]See also BAND, BREED, BROOD, CHOIR, CITIZEN, CREW, FLOCK, FRY, HERD, HOST, INHABITANT, KIND, NATION, PEOPLE, RACE, SEED, SHOAL, SQUADRON, TRAIN, TRIBE, TROOP.

Legion—*continued*

1596   Emongst the Angels, a whole legione
         Of wicked Sprights did fall from happy blis.
             —Spenser *F. Q.* III. ix. 2.

1600   But sittest, crown'd with stars' immortal rays,
         In heaven, where legions of bright angels sing.
             —E. Fairfax *Tasso* I. ii.

1605   And neuer more the nimble painted Legions
         With hardy wings had cleft the ayrie Regions.
             —Sylvester *Div. Wks.* (*Arke*) 387.

1613   Those fell legions,
         That walk the mountains and Silvanus' regions.
             —W. Browne *Brit. Past.* I. i. 451–2.

1633   Yet could his [the dragon's] bat-ey'd legions eas'ly see
         In this dark Chaos; they the seed of night.
             —P. Fletcher *Purple Isl.* XII. xxiii.

1638   He heard a sound of words, and looking out,
         He saw a legion of the monkish rout.
             —Whiting, in *CP* III. 529.

1647   Him [Christ], whom his drowsy sons did leave
         Sleepless, aërial legions triumph to receive!
             —Hall, in *CP* II. 214.

1652   Who, where they come, with purer rays of light,
         Dazzle thy bat-ey'd legions quite,
         Rage, Impudence, and Ignorance, the imps of Night.
             —Benlowes *Theoph.* X. xvi.

1667   The Powers Militant,
         That stood for Heav'n, in mighty Quadrate joyn'd
         Of Union irresistible, mov'd on
         In silence thir bright Legions.
             —Milton *P. L.* VI. 61–4.

1668   When, Lo! a scorching wind from the burnt Countrys blew,
         And endless Legions with it drew
         Of greedy Locusts.
             —Cowley 225.

1675   Him [Orion], as through Heaven he marches, follow All
         The starry Legions as their General.
             —Sherburne *Sphere* 32.[1]

---

[1]Sherburne's note: "The Southern Constellations are here said to follow Orion, as Souldiers, their General: and Scripture it self hath reduc'd the Stars into a Military Order, and call'd them στρατιὰν τῶν ὠρανῶν, *Militiam Cœli*, The Host of Heaven."

Legion—*continued*

1686   For Lucifer and all his legions are o'erthrown.
            —Flatman, in *CP* III. 377.

1722   All o'er the Seas the thronging Legions spread.
            —Diaper *Oppian's Hal*. I. 1324.

Liquid air[1]

> εἰ δ' ἄγε τοι λέξω πρῶθ' ἥλικά τ' ἀρχήν,
> ἐξ ὧν δῆλ' ἐγένοντο τὰ νῦν ἐσορῶμεν ἅπαντα,
> γαῖά τε καὶ πόντος πολυκύμων ἠδ' ὑγρὸς ἀήρ
> Τιτὰν ἠδ' αἰθὴρ σφίγγων περὶ κύκλον ἅπαντα.
>
>   —Empedocles (Diels, Fr. 38). (Come, I
> will make known to you the first, primeval ele-
> ments, from which have arisen all that we now
> behold, the earth and the sea of many waves
> and the liquid air and the Titan, Aether, who
> circles the entire globe.)

Si non fecundas vertentes vomere glaebas
Terraique solum subigentes cimus ad ortus,
Sponte sua nequeant liquidas existere in auras.
    —Lucretius V. 210–12.

Semper enim, quodcumque fluit de rebus, id omne
Aeris in magnum fertur mare.
    —*Ibid*. V. 275–6.

Apparet liquido sublimis in aëre Nisus.
    —Virgil *Geo*. I. 404.

Subitas candescere flammas
Aera per liquidum tractosque perire cometas
Rara per ingentis uiderunt saecula motus.
    —Manilius I. 814–16.

Hic rerum solers summusque archangelus alto
Aëra per liquidum leuibus circundatus alis,
Velocesque mouens ignito corpore pennas,
Nulli conspectis ad terram motibus ibat.
    —Avitus *Orig. Mundi* 54.

1505   Ut [sol] lustraret olympum
      Et terras simul et magnas liquidi aeris oras.
          —Pontano *Urania* I. 246–7.

1549   L'oyseau par sentier incongnu
      Tente le premier navigaige
      Des ailes, que sa mere guyde,
      L'asseurant parmy l'air liquide.
          —Du Bellay III. 112.

---

[1]See also ELEMENT, FLUID, SWIM.

Liquid air—*continued*

1585   La flamme chaude-seche en l'onde froide-humide,
La terre froide-seche en l'air chaud et liquide
Ne se mue aisement.
     —Du Bartas *I Sem.* II. 237–9.

1596   As when the daughter of Thaumantes faire,
Hath in a watry cloud displayed wide
Her goodly bow, which paints the liquid ayre.
     —Spenser *F. Q.* V. iii. 25.

1600   There on the table was all dainty food
That sea, that earth, or liquid air could give.
     —E. Fairfax *Tasso* XV. lviii.

1614   Loading the tables with all sortes of meat,
Which yielded are on earth or liquid aire.
     —Mure I. 91.

1633   The wanton boy had dreamt that latest night,
That he had learnt the liquid aire dispart,
And swimme along the heav'ns with pineons light.
     —P. Fletcher *Purple Isl.* XI. xxiii.

1647   The Nights nimble net
That doth encompasse every opake ball,
That swim's in liquid aire, did Simon nought apall.
     —More *Psychozoia* III. ii.

1656   Du sommet de la roche, en roidissant son aisle,
Par les liquides airs il s'eslance vers elle.
     —Chapelain *Pucelle* 187.

1667   And God made
The Firmament, expanse of liquid, pure,
Transparent, Elemental Air.
     —Milton *P. L.* VII. 263–5.

1668   Through liquid Air, heav'ns busie Souldiers fly.
     —Cowley 330.

1674   Liquidasque per auras
Aereum immensum, Doctissime, detegis orbem.
     —Anon., in Mayow *Tract.* b.

1698   But, if a blast of wind
Without, or vapors issue from behind,
The leafs are borne aloft in liquid air.
     —Dryden *Aen.* III. 569–71.

1712   To happy Purpose they [magnetic effluvia] their
       Vigour spend,
For these Contentions in the Balance end,
Which must in liquid Air the Globe suspend.
     —Blackmore *Creation* I. 307–9.

Liquid air—*continued*

1716   Mais la Terre, au contraire, inactive & pesante,
Et qui sous nos yeux se présente,
Comme un mélange épais, materiel, obscur,
Forme un Globe grossier dans l'Air liquide & pur.
—Genest *Prin. Phil.* 81–2.

Aer vero bene temperatus et humidus [ὑγρότερος] et ventus austrinus commodissime [myrtus] alunt.—Theophrastus *De Causis Plant.* II. viii. 1.

The air, which extends around us, is soft and by its nature liquid [ὑγρὸν].—Basil *Opera* (1721) I. 33.

1515   Enimuero lune corpius haud absumi cum ipsa decrescit / argumento dilucido sunt ea quae cernimus licet. n. tibi liquido in aere [ἐν καθαρῷ τῷ ἀέρι¹].—Argyropolus *Basil* XXVI–XXVII.

1581   L'air n'a nulle couleur de sa propre nature, qui est aussi liquide & transparente.—Daneau (translating Damascene) *Phys. Fran.* 419.

1604   Non minus quadraginta stadiorum à terrâ altitudinem esse, in quâ nubila, ac venti, nubésque proueniant. Inde purum liquidúmque, & imperturbatæ lucis Aërem: sed à turbido ad Lunam, vicies centum millia stadiorum. Ima ergo pars, ad XL. stadia attollitur; mediam non definit; vltima & liquida amplissima, ad multa millia.—Lipsius *Physiol. Stoic.* 111.

1630   Cet air a esté despouïllé de cette subtilité liquide qui faisoit qu'il n'adherast a chose aucune, & s'est rendu grossier, pesant & adherable. —Rey *Essais* 70.

1643   The one moves himself by his finnes, the other by his wings. The one cuts and glideth through the liquid aire, the other shoots and darteth through the humid water.—Swan *Spec. Mundi* 383.

1644   [Certain atoms of fire] being more dense then the ayre in which they are carryed, must of necessity cutt their way through that liquide and rare medium.—Digby *Two Treat.* 80.

1650   A little before I said, that all things were made of the liquid aire, or the vapour, which the Elements by a perpetuall motion distill into the bowells of the earth.—French *Sandivogius* 12.

1656   [The middle region], wherein the clouds and winds are generated, is, according to Possidonius, forty furlongs above the earth. Next to it is the pure and liquid aire of untroubled light.—Stanley *Hist. Phil. 8th Part* 109.

1662   The Winde according to Hypocrates, is a flowing Water of the Air.— Chandler *Van Helmont* 78.

1664   Apres la flâme il n'y a rien de plus liquide que l'air.—Descartes *Monde* (*Lumière* 27).

---

¹Migne *Patr. Gr.* XXIX. 124.

Liquid air—*continued*

1666 Radij per lineas rectas. In diversorum diaphanorum communi superficie frangitur radius. aliqui reflectuntur. solidi et liquidi, liquidum
aer at aqua.—Huyghens XIII. 737.

1672 On donne ordinairement le nom d'air à toute cette matiere liquide &
transparente dans laquelle nous vivons, & qui est répanduë de tous
costez alentour du Globe composé de la terre & de l'eau.—Rohault
Traité Phys. II. 188.

Ainsi, l'air doit toûjours estre liquide, & ne doit jamais se durcir,
comme nous voyons qu'il arrive à l'eau lors qu'elle se gele.—*Ibid.* II. 190.

1685 And first the Air being a Fluid, we are to take notice of those properties
which it has in common with other fluids.—*Phil. Trans.* XV. 992.

1694 The parts of the Air, as well as of other liquid Bodies, by their beating
against each other . . . must needs produce a Sound.—Blome *Le Grand*
II. 38.

Liquid fire

Namque canebat uti magnum per inane coacta
Semina terrarumque animaeque marisque fuissent
Et liquidi simul ignis.
        —Virgil *Ecl.* VI. 31–3.

Hac etiam fit uti de causa mobilis ille
Devolet in terram liquidi color aureus ignis,
Semina quod nubes ipsas permulta necessust
Ignis habere.
        —Lucretius VI. 204–7.

1622 Wash me in steep-down gulfs of liquid fire!
        —Shakespeare *Oth.* V. ii. 280.

1648 By all thy brim-fill'd Bowles of feirce desire
By thy last Morning's draught of liquid fire.
        —Crashaw 327.

1667 Nigh on the Plain in many cells prepar'd,
That underneath had veins of liquid fire
Sluc'd from the Lake.
        —Milton *P. L.* I. 700–2.

1698 Thus, when a flood of fire by wind is borne,
Crackling it rolls, and mows the standing corn.
        —Dryden *Aen.* II. 406–7.

1627 The powder in shot, being dilated into such a flame as endureth not
compression, moveth likewise in round, (the flame being in the nature
of a liquid body) sometimes recoiling, sometimes breaking the piece,
but generally discharging the bullet.—Bacon *Works* IV. 164.

Liquid fire—*continued*

1644 Fire is not like a standing poole, which continueth full with the same water; and as it hath no wast, so hath it no supply: but it is a fluent and brookelike current.—Digby *Two Treat.* 43.

1651 Flamma, est fluxus ignis; flatus, aëris; flumen, aquæ.—W. Harvey *Gener. Animal.* 247.

1661 Ignis subterraneus, qvi à Spiritu ignito accenditur, nec tàm sulfure, qvàm bitumine vivit: haecǵue illa natura est, qvæ voracitatem in toto mundo avidissimam sine damno sui pascit. Crassa aliqvando flamma, liqvidior qvandoǵve & valdè lucens, exurens nonnumqvam, impotens sæpè.—Jonston *Not. Reg. Min.* 4–5.

1664 La flâmme dont i'ay dé ja dit que les parties sont perpetuellement agitées, est non seulement liquide, mais aussi rend liquide la pluspart des autres corps.—Descartes *Monde* (*Lumière* 26).

1674 That Torrent of melting Minerals, which boiled over the Crucible (if I may so speak) upon the late Conflagration in Sicily, and poured it self into the adjacent Plains. This liquid Fire, as it cooled, condensing, became crusty at top.—*Phil. Trans.* IX. 170.

1686 [Phosphorescent water] being dash't with Oars, it seems to run off them, just like liquid fire.—Plot *Stafford.* 117.

1690 Et je ne crois pas que ce mouvement [de la lumière] se puisse mieux expliquer, qu'en supposant ceux d'entre les corps lumineux qui sont liquides, comme la flame, et apparemment le soleil, & les étoiles, composez de particules qui nagent dans une matiere beaucoup plus subtile, qui les agite avec une grande rapidité.—Huyghens XIX. 469.

1718 Fire is a particular Fluid Matter, like Water or Air, which, like those, adheres to many Bodies, and adds something to the Composition thereof.—J. Chamberlayne *Nieuwentyt* II. 594.

Liquid light[1]

Largus iter liquidi fons luminis, aetherius sol,
Inrigat adsidue caelum candore recenti
Suppeditatque novo confestim lumine lumen.
—Lucretius V. 281–3.

τῇ μὲν ξανθὸς ἴασπις ἐπέτρεχε, τῇ δὲ Σελήνης
εἶχε λίθον πάνλευκον, ὃς εὐκεράοιο θεαίνης
λειπομένης μινύθει καὶ ἀέξεται, ὁππότε Μήνη
ἀρτιφαὴς σέλας ὑγρὸν ἀποστίλβουσα κεραίης
Ἠελίου γενετῆρος ἀμέλγεται αὐτόγονον πῦρ.
—Nonnos *Dionys.* V. 162–6. (One wing was covered with yellow jasper, one had the allwhite stone of Selene, which fades as the

---

[1]See also AETHER.

Liquid light—*continued*

horned goddess wanes, and waxes when
Mene newkindled distils her horn's liquid
light and milks out the self-gotten fire of
Father Helios.—Tr. Rouse.)

1655   Thy heav'ns (some say)
Are a firie-liquid light,
Which mingling aye
Streames, and flames thus to the sight.
    —H. Vaughan 421.

1667   Of Light by farr the greater part he took,
Transplanted from her cloudie Shrine, and plac'd
In the Suns Orb, made porous to receive
And drink the liquid Light, firm to retaine
Her gather'd beams, great Palace now of Light.
    —Milton *P. L.* VII. 359–63.

1668   Of Lemon Trees, which there did proudly grow,
And with bright stores of golden fruit repay
The Light they drank from the Suns neighb'ring ray.
    —Cowley 256.

1741   Tum quot Luna solet, totidem Lux mimica vultus
Induit; ingénti tum solis lampade cyclo
Mentitur: liquidi tremulum quoque luminis æquor
Crispatur longè, dulcique volumine ludit.
    —Anon., in *Mus. Angl.* (5th ed.) II. 216.

1746   But yonder comes the powerful king of day
Rejoicing in the east.   The lessening cloud,
The kindling azure, and the mountain's brow
Illumed with fluid gold,[1] his near approach
Betoken glad.
    —Thomson *Summer* 81–5.

Liquid sky[2]

Contemplor
Inde loci liquidas pilatasque aetheris oras.
    —Ennius *Sat.* 3–4.

Inde mare inde aer inde aether ignifer ipse
Corporibus liquidis sunt omnia pura relicta.
    —Lucretius V. 498–9.

Huius apes summum densae (mirabile dictu)
Stridore ingenti liquidum trans aethera vectae.
    —Virgil *Aen.* VII. 64–5.

---

[1]The 1727 edition has "ethereal gold."
[2]See also AETHER.

Liquid sky—*continued*

1596   More swift, then swallow sheres the liquid skie.
        —Spenser *F. Q.* II. vi. 5.

        Like as a fearefull Doue, which through the raine, . . .
        Doubleth her haste for feare to be for-hent,
        And with her pineons cleaues the liquid firmament.
        —*Ibid.* III. iv. 49.

1627   The earth of all the low'st, yet middle lies;
        Nor sinks, though loosely hang'd in liquid skies.
        —P. Fletcher *Locusts* V. xxii.

1640   Above all these he plac't the liquid Skies;
        Which, void of earthly dregs, did highest rise.
        —Sandys *Ovid's Met.* 2.

1668   Where never Fish did fly,
        And with short silver wings cut the low liquid Sky.
        —Cowley 185.

1672   So Venus moves, when to the Thunderer,
        In smiles or tears, she would some suit prefer;
        When with her cestus girt,
        And drawn by doves, she cuts the liquid skies.
        —Dryden *II Conq. Gran.* II. iii, in *Works* IV. 151–2.

1697   Wings raise my feet, I'm pleas'd to mount on high,
        Trace all the Mazes of the liquid Sky.
        —Creech *Manilius* (Bk. I) 2.

1713   Not half so swift the trembling doves can fly,
        When the fierce eagle cleaves the liquid sky.
        —Pope *Win. For.* 185–6.

1598 In quo per omnes, quos designavi, Cometas liquidò demonstrabo; in quibusdam apertiùs, quibusdam verò, prout commoditas concessit, eos omnes in Æthereâ Mundi regione versatos fuisse, & nequaquam Sublunari Aëre, ut hactenus nobis frustrà tot seculis persuasit Aristoteles, atque eius sectatores . . . quarum hæc præcipua est, quod ex Cometis, quos reverâ Æthereos esse probo, totum Cœlum limpidissimum & liquidissimum esse, nullisque duris & realibus orbibus refertum, satis constare potest.—Brahe *Astr. Mech.* G.

1620 Cometas per omnes cæli partes proprijs motibus discurrere: solent nonnulli recentiores de cæli duritiæ, vel fluiditate nonnulla conijcere; quod eis videatus sine cæli liquiditate non posse prædicta saluari, posito enim cælo duro non vident qua ratione Mercurius, Venus, & Mars, per cælum solis susque deque vagari possint.—Blancanus *Sph. Mundi* 304.

1651 The Skie is the most liquid part of the whole world, and therefore transparent, and most moveable.—Comenius *Nat. Phil. Ref.* 89.

Liquid sky—*continued*

1660　Quod sì, vt solares maculæ demonstrant, Sol circa proprium centrum vertitur, quid est cur astra extrinseco, non proprio, & insito motu in liquido æthere ferantur?—Du Hamel *Astr. Phys.* 75.

Omitto etiam Solem quinque planetarum motus regere, ac moderare, quod explicari minimè potest, nisi cælum fluidum, ac liquidum statuamus.—*Ibid.* 77.

1670　From all which, the Author [Pietro M. Cavina] deduceth these Conjectures. 1. That the Heaven of the Fixt Stars is liquid.—*Phil. Tran.* V. Gg₄.

1696　*Liquidum*] Purum & ab omni fæce remotum.—Freind's note on *Ovid Met.* I. 67.

Liquid water[1]

> γίγνετο δ' ὑγρὸν ὕδωρ καὶ δένδρεον ὑψιπέτηλον.
> —Homer *Odys.* IV. 458. (Then he turned into liquid water,[2] and into a tree, high and leafy.)

> συντέμνει δ' ὅρος
> ὑγρᾶς θαλάσσης.
> —Aeschylus *Suppl.* 258–9. (The boundary of the liquid sea restrains my realm.—Tr. Smyth.)

> In saxis ac speluncis permanat aquarum
> Liquidus umor et uberibus flent omnia guttis.
> —Lucretius I. 348–9.

> Non liquidi gregibus fontes, non gramina deerunt.
> —Virgil *Geo.* II. 200.

> Liquidarum et lapsus aquarum
> Prodit cærulea dispersas luce figuras.
> —Ausonius *Mosella* 61–2.

> Fluminis ut liquidi caperent miranda lauacra.
> —Juvencus *Evangel.* I. 311.

> Aedibus in mediis puro fluit agmine flumen,
> Quod rigat insignes liquidis de fluctibus hortos
> Quadrifidosque secat undanti ex fonte meatus.
> —Cyprianus Gallus *Genes.* 54–6.

---

[1]See also CRYSTAL WATER.

[2]ὑγρός may be translated *humid* as well as *liquid*, and it is often difficult to establish the exact meaning of the Greek epithet. But Henri Estienne, without giving his references, provides some striking evidence to prove that the phrase ὑγρὸν ὕδωρ may be taken to mean *liquid water:* "ὑγρὸν ὕδωρ autem ad differentiam τοῦ πηγετοῦ seu πάγου, glaciei. ea enim est humor frigore concretus."—*Thesaurus* III. 1725.

Liquid water—*continued*

1505   Vos o, quæ liquidos fontes, quæ flumina, nymphæ
        Naiades, colitis.
            —Pontano *Hesper.* I. 1–2.

1555   Et propter liquidas vndas, & læta fluenta
        Sunt molles herbæ, prostrata cubilia somno.
            —Bodin(?) *Oppian* 2.

1578   Et elles, d'ordre le suivant,
        Fendoient le grand vague liquide.
            —Ronsard III. 55.

1585   Vous croiriez estre vuide
        L'espace qui depart la terre et l'eau liquide
        Du ciel sans fin rouant.
            —Du Bartas *I Sem.* II. 873–5.

1596   Some of them washing with the liquid dew
        From off their dainty limbes the dustie sweat.
            —Spenser *F. Q.* III. vi. 17.

1605   For as in liquid cloudes (exhaled thickly)
        Water and Ayre (as moist) doe mingle quickly.
            —Sylvester *Div. Wks.* (*Deceipt*) 306.

1613   Whoso hath seen young lads (to sport themselves)
        Run in a low ebb to the sandy shelves, . . .
        Or liquid water each to other bandy.
            —W. Browne *Brit. Past.* I. v. 3–7.

1627   With blood, and warres the ice and liquid snowes
        Are thaw'd.
            —P. Fletcher *Locusts* III. xii.

1648   And beasts and painted birds, which liquid springs
        Inhabit.
            —Fanshawe *Virgil* 63.

1651   There with its liquid streams the neighbouring Lake
        A Luke-warm Bath for her fair Limbs did make.
            —Sherburne *Salmacis* 9.

1674   Whose drink was only from the liquid brook.
            —Milton *S. A.* 557.

1692   Obreptat pronus ripæ, lapsuque silenti
        Ex inclinato pendentem vimine ofellam
        In liquidas demittit aquas.
            —Ford, in *Mus. Angl. Anal.* (1st ed.) 134.

1698   With headlong haste they leave the desert shores,
        And brush the liquid seas with lab'ring oars.
            —Dryden *Aen.* IV. 837–8.

Liquid water—*continued*

1713   The liquid Drops, that ooze from weeping Trees,
            And sparkling Stones, with Star-like Lustre please.
            —Diaper *Dryades* 7.

1716   Nous verrons comment l'Eau liquide
            Dans le froid de l'Hyver souvent peut se durcir.
            —Genest *Prin. Phil.* 141.

1601   Some [clouds] are fruitfull to bring forth moisture, that is turned into
        liquid raine: others to yeeld an humour either congealed into frosts, or
        gathered and thickened into snow, or els frozen and hardened into
        haile.—Holland *Pliny* I. 19 (Bk. II, chap. xxxix).

1612   Duplex igitur effectus à Mose exponitur: unus, quòd aër expansus
        fuit, qui priùs in materiâ illâ informi sic fuit confusus, ut planè aër dici
        non potuerit: alter, quòd hac distentione & diductione, sive (ut Physici
        loquuntur) subtiliatione aëris, posteà ex mandato Dei idem aër dis-
        tentus egit in elemento liquido aquæ, eamque dispescuit in duas sedes
        ordinarias.—Alsted *Syst. Phys.* 38.

1630   Aqua est liquida, vel concreta. Illa communiter aqua, hæc glacies
        dicitur.—Alsted *Encyclo.* I. 697.

1644   Lachrymam dixi supra succum esse qui ab incisione & sponte defluit.
        Is vel concretus, vel liquidus est. Concretus Thus, myrrha, liquidus,
        abietis, pini.—Bodaeus *Theophrastus* 968.

1657   In the vallies of Chile in their season fall great dews (which collect and
        harden) like bread tempered with Sugar or Marchpane (Mark, they
        fall liquid dews) which is as wholesome as that which they call Manna:
        By all which instances, it appears that Manna is first a liquid dew, and
        after inspissated by a vertue of the tree, or plant on which it falls.—
        Purchas *Theat. Insects* 133.

1661   The liquid juyce, which is diffused through the parts of the Wood, is in
        a continual agitation, which in Des-Cartes his Philosophy is the cause
        of fluidity.—Glanvill *Van. Dogm.* 52.

1675   And what if we should indeed suspect all Earth to be arrant salt, nay
        glass; and that glass, how hard soever, the offspring and child of water,
        the most fluid, crystalline, sincere, and void of all other qualities? It
        is not impossible, I think, but by the different texture of its parts, even
        that liquid element may be brought to the consistence of a most different
        body to what it appears.—Evelyn *Terra* 19.

1684   Hinc aqua humida quidem est, vel quia madefacit, vel quia alienis
        corporum figuris sese accomodat, sed proprie liquida dicitur, quod in
        plano declivi fluat. Est enim aer spirabilis potius, quam liquidus: &
        licet in sensu Aristotelico sit humidissimus, humor tamen dici non
        potest. Sed aqua liquida est & fluida, ac medium nacta est statum
        inter ea quæ dura dicuntur, & spirabilia.—Du Hamel *Phil. Vetus et
        Nova* 70.

Liquid water—*continued*

1698 In August I have observed the Clusters both Green and Ripe of *Periclymenum Ger.* very Leaky; which upon nearer and heedful Inspection I found to be a thin clammy Juice, or Liquid Gum, which falls down upon the Leaves, and keeps its Liquid Form there.—*Phil. Trans.* XIX. 373.

1719 Il faut considerer que la superficie du Globe de la Terre, est terminée par la superficie des Eaux de la Mer qui est un corps liquide & fluide. —Roubais *Diss. Phys.* 45.

Lively

1567 And to thintent with lively things eche Region for to store,
      The heavenly soyle, to Gods and Starres and Planets first
          he gave.
          —Golding *Ovid's Met.* I. 82–3.

1596 His blessed body spoild of liuely breath,
      Was afterward, I know not how, conuaid
      And fro me hid.
          —Spenser *F. Q.* I. ii. 24.

1605 Thou radiant Coach-man, running endlesse course
      Fountaine of Heat, of Light the liuely source.
          —Sylvester *Div. Wks.* (*4th Day*) 133.

1622 Not from the quickned Mine, by the begetting Sunne
      Giving that naturall power, which by the vig'rous sweate,
      Doth lend the lively Springs their perdurable heate
      In passing through the veines, where matter doth not need.
          —Drayton *Poly-Olb.* III. 208–11.

1633 That his hot bloud, driv'n from the native seat,
      Leaves his faint coward heart empty of lively heat.
          —P. Fletcher *Purple Isl.* VIII. xiv.

1642 For no hot Frenchman, nor high Tuscan blood,
      Whose panting veins do swell with lively heat,
      In Venus' breach more stoutly ever stood.
          —Kynaston *Leo. and Syd.* 1583–5.

1651 [He] a cheerful Emrauld drew;
      Cheerfull, as if the lively stone had sence.
          —Davenant *Gond.* III. iv. 45.

1667 [I] sometimes ran
      With supple joints, as lively vigour led.
          —Milton *P. L.* VIII. 268–9.

1700 And Emily attir'd in lively green.
          —Dryden *Pal. and Arc.* II. 228.

Living

NOTE.—*Living* is a much more frequent epithet in poetry than *lively* or *live*, and is so much used to translate the Latin *vivus* that I have chosen to present under it the passages from Latin, French, Italian, and Portugese poets which contain *vivus* or its equivalent.

Fronte sub adversa scopulis pendentibus antrum,
Intus aquae dulces vivoque sedilia saxo,
Nympharum domus.
—Virgil *Aen.* I. 166–8.

Nunc et de caespite uiuo
Frange aliquid, largire inopi, ne pictus oberret
Caerulea in tabula.
—Persius VI. 31–3.

Vulcano condicta domus, quam subter eunti
Stagna sedent, venis oleoque madentia vivo.
—Gratius *Cyneg.* 433–4.[1]

Nec cessant a caede manus, si sanguine uiuo
Est opus, erumpant iugulo qui primus aperto.
—Lucan VI. 554–5.

Uiuax flamma uiget, seu caua testula
Sucum linteolo suggerit ebrio.
—Prudentius *Cath.* V. 17–18.

Venient cito saecula, cum iam
Socius calor ossa reuisat
Animataque sanguine uiuo
Habitacula pristina gestet.
—*Ibid.* X. 37–40.

1572   Vi claramente visto o lume viuo.
            —Camoens *Lus.* 82b.

1578   Rien n'est si dur qu'une roche massive,
            Rien n'est si mol qu'une fontaine vive.
            —Ronsard IV. 234.

1585   Vives, s'alloient jetter sous les funestes lames
            De leurs blesmes espoux: loyales, ne pouvant,
            Leurs maris estans morts, humer plus l'air vivant.
            —Du Bartas *I Sem.* V. 200–2.

---

[1]Vlitius' note: "Vivum liquorem & oleum, quia ἐπινήχα, i. supernatat, & perpetuo movetur. Ut vivum argentum, quod vernacula nostra mobile, sive agile dicimus, eadem ratione . . . . *Vivum oleum* etiam dici potuit hoc liquidi bituminis genus, quia diutissime ardet . . . . Tertia insuper causa dari potest, cur *vivum oleum* dicatur hoc loco, quod non artificiale, sed naturale fit. Ut *vivi lacus* Georg. II. *vivoque sedilia saxo.* Aeneid. I."—*Poetae Latini Rei Venaticae* I. 172.

Living—*continued*

1595   More then most faire, full of the liuing fire,
        Kindled aboue vnto the maker neere.
          —Spenser *Amor.* viii.

1602   Fiumi, laghi, ruscei, fontane viue.
          —Valvasone *Caccia* II. xxviii.

1610   About the holy Cittie rowles a flood
        Of moulten chrystall, like a sea of glasse,
        On which weake streame a strong foundation stood,
        Of living Diamounds the building was.
          —G. Fletcher *Christs Triumph after Death* xxxviii.

1620   Ie vous fay deux presens en ce present icy,
        Dont l'vn c'est vn Crystal taillé par artifice.
        L'autre vn ardant desir de vous rendre seruice,
        A ce Crystal semblable et dissemblable aussi.
        Semblable d'vne part, en ce qu'il est ainsi
        Pur, et net, et luisant, et sans tache et sans vice,
        Et que vostre vertu, sa mere et sa nourrice,
        L'a dans sa viue roche en constance endurcy.
          —Bertaut *Œuv. Poét.* 293.

1623   Is 't night's predominance or the day's shame
        That darkness does the face of earth entomb,
        When living light should kiss it?
          —Shakespeare *Macbeth* II. iv. 8–10.

1633   In midst of both [humors of the eye] is plac't the Crys-
          tall pond;
        Whose living water thick, and brightly shining, . . .
        The divers forms doth further still direct.
          —P. Fletcher *Purple Isl.* V. xxix.

1640   The Nymphs by their own rivers sweare:
        And sit on benches made of living stone.
          —Sandys *Ovid's Met.* 90.

1651   The living Metal, held so volatile
        By thy dull world, this Chymick Lord can fix!
          —Davenant *Gond.* I. v. 29.

1656   Autour d'elle s'espand vne viue clarté.
          —Chapelain *Pucelle* 224.

1667   Th' Angelic throng
        Disperst in Bands and Files thir Camp extend
        By living Streams among the Trees of Life.
          —Milton *P. L.* V. 650–2.

1668   Through the soft wayes of Heaven, and Air, and Sea,
        Which open all their Pores to Thee [Light];

Living—*continued*

Like a cleer River thou dost glide,
And with thy Living Stream through the close Chan-
nels slide.
—Cowley 447.

1675 The Waters now are truly living made,
But how is this? Th' Almighty Word has said;
He said, Now let the Waters living be.
—Traherne 241.

1690 This is the living coal, that, burning in me,
Would flame to vengeance, could it find a vent.
—Dryden *Don S.* I. i, in *Works* VII. 340.

1713 Who now shall charm the shades where Cowley strung
His living harp, and lofty Denham sung?
—Pope *Win. For.* 279–80.

1612 Argentum vivum est aqua terrea.—Alsted *Syst. Phys.* 154.

1637 Ce qu'il y a de plus remarquable en tout cecy, c'est la generation des
esprits animaux, qui sont comme vn vent tres subtil, ou plutost comme
vne flame tres pure & tres viue.—Descartes *Œuvres* VI. 54.

1650 Then take water of salt-nitre, which comes from our earth, in which
there is a river of living water, if thou diggest the pit knee deep, therefore take water out of that, but take that, which is clear.—French
Sandivogius 31.

1651 Aër etiam suo merito spiritus dicitur, siquidem hic à spirando nomen
sumpsit; & Aristoteles disertis verbis fatetur, vitam quandam, atque
ortum & interitum vel flatuum esse. Denique & fluminis aqua, viva
appellatur.—W. Harvey *Gener. Animal.* 247.

1656 For Epicurus did not admit of any Soul to reside in Plants, but held,
that they were governed and grew by vertue of a certain nature not
vegitable, proper to them alone, and yet affirmed, that they live, that
is, enjoy a peculiar motion, as the water of Chrystal springs, the fire
which we excite to a flame, is called *living water*, and *living fire.*—Evelyn
Lucretius 153.

1662 The white or boyling Sand *Quellem*, doth shew it self in a living and
vitall Soil.—Chandler *Van Helmont* 50.

1667 *Eau viue.* Aqua viua, iugis, perennis. *Eau morte, croupissante.* Aqua
reses, pigra, stagnans.—Pomey *Indic. Univers.* 59.

1677 When these *animalcula* or living Atoms did move, they put forth two
little horns, continually moving themselves.—*Phil. Trans.* XII. 821.

1678 I presumed it might be worth while to try whether his Phosphorus did
shine by virtue of a kind of real or (if I may so call it) living flame.—
Hooke *Cometa*, in Gunther *Early Science in Oxford* VIII. 279.

Living—*continued*

1686 Where the waters flow from quick and living springs, the Mines are work't on high or open Countrys.—Plot *Stafford*. 37.

1698 The principle Matter of all Metals in their Mines, is a dry Water, which they call *Aqua Viva*, or *Argentum vivum*, and *Spiritus fœtens*, otherwise called Sulphur.—Hortolanus *Golden Age* 116.

Lucid

E tenebris autem quae sunt in luce tuemur
Propterea quia, cum propior caliginis aer
Ater init oculos prior et possedit apertos,
Insequitur candens confestim lucidus aer
Qui quasi purgat eos ac nigras discutit umbras
Aeris illius.
—Lucretius IV. 337–42.

At si, cum referetque diem condetque relatum,
Lucidus orbis erit, frustra terrebere nimbis
Et claro silvas cernes Aquilone moveri.
—Virgil *Geo*. I. 458–60.

Lunaque non gracili surrexit lucida cornu
Aut orbis medii puros exesa recessus.
—Lucan V. 546–7.

Patet ecce fidelibus ampli
Via lucida iam paradisi.
—Prudentius *Cath*. X. 161–2.

1572 La neste tempo o lucido Planeta,
Que as horas vay do dia distinguindo,
Chegaua aa dejejada, & lenta Meta.
—Camoens *Lus*. 19.

1585 Quî tandem ab igne non cremante Numinis,
Quò abesse propiùs angelus quiuis solet,
Non hoc magis stupescet attonitus metu,
In fulgida & sacra Deo caligine
Non lucidum ignem nactus & flammam simul?
—Morellus *Pisidas* 1471–5.

1591 Streight with his azure wings he cleau'd
The liquid clowdes, and lucid firmament.
—Spenser *Hubberd* 1258–9.

1592 Ma 'n mezzo mormorando un vivo fonte
Lucido sorge, e trasparente, e puro.
—Tasso *Mondo Creato* V. 1336–7.

1615 De quien timido Athlante a mas lucida,
A region mas segura se leuanta.
—Góngora II. 228–9.

Lucid—*continued*

1667   Fair Damascus, on the fertil Banks
           Of Abbana and Pharphar, lucid streams.
           —Milton *P. L.* I. 468–9.

1674   Spirit, who art thou, and from whence arrived?
           (For I remember not thy face in heaven)
           Or by command, or hither led by choice?
           Or wander'st thou within this lucid orb?
           —Dryden *State of Inn.* II. i, in *Works* V. 137.

1675   Round is the Moon to sight,
           And with a swelling Body barrs the Light;
           Hence never wholly Lucid is her Ball,
           When the Sun's Beams on it obliquely fall.
           —Sherburne *Sphere* 16.

1692   And move as swift and active as a Ray
           Shot from the lucid spring of day!
           —Norris 136.

1714   He summons strait his Denizens of Air;
           The lucid Squadrons round the Sails repair.
           —Pope *Rape of the Lock* II. 55–6.

1746   Nor is the stream
           Of purest crystal, nor the lucid air,
           Though one transparent vacancy it seems,
           Void of their unseen people.
           —Thomson *Summer* 308–11.

Ab aethere lucidissimo aër in terram vsque diffusus est, agilior quidem, tenuior, & altior terris nec minus aquis, caeterum aethere spissior grauiorque, frigidus per se, & obscurus.—Seneca *Quaest. Nat.* II. x. 1.

1600   Etenim cum lux qualitas quædam sit, temperamentum seu corporis proprietatem consequens quod de omnibus lucidis corporibus (cœlesti excepto) intelligas.—H. Fabricius *De Visione* 44.

1615   Light is properly called that which is in a lucide or bright bodie, as in the Sunne and in other Starres.—Crooke *Body of Man* 684.

1634   Quòd radij lucidi ab oppositis extremitatibus oræ Solis delapsi.— Kepler *Plutarch* 150.

1646   I said that the eye could not be still deceived in its sight or judgement of a lucid body, which is its prime and proper object.—Rosse *New Planet* 78.

1656   Of lucid Meteors appearing in the clouds, are Haloes, Rainbowes, Parelies, and Streaks.—Stanley *Hist. Phil. 6th Part* 65.

1661   I hold that the surface of the water would appear lucid [lucida[1]], because that it is smooth and transparent.—Salusbury *Math. Coll.* 55.

---

[1]Galileo *Dial.* 62.

Lucid—*continued*

1674 And as for the Bipartition of the Sensitive Soul into two principle members as it were, or active fourses; vix. the Fiery part, upon which Life depends; and the Lucid, from whence all the faculties Animal are, like so many distinct rayes of light, derived: I will not affirm it to be very ancient.—Charleton *Nat. Hist. Passions* bb₇₋₈.

1683 For the putting the Retina in water is . . . to magnifie the Image of it by a double refraction of the lucid raies.—*Phil. Trans.* XIII. 174.

1684 Ignis vero calidus est & siccus, lucidus, subtilis & actuosus.—Du Hamel *Phil. Vetus et Nova* II. 56.

1694 Yea sometimes, tho' there be no Lucid Body to affect the neighbouring Air; yet sometimes some sharp Humour or Vapor, only moving the Filaments of the Retina, causeth an appearance of Light to the Eye. —Blome *Le Grand* II. 44.

1704 And if Rays of all sorts, flowing from any one lucid point in the Axis of any convex Lens, be made by the Refraction of the Lens to converge to points not too remote from the Lens, the Focus of the most refrangible Rays shall be nearer to the Lens than the Focus of the least refrangible ones.—Newton *Opt.* (Bk. I) 61.

Matter

Haud igitur redit ad nilum res ulla, sed omnes
Discidio redeunt in corpora materiai.
    —Lucretius I. 248–9.

Siue parens rerum, cum primum informia regna
Materiamque rudem flamma cedente recepit,
Fixit in aeternum causas.
    —Lucan II. 7–9.

1585 La matiere du monde est ceste cire informe,
Qui prend sans se changer toute sorte de forme.
    —Du Bartas *I Sem.* II. 193–4.

1593 Subject and servile to all discontents,
As dry combustious matter is to fire.
    —Shakespeare *V. and A.* 1161–2.

1605 Almightie Father, as of waterie matter
It pleas'd thee make the people of the Water.
    —Sylvester *Div. Wks. (6th Day)* 208.

1646 But clammy matter doth deny
A clear discovery.
    —Hall, in *CP* II. 209.

1656 And new recruits
Cherish Etherial Fires, which in no wise
Could be, unless abundant matter rise
From infinite.
    —Evelyn *Lucretius* 73–5.

Matter—*continued*

1667   Thus God the Heav'n created, thus the Earth,
         Matter unform'd and void.
                 —Milton *P. L.* VII. 232–3.

         Ere this diurnal Starr
         Leave cold the Night, how we his gather'd beams
         Reflected, may with matter sere foment,
         Or by collision of two bodies grinde
         The Air attrite to Fire.
                 —*Ibid.* X. 1069–73.

1675   Whither as Earth transpires its Native fumes,
         Those humid Spirits the hot Air consumes,
         When a long Drouth from Clouds hath clear'd the Sky
         And Heav'n by the Sun's scorching Beams grows dry;
         Whence fitting Aliment is snatch'd by Fire,
         And Matter like to Tinder flames acquire.
                 —Sherburne *Sphere* 60.

1716   Bien que notre Air se meuve pesament
         Près de la Matiere étherée,
         Pour l'Onde, & pour la Terre il est un Corps leger.
                 —Genest *Prin. Phil.* 108.

         Terra et pars est mundi et materia.—Seneca *Nat. Quaest.* II. v. 1.

1588   Ergo materiam omnium Cometarum prorsus Cœlestem esse iudico,
         siquidem etiam omnes in ipso Cœlo generantur.—Brahe *Mundi Æth.* 254.

1614   And as waters were the matter of air, of the firmament, and of the
         lower and upper waters, and of the seas, and creatures therein.—
         Raleigh *Hist. of the World,* in *Works* II. 15.

1621   The whole herbe and root is full of clammie white iuyce like milk, and
         of a very loathsome stinkinge smell, which on the stalks sometimes
         turneth into a yealowish gummie matter.—Goodyer, in Gunther *Early
         Brit. Bot.* 159.

1630   La pesanteur est tellement joincte à la premiere matiere des elements,
         qu'elle n'en peut estre deprinse.—Rey *Essais* 25.

1644   Dicentes illam nihil esse in pellucido corpore, præter actionem, aut
         inclinationem ad motum, materiæ cujusdam subtilissimæ, omnes illius
         poros replentis; & cogitandum poros omnium corporum pellucidorum
         adeo æquales & rectos esse, ut facillimè hanc materiam subtilem sine
         morâ & offensione transmittant.—Descartes *Œuvres* VI. 635.

1651   It is plain that sundry winds may arise in sundry places together, ac-
         cording as matter of exhalations is afforded here and there, and occa-
         sion to turn it self hither or thither.—Comenius *Nat. Phil. Ref.* 108.

1665   He finds the Matter of Comets to be in the Æther it self, making the
         Æther and the Air to differ onely in purity.—*Phil. Trans.* I. 106.

Matter—*continued*

1673 Il faut premierement supposer que la matiere du Tonnerre, est une espece de bitume composé du meslange de plusieurs particules ou exhalaisons subtiles.—Mariotte *Percussion* 216.

1688 Beyond the Air is the Celestial Matter, incomparably more pure and subtile, and much more agitated than the Air.—Glanvill *Fontenelle* 32.

1690 La rareté des corps transparens estant donc telle que nous avons dit, l'on conçoit aisement que les ondes puissent estre continuées dans la matiere etherée qui emplit les interstices des particules.—Huyghens XIX. 483.

1700 Being sadly affrighted with the Thunder and Lightning (for part of the Sulphurous Matter came down the Chimney, and fill'd the House with a strong Scent, like that of Gunpowder after firing) she leaves the House.—*Phil. Trans.* XXI. 52.

1712 [Quinces] seemed to consist as much of a Woody Matter as of the usual Substance of this Fruit: as in the former Instance there seem'd to be a Leafy Matter, if I may so call it, intermixt with that of the Fruit.— Morton *Northampton.* 394.

1718 Fire is a particular Fluid Matter, like Water or Air, which, like those, adheres to many Bodies, and adds something to the Composition thereof.—J. Chamberlayne *Nieuwentyt.* II. 594.

Nation[1]

        Adorat haec brutum pecus,
        Indocta turba scilicet,
        Adorat excors natio,
        Uis cuius in pastu sita est.
           —Prudentius *Cath.* XI. 81–4.

1596   Euen all the nation of vnfortunate
        And fatall birds about them flocked were.
          —Spenser *F. Q.* II. xii. 36.

1605   The scaly Nation
        That in the Ocean haue their habitation.
          —Sylvester *Div. Wks.* (*Eden*) 273.

1609   Miembros de algun nauio de vendeja,
        Patria comun de la nacion bermeja.
          —Góngora I. 302.

1610   But nettles, kixe, and all the weedie nation,
        With emptie elders grow, sad signes of desolation.
          —G. Fletcher *Christs Triumph over Death* l.

---

[1]See also BAND, BREED, BROOD, CHOIR, CITIZEN, CREW, FLOCK, FRY, HERD, HOST, INHABITANT, KIND, LEGION, PEOPLE, RACE, SEED, SHOAL, SQUADRON, TRAIN, TRIBE, TROOP.

Nation—*continued*

1627   And as the scaly nation they invade,
        Were snar'd themselves.
          —P. Fletcher *Locusts* III. xxi.

1652   Love, thou canst ocean-flowing storms appease;
        And such o'ergrown Behemoths please,
        As tax the scaly nation, and excise the seas.
          —Benlowes *Theoph.* III. xcix.

1672   By all the heavenly nations she is blest.
          —Dryden *II Conq. Gran.* II. iii, in *Works* IV. 152.

1684   When men usurp it [modesty] from the female nation,
        'Tis but a work of supererogation.
          —Dryden *Epilogue to The Princess of Cleves* 21–2.

1698   Around the forest flies the furious blast,
        And all the leafy nation sinks at last.
          —Dryden *Aen.* X. 570–1.

1722   In oozy Beds the scaly Nations sleep.
          —J. Jones *Oppian's Hal.* IV. 692.

1734   Who taught the nations of the field and wood
        To shun their poison and to choose their food?
          —Pope *Man* III. 99–100.

1746   The furry nations harbour—tipt with jet,
        Fair ermines spotless as the snows they press.
          —Thomson *Winter* 811–12.

Native (*adjective*)[1]

χρύσειον δ' ἐκόμησε γενέθλιον ἔρνος ἐλαιής.
          —Callimachus *Hymn* IV. 262. (And
golden foliage [Delos] thy natal olive tree
put forth.)

Et quoniam docui mundi mortalia templa
Esse et nativo consistere corpore caelum.
          —Lucretius VI. 43–4.

Luminis exigui fuerat prope templa recessus,
Speluncae similis, nativo pumice tectus.
          —Ovid *Met.* X. 691–2.

Nec sonat Oebalius caveae favor ad iuga nota
Taygeti, lavitur patrios ubi victor ad amnes.
          —Valerius Flaccus *Argon.* IV. 228–9.

εἰ μὴ χωομένη πάλιν Ἄρτεμιν εἰς φυτὸν ὕλης
τόξον ἐμὸν μετάμειψεν.
          —Nonnos *Dionys.* V. 507–8. (Unless Ar-
temis in her anger has changed my bow
back to its native wood.—Tr. Rouse.)

---

[1]See also ELEMENT (NATIVE).

Native (*adjective*)—*continued*

1585   Cela se void à l'œil dans le bruslant tison:
        Son feu court vers la ciel sa natale maison.
           —Du Bartas *I Sem.* II. 59–60.

1592   Fu chi pensò ch' alta cagione il Sole
        Fosse di ciò che 'n lei s'appiglia o nasce,
        Lo qual la scalda con gli ardenti raggi,
        E 'l suo natio vigor dal suo profondo
        Con quel vital calore attragge in alto.
           —Tasso *Mondo Creato* III. 862–6.

1596   And lyke the natiue brood of Eagles kynd.
           —Spenser *Heav. Beauty* 138.

1605   This in a Fire-brand may we see, whose Fier
        Doth in his flame toward's natiue Heau'n aspier.
           —Sylvester *Div. Wks.* (*2d Day*) 33.

1614   Then did Pallas call
        Telemachus, (in bodie, voice, and all
        Resembling Mentor) from his natiue nest.
           —Chapman *Odys.* 29.

1622   A purple blush with native tincture dyed
        My cheek's late lily in a deepest red.
           —Hannay *Sher. and Mar.* I. 433–4.

1633   Pace with her native streame, this fish doth keepe,
        And journeyes with her, towards the glassie deepe.
           —Donne *Progr. of the Soule* 251–2.

1640   Now them [nymphs] to Sea their native current bore.
           —Sandys *Ovid's Met.* 204.

1647   Then when above its native orb it came,
        And reacht the lesser lights o'th'sky, this flame
        Contracted to a starre should wear thy name.
           —Stanley *Poems and Trans.* (*Poems* 4).

1648   Since they [people] sometime,
        Forsake ne're more to see't, their Native Clime.
           —Sherburne *Seneca's Answer* 28.

1651   There stands a Wood
        Where Lovers Myrtles, and the Poets Bays,
        Their spreading Tops to Native Arbors raise.
           —Sherburne *Salmacis* 8.

1667   But have I now seen Death?   Is this the way
        I must return to native dust?
           —Milton *P. L.* XI. 462–3.

1687   A limpid stream drawn from the native source.
           —Dryden *Hind and Panther* 1186.

Native (*adjective*)—*continued*

1698   Nor can the groveling mind,
In the dark dungeon of the limbs confin'd,
Assert the native skies, or own its heav'nly kind.
    —Dryden *Aen.* VI. 995–7.

Ooze and Oozy

1622   Upon a thousand Swannes the naked Sea-Nymphes ride
Within the ouzie Pooles, replenisht every Tide.
    —Drayton *Poly-Olb.* II. 37–8.

1623   I wish
Myself were mudded in that oozy bed
Where my son lies.
    —Shakespeare *Tempest* V. i. 150–2.

1633   Cleer Jordan's Selfe, in his dry oazie Bed,
Blushing for shame, was fain to hide his dead.
    —Sylvester *Div. Wks.* (*Beth. Rescue*) 481.

1667   But they, or under ground, or circuit wide
With Serpent errour wandring, found thir way,
And on the washie Oose deep Channels wore.
    —Milton *P. L.* VII. 301–3.

1678   Sea-horses floundering in the slimy mud,
Tossed up their heads, and dashed the ooze about them.
    —Dryden *All for Love* I. i, in *Works* V. 343.

1680   The Fishes to their Banks or Ouze repair'd.
    —Otway *Orphan* III. i. 499.

1698   Old Tiber roar'd, and, raising up his head,
Call'd back his waters to their oozy bed.
    —Dryden *Aen.* IX. 151–2.

1705   Gods may descend in Factions from the Skies,
And Rivers from their Oozy Beds arise.
    —Addison *Campaign* 23.

1713   In that blest moment from his oozy bed
Old father Thames advanced his rev'rend head.
    —Pope *Win. For.* 329–30.

Orb[1]

ὡς αὐγὴ τύψασα σεληναίης κύκλον εὐρύν.
    —Empedocles (Diels, Fr. 43). (As
the sunbeam striking the broad orb of
the moon.)

---

[1]See also BALL, GLOBE, SPHERE.

Orb—*continued*

καὶ πημάτων ὕψιστον, ὧν κράντης χρόνος,
μήνης ἑλίσσων κύκλον, αὐδηθήσεται.
—Lycophron *Alex.* 305-6. (And
crown of all my woes that Time, wheeling
the moon's orb, shall be said to bring to
pass.)

Et quantos radios iacimus de lumine nostro,
Quis hunc convexum caeli contingimus orbem,
Sex tantae poterunt sub eum succedere partes
Bina pari spatio caelestia signa tenentes.
—Cicero *Aratus' Phaen.* 559-62.

Medio cursu flatus aquilonis et austri,
Distinet aequato caelum discrimine metas
Propter signiferi posituram totius orbis.
—Lucretius V. 689-91.

Astriferum iam velox circulus orbem
Torsit et amissae redierunt montibus umbrae.
—Statius *Theb.* II. 400-1.

Κριὸν ἀνεστυφέλιξε, μεσόμφαλον ἄστρον Ὀλύμπου,
γείτονος εἰαρινοῖο πυραυγέος ὑψόθι κύκλου
ἀμφιταλαντεύοντος ἰσόζυγον ἦμαρ ὀμίχλῃ.
—Nonnos I. 181-3. (He buffeted the Ram,
that midnipple star of Olympos, who balances with
equal pin day and darkness over the fiery orb of his
spring-time neighbour.—Tr. Rouse.)

1594   By earth, the common mother of vs all,
By heauen, and all the moouing orbes thereof.
—Marlowe *Edw. II* 1437-8.

1605   'Tis question-lesse the Orbe of Earth and Water
Is the least Orbe in all the All-Theater.
—Sylvester *Div. Wks.* (*3d Day*) 90.

1616   Faire Diane, from the Hight
Of Heauens first Orbe who chear'st this lower Place.
—Drummond I. 133.

1620   La que dulcemente abreuia
En los orbes de sus ojos
Soles con flechas de luz,
Cupidos con raios de oro.
—Góngora II. 341.

1628   Thou, by whose pow're the spheares are rold,
Earth's hanging orbe who dost vphold.
—Mure I. 173.

Orb—*continued*

1633   This various vast Orb, which the World wee call.
           —Sylvester *Div. Wks.* (*Hymn of Almes*) 515.

1648   His [a serpent's] poys'nous length in round
           And complicated Orbs he folds.
           —Sherburne *Medea* 38.

1659   His tortured ghost might go
           Beyond that orb of atoms that attend
           Mortality.
           —W. Chamberlayne *Phar.* I. iii. 80–2.

1667   This round World, whose first convex divides
           The luminous inferior Orbs, enclos'd
           From Chaos and th' inroad of Darkness old.
           —Milton *P. L.* III. 419–21.

1671   All otherwise to me my thoughts portend,
           That these dark orbs no more shall treat with light.
           —Milton *S. A.* 590–1.

1675   Stretch'd through thin Air the subtle Axis lies,
           Whose distant Poles the Ballanc'd Fabrick hold;
           Round this the Star-imbellish'd Orbs are rowl'd.
           —Sherburne *Sphere* 22–3.

1690   I saw him, as he terms himself, a sun
           Struggling in dark eclipse, and shooting day
           On either side of the black orb that veiled him.
           —Dryden *Don S.* I. i, in *Works* VII. 336.

1712   Then let Gassendus chuse what Frame he please,
           By which to turn the Heav'nly Orbs with Ease.
           Blackmore *Creation* I. 397–8.

1713   Now Night in silent State begins to rise,
           And twinkling Orbs bestrow th' uncloudy Skies.
           —Gay *Rural Sports* 14.

1543   De Revolutionibus Orbium cælestium, Libri VI.—Copernicus (in title).

1602   An orbe, called in Latine *Orbis*, which is as much to say, as a round hoope or sphere, hauing breadth and thickenesse, and sometime it is taken for a circle.—Blundeville *Theor. Planets* 1.

1612   Orbis est sphærica quædam cæli series. Estque vel empyreus, vel ætherius.—Alsted *Syst. Phys.* 125.

1621   The firmament is the orbe of the moueable heauen: contayning the world, which consisteth of Ethereall and elementall parts.—Widdowes *Nat. Phil.* 5.

1632   Astronomi eccellenti sono state osseruate molte Comete generate, e disfatte in parti più alte dell' Orbe lunare.—Galileo *Dial.* 43.

Orb—*continued*

1634 Libellus De Facie, Quæ in Orbe Lunæ Apparet.—Kepler *Plutarch* (translating the title: Περὶ τοῦ ἐμφαινομένου προσώπου τῷ κύκλῳ τῆς σελήνης).

1659 While discoursing about the variety of the Suns rising, he made it appear, that the Sun and the World (*i.e.* the Starry Orb) were not carryed the same, but quite contrary wayes; and consequently, that that part of the Heavens which was the West or Occident of the Starry Orb, was the very rising, or Orient of the Solary.—Moxon *Disc. Astr.* 9.

1668 And from his Observations of the new Star of 1572, and six others in his time, he [Tycho] asserted Comets into their place among Heavenly Bodies, shattering all the Solid Orbs to pieces.—Glanvill *Plus Ultra* 41.

1678 The Earth moves in an annual orb about the Sun.—Hooke *Cometa*, in Gunther *Early Science in Oxford* VIII. 241.

1687 Diximus Cometas esse genus Planetarum in Orbibus valde excentricis circa Solem revolventium.—Newton *Principia* 508.

1695 That there is a mighty Collection of Water inclosed in the Bowels of the Earth, constituting an huge Orb in the interiour or central Parts of it; upon the Surface of which Orb of Water the terrestrial Strata are expanded. That this is the same which Moses calls the Great Deep, or Abyss: the ancient Gentile Writers, Erebus, and Tartarus.—J. Woodward *Nat. Hist. Earth* 117.

Paint[1]

> Concharumque genus parili ratione videmus
> Pingere telluris gremium.
> —Lucretius II. 374–5.

> Omne adeo genus in terris hominumque ferarumque
> Et genus aequoreum, pecudes pictaeque volucres.
> —Virgil *Geo.* III. 242–3.

> Orbe peregrino caelum depingitur astris.
> —Manilius I. 445.

> Quamuis innumero sidere regiam
> Lunarique polum lampade pinxeris.
> —Prudentius *Cath.* V. 5–6.

> Iam si prædulceis delectat carpere somnos
> Mollibus in pratis, pictaque recumbitur herba.
> —Avitus *Orig. Mundi* 18.

> Li fior dipinti e la novella erbetta,
> Ch'e' prati fan di ben mille colori.
> —Boccaccio *Filostr.* VII. lxiii.

---

[1]See also RAY (OF LIGHT).

Paint—*continued*

1505   Aera quin etiam pictæ petiere volucres
        Armatæ accurvis rostris atque unguibus uncis.
            —Pontano *Urania* I. 1076–7.

1572   Pintando estaua ali Zefiro, & Flora
        As violas da cor dos amadores.
            —Camoens *Lus.* 154b.

1578   Et sur les bords tousjours l'herbe verdoye
        Sans qu'on la fauche, et tousjours diaprez
        De mille fleurs s'y peinturent les prez.
            —Ronsard IV. 59.

1585   Mais quand, vers son declin, du soleil le visage
        Flamboye vis à vis d'un humide nuage
        Qui ne peut soustenir l'eau dont il est enceint,
        Plus long temps dans le flanc sa claire force il peint
        Dessus l'humide nue, et d'un pinceau bisarre
        La courbeure d'un arc sur noz testes bigarre.
            —Du Bartas *I Sem.* II. 717–22.

1588   Al Tajo mira en su humido exercicio
        Pintar los campos i dorar la arena.
            —Góngora I. 105.

1592   Avea la dotta man del Mastro eterno
        De' bei fiori di stelle 'l ciel dipinto.
            —Tasso *Mondo Creato* V. 29–30.

1596   [Nature] Which feedes each liuing plant with liquid sap,
        And filles with flowres faire Floraes painted lap.
            —Spenser *F. Q.* II. ii. 6.

1611   And God almighty rightly did Ordain
        One all Divine, one Heav'nly, one Terrene;
        Decking with Vertues one, with Stars another,
        With Flowrs and Fruits, and Beasts, and Birds the other:
        And play'd the Painter, when he did so gild
        The turning Globes; blew'd Seas, and green'd the field,
        Gaue precious Stones so many-coloured lustre,
        Enameld Flowrs, made Metals beam and glister:
        The Caruer, when he cut in leaues and stems
        Of Plants, such veins, such figures, files and hems:
        The Founder, when he cast so many Forms
        Of winged Souls, of Fish, of Beasts, of Worms.
            —Sylvester *Div. Wks. (Magnif.)* 582.

1622   But it invales it selfe, and on it either side
        Doth make those fruitfull Meads, which with their painted
                pride
        Imbroader his proud Banke.
            —Drayton *Poly-Olb.* XIV. 91–3.

Paint—*continued*

1630   But now an opall hew
        Bepaintes Heauens Christall.
           —Drummond II. 18.

1647   All at the painted field arrive, where these
        With severall flowers their severall fancies please.
           —Stanley *Poems and Trans.* (*Trans.* 7).

1659   The Earth—his lovely mistress—clad in all
        The painted robes the morning's dew let fall.
           —W. Chamberlayne *Phar.* II. iv. 411–12.

1667   Ye Mists and Exhalations that now rise
        From Hill or steaming Lake, duskie or grey,
        Till the Sun paint your fleecie skirts with Gold.
           —Milton *P. L.* V. 185–7.

        The smaller Birds with song
        Solac'd the Woods, and spred thir painted wings.
           —*Ibid.* VII. 433–4.

1668   Men doubt, because they stand so thick i' th' skie,
        If those be Stars which paint the Galaxie.
           —Cowley 17.

1668   All the Worlds bravery that delights our Eyes
        Is but thy [Light's] sev'ral Liveries,
        Thou the Rich Dy on them bestowest,
        Thy nimble Pencil Paints this Landskape as thou go'st.
           —Cowley 446.

1675   'Twixt the Ecliptick and the latent Bears,
        Which 'bout the creaking Axis turn the Sphears,
        Heaven's stranger Orbe with these Stars painted shines,
        Which Antient Poets call'd the Southern Signs.
           —Sherburne *Sphere* 37.

1686   Heaven's famed Vandyke, the Sun, he paints—'tis clear—
        Twelve signs throughout the zodiac every year:
        'Tis he, that at the spicy spring's gay birth
        Makes pencils of his beams and paints the Earth;
        He limns the rainbow when it struts so proud
        Upon the dusky surface of a cloud.
           —Flatman, in *CP* III. 412.

1700   The painted birds, companions of the spring.
           —Dryden *Flower and Leaf* 46.

1713   The wat'ry landscape of the pendent woods,
        And absent trees that tremble in the floods:
        In the clear azure gleam the flocks are seen,
        And floating forests paint the waves with green.
           —Pope *Win. For.* 213–16.

Paint—*continued*

1716　　　Et qu'on place un Velin au lieu de la Retine,
　　　　　Où les Rayons unis se puissent arrêter,
　　　　　Des Objets du dehors nous avons la Peinture;
　　　　　Le Velin en reçoit les fidelles Portraits,
　　　　　Ainsi que dans notre Oeil chaque Objet s'y figure,
　　　　　Avec ses couleurs & ses traits.
　　　　　　　—Genest *Prin. Phil.* 228.

1515　Segetes planis in Regionibus inundantes: prata per uirescentia: copiaque
　　　florum uarietateque depicta.—Argyropolus *Basil* VIIIb.

1567　Kalophanus is a kinde of stone black, yet be painted with other colours,
　　　which being carried in the mouth is saide to clarifie the voice, and to
　　　helpe them that be hoarse, as the Lapidarie witnesseth.—Maplet
　　　Greene Forest 28.

1634　Et colores iridis vtriusque, cum suâ differentiâ claritatis, sunt reale
　　　quid, nequaquam verò visûs opus: pingunt enim se non tantùm in
　　　oculo, sed etiam in albo pariete in obscuro.—Kepler *Plutarch* 154.

1637　I'ay obserué que les rayons, passant par cete ouuerture & de là s'allant
　　　rendre sur vn linge ou papier blanc F G H, y peignent toutes les couleurs
　　　de l'arc-en-ciel.—Descartes *Œuvres* VI. 330.

1646　Fit inquam receptis speciebus in tunica retina quam vitreus humor in
　　　fundo oculi distendit quasi linteum seu chartam mundam in qua
　　　obiectorum species appellant, eoque perfectius depingantur quo me-
　　　lioris & aptioris erit configurationis crystallinus humor qui in vueæ
　　　foramine lentis vicem obtinet, per quam eiusmodi species traiectæ in
　　　fundum oculi veluti in cameræ occlusæ parietem deferantur.—Niceron
　　　Thaum. Opt. 17.

1664　If the Sun-beams be in a convenient manner trajected through a Glass-
　　　prism, and thrown upon some well-shaded Object within a Room, the
　　　Rainbow thereby Painted on the Surface of the Body that Terminates
　　　the Beams, may oftentimes last longer than some Colours I have
　　　produc'd in certain Bodies.—Boyle *Exper. Colour* 77.

1665　Neque hîc ejusdem [Naturæ] stetit industria, sed altius assurgens, sua
　　　in gemmato regno cœlorum finxit tentoria, quæ & Sole, Luna, Stellis
　　　miro ordine vestivit: Deinde ad opticam progressa, flumina, sylvas
　　　prata, montes, maria, ad exactam prospectivæ amusim in multis
　　　lapidibus ita depinxit, ut nullius Optici manum ultra suam industriam
　　　desiderare voluisse videatur.—Kircher *Mundus Subt.* II. 22.

1670　Place by night a lighted Candle very near your Eies, and cause a dog,
　　　distant from the candle 8 or 10 paces, to look upon you, then you shall
　　　see in his eyes, a light sufficiently bright, which I hold to proceed from
　　　the reflexion of the light of the Candle, whose image is painted on the
　　　Choroeides of the dog.—*Phil. Trans.* V. H$_2$b.

Paint—*continued*

1672 So the ray HM moves swifter from the glass after its emersion at M, than either GL, FK, or EI, and retaining a greater propensity to the way it made in the free air is less refracted, and painted nearer the perpendicular than they.—Flamsteed, in Rigaud II. 135.

1704 When a Man views any Object . . . the Light which comes from the several Points of the Object is so refracted by the transparent skins and humours of the Eye . . . as to converge and meet again at so many Points in the bottom of the Eye, and there to paint the Picture of the Object upon that skin (called the *Tunica Retina*) with which the bottom of the Eye is covered. For Anatomists when they have taken off from the bottom of the Eye that outward and most thick Coat called the *Dura Mater*, can then see through the thinner Coats the Pictures of Objects lively painted thereon. And these Pictures propagated by Motion along the Fibres of the Optick Nerves into the Brain, are the cause of Vision.—Newton *Opt.* (Bk. I) 10.

The Light reflected from the Book might be made to converge and meet again at the distance of six Feet and two Inches behind the Lens, and these paint the Species of the Book upon a Sheet of white Paper much after the manner of the second Experiment.—*Ibid.* 36.

1709 There is, at this Day, no one Ignorant, that the Pictures of External Objects are painted on the Retina, or Fund of the Eye. That we can see no thing which is not so Painted . . . . The Objects are Painted in an inverted Order on the Bottom of the Eye: The upper part of any Object being Painted on the lower part of the Eye, and the lower part of the Object, on the upper part of the Eye.—Berkeley *Theory Vis.* 100.

1718 The Rays coming from an Object, and falling upon a flatter Glass, do paint the Image further backwards than when the Glass is more Convex.—J. Chamberlayne *Nieuwentyt.* I. 235.

Passage[1]

Undique quandoquidem per caulas aetheris omnis
Et quasi per magni circum spiracula mundi
Exitus introitusque elementis redditus extat.
    —Lucretius VI. 492–4.

Multa foramina cum veriis sint reddita rebus,
Dissimili inter se natura praedita debent
Esse et habere suam naturam quaeque viasque.
    —*Ibid.* 981–3.

Quaecumque foramina nouit
Umor, ab his largus manat cruor.
    —Lucan IX. 811–12.

Aut ideo spirant mediaque ex arce cerebri
Demittunt geminas sociata foramina nares.
    —Prudentius *Hamart.* 312–13.

[1]See also BUXOM, CLEAVE, CUT, VENT, YIELDING.

Passage—*continued*

1593   Once more the ruby-colour'd portal open'd,
Which to his speech did honey passage yield.
    —Shakespeare *V. and A.* 451–2.

As when the wind, imprison'd in the ground,
Struggling for passage, earth's foundation shakes.
    —*Ibid.* 1046–7.

1596   The waues obedient to their beheast,
Them yielded readie passage, and their rage surceast.
    —Spenser *F. Q.* III. iv. 31.

1605   [The crane's] pointed Bill cuts passage through the skies.
    —Sylvester *Div. Wks.* (*5th Day*) 182.

1614   The wepon, foaming in her luk-warme blood,
Maide open passage to the gushing flood.
    —Mure I. 141.

1622   The quaking Aspen light and thin
To th' air light passage gives.
    —Hannay *Philo.* 9–10.

1633   Much as an one-ey'd room, hung all with night,
(Onely that side, which adverse to his eye
Gives but one narrow passage to the light).
    —P. Fletcher *Purple Isl.* V. xxxvi.

1640   But now the loade above his stature climes,
And choakes the passage of his breath.
    —Sandys *Ovid's Met.* 225.

1651   Yet lights last Rays were not intirely spent;
For they discern'd their passage through a Gate.
    —Davenant *Gond.* I. vi. 69.

1659   Hoarsnesse and sores the throat did fill,
And stopt the passages of speech and life.
    —Sprat *Plague* B₄b.

1665   Much more our Souls then, when they go from hence,
And back unto the Elements dispense
All that built up our frail and earthly frame,
Shall through each pore & passage make their breach.
    —Herbert of Cherbury 83–4.

1668   So stars appear to drop to us from skie,
And gild the passage as they fly.
    —Cowley 46.

1671   O that torment should not be confin'd
To the bodies wounds and sores
With maladies innumerable

Passage—*continued*

> In heart, head, brest, and reins;
> But must secret passage find
> To th' inmost mind.
> —Milton *S. A.* 606–11.

1676   [Let] My sorrow to my eyes no passage find.
> —Dryden *Aureng-Zebe* V. i, in *Works* V. 293.

1698   The spear flew hissing thro' the middle space,
> And pierc'd his throat, directed at his face;
> It stopp'd at once the passage of his wind,
> And the free soul to flitting air resign'd.
> —Dryden *Aen.* X. 481–4.

1705   But if the rushing Wave a Passage finds,
> Enrag'd by Watry Moons, and warring Winds,
> The trembling Peasant sees his Country round
> Cover'd with Tempests, and in Oceans drown'd.
> —Addison *Campaign* 10.

1716   A des Corps dont les Cieux, les Airs sont penetrez,
> Depuis le haut Sommet des Lambris étherez,
> Dans ses pores la Terre aussi donne passage.
> —Genest *Prin. Phil.* 94–5.

1601   The Arteries [are] the passages of the spirit and life . . . . Neither doe they all containe within them vitall spirit.—Holland *Pliny* I. 345 (Bk. XI, chap. xxxvii).

1622   It seemed to be a disease [of the eyesight], called in Greeke, *Symptosis*, in Latine, *Concidentia:* this came of drynesse of the brain, whereby the sinewes were withered and gathered together, and wrinkled, the holes or pory passages thereof were stopped.—Banister *Guillemeau* d_{12}–e_1.

1634   The Hearing hath for its Organe the Eare and Auditory passage, which goes to the stony bone furnished with a Membrane investing it, an Auditory Nerve, and a certaine inward spirit there conteined.—T. Johnson *Parey* 24.

1646   And therefore waters frozen in Pans, and open Glasses, after their dissolution do commonly leave a froth and spume upon them, which are caused by the airy parts diffused in the congealable mixture which uniting themselves and finding no passage at the surface, do elevate the mass, and make the liquor take up a greater place then before. —T. Browne II. 91–2.[1]

1651   Most mountains are stony, (and yield metals;) because the subterrane fire (on the third day of the creation) swelling the earth here, made it self many channels and passages, breathing through which, it doth variously exhale, melt, mix and boile the matter: which is not done so copiously under plains.—Comenius *Nat. Phil. Ref.* 146.

---

[1]Quoted from the 1672 edition.

Passage—*continued*

1653   That argument which Galen brings for the passages of the blood through the right ventricle out of the *vena cava* into the lungs, we may more rightly use for the passages of the blood out of the veins through the heart into the arteries, changing only the terms.—W. Harvey *Anat. Exer.* 54.

1661   For the *meatus*, or passages [of spirits in the body], through which those subtill emissaries are conveyed to the respective members, being so almost infinite, and each of them drawn through so many meanders, cross turnings, and divers roades, wherein other spirits are continually a journeying; it is wonderfull, that they should exactly perform their regular destinations without losing their way in such a wilderness.— Glanvill *Van. Dogm.* 24.

1664   Les arteres & les nerfs s'ouvriroient, & donnans ainsi passage à ce peu d'esprits animaux, qui sans cela auroient esté employez à d'autres vsages, ils pourroient mouvoir quelques membres.—Descartes *Monde* (*Fièvre* 13).

1670   He examines the Torricellian Experiment, not admitting that to be an Instance of Vacuity, but esteeming, that a great force of Introsuction (so he calls it) makes temporary pores and pervious passages.—*Phil. Trans.* V. O₃.

1674   There is a ready passage of the blood out of the arteries into the veins. —*Phil. Trans.* IX. 136.

1687   The Heart, is deficient many ways; it may be stopped and suffocated for want of Air and respiration, for the Atoms of Light implanted in the Heart at the time of a Man's Conception, (the commerce of the Solar Spirits being intercepted for want of Air,) do sometimes suddenly stand still, they flye away, finding a passage through a solution of the continuum or through Pores made fit by a burning Feaver in the Heart, all the Water of the *Pericardium* being dryed up: Thick and viscous Blood does sometimes stop the motion of these Vital Atoms. Poyson also does by its acute Particles pierce through the Heart, and give an exit to those Spirits of Light, which are tyed to those which the Sun bestows upon us, and are attracted by them, returning thither from whence they came.—Midgley *Nat. Phil.* 331–2.

1695   The [subterranean] Fire it self, which, being thus assembled and pent up, is the Cause of all these Perturbations, makes its own way also forth, by what Passages soever it can get vent.—J. Woodward *Nat. Hist. Earth* 139.

1704   That in the passage of Light out of Glass into Air there is a reflexion as strong as in its passage of Air into Glass.—Newton *Opt.* (Bk. II) 65.

1718   And to the End, that the Countenance should not always appear Weeping and cover'd with Tears, that there are Passages contrived, by which this Humour at the usual Times can be discharged into the Nostrils.—J. Chamberlayne *Nieuwentyt* I. 216.

Passage—*continued*

1718   Fire can also pass thro' Water, and produce a Flame upon it, without
being extinguished therewith: It can't be objected, that there are not
sufficient Pores or Passages in the Water for it.—*Ibid.* II. 622.

Pearl[1]

1544   Tu vois ma face emperlée de gouttes.
    —Scève 68.

1585   Les fleurs
Que la flairante Aurore emperle de ses pleurs.
    —Du Bartas *I Sem.* III. 943–4.

1594   This plot of death when sadly she had laid,
And wip'd the brinish pearl from her bright eyes.
    —Shakespeare *Lucrece* 1212–13.

1596   Now gan the humid vapour shed the ground
With perly deaw.
    —Spenser *F. Q.* III. x. 46.

1598   As shee spake,
Foorth from those two tralucent cisterns brake
A streame of liquid pearle, which downe her face
Made milk-white paths.
    —Marlowe *Hero and Leander* I. 295–8.

1600   The manna on each leaf did pearled lie.
    —E. Fairfax *Tasso* XVIII. xxiv.

1600   To-morrow night, when Phœbe doth behold
Her silver visage in the wat'ry glass,
Decking with liquid pearl the bladed grass.
    —Shakespeare *M. N. D.* I. i. 209–11.

1605   Or whether th' upper Clouds moist heauines,
Doth with his waight the vnder Cloud oppresse,
And so one humour doth another crush,
Till to the ground their liquid pearles doo gush.
    —Sylvester *Div. Wks.* (*2d Day*) 49.

1605   Like as the Vine
Vntimely cut, weepes at her wound, her wine,
In pearled teares.
    —Sylvester *Div. Wks.* (*3d Day*) 85.

1613   La vista saltearon poco menos
De el huesped admirado
Las no liquidas perlas.
    —Góngora II. 95–6.

1616   The Cloudes for Ioy in Pearles weepe downe their Showrs.
    —Drummond I. 61.

---

[1]See also TEAR, and the periphrases for *tears*, pp. 388–9.

Pearl—*continued*

1622   Comes Irt, of all the rest, though small, the richest Girle,
Her costly bosome strew'd with precious Orient Pearle,
Bred in her shining Shels, which to the deaw doth yawne,
Which deaw they sucking in, conceave that lusty Spawne.
    —Drayton *Poly-Olb.* XXX. 115-18.

1630   Whilst-Ropes of liquid Pearle still load my laboring Oares.
    —Drayton *Nimph.* VI. 163.

1633   And with the rising Sunne banquet on pearled dew.
    —P. Fletcher *Purple Isl.* VI. lxxvii.

1648   Like to the Summers raine;
Or as the pearles of Mornings dew.
    —Herrick 125.

1651   Fore the entry of the Grot
With streams of liquid Pearl, (the humid Son
Of some large Torrent) a small Brook does run.
    —Sherburne *Salmacis* 2.

1652   Scenting 'bove thousand precious ointments, shed
On consecrated Aaron's head;
Above pearl'd dew on Hermon's ever-fragrant bed.
    —Benlowes *Theoph.* VI. xxi.

1667   Innumerable as the Starrs of Night,
Or Starrs of Morning, Dew-drops, which the Sun
Impearls on every leaf and every flouer.
    —Milton *P. L.* V. 745-7.

1678   Come, and the liquid pearls descry,
Which glittering 'mong the flowers lie.
    —K. Philips, in *CP* I. 605.

1687   The rivers are at liberty,
And their just tribute pay,
Of liquid pearls, and crystal to the sea.
    —Ayres, in *CP* II. 311.

1698   For him the lofty laurel stands in tears,
And hung with humid pearls the lowly shrub appears.
    —Dryden *Ecl.* X. 19-20.

1709   Now hung with pearls the dropping trees appear.
    —Pope *Winter* 31.

1722   Air when too gross will falling Drops increase,
And hang in lucid Pearls on weeping Trees.
    —Diaper *Oppian's Hal.* I. 696-7.

1664   The rest of the Tree doe indeed contain the like Terebinthine sap, as
appears (upon any slight incision of bark on the stem, or boughs) by a
small crystaline pearl which will sweat out.—Evelyn *Sylva* 55.

Pearl—*continued*

1667　In the Valley of Lancy . . . grows a Plant like the Doronicum . . . near the roots whereof you may find pure Quicksilver, running in small grains like Pearls.—*Phil. Trans.* II. 494.

1677　By Authors they are called Stalagmites, and seem either to be generated of pearls of dew, setled on the stones as they lie in the Fields.—Plot *Oxford*. 95.

1697　The red Threads of *Rorella* end, or are toped with little Bags; which being compressed do yield a Purple Juice . . . and those small Buttons on the very tops of those Threads, are encompassed with small Transparent Pearls or Drops of a liquid Gum.—*Phil. Trans.* XIX. 373.

1698　On the top-most Leaves of *Lactuca syl. costa spinosa, C. B.* in July, many small Drops or Pearls of an Oily Juice, coagulated and hardned Rosinlike, are plain to be discerned.—*Phil. Trans.* XIX. 380.

People[1]

Praeterea genus horriferum natura ferarum
Humanae genti infestum terraque marique
Cur alit atque auget?
　　—Lucretius V. 218–20.

Eum vasti circum gens umida ponti
Exsultans rorem late dispergit amarum.
　　—Virgil *Geo.* IV. 430–1.

Praecipue, medio cum luna implebitur orbe,
Certa nitent mundo tum lumina; conditur omne
Stellarum uulgus, fugiunt nisi nomine dignae.
　　—Manilius I. 469–71.

Nec non et uasti circum gens umida ponti
Iam sole infuso, iam rebus luce retectis
Exultam rorem late dispergit amarum.
　　—Proba *Cento* 88–90.

Exilit inde volans gens plumea laeta per auras
Aera concutiens pennis crepitante volatu.
　　—Dracontius *Laud. Dei* I. 242–3.

Quodque caret proferre aliquam de gurgite gentem
Squamigeram leuique cute uel cortice saeptam
Uel crispam conchae et duplici conpagine clausam.
　　—Incertus *Sodoma* 143–5.

1555　Dispersas ponti gentes, aciesque natantum
Squamigeras, almæ varium genus Amphitrites,
Antonine canam.
　　—Lippius *Oppian's Hal.* 1.

---

[1]See also BAND, BREED, BROOD, CHOIR, CITIZEN, CREW, FLOCK, FRY, HERD, HOST, INHABITANT, KIND, LEGION, NATION, RACE, SEED, SHOAL, SQUADRON, TRAIN, TRIBE, TROOP.

People—*continued*

ante 1573   Les peuples froidureux qui combatent sur l'eau.
        —Jodelle 242.

1578   Adieu, peuples ailez, hostes Strymoniens,
        Qui volant de Thrace aux Aethiopiens,
        Sur le bord de la mer encontre les Pygmées.
        —Ronsard IV. 440.

1584   Et les peuples nageurs et les troupes volantes.
        —Du Bartas *Eden* 574.

1585   Quand, formant l'univers, sa tout-puissante voix
        Pour le peuple brillant [étoiles] fit de si belles loix.
        —Du Bartas *I Sem.* IV. 195–6.

1592   E giusta legge affrena
        I popoli natanti.
        —Tasso *Mondo Creato* V. 453–4.

1596   The woodborne people fall before her flat,
        And worship her as Goddesse of the wood.
        —Spenser *F. Q.* I. vi. 16.

1605   Nor euer did the pretie little King
        Of Hunnie-People, in a Sun-shine day
        Lead to the field in orderly aray
        More busie buzzers.
        —Sylvester *Div. Wks. (Fur.)* 338.

1613   Entre vn vulgo nadante, digo apenas
        De escama.
        —Góngora II. 101.

1616   The feathred People, and their Eagle Kings.
        —Drummond I. 103.

1630   The honny People leaue their golden Bowres.
        —Drummond II. 21.

ante 1640   Ere th'astonisht Spring
        Heard in the ayre the feather'd people sing.
        —Habington *Castara* 74.

1651   And see how the Mute People of the Floud,
        With Ebon Backs, and Silver Bellies scudd.
        —Sherburne *Salmacis* 8.

1656   Aux Peuples escaillés il donne en vain la chasse.
        —Chapelain *Pucelle* 123.

1674   The ethereal people flocked for news in haste.
        —Dryden *State of Inn.* V. i, in *Works* V. 168.

1686   The scaly people their resentments show'd
        By pleas'd levoltoes on the wond'ring flood.
        —Flatman, in *CP* III. 371.

People—*continued*

1692   Nimis beatus ille qui tremulam manu
Arundinem scita regit,
Epulisque gentes fascinans aquatiles
Rictu fugaces protrahit.
     —Ford, in *Mus. Angl. Anal.* (1st ed.) 139.

1703   Vn Hameau craint il des sieges?
On n'y connoit point les pieges
Du cruel Age de Fer;
Et si quelque main traitresse
Parmi les guerets en dresse
Ce n'est qu'au Peuple de l'air.
     —Cléric *Jeux Floraux* C$_{1-2}$.

1726   Thither, the houshold, feathery, People croud,
The crested Cock, with all his female Train.
     —Thomson *Winter* 126–7.

1741   Variisque colorum
Naturâ pictrice nitet Gens florea fucis.
     —Anon., in *Mus. Angl.* (5th ed.) II. 231.

Plough[1]

    Et nunc Pristis habet, nunc victam praeterit ingens
Centaurus, nunc una ambae iunctisque feruntur
Frontibus et longa sulcant vada salsa carina.
     —Virgil *Aen.* V. 156–8.

1614   Against the ship sides, that now ranne, and plowd
The rugged seas vp.
     —Chapman *Odys.* 30.

1618   Hebbero piume tutti, e apriro l'ale
Per solcar l'aria lucida e leggiera.
     —Murtola *Creat. Mondo* V. xiii. 2.

1622   Next Malgo, who againe that Conquerors steps to tread,
Succeeding him in Raigne, in conquests so no lesse,
Plow'd up the frozen Sea.
     —Drayton *Poly-Olb.* XIX. 172–4.

1633   Vain men, too fondly wise, who plough the seas,
With dangerous pains another earth to finde.
     —P. Fletcher *Purple Isl.* I. xxxvi.

1655   And you shall spye ploughing the Ocean
Your Argonauts.
     —Fanshawe *Lus.* I. xviii.

1690   So should my honour, like a rising swan,
Brush with her wings the falling drops away,
And proudly plough the waves.
     —Dryden *Don S.* V. i, in *Works* VII. 453.

---

[1]See also CLEAVE, CUT.

Pole[1]

ἐγὼ δ'
'Ελένην Δίοις μελάθροις πελάσω,
λαμπρῶν ἄστρων πόλον ἐξανύσας.
—Euripides *Orestes* 1683–5. (I
will bear Helen to the Mansions
of Zeus, on reaching the firmament [pole] of the shining stars.)

Principio magnus caeli si vortitur orbis,
Ex utraque polum parti premere aera nobis
Dicendum est extraque tenere et claudere utrimque.
—Lucretius V. 510–12.

Nam neque erant astrorum ignes nec lucidus aethra
Siderea polus, obscuro sed nubila caelo.
—Virgil *Aen.* III. 585–6.

Sed prius eoae quaerunt tua lumina terrae,
Post medio subiecta polo quaecumque coluntur.
—Manilius I. 224–5.

Per poli liquentis axem fulgor auri absconditur.
—Prudentius *Peristep.* I. 88.

Hic gens ardentem cæli subterjacet axem,
Quam candor fervens albenti ex æthere fuscat.
—Avitus *Initio Mundi* 196–7.

1505   Tanta mole ruit tantaque impulsa ruina
Fumida vis, procul acta polo atque e nube profunda.
—Pontano *Meteor.* 647–8.

1551   Crois-tu se paistre les vers
Du nom de celle qui vole
Admirable en l'Univers
De l'un jusqu'à l'autre pole?
—Du Bellay IV. 65.

1572   La onde mais debaxo està do Polo,
Os montes Hyperboreos aparecem.
—Camoens *Lus.* 39.

1591   Changes le jour en nuict, tiens sous ta clef les vents,
Rens fixe le soleil et les poles mouvans.
—Du Bartas *Troph.* 573–4.

1594   The God that framde the fixed pole, and Lamps of
         gleaming light,
The azure skies, and twinkling Starres, to yeeld this
         pleasant sight.
—Willoughby *Avisa* 177.

---

[1]Not in Homer, Empedocles, or Ennius.

Pole—*continued*

1605   True Atlasses: You Pillars of the Poles
Empireall Pallace.
—Sylvester *Div. Wks.* (*Colom.*) 491.

1614   Whil Phoebus' steeds abowt the Poles do praunce.
—Mure I. 87.

1637   She has sought thee forth
Through both the poles and mansions of the north.
—Marmion *Cup. and Psy.* II. i. 31–2.

1645   And the slope Sun his upward beam
Shoots against the dusky Pole.
—Milton *Comus* 98–9.

1659   Love, by whose motion on the pole of merit
This bright orb turned.
—W. Chamberlayne *Phar.* II. v. 8–9.

1674   Eternity stands permanent and fixed,
And wheels no longer on the poles of time.
—Dryden *State of Inn.* V. i, in *Works* V. 176–7.

1697   And that the Stars in constant order roll,
Hang there, nor fall, and leave the liquid Pole;
'Tis not from Chance.
—Creech *Manilius* (Bk. I) 22.

1713   Tempt icy seas, where scarce the waters roll,
Where clearer flames glow round the frozen pole.
—Pope *Win. For.* 389–90.

Ponderous

1562   Car du pondereux globe equalibrant au tiers
Les cieux hauts elle voit plus grands de maints quartiers.
—Scève 254.

1604   The sepulchre,
Wherein we saw thee quietly inurn'd,
Hath op'd his ponderous and marble jaws.
—Shakespeare *Hamlet* I. iv. 48–50.

1616   To place this pondrous Globe of Earth so euen,
That it should all, and nought should it vphold.
—Drummond I. 87.

1622   The Dane prepares his Axe, that pond'rous was to feele.
—Drayton *Poly-Olb.* XII. 261.

1627   The ponderous earth out of her center tost
Her middle place in the worlds orbe has lost.
—May *Lucan* Lb.

Ponderous—*continued*

1630   This in one hand a pondrous Sword doth hold.
          —Drummond II. 39.

1640   With-held; both by diverting her pursuit;
          And with the burden of the ponderous fruit.
          —Sandys *Ovid's Met.* 191.

1656   For every place and space we empty call,
          Bee't Medium or no, it must yeeld all
          Alike to pond'rousness, even wheresoe're
          Its motion drives; nor any place is there
          Whither, when heavy bodies are arriv'd,
          They can in Vacuum stand of weight depriv'd.
          —Evelyn *Lucretius* 77.

1667   His ponderous shield
          Ethereal temper, massy, large and round.
          —Milton *P. L.* I. 284–5.

1686   Regardless of those pond'rous little things
          That discompose th' uneasy heads of kings.
          —Flatman, in *CP* III. 336.

1693   Earth sinks beneath, and draws a numerous throng
          Of ponderous, thick, unwieldy seeds along.
          —Dryden *Ovid's Met.* I. 36–7.

1712   Those who ascribe this one determin'd Course
          Of pondrous Things to Gravitating Force,
          Refer us to a Quality occult.
          —Blackmore *Creation* I. 136–8.

1728   As, forced from wind-guns, lead itself can fly,
          And pond'rous slugs cut swiftly thro' the sky.
          —Pope *Dunc.* I. 181–2.

1600   Cardinalis etiam Cusanus non est contemnendus: "Habet inquit ferrum in magnete quoddam sui effluxus principium, & dùm magnes per sui præsentiam excitat ferrum graue & ponderosum."—W. Gilbert *Magnete* 64.

1620   [Waters from lead pipes] are troublesome to the stomacke, and ponderous to all the bowels.—Venner *Via Recta* 10.

1630   Le priuilege que la nature a departi aux choses pondereuses & fluides de chasser haut celles qui le sont moins, en s'enfonçant tousiours dedans icelles.—Rey *Essais* 55.

1650   The foure Elements in the first operation of Nature doe by the help of the Archeus of Nature distill into the center of the earth a ponderous, or heavy Vapour of water, which is the seed of Metalls.—French *Sandivogius* 19.

Ponderous—*continued*

1653 Saturn is more ponderous then Jupiter, and Jupiter then Mars.—
Dariott *Redivivus* 49.

1661 Ponderous matters descend towards the Centre, with a right motion.—
Salusbury *Math. Coll.* 22.

1664 [For planting] Chuse your Seed of that which is perfectly mature,
ponderous and sound.—Evelyn *Sylva* 4.

1679 For this [air], as in reason it ought to be esteemed the most ponderous
part of the atmosphere, because the lowest, so it betrays its ponderosity
by making vapours ascend readily in it, by sustaining mists and clouds
of snow, and by buoying up gross and ponderous smoke.—Newton, in
Rigaud II. 418.

1687 [Mechanics] teacheth in general, how to find out the ponderousness of
every thing, and how to move things with little strength. [Hæc ars
docet in genere modum reperiendæ ponderationis].—Abercromby
Acad. Sci. 112, 113.

1695 The Pebles, *Pyritæ*, Amber, or other like Nodules, which happened to
be reposed in those Cliffs, amongst the Earth so beaten down, being
hard, and not so dissoluble, and likewise more bulky and ponderous,
are left behind upon the Shores, being impeded, and secured, by that
their bulk and weight, from being born along with the Terrestrial
Matter into the Sea.—J. Woodward *Nat. Hist. Earth* 220.

1700 The mineral Matter is a great deal of it not only gross and ponderous,
but scabrous and inflexible.—*Phil. Trans.* XXI. 211.

Prey

ὦ πταναὶ θῆραι χαροπῶν τ'
ἔθνη θηρῶν, οὓς ὅδ' ἔχει
χῶρος οὐρεσιβώτας.
—Sophocles *Philoct.* 1146–8.
(Ye feathered prey, and ye nations of bright-eyed beasts who
dwell in this place, roaming the
hills.)

1572 Ia sica vencedor o Lusitano
Recolhendo os trofeos & presa rica.
—Camoens *Lus.* 46b.

1592 O su per l'onde, e dentr' a l'onde istesse
Cercan l'umida preda, e 'l cibo usato
De gli animai squamosi e de gli alati.
—Tasso *Mondo Creato* III. 476–8.

1595 Into a forest wide and waste he came
Where store he heard to be of saluage pray.
—Spenser *Astro.* 93–4.

Prey—*continued*

1605   Vn-stor'd of dinner, till the morrow-day;
          Pleas'd with an Apple, or some lesser pray.
              —Sylvester *Div. Wks.* (*Handie-Crafts*) 361.

1613   And these [fish] haue wider mouths to catch and take
          Their flying pray.
              —Dennys *Secrets of Angling* C₈.

ante 1642   He wishes some incensèd boar his prey.
              —Godolphin, in *CP* II. 253.

1659   Who now, befriended
          With the protecting darkness, hastes away,
          Swift as desire, with the fair trembling prey.
              —W. Chamberlayne *Phar.* II. i. 188–90.

1667   The onely two of Mankinde, but in them
          The whole included Race, his purposd prey.
              —Milton *P. L.* IX. 415–16.

1668   A Bear and Lyon by fierce hunger led,
          Broke from the wood, and snatcht my Lambs away;
          From their grim mouths I forc'ed the panting prey.
              —Cowley 337.

1686   He, like an eagle, soar'd aloft,
          To seize his noble prey.
              —Flatman, in *CP* III. 306.

1698   Ascanius, who, before this day,
          Was wont in woods to shoot the savage prey.
              —Dryden *Aen.* IX. 802–3.

1714   Slight Lines of Hair surprize the Finny Prey.
              —Pope *Rape of the Lock* II. 26.

1722   The rav'nous Eagle, and the noisy Mew
          Fearless thro' Waves the scaly Prey pursue.
              —Diaper *Oppian's Hal.* I. 708–9.

Purple

NOTE.—Nicholas Tindal, editor of Spence's *Polymetis*, wrote: "The meaning of *purpureus* is not settled. It is used of fire, swans, and snow."[1] But though the English equivalent, especially in its poetical application, does not always have a precise significance, certain of its uses as a color term in time determined the meaning it has now. It is possible that the constant use of *purple* to describe blood, arterial or otherwise, in prose writings had something to do with this limitation of meaning. Ioannes Bodaeus, a seventeenth-century editor of Theophrastus who had need of a precise term, was obliged to refer at length

---

[1] Joseph Spence, *Polymetis* (London, 1802), p. 76, note 1.

Purple—*continued*

to many ancient poets to get at the sense of the word in his author; it may
be useful to observe his conclusions as well as his method:

Purpureum veteres ponunt, vel pro colore purpureo, qui duplex est, ut mox dicam;
vel pro vivaci, excellentique. Id quod probatu non difficile est . . . . Anacreon
Poëta Venerem πορφυρᾶν vocavit, quod esset splendida, venusta. Hoc etiam
sensu apud ipsum legitur Dioscoridem, uti cap. XCIX. de bitumine. Ἔστι δὲ καλὴ
ἡ πορφυρειδῶς στίλβουσα, *probatur purpuræ modo splendens.* Purpureum bitumen
videre nondum licuit.[1]

ὡς Αἴας ἐπέτελλε πελώριος, αἵματι δὲ χθὼν
δεύετο πορφυρέῳ.
> —Homer *Il*. XVII. 360–1. (Thus mighty
> Aias charged them, and the earth grew wet
> with purple blood.)

ἴων ξανθαῖσι καὶ παμπορφύροις ἀκτῖσι βεβρεγμένος ἁβρὸν
σῶμα.
> —Pindar *Ol*. VI. 55–6. (Its dainty form steeped in
> the golden and the deep-purple light of pansies.—Tr. Sandys.)

Largior hic campos aether et lumine vestit
Purpureo.
> —Virgil *Aen*. VI. 640–1.

Qui color infectis adversi solis ab ictu
Nubibus esse solet aut purpureae Aurorae,
Is fuit in vultu visae sine vesta Dianae.
> —Ovid *Met*. III. 183–5.

1585   La figue jette-laict, la cerise pourpree.
> —Du Bartas *I Sem*. III. 497.

1592   Per non turbar co' lor torbidi spirti
Del bell' aer purpureo 'l dolce aspetto.
> —Tasso *Mondo Creato* V. 1410–11.

1613   El huerto le da esofras, a quien debe
Si purpura la rosa, el lilio nieue.
> —Góngora II. 95.

1622   With purple red,
All overspread,
Sweet virgin shame did make her.
> —Hannay *Philo*. 446–8.

1623   The red rose and the white are on his face,
The fatal colours of our striving houses;
The one his purple blood right well resembles.
> —Shakespeare *III Henry VI* II. v. 97–9.

---

[1] *Hist. Plant.* (Amsterdam, 1644), 867. A good modern discussion of the ancient
use is to be found in Alice E. Kober's *The Use of Color Terms in the Greek Poets* (Geneva, N. Y.: W. F. Humphrey, 1932), 93–100.

Purple—*continued*

1638 Moist clouds long since have washed the purpled grass.
   —Whiting, in *CP* III. 550.

1645 Throw hither all your quaint enameld eyes,
   That on the green terf suck the honied showres,
   And purple all the ground with vernal flowres.
   —Milton *Lyc.* 139–41.

1655 The purpled Sea there boyling o're with blood.
   —Fanshawe *Lus.* X. xxix.

1678 In the full vintage of my flowing honours,
   Sat still, and saw it prest by other hands.
   Fortune came smiling to my youth, and wooed it,
   And purple greatness met my ripened years.
   —Dryden *All for Love* I. i, in *Works* V. 354.

1692 Unde hinc purpureus venas, hinc lacteus imber
   Irrigat; in fontes quæ causa recedere jussit
   Sanguinis assiduo remeantia flumina motu.
   —Fell, in *Mus. Angl. Anal.* (1st ed.) 49.

1698 Let oaks now glitter with Hesperian fruit,
   And purple daffodils from alder shoot.
   —Dryden *Ecl.* VIII. 72–3.

1700 He turn'd the point; the sword, inur'd to blood,
   Bor'd his unguarded breast, which pour'd a purple flood.
   —Dryden *Cymon* 603–4.

1709 Why sit we sad, when Phosphor shines so clear,
   And lavish Nature paints the purple year?
   —Pope *Spring* 27–8.

1714 Pale Spectres, gaping Tombs, and Purple Fires.
   —Pope *Rape of the Lock* IV. 44.

1657 The flowers [of the almond tree] are of a paler Purple Colour then the
   Peach blossoms.—Coles *Adam in Eden* 150.

1664 Sanguis enim extravasatus, cùm sponte suâ in partes secedit, hic liquor
   à crassamento purpureo dijunctus, eidémque innatans, limpidus apparet.—Willis *Cerebri Anat.* 255.

1669 Quocirca cum ita se res habeat, proximo in loco videndum est, cui
   tandem sanguis acceptum refert quòd colore tam rutilo & purpureo
   penitus imbuatur: Atque hoc pulmonibus totum tribuendum est,
   siquidem expertus sum sanguinem, qui totus venosi instar atro colore
   pulmones intrat, arteriosum omninò & floridum ex illis redire; si enim
   abscissâ arteriore parte pectoris & folle in asperam arteriam immisso
   pulmonibus continenter insufflatis, &, quo liber per eos aëri transitus
   fiat, acu simul undique perforatis, vena pneumonica prope auriculam
   sinistram pertundatur, sanguis totus purpureus & floridus in admotum

Purple—*continued*

vasculum exiliet; atque quamdiu pulmonibus recens usque aër hoc modo suggeritur, sanguis ad plures uncias, imo libras per totum coccineus erumpet, non aliter quàm si arteriâ pertusâ aliquâ exciperetur. —Lower *Tract. Corde* 166–7.

1674 Nor doth the disorder cease here, but extend itself to the upper region also, to the brain; where the Spirits being put into confusion, and the arteries surcharged with too great an afflux of blood from the oppressed heart; the palace of the Soul itself is brought into danger of a purple deluge.—Charleton *Nat. Hist. Passions* 156.

1682 *Crocus purpureus minor*, the small purple Crocus.—S. Gilbert *Flor. Vade-Mecum* 17.

1697 The red Threads of *Rorella* end, or are toped with little Bags; which being compressed do yield a Purple Juice.—*Phil. Trans.* XIX. 373.

1718 That all Metals being placed in the Focus of the Burning-Glass, will run into Glass; and that Gold in its Vitrification, assumed a fine Purple Colour.—J. Chamberlayne *Nieuwentyt* II. 563.

Race[1]

1567 There is no moe but thou and I of all the mortall race.
    —Golding *Ovid's Met.* I. 418.

1585 De mesme tu formas d'une terrestre masse
    Des fragiles humains la limonneuse race.
    —Du Bartas *I Sem.* VI. 485–6.

1590 Of all the race of siluer-winged Flies
    Which doo possesse the Empire of the aire.
    —Spenser *Muio.* 17–18.

1600 Of Sophia fair thou never wert the child,
    Nor of the Azzaine race ysprung thou art.
    —E. Fairfax *Tasso* XVI. lvi.

1605 And let loose Auster, and his lowring race.
    —Sylvester *Div. Wks.* (*2d Day*) 71.

1611 From Enes, where the race of mules, fit for the plough
       is bred.
    —Chapman *Il.* 33.

1622 Those great race of Hounds, the deepest mouth'd of all.
    —Drayton *Poly-Olb.* XXVII. 219.

1633 The first was Errour false, who multiplies
    Her num'rous race in endlesse progenies.
    —P. Fletcher *Purple Isl.* VII. xli.

---

[1]See also BAND, BREED, BROOD, CHOIR, CITIZEN, CREW, FLOCK, FRY, HERD, HOST, INHABITANT, KIND, LEGION, NATION, PEOPLE, SEED, SHOAL, SQUADRON, TRAIN, TRIBE, TROOP.

Race—*continued*

1640 Such a grace
Great Neptune gave; the root of Neleus race.
  —Sandys *Ovid's Met.* 226.

1651 And Vertue's claim exceeds the right of blood,
As Souls extraction does the Bodies Race.
  —Davenant *Gond.* III. iv. 10.

1667 Shall we then live thus vile, the race of Heav'n
Thus trampl'd?
  —Milton *P. L.* II. 194–5.

1668 And in the silken Beds [frogs] their slimy Members place;
A Luxurie unknown before to all the Watry Race.
  —Cowley 222.

1675 What time th' inraged Earth a Giant Race
'Gainst Heaven produc'd.
  —Sherburne *Sphere* 35.

1698 Undoubted offspring of ethereal race!
  —Dryden *Aen.* VIII. 51.

1713 Our plenteous streams a various race supply.
  —Pope *Win. For.* 141.

1728 Then comes the tulip-race, where beauty plays
Her gayest freaks.
  —Thomson *Spring* 539–40.

1733 Where loud-tongu'd Virgins vend the scaly Race.
  —Whitehead *State Dunces* 10.

Ray (*of light*)[1]

Nubila cum longo cessant depulsa sereno
Et solis radiis arescit torridus aer.
  —Manilius I. 819–20.

Occurrunt celsis inmissa foramina tectis,
Quae iaciant claros antra super radios.
  —Prudentius *Peristep.* XI. 161–2.

1552 Aux rayons du beau jour
Qui luyt au ciel, ton eternel sejour.
  —Du Bellay IV. 111.

1585 Dieu fait que le soleil, et les astres de mesme,
Bien qu'ils soient tres-ardens, ne se bruslent eux mesme,
Que leurs rayons brillans d'un triste embrasement
N'anticipent le jour du dernier jugement.
  —Du Bartas *I Sem.* VII. 155–8.

---

[1]See also BEAM, PAINT.

Ray (*of light*)—*continued*

1592   Fu chi pensò ch' alta cagione il Sole
Fosse di ciò che 'n lei s'appiglia o nasce,
Lo qual la scalda con gli ardenti raggi.
—Tasso *Mondo Creato* III. 862–4.

1596   And face all tand with scorching sunny ray.
—Spenser *F. Q.* I. vi. 35.

1605   And supping-vp still with his thirstie Rayes,
All the fresh humour in the floating Seas.
—Sylvester *Div. Wks.* (*3d Day*) 83.

1606   Por las ondas que doran
Los raios de la luz dexan sus cueuas.
—Góngora I. 272.

1610   As when the cheerfull Sunne, elamping wide,
Glads all the world with his uprising raye.
—G. Fletcher *Christs Victorie in Heaven* xli.

1633   The pitchie vapours choke the shining ray.
—P. Fletcher *Purple Isl.* XII. xxii.

1642   Her tresses flow'd like waves of liquid gold,
Burnisht by rising Titan's morning ray.
—Kynaston *Leo. and Syd.* 108–9.

1659   Commanded parties, which ere night shut in
Light's latest rays, did furiously begin.
—W. Chamberlayne *Phar.* II. ii. 183–4.

1667   The Sun, who scarce up risen
With wheels yet hov'ring o're the Ocean brim,
Shot paralel to the earth his dewie ray.
—Milton *P. L.* V. 139–41.

1682   So Reason's glimmering ray
Was lent, not to assure our doubtful way,
But guide us upward to a better day.
—Dryden *Rel. Laici* 5–7.

1698   The rattling sound
Of mimic thunder, and the glitt'ring blaze
Of pointed lightnings, and their forky rays.
—Dryden *Aen.* VI. 789–91.

1716   Comparons les Rayons à de petites Balles,
Ou concevons qu'ils sont autant de Dards,
Qui dans leur Cours direct viennent sans intervalles
Toucher, & fraper nos Regards.
—Genest *Prin. Phil.* 177.

1722   Matter by slow Gradations downward sinks;
And intermediate Changes gently pass

Ray (*of light*)—*continued*

> From lightsome Æther to the dullest Mass.
> Or climb by the same Steps from lumpish Clay
> To the bright Liquid, and the fine-spun Ray.
> —Diaper *Oppian's Hal.* I. 683–7.

1596   Quid est radius? Est lucida qualitas à corpore lucenti emissa: lucidum autem est non modò luminosum, sed etiam splendidum: neque tamen admittendum est, omne corpus radios habere, vt quibusdam videtur. —Bodin *Theat.* 450.

1600   Sic omnes stellæ immutant suos luminis radios in superficie telluris, admirabili hac magnetica axis telluris inflexione.—W. Gilbert *Magnete* 235.

1626   Nam si lapides Indiæ vel Hyberniæ hexagonios sumamus & si eos teneamus contra radios solis per fenestram vel foramen aliquod penetrantes, in vmbra seu aere vmbroso, percipiemus iuxta radios omnes colores iridis eodem ordine, quo in arcu cælesti disponuntur.—Fludd *Meteor Cosmica* 136.

1632   Dal che segue di necessità, che sopra qualsiuoglia parte di qualunque superficie opposta a quella, che riceue i raggi primarii incidenti, peruengano raggi reflessi, & in conseguenza l'illuminazione. Seguene ancora, che il medesimo corpo, sul quale vengono i raggi illuminanti, rimirato da qualsiuoglia luogo si mostri tutto illuminato, e chiaro: e però la Luna per esser di superficie aspra, e non tersa, rimanda la luce del Sole verso tutte le bande, & a tutti i riguardanti si mostra egualmente lucida.—Galileo *Dial.* 70.

1644   Et experientia me docuit, medium L, qui crystallinus humor dicitur, præterpropter eamdem refractionem producere quam vitrum aut crystallus, & duos reliquos paulo minorem, fere qualem aqua communis: unde fit ut faciliùs medius quàm reliqui duo, & adhuc faciliùs hi quàm aër luminis radios admittant.—Descartes *Œuvres* VI. 596.

1658   In regionibus torridis, videtur densari frigus per antiperistasin; adeo ut, si quis se recipiat ex campo aperto et radiis solaribus sub arbore patula, statim cohorreat.—Bacon *Works* IV. 107.

1674   Radii lucis (hoc est lucidi transitûs aut impulsûs quales descripsimus tramites) in eodem existentes similari medio directi sunt. Hoc è dictis abunde patet. Quin indè Corollarii vice deducitur radios quoad rem ipsam, Physicéque loquendo figurà prismaticos esse, vel cylindricos. Nempe corpusculum illud quodpiam in lucidi superficie positum, à quo radius originem suam ducit, dum à primo suo loco ceu base defertur aut totâ suâ superficie contiguum sibi corpus rectà propellit, figuræ suæ (vel impulsi saltem corporis figuræ) congruum designat, super hac vel illa base constitutum, solidum longum, exile, teres, quale cylindrus, aut prisma. Proinde quando Mathematicè rem tractamus, istos radios pro rectis lineis habere possumus; tum quia reverà sunt adeò tenues &

Ray (*of light*)—*continued*

recti; tum quia plerumque pro cylindricis ejusmodi seu prismaticis figuris ipsarum axes ità sumi possunt, ut nihil indè ratiocinio Mathematico derogetur.—Barrow *Lect. Optic.* 15.

1676 For assuming the rays of light to be small bodies emitted every way from shining substances, those, when they impinge on any refracting or reflecting superficies, must as necessarily excite vibrations in the æther as stones do in water when thrown into it.—Newton, in D. Brewster I. 391.

1690 Car un rayon visible de lumiere, quelque mince qu'il soit, a tousjours quelque épaisseur.—Huyghens XIX. 479.

1698 If an Object be placed so much nigher to the Eye then the focus of a Spher, as to be within its Surface, the Rays of Light must come too much Diverging to shew the Objects they come from distinctly.—*Phil. Trans.* XIX. 285.

1704 Rays, or Beams of the Sun, or Rays of Light, are either according to our Atomical Hypothesis, those very minute Particles or Corpuscles of Matter, which continually issuing out of the Sun, do thrust on one another all around in Physically short Lines; . . . or else as the Cartesians assert, they are made by the Action of the Luminary on the Contiguous Æther and Air, and so are propagated every way in strait Lines, through the Pores of the Medium.—Harris *Lex. Tech.* (under *Rays*).

1729 But perhaps some may think, that this Train of Matter which is extended from one Point of the luminous Body, to a Point of the Object which it illuminates, and which is called a Ray of Light, may more properly be compared to a Thread than to a Stick, because its Parts are not so firmly connected together, as those of a Stick are.—Clarke *Rohault* I. 207.

Ray (visual ray)

NOTE.—The conception of a visual ray coming forth from the eye is generally known, but it seems proper to describe the theory here in order to suggest that belief in a world in which the sight of each person was conceived of as a tactile thing must have strongly qualified thoughtful contemplation of the appearance of material objects. Such a discussion is also pertinent in showing how this theory of sight survived, and how some of the terms that were developed in its exposition were found serviceable by writers who proposed theories supported by later discoveries. With a background of this sort it will be possible to learn more precisely what was meant in various poetic uses.

Accepting the theory that beams went out from the eye and brought back to a person's sight the thing they found, one would feel differently than a Newtonian, say, about the lines in Shakespeare:

> The deep-green em'rald, in whose fresh regard
> Weak sights their sickly radiance do amend.[1]

---

[1] *Lover's Complaint* 213–14.

Ray (visual ray)—*continued*

And, of course, this theory was the very means for the expression of a kind of fierce detachment in Donne:

> Our hands were firmely cimented
>> With a fast balme, which thence did spring,
> Our eye-beames twisted, and did thred
>> Our eyes, upon one double string;
> So to'entergraft our hands, as yet
>> Was all the meanes to make us one,
> And pictures in our eyes to get
>> Was all our propagation.[1]

Shadwell treats the same idea humorously: "You might observe, whenever he star'd upon them, they would steal a look at us; and by stealth have often twisted Eye-beams with us."[2]   In Milton there is the famous reflection:

> For inward light alas
> Puts forth no visual beam.[3]

William Chamberlayne worked out the idea elaborately:

> But now, broke through the epileptic mist
> Of amorous rapture, rallied spirits twist
> Again their optic cordage; whose mixed beams
> Now separate, and on collateral streams
> Dispersed expressions of affection bore
> To each congratulating friend.[4]

Beare ascribes the origin of this theory to Alcmaeon and Empedocles and says:

Almost all the early attempts at a theory of vision agree in regarding the 'pupil' of the eye as a matter of primary importance for visual function.

Another fact which greatly influenced this branch of study was that when the eyeball is pressed, or moved hastily, in darkness, a flash of light is seen within the eye.   From this was drawn the conclusion that the eye has within it a native fire, and that on this native fire, not less than upon the image in the pupil, its faculty of vision somehow depends.

A third fact which formed a basis of visual theory was that the interior of the eye is found to contain aqueous humours—roughly called 'water' by the Greeks. The functions of the retina being altogether unknown, and the optic nerves being perhaps better known, but certainly not known in their true character, the primary business of the early psychologists who treated of vision seemed to be, to determine the parts played in vision by the *image*, the *fire*, and the *water*, respectively.   As regards the assumed intra-ocular fire, the question was frequently agitated, whether its rays went forth from the eye as from a luminary, and (either by themselves or in combination with a column of light proceeding from the object) as it were *apprehended* the object of vision, and brought it within the purview of 'the soul'; or whether the fire merely lurked within the periphery of the eye, and there seized

---

[1]*Extasie* 5–12.
[2]*Squire of Alsatia* II. i, in *Works* IV. 226.
[3]*S. A.* 162–3.
[4]*Phar.* IV. ii. 544–9.

Ray (visual ray)—*continued*

the image which, coming to it from outside, was reflected in the aqueous interior, as if in a mirror.[1]

An important presentation occurs in Plato:

And of the organs they [the gods] constructed first light-bearing eyes, and these they fixed in the face for the reason following. They contrived that all such fire as had the property not of burning but of giving a mild light should form a body akin to the light of every day. For they caused the pure fire within us, which is akin to that of day, to flow through the eyes in a smooth and dense stream; and they compressed the whole substance, and especially the centre, of the eyes, so that they occluded all other fire that was coarser and allowed only this pure kind of fire to filter through. So whenever the stream of vision [τὸ τῆς ὄψεως ῥεῦμα] is surrounded by mid-day light, it flows out like unto like, and coalescing therewith it forms one kindred substance along the path of the eyes' vision, wheresoever the fire which streams from within collides with an obstructing object without. And this substance, having all become similar in its properties because of its similar nature, distributes the motions of every object it touches, or whereby it is touched, throughout all the body even unto the Soul, and brings about that sensation which we now term "seeing."[2]

Aristotle at one place[3] rejected this thesis, but he apparently made use of it at other times without demur.[4]

Some form of the theory was developed by Ptolemy, and no other explanation achieved much importance until Descartes presented his. Throughout the seventeenth century there were survivals of the old belief, but for the more advanced scientists a quite different debate arose, concerned with the corpuscular and undulatory theories of light. It is at least curious that, when discussion had left the early, crude notions far behind, the phrase *visual ray* survived to mean something quite different.

ὅσσον δ' ὀφθαλμοῖο βολῆς ἀποτέμνεται αὐγή.
—Aratus *Phaen.* 541. (As long as is the ray cast to heaven from the glance of the eye.—Tr. G. R. Mair.)

1585 Hic altor ignis omnium, qui vesperum
Cùm subter est terram facit, supra at diem.
Hic orbis est speculum, vel è contrario,
Scintilla visus, splendor vnde luminum,
Vel fulgor emicans procul, peregrina vel
Vtcunque res inducta, visum perficit.
  —Morellus *Pisidas* 8b.

---

[1]*Greek Theories of Elementary Cognition from Alcmaeon to Aristotle* (Oxford, 1906) 9–10.
[2]*Timaeus* 45B–D (*LCL* 101–3).
[3]*De Sensu et Sensili* 438a25, in *Opera* III. 478.
[4]See, for example, *Meteor.* 373b2–10, in *Opera* III. 601–2.

Ray (visual ray)—*continued*

1595   Betwixt mine Eye and obiect, certayne lynes,
             Moue in the figure of a Pyramis,
             Whose chapter in mine eyes gray apple shines,
             The base within my sacred obiect is.
                  —Chapman *Ovids Banquet* lxiv, in *Poems*.

1614   And Sleepe bereft vs of our visuall light.
                  —Chapman *Odys*. 62.

1638   They thought no eye a saucy ray durst dart.
                  —Whiting, in *CP* III. 470.

1655   As through the Ayre his visual Raies disperse,
             Hee sees, farr off, from high and antient Mountains,
             Melt down a payre of deep and crystall Fountains.
                  —Fanshawe *Lus*. IV. lxix.

1659   Though it [love] with twisted eye-beams strengthened
                  grew
             At every interview.
                  —W. Chamberlayne *Phar*. III. i. 110–11.

1667   And the Aire,
             No where so cleer, sharp'nd his visual ray
             To objects distant farr.
                  —Milton *P. L.* III. 619–21.

1700   So long her earnest eyes on his were set,
             At length their twisted rays together met.
                  —Dryden *Sig. and Guis*. 63–4.

1739   [The jewelled eyes of the Trojan horse:]
             There flaming Amethysts their light display,
             And sparkling Beryls form the visual ray.
                  —Merrick *Tryphiodorus* 96–7.

1504   Visionem fieri per egressum spiritus visibilis ab oculo ad rem visam.—
             Reisch *Margar. Phil.* gg₃.

             Radium visualem speciem rei visibilis dicimus. non ut lineam aut
             superficiem mathematicam profundo carentem: sed corporalem &
             pyramidalem: cuius basis in re visa & conus in oculo vidente est.—
             Ibid. hh.

ante   There is added to this rare heith a mervelous sensible deceipt of the
1590   behoulder, for it seameth not to be by the half so high, to take the
             vewe thereof from the foundation.   I attribute this to the smale hould
             the beames of the eyes can have on the stones of this buildinge, beinge
             everie waie (as I before have mencioned) perflatiles, and the force of
             the sight beinge divided into so many and sundry partes (by the meanes
             of those chiones it lighteth on when any man looketh up to the tower,)
             is made more weake and feable, and, therefore, cannot by reflection
             bringe backe to the eyes the perfect forme of the object; for the sence

Ray (visual ray)—*continued*

of seeing beinge the servaunt of the mynde, dooth represent the eyes
(which be, as Plato termeth them, *ad animam perforatæ fenestræ*,) the
trew shape of that thinge it was commaunded to behould, sendinge
forthe his beames, as bailifs, to arest the object to appeare before reason
that keapeth his coort in man's mynde; which, beinge vearye swifte,
escapeth, and is not attayned to by pursute; and by that reason, lookinge
on a whirlinge wheele, wee discerne not the spookes thereof, nor on
birdes flyinge wee see no fethers; or yf the object be veary farr of, as
out of his bailiwike, he retoorneth *non est inventus;* and therefore we
attaine not by sight the grasse that groweth on mountaines farr of, nor
discern branches though wee behould the trees; or if they be but informed by others, then they reporte falsly.—Stephen Powle, in Halliwell *Progr. of Science* 23–4.

1596   Quid autem absurdius, quàm in vniuersum cœleste hemisphærium ab
oculis emitti radiorum vim infinitam, idq́ue momento vsque ad sydera,
& ab illis eodem momento ad oculos reflecti?—Bodin *Theat.* 451.

1622   Seeing beames come from the Eye.   Three things are required for
sight: That the beames associate the Ayre.   That seeing spirits slide
not out.   That the visible spirits be vnited with the Ayre.—Banister
Guillemeau b₁b.

1632   Ma di vno, costituito sopra la superficie terrestre, il raggio, che dall'
occhio suo andasse fino al centro del globo lunare, non passerebbe per
l'istesso punto della superficie di quella, per il quale passa la linea
tirata dal centro della Terra a quel della Luna, se non quando ella gli
fusse verticale: ma posta la Luna in oriente, ò in occidente, il punto
dell' incidenza del raggio visuale, resta superiore a quel della linea,
che congiugne i centri, e però si scuopre qualche parte dell' emisferio
lunare verso la circonferenza di sopra, e si nasconde altrettanto della
parte di sotto.—Galileo *Dial.* 58.

1634   Itaque sicut [arcum cœlestem] vos putatis radio visorio [τῆς ὄψεως[1]]
versus Solem repercusso in nube co[n]spici.—Kepler *Plutarch* 101–2.

1651   Optica est Scientia de modo visionis, & visibilitate quatenus ea per
radios visuales, & vmbras à radijs terminatas fieri potest.—Ricciolus
Almagest. Nov. I. 2.

1663   You must apprehend the optick spirits to be a thin continuous body,
equally interwoven through all its parts with a proportion of thin yet a
little condensed fire.—G. Harvey *Prin. Phil.* II. 152.

1669   We can hear in the dark, Immured, and by curve Lines, that is, Sound
can pass to the Ears, where visual Rayes cannot to the Eye.—Holder
Elem. Speech 2.

1676   Since the Satellites have the center of Jupiter for the center of their
particular motions, and that the circles by them described are not di-

---

[1]Plutarch 921a.

Ray (visual ray)—*continued*

rectly opposit to the Earth nor the Sun, there is always a part of each
of those circles inferior to Jupiter, and another superior to him, and
this, being compared to the center of the apparent disque of Jupiter,
is sometimes turned to the South, sometimes to the North, by a perpetual change of inclination to our visual ray.—*Phil. Trans.* XI. 681.

1687   The visuel Rays [Radii visorii], are the streight lines, by which the
frame of the visible Object is in a manner carried to the eye.—Abercromby *Acad. Sci.* 138, 139.

1690   Mais je m'etonne . . . ne trouvant pas que personne ait encore expliqué
probablement ces premiers, & notables phenomenes de la lumiere,
sçavoir pourquoy elle ne s'étend que suivant des lignes droites, &
comment les rayons visuels, venant d'une infinité de divers endroits,
se croisant sans s'empêcher en rien les uns les autres.—Huyghens
XIX. 459.

1700   The Perpendicular End of the Cylinder DC was clos'd with an Object
Glass of a 76th. Foot Telescope, *oo;* and the other End AB, with a well
polisht flat Glass *ff;* which was carefully chosen to transmit the Object
distinct enough notwithstanding its Obliquity to the Visual Rays.—
Phil. Trans. XXI. 340.

Region[1]

Terraque ut in media mundi regione quiescat,
Evanescere paulatim et decrescere pondus
Convenit.
    —Lucretius V. 534–6.

Arma inter nubem caeli in regione serena
Per sudum rutilare vident et pulsa tonare.
    —Virgil *Aen.* VIII. 528–9.

Circumque feratur
Aeterna cum luce dies, qui tempora monstrat
Nunc his nunc illis eadem regionibus orbis.
    —Manilius I. 189–91.

Et ver autumno, brumae miscebitur aestas,
Atque eadem regio vesper et ortus erit.
    —Ovid *Ibis* 37–8.

Nam quantum subiecta situ tellus iacet infra
Diuiditurque ab humo conuexi regia caeli.
    —Prudentius *Sym.* II. 125–6.

1505   Et quoniam tres in partes distinguitur in aer,
Prima æque patiens est frigoris atque caloris,
Alternasque vices alterna sorte rependit,
Vere tepens, æstate calens, eadem horrida bruma;

---

[1]See also CLIMATE AND CLIME, EMPIRE, KINGDOM, REIGN.

Region—*continued*

        Proxima, ab inflexu radiorum amota, malignum
        Frigus et algentem late complexa rigorem,
        In quam cœruleus passim vapor actus inerrat,
        Unde cadunt himbres, unde et nix concitat alas;
        Ultima torrenti semper sitit usta calore,
        Flammarum consueta vagos involvere tortus.
        Halitus ille igitur longe validusque potensque
        Huc penetrat, superatque hiemes et frigora victor.
        —Pontano *Meteor.* 551–62.

1544   L'Aulbe estaingnoit Estoilles a foison,
        Tirant le jour des regions infimes.
        —Scève 31.

1578   Trassant de l'air venteux la region humide.
        —Ronsard VI. 177.

1585   Des astres tournoyans l'influance diverse
        Passe de part en part sans nul empeschement
        Le difane corps du plus chaud element,
        Les regions de l'air, le transparant de l'onde.
        —Du Bartas *I Sem.* II. 350–3.

        La rosee, le vent, et la pluye, et le glas
        Se creassent en l'air moitoyen, haut et bas.
        —*Ibid.* II. 459–60.

1590   Which threatned more than if the region
        Next vnderneath the Element of fire,
        Were full of Commets and of blazing stars.
        —Marlowe *Tambur.* 4199–4201.

1605   Th' Aerie Regions euer-lasting Frost.
        —Sylvester *Div. Wks.* (*2d Day*) 53.

1609   And first, she past the region of the ayre,
        And of the fire, whose substance thin and slight,
        Made no resistance.
        —Spenser *F. Q.* VII. vi. 7.

1613   Tyranno el Sacre de lo meno puro
        Desta primer region, sañudo espera
        La desplumada ia, la breue esphera.
        —Góngora II. 118.

1620   Deese engendre-amours, germeuse Citheree,
        Qui par les regions de la voulte Etheree
        Fais ta ronde eternelle en ton char radieux.
        —Hesteau *Poème Phil.* 58.

1633   She carries no desire to know, nor sense,
        Whether th'ayres middle region be intense;

Region—*continued*

For th'Element of fire, she doth not know,
Whether she past by such a place or no.
—Donne *Progr. of the Soule* (*2d Anniver.* 191–4).

1640   As when a Spring-conducting pipe is broke,
The waters at a little breach breake out,
And hissing, through the aiery Region spout.
—Sandys *Ovid's Met.* 66.

1651   To Streets (the People's Region) early Fame
First brought this grief, which all more tragick make.
—Davenant *Gond.* II. ii. 1.

Me thinks, they through the Middle Region come;
Their Chariots hid in Clouds of Dust below.
—*Ibid.* III. iii. 19.

1656   When as his body dead, perhaps his soul
May transmigrate into some winged foul,
And Feather'd so may sore aloft, and fly
With nimble plumes amid the middle sky.
—T. Harvey *Mantuan* 17.

1668   Is there no temperate Region can be known,
Betwixt their Frigid, and our Torrid Zone?
—Denham *Cooper's Hill* 139–40.

1671   For Satan with slye preface to return
Had left him vacant, and with speed was gon
Up to the middle Region of thick Air.
—Milton *P. R.* II. 115–17.

1693   And as five zones th' ethereal regions bind,
Five, correspondent, are to earth assign'd.
—Dryden *Ovid's Met.* I. 52–3.

1698   Jove's bird comes sousing down from upper air.
—Dryden *Aen.* IX. 762.

1712   Hence the Melodious Tenants of the Sky,
.   Which haunt Inferior Seats, or soar on high,
With Ease thro' all the Fluid Region stray.
—Blackmore *Creation* II. 651–3.

1716   Dans les Régions Planetaires
Les Globes décrivant leurs Routes circulaires.
—Genest *Prin. Phil.* 89.

1515 Audium equidem quendam eorum [piscium]: qui maritimis in regionibus uersantur Equoreum Herniaceum commemorantem.—Argyropolus
Basil XXXIIII.

Region—*continued*

1547 Regiones aeris in quibus meteora fiunt, tres statuuntur: suprema cali-
dissima, media frigidissima, & infima quæ supra terræ & aquæ superficiem iacet, temperata, magis minúsue, prout Sol ad nos accedit, uel
recedit.—Mizaldus *Meteor.* 8.

1555 [Snow] is a moyst vapour, drawen vp to the middle region of the ayre,
then thycked, and frosen into the body of a cloude. So congelated,
descendeth.—Dygges *Prognost.* 28.

1571 In the hyghest region, be generated Cometes or blasing starres, and
suche lyke of diuerse sortes. In the midle region cloudes, rayne,
stormes, wyndes. &. In the lowest region, dewe, frost, horefrost,
mistes, bryght rods.—Fulke *Meteors* A₆.

1588 Vnde verò hæc materia illis [cometis] in Ætherea Mundi Regione
suppetat.—Brahe *Mundi Æth.* 254.

1600 Cur magnes in polis suis diuersâ ratione robustior sit; tam in borealibus
regionibus, qùam australibus.—W. Gilbert *Magnete* 105.

1614 The ayre passeth and spreadeth it selfe from the ætheriall & cleere
region, as farre as the earth, more swift, more subtile, and higher then
the earth and waters.—Lodge *Seneca* 782.

1623 In mediam aeris regionem feruntur halitus, ibique in nubes coguntur,
quæ decidunt & fœcundant terram. Cerebrum est analogum mediæ
isti aeris regioni, quique vapores è visceribus delati inibi frigescunt,
indeque velut in pluuias soluti destillant.—Alsted *Theol. Nat.* 594.

1630 Il y auoit un canal depuis le centre de la terre iusques bien auant dans
la region du feu.—Rey *Essais* 20.

1644 La region superieur est celle qui est proche de la region du feu & la
touche . . . . Sa chaleur est aidée par le voisinage de la region du feu.
—Du Moulin *Phys.* 76–7.

1651 For there is nothing to the contrary, why we should not hold, that they
[celestial waters] also exhale, and are spread abroad into the thinner
region of the stars.—Comenius *Nat. Phil. Ref.* 128.

1657 The Method which I shall follow in this ensuing Treatise, shall be
according to that which Anatomists use in Mans body, which they
divide into four parts, viz. The upper, middle, and lower Regions;
and lastly, the Limbs.—Coles *Adam in Eden* 1.

1668 We have travell'd those upper Regions by the help of our Tubes.—
Glanvill *Plus Ultra* 113.

1675 Anaxagoras would have these kind of Meteors to be sparkles falling
from the fiery Region.—Sherburne *Sphere* 61.

1683 Nor is there scarce any part of Nature more full of Wonders than these
liquid Regions.—Tryon *Way to Health* 142.

Region—*continued*

1687   The World is the Highest Heaven, and whatever it contains, it is
       divided into the Sublunary Region, and the Cœlestial [regionem sub-
       lunarem, & cœlestem].—Abercromby *Acad. Sci.* 44, 45.

1693   The Airy regions every where at the same height would be equally re-
       plenished with the proportion of Water it would contain, regard being
       only to be had to the different degree of warmth, from the nearness or
       distance of the Sun.—*Phil. Trans.* XVII. 470.

1709   The greater the quantity of Vapours raised is, and withal the more
       intense the Cold of those airy Regions, the greater is the quantity of
       Rain.—*Phil. Trans.* XXVI. 342–3.

1719   La moienne Region de l'Air demeure assez tranquile dans le même
       tems que sa partie inferieure est agitée par des Vents violents.—Roubais
       Diss. Phys. 16–17.

Reign[1]

       Tenet ille immania saxa,
       Vestras, Eure, domos; illa se iactet in aula
       Aeolus et clauso ventorum carcere regnet.
           —Virgil *Aen.* I. 139–41.

       Totus iam denique mundus
       Axis & unda fuit, nam cunctis morte subactis
       Regnabant pelagi syluoso gurgite monstra.
           —Avitus *Orig. Mundi* 65.

1572   Quero que aja no reino Neptunino
       Onde eu nasci, progenie forte & bella.
           —Camoens *Lus.* 151b.

1596   Like as a fearefull Doue, which through the raine,
       Of the wide aire her way does cut amaine.
           —Spenser *F. Q.* III. iv. 49.

1600   Acquainted well with all the damned rout
       Of Pluto's reign, ev'n from his tender age.
           —E. Fairfax *Tasso* IV. xx.

1613   Clarissimo ninguno
       De los que el Reino muran de Neptuno.
           —Góngora II. 110.

1638   If in the reign of silent night abroad
       She rang'd, the Empress of the lowest sphere,
       Amazed at her perfections, left her road.
           —Whiting, in *CP* III. 440.

---

[1]See also EMPIRE, KINGDOM, REGION.

Reign—*continued*

1647   Malignant Stars, and furious winds may raigne,
        Burying the ships in the vast watry plaine.
                —Stanley *Oronta* 6.

1656   Entre le haut des Cieux, & le bas de la Terre,
        Dans la plaine estendüe où regne le Tonnerre,
        Habite la Terreur.
                —Chapelain *Pucelle* 116.

1671   Princes, Heavens antient Sons, Æthereal Thrones,
        Demonian Spirits now, from the Element
        Each of his reign allotted, rightlier call'd,
        Powers of Fire, Air, Water, and Earth beneath.
                —Milton *P. R.* II. 121–4.

1698   Escap'd the dangers of the wat'ry reign,
        Yet more and greater ills by land remain.
                —Dryden *Aen.* VI. 129–30.

1713   As bright a Goddess, and as chaste a Queen;
        Whose care, like hers, protects the sylvan reign.
                —Pope *Win. For.* 162–3.

Rural

1578   De sa Mere l'apprentif
        Peut de son luc deceptif
        Tromper les bandes rurales.
                —Ronsard III. 379.

1596   Who when they heard that pitteous strained voice,
        In hast forsooke their rurall meriment.
                —Spenser *F. Q.* I. vi. 8.

1602   The Rurall rout,
        All round about,
        Like Bees came swarming thicke, to heare him sing.
                —A. W., in *Poet. Rhaps.* I. 40.

1613   Shrill as a thrush upon a morn of May,
        (A rural music for an heavenly train).
                —W. Browne *Brit. Past.* I. iii. 398–9.

1640   Who oft deceiv'd the Satyrs that pursu'd,
        The rurall Gods, and those whom Woods include.
                —Sandys *Ovid's Met.* 7.

1652   Oracle of rural loves!
        Speaking shade! soul of the Groves!
                —Stanley *Poems* 196.

1667   The smell of Grain, or tedded Grass, or Kine,
        Or Dairie, each rural sight, each rural sound.
                —Milton *P. L.* IX. 450–1.

Rural—*continued*

1668   Nay the Birds rural musick too
                Is as melodious and free,
                As if they sung to pleasure you.
                    —Cowley 70.

1687   With rural pipe himself can please,
                And charm his wand'ring sheep.
                    —Ayres, in *CP* II. 332.

1698   Of oaken twigs they twist an easy bier,
                Then on their shoulders the sad burden rear.
                The body on this rural hearse is borne.
                    —Dryden *Aen.* XI. 95–7.

1713   The rural Pow'rs confess'd their meaner Lays,
                When Thyrsis sung, and own'd his juster Praise.
                    —Diaper *Dryades* 4.

Rustic

1544   Or passeront maintz siecles & saisons,
                Et les outilz des rustique maisons
                Se changeront auant (ie te promectz)
                Qu' un si clair uiz se mire en toy iamais.
                    —J. Martin *Sannazaro* 105.

1578   Ainsi servant à tous par si belle pratique,
                Eussions gaigné les cœurs de la troupe rustique.
                    —Ronsard V. 238.

1585   De la douce musette, elle boult, elle dance,
                Suyvant de point en point la rustique cadance.
                    —Du Bartas *I Sem.* III. 237–8.

1596   With whom he myndes for euer to remaine,
                And set his rest amongst the rusticke sort.
                    —Spenser *F. Q.* VI. x. 2.

1605   The rauisht Fountaine falls to daunce and bound,
                Keeping true Cadence to his rustike sound.
                    —Sylvester *Div. Wks.* (*3d Day*) 84.

1640   Sad Achelous now his rustick face
                And maymed head within the current shrouds.
                    —Sandys *Ovid's Met.* 164.

1656   There's now no need to follow rustick Pan,
                Or any rural Gods.
                    —T. Harvey *Mantuan* 78.

1667   Ith' midst an Altar as the Land-mark stood
                Rustic, of grassie sord.
                    —Milton *P. L.* XI. 432–3.

Rustic—*continued*

1678   See, see, how from the thatchèd rooms
                  Of these our artless cabins, comes
                  A rustic troop of jolly swains.
                  —K. Philips, in *CP* I. 605.

Scaly kind

NOTE.—A single quotation from Creech (1697) may serve as an illustration of the poetical use of the epithet *scaly* in the description of fish:

          And He that then is born shall be inclin'd
          To spoil the Sea, and kill the Scaly Kind.[1]

It does not seem necessary to give here the innumerable examples of the term in poetry which will be found under the periphrases for *fish* (see pp. 367–70). It is necessary, however, to establish the meaning of the epithet in scientific writing before listing the prose uses of the word.

Scaly as an epithet in the scientific description of fishes derived from a scheme of classification which came down from Aristotle and endured to the time of John Ray, in the later seventeenth century, when, indeed, it was modified rather than displaced.   Aristotle first divided animals into two groups, those with, and those without, blood.   The animals with blood were subdivided into three classes, quadrupeds, birds, and fish.   These three classes were also regarded as *vivipares* and *ovipares*. 'Ιχθύες were either fish or whales. The bloodless animals were separated into those with soft outsides (mollusks) and those with soft insides (crustaceans, testaceans, and insects).[2]   Within these primary divisions means existed for distinguishing smaller groups.   Fish, for instance, were classified and named according to the nature of their habitats.   Walter Charleton, in his distinguished book *Onomasticon Zoicon* (1668), used this method:

MARINI seu *Pelagii*, ut ab iis initium capiamus, sunt vel (I.) πετραῖοι, *Saxatiles*, qui inter saxa & promontoria vivunt . . . .   (2.) Αἰγιαλώδες, *Littorales*, qui non in aquis profundis, sed circa Littora versantur: (3.) Πελάγιοι, *Pelagii*, in alto mari degentes.[3]

Aristotle, also, distinguishes among fish by their skins.   The same scheme was adopted by Charleton: " *Tegumentorum* ratione, quidam *Squammosi* sunt; quidam *Cute* tecti, eaque vel *Aspera*, vel *Lævi*."[4]   The epithet *squammosi*, then, applied to river fishes (*fluviatiles*), distinguishes scaly ones from smooth ones, such as eels, and, applied to other classes, distinguishes scaly fish from those with other types of skin.   So we find Robert Plot writing in 1686: "But for *breeding* and *living*, there is no fish so wonderfull amongst all the *scaly* or *shelly* kinds, as there is amongst the smooth ones, viz. the common *Eele* . . . ."[5]

---

[1]*Manilius* (Bk. V) 81.

[2]See Léon-Henri-Marie Carleer, *Examen des Principales Classifications Adoptées par les Zoologistes* (Brussels, 1861) 10, 14.

[3]P. 120.   For Aristotle's classification see *De Animal. Hist.* 488b7, in *Opera* III. 4.

[4]P. 119.   Compare *De Animal. Hist.* 505a25, in *Opera* III. 28.

[5]*Stafford.* 242.   Bradley was speaking of fish when he wrote "the *Squameous* or *Scaley* Kind," but one of his chapter headings used the same epithet for reptiles:

Scaly kind—*continued*

Piscium feminae maiores quam mares. in quodam genere omnino non sunt mares, sicut erythinis et channis, omnes enim ovis gravidae capiuntur. vagantur gregatim fere cuiusque generis squamosi.—Pliny *Nat. Hist.* IX. xxiii. § 56.

1552   *Cortex, φωλίς. Squama, λεπίς.* Cortice autem integuntur quæ ouipara sunt pedestria, appellanturque φολιδωτὰ: squama uero pisces tantum, sicuti penna aues.—Wotton *Differ.* 16b.

1596   Sunt enim piscium duo summa genera, alterum quidem læue, alterum scabrum: huius item quattuor genera, scilicet testaceum, crustaceum, squammatum, & aculeatum.—Bodin *Theat.* 322.

1601   The creatures that breed and live in the water, bee not all covered and clad alike: for some have a skin over them, and the same hairie, as the Seales and Water-horses. Others have but a bare skin, as the Dolphins. There be againe that have a shell like a barke, as the Tortoises: and in others, the shell is as hard as the flint, and such be the oysters, muscles, cockles, and winkles. Some be covered with crusts or hard pills, as the locusts: others have besides them, sharpe prickes, as the Vrchins. Some be skaled, as fishes.—Holland *Pliny* I. 242 (Bk. IX, chap. xii).

1606   Quartus ordo continet Pisces compressos, squamosos, & litorales, vt Aurata ab auri colore, Sparus, Cantharus.—Daneau *Phys. Christ.* 206b.

1621   Fishes are soft, or hard: the soft haue scales, or onely a skin. Of the scalie be the Carpe, the Pearch. Of the slimie be Eelles.—Widdowes *Nat. Phil.* 63.

1631   Piscis est animal in aquis, & sub aquis degens. & propriè pro eo vsurpatur, quod squamis tegitur, vt ex Plinio constat lib. 9. ca. 12. Græcis ἰχθὺς. Omnia autem in aquis degentia aquatilia nuncupantur, & distinguuntur à terrestribus animalibus. Sunt autem tegmina aquatilium varia. alia enim corio & pilis operiuntur, vt vituli, hippotami: alia corio tantum, vt Delphini: cortice, vt testudines: silicum duritie, vt conchæ, ostrea. Crustis, vt locustæ: Spinis, vt Echini; Squamis, vt pisces. Quamuis Piscium nomen aliquando sit generale pro quouis aquatili.—Beierlynck *Theat.* VI. 355.

"Of SERPENTS, the CROCODILE, LIZARD, CAMELION, and others of the Scaley Tribe, which are Amphibious, and Inhabitants of the Land."—*Works of Nature* (1726) 71. The ambiguity was probably a matter of translation.

According to Aristotle, most fishes were λεπιδωτοί (*squamati*), whereas serpents were φολιδωτοί (*squarrosi*) (*De Animal Hist.* 505a25 and 490b24, in *Opera* III. 28 and 7). Though he generally used the epithet with a noun, as οἱ ἰχθύες οἱ λεπιδωτοί (*De Gener. Animal.* 733a28, in *Opera* III. 346), he sometimes employed it without a noun as a synonym for fish: πολλοῖς τῶν λεπιδωτῶν (*De Part. Animal.* 670b2, in *Opera* III. 265). He also used τὰ φολιδωτὰ without a noun (*De Respir.* 475b22, in *Opera* III. 544).

Seneca may have been taking advantage of the same ambiguity when he called serpents "squamifera turba" (*Medea* 685). Sherburne's translation was "scaly Multitudes" (*Medea* [1648] 38).

Scaly kind—*continued*

1661 Fishes, which are, 1. Marine, and these are either pelagious, living in the main sea, and either scaled; as the Linge ... or smooth, as the tunie ... or saxatile, living neer stones, and are squammose.—Lovell *Panzoologico*. A₆b.

1667 Nec libenter pisces, ut & reliqui greges animalium, ex nativis suis locis demigrant longinque, sed amant commorari, velut in patria & ad-haerere suae agnatae familiae, in genitalibus suis aquis, gentilique salo. Unde fit ut in diversis aquis diversae species generis squamati inveniantur, & piscatu educantur.—Milius *Orig. Animal.* 53.

1674 Fluviatiles: River Fishes, and such as live in standing pools and ponds of Water.   Squamosi; Scaly.—Ray *Eng. Words* 110.

1677 A Fish of the squammous kind, which they call a Finscale.—Plot *Oxford.* 184.

1712 The Fish here called a Shallow, found in the Cherwell and other of our Rivers, as also in Ponds, as at Astwell, a Scaly Fish, in shape betwixt a Roache and a Bream.—Morton *Northampton.* 419.

1726 The Squameous or Scaley Kind of them lay their Eggs or Spawn in shallow Water.—Bradley *Works of Nature* 59.

Scour

1596 Vnwont with heards to watch, or pasture sheepe,
But to forray the land, or scoure the deepe.
    —Spenser *F. Q.* VI. xi. 40.

1600 Some troops of horse that lightly armed ride,
He sent to scour the woods and forests main.
    —E. Fairfax *Tasso* I. lxxiv.

1611 Hee ierks his Iades, and makes them scour amain,
Through thick and thin, both over Hill and Plain.
    —Sylvester *Div. Wks.* (*Decay*) 621.

1613 The Midland Sea so swiftly was she scouring,
The Adriatic gulf brave ships devouring.
    —W. Browne *Brit. Past.* II. i. 923–4.

1640 Then down the Hill of Heaven they scoure amain.
    —Sandys *Ovid's Met.* 26.

1659 The field, scoured by the beastly rage
O' the savage clowns, had left no foe to engage.
    —W. Chamberlayne *Phar.* II. i. 323–4.

1667 Puts on swift wings, and toward the Gates of Hell
Explores his solitary flight; som times
He scours the right hand coast, som times the left.
    —Milton *P. L.* II. 631–3.

Scour—*continued*

1682   They steal not, but in squadrons scour the plain.
                —Dryden *Medal* 243.

1698   Full thirty ships transport the chosen train
                For Troy's relief, and scour the briny main.
                —Dryden *Aen.* X. 306–7.

1713   The Dewlap'd Bull now scow'rs throughout the Plains.
                —Gay *Rural Sports* 13.

Scud

1600   The fleecie Flocks doo scud and skip.
                —W. H., in *Eng. Helicon* I. 67.

1605   As through the Oceans cleere and liquid Flood
                The slipperie Fishes vp and downe doo scud.
                —Sylvester *Div. Wks.* (*2d Day*) 67.

1613   The trout within the weeds did scud.
                —W. Browne *Brit. Past.* I. ii. 153.

1622   The darling daughter borne of loftie Penigent,
                Who from her fathers foot, by Skipton downe doth scud,
                And leading thence to Leeds, that delicatest Flood.
                —Drayton *Poly-Olb.* XXVIII. 54–6.

1648   Then let thy active hand scu'd o're the Lyre.
                —Herrick 67.

1652   The pleasant grove triumphs with blooming May,
                While Melancholy scuds away.
                —Benlowes *Theoph.* XII. lxix.

1667   And scudding thence, while they their horn-feet ply,
                About their sires the little silvans cry.
                —Dryden *Ind. Emp.* II. i, in *Works* II. 343.

1675   Whilst the glad Fish to the lov'd Waters scud.
                —Sherburne *Sphere* 22.

Seed[1]

NOTE.—Aristotle reports that Anaxagoras considered the four elements to be really collections of all kinds of seeds. Each element was πανσπερμία.[2] Epicurus and Democritus adopted this theory, but for them the words σπέρματα and *semina* signified atoms.[3] Lucretius denied any essential distinction between the living and the nonliving, and consequently his use of *semina* was

---

[1]See also BAND, BREED, BROOD, CHOIR, CITIZEN, CREW, ELEMENT, FLOCK, FRY, HERD, HOST, INHABITANT, KIND, LEGION, NATION, PEOPLE, RACE, SHOAL, SQUADRON, TRAIN, TRIBE, TROOP.

[2]*De Gener. et Corrupt.* 314a29, in *Works* II. 432.

[3]See Katharine C. Reiley, *Studies in the Philosophical Terminology of Lucretius and Cicero* (New York, 1909) 39–40.

Seed—*continued*

free from the notion that each seed is an animalcule. But in the passage of
time, with the acceptance of the theory of a universe based on the interaction
of the four elements and with teleological beliefs generally and strongly held,
it was difficult to maintain the bare Lucretian notion. Fracastoro, for example, studied Lucretius to good effect, and learned much to help him
to attack the problem of contagious disease. The phenomena of life appeared
to him as the products of atomic activity, but for many of those following
Fracastoro "atoms" became in their turn animalcules.[1]

The poetic use of the word *seed* in the seventeenth century may be referred
very often to some development of these ancient theories. Such allusions will
be partly explained by the quotations from scientific writers that follow, but
at this place slightly more extended comment may prove helpful as a gloss
to certain poetic uses.

Cowley's line, for example, "Clouds where seeds of Thunder ly,"[2] is to be
explained according to Epicurean theory:

For that the nature of thunder is fiery is manifest, even because it often burneth
the houses upon which it is darted, and for that it leaveth behind it a stench like
brimstone. That it is generated within the clowds, is evident, for that it never
thunders when the sky is clear . . . . Lastly, that many little bodies or seeds, as
it were, of fire, are contained within a clowd, may be argued, as well from the
effect, as for that amongst the little bodies of a cloud rising up from beneath, are
intermingled, not onely watery, but fiery also, and of other sorts. Withall, it
cannot be, but that the clowd must receive many things from the beams of the
Sun. When therefore the blast or wind which drove the clowds together, hath
intermingled it self with the seeds of fire, that are in the bosom, as it were, and
cavity of the cloud, there is caused a whirling or vortex within it, which being
carried about very rapidly, groweth hot by motion; and either by intension of this
heat, or the contagion of some other fire, breaketh out into perfect thunder, and
tearing the clowd is darted forth.[3]

The phrase *seeds of fire* may be explained by Sherburne's note on his translation of Manilius:

> Whether from fiery Seeds inclos'd in Earth,
> And thence emitted, Comets draw their Birth:

Comets to come from a sulphureous unctuous ignescent matter exhaling from the
Earth and Sea, &c. *Vide Aristotel. Meteor. l.i. c.7.* and 10.[4]

And for the theory that stars were seeds of fire scattered by the sun, Sherburne
gives as authorities Xenophanes and Minucius Felix.[5]

One further development of the seminal theory may be mentioned here,
since it is rather strange to modern readers. This is the notion that minerals
grow from seed. There are any number of references to the idea in neoclassic
poetry. One such description occurs in Dryden:

---

[1]See Charles Singer, *From Magic to Science* (London: E. Benn, 1928), 8.
[2]*Poems* 330.
[3]Stanley *Hist. Phil. III* (5th Part 220).
[4]*Sphere* 62.
[5]*Ibid.* 14.

Seed—*continued*

> As those who unripe veins in mines explore,
> On the rich bed again the warm turf lay,
> Till time digests the yet imperfect ore,
> And know it will be gold another day.[1]

This theory will be explained in the following quotations, but it may be remarked here that such a notion did not belong merely to the older science but was restored and given increasing importance at the end of the seventeenth century, by Tournefort.[2]

ὡς δ' ὅτε τις δαλὸν σποδιῇ ἐνέκρυψε μελαίνῃ
ἀγροῦ ἐπ' ἐσχατιῆς, ᾧ μὴ πάρα γείτονες ἄλλοι,
σπέρμα πυρὸς σώζων, ἵνα μὴ ποθεν ἄλλοθεν αὔοι.
—Homer *Odys.* V. 488–90. (As a man hides
a brand beneath the dark embers in an outlying
farm, a man who has no neighbours, and so saves
a seed of fire, that he may not have to kindle it
from some other source.—Tr. A. T. Murray.)

σύ τ', 'Ινάχειον σπέρμα, τοὺς ἐμοὺς λόγους
θυμῷ βάλ'.
—Aeschylus *Prom.* 705–6. (And thou,
O seed of Inachus, take my words to heart.)

Ergo fervidus hic nubem cum perscidit atram,
Dissipat ardoris quasi per vim expressa repente
Semina quae faciunt nictantia fulgura flammae.
—Lucretius VI. 180–2.

τῆς κηρύλου δάμαρτος ἀπτῆνα σπόρον.
—Lycophron *Alex.* 750. (The
tiny unfledged seed of the halcyon's
bride.)

At rabidae tigres absunt et saeva leonum
Semina.
—Virgil *Geo.* II. 151–2.

Ut uoluit credi, qui primus moenia mundi
Seminibus struxit minimis inque illa resoluit.
—Manilius I. 486–7.

Natus homo est, sive hunc divino semine fecit
Ille opifex rerum, mundi melioris origo,
Sive recens tellus seductaque nuper ab alto
Aethere cognati retinebat semina caeli.
—Ovid *Met.* I. 78–81.

---

[1]*Ann. Mir.* cxxxix. For other allusions to this theory see W. Browne *Brit. Past.*
II. v. 99–102; May *Lucan* R₂; Davenant *Gond.* II. iv. 14; Thomson *Summer* 1107;
Pope *Win. For.* 393–6.

[2]See Honoré Maria Lauthier, *Lettre à Monsieur Begon . . . Contenant un Abregé de
la Vie de M. De Tournefort* (Paris, 1717), 22.

Seed—*continued*

> Promissus Abrahae patri
> Eiusque in aeuum semini.
> —Prudentius *Cath.* XII. 43–4.

> Now, ladi bryghte, sith thou canst and wilt
> Ben to the seed of Adam merciable.
> —Chaucer *A B C* 181–2.

ante
1557

> Ce petit Dieu, qui enflamme
> Des Dieux le plus furieux,
> Enferma dedans tes yeux
> Les semences de sa flamme.
> —Du Bellay V. 286.

1558

> Les semences qui sont meres de toutes choses,
> Retourneront encor' à leur premier discord,
> Au ventre du Chaos eternellement closes.
> —Du Bellay II. 22.

1578

> O germe de Venus, enfant Idalien.
> —Ronsard II. 189.

1584

> C'est donques à bon droict que l'humaine semence
> Porte de son peché la dure penitence.
> —Du Bartas *Impost.* 593–4.

1596

> Be it worthy of thy race and royall sead.
> —Spenser *F. Q.* III. ii. 33.

1605

> I'le kindle warre betweene the Womans seed
> And thy fell race.
> —Sylvester *Div. Wks.* (*Deceipt*) 316.

1611

> Nor sate great Iuno ignorant, when she beheld, alone,
> Old Nereus siluer-footed seed, with Ioue.
> —Chapman *Il.* 12.

1627

> Happy who quells that rising Babel seed!
> —P. Fletcher *Locusts* V. xl.

1638

> But know at first 'twas but an homely weed,
> Her presence made it holy, not its seed.
> —Whiting, in *CP* III. 473.

1640

> Iustling the stones, and minerals which have
> The seede of fire, inkindled with their rage.
> —Sandys *Ovid's Met.* 274.

1656

> With open shells in seas, on heauenly due
> A shining oister lushiouslie doth feed,
> And then the Birth of that ætheriall seed
> Shows, when conceau'd, if skies lookt darke or blew.
> —Drummond II. 185.

Seed—*continued*

1667   In this deep quiet, from what source unknown,
Those seeds of fire their fatal birth disclose;
And first, few scatt'ring sparks about were blown,
Big with the flames that to our ruin rose.
—Dryden *Ann. Mir.* ccxvii.

1668   Not Winds to Voyagers at Sea,
Nor Showers to Earth more necessary be,
(Heav'ens vital seed cast on the womb of Earth
To give the fruitful Year a Birth).
—Cowley 182.

1671   For never was from Heaven imparted
Measure of strength so great to mortal seed.
—Milton *S. A.* 1438–9.

1697   For Earthy Mists involving Seeds of Flame
May rise on high, and fiery Comets frame.
—Creech *Manilius* (Bk. I) 34.

1700   Great was th' effect, and high was his intent,
When peace among the jarring seeds he sent.
Fire, flood, and earth, and air by this were bound.
—Dryden *Pal. and Arc.* III. 1026–8.

1712   Here in their Beds the finish'd Minerals rest,
There the rich Wombs the Seeds of Gold digest.
—Blackmore *Creation* I. 456–7.

1604   Plutarchus clarissimè: τὸ πῦρ σπέρμα λέγουσιν εἶναι τοῦ κόσμου: Ignem semen aiunt Mundi.—Lipsius *Physiol. Stoic.* 135.

1606   Omnium igitur metallorum mater communis est ipsa Terra, quemadmodum & Iob. 28. vers. 1. & 2. & Deut. 8. vers. 9. perspicuè demonstratur. Nam illa suppeditat communem omnibus materiam, quâ constant, nempe halitum quendam viscosum, sed humidiorem tamen eo, ex quo lapides concrescunt. Hic igitur viscosus halitus lapideo humidior in locis subterraneis & in mediis ipsius terræ visceribus vi quadam syderum & calore Solis è Terra exprimitur primum: postea verò frigore in eadem terra concrescit, & cum sicco terrestri permiscetur, ac agglutinatur. Vnde fit, vt pro diuersa ratione istius mixtionis, diuersa quoque ex eodem illo lento, pingui & viscoso humore metallorum genera nascantur atque producantur.—Daneau *Phys. Christ.* 103.

1630   Semen illud Solis est lumen, quod in aëra spargitur.—Alsted *Encyclo.* 691.

1650   [Water] is the menstruum of the world, which penetrating the Aire, by means of heat, drawes along with it selfe a warm vapour, which causeth a naturall generation of those things, which the Earth, as a matrix is impregnated withall, and when the matrix receives a due proportion of Seed, of what kind soever, it proceeds, and Nature workes without intermission to the end.—French *Sandivogius* 86.

Seed—*continued*

1651   Now the seed (kernell or graine) is nothing else, but the image of the whole plant, gathered together into a very small part of the matter; from whence, if need be, the same plant may be produced again.— Comenius *Nat. Phil. Ref.* 154.

1655   It is even so with the World, for it was originally made of a seed, of a seminall viscuous Humidity or Water, but that Seed (as we have said in our Aphorisms) disappeared in the Creation, for the Spirit of God that moved upon it that transform'd it, and made the World of it. Howsoever that very World doth now yield and bring forth out of its own Body a secondary seed, which is the very same in Essence and substance with that primitive generall seed whereof the World was made.   And if any man shall ask, what use Nature makes of this generall seed, and wherefore she yields it?   I answer, that it is not to make another World of it, but to maintain that World with it which is made already; For God-Allmighty hath so Decreed, that his Creatures are nourished with the very same matter whereof they were formed.— T. Vaughan *Euphrates* 24–5.

For this thing is not Water, otherwise than to the sight, but a coagulable fat Humidity, or a mixture of Fire, Aire, and pure Earth, overcast indeed with Water, and therefore not seen of any, nor known but to few . . . .   In the Bowells of the Earth it is congealed by a sulphurious heat into Metalls, and if the place of its congelation be pure, then into a bright Metall, for this Sperme is impregnated with light, and is full of the Star-fire, from whence all Metalls have their Lustre.   The same might be said of Pearles and Precious Stones, this starrie seed being the Mother of them all; for when it is Minerallised by it self, and without any sæculent mixture, then *Vomit igniculos suos*, it sheds and shoots its Fires, and hath so much of Heaven, that if we did not know the Conspiracy, we should wonder how it could love the Earth.—*Ibid.* 27–9.

1656   In the Earth are contained the seeds and seminal virtues of all Elementary bodies.—Culpeper *Treat. Aurum Potab.* 35–6.

1659   The Sun is a kind of fountain, into which there flow together from beneath on every side perpetuall rivolets; for the seeds of heat throughout the whole world flow so into the Sun, as that immediately from him, as from one fountain or head, both heat and light overfloweth every way.—Stanley *Hist. Phil. III* (*5th part* 215).

1664   First, then, we have not those narrow conceptions of these subtle Spirits to think that they are onely included within the Bodies of Animals, or generated (much less created) there, but we doe believe that they are universally diffused throughout all Bodies in the World, and that Nature at first created this aetherial substance or subtle particles, and diffused them throughout the Universe, to give fermentation and concretion to Minerals; vegetation and maturation to Plants; life, sense, and motion to Animals; And indeed, to be the main (though invisible)

Seed—*continued*

Agent in all Natures three Kingdoms, Mineral, Vegetal, and Animal. —Power *Exper. Phil.* 61.

1674 Terram Semine quodam Universali, omnia fœcundante, imprægnari, jam olim recepta opinio est.—Mayow *Tract.* 7.

1693 All Vegetables we see do proceed *ex Plantula*, the Seeds of Vegetables being nothing else but little Plants of the same kind folded up in Coats and Membranes: and from hence we may probably conjecture that so curiously an organized Creature as an Animal, is not the sudden product of a Fluid or *Colliquamentum*, but does much rather proceed from an Animalcle of the same kind, and has all its little Members folded up according to their several Joynts and Plicatures, which are afterwards enlarged and distended, as we see in Plants.—*Phil. Trans.* XVII. 476.

1721 It seems, therefore, to me consonant to the Scripture, That God Almighty did at first create the Earth or Terraqueous Globe, containing in itself the Principles of all simple inanimate Bodies, or the minute and naturally indivisible Particles of which they were compounded, of various but a determinate number of Figures ... and these variously and confusedly commixed, as though they had been carelessly shaken and shuffled together; yet not so, but that there was Order observed by the most Wise Creator in the Disposition of them. And not only so, but that the same Omnipotent Deity did create also the Seeds or Seminal Principles of all Animate Bodies, both Vegetative and Sensitive; and dispers'd them, at least the Vegetative, all over the superficial Part of the Earth and Water. And the Notion of such an Earth as this is, the Primitive Patriarchs of the World delivered to their Posterity, who, by degrees annexing something of Fabulous to it, imposed upon it the Name of Chaos. The next Work of the Divine Power and Wisdom was the Separation of the Water from the dry Land and Raising up of the Mountains . . . . To which follows the Giving to both Elements a Power of hatching, as I may so say, or quickening and bringing to Perfection the Seeds they contained; first the more imperfect, as Hearbs and Trees; then the more perfect, Fish, Fowl, Four-footed Beasts, and creeping Things or Insects.—Ray *Physio-Theol.* 6–7.

Shoal[1]

1579 I sawe a shole of shepeheardes outgoe.
—Spenser *S. C.: May* 20.

1605 But th' Art of Man, not onely can compack
Features and formes that life and motion lack;
But also fill the Aire with painted shoales
Of flying Creatures (artificiall Fowles).
—Sylvester *Div. Wks. (6th Day)* 221.

---

[1]See also BAND, BREED, BROOD, CHOIR, CITIZEN, CREW, FLOCK, FRY, HERD, HOST, INHABITANT, KIND, LEGION, NATION, PEOPLE, RACE, SEED, SQUADRON, TRAIN, TRIBE, TROOP.

Shoal—*continued*

1622   He [the cormorant] under water goes, and so the
        Shoale pursues.
        —Drayton *Poly-Olb.* XXV. 131.

1633   A vagrant rout (a shoal of tatling daws).
        —P. Fletcher *Purple Isl.* VIII. xxii.

1647   And the Furies in a shole
        Come to fright a parting soule.
        —Herrick 348.

1659   Like a shoal of smaller fishes made
        So bold by number that they durst invade
        The big-bulked whale.
        —W. Chamberlayne *Phar.* III. v. 13–15.

1667   Forthwith the Sounds and Seas, each Creek & Bay
        With Frie innumerable swarme, and Shoales
        Of Fish that with thir Finns & shining Scales
        Glide under the green Wave.
        —Milton *P. L.* VII. 399–402.

1675   For streight the mighty Product of the Deep,
        As if awaken'd from their watry Sleep,
        Did now in numerous Shoals themselves display.
        —Traherne 241.

1690   Our lean faith
        Gives scandal to the Christians; they feed high:
        Then look for shoals of converts, when thou hast
        Reformed us into feasting.
        —Dryden *Don S.* I. i, in *Works* VII. 329.

1722   No Robber [fish] comes that preys on weaker Shoals.
        —Diaper *Oppian's Hal.* I. 1024.

Slide[1]

1591   And where the christall Thamis wont to slide
        In siluer channell, downe along the Lee.
        —Spenser *Ruines of Time* 134–5.

1600   Along their watery cheeks warm tears down slide.
        —E. Fairfax *Tasso* III. vii.

1614   Ships, hulks, and galleyes slide along the shore.
        —Mure I. 123.

1622   Melandidar, that brings
        Her flowe, where Conway forth into the Sea doth **slide**.
        —Drayton *Poly-Olb.* X. 42–3.

1633   A thousand Sail slide on the sleeping Wave.
        —Sylvester *Div. Wks.* (*Beth. Rescue*) 483.

---

[1]See also GLIDE.

Slide—*continued*

1642   And there a while abide,
          Where the deep Eagh and fishfull Dergh do slide.
          —Kynaston *Leo. and Syd.* 2932–3.

1651   [Nature] Fishes learns through streams to slide.
          —Stanley *Anacreon* 3.

1653   Fowl of the Heavens, and Fish that through the wet
          Sea-paths in shoals do slide.
          —Milton *Ps. viii* 21–2.[1]

1668   On no smooth Sphear the restless seasons slide.
          —Cowley 251.

1686   How smooth and pleasant is his way,
          Whilst Life's Meander slides away.
          —Flatman, in *CP* III. 319.

1700   Beneath the sliding sun thou runn'st thy race.
          —Dryden *Pal. and Arc.* III. 131.

Sluice[2]

NOTE.—I have found no passages in scientific writing that use the word *sluice* when describing the passage of tears from the eyes, but there are certain scientific uses of *foramen, conduit,* and *canal* which suggest a literal basis for the more extravagant poetic term and which are illustrated in the prose quotations below.

1593   She vail'd her eyelids, who, like sluices, stopt
          The crystal tide.
          —Shakespeare *V. and A.* 956–7.

1605   My Mouth, thine Eares, doth euer chastly vse
          With putting in hot Seed of actiue Loue;
          Which, streight thine Ear conueyeth (like a Sluce)
          Into thy Mouth.
          —John Davies of Hereford *Wit. Pilgr.* D.

1622   Each eye a tear-evacuating sluice.
          —Hannay *Sher. and Mar.* I. 603.

1633   As, when the Heav'ns, opening their Sluces wide,
          Poure sodain Showers, surrounding every side.
          —Sylvester *Div. Wks.* (*Beth. Rescue*) 482.

---

[1]Milton's use of *slide* (*Lyc.* 86) is referred to Ovid's "Ut celer admissa labitur amnis aquis" (*Am.* I. viii. 50) by A. S. Cook, "Four Notes," *Studies in Philology,* XVI (1919), 184–5. *Lapsus* must also have served as a model for later use. Milton's "liquid Lapse of murmuring Streams" (*P. L.* VIII. 263) is comparable to Horace's "fluminum lapsus" (*Odes* I. xii. 10).

[2]See also CONDUIT.

Sluice—*continued*

1648   Forbeare
        (In my short absence) to unsluce a teare.
            —Herrick 14.

1652   Eyes, keep your sluices ope; Heav'n best by tears is woo'd.
            —Benlowes *Theoph.* II. lxiv.

1667   Two other precious drops that ready stood,
        Each in thir chrystal sluce, hee ere they fell
        Kiss'd as the gracious signs of sweet remorse.
            —Milton *P. L.* V. 132–4.

1676   Give sorrow vent, and let the sluices go.
            —Dryden *Aureng-Zebe* V. i, in *Works* V. 285.

1681   Ope then mine Eyes your double Sluice,
        And practise so your noblest Use.
            —Marvell *Eyes and Tears* 45–6.

1692   The common Sluces of the Eyes
        To vent his mighty Passion won't suffice.
            —Norris 2.

1700   How lambent Flames from life's bright Lamp arise,
        And dart in emanations through the eyes;
        While from each Sluice, a briny Torrent pours,
        T' extinguish feav'rish Heats with ambient Show'rs.
            —Garth *Dispensary* 3.

1712   How the bright Sluces of Etherial Light
        Now shut, defend the Empire of the Night.
            —Blackmore *Creation* VII. 599–600.

1600   Propter quam causam natura sapientissima duplicem viam ad lacrymas
        expurgandas parauit, vna est per oculorum utrosque angulos, alia per
        nares. Etenim in vtraque extremitate tarsorum superna scilicet &
        inferna, bina in vnoquoque angulo foraminula apparent tam exigua
        atque angusta, vt vix in viuentium corporibus, aspectabilia sint; in
        cadaueribus autem omninò sensum effugiant: per quæ lacrymæ cum
        effunduntur exeunt, potissimùm autem per internum angulum quo vt
        decliuiore vtitur natura ad lacrymarum effluxum. alia autem atque
        adhuc patentior via nares sunt, in quarum summitate ad internum angu-
        lum foramina in osse insculpuntur tàm magna vt quiuis ea admiretur:
        quæ si attentè intuearis, insignes quidam canales tibi videbuntur eo loci
        ad hunc vsum excauati vt lacrymæ per nares expurgentur: quin etiam
        ductum quendam neruosum ab oculis in eiusmodi foramina ingredi
        videbis, quasi accomodatum canalem ad lacrymas in nares deriuandas.
        —H. Fabricius *De Visione* 25.

1622   The eyes are indued with two sorts of nerues or sinews, whereof the first
        are called *optici* in Greeke, and *visuales* in Latine, which is in English,
        sinewes pertaining to sight, whereof either eye hath one proper vnto it,

Sluice—*continued*

which differ from other sinewes, because they are neither of so sound and firme substance, but soft, and within full of little holes (albeit this hollownesse is not so euident in them that are dead) which are as small Conduit pipes and little gutters.—Banister *Guillemeau* A₁₀.

1622   The second vse [of glandulous flesh in the eye] is, to couer the little conduit in the corner of the eye, by the which the excrements and naturall superfluities are conueyed into the nose. This excrement is a thinne liquid humour, which floweth out in weeping, or laughing, and whensoeuer the braine doth dis-burthen it selfe of these superfluities. —*Ibid.* I₁₁₋₁₂.

1632   Est enim illic Foramen in inferioris palpebræ tarso, magnitudine quidem exiguum, sed profunditate summum, ex quo lachrymæ emanant. —Spigel *Hum. Cor.* 5.

1718   To the end that the external Membrane of the Eyes may not be dryed up, and wrinkled by the Air, and so not only the Motions of the Eyelids, but likewise the Sight it self obstructed; that there are Glands placed in one Corner of the Eye, and over it, which by several little Tubes, shed a continual Moisture upon the Eye, to make it smooth, and to secure the Membrane from too great a Dryness. And to the End, that the Countenance should not always appear Weeping and cover'd with Tears, that there are Passages contrived, by which this Humour at the usual Times can be discharged into the Nostrils. And the same Humour in extraordinary Occasions, being changed into a flood of Tears, we are then much more sensible of the Course of them into the Nostrils.—J. Chamberlayne *Nieuwentyt* I. 215–16.

Sounding

NOTE.—The full significance of *sounding* and of *vocal* can only be known through a study of the older theories of the nature of sound. A few of the more important concepts may be briefly indicated here.

According to Aristotle:

Voice . . . is a sound made by a living animal, and even then not with any part of it taken at random. But, since sound only occurs when something strikes something else in a certain medium, and this medium is the air, it is natural that only those things should have voice which admit the air . . . . So it is necessary that during respiration the air should be breathed in. So the blow given to the air breathed in by the soul in these parts against what is called the windpipe causes the voice. For not every sound made by a living creature is a voice, as we have said (for even those who cough are making a sound with their tongue), but that which strikes must possess a soul, and have some mental picture; for the voice is a sound which means something.[1]

Sound, itself, in the opinion of Pythagoras and Plato as well as of Aristotle, was incorporeal, "for it is not the air, but the figure bounding the air, or its

---

[1] *On the Soul* 420b10, 25–30 (LCL 117–19).

Sounding—*continued*

surface, that, in virtue of a certain sort of shock, becomes vocal sound."[1] For Democritus, however, sounds were "particles thrown off by the sonant body and conveyed by the medium of the air to the ear, and through it 'to the soul'."[2]

Both of these notions survived in the seventeenth century, but the theory was also developed that only certain particles in the air served to propagate sound. Gassendi conceived that certain atoms performed this function, and Derham followed the belief that sound might be conveyed by either material or ethereal particles.[3]

In poetry, too, descriptions occur that indicate an interest in the means through which sound is conveyed, and frequently it is clear that some scientific theory is being more or less explicitly followed. In Avitus, for example, we find:

> Flexilis artatur recavo sic lingua palato,
> Pressus ut in cameram pulsantis verbere plectri
> Percusso resonet modulatus in aere sermo.[4]

Chaucer based his speculation on Boethius and Vincent of Beauvais:

> Soun is noght but air y-broken,
> And every speche that is spoken,
> Loud or privee, foul or fair,
> In his substaunce is but air.[5]

Milton, for the purposes of description at least, seemed to make use of the incorporeal theory:

> I hear the sound of words, thir sense the air
> Dissolves unjointed e're it reach my ear.[6]

An anonymous poem of the eighteenth century is obviously a scientific essay in verse; two or three lines will indicate the nature of its contents:

> Namque ubi per patulas, facili jam tramite fauces
> Rasit iter liquidum Sonus, oris protinus hæret
> Vestibulum ante ipsum, & labrorum in limine primo
> Sistit.[7]

For the better understanding of *sounding* and *vocal* in verse certain of the prose passages below have been included because they further illustrate theories underlying the choice of words.

---

[1] See John I. Beare, *Greek Theories of Elementary Cognition from Alcmaeon to Aristotle* (Oxford, 1906) 107.

[2] *Ibid.* 99.

[3] See A. Wolf, *A History of Science, Technology, and Philosophy in the 16th & 17th Centuries* (London: Allen and Unwin, 1935) 288.

[4] *Initio Mundi* 87–9.

[5] *Hous of Fame* II. 257–60 (Skeat).

[6] *S. A.* 176–7.

[7] *Mus. Angl.* (5th ed.) 208.

Sounding—*continued*

ἐπεὶ ἦ μάλα πολλὰ μεταξὺ
οὔρεά τε σκιόεντα θάλασσά τε ἠχήεσσα.
—Homer *Il.* I. 156–7. (For full
many things lie between us—shadowy
mountains and sounding sea.)

ἀλλὰ σὺ τῆσδ᾽ ἀφ᾽ ὁδοῦ διζήσιος εἶργε νόημα
μηδέ σ᾽ ἔθος πολύπειρον ὁδὸν κατὰ τήνδε βιάσθω,
νωμᾶν ἄσκοπον ὄμμα καὶ ἠχήεσσαν ἀκουήν
καὶ γλῶσσαν.
—Parmenides (Diels, Fr. 1. 33–6). (Keep your
mind from this way of thinking, and see to it that
custom does not drive you into a tangled path,
guided by sightless eyes, a sounding ear and
tongue.)

At tuba terribilem sonitum procul aere canoro
Increpuit, sequitur clamor caelumque remugit.
—Virgil *Aen.* IX. 503–4.

Gaudete, o celeres, subnixae nubibus altis,
Quae mare, quae viridis silvas lucosque sonantis
Incolitis.
—Virgil *Ciris* 195–7.

Si domitam Iericon lituis atque aere canoro
Rursus in antiquos patitur consurgere muros.
—Prudentius *Hamart.* 480–1.

1567   And bade him take his sounding Trump and out
           of hand too blow.
           —Golding *Ovid's Met.* I. 391.

1572   A canora trombeta embandeirada
           Os corações aa paz acostumados.
           —Camoens *Lus.* 55b.

1584   Tandis qu'environné des enfumez Cyclopes
           Il coule tout en eau, qu'il lasse ses Steropes,
           Et ses Brontes my-nus, qu'il va, subtil, hastant
           Sous leurs sonnantes mains l'ouvrage bluetant,
           Jubal ne perd point tems.
           —Du Bartas *Art.* 485–9.

1591   And the sweet waues of sounding Castaly
           With liquid foote doth slide downe easily.
           —Spenser *Virg. Gnat.* 23–4.

1592   Ma solo aperto un varco
           Lascia al precipitoso uscir de l'acque,
           Che per sassoso calle al mar sonante
           Corrono.
           —Tasso *Mondo Creato* III. 489–92.

Sounding—*continued*

1595   And as guilt Atoms in the sunne appeare,
        So greete these sounds the grissells of myne eare,
        Whose pores doe open wide to theyr regreete,
        And my implanted ayre, that ayre embraceth
        Which they impresse; I feele theyr nimble feete
        Tread my eares Labyrinth.
           —Chapman *Ovids Banquet* xxi–xxii, in *Poems.*

1600   Another stroke he lent him on the brow,
        So great that loudly rung the sounding steel.
           —E. Fairfax *Tasso* VII. xlii.

1605   Which [her voice] when she tunes to Siluer-sound-
           ing strings,
        Hir voice much more then Siluer-sounding rings.
           —John Davies of Hereford *Wit. Pilgr.* N₂.

1613   De estrellas fijas, de Astros fugitiuos,
        Que en sonoroso humo se resueluen.
           —Góngora II. 88.

1616   Till round the world in sounding coombe and plain,
        The last of them tell it the first again.
           —W. Browne *Brit. Past.* II. i. 196–7.

1622   The sounding brass so beat the walls,
        Glib Echo answering the calls.
           —Hannay *Philo.* 1476–7.

1633   The sounding Echo back the musick flung.
           —P. Fletcher *Purple Isl.* XII. lxxxviii.

1640   Struck by his sprawling feet, wide open flye
        The sounding doores.
           —Sandys *Ovid's Met.* 259.

1652   As, in a sounding quire the well-struck concert plays.
           —Benlowes *Theoph.* VI. lxv.

1667   Highly they rag'd
        Against the Highest, and fierce with grasped arm's
        Clash'd on their sounding shields the din of war.
           —Milton *P. L.* I. 666–8.

1679   Give, with thy trumpet, a loud note to Troy,
        Thou noble champion, that the sounding air
        May pierce the ears of the great challenger,
        And call him hither.
           —Dryden *Tro. and Cres.* IV. ii, in *Works* VI. 354.

1687   Before the sounding ax so falls the vine.
           —Dryden *Hind and Panth.* 439.

Sounding—*continued*

1711   But when loud surges lash the sounding shore,
              The hoarse rough verse should like the torrent roar.
                   —Pope *Criticism* II. 168–9.

Praeter haec natura aptus aër ad voces: quidni, cum vox nihil aliud
est quam ictus aër?—Seneca *Nat. Quaest.* II. xxix.

1596   Quid est metallum sonans?   Est æris & stamni confusio, quibus aliquid
         plumbi nigri admiscetur, vt mollior sit & gratior sonus.—Bodin *Theat.*
         257.

1623   Aer est vehiculum luminis, vocis, sonorum, & imaginum, quæ in sensus
         feruntur, & denique volatilium.—Alsted *Theol. Nat.* 310.

1644   Like the iacke of a virginall, which stricketh the sounding corde.—
         Digby *Two Treat.* 276.

1651   The audible quality is called sound; which is a cleaving of the air
         sharply stricken, flowing every way.   Every motion of the air doth not
         give a sound, but that motion whereby the air is suddenly divided and
         parted.   Now a sound is either acute or obtuse; pleasing or displeasing;
         according as the body, that smiteth the air, is acute or obtuse, smooth
         or rough.   The naturall kinds of sound are: *tinkling*, when the air blows
         through some sharp thing.   *Murmur* of running water: *ratling* of thunder:
         rustling of leaves: *bellowing* or *lowing* of Oxen: *roaring* of lions: *hissing* of
         serpents: and the voices of other living creatures.—Comenius *Nat. Phil.*
         Ref. 64–5.

         Hearing hath the ear for its Organ; which containes the hole to the
         brain, together with a gristly border winding about like the shell of a
         snaile, adjoyned without to receive the motion of the aire when [it] is
         stricken, and turne it inward: but within at the center of the windings
         is a little drum, with a little bit of flesh standing by it, like a hammer;
         which being beaten with the aire that enters, beats the drum also, which
         the spirit perceiving, judges of the greatnesse or smalnesse, nearnesse or
         distance of the thing beaten with the aire: and by multiplied experience,
         knows what it is that moves the aire, and of what sort.—*Ibid.* 186.

         The sound of a bell, doth not sticke in the aire, but is wheeled about
         in the sounding bell.—*Ibid.* 187.

1655   At in generatione soni, in prima collisione vel diffractione, aeris pars
         eadem per spatium notabile, et quidem notabili velocitate excutitur et
         loco pellitur; et mox, propter remotiorum partium laxiores orbes dissi-
         patus, languescit motus ejus.   Itaque excussum aerem, qui sonum
         efficit, excipiens ventus totum movet, secundus quidem propius ad
         aurem, adversus vero ab aure longius; et proinde fit, ut vento flante ab
         objecto audiatur sonus tanquam e loco propinquiore; flante in con-
         trarium, tanquam e loco remotiore.—Hobbes I. 404.

1656   [According to Zeno] Voice is Air, not composed of little pieces, but
         whole and continuous, having no vacuity in it . . . .   Voice is a body,

Sounding—*continued*

for it acteth, it striketh upon, and leaveth an impression in our Ear, as a seal in Wax.—Stanley *Hist. Phil. 8th Part* 114.

1669 All Tuneable Sounds, whereof Humane voice is one, are made by a regular vibration of the sonorous body, and Undulation of the Air, proportionable to the Acuteness or Gravity of the Tone.—Holder *Elem. Speech* 47.

1682 I can judge from whence an echo or other sound comes tho I see not ye sounding body, & this judgment depends not at all on ye tone.— Newton, in D. Brewster I. 425.

1684 We may also by a single stroak made upon Wood, Stone, or Metal, or any other sounding Body, judge how far off he is that gives the blow; telling the Vibrations between the stroak seen, and the hearing of the Noise.—R. Waller *Acad. Cimen.* 141.

1701 Le Son est formé par les vibrations des partis du corps sonore.—Sauveur *Prin. Acoust.* 2.

1704 Sound in a Bell or musical String, or other sounding Body, is nothing but a trembling Motion, and in the Air nothing but that Motion propagated from the Object, and in the Sensorium 'tis a Sense of that Motion under the form of sound.—Newton *Opt.* (Bk. I) 90.

Sphere[1]

NOTE.—It will hardly be necessary to list below the occurrences of *sphere* in scientific prose in the seventeenth century, but a brief description of the ancient theory of the heavens, first developed by Eudoxus, may be serviceable in indicating how the words *orb* and *sphere* were used interchangeably. According to Eudoxus,

Les étoiles fixes sont toutes serties en un corps solide que nous nommerons, *brevitatis causa*, un *orbe* ou une *sphère*, mais qui, en réalité, est une couche sphérique comprise entre deux surfaces sphériques concentriques à la Terre; cet orbe tourne d'Orient en Occident, avec une vistesse uniforme, autour d'un axe qui est l'axe du Monde; les pôles de cette rotation sont les pôles du Monde. La durée de révolution de cette sphère est ce que nous nommons le jour sidéral.[2]

And there is this comment by a seventeenth-century writer on the use of these words:

The Sphere is a round body, presenting the frame of the whole world, as the circles of the heaven and the earth; this is sometimes called a martial sphere, for the orbs of the planets are called their spheres, that is the circles in which they move.[3]

---

[1]See also BALL, GLOBE, ORB.
[2]Pierre Duhem, *Le Système du Monde, Histoire des doctrines cosmologiques de Platon à Copernic* (Paris, 1913) I. 114.
[3]W. Lilly *Erra Pater* 18–19.

Sphere—*continued*

ἀλλ' ὅ γε πάντοθεν ἶσος ⟨ἔην⟩ καὶ πάμπαν ἀπείρων
Σφαῖρος κυκλοτερὴς μονίηι περιηγέι γαίων.
—Empedocles (Diels, Fr. 28).   (The circular sphere,
exulting in the surrounding solitude, equal on all sides
and entirely limitless.)

1563   A God there is, that guyds the Globe,
And framde the fyckle Spheare.
—Googe 63.

1584   Puis il prend l'astrelabe, où la sphere est reduite
En forme tout plate.
—Du Bartas *Colom.* 601–2.

1592   E ne la spera de l'opaca Luna
È pura terra forse?
—Tasso *Mondo Creato* VII. 746–7.

1596   Ere flitting Time could wag his eyas wings
About that mightie bound, which doth embrace
The rolling Spheres, and parts their houres by space.
—Spenser *Heav. Love* 24–6.

1605   Th' ord'red motions of the spangled Spheares.
—Sylvester *Div. Wks.* (*1st Day*) 6.

1613   Ella, la misma pompa de las flores,
La esphera misma de los raios bellos.
—Góngora II. 77.

1622   And heere allow them place, beneath this lower Sphere
Of the unconstant Moone.
—Drayton *Poly-Olb.* V. 181–2.

1628   That Day shall rest Heauen's rolling spheares,
Earth's refluous tumults, deathes pale feares.
—Mure I. 156.

1638   I may as well go fathom all the spheres
As measure her disasters, count her tears.
—Whiting, in *CP* III. 506.

1648   And those bright Sparkes (like Gems in Rings of Gold)
Wee in their sev'rall Spheares inchac'd, behold.
—Sherburne *Seneca's Ans.* 2.

1656   And Sols bright flame fresh nourishments invite
In azure Sphears.
—Evelyn *Lucretius* 77.

1667   For of Celestial Bodies first the Sun
A mightie Spheare he fram'd.
—Milton *P. L.* VII. 354–5.

Sphere—*continued*

1675   'Twixt the Ecliptick and the latent Bears,
Which 'bout the creaking Axis turn the Sphears,
Heaven's stranger Orbe with these Stars painted shines,
Which Antient Poets call'd the Southern Signs.
    —Sherburne *Sphere* 37.

1698   Daphnis, the guest of heav'n, with wond'ring eyes,
Views, in the Milky Way, the starry skies,
And far beneath him, from the shining sphere,
Beholds the moving clouds, and rolling year.
    —Dryden *Ecl.* V. 86–9.

1734   Go, soar with Plato to th' empyreal sphere,
To the first good, first perfect, and first fair.
    —Pope *Man* II. 23–4.

Squadron[1]

1550   Les scadrons avantureux
Des abeilles fremissantes
Forment leur miel savoureux.
    —Du Bellay IV. 12.

ante   Tu vins lacher sur moy un esquadron nouveau
1573   De vices monstrueux, qui mes vertus m'emblerent.
    —Jodelle 172.

1578   Tous animaux,
Les emplumez, les escadrons des eaux.
    —Ronsard IV. 209.

1585   Du ciel flottant les escadres isnelles.
    —Du Bartas *I Sem.* II. 318.

1592   E mille appariranno e mille ardenti
D'esercito divin falangi e squadre.
    —Tasso *Mondo Creato* VII. 300–1.

1596   They [angels] for vs fight, they watch and dewly ward,
And their bright Squadrons round about vs plant.
    —Spenser *F. Q.* II. viii. 2.

1605   Heau'ns glorious Hoast in nimble squadrons flies.
    —Sylvester *Div. Wks.* (*1st Day*) 21.

1607   Al jauali en cuios cerros
Se leuanta vn esquadron
De cerdas, si ya no son
Caladas picas sin hierros.
    —Góngora I. 286.

---

[1]See also BAND, BREED, BROOD, CHOIR, CITIZEN, CREW, FLOCK, FRY, HERD, HOST, INHABITANT, KIND, LEGION, NATION, PEOPLE, RACE, SEED, SHOAL, TRAIN, TRIBE, TROOP.

Squadron—*continued*

1614   The skailly squadrones of the liquid lakes.
          —Mure I. 132.

1630   The spotlesse Sprightes of light,
          His Trophees doe extole,
          And archt in Squadrons bright,
          Greet their great victor in his Capitole.
          —Drummond II. 25.

1638   And as when Reynald, with his wily plot,
          Into the squadron of the geese is crept.
          —Whiting, in *CP* III. 530.

1647   Roses of gold on azure sowne,
          You sparkling Jewells of the night,
          Who silently encamp unknown,
          Your squadrons in their Tents of light.
          —Stanley *Ps. cxlviii* 4.

1657   And as Diseases subtilly do part
          Themselves in Squadrons; some invade the heart,
          Others the Head surprise; and others strive
          If not to kill, to make Us dye alive.
          —Anon., in Coles *Adam in Eden* a4.

1659   And now the spangled squadrons of the night,
          Encountering beams, had lost the field to light.
          —W. Chamberlayne *Phar.* IV. ii. 408–9.

1668   Till Moses lifting up his hand,
          Waves the expected Signal of his Wand,
          And all the full-charg'ed clouds in ranged Squadrons move.
          —Cowley 225.

1698   With such a tempest thro' the skies they [bees] steer,
          And such a form the winged squadrons bear.
          —Dryden *Geo.* IV. 447–8.

1722   Oft has the Wolf the bearded Squadrons [prawns] sought,
          And oft the luscious Food too dearly bought.
          —Diaper *Oppian's Hal.* II. 216–17.

Stem

1609   Yet many of their stemme long after did suruiue.
          —Spenser *F. Q.* VII. vi. 2.

1614   Æneas' vertue and his stemme preclare,
          Still in her ravisht minde, a place doth pleed.
          —Mure I. 95.

1623   This is a stem
          Of that victorious stock; and let us fear
          The native mightiness and fate of him.
          —Shakespeare *Henry V* II. iv. 62–4.

Stem—*continued*

1633 From out whose loyall blood
Th' Heroïck Stems of Royall Bourbon's bud.
—Sylvester *Div. Wks. (St. Lewis)* 535.

1645 Where ye may all that are of noble stemm
Approach, and kiss her sacred vestures hemm.
—Milton *Arcades* 82–3.

1672 From equal stems their blood both houses draw.
—Dryden *I Conq. Gran.* I. i, in *Works* IV. 42.

Store

1591 A mountain, whose
Tempestuous gulfe hath store,
Both of Saltpeeter and of Pitch.
—James I *Furies* 252–4.

1596 And throwing downe his load out of his hand,
To weet great store of forrest frute.
—Spenser *F. Q.* VI. vii. 24.

1600 At last they came where all his watery store
The flood in one deep channel did engrave.
—E. Fairfax *Tasso* XV. viii.

1611 In his faire Orchards midst, whose fruitfull store
Hath graç't his Table twenty years and more.
—Sylvester *Div. Wks. (Magnif.)* 554.

1617 Q^{ch}, (lyk the boundles ocean), swels no moir,
Tho springs and founts infuis thair liquid stoir.
—Mure I. 40.

1622 Faire Micklewood (a Nymph, long honor'd for a Chase,
Contending to have stood the high'st in Severns grace,
Or any of the Dryad's there bordring on her shore)
With her coole amorous shades, and all her Sylvan store.
—Drayton *Poly-Olb.* XIV. 197–200.

1651 There constantly the pregnant Earth unplow'd
Her fruitful store supplies.
—Stanley *Anacreon* 58.

1659 They drunk, and found they flam'd the more,
And only added to the burning store.
—Sprat *Plague* C$_2$.

1668 All Autumns store did his rich Spring adorn;
Like Trees in Par'dice he with Fruit was born.
—Cowley 378.

1685 Midway and Isis, you that augment me,
Tides that increase my watery store.
—Dryden *Alb. and Alban.* I. i, in *Works* VII. 254.

Store—*continued*

1698   Three rays of writhen rain, of fire three more,
             Of winged southern winds and cloudy store
             As many parts, the dreadful mixture frame.
                  —Dryden *Aen.* VIII. 567–9.

1709   Th' industrious bees neglect their golden store.
                  —Pope *Winter* 51.

Subtle[1]

             Hunc tibi subtilem cum primis ignibus ignem
             Constituit natura minutis mobilibusque
             Corporibus.
                  —Lucretius VI. 225–7.

1549   Telles sont les flammes subtiles
             Du feu, dont les vives scintiles
             Vont Dieux & hommes affolant.
                  —Du Bellay III. 24.

1567   The suttle ayre to flickring fowles and birdes he
                  hath assignde.
                  —Golding *Ovid's Met.* I. 85.

1572   No ar hum vaporzinho & sutil fumo
             E do vento trazido, rodearse.
                  —Camoens *Lus.* 82b.

1585   La plus subtile humeur qui flotte dans les mers
             Est des rais du soleil portee par les airs.
                  —Du Bartas *I Sem.* III. 123–4.

1593   And some the water ioye, to their desire,
             The subtile ayre contents another sort.
                  —W. Raleigh, in *Phœnix Nest* 81–2.

1596   An Egle, that with plumy wings doth sheare
             The subtile ayre.
                  —Spenser *F. Q.* III. vii. 39.

1610   Aunque dos catarriberas
             Me dixeron de vn nebli
             Que por la garça bebia
             Este elemento subtil.
                  —Góngora I. 426.

ante 1625   My cries shall beat the subtile air no more.
                  —W. Browne *Brit. Past.* III. i. 389.

1633   Or were it such gold as that wherewithall
             Almighty Chymiques from each minerall,
             Having by subtle fire a soule out-pull'd.
                  —Donne *Eleg.* XI. 43–5.

_____
[1]See also THIN AND THINNER.

Subtle—*continued*

1640
> Or if Bitumen doe the fire provoke;
> Or sulpher burning with more subtill smoke.
> —Sandys *Ovid's Met.* 274.

1647
> Fire, which above the aire hast seat,
> And dost both light, and lightnesse wear;
> So plac'd, as if thy subtle heat
> Did purify pale Cinthia's spheare.
> —Stanley *Ps. cxlviii* 7.

1654
> That the ill humour may by sweat perspire,
> And oyntment through the subtile pores retyre.
> —Wase *Gratius* B$_{10}$b.

1668
> The evil Spirits their charms obey,
> And in a subtle cloud they snatch the Rods away.
> —Cowley 221.

ante 1674
> And did, much like the subtil piercing Light,
> When fenc'd from rough and boistrous Storms by
>   night,
> Break throu the Lanthorn-sides.
> —Traherne 155.

1686
> The ether there
> So very pure, so subtil, and so rare,
> 'Twould a chameleon kill.
> —Flatman, in *CP* III. 303.

1698
> The soil exhaling clouds of subtile dews.[1]
> —Dryden *Geo.* II. 297.

1713
> The blended Elements, that long had strove,
> Would not so ready joyn in mutual Love:
> But, first, the purer Parts their Places took,
> And subtle Fire the meaner Mass forsook.
> —Diaper *Dryades* 28.

1716
> Que ce Corps, devenu plus leger, ou plus rare,
> En subtiles Vapeurs s'assemble, ou se separe,
> Pour un Etre pensant peut-on le recevoir?
> —Genest *Prin. Phil.* 21.

Ex quibus quoque procedunt radii, videntur magis quam ea, in quibus aliunde incidunt, ut ea quae videntur in aere subtili claro . . . manifestora apparent.—Ptolomy *Ottica* 13.

1576 But Dystillation, as writeth Ioannes Langius in his Epystles, is the seperating and running forth of a subtill moysture.—Baker *Gesner* 1.

---

[1]Virgil *Geo.* II. 217: "tenuem nebulam."

Subtle—*continued*

1581 Il y a donc certaines euaporations, qui se leuent de la terre & qui
continuellement montent & s'esleuent dedans l'Air, qui est sur nos
testes: lesquelles exhalations sont subtiles & inuisibles estans paruenues
en l'air, si ce n'est du matin.—Daneau *Phys. Fran.* 35.

1600 Electrica verò effluuia peculiaria, quæ humoris fusi subtilissima sunt
materia, corpuscula allectant.—W. Gilbert *Magnete* 57.

1612 Aër est elementum subtile, humidum & calidum, igne gravius, aquâ
& terrâ levius, respirationis & sonorum causa, à naturâ colore vacum.
—Alsted *Syst. Phys.* 37.

1621 Winde is a subtill smoake, beaten downeward by the cold in the middle
of the ayre.—Widdowes *Nat. Phil.* 19.

1637 Des esprits animaux, qui sont comme vn vent tres subtil, ou plutost
comme vne flamme tres pure & tres viue.—Descartes *Methode* 54–5.

1644 As when a thicke short guilded ingott of siluer is drawne out into a
long subtile wyre.—Digby *Two Treat.* 177.

1657 Nor is there any Element that God created more subtle or thin [than
air].—Pinnell *Croll* 40.

1662 That the Air is nothing but a Congeries or heap of small and (for the
most part) of flexible Particles . . . which are rais'd by the heat (especially that of the Sun) into that fluid and subtle Ethereall Body that
surrounds the Earth.—Boyle *Spring of Air* 14.

1675 Nous pouvons déja définir les Astres un amas de matiere tres-subtile,
dont toutes les parties sont fort agitées entr'elles.—Gadroys *Syst.* 212.

1687 With Cartesius they say, that there is much more of the *Materia Subtilis*
or subtile Matter, in thin Bodies, than there is in thick and condensed
Bodies.—Midgley *Nat. Phil.* 204.

1698 The means of its Production [the liquor Alchahest] is by reiterated
Solution, and an intervening Coagulation; and thus is the Subject
brought to the most subtle Atoms, of which in Nature it is capable.—
Hortolanus *Golden Age* 157.

1714 The finer and more subtile Air of the Hills.—Derham *Physico-Theol.* 72.

Swim[1]

        Expectant imbres, quorum modo cuncta natabant
        Inpulsu, et siccis uoltus in nubibus haerent.
        —Lucan IV. 330–1.

        ἐρετμώσας δὲ πορείην
        νηχομένων πτερύγων ἑτερόζυγι σύνδρομος ὁλκῷ
        πατρῴους ἀνέβαινεν ἐς ἀστερόεντας ὀχῆας.
        —Nonnos *Dionys.* XXXIII. 191–3. (Then

---

[1]Not used of motion in the air by Lucretius, Virgil, Spenser, or Milton. For
further illustration see LIQUID AIR.

Swim—*continued*

paddling his way with the double beat of his swimming wings he mounted to the starry barriers of his father.)

Vestiri colles et roscida prata,
Innarique aer pennis atque æquora caudis.
—Pontano *Urania* I. 972–3.

1585   Tout ainsi que ça-bas d'un branslement divers
Les oiseaux peinturez nagent entre deux airs.
—Du Bartas *I Sem.* IV. 115–16.

1600   Swift o'er the grass the rolling chariot swims.
—E. Fairfax *Tasso* IV. lv.

1605   The painted Birds betweene two aiers doo swim.
—Sylvester *Div. Wks. (4th Day)* 119.

1627   So when a sable cloud with swelling sayle
Comes swimming through calme skies.
—P. Fletcher *Locusts* IV. xvii.

1630   Thus singing through the Aire the Angels swame.
—Drummond II. 10.

1647   The Nights nimble net
That doth encompasse every opake ball,
That swim's in liquid aire, did Simon nought apall.
—More *Psychozoia* III. ii.

1668   The dismal Lightnings all around,
Some flying through the Air, some running on the ground,
Some swimming o're the waters face.
—Cowley 225.

ante   O'r which, without a Wing,
1674   Or Oar, he dar'd to swim,
Swim throu the Air
On Body fair.
—Traherne 184.

1716   On void que dans l'Ether une Planete nage,
Par son poids, par sa masse y prend certain étage.
—Genest *Prin. Phil.* 91.

1743   Of all th' enamell'd race, whose silv'ry wing
Waves to the tepid zephyrs of the spring,
Or swims along the fluid atmosphere.
—Pope *Dunc.* IV. 421–3.

1581   Ainsi voyons nous que les oiseaux vont & nagent par l'air, en le fendant de leurs æles, comme les poissons font l'eau.—Daneau *Phys. Fran.* 284.

Swim—*continued*

1637 Ce trou n'est pas tousiours de mesme grandeur, & la partie E F de la peau en laquelle il est, nageant librement en l'humeur K, qui est fort liquide, semble estre comme vn petit muscle, qui se peut estrecir & eslargir a mesure qu'on regarde des obiets plus ou moins proches.— Descartes *Œuvres* VI. 107.

1644 Smoake is nothing else, but a company of litle round bodies, swimming in the ayre.—Digby *Two Treat.* 115.

1655 Præterea, quoniam globus telluris ætheri, a solis motu pulso, innatat, partes ætheris telluri impingentes undequaque per ipsius telluris superficiem expandentur.—Hobbes I. 383.

1657 So at the Creation did the bodies of the Stars grow out of Heaven, swiming in their Orbs as birds fly in the Aire.—Pinnell *Croll* 40.

1666 Mixtures of Snow and Salt, being put into Glasses or other Vessels, the aqueous vapors, that swim to and fro in the Air, and chance to glide along the sides of the Vessels, are by the coldness thereof condens'd into Water.—*Phil. Trans.* I. 257.

1677 When [sulphur] contains some spirituous and aery Particles, it swims upon the water, as the Aromatick subtil Oils of Rose-mary, Sage, Turpentine, and others.—Glaser *Compl. Chym.* 6–7.

1682 The Seeds of some Plants, as of Mosses, (which, through their smallness, will ascend like Moths in the Sun) may fly or swim for some time, in the Aer.—Grew *Phil. Hist. Plants* 8.

1694 The Cause of these Changes is the motion of that Planet [Venus], which swiming in the fluid Heaven, makes its circumvolution about the Sun.—Blome *Le Grand* II. 61.

1696 Part of the Alcaly sucks up the Acid which the Flint contains for Lime or Calx, and it swims a top of the slaked Flint.—Tachenius *Hippocrates* 10.

1738 Gassendus asserts, that Bodies receive the Impressions of Cold from Nitrous Exhalations swimming in the Air.—Pointer *Weather* 181.

1764 *Natans* Folium [*nato*, to swim] applied to aquatic plants; swimming on the surface of the water, as in the *Nymphæa*, Potomogeton.—Berkenhout *Bot. Lex.* (under *Natans*).

Sylvan

1579   Here han the holy Faunes resourse,
         And Syluanes haunten rathe.
            —Spenser *S. C.: July* 77–8.

1600   The wicked sprites in sylvan pinfolds were.
            —E. Fairfax *Tasso* XIII. xx.

1616   And if thou chance to see that lovely boy
         (To look on whom the sylvans count a joy).
            —W. Browne *Brit. Past.* II. iii. 37–8.

Sylvan—*continued*

1622   Once were we two faire Nymphs, who fortunatly prov'd,
The pleasures of the Woods, and faithfully belov'd
Of two such Sylvan gods, by hap that found us here;
For then their Sylvan kind most highly honoured were.
          —Drayton *Poly-Olb.* XXII. 43–6.

1640   A Cave, inviron'd with a sylvan shade,
Distilling streames.
          —Sandys *Ovid's Met.* 258.

1659   They're past
That sylvan labyrinth, and with that had cast
Their greatest terror off.
          —W. Chamberlayne *Phar.* IV. ii. 404–6.

1667   Cedar, and Pine, and Firr, and branching Palm,
A Silvan Scene, and as the ranks ascend
Shade above shade, a woodie Theatre.
          —Milton *P. L.* IV. 139–41.

1667   The frighted satyrs, that in woods delight,
Now into plains with pricked-up ears take flight;
And scudding thence, while they their horn-feet ply,
About their sires the little silvans cry.
          —Dryden *Ind. Emp.* II. i, in *Works* II. 342–3.

1698   There, while I went to crop the sylvan scenes,
And shade our altar with their leafy greens,
I pull'd a plant.
          —Dryden *Aen.* III. 34–6.

1713   'T is yours, my Lord, to bless our soft retreats,
And call the Muses to their ancient seats;
To paint anew the flowery sylvan scenes,
To crown the forests with immortal greens.
          —Pope *Win. For.* 283–6.

Enough for me, that to the list'ning swains
First in these fields I sung the sylvan strains.
          —*Ibid.* 433–4.

Tear[1]

Pars intra saepta domorum
Narcissi lacrimam et lentum de cortice gluten
Prima favis ponunt fundamina, deinde tenacis
Suspendunt ceras.
          —Virgil *Geo.* IV. 159–62.

Flet tamen: et tepidae manant ex arbore guttae.
Est honor et lachrymis.
          —Ovid *Met.* X. 500–1.

---

[1]See also PEARL.

Tear—*continued*

Nectar de liquido uertice feruidum
Guttatim lacrimis stillat olentibus.
—Prudentius *Cath.* X. 21–2.

1579   I see your teares, that from your boughes doe raine,
Whose drops in drery ysicles remaine.
—Spenser *S. C.: Jan.* 35–6.

1592   When first I saw the sunne the day begin,
And dry the Mornings tears from hearbs and grasse.
—Greene *Groats-Worth of Witte* 49.

1605   As the thorough-seasoned Butte
Wherein the teares of pressed Grapes are put.
—Sylvester *Div. Wks. (Eden)* 273.

1616   Trees, euen hard Trees, through Rine distill their Teares.
—Drummond I. 118.

1640   From these cleere dropping trees, teares yearely flow:
They, hardned by the Sunne, to Amber grow.
—Sandys *Ovid's Met.* 28.

1646   There is no need at all
That the Balsame-sweating bough
So coyly should let fall,
His med'cinable Teares.
—Crashaw *Weeper* xii.

1659   The brown bowls stand
With amber liquor filled, whose fruitful tears
Dropped loved Ismander's health, till it appears
In sanguine tincture on their cheeks.
—W. Chamberlayne *Phar.* IV. ii. 565–8.

1698   First let 'em sip from herbs the pearly tears
Of morning dews.
—Dryden *Geo.* III. 505–6.

1712   The fragrant Trees, which grow by Indian Floods,
And in Arabia's Aromatic Woods,
Owe all their Spices to the Summer's Heat,
Their gummy Tears, and odoriferous Sweat.
—Blackmore *Creation* II. 245–8.

Quin etiam silvestris papaveris, cum iam ad excipiendam lacrimam maturum est, manipellus qui manu conprehendi potest, in vas demittitur.—Celsus V. 25. 4.

Primum favos construunt, ceram fingunt, hoc est domos cellasque faciunt, dein subolem, postea mella, ceram ex floribus, melliginem a lacrimis arborum quae glutinum pariunt.—Pliny *Nat. Hist.* XI. v. § 14.

Tear—*continued*

1515   Vna nimirum aqua per fibres eadem atque radices attracta: alio modo radices alio caducis corticem: alio lignum: alio medullam alit: & folium fit: & in ramos surculosque diffunditur: & incrementa frugibus praestat lachryme denique succusque stirps eadem ex causa manant.—Argyropolus *Basil* XXIIIIb.

1554   Cancamum Arabici ligni lacryma est, myrrhæ quodammodo similis, uirosi gustus, quam ad suffimenta usurpant.—Matthiolus *Dioscorides* 45.

1567   The bark of this [Balme] Tree must first be stricken and hewen with Iron wedges, before it yeeldeth any fruit, whereby it being so wounded, by and by droppeth and distilleth a certaine humor, in a maner tear-like, which humor thus issued through the coldenesse or other affection of the Air about it, drieth to a kinde of Gum.—Maplet *Greene Forest* 62.

1606   Nonnulli certè Resinæ nomine generaliter & Gummi & Picem & resinam & Lachrymam & quidquid oleaginosi liquoris ex arboribus colligitur.—Daneau *Phys. Christ.* 133b.

1627   It is not unlike that the sap and tears of some trees may be sweet.—Bacon *Works* IV. 435.

1629   Lachryma verò est is humor, qui statim desecto caudice vel ramo, aut aliquibus tantùm, ipso ligno prosilit, & apparet: vulgus locat *la seue.*—Stephanus *Præd. Rust.* 121.

1644   Quibusdam etiam [humoribus] in lachrymæ [δακρυώδης] modum gignitur; ut abieti, pino, terebintho, larici, piceæ, amygdalæ, ceraso, pruno, junipero, ulmo, spinæ Ægyptiæ: nam ea quoque fert gummi, verum non ex cortice, sed in vase. Adde illas, quæ thus, quæ myrrham præstant: lachrymis enim hæc quoque annumerantur. Ad hæc balsamum, & chalbanam, & si quid aliud simile sit.—Bodæus *Theophrastus* 964.

   Quid gummi sit, docet Galenus lib. VII. Simpl. Κόμμι δάκρυον . . . ; *Gummi lachryma* est congelata, concretaque in truncis arborum, ipsam producentium, velut resina quoque in multis visitur, quæ resinam proferre possunt. Lachrymam dixi supra succum esse qui ab incisione & sponte defluit. Is vel concretus, vel liquidus est.—*Ibid.* 966.

1655   Cancamum is the Lachryma of an Arabick tree resembling Myrrhe.—Goodyer *Dioscorides* 21.

1657   Amongst teares or exudations many things take place, as the water that flowes from a vine cut, the milk of all Tithymalls, and the thick juice of Poppies, which when it is congealed is called Opium. In many plants therefore the barke onely is wounded, and thence distills δάκρυον, that is tears, into a bason, or some such vessell hanged for the purpose.—Tomlinson *Renodaeus* 79.

1663   Lachrymal humours are fluidities proceeding out the pores of a plant through διαπέδεσις, or transudation, pressed out . . . among these some are more aqueous, concreasing afterwards into a gumme, others like Pitch changing into Rozin.—G. Harvey *Prin. Phil.* II. 273.

Thin and Thinner[1]

NOTE.—*Thin* and *thinner*, applied to air, are common epithets in eighteenth-century verse, but the significance of their use may be somewhat pointed by a few quotations among the following passages that use the term *thickness* in regard to air when it is filled with vapors or exhalations.

φῶς δ᾽ ἔξω διαθρῶισκον, ὅσον ταναώτερον ἦεν,
λάμπεσκεν κατὰ βηλὸν ἀτειρέσιν ἀκτίνεσσιν.
　　　　—Empedocles (Diels, Fr. 84). (The light
darts forth, as something thinner, and brightens
the firmament with flashing beams.)

Nam per aquas quaecumque cadunt atque aera rarum,
Haec pro ponderibus casus celerare necessest
Propterea qui corpus aquae naturaque tenvis
Aeris haut possunt aeque rem quamque morari,
Sed citius cedunt gravioribus exsuperata.
　　　　—Lucretius II. 230–4.

Tali Cyllenius ore locutus
Mortalis visus medio sermone reliquit
Et procul in tenuem ex oculis evanuit auram.
　　　　—Virgil *Aen.* IV. 276–8.

Cum libet, in gelidum flabrali frigore uentum
Spiritus existit tenuis et sibilat aër.
　　　　—Prudentius *Apoth.* 841–2.

ἡ δὲ παχυνομένη νεφέων ὤδινε καλύπτρην,
σεισαμένη δὲ πάχιστον ἀραιοτέρῳ δέμας ἀτμῷ,
ἂψ ἀναλυσαμένη μαλακὸν νέφος εἰς χύσιν ὄμβρου.
　　　　—Nonnos *Dionys.* II. 502–4. (This thickens
and produces the cloudy veil; then shaking the
thick mass by means of the thinner vapour, it
dissolves the fine cloud again into a fall of rain.
—Tr. Rouse.)

Ὦ λεπτόσωμον ἐκχέων τὸν ἀέρα;
　　　　—Pisidas *Hex.* 204. (Thou
dost pour forth the thin-bodied
air.)

1596　　A litle smoke, whose vapour thin and light,
　　　　Reeking aloft, vprolled to the sky.
　　　　　　—Spenser *F. Q.* III. vii. 5.

1611　　Through the thin air, the winged shaft doth sing.
　　　　　　—Sylvester *Div. Wks.* (*Decay*) 228.

---

[1]See also SUBTLE.

Thin and Thinner—*continued*

1622   The angry Armies meet, when the thin ayre was rent,
With such re-ecchoing shouts, from either Souldiers sent.
—Drayton *Poly-Olb.* XXII. 1459-60.

1633   Thinner then burnt aire flies this soule.
—Donne *Progr. of the Soule* 173.

1633   The Cities [the heart's] left side, (by some hid direction)
Of this thinne aire, and of that right sides rent,
(Compound together) makes a strange confection.
—P. Fletcher *Purple Isl.* IV. xxi.

1638   The earth, resolved to water, rarefies
Into pure air; the thinner water flies;
The purer air assumes a scorching heat.
They, back returning, orderly retreat:
Those subtle sparks converted are to breath,
The spissy air, being doomèd unto death,
Turns into sea, earth's made a thick'ned water.
—Whiting, in *CP* III. 547-8.

1640   Nor hung the self-poiz'd Earth in thin Ayre plac'd.
—Sandys *Ovid's Met.* 1.

1647   Ascending thus with joy, as thou dost fare
Through the thin Sky.
—More *Triumph* 21-2.

1659   Exalted by
Clear aqueducts, in showers it from those high
Supporters falls; now turned into a thin
Vapour, in that heaven's painted bow is seen.
—W. Chamberlayne *Phar.* II. iv. 243-6.

1667   Fish within thir watry residence,
Not hither summond, since they cannot change
Thir Element to draw the thinner Aire.
—Milton *P. L.* VIII. 346-8.

1675   And in a liquid Plain the Waters spread,
Whence hungry Air is by thin Vapours fed.
—Sherburne *Sphere* 13.

1713   Into the thinner Element he's [the fish is] cast,
And on the verdant Margin gasps his Last.
—Gay *Rural Sports* 4.

1722   [The fish] Resign'd with painful Expectation waits,
Till thinner Element compleats his Fates.
—J. Jones *Oppian's Hal.* III. 149-50.

Air is thinner and less corporeal [λεπτότερον καὶ ἀσωματώτερον] than water.—Aristotle *Nat. Auscult.* 215b4, in *Opera* II. 295.

Thin and **Thinner**—*continued*

Sed in olfactu difficultas singularis evenit: olere enim ait magis tenuem aërem [τὸν λεπτὸν ἀέρα], acrius vero odorari ea, quæ densum quam quæ tenuem spirando attrahant.—Theophrastus *De Sensu* VI (35).

1614   The ayre passeth and spreadeth it selfe from the ætheriall & cleere region, as farre as the earth, more swift, more subtile, and higher then the earth and waters, yet more thicke and waighty then that region, being of himselfe colde and obscure; his light and heate are borrowed from another place, yet in euery place he is not like himselfe, for he is changed by his neighbours.   The higher part thereof is driest, hottest, and for this cause also the most thinnest, by reason of the vicinitie of eternall fires, and those so many motions of starres, and the continuall reuolution of the heauens.   That lower part, which is neerest vnto the earth is thicke and obscure, by reason that it intertayneth the exhalations of the earth.—Lodge *Seneca* 782.

1621   Raritas or Thinnes is that which hath hollow parts or spongie, as a sponge, cloudes &c.—Widdowes *Nat. Phil.* 3.

1627   In air, the thinner or drier air carrieth not the sound so well as the more dense; as appeareth in night sounds, and evening sounds, and sounds in moist weather and southern winds.—Bacon *Works* IV. 273.

1637   But before all things hee separated according to the degrees both of thickenesse and rarenesse, this Chaos into foure kinds.   He made the thinnest part [la plus subtile] bright, and hot, and called it fire, or light. Another likewise, thinne, cleare, and moist, he called aire [Aliam iterum tenuem, pellucidam, et humidam].—Comenius *Gate of Tongues* 4.

1661   If our sight represent a Staff as crooked in the water; the same faculty rectifies both it, and us, in the thinner Element.—Glanvill *Van. Dogm.* 71.

1670   The Creator began to subdivide the third rank, or the Elementary matter . . . by gathering together into one place all the Elementary Aqueous particles, which he call'd Seas; so that the Dry began to appear, which he called Earth; resolving and raising upwards into vapors and exhalations the thinner particles, thence to produce Air and Fire. —*Phil. Trans.* V. K₃b.

1687   Lay an Image, or any other visible object, in the bottom of a Vessel, and then go back till it vanish out of your sight; now if you fill this Vessel with water, it shall presently be visible again, because the Ray coming from your eye, breaks downwards in the superficies of the water, as the same going streight up to the superficies of the water deviates from the perpendicular, because of the thinner air [ob tenuiorem aerem] towards the eye, which renders the object visible again. —Abercromby *Acad. Sci.* 64–6, 67.

1696   Et liquidum spisso secrevit ab aëre cælum.   Ovid *Met.* I. 23.   *Spisso:* Respectu ætheris, scilicet, propter vapores è terra in aërem ascendentes. —Freind's note on Ovid *Met.* (p. 4).

Thin and Thinner—*continued*

1696   The Constitution of the Antediluvian Air was Thin, Pure, Subtile, and Homogeneous.—Whiston *New Theory* 182.

1704   Had the rays been perpendicular to the Glasses, the thickness of the Air at these Rings would have been less in the proportion of the Radius to the secant of 4 degrees.—Newton *Opt.* (Bk. II) 10.

Train[1]

1563   Wher lyes ye rowt,
Of Cruell Cupides trayne.
    —Googe 122.

1578   Ils faillent de laisser le chemin de leurs peres,
Pour ensuivre le train des sectes estrangeres.
    —Ronsard VI. 279.

1596   Soone after whom the louely Bridegroome came,
The noble Thamis, with all his goodly traine.
    —Spenser *F. Q.* IV. xi. 24.

1605   The nimble winged traine
That cleaue the Aire.
    —Sylvester *Div. Wks.* (*Tri. Faith*) 573.

1616   More happy deem I thee, lamented swain,
Whose body lies among the scaly train.
    —W. Browne *Brit. Past.* II. i. 285–6.

1622   Proude Tamer swoopes along, with such a lustie traine
As fits so brave a flood two Countries that divides.
    —Drayton *Poly-Olb.* I. 205–6.

1630   Nor Sheepheard hastes, when frays of Wolues arise,
So fast to Fold to saue his bleeting Traine.
    —Drummond II. 7.

1637   Salacia heavy with her fishy train,
And Nereus' daughters came to entertain.
    —Marmion *Cup. and Psy.* I. i. 117–18.

1651   Behold the King, with such a shining Traine
As dazles sight, yet can inform the Blind.
    —Davenant *Gond.* III. iii. 18.

1659   No, they' [the Persians] are a base and a degenerate Train.
    —Sprat *Plague* C$_4$b.

1675   And darted Flames swift Arrows imitate,
When the dry Train [of a comet] runs in a narrow Strait.
    —Sherburne *Sphere* 61.

---

[1]See also BAND, BREED, BROOD, CHOIR, CITIZEN, CREW, FLOCK, FRY, HERD, HOST, INHABITANT, KIND, LEGION, NATION, PEOPLE, RACE, SEED, SHOAL, SQUADRON, TRIBE, TROOP.

Train—*continued*

1682   And frogs and toads, and all the tadpole train,
        Will croak to Heav'n for help from this devouring crane.
          —Dryden *Medal* 304–5.

1712   See, how the Streams advancing to the Main
        Thro' crooked Channels draw their Chrystal Train.
          —Blackmore *Creation* I. 599–600.

1713   Let old Arcadia boast her ample plain,
        Th' immortal huntress, and her virgin train.
          —Pope *Win. For.* 159–60.

Tribe[1]

1640   As for the Ladies they
        Pos'd with the Medley of thy Language, say
        Th' art a meere Scholler, and the Scholler swears
        Thou art of any tribe rather then theirs.
          —Randolph *Poems* 121.

1655   In fine De Game goes not: the Regidore
        Forbids, in favour of that barb'rous Tribe.
          —Fanshawe *Lus.* VIII. lxxxiv.

1667   O flours,
        That never will in other Climate grow,
        My early visitation, and my last
        At Eev'n, which I bred up with tender hand
        From the first op'ning bud, and gave ye Names,
        Who now shall reare ye to the Sun, or ranke
        Your Tribes, and water from th' ambrosial Fount?
          —Milton *P. L.* XI. 273–9.

1722   The various Finny Tribes, that swifter glide,
        Array'd in silver Scales, and spotted Pride.
          —Diaper *Oppian's Hal.* I. 1077–8.

1727   Prone to the lowest vale the aerial tribes
        Descend.
          —Thomson *Summer* 1121–2.

1757   With curious eye observe,
        In what variety the tribe of salts,
        Gums, ores, and liquors, eye-delighting hues
        Produce, abstersive or restringent.
          —Dyer *Fleece* II. 570–3.

1627 There be two great families of things. You may term them by several
names; sulphureous and mercurial, which are the chemist's words (for
as for their *sal*, which is their third Principle, it is a compound of the
other two); inflammable and not inflammable; mature and crude; oily

---

[1]See also BAND, BREED, BROOD, CHOIR, CITIZEN, CREW, FLOCK, FRY, HERD, HOST, INHABITANT, KIND, LEGION, NATION, PEOPLE, RACE, SEED, SHOAL, SQUADRON, TRAIN, TROOP.

Tribe—*continued*

and watery.   For we see that in subterranies there are, as the fathers
of their tribes, brimstone and mercury; in vegetables and living creatures there is water and oil.—Bacon *Works* IV. 331.

1629   Vnto the former Starre-flowers, must needes bee ioyned another tribe
or kindred, which carry their straked flowers Starre-fashion, not spike-
wise, but in a tuft or vmbell thicke thrust or set together.—Parkinson
Par. Terr. 141.

1644   Hauing thus brought on the course of nature as high as liuing creatures
(who[s]e chiefe specieses or diuision, is those that haue sense) and hauing
declared the operations which are common to the whole tribe of them,
which includeth both plants and animals.—Digby *Two Treat.* 242.

1651   The whole multitude of creatures, is ranked into these seven Classes, or
great Tribes . . . Elements, Vapours, Concretes, Plants, Living Creatures, Men, Angels.—Comenius *Nat. Phil. Ref.* 239–40.

1668   Plant, Vegetable.   Special kinds; denoting either, that tribe of Plants
that are most small, tender and numerous; Or those kinds, amongst
these, which are commonly fed upon by beasts, &c.—Wilkins *Real
Character* 54.

1674   All volatil Salts, although the Tribes and Concrets that afforded them
were exceeding different and distant . . . are brought unto a perfect
agreement in some few common properties.—*Phil. Trans.* IX. 172.

1680   Vegetables being the largest Genus in Nature, comprehendeth the
greatest part by far of *Materia Medica,* or things used for Physic.   These
are to be known in all their Parts, by Name, as also as digested into
Tribes, and Families.—Merrett *Compl. Phys.* 3.

1683   All sublunary Bodies, or Concrets, about which this Art is conversant,
are divided into three Families or Tribes; viz. Animal, Vegetal, and
Mineral.—Mackaile *Divers. Salts* 1.

1698   It being peculiar to this Tribe of Animals alone, for any thing yet
known to the contrary, that its progressive motion is by turning or
rolling upon its Spines.—*Phil. Trans.* XIX. 198.

1700   For want of fresh support and Nutriment [trees] shed their Leaves,
unless secured by a very firm and hardy Constitution indeed, as our
ever-Greens are.   Next the Shrubs part with theirs: and then the Herbs
and lower Tribes.—*Phil. Trans.* XXI. 225.

1712   Of all the Winged Tribe, there are the most frequent and observable
Irregularities in the Eggs of Domestick Fowl, those especially of the
Poultry-kind.—Morton *Northampton.* 432.

1714   Having as briefly as well I could dispatched the Tribe of the Quadrupeds, I shall next take as brief and transient a View of the Feather'd
Tribe.—Derham *Physico-Theol.* 335.

1735   I could, had I Time, have named to you a far greater Number of remarkable Peculiarities in the Nature of the finny Tribe.—B. Martin
Phil. Gram. 306–7.

Troop[1]

1578 De L'air la vagabonde troupe
T'obeyst et celle qui coupe
Du ventre le marbre des flots.
 —Ronsard III. 7.

1579 The vaunting Poets found nought worth a pease,
To put in preace emong the learned troupe.
 —Spenser *S. C.: Oct.* 69–70.

1584 Et les velus troupeaux et les troupeaux laineux.
 —Du Bartas *Arche* 484.

1605 Viòla en las seluas vn dia
En vna virginal tropa
De seguaces de Diana.
 —Góngora I. 247.

1605 And there, that tree from of whose trembling top
Both swimming shoales, and flying troupes doe drop.
 —Sylvester *Div. Wks.* (*Eden*) 292.

1616 The feathred Troupes, that flie and sweetly sing.
 —Drummond I. 70.

1637 A troop of Tritons were straight sounding heard.
 —Marmion *Cup. and Psy.* I. i. 115.

1640 About her, all our winged troops repayre;
And, with invectives, chace her through the Ayre.
 —Sandys *Ovid's Met.* 30.

1656 Ainsi lors que de loups vne trouppe enragée
A du belant trouppeau la closture assiegée.
 —Chapelain *Pucelle* 126.

1667 For that fair femal Troop thou sawst, that seemd
Of Goddesses, so blithe, so smooth, so gay.
 —Milton *P. L.* XI. 614–15.

1687 The wanton Cupids in a troop descend.
 —Ayres, in *CP* II. 285.

1707 Deja dans la Plaine fleurie,
Le Berger laisse errer ses Troupeaux bondissants.
 —La Motte *Odes* 147.

1746 The gay troops begin
In gallant thought to plume the painted wing.
 —Thomson *Spring* 584–5.

---

[1]See also BAND, BREED, BROOD, CHOIR, CITIZEN, CREW, FLOCK, FRY, HERD, HOST, INHABITANT, KIND, LEGION, NATION, PEOPLE, RACE, SEED, SHOAL, SQUADRON, TRAIN, TRIBE.

Tuft

1578   Tout seul me suis perdu par les rives humides
        Et par les bois tofus, les Pierides.
            —Ronsard VI. 339.

1597   There stands the castle, by yon tuft of trees.
            —Shakespeare *Rich. II* II. iii. 53.

1605   The Reaper, panting both for heat and paine,
        With crooked Rasor shaues the tufted Plaine.
            —Sylvester *Div. Wks.* (*4th Day*) 137.

1613   A tuft of trees grew circling in a rank.
            —W. Browne *Brit. Past.* I. iii. 388.

1638   Air's fleeting tuns crystalline streams distil,
        To wash the grassy-tufted tapestry.
            —Whiting, in *CP* III. 467.

1640   Or when lowd Eurus breakes
        Through tufted Pines.
            —Sandys *Ovid's Met.* 276.

1656   Like a field Larke he looks with tufted Crown.
            —T. Harvey *Mantuan* 64.

1667   With high Woods the Hills were crownd,
        With tufts the vallies & each fountain side.
            —Milton *P. L.* VII. 326–7.

1698   [Bees] near a living stream their mansion place,
        Edg'd round with moss and tufts of matted grass.
            —Dryden *Geo.* IV. 23–4.

1713   And 'midst the desert fruitful fields arise,
        That crown'd with tufted trees and springing corn,
        Like verdant isles, the sable waste adorn.
            —Pope *Win. For.* 26–8.

1622?   The eare [of capon's-tail grass] is almost a foot in length, composed of
        many small and slender hairy tufts, which when they come to maturitie
        looke a grayish or whitish colour, and do very well resemble a Capons
        taile.—T. Johnson (?), in Gunther *Early Brit. Bot.* 171.

1625   For the main garden, I do not deny but there should be some fair
        alleys, ranged on both sides, with fruit-trees, and some pretty tufts of
        fruit-trees and arbours with seats, set in some decent order.—Bacon
        Essays (*Of Gardens*) 329.

1657   The ordinary Oats groweth up with divers tall joynted stalks and leaves,
        somewhat resembling Wheat, bearing at the tops, a large spread tuft,
        of many pointed Aglets, hanging down like small winged Birds.—Coles
        Adam in Eden Mmb.

1664   Thus your *Coryletum* or Copse of Hasels being planted about Autumn,
        may (as some practice it) be cut within three or four inches of the

Tuft—*continued*

ground the Spring following, which the new Cion will suddenly repair in clusters and tufts of fair poles of twenty, and sometimes thirty foot long.—Evelyn *Sylva* 35.

1682 The Leaves of divers Flowers at their Basis have an hairy Tuft; by which Tufts the Concave of the Empalement is filled up.—Grew *Anat. Plants* 36.

1687 Plant strawberries (especially the large sort) in tufts at a foote distance so as you may stirr & strew rich earth about them, and water them well. Thus will one tuft produce more & better fruite than where planted so thick together.—Evelyn *Gardiner* 26.

1712 And so down to Oundle, almost every Town has its Tufts, or Groves [of Wyche-Elms].—Morton *Northampton.* 30.

Vapor[1]

Sol si perpetuo siet,
Flammeo vapore torrens terrae fetum exusserit,
Nocti ni interveniat, fructus per pruinam obriguerint.
—Pacuvius *Trag.* 26–8.

Quod genus in somnis sopiti ubi cernimus alte
Exhalare vaporem altaria ferreque fumum.
—Lucretius III. 431–2.

Cumque sit ignis aquae pugnax, vapor umidus omnes
Res creat.
—Ovid *Met.* I. 432–3.

Quoque minus possent siccos tolerare uapores
Quaesitae fecistis aquae.
—Lucan IV. 305–6.

Tristis cometa intercidat
Et, si quod astrum Sirio
Feruet uapore, iam dei
Sub luce distructum cadat.
—Prudentius *Cath.* XI. 21–4.

ἤδη γὰρ περίφοιτος ἀπὸ χθονίου κενεῶνος
ξηρὸς ἀερσιπότητος ἀνέδραμεν ἀτμὸς ἀρούρης,
καὶ νεφέλης ἔντοσθεν ἐελμένος αἴθοπι λαιμῷ
πνίγετο θερμαίνων νέφος ἔγκυον.
—Nonnos *Dionys.* II. 482–5. (For already from the underground abyss a dry vapour diffused around rose from the earth on high, and compressed within the cloud was stifled in the fiery gullet, heating the pregnant cloud.
—Tr. Rouse.)

---

[1]See also EXHALATION, EXHALE.

Vapor—*continued*

1572 Eu o vi certamente (& nano presumo
      Que a vista me enganaua) leuantar se,
      No ar hum vaporzinho & sutil fumo
      E do vento trazido, rodearse.
            —Camoens *Lus.* 82b.

1585 Idem aridi fœtus satorum vt sint facit,
      Reddit liquorum idem vapores humidos [Ὑγρὰς τὰς ἰκμάδας],
      Hos namque miscet cursibus per aërem.
      Viæḉue comes vdo calens adiungitur,
      Vt temperatum misceatur in modum,
      Hæc qualitatum summitas, quæ ipsis inest:
      Ne rapidè adurat omnia immodicus calor,
      Cùm nullus adsit intus vuidus vapor [Ὑγρᾶς ἰκμάδος]:
      Neu humoribus redundet iste neutiquam
      Cursus liquore destitutus humido.
      At veluti bini ad vnicum artifices opus:
      Vapor quidem humectat, parítque gramina,
      Et gignit Autumni asperos fœtus grauis.
            —Morellus *Pisidas* 294–306.

1585 Je sçay qu'on tient qu'alors que la vapeur humide
      Qui part tant du doux flot que du flot nereide,
      Et l'ardante vapeur montent ensemblement
      Dans l'estage second du venteux element.
            —Du Bartas *I Sem.* II. 645–8.

1596 Now gan the humid vapour shed the ground
      With perly deaw.
            —Spenser *F. Q.* III. x. 46.

1605 But if the Vapour brauely can aduenture
      Vp to th'eternall seat of shiuering Winter,
      The small thin humour by the cold is prest
      Into a Cloud, which wanders East and West
      Vpon the Winds wings, till in drops of Raine
      It fall into his Grandames lap againe.
            —Sylvester *Div. Wks.* (*2d Day*) 49.

1611 Boreas and the ruder winds (that vse to driue away
      Aires duskie vapors, being loose, in many a whistling gale).
            —Chapman *Il.* 74.

1620 Tesmoigne sa puissance, ô toy voûte azuree,
      Qui de mille yeux ardans as le front esclaircy:
      Et vous grands arrousoirs de la terre alteree,
      Vapeurs dont le corps rare est en pluye épaissy.
            —Bertaut *Œuv. Poét.* 23.

1633 As when the Sunne in midst of summers heat
      Draws up thinne vapours with his potent ray.
            —P. Fletcher *Purple Isl.* XI. xi.

Vapor—*continued*

1655   From the Ocean breathed
        A little Vapour, or aeriall Fume,
        With the curld wind (as by a Turnor) wreathed.
        —Fanshawe *Lus*. V. xix.

1667   Thus fighting fires a while themselves consume,
        But straight, like Turks, forc'd on to win or die,
        They first lay tender bridges of their fume,
        And o'er the breach in unctuous vapors fly.
        —Dryden *Ann. Mir*. ccxlvi.

1667   A wandring Fire
        Compact of unctuous vapor, which the Night
        Condenses, and the cold invirons round.
        —Milton *P. L*. IX. 634–6.

1668   He [Gabriel] cuts out a silk Mantle from the skies,
        Where the most sprightly azure pleas'd the eyes.
        This he with starry vapours spangles all,
        Took in their prime e're they grow ripe and fall.
        —Cowley 304.

1675   Nor suddain Flames breaking through Skies admire,
        Nor frequent Coruscations by Earths hot
        Exhaling Vapours in the Aire begot.
        —Sherburne *Sphere* 62.

1681   What tho' his birth were base, yet comets rise
        From earthy vapors, ere they shine in skies.
        —Dryden *Abs. and Achit*. I. 636–7.

1708   Th' infernal Winds, 'till now
        Closely imprison'd, by Titanian Warmth,
        Dilating, and with unctuous Vapours fed,
        Disdain'd their narrow Cells.
        —J. Philips *Cyder* I. 197–200.

1713   Bright lambent Flames, and kindled Vapours rise,
        Sweep glaring thro' the Dusk, and strike the wond'ring
           Eyes.
        —Diaper *Dryades* 7.

Why is it that, when considerable vapour [ἀτμὸς] arises from the earth by the action of the sun, the year is inclined to plague?—Aristotle *Problem*. 862a4, in *Opera* IV. 112.

Sunt autem stellae natura flammeae; quocirca terrae, maris, aquarum vaporibus aluntur iis, qui a sole ex agris tepefactis et ex aquis excitantur, quibus altae renovataeque stellae atque omnis aether refundunt eadem et rursum trahunt indidem.—Cicero *De Nat. Deo*. II. xlvi. 118.

1504   Aquosarum impressionum materia est vapor. Causa effectiua remota calor solis & astrorum.—Reisch *Margar. Phil*. dd$_5$.

Vapor—*continued*

1515 Atque in firmamento cœli / idest in aere / ut antea disseruimus / qui
ueluti cœlum conspicitur: & dentior est atque crassior: quam ethereum
corpus ob exhalationes: quæ hinc ad illum uaporesque feruntur.—
Argyropolus *Basil* XXXIX.

1555 [Snow] is a moyst vapour, drawen vp to the middle region of the ayre,
then thycked, and frosen into the body of a cloude.—Dygges *Prognost.* 28.

1614 The earthly vapour is drie and resembleth smoake, whence arise the
windes, the thunders, and lightnings. That of the waters is moyst,
and converteth it selfe into raines and snowes.—Lodge *Seneca* 783.

1622 Vapores ex mari, et amnibus, et paludibus inundatis, longe majorem
copiam gignunt ventorum, quam halitus terrestres. Attamen, qui a
terra et locis minus humidis gignuntur venti, sunt magis obstinati et
diutius durant, et sunt illi fere qui dejiciuntur ex alto; ut opinio veterum
in hac parte non fuerit omnino inutilis; nisi quod placuit illis, tanquam
divisa hæreditate, assignare vaporibus pluvias, et ventis solummodo
exhalationes; et hujusmodi pulchra dictu, re inania.—Bacon *Works* III.
258.

1637 Waterish vapors [*vapores aquosi*] are continually carried upward. Out
of them thickned is made a cloud, or if it falls downward, a mist, or a
little white cloud. From thence it raines, it snowes, it hailes.—Comenius *Gate of Tongues* 8.

1639 All treasure and riches are nothing but congealed vapours: for what is
corne, and fruits, the chiefest of all riches, but the fatnesse of the earth;
Iacobs blessing elevated by the heate of the Sunne and turned into
vapour by the helpe of the Vniversall spirit of the world, then drawne
together by the Adamantine vertue of the Seeds, and Plants, and so
congealed into the same forme?—Plattes *Infin. Treas.* C_{3-4}.

1651 This falling star is made of a grosse vapour; and by reason of its grossenesse hanging together like a cord.—Comenius *Nat. Phil. Ref.* 132.

1660 Quid verò aliud est nubes, nisi vapor qui in alto aëre suspenditur?—
Du Hamel *Meteor. et Fossil.* 43.

1661 That Comets are of nature Terrestrial, is allowable: But that they are
materiall'd of vapours, and never flamed beyond the Moon; were a
concession unpardonable.—Glanvill *Van. Dogm.* 174–5.

1676 In the Earth there are Mines in that abundance as continually to
furnish Vapors capable, when condensed, to entertain and feed the perpetual course of those waters in Springs that dry not up.—*Phil. Trans.*
XI. 612.

1691 An Account of the Circulation of the watry Vapours of the Sea, and
of the Cause of Springs.—*Phil. Trans.* XVII. 468.

1704 The *Ignis Fatuus* is a vapour shining without heat.—Newton *Opt.* (Bk.
III) 134.

Vapor—*continued*

1718   The Aqueous Vapours which arise from the Seas, Rivers, and Marshy
       Grounds, being got to the Middle Region of the Air, form Clouds there
       and grow cold.—Desaguliers *Mariotte* 13.

1726   Vapores autem, qui ex sole & stellis fixis & caudis cometarum oriuntur,
       incidere possunt per gravitatem suam in atmosphæras planetarum &
       ibi condensari & converti in aquam & spiritus humidos, & subinde
       per lentum calorem in sales & sulphura & tincturas & limum & lutum
       & argillam & arenam & lapides & coralla & substantias alias terrestres
       paulatim migrare.—Newton *Principia* (3d ed.) 526.

Vent[1]

1593   An oven that is stopp'd, or river stay'd,
       Burneth more hotly, swelleth with more rage;
       So of concealed sorrow may be said,
       Free vent of words love's fire doth assuage.
           —Shakespeare *V. and A.* 331–4.

1600   At length her sorrows wax'd so big within her,
       They strove for greater vent.
           —Chalkhill *Thea. and Clear.* 47–8.

1611   The late iarre, in which he thunderd threats
       Against Achilles, still he fed, and his affections heats
       Thus vented to Talthybius.
           —Chapman *Il.* 8.

1622   Oft whispering our deare loves, our thoughts oft did we vent.
           —Drayton *Poly-Olb.* XXII. 50.

1633   Here first the purple fountain making vent,
       By thousand rivers through the Isle dispent.
           —P. Fletcher *Purple Isl.* III. vii.

1640   He hist, when he his sorrowes sought to vent.
           —Sandys *Ovid's Met.* 70.

1651   I' th' midd'st of this vast Cave, (which seems to prop
       With it's arch'd back th' whole Mountain) tow'rd the top
       Opens a spacious Vent; through which, it's flight,
       The damp Air takes, Entrance, the Suns warm light.
           —Sherburne *Salmacis* 2.

1667   He ceas'd, discerning Adam with such joy
       Surcharg'd, as had like grief bin dew'd in tears,
       Without the vent of words, which these he breathd.
           —Milton *P. L.* XII. 372–4.

1687   Some vent their sighs to th' air, and ease do find.
           —Ayres, in *CP* II. 278.

---

[1]See also PASSAGE.

Vent—*continued*

1690 This is the living coal, that, burning in me,
Would flame to vengeance, could it find a vent.
  —Dryden *Don S.* I. i, in *Works* VII. 340.

1698 Then thro' his breast his fatal sword he sent,
And the soul issued at the gaping vent.
  —Dryden *Aen.* X. 848–9.

1567 Ematites [a stone] . . . so named for that it resolueth and chaungeth oft
into a bloudie colour: and is called of some stench bloud, for that it
stoppeth his vent or course of flowing.—Maplet *Greene Forest* 20–1.

1621 An Earthquake is a fume, contained in the earth: when it findeth no
vent, it shaketh it, & is made according to the breadth or depth of the
earth.—Widdowes *Nat. Phil.* 19.

1650 And by how much the greater are the pores of the earth, by so much
the better is the place purified. Since therefore by such a breathing
place or vent, a greater heat, and a greater quantity of water passeth,
therefore the sooner is the earth depurated.—French *Sandivogius* 14.

1683 Likewise I observed that dividing this part [of the worm] there issued
out a copious *Ichor;* which is naturally discharged by some Pores or
small Vents in the Skin.—*Phil. Trans.* XIII. 155.

1686 There are many Lakes in the World of Salt water, that have no subterraneous Vents into the Sea.—Plot *Stafford.* 71.

1696 Even so the greater World has Minerals, Metals, Stones, Waters, &c.
and hath Analogous Motions, and its Vapours pent up, and having no
vent may ferment, and may give rise to hot Baths, and other mineral
Waters.—*Phil. Trans.* XIX. 216.

1714 Nay, if the Hypothesis of a central Fire and Waters be true, these Out-
lets seem to be of greatest Use to the peace and quiet of the Terraqueous
Globe, in venting the Subterraneous Heat and Vapours.—Derham
Physico-Theol. 69.

1725 From what has been said upon this head, we may easily form a right
notion of suppuration: to effect which, we must indeed stop the pores,
so as to leave no vent thro' the skin.—Freind *Hist. Phys.* I. 71.

Verdant

1596 And streames of purple bloud new dies the verdant fields.
  —Spenser *F. Q.* I. ii. 17.

1600 Out of the rift red streams he trickling see
That all bebled the verdant plain around.
  —E. Fairfax *Tasso* XIII. xli.

1622 And varying her cleere forme a thousand sundry wayes,
Streakes through the verdant Meads.
  —Drayton *Poly-Olb.* XXII. 26–7.

Verdant—*continued*

1647   Loves Queene to morrow, in the shade
        Which by these verdant Trees is made,
        Their sprowting tops in wreathes shall bind.
            —Stanley *Poems and Trans*. (*Trans*. 37).

1656   The skies are clear and warm; the verdant earth
        Is clad in green, the Birds with vernal song
        Now clear the fields, and all are big with yong.
            —T. Harvey *Mantuan* 11.

1667   The parting Sun
        Beyond the Earths green Cape and verdant Isles
        Hesperean sets, my Signal to depart.
            —Milton *P. L.* VIII. 630–2.

1678   Agèd stooping trees,
        Whose verdant shadow does secure
        This place a native furniture.
            —K. Philips, in *CP* I. 606.

1687   Clear is the air, and verdant is the grass.
            —Ayres, in *CP* II. 276.

1698   The verdant fields with those of heav'n may vie.
            —Dryden *Aen*. VI. 869.

1709   For her the flocks refuse their verdant food.
            —Pope *Winter* 37.

1744   Dew-dropping Coolness to the shade retires;
        There, on the verdant turf or flowery bed,
        By gelid founts and careless rills to muse.
            —Thomson *Summer* 206–8.

Vital[1]

NOTE.—It may be helpful to review here something of an earlier theory of the nature of life in order to supply a context for the use of the epithet *vital* in poetry. For it appears that this adjective, applied to the air and to parts of the human body, is characteristic of neoclassic poetry, and that its use is frequently consistent with one rather comprehensive theory, which is more exactly referred to, of course, by some poets than by others. Moreover, though this theory derives from the classical writers, it seems not to have been commonly referred to before the sixteenth century; the literature of the Middle Ages makes surprisingly little reference to it.[2]

Galen provided the framework for Renaissance theories of the nature and means of life, and when modifications of his ideas were made, and even when his ideas were discredited, there remained much for which his explanation

---

[1] See also AETHER, ELEMENT, and the periphrases for *death*, pp. 364–6.
[2] P. Ansell Robin, *The Old Physiology in English Literature* (London, 1911) 146–7.

Vital—*continued*

was at least as good as any other. For the rest, many of his notions survived when they should rightly have been forgotten.

Singer gives the following brief account of Galen's physiology:

The basic principle of life in the Galenic physiology was a *spirit* or *pneuma* drawn from the general World-spirit in the act of breathing. It entered the body through the windpipe or *trachea* and so passed to the lung and thence, through the *arteria venalis*—which we now call the 'pulmonary vein'—to the left ventricle of the heart, where it encountered the blood . . . . But what was the origin of the blood? . . . Galen believed that the food-substance from the intestines was carried as 'Chyle' by the portal vein to the liver. There it was converted into blood and endowed with a particular pneuma, the *Natural Spirit*, which bestowed the power of growth and nutrition. Part of this lower-grade blood was carried from the liver to the right ventricle, where it gave off impurities by way of the *vena arterialis*, our 'pulmonary artery,' to the lungs, whence they were exhaled in the breath. The venous blood, thus continuously purified, ebbed to and fro in the veins for purposes of ordinary nutrition. A very small part of this venous blood passed through invisible pores in the muscular septum to the left ventricle. There it mixed with air drawn in from the lung by way of the *arteria venalis*, our 'pulmonary vein.' From this mixture was produced a higher-grade blood, the arterial blood, instinct with the principle of life and charged with a second kind of pneuma, the *Vital Spirit*. Blood containing this second kind of pneuma ebbed to and fro in the arteries endowing the various organs with function. Such as reached the brain became there charged with the noblest essence of all, the third pneuma, the *Animal Spirit* or breath of the soul. The *Animal Spirit* was carried from the brain by the nerves —believed to be hollow—and through them initiated the higher functions of the organism, including motion and sensation.[1]

Galen, of course, developed the notions of Hippocrates, and succeeding writers made such changes as they were inclined to. For the Stoics the pneuma was a material substance in the air, an aether.[2] Democritus, however, thought that small particles in the air enter the body in breathing and thereby replenish the soul, which is formed of the same sort of particles. According to him the soul was identical with the heat of the body; when breathing stopped, the soul escaped.[3] Lucretius, in the passage quoted below, seems to refer to this conception.

These are variations which are important—or were once—and yet all the theories agree on a conception of a kind of world soul, the source of all life. For some this source was spirit, for others, the light of the sun. Materialists and Christians alike were able to adapt the theory to their philosophies. The prose passages given below reflect these adaptations and also show how what is known as modern science wrestled with some of these complex ideas.

Est igitur calor ac ventus vitalis in ipso
Corpore qui nobis moribundos deserit artus.
—Lucretius III. 128–9.

---

[1] *A Short History of Medicine* (New York: Oxford University Press, 1928) 57–8.
[2] Robin, *op. cit.* 144–5.
[3] Aristotle *On Respiration* 472a5, in *Opera* III. 539.

Vital—*continued*

Quisquis es, haud, credo, invisus caelestibus auras
Vitalis carpis, Tyriam qui adveneris urbem.
—Virgil *Aen.* I. 387–8.

Quo perit usus aquae suco corruptus amaro,
Vitali sale permutant redduntque salubre.
—Manilius V. 691–2.

Totque foraminibus penetrati corporis exit
Fibrarum anhelans ille uitalis calor.
—Prudentius *Peristep.* IX. 91–2.

καὶ διὰ μυκτήρων φυσίζοος ἔρρεεν ἀήρ:
—Tryphiodorus 77. (Through
the nostrils [of the Trojan horse]
flowed the life-giving air.—Tr. A.
W. Mair.)

Quantum vitalis natura tetendit in axes,
Tantum virtuti pervia terra tuae.
—Rutilius *De Reditu Suo* 61–2.

Quod tamen amisso dudum peccatur honore,
Ascribam tibi, prime pater, qui semine mortis
Tollis succiduae vitalia germina proli.
—Avitus *Initio Mundi* 6–8.

Cur non magis quæ Virgo partum pepererit,
Faciet fidem nullo editæ prolis satu,
Vitalis auræ [ζωοποιοῦ Πνεύματος¹] plena cùm esset spiritu?
—Morellus *Pisidas* 1123–5.

1563   And in this race with famous ende,
To do his Countrey good,
Gaue Onset fyrst vpon his Foes,
And lost his vitall blud.
—Googe 71.

1572   Que por se sustentar em toda idade,
Tudo faz a vital necessidade.
—Camoens *Lus.* 138b.

1578   Mais privé d'action demeure froid et palle,
Sans force et mouvement et sans humeur vitalle.
—Ronsard V. 53.

1585   Car les vitaux rayons des astres flamboyans
Versent esparsement sur les airs ondoyans.
—Du Bartas *I Sem.* II. 339–40.

1591   What man henceforth, that breatheth vitall ayre,
Will honour heauen, or heauenlie powers adore?
—Spenser *Daph.* 197–8.

---

¹Migne *Patr. Gr.* XCII. 1522.

Vital—*continued*

1592   Anch' ei presente a l'opra
        Spirando gia forza e virtude a l'onda,
        D'uccello in guisa, che da frale scorza
        Col suo caldo vital covata e piena,
        Trae non pennato 'l figlio, e quasi informe.
          —Tasso *Mondo Creato* I. 528–32.

1600   And dried up the vital moisture was
        In trees, in plants, in herbs, in flowers, in grass.
          —E. Fairfax *Tasso* XIII. lvii.

1603   To keepe Lifes breath (at point to part) intire,
        And blowe the sparkes that kindle vitall fire.
          —John Davies of Hereford *Micro.* 52.

1605   O, how shall I on learned Leafe forth-sett
        That curious Maze, that admirable Nett,
        Through whose fine folds the spirit doth rise and fall,
        Making it's powers, of Vital, Animal.
          —Sylvester *Div. Wks.* (*6th Day*) 214.

1610   I de el balsamo vital
        Que suda Ciudad Réàl.
          —Góngora I. 445.

1622   And Devonshire that day
        Drew his last vitall breath.
          —Drayton *Poly-Olb.* XXII. 1337–8.

1633   This World, in that great earthquake languished;
        For in a common bath of teares it bled,
        Which drew the strongest vitall spirits out.
          —Donne *Anat. of the World* 11–13.

1640   A death-resembling cold
        Beseig'd her heart, and vitall heat controld.
          —Sandys *Ovid's Met.* 168.

1651   Love's vital heat does last, whilst Love is true.
          —Davenant *Gond.* III. ii. 64.

1659   Hold! Heavens hold! Why should your Sacred fire,
        Which doth to all things life inspire,
        By whose kind beams you bring
        Each year on every thing,
        A new and glorious Spring,
        Which doth th' original Seed
        Of all things in the womb of earth that breed,
        With vital heat and quick'ning seed,
        Why should you now that heat imploy,
        The Earth, the Air, the Fields, the Cities to annoy?
        That which before reviv'd, why should it now destroy?
          —Sprat *Plague* B$_2$.

Vital—*continued*

1667   On the watrie calme
             His brooding wings the Spirit of God outspred,
             And vital vertue infus'd, and vital warmth
             Throughout the fluid Mass.
                 —Milton *P. L.* VII. 234–7.

1668   My much-wrong'd Husband speechless lies within,
             And has too little left of vital breath
             To know his Murderers, or to feel his Death.
                 —Cowley 256–7.

1684   The Breast it strook where Life maintains her Seat,
             And labouring Lungs still fan the vital Heat.
                 —Creech *Theocritus* 147.

1692   Atque inspirato vitales aere flammas
             Suscitat, & raptim cœlesti accenditur igne.
                 —Grovius, in *Mus. Angl. Anal.* (1st ed.) 156.

1698   [Eurydice] Longing the common light again to share,
             And draw the vital breath of upper air.
                 —Dryden *Geo.* IV. 698–9.

1709   So may kind rains their vital moisture yield,
             And swell the future harvest of the field.
                 —Pope *Winter* 15–16.

1757   Wide as the Atlantic and Pacific Seas,
             Or as air's vital fluid o'er the globe.
                 —Dyer *Fleece* IV. 695–6.

1515   Aiebat igitur ille Syrorum linguam indicatiorem esse: & ob affinitatem
         quam habet cum hebraica lingua: sententias aliquo modo scripturarum
         magis attingere: Itaque talem huiusce dicti sententiam esse dicebat:
         Verbum hoc: ferebatur: profouebat / uitalemque [ζωτικήν] fecundi-
         tatem: aquarum nature prebebat / sumunt / atque interpretantur in-
         cubantis auis effigie uimque uitalem quandam imprimentis in ea quæ
         ab ipsa fouent: Talem hanc uocem asserimus sententiam indicare super
         aquas inque spiritum dei ferre / idest ad fecunditatem uitalem aquae
         naturam sanctum spem preparare.—Argyropolus *Basil* Xa–b.

1601   Aire: even all that portion of the whole, which seeming like a void and
         emptie place, yeeldeth this vitall spirit whereby all things do live.—
         Holland *Pliny* I. 18 (Bk. II, chap. xxxviii).

1609   Et sicut in Humano corpore Cor est scaturgio vitalis spiritus & sanguinis,
         omnibus reliquis membris motum & vigorem impartiens: Ita Sol Cor
         Cœli vicissim tanquam omnium Virtutum Elementarium Dominus per
         universam Naturam suos spargit & infundit radios.—Croll *Basil. Chym.*
         208.

1615   Sanguis enim uitalis, ut qui uehementer per totum corpus circunfundi
         debet, iurè tum ex crassiori sanguine tum ex aere, quo tenuior &

Vital—*continued*

fluxilis magis efficiatur, suam generationem adeptus est.—H. Fabricius
Respir. 6.

1627 As for living creatures, it is certain their vital spirits are a substance
compounded of an airy and flamy matter; and though air and flame
being free, will not well mingle; yet bound in by a body that hath
some fixing, they will.—Bacon *Works* IV. 177.

1650 For we must know that the winter is the cause of putrefaction, seeing it
congeals the Vitall spirits in trees.—French *Sandivogius* 17.

1651 Wee finde by experience, that bread, wine and water, yea aire, are
vitall to those that feed upon them, but whence have they that vital
force, I pray you, if not from this diffused soule?—Comenius *Nat. Phil.
Ref.* 23.

The Spirit of a plant is called a vegetable, or vitall spirit; which puts
forth its virtue three manner of wayes; in nutrition, augmentation, and
generation.—*Ibid.* 150.

For joy is a motion, wherein the spirit poureth forth it self at the sense
of a pleasant object, as though it would couple it self with the thing
that it desireth.   Thence that lively colour in the face of a joyful man
from the vital spirit, flowing thither with a most pure portion of the
blood.—*Ibid.* 192.

1651 Vita igitur in sanguine consistit, (utì etiam in sacris nostris legimus)
quippe in ipso vita atque anima primùm elucet, ultimóque deficit . . . .
Et cuilibet cernere est, sanguinem ultimò calorem (pulsûsque vitæque
autorem) in se retinere: quo semel prorsus extincto, ut jam non ampliùs
sanguis est, sed cruor; ità nulla postliminio ad vitam revertendi spes
reliqua.—W. Harvey *Gener. Animal.* 151.

Sanguis itaque est spiritus, ob eximias ejus virtutes, & vires; est etiam
cælestis, siquidem in illo spiritu hospitatur natura (nempe anima)
respondens elemento stellarum; id est, aliquid cœlo analogum, cœli
instrumentum, cœli vicarium.—*Ibid.* 248.

1653 This indeed is the chief use and end of the Circulation of the blood,
for which cause the blood, by its continual course and perpetual influence, is driven about; namely, that all the parts depending upon it
by their first innate warm moisture might be retained in life, and in
their own vital and vegetative essence, and perform all their functions,
whilst (as the Naturalists say) they are sustained and actuated by natural heat, and vital spirits.—W. Harvey *Anat. Exer.* 134-5.

1662 Therefore the Eternall would have the Heaven to contain Waters above
it, and as yet something more (by reason whereof it is called Heaven)
that which we call, the Air, the Skie, or Vitall Air.—Chandler *Van
Helmont* 48.

1668 'Tis the more subtile and nitrous particles, the Air abounds with, that
are through the Lungs communicated to the Bloud: And this Aereal

Vital—*continued*

Niter he [Mayow] makes so necessary to all life, that even the Plants themselves do not grow in the Earth, that is deprived thereof, which yet, being exposed to the Air, and afresh impregnated by that fertilizing salt, becomes fit again to nourish those Plants.—*Phil. Trans.* III. 833.

1674 It is not obscure, that the Existence of this Corporeal Soul depends intirely upon the Act, or Life of it: and in this very respect, seems exactly like to common Flame, and to that alone; inasmuch as the substance of both ceases to be, in the very instant it ceaseth from Motion, wherein the very life of both doth consist; nor can either of the two be, by any means whatever, redintegrated, so as to be numerically the same thing it was. From whence it seems a genuine consequence, that the Essence, or Being of a Sensitive Soul, hath its beginning wholly from life, and from the accension or kindling of a certain subtile and inflammable matter. To render this yet more plain; when in the Genital matter, swarms of active, and spirituous, chiefly Sulphureous particles, predisposed to animation, have met with a less number of Saline particles, in a convenient focus; being as it were kindled, sometimes by another Soul (as in all Viviparous Animals) viz. of the Generant, somtimes by their own rapid motion (as it happens in Oviparous) they conceive life, or break forth into a kind of flame, which thenceforth continues to burn so long as it is constantly fed with sulphureous fewel from within, and nitrous from without; but instantly perisheth, when either through defect of such aliment, or violence from external agents, it comes once to be extinct. This Act of the Corporeal Soul, or enkindling of the vital matter, is in more perfect Animals, such as are furnished with hot blood, so manifestly accompanied with great heat; fuliginous exhalations, and other effects of fire, or flame; that it is difficult for even the most Sceptical person in the World to doubt, that the blood is really in a continual burning, and that life is rather Flame it self, than only like it.—Charleton *Nat. Hist. Passions* 14–16.

1674 The Igneous and Vivifying Spirit, lodged by the Creator in the Sun, and convey'd to the several bodies of the Universe by the Air and Wind, imbued with those vital and benign rayes of the Solar Globe. —*Phil. Trans.* IX. 64.

1676 [A certain ethereal substance bears] much the same relation to æther which the vital aërial spirit requisite for the conservation of flame and vital motions does to air.—Newton, in D. Brewster I. 394.

1685 Or else it may be a humour in this Animal [a kind of shellfish], which by its Vitall energie, as the spring of life and motion, supplies the want of heart, liver, blood, &c.—*Phil. Trans.* XV. 1284.

1694 The difference between the Animal and Vital Spirits is very small, or to speak properly none at all. For the Animal Spirit is nothing else, but the Vital better depurated, and freed from its grosser Particles in the Brain. Yet they are distinguish'd in this, that the Vital Spirit, being diffused with the Blood throughout the whole Body, doth pro-

Vital—*continued*

mote and execute the Vital Functions, viz. Nutrition, Accretion, and Generation: Whereas the Animal Spirits, collected in the Brain, and from thence diffused through the Nerves into the Organs, are chiefly subservient to the Animal Functions, viz. Sense and Motion.—Blome *Le Grand* I. 254.

1704 Vital Faculty, is an Action whereby a Man lives, which is performed, whether we design it or no.—Harris *Lex. Tech.* (under *Vital Faculty*).

1738 The Species of Quadrupeds and Fowls are not to be compar'd, for Number, to Fishes and Insects; there being in all Probability (by what I have observ'd) above a hundred Species of these latter Creatures, whose Vital Juice is Cold, to one of the former: But because we most converse with those whose Vital Juice is Hot, we are apt to think the same of all.—Pointer *Weather* 152.

Vocal[1]

Nunc te vocales impellere pollice chordas.
　　—Tibullus II. v. 3.

Adspicit hunc trepidos agitantem in retia cervos
Vocalis nymphe.
　　—Ovid *Met.* III. 356–7.

Stupet omine tanto
Defixus senior, divina oracula Phoebi
Agnoscens monitusque datos vocalibus antris.
　　—Statius *Theb.* I. 490–2.

1622 For, with their vocall sounds, they [other birds] sing
　　　to pleasant May;
Upon his dulcet pype the Merle doth onely play.
　　—Drayton *Poly-Olb.* XIII. 61–2.

1638 O Fountain Arethuse, and thou honour'd floud,
Smooth-sliding Mincius, crown'd with vocall reeds.
　　—Milton *Lyc.* 85–6.

1640 The vocall Nymph [Echo], this lovely Boy did spy.
　　—Sandys *Ovid's Met.* 50.

1648 He [Orpheus] from the vocall Muse that springs,
At sound of whose Harmonious strings,
The rapid streames their motions ceast.
　　—Sherburne *Medea* 36.

1651 When I see in the ruines of a sute
Some nobler brest, and his tongue sadly mute
Feed on the Vocall silence of his Eye.
　　—H. Vaughan 45.

---

[1]See Sounding for a brief account of the older theories of the nature of sound.

Vocal—*continued*

1659   Ere dissolving tears allowed
                A vocal utterance, as intended words
                Something contained too doleful for records,
                Both sighed, both wept.
                    —W. Chamberlayne *Phar*. V. iii. 240–3.

1667   He glad
                Of her attention gaind, with Serpent Tongue
                Organic, or impulse of vocal Air,
                His fraudulent temptation thus began.
                    —Milton *P. L.* IX. 528–31.

1692   And you fair Rivers that as swiftly flow,
                You who so often have been vocal made
                By swains that pipe and sing under the shade.
                    —Norris 45.

1698   The pines of Mænalus, the vocal grove,
                Are ever full of verse, and full of love.
                    —Dryden *Ecl.* VIII. 31–2.

1709   But tell the reeds, and tell the vocal shore,
                Fair Daphne's dead, and music is no more!
                    —Pope *Winter* 59–60.

Praeter haec natura aptus est aer ad uoces. Quidni, cum uox nihil aliud sit, quam ictus aer? Debent ergo nubes utrimque conseri, et cauae, & intentae. Vides enim quanto uocaliora sint uacua quam plena, quanto intenta quam remissa.—Seneca *Nat. Quaest.* II. xxix.

Cyrenis mutae fuere ranae, inlatis e continente vocalibus duret genus earum.—Pliny *Nat. Hist.* VIII. lxxxiii. 227.

1552   Pisces uocis quidem espertes sunt, ut diximus, sed sonos quosdam stridoresque mouent, qui uocales esse existimantur, ut lyra, ut chromis, de qua suprà dictum abunde est: his enim quasi grunnitus quidam emittitur.—Wotton *Differ.* 163.

1615   For euen as if you cast a stone into a pond there will circles bubble vp one ouertaking and moouing another: so it is in the percussion of the Ayre; there are as it were certaine circles generated, vntil by succession they attaine vnto the Organ of Hearing. Auicen very wittily calleth this continuation of the strucken Ayre *vndam vocalem*, a vocall waue.— Crooke *Body of Man* 696.

1656   Voice is the impulsion of air attracted by respiration, and forced against the vocall artery by the soul, which is in the lungs, with some intent of signification.—Stanley *Hist. Phil. 6th Part* 71.

1661   And the spirits for their liquidity are more uncapable then the fluid Medium, which is the conveyer of Sounds, to persevere in the continued repetition of vocal Airs.—Glanvill *Van. Dogm.* 38.

Vocal—*continued*

1669   The Larynx both gives passage to the Breath, and also, as often as we please, by the force of Muscles, to bear the sides of the Larynx stiffe and near together, as the Breath passeth through the Rimula, makes a vibration of those Cartilaginous Bodies which forms that Breath, into a Vocal sound or Voice, which by the Palate, as a Chelis or shell of a Lute, is sweetened and augmented.—Holder *Elem. Speech* 23.

1676   'Tis a real Truth (though I must here be more sober than to mention it in good earnest,) that (sometimes) the stateliest Trees will familiarly treat, and answer distinctly to all the Discourses, Noise and Voices of the Family, from the softer whisper to the loudest raillery, with vocal imitation.—*Phil. Trans.* XI. 645.

Yielding[1]

     Cedere squamigeris latices nitentibus aiunt
     Et liquidas aperire vias, quia post loca pisces
     Linquant, quo possint cedentes confluere undae.
         —Lucretius I. 372–4.

     Seu te discus agit (pete cedentem aëra disco).
         —Horace *Sat.* II. ii. 13.

     Inde Cythera petit, Boreaque urguente carinas
     Graia fugit, Dictaea legit cedentibus undis
     Litora.
         —Lucan IX. 37–9.

1596   So to a fish Venus herselfe did change,
     And swimming through the soft and yeelding waue,
     With gentle motions did so smoothly range
     As none might see where she the water draue.
         —Sir John Davies *Orchestra* lxxxiv.

1597   Be he the fire, I'll be the yielding water.
         —Shakespeare *Rich. II* III. iii. 58.

1600   Their humble song the yielding air doth beat.
         —E. Fairfax *Tasso* XI. v.

1616   The while his tough hoof tore
     The yielding turf.
         —W. Browne *Brit. Past.* II. i. 763–4.

1622   As when a man doth throw
     An Axtree, that with sleight deliverd from the toe
     Rootes up the yeelding earth.
         —Drayton *Poly-Olb.* I. 497–9.

1638   His eyes shot Cupids at my yielding heart,
     But his firm breast repelled my feeble dart.
         —Whiting, in *CP* III. 503.

---

[1]See also BUXOM, CLEAVE, CUT, LIQUID AIR, PASSAGE, THIN AND THINNER.

Yielding—*continued*

1640   Then swiftly through the yeelding ayre they glide.
           —Sandys *Ovid's Met.* 107.

1651   [Nature] Fishes learns through streams to slide:
          Birds through yeelding air to glide.
           —Stanley *Anacreon* 3.

1656   That Waters yeeld to shoving fish (say they)
          When gliding through they cut the liquid way.
           —Evelyn *Lucretius* 35.

1667   Deep in their hulls our deadly bullets light,
          And thro' the yielding planks a passage find.
           —Dryden *Ann. Mir.* lx.

1668   Michael, the warlike Prince, does downwards fly
          Swift as the journeys of the Sight,
          Swift as the race of Light,
          And with his Winged Will cuts through the yielding sky.
           —Cowley 227.

1675   We then through yielding Aire, and mount the Skies.
           —Sherburne *Sphere* 2.

1686   With painted oars the youths begin to sweep
          Neptune's smooth face, and cleave the yielding deep.
           —E. Waller *Danger at St. Andrews* 41–2.

1691   For he's a puling sprite.
          Why didst thou choose a tender airy form,
          Unequal to the mighty work of mischief?
          His make is flitting, soft, and yielding atoms.
           —Dryden *King Arthur* I. ii, in *Works* VIII. 148.

1698   For wedges first did yielding wood invade.
           —Dryden *Geo.* I. 216.

           A lance of tough ground ash the Trojan threw,
          Rough in the rind, and knotted as it grew:
          With his full force he whirl'd it first around;
          But the soft yielding air receiv'd the wound.
           —Dryden *Aen.* IX. 1003–6.

1627   The cause of all vivification is a gentle and proportionable heat, working upon a glutinous and yielding substance.—Bacon *Works* V. 115.

1633   Being suppurate, and turned to Pus, the Tumor is soft, yeelding, and growing to a point.—Banester *Tumors* 3.

1643   The place of fishes is the water; the place of fowls the aire: both which are diaphanous, clear, moist, and easie yielding elements.—Swan *Spec. Mundi* 382.

Yielding—*continued*

1644 Water, oyle, milke, honey, and such like substances will . . . yield easily to any harder thing that shall make its way through them.—Digby *Two Treat.* 16.

1661 The making of one hole in the yeelding mud, defaces the print of another near it.—Glanvill *Van. Dogm.* 35.

1676 It will not be amiss to take notice, that either the surface of the Air it self, as thin and yielding a Fluid as it is, or the surface of a Solid, contiguous to included Air, or some interposed subtile matter, may reflect the Incident beams of Light more strongly than most men would expect.—*Phil. Trans.* XI. 801.

1680 Nor is the Hardness and Brittleness of Salt more difficult for Nature to introduce into such a yeelding body as Water, than it is for her to make the Bones of a Chick out of the tender Substance of the Liquors of an Egg.—Boyle *Scept. Chym.* 163.

1684 By which resurge [water] quickens and hastens the motion of the air rouling over it, and by it's yielding preserves it in it's Arch'd Cycloidical or Eliptical Figure.—*Phil. Trans.* XIV. 478.

1698 Tho' the smallness of these [gravitational] Forces, in respect of the Gravitation towards the Earths Center, renders them altogether imperceptible by any Experiments we can devise, yet the Ocean being fluid and yielding to the least force, by its rising shews where it is less prest, and where it is more prest by its sinking.—*Phil. Trans.* XIX. 450.

Zone[1]

> Quinque tenent caelum zonae: quarum una corusco
> Semper sole rubens et torrida semper ab igni.
> —Virgil *Geo.* I. 233-4.

> Utque duae dextra caelum totidemque sinistra
> Parte secant zonae, quinta est ardentior illis,
> Sic onus inclusum numero distinxit eodem
> Cura dei, totidemque plagae tellure premuntur.
> —Ovid *Met.* I. 45-8.

> At, qua lata iacet, uasti plaga feruida regni
> Distinet Oceanum zonaeque exusta calentis.
> —Lucan IV. 674-5.

> ἐν δέ τε τείρεα πάντα, τά περ πολυφεγγέι κόσμῳ
> μιτρώσας στεφανηδὸν ἕλιξ ποικίλλεται αἰθὴρ
> ἑπτὰ περὶ ζώνῃσι.
> —Nonnos *Dionys.* XXV. 394-6. (All the constellations were there which adorn the upper air, surrounding it as with a crown of many shining jewels throughout the seven zones.— Tr. Rouse.)

[1]See also BELT, CLIMATE AND CLIME.

Zone—*continued*

1572 Entre a Zona que o Cancro senhorea,
Meta Septentrional do Sol luzente,
E aquella, que por fria se arrecea
Tanto, como a do meyo por ardente.
  —Camoens *Lus.* 39.

1604 Let them throw
Millions of acres on us, till our ground,
Singeing his pate against the burning zone,
Make Ossa like a wart!
  —Shakespeare *Hamlet* V. i. 303–6.

1605 To part the Earth in Zones and Climats euen.
  —Sylvester *Div. Wks. (Colum.)* 477.

1616 Let Icarus alone
To scorch himself within the torrid zone.
  —W. Browne *Brit. Past.* II. i. 887–8.

1617 De mas coronas
Ceñido que sus orbes dos de zonas.
  —Góngora II. 270.

1628 Whose vessels have, by our protection, gone
Past both the Tropicks, and through every Zone.
  —Wither *Britain's Remembrancer* 18.

1633 Off with that girdle, like heavens Zone glittering.
  —Donne *Eleg.* XIX. 5.

1642 Inhabitants of the cold frozen zone,
Call'd Leucomori, for six months seem dead.
  —Kynaston *Leo. and Syd.* 1045–6.

1651 Love's Torrid Zone, their hearts.
  —Davenant *Gond.* II. vii. 73.

1667 Scarce the Sun
Hath finisht half his journey, and scarce begins
His other half in the great Zone of Heav'n.
  —Milton *P. L.* V. 558–60.

1668 That to rich Ophirs rising Morn is knowne,
And stretcht out far to the burnt swarthy Zone.
  —Cowley 328.

1698 But we must beg our bread in climes unknown,
Beneath the scorching or the freezing zone.
  —Dryden *Ecl.* I. 85–6.

Thales and Pythagoras and his followers divide the globe of the whole sky into five circles which they call zones [ζώνας].—Plutarch *De Plac. Phil.* 888c1.

Zone—*continued*

1569   On feint au ciel cinq ceintures, que les Latins appellent Zones, par lesquelles on diuise la rondeur de la terre: Les deux sont froides, les deux temperées, & l'autre chaulde.—Chastel *Gomara* 3.

1581   Ils disent dauantage, qu'il y a sept Zones, espaces, ou cercles au ciel: entre lesquels les vns sont plus hauts, que les autres. Que le ciel donc est d'une nature fort mince, & qu' en chacune Zone, ou cercle du ciel neantmoins, qu'il y a vne estoille fichee, qui s'appelle Planete.— Daneau (translating Damascene) *Phys. Fran.* 402.

1612   We respect the deuision of all the earth into fiue parts called in Latin *Zonæ*, correspondent to the diuision of the heauens by fiue circles.— Cogan *Haven of Health* vb.

1627   Under the line the sun crosseth the line, and maketh two summers and two winters; but in the skirts of the torrid zone it doubleth and goeth back again, and so maketh one long summer.—Bacon *Works* IV. 351.

1651   Zonæ apud Cosmographos sunt fasciæ in Sphæræ cælestis aut terrestris superficie, sed præcipuè terrestris, à circulis Tropicis, aut Polaribus, aut vtrisque terminatæ.—Ricciolus *Almagest. Nov.* I. 21–2.

1659   A Zone is a space of Earth contained between two Parrallels.—Moxon *Tutor Astr.* 27.

1663   They proclaime the Solar or other intense heat to discusse and disperse the exhalations in the torrid Zone.—G. Harvey *Prin. Phil.* II. 380.

1676   He considers, why the *Uvea* or *Choroides* is black in Men, but of divers colours in Brutes; why the Northern Nations have generally grey, but those of the Torrid zone, black eyes.—*Phil. Trans.* XI. 746.

1687   There are five Zones, one Torrid, two Temperate, and two Cold ones. —Abercromby *Acad. Sci.* 50.

1696   Cœlum dividunt Astronomi secundum latitudinem: in quinque Zonas seu partes. Quarum media inter Tropicos quos Sol non transgreditur Torrida dicitur; duæ quæ ab istius dextra versus Polum Arcticum, & sinistra versus Antarcticum porriguntur Temperatæ; totidemque frigidæ quæ Polos seu mundi cardines tangunt: Volueruntque iidem Astronomi his Cœli Zonis similes terræ respondere.—Freind's note on Ovid *Met.* (p. 6).

1718   It is well known, that all the Geographers do divide the Superficies of this Globe into five Zones.—J. Chamberlayne *Nieuwentyt* II. 579.

Periphrases

THE most common form of periphrasis in eighteenth-century English poetry is the two-word phrase made up of a noun and an adjective. Ordinarily the two words are in juxtaposition, the noun bears a collective meaning, and the phrase is introduced by the definite article. This is the form Professor Greenough used to call "the Periphrastic Kind." The following list is largely restricted to this sort of periphrasis as it is used in the description of the natural world.

What have appeared to me as the most popular subjects of periphrasis are listed in alphabetical order. Under each heading is given a representative selection of periphrases on the subject to be found in the works of different poets. The poets represented are cited in roughly chronological order. While not exhaustive, the citations offer a fair indication of the extent to which the various poets used this form. It is hardly necessary to repeat that the emphasis of the collection is upon the literature written before the time of Dryden; examples of periphrases from the eighteenth century may easily be supplied by the reader.

For an explanation of the system of abbreviations see page xiv. In the interests of brevity, where two or more examples in succession are drawn from the same work the title is not repeated.

Air

Du Bartas.—venteux element, *Furies* 224.

Spenser.—fine element, *F. Q.* I. v. 28.

Middleton.—airy kingdom, *Prol. to Micro-Cynicon*, in *Works* V. 483.

Sylvester.—Storm-breed Element, *1611* 605.

Góngora.—elemento subtil, I. 426. diaphano elemento, II. 118.

Sandys.—ayrie region, *Ovid's Met.* 260.

Sherburne.—airy Regions, *Medea* 54.

Air—*continued*

BENLOWES.—aerial plain, *Theoph.* V. xlii.

BUTLER.—Airy Empire, *Hudibras* II. iii (p. 158).

DRYDEN.—airy palaces, *Geo.* I. 559.

POPE.—airy wastes, *Win. For.* 167.

Angels

PRUDENTIUS.—christicolis,[1] *Cath.* III. 56. aërios ministros, *Hamart.* 166.

BUCHANAN.—Aethereos animos, *Mem.* 271.

SCÈVE.—au Ciel residentz, 26.

DU BELLAY.—bandes du ciel, IV. 23. trouppes divines, IV. 82.

CAMOENS.—coros soberanos, *Lus.* 70. sancto coro, 89b. celestes Coros, 164.

RONSARD.—troupes Celestes, V. 20.

DU BARTAS.—exercite des cieux, *I Sem.* I. 542. bourgeois de la province astree, V. 1000. esprits ailez, VII. 181. citoyens du ciel, *Eden* 204. troupe celeste, *Lepan.* 41. astreuse phalange, 80. courriers emplumez, 612. citadins porte-aisles, 623. troupes immortelles, 624. bandes emplumees, 667.

VALVASONE.—angeliche genti, *Angel.* I. xcii.

TASSO.—cittadini del celeste regno, *Mondo Creato* IV. 674. angeliche squadre, IV. 761.

E. FAIRFAX.—wingéd warrior, *Tasso* IX. lx.

SYLVESTER.—blessed Legions, *1605* 286. bright-winged Bands, *1611* 596. heav'nly Quire, *1633* 396. winged Heralds, 413. Celestiall Bird, 414. sacred Torch-man, 414.

Angels—*continued*

Heav'nly Warder, 417. winged Watch-man, 418. Heav'ns bright Messenger, 432. Cœlestiall Herald, 432. immortall Quier, 441. sacred Bands, 456. heav'nly Hoast, 487. Heav'ns harmonious Quire, 562.

MURE.—blest cœlestiall crew, I. 166. blessed Bands, I. 179. cœlestiall Quire, I. 189.

DRUMMOND.—deniz'd Citizen of Skie, II. 32.[2] Heauens ancient Denizones, II. 50. immortall People of the Skies, II. 201.

BENLOWES.—Heav'n's quire, *Theoph.* I. xxx. celestial quire, II. lxxxv. indegenae of Heav'n, V. lxi. enthean quire, VI. xlviii. heav'nly choristers, VII. lxi.

FANSHAWE.—Quires Angelicall, *Lus.* VI. lxxxi. celestial Quires, X. xx.

CHAPELAIN.—soldats ailés, *Pucelle* 114. bande celeste, 117.

MILTON.—spangled host, *Nativity* 21. heav'nly brood, *Fair Inf.* 55. golden-winged hoast, 57. winged Warriours, *Circum.* 1. glistring Guardian, *Comus* 218. heav'nly habitants, 458. aerie crowd, *P. L.* I. 775. Celestial vertues, II. 15. Aerie Knights, II. 536. Sanctities of Heaven, III. 60. Heav'nly Quire, III. 217. winged messengers, III. 229. winged Warriour, IV. 576. Angelic Squadron, IV. 977. Celestial Ardors, V. 249. angelic Quires, V. 251. Angelic Vertue, V. 371. winged Hierarch, V. 468. Angelic Host, V. 535. Angelic throng, V. 650. Heav'ns Host, V. 710. Celestial Quires, VII. 254. glorious Train, VII. 574.

---

[1] This word may be properly compared with *caelicolum;* see Ennius *Ann.* 491.

[2] Compare Mure's phrase for Christ, "Endenizde citizen of skies" (I. 171).

Angels—*continued*

Ethereal Messenger, VIII. 646. flaming Ministers, IX. 156. Angelic Guards, X. 18. ethereal People, X. 27. heav'nly Audience, X. 641. bright Minister, XI. 73. Sons of Light, XI. 80. flaming Warriours, XI. 101. heav'nly Bands, XI. 208. great Visitant, XI. 225. heav'nly Host, XI. 230. Celestial Guide, XI. 785. Host of Heaven, *P. R.* I. 416. Angelic orders, *S.A.* 672. aligeræ turmæ, *Eleg.* III. 65.

COWLEY.—white and radiant crew, 37. heav'ns busie Souldiers, 330.

FLATMAN.—celestial quire, *CP* III. 377.

DRYDEN.—heaven's bright host, *State of Inn.* I. i, in *Works* V. 127. winged warriors, IV. i (V. 151). hymning guards, IV. i (V. 164). ethereal people, V. i (V. 168). Heaven's winged messenger, V. i (V. 174). heavenly nation, *II Conq. Gran.* II. iii (IV. 152). ethereal crowd, *All for Love* V. i (V. 424).

THOMSON.—quire celestial, *Summer* 190.

Animals

AESCHYLUS.—ἀγρόνομων θηρῶν [field-dwelling beasts], *Agam.* 142–3.

SOPHOCLES.— θῆρ' ὀρειβάτην [mountain-ranging beast], *Philoct.* 955.

EURIPIDES.— φύσιν ὀρεσκόων [mountain-dwelling brood], *Hippol.* 1277.

CALLIMACHUS.— γενέθλη τετραπόδων [four-footed breed], *Hymn* III. 130–1.

PACUVIUS.—Quadrupes agrestis, 4.

LUCRETIUS.—fera saecla ferarum, III. 753. silvestria saecla ferarum, V. 967.

VIRGIL.—agmen ferarum, *Ciris* 308.

Animals—*continued*

OPPIAN. — ἄφρονα φῦλα [senseless tribes], *Cyneg.* II. 398. χερσαίησιν ἀγέλησιν [herds of the land], *Hal.* III. 442.

Orphica. — βιοθρέμμονα φῦλα [life-bearing tribes], *Hymn* XXXIV. 19. φῦλα τετραπόδων [tribes of four-footed creatures], LXXVIII. 10–11.

PRUDENTIUS.—brutum pecus, *Cath.* XI. 81. excors natio, XI. 83. uago grege, *Peristep.* XI. 93.

NONNOS.— στίχας ὕλης [troops of the forest], *Dionys.* XIV. 9.

AVITUS.—Quadrupedum greges, *Orig. Mundi* 63.

DU BARTAS.—citadins des autres elemens, *I Sem.* III. 476. champestre brigade, IV. 408. bestes forestieres, V. 907. sauvage bande, VI. 310. hostes des bois, des ondes et des airs, VI. 420. hostes des forests, VI. 930. rebelles bandes, *Furies* 165. velus troupeaux, *Arche* 484. hostes de la terre, *Bab.* 408. peuples et du sec et du moitte element, 420.

SPENSER.—brutish nation, *Astro.* 98. [Cf. saluage nation, *F. Q.* I. vi. 11. woodborne people, I. vi. 16.]

SYLVESTER.—brutish Band, *1605* 192. rude guestes of Aire, and Woods and Water, 206. wandring Heards Of Forrest people, 224. irefull Droues that in the Desarts roare, 227. earthly Bands, 396. Flocks and Droues couer'd with wooll and haire, 404. Forrest - haunting Heards, 425. inhabitants of Sea, and Earth, and Ayre, 426. Legions of Groue-haunting Heards, *1611* 626. savage heards, *1633* 596.

W. BROWNE.—forest's citizens, *Brit. Past.* I. i. 510. savage brood, II. i. 592.

MURE.—brutish bands, I. 132. savage citizens, I. 132.

Animals—*continued*

DRAYTON.—wild and frightfull Heards, *Poly-Olb.* XIII. 87. Bestiall Rout, XXX. 6.

DRUMMOND.—sauage brood, II. 12. Earths ruthlesse brood & harmelesse Heards, II. 57. Woods wilde Forragers, II. 57. woods Burgesses, II. 214.

DAVENANT.—brute heard, *Love and Honour* I. i. 250. Furr'd and Horned Subjects, *Gond.* II. vi. 61.

FANSHAWE.—bruit Creatures, *Lus.* X. vi.

MILTON.—fourfooted kindes, *P. L.* IV. 397. bestial herds, IV. 754. brutal kind, IX. 565.

COWLEY.—panting prey, 337.

DRYDEN.—furred and feathered kind, *State of Inn.* III. i, in *Works* V. 143. savage kind, *I Conq. Gran.* I. i (IV. 36). savage race, *Aureng-Zebe* III. i (V. 254). bestial citizens, *Hind and Panth.* 167. furry spoils, 267. sylvan subjects, 515. furry sons, 1319. four-foot kind, *Lucretius* IV. 273. savage herd, *Don S.* II. i, in *Works* VII. 360. bulky herd of nature, V. i (VII. 466). dumb creation, *Cleom.* V. ii (VIII. 345). savage prey, *Aen.* IX. 803. frighted sylvans, XII. 763.

POPE.—lords of empty wilds and woods, *Win. For.* 48. nations of the field and wood, *Man* III. 99.

DIAPER.—Natives of the shelt'ring Wood, *Dryades* 22.

THOMSON.—furry nations, *Winter* 811.

Bees

VIRGIL.—parvos Quirites, *Geo.* IV. 201.

CLAUDIAN.—mellifer exercitus, *Proserp.* II. 127.

Bees—*continued*

NONNOS. — φιλοσμήνου τοκετοῖο [the hive-loving brood], *Dionys.* XIII. 272.

DU BARTAS.—escole De l'essaim donne-miel, *I Sem.* VII. 555–6. peuple amasse-miel, *Furies* 292.

SHAKESPEARE.—singing masons, *Hen. V* I. ii. 198.

SYLVESTER.—Hunnie-Flies, *1605* 251. Hunnie-People, 338. busie buzzers, 338.

GÓNGORA.—plebeio enxambre, II. 98.

DRUMMOND.—honny People, II. 21. honey Flies, II. 201.

WHITING.—honey - making waxen - thigh'd Inhabitants of Hybla's fragrant vales, *CP* III. 440.

STANLEY. — wing'd Confectioners, *Anacreon* 67.

CLEVELAND.—airy freebooter, *CP* III. 79.

CHAPELAIN.—volans Citoyens, *Pucelle* 448.

DRYDEN.—frugal kind, *Geo.* IV. 17. trading citizens, 20. laden host, 41. industrious kind, 53. winged nation, 73. wand'ring gluttons, 166. little citizens, 295. lab'ring kind, 401. winged squadrons, 448.

THOMSON.—busy nations, *Spring* 510. little chymist, 513. happy people in their waxen cells, *Autumn* 1176. tender race, 1181.

Birds

SOPHOCLES. — πτηνῶν ἀγέλαι [herds of winged creatures], *Ajax* 168. πταναὶ θῆραι [winged prey], *Philoct.* 1146.

EURIPIDES.—αἰθέρος τέκνοις [offspring of the aether], *Electra* 897.

ARISTOPHANES. — φῦλα πτερυγοφόρ' [feathered tribes], *Birds* 1756–7. πτηνῶν γένη [race of winged creatures], *Thesmo.* 46.

Birds—*continued*

ENNIUS.—genus altivolantum, *Ann.* 81.

LUCRETIUS.—genus alituum, V. 1078.

VIRGIL.—agminis aligeri, *Aen.* XII. 249.

MANILIUS.—aerios populos, V. 368. alituum genus, V. 369.

STATIUS.—aeriae gentis, *Silvae* II. iv. 24.

LACTANTIUS.—Alituum choro, *Phoen.* 157.

CLAUDIAN.—alituum cohors, *Phoenix* 77.

PRUDENTIUS.—plumigeram seriem, *Cath.* III. 44.

DRACONTIUS.—gens plumea, *Laud. Dei* I. 242.

PONTANO.—alituum genus, *Meteor.* 1498.

CAMOENS.—siluestres couas, *Lus.* 115.

RONSARD.—De l'air la vagabonde troupe, III. 7. bande ailée, III. 79. escadron qui volle, IV. 440. peuples ailez, IV. 440. troupes esmaillées, VI. 69. Peuple emplumé, VI. 395.

DU BARTAS.—bandes ailees, *I Sem.* I. 388. du ciel flottant les escadres isnelles, II. 318. chantres ailez, IV. 620. pipeur escadron, V. 138. escadre plumeuse, V. 712. la troupe Qui de l'air orageux les plaines entrecoupe, V. 903–4. volant exercite D'animaux bigarrez, VI. 835–6. troupeaux emplumez, VI. 1019. peuple volant, VII. 86. troupes volantes, *Eden* 574. chantres volans, *Furies* 165. hostes des airs, *Arche* 236. chantres peints, *Bab.* 200. peuples emplumez, *Schisme* 400. postes emplumez, *Magnif.* 1066. de l'air les troupes grivelees, *Decad.* 225.

JAMES I.—flying songsters sweet, *Furies* 348.

Birds—*continued*

TASSO.—animai pennuti, *Mondo Creato* V. 735.

CHALKHILL.—airy choir, *Thea. and Clear.* 13.

E. FAIRFAX.—feather'd fellows, *Tasso* XVI. xiii.

JOHN DAVIES OF HEREFORD.—melodious nimble-winged Quiers, *Micro.* 159.

MIDDLETON.—winged passengers, V. 555. tree-quiristers, V. 603.

SYLVESTER.—Aires nimble - winged guests, *1605* 42. Swift-winged Singers, 137. flying multitude, 183. Aerie flokes, 185. feathered Flocks, 227. winged Consorts, 234. winged Legions, 237. flying troupes, 292. fethered singers, 334. Airie peoples, 378. nimble painted Legions, 387. ayrie broods, 396. painted Singers, 418. winged quiars, 422. downie feathered Yong, 438. nimble winged traine, 573. winged people, *1611* 602. winged Myriades, *1633* 596. Forrest Quier, 613.

CHAPMAN.—airie brood, *Il.* 25.

GÓNGORA.—Citharas de pluma, II. 71. Monarchia canora, II. 83. Aladas Musas, II. 99. Organos de pluma, II. 104. Insidia ceua alada, II. 112. turba fugitiua, II. 117. genero alado, II. 117.

W. BROWNE.—wood's sweet quiristers, *Brit. Past.* I. ii. 425. flitting pinionists of air, I. iv. 694. woods' most sad musicians, I. v. 45. artless songsters, II. ii. 543. quaint musicians, II. ii. 559.

BERTAUT.—brigade emplumée, *Œuv. Poét.* 517.

DRAYTON.—feath'red Sylvans, *Poly-Olb.* XIII. 44. mirthfull Quires, XIII. 51. chaunting Fowles, XIII. 77. feathered flocks, XXV. 198.

Birds—*continued*

HANNAY.—Nature's Quiristers, *Philo.* 471.

DRUMMOND.—wing'd Musicians, I 65. feathred Troupes, I. 70. feathred People, I. 103. feather'd Syluans, I. 142. painted Singers, II. 21. Aires Quiresters, II. 142.

DONNE.—free inhabitants of the Plyant aire, *Progr. of the Soule* 215.

P. FLETCHER.—winged shoals, *Purple Isl.* VIII. xxii.

WHITING.—chirping choristers, *CP* III. 440.

CAREW.—chirping minstrels, 1. chirping Wood-choir, 46.

RANDOLPH.—sweetest Chanters, *Poems* 76.

SANDYS.—winged troops, *Ovid's Met.* 30.

HALL.—choristers of air, *CP* II. 224.

STANLEY.—winged Choristers, *Ps. cxlviii* 10. living galleys of the aire, 11.

BOSWORTH.—warbling chanters, *Arcad. and Seph.* (*Proem* 41). silvan warblers, I. 690. woods' chanters, *To Mr. Emely* 42.

DAVENANT.—Feather'd kinde, *Gond.* II. vi. 57. Nature's Voluntary Quire, II. vi. 81.

BENLOWES.—air-minstrels, *T h e o p h.* III. xxxiii. sirens of the grove, III. xxxiii. wing'd, hoof'd, finny droves, X. x. traceless minstrels, XII. lii. painted quire, XII. lxix. aery choristers, XIII. xi.

K. PHILIPS.—Feather'd musician, *CP* I. 605. wingèd quire, I. 609.

CLEVELAND.—winged choristers, *CP* III. 35.

FANSHAWE.—feather'd-Minstrels, *Lus.* IX. lix. little Chirpers, IX. lxiii.

KING.—feather'd chorister, *CP* III. 183.

Birds—*continued*

MILTON.—callow young, *P. L.* VII. 420. Aierie Caravan, VII. 428.

COWLEY.—woods Poetick Throats, 58. Flying prey, 162.

OTWAY.—Feather'd kind, *Orph.* V. i. 239.

FLATMAN.—wingèd choir, *CP* III. 352.

AYRES.—wing'd inhab'tants of the wood, *CP* II. 288. Feather'd Atom, II. 303.

W. CHAMBERLAYNE.—feathered heroes, *Phar.* IV. i. 240.

DRYDEN.—airy choristers, *Thren. Aug.* 366. feathered kind, *State of Inn.* III. i, in *Works* V. 143. feather'd Nimrods, *Hind and Panth.* 2568. callow care, *Geo.* I. 562. unfeather'd innocence, IV. 745. wing'd inhabitants of air, *Aen.* III. 463. rural poet, *Flower and Leaf* 125.

CLÉRIC.—Peuple de l'air, *Jeux Floraux* C_2.

POPE.—feather'd quires, *Autumn* 24. feather'd people, *Win. For.* 404.

J. HUGHES.—Feather'd Brood, *Ode to Creator* 4.

DIAPER.—feather'd World, *Oppian's Hal.* I. 39. feather'd Pillagers, I. 276. feather'd Wantons, I. 783. downy Songsters, I. 1232. feather'd Race, II. 168.

THOMSON.—feathery people, *Winter* 87. feathered game, 793. plumy nations, *Summer* 737. aerial tribes, 1121. plumy people, *Spring* 165. gay troops, 584. tuneful nations, 594. coy quiristers, 597. glossy kind, 617. fearful kind, 689. soft tribes, 711. feathered youth, 729. plumy burden, 747. soaring race, 753. gentle tenants of the shade, 789. feathered eddy, *Autumn* 840. merry minstrels, *Castle of Ind.* I. x. 1. swarming songsters, I. x. 2.

Blood

LUCRETIUS.—ruber umor, IV. 1051.

NONNOS.—φονίην ἐέρσην [gory dew], Dionys. XVII. 360.

DU BARTAS.—fils rouges, Furies 326. ame rouge, Troph. 320.

SHAKESPEARE.—purple sap, Rich. III IV. iv. 277.

E. FAIRFAX.—purple flood, Tasso XII. lxxxiii.

SYLVESTER.—crimsen streames, 1605 339. ruddy soule, 1611 523. crimsin tears, 650. Crimsin Flood, 1633 504.

GÓNGORA.—Humor purpureo, II. 300.

CHAPMAN.—purple licour, Odys. 44.

MURE.—crimson flood, I. 74.

DRUMMOND.—purple flood, II. 13.

P. FLETCHER.—purple wine, Purple Isl. XI. xlii.

WHITING.—sanguine liquor, CP III. 448. sanguine flood, III. 518.

GODOLPHIN.—purple flood, CP II. 251.

HALL.—scarlet sweat, CP II. 217.

BENLOWES.—purple ocean, Theoph. IV. xii. purple riv'lets, XIII. lxxv.

W. CHAMBERLAYNE.—purple flood, Phar. I. ii. 315.

FLATMAN.—crimson flood, CP III. 314.

GROVIUS.—vitalem liquorem, Mus. Angl. Anal. (1st ed., 1692) 146.

DRYDEN.—sanguine torrent, Don S. I. i, in Works VII. 324. purple vomit, Cleom. I. i (VIII. 285). crimson flood, Aen. X. 1117.

DIAPER.—vital Flood, Oppian's Hal. II. 151.

J. JONES.—vital Tides, Oppian's Hal. IV. 679.

ARMSTRONG.—vital fluid, Health II. 16.

Body

LUCAN.—conpages humana, V. 119.

PRUDENTIUS.—conpage terrea, Peristep. V. 302.

AVITUS.—lutea compagine, Carm. V. 288, in Œuvres.

SCÈVE.—superbe Machine, 29.

RONSARD.—despouille mortelle, II. 168. manteau terrien, V. 17.

DU BARTAS.—despouille sacree, I Sem. V. 999. vase estroit, Eden 340. mesche vitale, Magnif. 51. estroite maison, 1226.

TASSO.—terreno albergo, Mondo Creato VII. 594.

SPENSER.—fleshly ferme, F. Q. III. v. 23. mortall frame, Love 113.

CHALKHILL.—earthly mansion, Thea. and Clear. 1950.

SYLVESTER.—fraile Earthen Masse, 1605 244. house of clay, 296. earthly clod, 381. grosse fleshly lump, 649. earthly TEMPLE, 1611 587. frame of flesh, 1633 640.

BERTAUT.—despoüille mortelle, Œuv. Poét. 196.

DRUMMOND.—earthly Iaile,[1] II. 47.

CAREW.—clayey tenement, 51.

E. WALLER.—soul's dark cottage, Last Verses 13. frail tenement of clay, Sev. Petitions 26.

DAVENANT.—private tenement, S. of Rhodes I. ii. 141. fleshy Robes, Gond. I. iii. 46.

BENLOWES.—load of clay, Theoph. I. lxxxvi. cloisters of their flesh, VI. xix. brittle sheds of clay, XI. lxxxviii.

FANSHAWE.—brittle Earthen Wall, Lus. IX. xci.

HAMMOND.—Man's fleshy boat, CP II. 513.

[1]This phrase may mean the earth instead of the body.

Body—*continuea*

W. CHAMBERLAYNE.—warm tenements of breath, *Phar.* IV. i. 27.

MILTON.—House of mortal Clay, *Nativity* 14. earthly mould, 138. humane weed, *Fair Inf.* 58. hairy strength, *L'A.* 112. fleshly nook, *Il. P.* 92. earthy load, *Son. XIV* 3. Earthy grosnes, *Time* 20. Sin-worn mould, *Comus* 17. earthie Charge, *P. L.* IX. 157. corporeal Clod, X. 786. fleshly Tabernacle, *P. R.* IV. 599. mole carneâ, *In Obit. Præs. Eli.* 37.

DRYDEN.—mortal frames, *Ind. Emp.* II. i, in *Works* II. 342. tenement of earth, *Amboyna* V. i (V. 86). lump of senseless clay, *All for Love* V. i (V. 432). tenement of clay, *Abs. and Achit.* I. 158. corporeal frame, *Lucretius* II. 24. earthly prison, *Don S.* III. i, in *Works* VII. 376. mortal frame, *Aen.* IV. 486. earthly mold, *Flower and Leaf* 483.

Bullets

CAMOENS.—ferrea pela, *Lus.* 165.

WHITING.—leaden globes, *CP* III. 488.

FANSHAWE.—Vulcans horrid Balls, *Lus.* II. lxix. Iron Ball, X. xxviii. thund'ring Ball, X. xlvi. sulphureous Balls, X. lv.

POPE.—leaden death, *Win. For.* 132.

Cannon shot

DU BARTAS.—salpetré foudre, *I Sem.* II. 433. foudreuse tempeste, *Lepan.* 462.

MILTON.—chaind Thunderbolts and Hail Of Iron Globes, *P. L.* VI. 589-90.

J. PHILIPS.—globous Irons, *Blenheim* 147.

Cattle

SOPHOCLES.— ἀφόβοις θηρσὶ [tame beasts], *Ajax* 366.

Cattle—*continued*

ACCIUS.—agrestis cornutos, 510.

PACUVIUS.—cornifrontes armentas, 2.

LUCRETIUS.—buceriae greges, II. 663. bucera saecla, V. 866.

NONNOS.—κερόεσσαν γενέθλην [horned generation], *Dionys.* XIV. 202.

Robin Hood.—horned beasts, xxii.

CHALKHILL.—milky droves, *Thea. and Clear.* 36.

SHAKESPEARE.—horned herd, *Ant. and Cleo.* III. xiii. 128.

SYLVESTER.—hungrie fodder-eaters, *1605* 118. domestick droves, *1633* 596.

DRAYTON.—stragling Heards, *Poly-Olb.* IV. 222.

POPE.—lowing herds, *Summer* 86.

THOMSON.—milky drove, *Autumn* 1265.

Corn

PONTANO.—lætam cererem, *Urania* II. 532. cerealia munera, II. 890.

DU MONIN.—de Ceres les émaillés cheueus, *Manip. Poet.* 15.

DU BARTAS.—espics barbotez, *I Sem.* VII. 498. despouilles blondes, *Magnif.* 279.

SYLVESTER.—bearded eares, *1605* 248. flowerie graine, 248. golden Treasures of the Plains, *1633* 603.

MAY.—yellow Ceres, *Lucan* Gb.

CAREW.—yellow Goddess, 127.

STANLEY.—hopefull treasure of the yeare, *Ps. cxlviii* 7.

MILTON.—bearded Grove, *P. L.* IV. 982. cornie Reed, VII. 321.

DRYDEN.—bearded product of the golden year, *Geo.* I. 113. foodful store, I. 204. bearded harvest, II. 746. yellow prey, *Aen.* IV. 585.

POPE.—bearded grain, *Win. For.* 370.

DIAPER.—yellow Harvest, *Oppian's Hal.* II. 47.

Corn—*continued*

THOMPSON.—breathing harvest, *Summer* 363. gifts Of yellow Ceres, *Liberty* I. 158–9.

JAGO.—bearded Store, *Edge-Hill* III. 602.

Death

NOTE.—Many of the apparently flamboyant accounts in poetry of people dying can be shown to be rather accurate descriptions of the physiology of death in the terms of an old theory. That theory is stated explicitly by Lucretius:

> est igitur calor ac ventus vitalis in ipso corpore qui nobis moribundos deserit artus.[1]

That is, in the loss of blood the vital breath (in some terms a physical substance) was also lost. As Pliny puts it: "In bloud consisteth a great portion and treasure of life. When it is let out, it carieth with it much vitall spirit."[2] Further, the identification of life with heat was the means by which the ancient atomists were able to explain how life left the body. Aristotle, in partial disagreement, describes the conclusions of Democritus in this way:

Democritus states that among animals that breathe there is a result of their breathing, and alleges that it prevents the soul from being crushed out; but he nowhere says that this is why nature has invented breathing; for generally speaking, like other natural philosophers, he never reckons upon any reason of this kind. But he does identify the soul with the heat, regarding both as first forms of spherical particles. So he contends that when these particles are being crushed by the surrounding air, which is pressing them out, breathing inter-

---

[1] III. 128–9.
[2] Holland *Pliny* I. 346 (Bk. XI, chap. xxxviii).

Death—*continued*

venes to help them. For in the air are a large number of these particles, which he calls mind and soul; so that when breathing takes place and the air enters, these enter too and check the crushing, preventing the soul which is in the animal from passing out. For this reason upon breathing in and breathing out depend life and death; for when the surrounding air by its crushing action wins the mastery, and nothing entering from the outside can check it, as breathing is impossible, death then comes to living creatures; for he considers that death is the passing out of such forms from the body owing to the pressure of the surrounding air.[3]

There is here, of course, a reference to a kind of world soul, and such in fact was one of the cardinal principles of Galen's physiology.[4] Through inhalation this vital heat is tempered and kept under control.[5] When breathing once stops, the soul finds a way to escape, through a wound if there is one, or through the mouth.

Such speculation concerning the presence and escape of life derived from the knowledge that the continuance of life depended on the normal functioning of the heart and of the blood. For it was in the veins, through which the blood passed, that the vital spirits also passed. And it is interesting to observe in this connection how death might come about through the effect of emotion upon the heart. One writer in the seventeenth century explains, for example, how joy causes the heart to dilate. And in the extreme case,

upon extraordinary dilatation of the floud-gates of the heart by immoderate

---

[3] Aristotle *On Respiration* 472a5 (LCL *On the Soul* 435–7).
[4] See p. 343.
[5] See Comenius *Nat. Phil. Ref.* 177.

Death—*continued*

joy, the current of blood both out of the *Vena cava*, and from the *arteria venosa*, may pour itself with so much violence, and in so great a quantity, into the ventricles thereof, that the heart, unable to discharge itself soon enough of that oppressing deluge, by retruding its valves, may be suffocated, its motions stopped, and the Vital Flame in a moment extinguished.[1]

And according to this writer, also, the particles of the soul escape when the heart stops beating.[2] Virgil, too, seems to have had knowledge that the vital flame ("calor") left the body under excessive emotion. As Dryden translates:

> Astonish'd at the sight, the
> vital heat
> Forsakes her limbs; her veins
> no longer beat.[3]

VIRGIL

Vomit ille animam et cum sanguine
mixta
Vina refert moriens.
—*Aen.* IX. 349–50.

DU BARTAS

Du bout de sa lame
Asseuré, fait sortir à fils rouges son
ame.
—*Furies* 325–6.

SHAKESPEARE

Her contrite sighs unto the clouds
bequeathed
Her winged sprite, and through her
wounds doth fly
Life's lasting date from cancell'd
destiny.
—*Lucrece* 1727–9.

---

[1]Charleton *Nat. Hist. Passions* 143.
[2]*Ibid.* 14.
[3]*Aen.* III. 397–8. Virgil's line reads: "calor ossa reliquit" (308). See Lucretius, also, III. 231–6.

Death—*continued*

SPENSER

Whiles sad Pyrochles lies on senselesse
ground,
And groneth out his vtmost grudging
spright,
Through many a stroke, and many a
streaming wound.
—*F. Q.* II. v. 36.

P. FLETCHER

There lies the grunting swine,
And spues his liquid soul out in his
purple wine.
—*Purple Isl.* XI. xlii.

SANDYS

Flames and pains increase:
Again they languish; and together
cease.
To liquid aire his vanisht spirits turn:
The sable coales in shrouds of ashes
mourn.
—*Ovid's Met.* 158.[4]

CHAPELAIN

Le grand corps de Norgale,
Parmy son sang fumeux, sa dure vie
exhale.
—*Pucelle* 64.

W. CHAMBERLAYNE

He falls, and from each purple
sallyport
Of wounds, tired spirits, in a thick
resort,
Fly the approach of death.
—*Phar.* IV. i. 393–5.

MILTON

He fell, and deadly pale
Groand out his Soul with gushing
bloud effus'd.
—*P. L.* XI. 446–7.

DRYDEN

Bring water; bathe the wound; while
I in death

---

[4]See Ovid *Met.* VIII. 401–2: "glomerataque sanguine multo viscera lapsa fluunt."

Death—*continued*

Lay close my lips to hers, and catch
the flying breath.
—*Aen.* IV. 982–3.

The streaming blood distain'd his
arms around,
And the disdainful soul came rushing
thro' the wound.
—*Ibid.* XII. 1376–7.

Deer

Note.—With the poetic periphrases
for *deer* given below we may compare
Plot's definition: "*Deer* (which are
also reckon'd amongst the horned
Animals that chew the Cudd)"[1] and
Morton's description: "The Deer-
Kind . . . are bifulcous and Ruminant,
or such as chew the Cud, and also the
Males of them are cornigerous, but
their Horns are solid, branched, and
deciduous."[2]

SOPHOCLES.—στικτῶν θηρῶν [dappled
beasts], *Philoct.* 184–5.

OPPIAN. — βαλίων θηρῶν [dappled
beasts], *Cyneg.* II. 314.

RONSARD.—cornus troupeaux, III.
211.

SHAKESPEARE.—dappled fools, *A. Y.
L. I.* II. i. 22.

W. BROWNE.—speckled herd, *Brit.
Past.* II. iv. 639.

DRAYTON.—Burgesse of the Wood,
Poly-Olb. XVIII. 66.

DENHAM.—horned hoast, *Cooper's Hill*
236.

JAGO.—horned Tribes, *Edge-Hill* IV.
173.

Dew

CATULLUS.—roscido umore, LXI.
24–5.

SPENSER.—deawy humour, *F. Q.* VI.
ix. 13.

---

[1]*Stafford.* 258.   [2]*Northampton.* 452.

Dew—*continued*

SHAKESPEARE.—liquid pearl, *M. N.
D.* I. i. 211.

SYLVESTER.—Sommers sweet-distill-
ing drops, *1605* 387.   purled Pearls,
1633 519.

DRAYTON.—moyst pearle, *Poly-Olb.*
XIII. 123. liquid pearle, XXI.
100.

MILTON.—Orient Pearle, *P. L.* V. 2.
pearly grain, V. 430.

DRYDEN.—dewy bev'rage, *Geo.* II.
294.

The Earth

Note.—Compare with the poetic
periphrases given below the following
prose phrases: "globo terrestre" (Galileo *Dial.* 52); "terrestriall Globe"
(Howell *Dodon. Grove* 30); "inferiour
world" (Comenius *Nat. Phil. Ref.*
128); "Globo Terraqueo" (Ricciolus
Almagest. Nov. I. 47); "inferiour
Globe" (Pinnell *Croll* 95); "terraque-
ous Globe," "terrestrial Globe" (Boyle
Examen of Hobbes 14, 27); "Mundum
Terrenum" (Kircher *Mundus Subt.* I.
65); "Terraqueous Globe" (*Phil.
Trans.* I. 265); "Terrestrial Globe"
(Wilkins *Real Character* 54); "sub-
lunary world" (Plot *Stafford.* 83);
"Terraqueous Globe" (Hooke *Cometa,*
in Gunther *Early Science in Oxford*
VIII. 294); "Terrestrial Sphere"
(Ray *Physio-Theol.* 87).

PRUDENTIUS.—sfera mobilis atque ro-
tunda, *Apoth.* 210.

SCÈVE.—Machine ronde, 22.

DU BELLAY.—voulte ronde, II. 141.
masse ronde, V. 407.

RONSARD.—machine ronde, V. 352.

DU BARTAS.—mere feconde, *I Sem.* I.
199. humain theatre, I. 512.
rond du plus bas element, II. 344.
basse rondeur, III. 427. ronde

The Earth—*continued*

machine, *Furies* 101. Des fragiles humains le diapré sejour, *Art.* 599. rond edifice, *Voc.* 98. rond bastiment, *Lepan.* 259.

Du Monin.—globe Terrien, *Urano.* 9. seiour rond, 18.

Tasso.—Gran teatro e volubile e rotante, *Mondo Creato* VII. 17.

James I.—Fabrique large and round, *Furies* 221.

Shakespeare.—mortal round, *V. and A.* 368. terrestrial ball, *Rich. II* III. ii. 41. world's globe, *II Henry VI* III. ii. 406. goodly frame, *Ham.* II. ii. 310. Tellus' orbed ground, III. ii. 166. great globe, *Temp.* IV. i. 153.

Sylvester.—flowerie-mantled Stage, *1605* 77. Mansion of Mankinde, 89. This glorious Buildings goodly Pedestall, 108. our Grandames fruitfull panch, 177. All-Theater, 206. Earthly Ball, 208. our Element, 247. Diaprie Mansions where man-kind doth trade, 379. Mundane Spheare, 478. terrestrial clod, 626. nether Ball, *1611* 556. massie Ball, *1633* 393. wretched Frame, 434. Earthly Stage, 487. round Theater, 515. fickle Frame, 596.

Chapman.—flow'ry sphere, *Il.* I. 84.

Drummond.—flowrie Globe, I. 120. great Round, II. 27. flowrie Orbe, II. 45.

Drayton.—terrestriall Globe, *Poly-Olb.* VIII. 114. mightie Round, XIX. 332. earthly Ball, XIX. 365.

Whiting.—massy globe, *CP* III. 482.

Fanshawe.—Globe of Neptune and of Ceres yellow, *Lus.* VIII. xxxii. Universall Frame, X. lxxix. World's great Fabrick, X. lxxx.

Milton.—firm opacous Globe Of this round World, *P. L.* III. 418–9.

The Earth—*continued*

great Round, VII. 267. Centric Globe, X. 671.

Cowley.—worlds vast ball, 261.

Dryden.—new-made orb, *State of Inn.* II. i, in *Works* V. 136. gay frame, II. i (V. 136). ball of earth and water mixt, II. i (V. 138). new-created frame, III. i (V. 150). drunken globe, *Aureng-Zebe* III. i (V. 244). terrestrial ball, *Ovid's Met.* I. 7. earthly ball, I. 61. goodly ball, *Ecl.* VI. 52. earth's compacted frame, *Aen.* VI. 980.

Pope.—congregated Ball, *Horace I Ep.* vi. 5.

Blackmore.—terrestrial Ball, *Creation* II. 90.

Thomson.—inferior world, *Summer* 1781.

Dyer.—globe terraqueous, *Fleece* IV. 656.

Fish[1]

Aeschylus. — ἀναύδων παίδων τᾶς ἀμιάντου [the voiceless children of the stainless sea], *Pers.* 577–8.

Sophocles.—πόντου εἰναλίαν φύσιν [brood of the briny sea], *Antig.* 342.

Euphro.—Νηρείων τέκνων [offspring of Nereus], *Comic. Attic. Frag.* (ed. Kock) III. 321.

Empedocles. — θαλασσονόμων [sea-dwellers], Diels, Fr. 76.

Pacuvius.—Nerei repandirostrum incurvicervicum pecus, 352.

Plautus.—squamoso pecu, *Rudens* 942.

Lucretius.—squamigerum genus, I. 162. squamigeri, I. 378. mutae natantes squamigerum pecudes, II. 342–3.

Virgil.—genus aequoreum, *Geo.* III. 243. genus omne natantum, III.

[1]See also Scaly kind, pp. 297–9.

Fish—*continued*

541. immania armenta, IV. 394–5. vasti gens umida ponti, IV. 430. pecus Amphitrites, *Ciris* 486.

MANILIUS.—squamigeri gregis, V. 659.

OPPIAN.—ἔθνεά τοι πόντοιο πολυσπερέας τε φάλαγγας παντοίων νεπόδων, πλωτὸν γένος ᾿Αμφιτρίτης [the nations of the sea and the far-scattered phalanxes of all kinds of finny ones, the swimming kind of Amphitrite], *Hal.* I. 1–2. ἀλίτροφα φῦλα [sea-bred tribes], I. 76. γένος ἄλμης [race of the sea], I. 111. ὅσοι ναίουσι θάλασσαν ζωοτόκοι [viviparous ones that dwell in the sea], I. 646–7. διερὸν στρατόν [watery army], II. 445. φῦλα Ποσειδάωνος ἐναύλων [tribes of the haunts of Poseidon], III. 5. πλωτῶν γένος [swimming kind], III. 183. νεπόδων στίχας [ranks of finny creatures], IV. 652. φῦλον ἅπαν νεπόδων τὸ πολύπλανον [the whole wandering tribe of finny creatures], *Cyneg.* II. 434. εἰναλίοις νεπόδεσσιν [finny creatures of the sea], III. 465.

INCERTUS.—squamosum agmen, *Iona* 86. gentem squamigeram, *Sodoma* 143–4.

AUSONIUS.—Squamigeri gregis, *Mosella* 83. pecus æquoreum, 135. cærula turba natantum, 141.

PRUDENTIUS.—squamosa agmina, *Peristep.* V. 444.

VICTOR.—Squammea turba, *Genes.* I. 123.

NONNOS. — ἀλίτροφα πώεα λίμνης [brine-bred flocks of the deep], *Dionys.* V. 182. ἰχθυόεσσαν γενέθλην [fishy offspring], XXVI. 273. εἰναλίης λιπογλώσσοιο γενέθλης [voiceless generation of the deep sea], XXVI. 281.

Fish—*continued*

EUGENIUS.—plebs squamosa, *Dubia* XX. 21–2.

PONTANO.—Neptunni pecus, *Urania* I. 1065. Æquoreus grex, III. 314. quæ æquora ponti Monstra colunt, *Meteor.* 58–9. grex Squamigerûm, 1498–9.

LIPPIUS.—Dispersas ponti gentes, aciésque natantum Squamigeras, almæ varium genus Amphitrites, *Oppian's Hal.* 1. squamigeros populos, 17.

DU BELLAY.—armez d'escailles, II. 23. marine trouppe, IV. 3.

CAMOENS.—gado de Proteo, *Lus.* 4. filhas de Nerêo, 22. cerulea companhia, 22.

JODELLE.—peuples froidureux, 242.

RONSARD.—troupe escaillée, III. 79. peuples escaillez, III. 183. tout ce qui habite D'escaillé dans la mer, IV. 115. escadrons des eaux, IV. 209. du vieillard Protée les troupeaux, IV. 422. bandes escaillées, VI. 69.

DU MONIN.—Squamiferos ciues, *Manip. Poet.* 6. bourgeois mariniers, 15. turmæ Squammigeræ, *Beresith.* 23.

DU BARTAS.—troupeaux escaillez, *I Sem.* II. 319. peuples sans poulmon, II. 342. bourgeois d'Amphitrite, II. 677. bourgeois de la plaine liquide, IV. 70. peuples escaillez, V. 22. nageurs citoyens de la venteuse mer, V. 30. moites citoyens, V. 69. citadins des flots, V. 165. goulus animaux que l'Amphitrite porte, V. 312. hostes de Neptune, V. 392. peuples vivans es provinces salees, V. 427. bandes escaillees, V. 428. bourgeois de Thetis, V. 535. bandes marinieres, V. 548. citadins des eaux,

Fish—*continued*

VI. 930. semence escailleuse, *Eden* 33. peuples nageurs, 574. muets troupeaux escaillez, *Furies* 163–4. branlante cité Des peuples escaillez, *Art.* 591–2. bourgeois des eaux, *Bab.* 408. race escaillee, *Lepan.* 485.

TASSO.—animai squamosi, *Mondo Creato* III. 478. squamose torme, V. 38. squammose gregge, V. 242. umidi natanti, V. 282. popoli natanti, V. 454. abitanti del mare ondoso, VI. 1873.

SPENSER.—flocking fry, *S. C.: Oct.* 14. finny droue, *F. Q.* III. viii. 29. Neptunes mightie heard, III. viii. 30.

CHALKHILL.—wat'ry inmates, *Thea. and Clear.* 28.

SYLVESTER.—scaly shoales, *1605* 10. innumerable Legions Of greedy mouthes that haunt the brynie Regions, 43. Sea-Citizens, 145. waterie Citizens, 151. Water's silent Colonies, 173. dyuing guests, 186. people of the Water, 208. Hoast that rowes In waterie Regions, 224. fruitfull-spawning Legions, 227. Ocean-peoples plenteous broods, 233. scaly Nation, 273. swimming shoales, 292. skalie Legions, 334. scaly folke, 378. Water-guests, 425. Ocean's fry, *1633* 596.

MURE.—Proteus' flocks, I. 69. skailly squadrones, I. 132.

MURTOLA.—squamosi armenti humidi, *Creat. Mondo* (1608) V. x. 4. squamose schiere, (1618) V. xii. 80.

W. BROWNE.—scaly train, *Brit. Past.* II. i. 286. finny coursers, II. i. 983. finny shoal, *Visions* I. 3.

GÓNGORA.—vulgo nadante, II. 101. escamada fiera, II. 102.

Fish—*continued*

DRAYTON.—finny Heard, *Poly-Olb.* II. 439. scalie brood, VII. 15. floating Fry, XXV. 125. new-spawn'd numerous Frie, XXVI. 223. Silver-scaled Sholes, *Nimph.* VI. 125.

DRUMMOND.—Proteus monstrous People, I. 7. Citizen of Thetis Christall Floods, I. 18. skalie Flockes, I. 69. People dombe, I. 146. Proteus Flockes, II. 28. humid Swimmers, II. 57.

P. FLETCHER.—scaly nation, *Locusts* III. xxi.

CAREW.—scaly herd, 25.

SHERBURNE.—Mute People of the Floud, *Salmacis* 8.

DAVENANT.—Seas deep Dwellers, *Gond.* II. v. 12.

H. VAUGHAN.—Scalie, shading familie, 40.

BENLOWES.—scaly nation, *Theoph.* III. xcix. scaly brood, XIII. liv.

CHAPELAIN.—Peuples escaillés, *Pucelle* 123. trouppeau müet, 123.

MILTON.—finny drove, *Comus* 115.

DRYDEN.—watery herd, *Cromwell* xxxv. scaly herd, *Ann. Mir.* xv. scaly nations, *Geo.* III. 806. scaly flocks, IV. 568. finny flocks, IV. 621. finny coursers, *Aen.* I. 211. fishy food, IV. 373. finny team, V. 1069.

FLATMAN.—scaly people, *CP* III. 371. scaly fry, III. 386.

FORD.—gregi silenti, *Mus. Angl. Anal.* (1st ed., 1692) 129. mutum natantûm gregem, 132. gens squamea, 133. grex squameus, 135. natio natatrix, 138. gentes aquatiles, 139.

AYRES.—silver finny race, Of slippery kind, *CP* II. 356.

CREECH.—Scaly Kind, *Manilius* (Bk. V) 81.

Fish—*continued*

BLACKMORE.—Finny Nations, *Creation* II. 150. Scaly Colonies, VII. 721.

POPE.—scaly breed, *Win. For.* 139. Finny Prey, *Rape of the Lock* II. 26.

DIAPER.—finny Race, *Dryades* 17. finny Herds, *Oppian's Hal.* I. 9. wat'ry Natives, I. 155. scaly Kind, I. 162. Sea-born Tribes, I. 706. scaly Prey, I. 709. moist Battalions, I. 735. moist Tribes, I. 968. Finny Tribes, I. 1077. scaly Nations, II. 1. floating Herd, II. 896.

J. JONES.—scaly Legions, *Oppian's Hal.* III. 81.

THOMSON.—copious fry, *Winter* 877. finny race, *Spring* 395. finny swarms, *Autumn* 922. watery breed, *Country Life* 54.

Flowers

AESCHYLUS.—γαίας τέκνα [children of the earth], *Pers.* 618.

VIRGIL.—Veneris florentia serta, *Dirae* 20.

HORACE.—ruris honorum, *Odes* I. xvii. 16.

RONSARD.—verds tresors de la plaine, III. 204.

DU BARTAS.—manteau fleuronné du plus bas element, *I Sem.* II. 480. peintes beautez, *Voc.* 27.

TASSO.—dipinte spoglie, *Mondo Creato* VII. 668.

SPENSER.—fields honour, *Muio.* 123. flowring pride, *Daphn.* 27.

SYLVESTER.—flowerie Mantle, *1605* 48. flowrie VER's inammeld tapistrie, 273. flowerie Fleece, 461. painted beauties, *1606* 2.

W. CHAMBERLAYNE.—flowery wealth, *Phar.* II. iv. 280. Earth's full-blown beauties, IV. iv. 187.

Flowers—*continued*

MILTON.—enameld eyes, *Lyc.* 139. vernal bloom, *P. L.* III. 43.

CREECH.—gawdy glories of the Spring, *Theocritus* 65.

DRYDEN.—flow'ry crops, *Geo.* IV. 433.

POPE.—rural dainties, *Spring* 99.

THOMSON.—flowery race, *Summer* 212. Summer's musky tribes, *Spring* 546.

ANON.—Gens florea, *Mus. Angl.* (5th ed., 1741) II. 231.

Goats

PACUVIUS.—caprigeno generi, *Paulus* 1.

LUCRETIUS.—cornigeras matres, II. 368. barbigeras pecudes, V. 900.

VIRGIL.—caprigenum pecus, *Aen.* III. 221.

OPPIAN.—κεραῇσι ἀγέλῃσιν [horned herds], *Hal.* IV. 330.

BODIN.—cornigeras gentes, *Oppian* 23.

DU BELLAY.—trouppeaux barbuz, IV. 186.

DU BARTAS.—troupeaus barbus, *Judit* II. 172.

SPENSER.—horned heard, *F. Q.* III. x. 47.

SANDYS.—bearded Heard, *Ovid's Met.* 7.

Hail

DU BARTAS.—bondissans balons d'une vapeur gelee, *Voc.* 250.

SYLVESTER.—balles of Icie stone, *1605* 50. Ice-pearls, *1606* 11.

FANSHAWE.—concrete raine, *Lus.* (*Petronius His Rapture*) 19.

DRYDEN.—harden'd rain, *Aen.* IX. 911.

Hive

VIRGIL.—pinguibus stabulis, *Geo.* IV. 14. rimosa cubilia, IV. 45. daedala tecta, IV. 179. cerea regna, IV. 202. sedem augustam, IV. 228. cerea castra, *Aen.* XII. 589.

Hive—*continued*

Du Bartas.—creuse logette, *Furies*
 294.

Sylvester.—waxen Citie, *1605* 338.
 Waxen Canapey, *1633* 484.

Sandys.—sexangular inclosure, *Ovid's*
 Met. 274.

Benlowes.—waxen cells, *Theoph.* XII.
 lxxv.

Milton.—Straw-built Cittadel, *P. L.*
 I. 773.

Dryden.—waxen lodgings, *Geo.* IV.
 81. waxen cities, 296. waxen
 work, 808.

Honey

Note.—In the older writers the distinction between honey and honey-
dew, or manna, was rarely made
with any accuracy, and even in the
seventeenth century the two substances were considered comparable
in nature. This is one of those
instances in which the advance of
knowledge has cut us completely off
from the common theory and language of earlier periods; we need to
be reminded of the older theorizing
to appreciate more adequately what
might otherwise appear grotesque
language in poetry. The identification of the two substances will be
readily observed in some of the prose
passages quoted below, and it will not
be necessary to discuss the theories in
themselves. For the rest, the prose
passages selected merely to illustrate
terminology seem to me to offer some
of the most striking instances of a
language that was once scientific, and
that now seems anything but that.

Bees gather wax [κήρωσιν] from the
tear [exudation, δακρύου] of trees;
honey [τμέλι] is what has fallen out of
the air, especially at the rising of the
constellations. . . . When it is mature
honey becomes thick; in its early form

Honey—*continued*

it is like water, and remains liquid
[ὑγρόν] for some days . . . . After
twenty days at the most it becomes
hard.—Aristotle *Animal. Hist.* 554a7, in
Opera III. 97.

Venit [mel] ex aere et maxime siderum
exortu, praecipueque ipso Sirio explen-
descente fit nec omnino prius vergili-
arum exortu, sublucanis temporibus.
itaque tum prima aurora folia arborum
melle roscida inveniuntur, ac si qui
matutino sub divo fuere, unctas liquore
vestis capillumque concretum sentiunt,
sive ille est caeli sudor sive quaedam
siderum saliva sive purgantis se aeris
sucus. utinamque esset purus ac liquidus et suae naturae, qualis defluit
primo!—Pliny *Nat. Hist.* XI. xii. § 30.

Et quant au miel, c'est vne humeur
semblable à la rosee du ciel, esparse sur
ces fleurs: laquelle humeur la mousche
à miel attire de sa bouche, & le met
dedans les troux & ruches de sa cire.—
Daneau (translating Basil) *Phys. Fran.*
(1581) 289.

Whosoever they are, that have occasion
to be abroad in the aire about the dawn-
ing of the morrow, they may evidently
perceive their clothes wet with a clammie humour of honie, yea, and their
haires glewed therewith together, if they
goe bare headed. Bee it what it will,
either a certaine sweat of the skie, or
some unctuous gellie proceeding from
the starres, or rather a liquor purged
from the aire when it purifieth it selfe;
would God wee had it so pure, so cleare,
and so naturall, and in the owne kind
refined, as when it descendeth first.—
Holland *Pliny* (1601) I. 315 (Bk. XI,
chap. xii).

A fat kind of dew like melting hony,
especially at the shining of Syrius being
gathered from leaues of trees, is Manna,
called also wilde honey, or meldewes.—
Widdowes *Nat. Phil.* (1621) 18.

Manna est pinguida aeris substantia,
quæ januis cœli apertis, & thesauro
diuino patefacto, è nubibus, mandato
diuino, more roris vel pruinæ in speciem

Honey—*continued*

minutam, & ad instar seminis Coriandri albi rotundam, succrescendo, in terras, ad voluntatem creatoris exercendam, descendit. — Fludd *Meteor. Cosmica* (1626) 98.

Quippe mense Maio, Iunio & Iulio, ambrosia quædam cælestis (melleum rorem vocant, ego melliginem appello) in plantarum folia delabitur, gustu suanissima, liquida, pura, & ipsum contra saccharum non ingrata.—Moufet *Theatr. Insect.* (1634) 24.

In the vallies of Chile in their season fall great dews (which collect and harden) like bread tempered with Sugar or Marchpane (Mark, they fall liquid dews) which is as wholesome as that which they call Manna: By all which instances, it appears that Manna is first a liquid dew, and after inspissated by a vertue of the tree, or plant on which it falls.—Purchas *Theatr. Insects* (1657) 133.

The Kinds of Dew:
   More Concrete; of a sweet tast: to which may be adjoyned that peculiar kind of physical Dew mixed with the Exudations of the Plant Ladanum. MANNA. LADANUM.
   More Liquid; gathered from Plants by Bees: to which may be adjoyned for its affinity, that other natural Body gathered likewise by Bees, and of a clammy consistence. HONEY. WAX.
—Wilkins *Real Character* (1668) 58.

Whether it did not exudate from the Plant it self; as I guess the Honey fall, or Gummy Dew, to be observed upon the Leaves of the Oake, &c. are nothing else?—*Phil. Trans.* XIX (1698). 374.

That clammy, sweet, Honey-like Juice, which is so frequently found upon the Leaves that are newly blasted, upon those of Fruit-Trees especially.—Morton *Northampton.* (1712) 333.

EURIPIDES.—ξουθᾶν πόνημα μελισσᾶν [the labor of the tawny bees], *Ipheg. Taur.* 165. ὀρείας ἀνθεμόρρυτον

Honey—*continued*

γάνος ξουθῆς μελίσσης [flower-flowing nectar of the mountain-ranging tawny bee], 634-5.

APOLLONIUS RHODIUS.—γλυκὺν καρπὸν [sweet harvest], *Argon.* I. 881-2.

VIRGIL.—liquido nectare, *Geo.* IV. 164. dulci nectare, *Aen.* I. 433.

PRUDENTIUS.—fauorum agrestium liquore, *Cath.* VII. 69-70.

NONNOS. — δαιδαλέην ὠδῖνα σοφῆς μελίσσης [the neat travail of the clever bee], *Dionys.* XXVI. 187.

PONTANO.—Cœlestem rorem, *Urania* I. 1112. ætherium rorem, II. 360. lectum e flore liquorem, II. 1298.

TASSO.—umor celeste rugiadose stille, *Mondo Creato* V. 941.

SYLVESTER.—delicious Deaw, *1633* 484.

GÓNGORA.—liquido oro, II. 83.

DRAYTON.—liquid gould, *Nimph.* III. 171.

MILTON.—liquid sweet, *P. L.* V. 25. mellifluous Dewes, V. 429.

DRYDEN.—golden dew, *Killigrew* 51. golden work, *Prol. to Amphitryon* 2. waxen labor of the bees, *Geo.* III. 688. liquid gold, IV. 50. gather'd glue, IV. 55. tenacious mass of clammy juice, IV. 58. golden juice, IV. 153. golden liquor, IV. 208. liquid nectar, IV. 240. golden flood, IV. 385. liquid store, *Aen.* I. 603. golden burthen, I. 605.

POPE.—golden store, *Winter* 51.

GAY.—fragrant Dew, *Rural Sports* 13. golden Treasures, 13. liquid Sweets, 13.

THOMSON.—luscious spoil, *Spring* 515.

Ice[1]

NONNOS.—μάρμαρον ὕδωρ [petrified or marble water], *Dionys.* III. 6.

---

[1]See also CRYSTAL WATER, pp. 130-3.

Ice—*continued*

πετρούμενον ὕδωρ [petrified water], XVIII. 234.

SYLVESTER.—crystall Crusts, *1633* 516.

CAREW.—icy cream, 1. Crystal cake, 16.

STANLEY.—cold fetters, *Ps. cxlviii* 8.

T. HARVEY.—Icie pavements, *Mantuan* 96.

Insects

OPPIAN.—ἀνιηραὶ θέρεος στίχες [the grievous hosts of harvest], *Hal.* II. 448.

PISIDAS. — Ἔθνος πτερωτὸν [winged nation], *Mundi Opificium* 1224.

SYLVESTER.—humming Creature, *1605* 253.

CHAPELAIN.—volante armée, *Pucelle* 50.

DRYDEN.—flying plague, *Geo.* III. 237.

DIAPER.—buzzing Squadrons, *Oppian's Hal.* II. 759.

THOMSON.—noisy summer-race, *Summer* 237. quivering nations, 344. frosty tribe, *Spring* 132.

DYER.—wingy swarm, *Fleece* I. 588.

Leaves

VIRGIL.—silvis honorem, *Geo.* II. 404.

DU BELLAY.—tresses verdoyantes, I. 108. perruque vive, III. 81.

RONSARD.—perruque verte, II. 461. teste ombreuse des bois, III. 185.

DU BARTAS.—fueilleux ornement, *Bab.* 144.

TASSO.—verde chioma, *Mondo Creato* III. 1157. frondose chiome, III. 1461.

SYLVESTER.—shadie locks of Forrests, *1605* 282. leafie robe, 416.

DRUMMOND.—leauie Lockes, II. 21.

Leaves—*continued*

DRYDEN.—shady honors, *Ovid's Met.* I. 768. leafy honors, *Aen.* II. 851. leafy nation, X. 571.

POPE.—growing honours, *Win. For.* 221.

Man

AESCHYLUS.—βρότειον σπέρμ' [mortal seed], Fr. 227 (399).

SOPHOCLES. — θνητὴ φύσις [mortal stock], Fr. 590. θνητῶν γένεθλα [generations of mortals], *Oed. Rex* 1424–5.

LUCRETIUS.—genus humanum, II. 342.

OVID.—mortale genus, *Met.* I. 188.

PRUDENTIUS.—mortale genus, *Hamart.* 406.

NONNOS.—βροτέη φύσις [the human race], *Dionys.* VII. 74.

CAMOENS.—gente humana, *Lus.* 117.

DU BARTAS.—semence humaine, *I Sem.* I. 428. roy des animaux, VI. 481. Des fragiles humains la limonneuse race, VI. 486. genre humain, *Colon.* 36. animaux marche-droict, 495.

TASSO.—animal che regna, *Mondo Creato* VI. 193.

SPENSER.—images of God in earthly clay, *F. Q.* I. x. 39.

SYLVESTER.—slimie Burgers of this Earthly Ball, *1605* 208. Earth's glorious Head, 208. fraile Engine of this earthen Type, 216. wretched clod, 394. vpright Creatures, 454. Worlds seed-remnant, 487. Adams race, *1633* 393. crooked kinde, 395. dustie Brood, 407. Adam's Progeny, 574.

MURE.—earth's fraile broode, I. 185.

DRUMMOND.—Adames Race, II. 60. earths tennants, II. 131.

Man—*continued*

MILTON.—this worlds brood, *Ps. iv* 27.
earthie Charge, *P. L.* IX. 157.
mortal seed, *S. A.* 1439.

DRYDEN.—human-kind, *Ovid's Met.*
I. 433.

POPE.—human Race, *Rape of the Lock*
II. 7.

Moon

EURIPIDES.—νυκτός ἀφεγγὲς βλέφαρον
[the dim eye of night], *Phoen.* 543.

VIRGIL.—aurea Phoebe, *Geo.* I. 431.

HORACE.—crescentem face Noctilu-
cam, *Odes* IV. vi. 38.

MANILIUS.—uaga Delia, I. 669.

SENECA.—noctium sidus, *Medea* 750.
face pallida, 792–3.

VALERIUS FLACCUS.—lampade Phoe-
bes, *Argon.* VII. 366.

OVID.—crescendo Phoebe, *Met.* I. 11.
lunaria cornua, II. 453. aurea
Phoebe, II. 723.

PONTANO.—phœbei luminis, *Urania* I.
838. aurato orbe, I. 842.

DU BELLAY.—l'œil palle de la nuit,
IV. 3.

DU BARTAS.—astre argenté, *I Sem.* I.
350. estoile argentine, III. 193.
flambeau delien, III. 200. estoille
cornue, IV. 436. grand Reine du
ciel, *Colom.* 651. flambeau guide-
nuicts, *Magnif.* 170. astre porte-
cornes, 352.

MARLOWE.—night-wandring pale and
watrie starre, *Hero and Leander* I. 107.

SHAKESPEARE.—moist star, *Ham.* I. i.
118.

SYLVESTER.—Horned Queene, *1605*
130. Nightly Brand, 223. Nights
dim Taper, *1611* 556. Night's-
Princesse, 561. silver-browd Diana, Queen of Night, *1633* 495.

WHITING.—monthly-hornèd queen,
CP III. 459.

Moon—*continued*

SANDYS.—Night-wandring Dian,
Ovid's Met. 273.

MILTON.—the hollow round Of Cynthia's seat, *Nativity* 102–3.

KYNASTON.—crescent - crownèd empress of the flood, *Leo. and Syd.* 1961.
Empress of the wat'ry wilderness,
3137.

OTWAY.—Ruling Planet of the Night,
Venice Preserved II. 178.

J. HUGHES.—[the sun's] pale Sister
of the Night, *Ode to Creator* 7.

Planets

NOTE.—Ricciolus has a passage which
illustrates sufficiently for most purposes the established terminology for
the description of planets:

Iam verò Stellæ illæ septem, quæ vario
& anomalo motu mutant subinde dis-
tantiam inter se se, & ab Ecliptica
vagantes & erraticæ, seu errones à
Latinis, πλανῆται à Græcis dicuntur;
reliquæ autem, quibus cœlum his su-
perius vndequaque rutilat, dicuntur
Fixæ seu *Inerrantes*.[1]

Certain phrases in scientific prose
are, however, worth special notice:
"globi errantes" (W. Gilbert *Magnete*
227); "globi celesti" (Galileo *Dial.*
72); "Erraticals" (Dariott *Redivivus*
253); "Errant Stars" (Moxon *Antiq.
Astron.* 25); "wandering Globes" (J.
Chamberlayne *Nieuwentyt* III. 839).

———

MANILIUS.—fulgentia sidera, I. 652.
sidera uaga, II. 742–3. uagae
stellae, V. 722.

MANETHON.—πλάνα φέγγη [wander-
ing lights], IV. 3, in *Poet. Bucol.*

CHAUCER.—erratick sterres, *Tro. and
Cris.* V. 1812.

RONSARD.—sept flames errantes, V.
35. sept Feux erratiques, VI. 109.

[1] *Almagest. Nov.* (1651) I. 393.

Planets—*continued*

Du Bartas.—sept feux errants, *I Sem.* IV. 295. flammes errantes, VI. 887. flambeaux vagabons, *Colom.* 611. torches vagabondes, 633.

Shakespeare.—wand'ring stars, *Hamlet* V. i. 279.

Sylvester.—Seauen Lights, *1605* 125. wandring Seauen, 479. erring Tapers, 489.

Milton.—luminous inferior Orbs, *P. L.* III. 420. wandring Fires, V. 177.

Cowley.—wandring Lights, 260.

Genest.—Globes errans, *Prin. Phil.* 126.

Rain

E. Fairfax.—falling liquor, *Tasso* XIII. lxxvii.

Sylvester.—liquid pearles, *1605* 49. liquid Show'rs, *1633* 458.

P. Fletcher.—liquid tears, *Purple Isl.* XI. xviii.

Rainbow

Du Bellay.—arc pluvieux, V. 105.

Ronsard.—Honneur de l'air, VI. 406.

Drayton.—Celestiall Bow, *Poly-Olb.* XXII. 80.

Sandys.—painted Bow, *Ovid's Met.* 208.

Milton.—humid Bow, *P. L.* IV. 151. showrie Arch, VI. 759.

Cowley.—Watry Bow, 331. Gawdy Heav'nly Bow, 444.

Thomson.—grand ethereal bow, *Spring* 204. amusive arch, 216.

Sea

Homer.—ὑγρὰ κέλευθα [watery ways], *Il.* I. 312. πόντος ἁλὸς πολιῆς [the deep of the hoary brine], XXI. 59. ἁλὸς εὑρέα κόλπον [the broad bosom of the brine], XXI. 125. ἰχθυόεντα κέλευθα [fishy ways],

Sea—*continued*

Odys. III. 177. πόντον ἀπείρονα κυμαίνοντα [the boundless surging deep], IV. 510. ἀλμυρὸν ὕδωρ [salt water], IV. 511. πουλὺν ὑγρήν [wide liquid], IV. 709. ἁλὸς πελάγεσσι [deeps of the brine], V. 335.

Hesiod.—ἀτρύγετον πέλαγος [barren deep], *Theog.* 131. γλαυκὴν δυσπέμφελον [the gray roughness], 440.

Aeschylus. — ἅλμην βρύχιον [deep brine], *Pers.* 397. δελφινοφόρον πεδίον πόντου [the dolphin-bearing plain of the sea], Fr. 72 (150).

Pindar.—'Ωκεανοῦ πελάγεσσι [streams of Ocean], *Pyth.* IV. 251.

Aristophanes.—ὑγρὸν πόντιον βάθος [the watery deep of the sea], *Peace* 140.

Timotheus. — πεδία πλόιμα [floating plains], *Pers.* 89.

Lycophron.—Τηθὺν [Tethys], *Alex.* 1069.

Livius Andronicus.—arua Neptuni, Baehrens 1. 18.

Ennius.—caerula prata, *Ann.* 143. Caeruleum sale, 385. aequora cana, 478. Imber Neptuni, 498. fluctus natantes, 596. marinas plagas, *Sat.* 65. aequora salsa, *Scen.* 367. Neptunus saevus, *Varia* 10.

Plautus.—caeruleos campos, *Trinummus* 833.

Cicero.—canos fluctus, *Aratus' Phaen.* 305. Neptunia prata, 373.

Lucretius.—Neptuni corpus acerbum, II. 472. aequora ponti, II. 772. aequore salso, III. 493. aequore alto, III. 784. altis aequoris undis, V. 374. ponti plaga caerula, V. 481. salso gurgite, V. 482. salsis lacunis, V. 794. marinis fluctibus, V. 1079–80. campos natantis, VI. 405.

Sea—*continued*

CATULLUS.—caeruleo ponto, XXXVI.
11. rapidum salum, LXIII. 16.
marmora pelagi, 88. liquidas
Neptuni undas, LXIV. 2. vada
salsa, LXIV. 6. caerula aequora,
LXIV. 7. candenti gurgite,
LXIV. 14. fluctus salis, LXIV.
67. pelagi vastos aestus, LXIV.
127. tremuli salis undas, LXIV.
128. gurgite lato, LXIV. 178.
horrida aequora, LXIV. 205–6.
spumantibus aequoris undis,
LXVIII. 3.

VIRGIL.—Thetim, *Ecl.* IV. 32. in-
fidum marmor, *Geo.* I. 254. Ti-
thoni croceum cubile, I. 447.
campi natantes, III. 198. umida
regna, IV. 363. magnum aequor,
IV. 388. aequor altum, IV. 528.
tumidum aequor, *Aen.* III. 157.
vastum aequor, III. 191. vasto
ponto, III. 605. undosum aequor,
IV. 313. vada salsa, V. 158.
salsos fluctus, V. 182. liquidas
undas, V. 859. immensa aequora,
VI. 355. campos liquentis, VI.
724. marmoreo aequore, VI. 729.
vada caerula, VII. 198. arva
Neptunia, VIII. 695. spumantem
pontum, IX. 103. campos salis,
X. 214. viridi sale, *Ciris* 461.
caeruleo regno, 483. liquido
aequore, 493. cano gurgite, 514.
aequoreo fluctu, *Culex* 357. trucem
pontum, *Catal.* IX. 47.

MANILIUS.—fluuidum aequor, I. 164.

OVID.—Amphitrite, *Met.* I. 14.
liquidas undas, I. 95. gurgite
caeruleo, II. 528. medii aequora
ponti, II. 872. apertum aequor,
IV. 527. aequoreae aquae, XI.
520. caeruleo ponto, XIII. 838.
fluctus aequorei, XV. 604–5.
caeruleas aquas, XV. 699. liquidi
ponti, *Fasti* IV. 575. liquido
aequore, V. 547. caeruleas undas,

Sea—*continued*

Ex Ponto II. x. 33. piscosis vadis,
Ars Amat. II. 82. Nereus caerulus,
Epist. IX. 14. aequoreas vias,
XVIII. 160.

LUCAN.—Oceani tumidas undas, I.
370. aequoreas undas, I. 401.
immensum aequor, I. 499. caeruleum aequor, II. 220. incerti
stagna profundi, II. 571. spumoso
aequore, II. 627. Tethyos aequora,
III. 233. sulcato gurgite, III. 551.
uasto profundo, III. 651. cano
aequore, IV. 587. tumidus pontus,
V. 217. aequora curua, V. 458–9.
placidus pontus, V. 638. latum
aequor, V. 707. placido profundo,
VI. 268. gurgite ponti, VII. 813.
tergo pelagi, IX. 341. stridentibus
undis, IX. 866. aequoreos sales,
X. 257.

VALERIUS FLACCUS.—spumantia regna, *Argon.* I. 194–5. tridentis regna,
I. 615–6. sale purpureo, III. 422.

OPPIAN.—κυματόεσσαν χύσιν [watery
flood], *Hal.* I. 4. ἅλμης ἰοειδέος
κέλευθα [the paths of the violet
brine], V. 103.

Orphica.—Τηθύος ἔσχατον ὕδωρ [the
uttermost water of Tethys], *Argon.*
335. ἀλμυρὸν ὕδωρ [briny water],
Hymn XVII. 6.

AUSONIUS.—liquidas vias, *Mosella* 150.
æquoream Tethyn, 281.

PRUDENTIUS.—uitreo aequore, *Peristep.* VII. 16.

NONNUS. — ἅλμης ὕδατος [watery
brine], *Dionys.* I. 75–6. βυθοῖο
ὕδατος [watery deep], XXVI. 239.

AVITUS.—uasto gurgite, *Orig. Mundi* 7.

PONTANO.—cœruleo æquore, *Urania*
I. 324. vasto gurgite, I. 430.
Cœruleos æstus, I. 833. liquentia
arva, I. 833. neptunnia arva, I.
931. cœruleo gurgite, II. 377.
spumosum æquor, II. 656. nep-

Sea—*continued*

tunnia regna, II. 667. cœruleis
undis, II. 983. vada salsa, III.
326. liquida æquora ponti, *Meteor*.
2.

SCÈVE.—undes sallées, 26. giron de
Thetys, 37.

DU BELLAY.—palais humides, I. 29.
giron humide, I. 107. sein de
Thetis, II. 20. flots marins, II. 72.
Neptune irrité, II. 95. campagnes
humides, II. 155. pléine humide,
II. 289. undes salées, III. 19.
onde azuree, III. 68. humide lict,
III. 85. champs de Neptune, IV.
89. plaines ondoyantes, IV. 113.
flotz escumeux, V. 223. flots
azurez, V. 343. champs ondoyans,
VI. 49. plaine azurée, VI. 298.
plaine salée, VI. 336. plus doux
element, VI. 363.

GOOGE.—Neptunes rayne, 102.

CAMOENS.—salso argento, *Lus*. 4.
ondas Neptuninas, 10b. humido
reino, 97b. fundo aquoso, 102b.
reino Neptunino, 151b. reino
fundo, 161b.

RONSARD.—plaine salée, I. 243. flots
poissonneux, II. 84. royaumes
humides, III. 37. plaines salées,
III. 38. champs escumeux, III. 49.
campagne humide, III. 50. plaines
humides, III. 80. flots de Thetis
salez, III. 157. ondeuses campaignes, III. 197. humide giron,
III. 222. humide monde, III. 242.
flot salé, IV. 61. element humide,
IV. 422. ondes marines, V. 17.
eaux azurées, V. 78. champ
escumeux et ondeux, V. 148. de
Thetis le sejour esmaillé, V. 149.
le doz escumeux des ondes em-
poullées, V. 201. espace humide,
V. 385. eschine mariniere, VI. 23.
marines campaignes, VI. 74. humides sillons, VI. 179. flots marins,
VI. 188. onde azurée, VI. 325.

Sea—*continued*

échine de l'eau, VI. 389. flots
Neptuniens, VI. 415. eaux pois-
sonneuses, VI. 420. escume marine,
VI. 422. eaux Tethiennes, VI. 445.
flots humides, VI. 446. humeur
mariniere, VI. 482.

DU BARTAS.—ondoyante plaine, *I
Sem*. I. 196. provinces salees, I.
208. matiere navale, I. 220.
royaumes salez, II. 320. champs
ondoyans, II. 472. ondeuse campaigne, II. 521. champs flotans,
III. 11. onde azuree, III. 154.
flottans seillons, III. 836. plaine
liquide, IV. 70. plaines poisson-
neuses, IV. 109. dos flotant de
l'azuré Neptune, IV. 134. ondeux
element, IV. 167. onde salee, V.
8. flottant giron de la perse
Thetis, V. 50. vagueux element,
V. 149. sein maternel, V. 158.
humide sejour, V. 166. regnes
flotans, V. 339. azur salé, V. 390.
climats ondoyans, V. 394. monde
salé, V. 433. plaine humide, V.
443. flo-flotant Neree, V. 451.
moite monde, V. 453. flot azuré,
V. 502. flotant cercueil, V. 510.
flots marins, V. 720. ondeuse
plaine, V. 731. flotantes pleines,
V. 852. regnes salez, VI. 422.
flotant neptun, VI. 451. ondeux
Neptune, *Eden* 138. sel azuré de
la campaigne humide, *Furies* 158.
bouillonnante plaine, 174. campagnes salees, *Magnif*. 380. vageuse
tumeur, 386. ondeuse Thetis,
Judit II. 236. verre flottant, *Yvry*
325. eschine de Neree, *Lepan*. 218.

JAMES I.—wavie raigne, *Furies* 65.
Neptune's fleeting plaine, 125.
azure salt of humide fielde, 333–4.
bulluring plaine, 367. humid
plaine, 1269.

TASSO.—salso elemento, *Mondo Creato*
III. 448. magioni umide algenti,

Sea—*continued*

V. 468. liquidi sentieri, V. 758.
umidi campi, V. 1592. ondosi
regni, VI. 187. umidi regni, VII.
269. ondoso grembo, VII. 908.

SPENSER.—Tethys bosome, *Rome* 270.
dreadfull deep, *Vanitie* 61. gulfe of
greedie Nereus, *Bellay* 179. swelling Tethys saltish teare, *F. Q.* I.
iii. 31. watrie wildernesse, I. iii.
32. swelling Neptune, II. vi. 10.
watery plaine, IV. xi. 24.

SHAKESPEARE.—bosom of the deep,
L. L. L. IV. iii. 31. main of waters,
Mer. of Ven. V. i. 97. wat'ry Neptune, *Rich. II* II. i. 63. Neptune's
empire, *Ham.* I. i. 119. Neptune's
salt wash, III. ii. 166. green
Neptune's back, *Ant. and Cleo.* IV.
xiv. 58. wat'ry main, *Son.* LXIV. 7.
foaming brine, *Temp.* I. ii. 211.
salt deep, I. ii. 253.

E. FAIRFAX.—heav'n's smooth looking-glass, *Tasso* XV. ix.

SYLVESTER.—wet Wildernes, *1605*
(sonnet before *Arke*). floating
Deepes, 48. waters gloomie Globe,
77. Mother Maine, 80. brinie
Ball, 81. Fish-full Waues of Neptunes Royall Seate, 83. Waters
wauing brine, 145. liquid Mansion, 146. liquid Liuings, 151.
siluer Brine, 154. moyst World,
160. Neptune's backe, 192. salt
kingdomes, 206. waterie World,
217. liquid Christal Regions, 227.
floating Water, 237. Neptunes
liquid Belt, 277. azure fore-head
of the liquid plaines, 333. brynie
Deepes, 462. richest azure of Seas
storm-full brine, 474. brynie glass,
1611 562. angrie Thetis, 614.
moist Cabin, *1633* 491.

MURTOLA.—humidi Solchi, *Creat.
Mondo* V. x. 5. humido chiostro,
V. xii. 36.

Sea—*continued*

DENNYS.—watry fort, *Secrets of Angling*
D₅.

GÓNGORA.—humido elemento, I. 58.
campo vndoso, II. 65. humido
templo de Neptuno, II. 68. Crystal
azul, II. 90. campos de Neptuno,
II. 91. vndosa campaña, II. 94.
marmol vndoso, II. 100. Reino de
Neptuno, II. 110. vndosa plata,
II. 283.

W. BROWNE.—liquid plain, *Inner
Temple Masque* 19. wat'ry Desert,
Brit. Past. II. i. 2.

CHAPMAN.—fishie world, *Odys.* 61.

MURE.—azure face of heaven's broad
looking-glasse, I. 65. glassie plaine,
I. 88. Neptun's azure bosome, I.
90. wat'ry plaine, I. 135. Neptun's back, I. 135. Neptun's empires, I. 136. azure plaine, I. 170.
liquid floare, I. 305.

BERTAUT.—Empire écumeux, *Œuv.
Poét.* 63. Royaumes humides, 121.
plaine azuree, 121. humide empire, 122. palais de Neree, 186.
ondeuse plaine, 249. onde sallee,
253. ondoyantes plaines, 261.
humides sillons, 261. campagne
ondeuse, 417.

DRAYTON.—watry Plaine, *Poly-Olb.* I.
431. watry kingdome, II. 441.
finnie Heaths, III. 347. watry
Court, V. 126. watry Realme,
XVI. 292. liquid wast, XIX. 232.
Neptunes liquid field, XXV. 151.
bracky Realme, *Nimph.* VI. 159.

MAY.—watry maine, *Lucan* D.

DRUMMOND.—watrie Plaines, I. 8.
Neptunes liquide Plaine, I. 47.
glassie Field, I. 152.

DONNE.—glassie deepe, *Progr. of the
Soule* 252. liquid path, 263.

CAREW.—angry main, 7. brackish
main, 56.

Sea—*continued*

SANDYS.—liquid Plaine, *Ovid's Met.* 1. wavy Monarchie, 28. Neptune's brine, 29. wavie fields, 206.

KYNASTON.—Thetis' glass, *Leo. and Syd.* 2705. wat'ry wilderness, 3137.

E.• WALLER.—liquid main, *To the King, On his Navy* 20. drowned ball, 24. watery field, *Instr. to a Painter* 227. Neptune's smooth face, *His Maj. Escaped* 42.

DAVENANT.—lower Ele'ment, *Gond.* I. vi. 30.

STANLEY.—watry plaine, *Oronta* 6. liquid plain, *Anacreon* 54.

BENLOWES.—glassy plains, *Theoph.* XII. cix.

FANSHAWE.—Neptune's curled head, *Virgil* 67. angry Brine, *Lus.* I. xviii. humid Green, I. lxxii. azure Waters Of Amphitrite, I. xcvi. Gulphs of Brine, II. cviii. Watry Ream, II. cxii. Salt Realm, X. cxx.

CHAPELAIN.—champs salés, *Pucelle* 12. moite prison, 121. plage escumeuse, 149. escume salée, 242. Empire liquide, 255. humide Element, 261. Camp liquide, 468.

EVELYN.—Azure deep, *Lucretius* 29.

COWLEY.—low liquid Sky, 185.

MILTON.—watry plain, *Ps. cxxxvi* 22. level brine, *Lyc.* 98. monstrous world, 158. watry floar, 167. unadorned boosom of the Deep, *Comus* 23. forhead of the Deep, 732. gloomy Deep, *P. L.* I. 152. vast and boundless Deep, I. 177. watry residence, VIII. 346. foaming deep, X. 301.

SHERBURNE.—watry Girdle of the Ambient Main, *Sphere* 18. floating Main, 39. watery Deep, 60.

DRYDEN.—wat'ry ball, *Ann. Mir.* xiv. wat'ry deserts, *Ind. Emp.* I. ii, in

Sea—*continued*

Works II. 337. boundless deep, *State of Inn.* I. i (V. 126). wat'ry plain, *Alb. and Alban.* II. iii (VII. 266). liquid main, *Lucretius* I. 24. watery bed, *Don S.* I. i, in *Works* VII. 340. wat'ry reign, *Aen.* I. 52. bosom of the deep, I. 65. boiling deep, I. 153. liquid empire, I. 198. liquid plains, I. 223. wat'ry deep, II. 48. floating field, V. 13. briny main, V. 186. liquid realms, V. 305. wat'ry waste, VII. 310. fields of Neptune, VIII. 920. liquid field, VIII. 930. wat'ry field, VIII. 938. liquid half of all the globe, IX. 160. glassy deep, X. 297.

CLÉRIC.—dos de Nérée, *Jeux Floraux* E₁b.

J. PHILIPS.—liquid Kingdoms, *Blenheim* 431.

POPE.—wat'ry plains, *Win. For.* 146. wat'ry waste, *Man* I. 106. liquid regions, *Il.* XIII. 50.

GENEST.—de Thetis le Sein humide, *Prin. Phil.* 48.

DIAPER.—wat'ry Sphere, *Oppian's Hal.* I. 533. liquid Wast, I. 541. wat'ry Roads, I. 1022. wat'ry Pastures, I. 1146. Liquid Worlds, II. 70. wat'ry Plain, II. 268. wavy Main, II. 275. wat'ry Vast, II. 308. liquid Fields, II. 327. liquid Realms, II. 895. unbounded Empire of the Main, II. 920.

J. JONES.—fluid Reign, *Oppian's Hal.* IV. 636.

THOMSON.—briny deep, *Summer* 167.

Serpents

SENECA.—squamifera turba, *Medea* 685.

RONSARD.—race serpentine, V. 15.

DU BARTAS.—bandes funestes De venins piolez, *Furies* 177–8.

Serpents—*continued*

SYLVESTER.—banefull creeping companies, *1605* 185. loathsome swarmes Of speckled poysons, 334.

CAREW.—viperous brood, 142.

SHERBURNE.—scaly Multitudes, *Medea* 38.

DRYDEN.—venom'd race, *Geo.* III. 629.

Sheep

SOPHOCLES.—λασίων θηρῶν [woolly beasts], *Philoct.* 184–5.

ENNIUS.—Balantum pecudes, *Ann.* 186.

ACCIUS.—pecus lanigerum, *Praetext.* 20.

LUCRETIUS.—balantum pecudes, II. 369. pigris balantibus, VI. 1132. lanigeras pecudes, VI. 1237.

VIRGIL.—balantum gregem, *Geo.* I. 272. lanigeros greges, III. 287. lanigeras pecudes, *Aen.* III. 642. pecora inertia, IV. 158. lanigeras bidentis, VII. 93.

OVID.—lanigeros greges, *Met.* III. 585. lanigerae pecudes, XIII. 781. lanigeri pecoris, *Fasti* II. 681.

DU BELLAY.—timides troupeaux, I. 91. troppeau champestre, IV. 196.

CAMOENS.—lanigeros carneiros, *Lus.* 31b.

RONSARD.—tropeau champestre, II. 87. lascif troupeau, III. 330. laineuse troupe, V. 251. troupeau porte-laine, V. 268. troupeaux frisez de fines laines, VI. 218.

DU BARTAS.—troupeaux laineux, *Arche* 484. belantes troupes, *Bab.* 289. troupeau porte-laine, *Troph.* 44. gras troupeaux, 971. troupeaux timides, *Yvry* 232.

TASSO.—umil gregge, *Mondo Creato* VI. 69.

WILLOUGHBY.—frisking flocke, *Avisa* 27.

Sheep—*continued*

SPENSER.—fleecie flockes, *F. Q.* III. vi. 15.

SYLVESTER.—bleating flocks, *1605* 421.

DRAYTON.—woolly flocks, *Poly-Olb.* II. 50.

W. BROWNE.—fleecy train, *Brit. Past.* I. i. 624. bleating charge, I. i. 684.

DRUMMOND.—bleeting Traine, II. 7.

WHITING.—fleecy train, *CP* III. 520.

BARLAEUS.—Lanigeri greges, *Poem.* II. 6.

STANLEY.—bleating flocks, *Poems and Trans.* (*Trans.* 47).

CHAPELAIN.—belant trouppeau, *Pucelle* 126.

T. HARVEY.—bleating Flocks, *Mantuan* 54.

MILTON.—nibling flocks, *L'A.* 72. fleecy wealth, *Comus* 503. chewing flocks, 539. bleating herds, *P. L.* II. 494. timerous flock, VI. 857. pasturing Herds, IX. 1109.

CREECH.—bleating flocks, *Theocritus* 43.

DRYDEN.—woolly breed, *Ecl.* I. 9. fleecy flocks, *Geo.* II. 270.

POPE.—fleecy care, *Spring* 19. rural care, *Summer* 35. panting flocks, 87. fleecy breed, *Winter* 82.

LA MOTTE.—Troupeaux bondissants, *Odes* 147.

THOMSON.—bleating kind, *Winter* 261. gentle tribes, *Summer* 417.

DYER.—fleecy tribe, *Fleece* I. 379.

Ships

HOMER.—ἁλὸς ἵπποι [horses of the sea], *Odys.* IV. 708.

CATULLUS.—pinea inflexae texta carinae, LXIV. 10.

VIRGIL.—nautica pinus, *Ecl.* IV. 38.

LYCOPHRON. — πεύκαισιν οὐλαμηφόροις [the warrior-bearing firs], *Alex.* 32.

Ships—*continued*

Du Bartas.—flotant chasteau, *Furies* 175. troupes marinieres, *Lep.* 313. exercite flottant, 348.

Sylvester.—winged waynes, *1605* 333. floating Castle, 334. floating Innes, 398.

Góngora.—Nadante vrna, II. 106.

W. Browne.—winged pines, *Brit. Past.* II. i. 220.

E. Waller.—winged castles, *Of Salle* 21.

Davenant.—floating forrests, *S. of Rhodes* I. 14.

Fanshawe.—winged Oak, *Lus.* VI. xxx.

Flatman.—floating groves, *CP* III. 309.

Dryden.—hollow wood, *State of Inn.* V. i, in *Works* V. 175. floating forests of the sacred pine, *Aen.* IX. 106.

Pope.—iron squadrons, *Win. For.* 363.

Shelley.—wingèd castles, *Hellas* 462.

Sky

Homer.—αἰθέρος ἀτρυγέτοιο [barren aether], *Demeter* 67.

Hesiod.—οὐρανοῦ ἀστερόεντος [starry heaven], *Works and Days* 548.

Pindar. — αἰθέρος ψυχρᾶς κόλπων ἐρήμων [the desolate bosom of the cold aether], *Olymp.* xiii. 88.

Euripides.—ταναὸν αἰθέρ' [outspread aether], *Orestes* 322.

Aristophanes.—βάθος κύκλου [heaven's highest vault], *Birds* 1715. τοὐρανοῦ τὸν κύτταρον [the vault of heaven], *Peace* 199. ἀστεροειδέα νῶτα αἰθέρος ἱερᾶς [the starry back of the divine aether], *Thesmo.* 1067–8.

Sky—*continued*

Ennius.—caeli[1] caerula templa, *Ann.* 49. magna templa caelitum commixta stellis ardentibus, *Scen.* 196. plagas caelestum, *Varia* 23.

Cicero.—lato tegmine caeli, *Aratus' Phaen.* 281. Igniferum aethera, 329. convexum caeli orbem, 560. Aetheris cavernis, *Scripta* IV. iii. 398.

Lucretius.—aetheris oris, II. 1000. aetheriis cavernis, IV. 391. signiferi orbis, V. 691. magni caerula mundi, V. 771. magni caelestia mundi templa, V. 1204–5. mundi magnum versatile templum, V. 1436. patuli aequora mundi, VI. 108. fulgentia caelestia templa, VI. 387–8.

Catullus.—templo fulgente, LXIV. 387.

Virgil.—arduus aether, *Geo.* I. 324. levem aethera, I. 406. caeli arcem, *Aen.* I. 250. aetheria plaga, I. 394. aethera apertum, I. 587. lucidus polus, III. 585–6. vasto aethere, V. 821. supera convexa, VI. 750. liquidum aethera, VII. 65. luminis oras, VII. 660. gelidi aetheris axe, VIII. 28. medium caeli orbem, VIII. 97. aetherios orbis, VIII. 137. sidera mundi, IX. 93. sideream sedem, X. 3. aetheris alti, XII. 181. aetherias arces, *Culex* 42. aetherio mundo, 102.

Manilius.—aetherias oras, I. 149. mundi arcem, I. 262. sidereus orbis, I. 281. conuexo Olympo, I. 539. altius aetherii circulus orbis,

[1]In this list the word *caelum* is not ordinarily considered an allowable term in periphrases for *sky*. It is worth remarking, however, that the word is derived from *cavus* by way of *cavilum*, and might very well be translated "vault of the sky."

Sky—*continued*

I. 802. nitidum mundum, I. 849. mundi flammea tecta, II. 118.

OVID.—candentem axem, *Met.* II. 297. summam arcem, II. 306. aetheriis sedibus, II. 512–13. oras aetherias, V. 511–12. aetherium axem, VI. 175. caelestibus oris, IX. 254. caelestes plagas, XII. 40. arces aetherias, XV. 858–9. convexa sidera, *Ex Ponto* IV. ix. 129–30. sideream mundi arcem, *Amores* III. x. 21. sidereas sedes, *Ars Amat.* II. 39. Caerulea via, *Epist.* XV. 106.

LUCAN.—aetheris sereni, I. 58. ardentem polum flammis, I. 527. aetherios recessus, VI. 445. alto aethere, VII. 447–8. signorum orbem, IX. 532. aetherio sulco, X. 502.

STATIUS.—astriferum orbem, *Theb.* II. 400. supera compage, VIII. 31.

VALERIUS FLACCUS.—Siderea arce, *Argon.* I. 498. effusis stellatus crinibus aether, II. 42. aetherias arces, V. 163. aeterni luminis arces, V. 409.

Greek Anthology. — ἄντυγος οὐρανίης [vault of heaven], IX. dcccvi. 6.

Orphica.—οὐρανοῦ ἀστερόεντος [starry heaven], *Hymn* XIII. 6. αἰθέρος γυάλοισι [caves of the aether], XIX. 16. κόσμος πολυδαίδαλος ἄστρων [the richly ornamented world of stars], XXVI. 8. ἀπείριτον αἰθέρα ·[the limitless aether], XXXIV. 11.

LACTANTIUS.—Stellifero polo, *Phoen.* 112.

PRUDENTIUS.—stelligeram aeream, *Cath.* V. 145. liquidum serenum, *Sym.* I. 414.

ENNODIUS.—astrigerum axem, *Carm.* I. i. 1.

DRACONTIUS.—Sidereus globus, *Carm. Deo* II. 5.

NONNOS. — ἄντυγα ἀστερόφοιτον

Sky—*continued*

᾿Ολύμπου [the starry vault of Olympus], *Dionys.* II. 262. ἄντυγας ἠερίας [aerial vaults], II. 535. αἰθέρος ἑπτάζωνον κενεῶνα [the sevenzoned vault of aether], III. 350.

PONTANO.—aerias arcis, *Urania* I. 70. iunonia regna, I. 70. medii aetheris oram, I. 236. aetheris alti, I. 537. astrigerum olympum, I. 573. aether Ignibus incandens, I. 639-40. Aeris campos, I. 647. Ætherium recessum, I. 936. Aerias plagas, I. 948. sidereas coeli arces, I. 961. coeli templa ardua, I. 965. liquidum aethera, I. 970. aetherios axes, II. 305. aetherios tractus, III. 96. liquidum inane, *Meteor.* 8.

SCÈVE.—chapelle ardente, 194.

DU BELLAY.—manoirs celestes, III. 45. palaiz supremes, III. 47. celeste campaigne, IV. 19. voûte du monde, IV. 23. voute etheree, V. 407. hauteur azuree, VI. 376.

RONSARD.—voute liquide, I. 97. voute estoillée, VI. 172. voute dorée, VI. 385. celeste plaine, VI. 387. voutes aitherées, VI. 434.

DU BARTAS.—ronde machine, I *Sem.* I. 119. pavillons astrez, I. 134. voustes estoilees, I. 387. lambris ardent, II. 410. cercles d'azur, II. 544. front celeste, II. 962. voute ætheree, II. 1006. azur des voutes estoillees, III. 14. plancher reluisant, IV. 64. doré firmament, IV. 288. celestes voyes, V. 664. province astree, V. 1000. astree machine, VII. 148. voute astree, VII. 436. De l'Olympe estoilé les estages, *Art.* 256. azur doré des pavillons du monde, 602. estincellante bale, *Colom.* 529. celestes provinces, 669. chapelle ardente, 696. celeste empire, *Magnif.* 387. azur ætheré, *Schisme* 108. voute cristaline, 568. voute empyree, *Lepan.* 261. plancher estoillé, 416.

Sky—*continued*

TASSO.—luminosi aperti campi, *Mondo Creato* V. 1373. stellanti chiostri, VI. 62.

SPENSER.—starry sphere, *F. Q.* I. x. 56.

SHAKESPEARE.—airy region, *Rom. and Jul.* II. ii. 21. vault of heaven, *II Henry IV* II. iii. 19. aerial blue, *Oth.* II. i. 39. azur'd vault, *Temp.* V. i. 43.

E. FAIRFAX.—spangled canopy, *Tasso* II. xcvi.

SYLVESTER.—Celestiall Arkes, *1605* 10. Heau'ns bright Arches, 64. azure Circle, 65. guilt azure Front Of firmest-Spheare, 131. Star-spangled Regions, 237. azure-spangled Regions, 286. celestiall roofes, 291. Heau'ns christal front, 330. bright Olympus starrie Canopie, 367. warbling Pole, 375. Arches starrie feeld, 378. azure-guilded Heau'ns Pauilions faire, 379. starrie welkin, 399. starrie Pole, 402. ætheriall thrones, 403. Heau'ns starrie Coach, 450. upper Loft, 480. Heau'ns bright Globe, 480. Ætherial Arch, 480. azure Christaline, 481. Azure steepe, 483. twinckling Globe, 487. goodly Seeling of a Waterie hew, 679. Seeling of this Globe, *1606* 5. Heau'ns starrefull Canapey, 30. happie Vault, *1611* 573. starrie floor, 575. Arches Crystalline, 607. Empyreal Round, 635. starry Temple, *1633* 393. Heav'nly Ball, 393. heav'ns Star-spangled ball, 396. That (liquid Crystall-like) strong Canapie, 475. heav'nly Vault, 491.

GÓNGORA.—campos de zaphiro, II. 53. muros liquidos, II. 118.

W. BROWNE.—earth's spangled canopy, *Brit. Past.* I. iii. 102.

Sky—*continued*

MURE.—cristall vaults, I. 128.

DRAYTON.—starry Frame, *Nimph.* III. 475.

DRUMMOND.—vaste Fieldes of Light, etheriall Plaines, II. 42. Seeling of the christall Round aboue, II. 50. airie Field, II. 62.

CAREW.—azure concave, 139.

WHITING.—azure firmament, *CP* III. 451.

SANDYS.—æthereall States, *Ovid's Met.* 29.

HALL.—fleeting vault, *CP* II. 209.

DAVENANT.—Heaven's vault, *Gond.* II. i. 28.

BENLOWES.—azure fields, *Theoph.* I. lxiii. studded orbs, VI. xxvi. Heav'nly Tent, VII. xxxvi. star-embroider'd hall, VIII. xlvii.

W. CHAMBERLAYNE.—heaven's spangled arch, *Phar.* III. iii. 12. spangled firmament, IV. iv. 271.

FANSHAWE.—heaven's pavilion, *Virgil* 31. azure Firmament, *Lus.* I. lviii. æthereal Hall, I. lxxiii. heav'nly Vault, II. lxx. Heaven's brazen Vault, II. xci. supernal Vault, IV. lxvii. great and spangled Canopy, X. lxxxix.

CHAPELAIN.—plaine estoillée, *Pucelle* 73. lambris estoillés, 253. voute azurée, 455.

EVELYN.—heavens cope, *Lucretius* 71.

MILTON.—arched roof, *Nativity* 175. bow'd welkin, *Comus* 1014. Heavens Azure, *P. L.* I. 297. Heavn's chearful face, II. 490. starry Sphear, III. 416. Sublunar Vault, IV. 777. Starrie Cope, IV. 992. Heav'ns wide Champain, VI. 2. mightie frame, VIII. 81.[1]

---

[1]Compare also the phrases "Crystallin Ocean" (*P.L.* VII. 271), "cleer Hyaline, the Glassie Sea" (*ibid.* VII. 619).

Sky—*continued*

COWLEY.—heavenly Vault, 171. Heav'ens fabrick, 262. Suns gilt Tent, 445.

SHERBURNE.—Cœlestial Frame, *Sphere* 38. Heavens azure Ceiling, 41. Heavens Waste, 48. Heavens azure Face, 49. Cœlestial Pavement, 50.

DRYDEN.—fields of light, *State of Inn.* I. i, in *Works* V. 126. vaulted arch, *Alb. and Alban.* III. i (VII. 278). starry walks, *Don S.* II. i (VII. 365). starry way, *Aen.* VI. 1084. starry frame, VIII. 181. fiery tracts, XII. 372.

POPE.—Fields of purest Æther, *Rape of the Lock* II. 77. yonder argent fields above, *Man* I. 41. empyreal sphere, II. 23. ethereal vault, III. 263. Vault of Air, *Horace I Ep.* vi. 5.

GENEST.—Voute étherée, *Prin. Phil.* 26. Voutes lucides, 38. Cercles etherez, 42. Espace enclos de Voutes étoilées, 79. celeste Lambris, 86. Lambris étherez, 94. Voute azurée, 234. Plaine étherée, 234.

THOMSON.—starry regions, *Summer* 1743.

Snow

DU BARTAS.—celeste laine, *I Sem.* II. 529. flocs de laine, *Art.* 144.

DU MONIN.—flocon laineus, *Urano.* 15b.

SYLVESTER.—heau'nly Wooll, *1605* 50. hoarie heapes, 80.

BENLOWES.—frosty cream, *Theoph.* IV. lxviii.

W. CHAMBERLAYNE.—winter's wool, *Phar.* I. iv. 300.

CONGREVE.—fleecy rain, *Mourning Bride* I. i (p. 425).

J. PHILIPS.—woolly Rain, *Cyder* II. 186.

Snow—*continued*

THOMSON.—heapy wreath, *Winter* 818. white abyss, 819. wintry load, *Summer* 1166.

Stars

ENNIUS.—ingentibus signis, *Ann.* 211.

CICERO.—sideribus claris, *Aratus' Phaen.* 404. Signa caelestia, 407. ardentia signa, 565. inlustria lumina, 626.

LUCRETIUS.—labentia signa, I. 2. nocturnas faces caeli sublime volantis, II. 206. palantia sidera, II. 1031. aetheris ignes, V. 448. lucida signa, V. 518. flammea corpora, V. 525. fervida signa, V. 628. noctis signa severa, V. 1190. noctivagae faces caeli, V. 1191. candida sidera, V. 1210.

CINNA.—ignes aetherios, Baehrens, Fr. 11, 2.

CATULLUS.—micantia sidera, LXIV. 206. magni lumina mundi, LXVI. 1. caelesti coetu, 37.

VIRGIL.—clarissima mundi lumina, *Geo.* I. 5–6. ignes nocturni, II. 432. aeterni ignes, *Aen.* II. 154.

MANILIUS.—mundi oculos, I. 133.

OVID.—sidereos ignes, *Met.* XV. 665.

LUCAN.—ignes caeli, VI. 337. aetheriae flammae, IX. 494.

VALERIUS FLACCUS.—luciferas faces, *Argon.* V. 370.

Orphica.—Νυκτὸς φίλα τέκνα μελαίνης [the dark night's own children], *Hymn* VII. 3.

NONNOS.—ἀστραίας φάλαγγας [starry battalions], *Dionys.* I. 224.

CYPRIANUS GALLUS.—sidereae cohortes, *Deut.* 197.

PONTANO.—stellanti lumine, *Urania* I. 429. vigilantia lumina flammæ Ætheriæ, I. 468–9. candenti lampade, II. 156. sidereis flammis,

Stars—*continued*

II. 765. geminatis ignibus, III. 85. globos flammarum, III. 89.

SCÈVE.—soubdains feuz du Ciel, 13. feux brillans, 194.

JODELLE.—lambeaux du ciel, 175; celestes flambeaux, 203.

DU BELLAY.—flambeaux ardens, I. 72. globes ardens, II. 282. celestes flammes, V. 387.

CAMOENS.—corpos lisos & radiantes, *Lus.* 175.

RONSARD.—celestes chandelles, III. 356.

DU MONIN.—genus Astræum, *Manip. Poet.* 5. luisantes chandelles, *Urano.* 18b.

DU BARTAS.—celestes chandeles, *I Sem.* I. 116. grand's touffes de feu, I. 239. medailles d'or, I. 546. clers brandons du ciel, II. 334. yeux de l'univers, II. 956. du ciel flamboyant les plus belles lumieres, III. 601. cloux qui brillent dans les cieux, IV. 55. yeux du ciel, IV. 62. corps spheriques, IV. 105. du ciel les medailles brillantes, IV. 137. flocons d'or, IV. 180. ardans yeux, IV. 180. peuple brillant, IV. 196. bagues d'or, IV. 201. corps estoillez, IV. 286. Du doré firmament les tremblantes chandelles, IV. 288. escussons ardemment reluisans, IV. 345. celestes chandelles, IV. 403. torches celestes, IV. 424. celestes corps, IV. 476. dorez flambeaux, VI. 496. torches brillantes, VI. 888. cloux d'or du viste firmament, VII. 445. brillantes merveilles, *Colom.* 50. luysans bataillons du celeste exercite, 326. de petits feux une troupe dore, *Magnif.* 988. ost estoilleux, *Yvry* 101.

SPENSER.—heauenly lampes, *F. Q.* III. ix. 53.

Stars—*continued*

SHAKESPEARE.—burning tapers of the sky, *Titus* IV. ii. 89. fiery orbs, *Cymb.* I. vi. 35.

SYLVESTER.—Celestiall Tapers, *1605* 41. Heau'ns bright Torches, 50. bright eyes of the Firmament, 64. Great-Worlds Torches, 71. Heau'ns bright Cressets, 118. Lampes dispersed in the Skies, 118. Heau'ns shining Hoast, 122. fixed Tapers, 125. Hoast of sparkes spred in the Firmament, 125. shields so shining cleere, 127. glist'ring Shields, 129. Hoast of th' vpper Twincklers bright, 134. glistring studs, 146. Heau'ns twinckling eyes, 196. Heau'ns heauie Globes, 236. guilt studs of the Firmament, 247. celestiall fires, 397. Twinckling Wonders of the Heau'ns, 471. Heau'ns bright Images, 472. flaming studs of many a twinkling Ray, *1611* 520. Millions of Tapers ouer all the Vault, 580. glittering studs of Gold, *1633* 393. glittering Signes, 469. Nightly Hoast, 482. twinkling Spangles, 484.

W. BROWNE.—lamps of heav'n, *Brit. Past.* I. iii. 148. bright ethereal fires, *Inner Temple Masque* 110.

MURE.—night's clear torches, I. 87. heavenly torches, I. 132.

DRAYTON.—Starry eyes of heaven, *Poly-Olb.* XXIII. 215.

DRUMMOND.—fixed Sparkes of Gold, I. 5. wandring Carbuncles, I. 5. golden Letters, I. 72. Firmaments bright Flowrs, II. 43. Heauens bright Eyes, II. 46. heauenlie Bodies, II. 59. Heavens brightest Tapers, II. 142.

BERTAUT.—yeux ardans, *Œuv. Poét.* 23. celestes flambeaux, 133.

Stars—*continued*

WHITING.—curlèd tapers of the firmament, *CP* III. 440. twinkling lamps, III. 505.

FANSHAWE.—golden Fry, *Lus.* III. xlv.

STANLEY.—sparkling Jewells of the night, *Ps. cxlviii* 4.

DAVENANT.—Lamps of Night, *Gond.* II. vi. 54.

BENLOWES.—starry troop, *Theoph.* III. xxxviii. sky-enchasèd diamonds, V. lxxv.

CHAPELAIN.—celestes flambeaux, *Pucelle* 295.

W. CHAMBERLAYNE.—spangled squadrons of the night, *Phar.* IV. ii. 408.

MILTON.—spangled host, *Nativity* 21. Starry Quire, *Comus* 112. shining Orbes, *P. L.* III. 670. living Saphirs, IV. 605. starrie Host, IV. 606. shining Globes, V. 259. Fires Ethereal, V. 417-18. starrie flock, V. 709. golden Lamps, V. 713. bright Luminaries, VIII. 98. Heav'nly fires, XII. 256. Æthereum pecus, *Nat. Non Pati Senium* 46. sydereis choreis, *Ad Patrem* 36.

COWLEY.—immortal Lights, 33. glittering Host, 212. starry vapours, 304. golden Worlds, 451.

SHERBURNE.—Heav'ns Eys, *Sphere* 12. starry Legions, 32. nameless Commons of the Sky, 38. golden Fires, 48.

FLATMAN.—glorious Lamps of light, *CP* III. 305.

DRYDEN.—rolling fires, *Rel. Laici* 4. nightly tapers, 8. lamps of heaven, *King Arthur* I. i, in *Works* VIII. 145.

GAY.—twinkling Orbs, *Rural Sports* 14.

GENEST.—Chiffres lumineux, *Prin. Phil.* 102.

POPE.—Heav'n's twinkling sparks, *Dunc.* II. 12.

Stars—*continued*

THOMSON.—lamps of heaven, *Summer* 180. radiant orbs, 1703. starry fires, *Autumn* 1104.

Sun

PINDAR.—ὁ γενέθλιος ἀκτίνων πατήρ [the father of the piercing beams], *Olymp.* vii. 70. ἀστέρος οὐρανίου [heavenly star], *Pyth.* iii. 75.

SOPHOCLES.—χρυσέας ἀμέρας βλέφαρον [the eye of golden day], *Antig.* 102-3. λαμπάδος ἱερὸν ὄμμα [the sacred eye of the torch], 879.

EURIPIDES.—ἡμερίαν ἀψῖδα [wheel of day], *Ion* 87-8.

ARISTOPHANES.—ὄμμα Αἰθέρος ἀκάματον [aether's unresting eye], *Clouds* 285.

ENNIUS.—candida lux, *Ann.* 90. albus iubar, 557. rota candida, 558. candentem facem, *Scen.* 280.

ACCIUS.—orbem flammeum radiatum solis, *Praetext.* 27-8.

CICERO.—Titanum suboles, *Aeschylus*, in *Scripta* IV. iii. 353. Phoebi fax, IV. iii. 399.

LUCRETIUS.—largus liquidi fons luminis, V. 281. aeternam lampada mundi, V. 402. solis rota altivolans, V. 432-3. alte lampade, V. 610. tremulum iubar ignis, V. 697. rosea face, V. 976.

VIRGIL.—Phoebeae lampadis, *Aen.* III. 637. crastinus Titan, IV. 118-19. roseus Phoebus, XI. 913. Hyperionis ardor, *Culex* 101. Phoebi aureus orbis, *Lydia* 40.

MANILIUS.—curru nitido, I. 738-9.

OVID.—Titan, *Met.* I. 10. ignifero axe, II. 59. mundi oculus, IV. 228. currus diurnos, IV. 630.

SENECA.—Phœbeæ facis, *Hippol.* 379.

LUCAN.—flammiger Titan, I. 415. Phaethon flagrantibus loris, II. 413.

Sun—*continued*

 igniferi orbis, III. 41. Phoebo siccante, IX. 315.

VALERIUS FLACCUS.—Hyperionius currus, *Argon.* II. 34–5. flammea iuga, III. 400–1. Phoebi surgentis orbem, III. 437.

Orphica.—Τιτὰν χρυσαυγής [golden-rayed Titan], *Hymn* VIII. 2. οὐράνιον φῶς [heavenly light], VIII. 2. κόσμου τὸ περίδρομον ὄμμα [circling eye of the world], VIII. 14. ζωῆς φῶς [light of life], VIII. 18.

PRUDENTIUS.—diurni sideris, *Peristep.* V. 246.

CHAUCER.—dayes honour, and the hevenes yë, *Tro. and Cris.* II. 904.

PONTANO.—Fons lucis, *Urania* I. 237. Igneus Titan, I. 355. candenti lampade, I. 472. Luciferi, III. 10.

SCÈVE.—du jour la clere pointe, 246.

GOOGE.—Golden Globe, 109.

DU BELLAY.—grand'lampe du jour, II. 80. torche etherée, IV. 163.

CAMOENS.—lucido Planeta, *Lus.* 19. luz do dia, 102b.

DU BARTAS.—fils tire-traits de la belle Latone, *I Sem.* I. 144. œil du monde, I. 455. clair brandon, I. 471. Lampe de l'univers, I. 485. flamboyant courrier, II. 469. doré brandon, II. 733. roy des flambeaux, III. 207. astre enfante-jours, IV. 8. torche journaliere, IV. 427. Fontaine de chaleur, IV. 508. Œil du jour, IV. 519. chaleureux Titan, IV. 661. des estoilles le roy, IV. 669. des astres l'honneur, IV. 749. astre cler, qui dore l'univers, IV. 782. brandon porte-jour, VII. 536. flambeau guide-jours, *Magnif.* 170.

TASSO.—sovran pianeta, *Mondo Creato* VII. 81.

Sun—*continued*

SHAKESPEARE.—fiery torcher, *All's Well* II. i. 165. Phœbus' cart, *Hamlet* III. ii. 165.

SYLVESTER.—Worlds bright Eye, *1605* 18. Prince of Starres, 82. Phœbus Torch, 83. Dayes glorious Prince, 115. Apollos glorie-beaming Carr, 128. Daies glorious Eye, 133. radiant Coach-man, 133. Starres-King, 139. Imperiall Starre, 139. Starrie-Prince, 141. match-les Maker of the Light, 141. chiefe of Planets, 142. Lampe which doth enlight the Whole, 143. Heau'ns greatest Light, 186. Eye of Heau'n, 196. Prince of Lights, 247. Heau'ns all-seeing eye, 314. Cynthias Brother, 362. bright day-star, 430. Heau'ns flaming Coach, 455. Load of Light, 479. Dayes glorious Torch, 489. Dayes Princely Planet, 490. glorious Gouernour of Day, *1606* 75. Worlds bright Eye, *1611* 546. Sol's blushing Eye, 546. Dance-guide Prince, 576. Dial, which doth houres direct, 639. Dayes daily Usher, *1633* 412. Flame-snorting Phlegon, 490. heav'ns bright champion, 602.

MURE.—Day-starre, I. 215. Dayes torch, II. 154.

BERTAUT.—grande lampe celeste, *Œuv. Poét.* 144.

DRUMMOND.—Lampe of Heauens Christall Hall, I. 8. Days golden Lamp, II. 50.

CAREW.—Planet of the Day, 39.

SANDYS.—Heaven's radiant Image, *Ovid's Met.* 25. Dayes burning eye, 186.

KYNASTON.—Heaven's glorious lamp of light, *Leo. and Syd.* 463.

DAVENANT.—bright officer of day, *Love and Honour* II. ii. 147. Lord of Day, *Gond.* II. iii. 32.

Sun—*continued*

SHERBURNE.—Heavens great Eye, *Salmacis* 7. gold Orb, *Sphere* 46.

BENLOWES.—circling charioteer of day, *Theoph.* I. lxiii.

FANSHAWE.—Phoebus' lamp, *Virgil* 17. glorious Guilder of the Pole, *Lus.* II. i. ever burning Lamp that rules the day, V. ii.

CHAPELAIN.—Flambeau du Monde, *Pucelle* 125. Oeil du Monde, 136. grand Globe de feu, 323.

MILTON.—gilded Car of Day, *Comus* 95. great Luminarie, *P. L.* III. 576. all-chearing Lamp, III. 581. prime Orb, IV. 592. great Light of Day, VII. 98. glorious Lamp, VII. 370. diurnal Starr, X. 1069. Luciferi regis, *Eleg.* III. 50.

DRYDEN.—lucid orb, *State of Inn.* II. i, in *Works* V. 137. world's eye, II. i (V. 137). globe of light, IV. i (V. 159). heaven's eye, *Aureng-Zebe* III. i (V. 243). day's bright lord, *Rel. Laici* 9. disk of Phœbus, *Ovid's Met.* XV. 284.

CHÂTRES.—celeste flambeau, *Preuves des Existences* 37.

POPE.—Phœbus' fiery car, *Win. For.* 147.

GENEST.—Astre du Jour, *Prin. Phil.* 130.

THOMSON.—king of day, *Summer* 81.

DESAGULIERS.—bright Globe, *Newt. Syst.* 3.

Tears[1]

NOTE.—The various poetical conceits for *tears* are so often fanciful that little is gained in any effort to work out their literal sense. Nevertheless, the fact that many writers identified the crystal humor of the eye with the

---

[1]See also CONDUIT, pp. 119–20, PEARL, pp. 269–71, and SLUICE, pp. 308–10.

Tears—*continued*

substance of tears, with or without adequate reason, demands that the student of such terms acquaint himself with some of the theories of the formation of tears. One may suspect often that the poetical phrases rest on the most crude and vague knowledge of theory as it is presented in the following prose quotations, but it is useful to determine so much:

Alij lacrymas nil aliud esse, nisi humoris potulenti portionem, quæ in cerebro, venisque oculorum, & præsertim venis angulorum oculi contineantur, quæ aut per compressionem, aut dilatationem illarum venarum erumpit.—Simoneta *Compend. Med.* (1594) 290–1.

Cum autem dictum ex Galeno fuerit, aqueum humorem eiusmodi tenue excrementum esse; dicendum adhuc est lacrymas cum aqueo humore par momentum habere. Etenim aqueus humor copia exiguus est: sunt enim tres quatuorue ad summum huius humoris guttæ. Sed crystallinus potissimùm & vitreus, cum purissima sint corpora, sicuti magnam crassi excrementi copiam secernunt, ita multò maiorem tenuioris secerni necessarium est. atque hoc lacrymæ sunt. Omitto nunc serosam humiditatem quam huic copiæ adiungi par est propter quam causam fortè ab Aristotele salsas esse lacrymas proditum est.—H. Fabricius *De Visione* (1600) 24.

Igitur aqueus [humor] est primo Crystallinus, non tamen fluidus vt aqua; sed compactus, vt aqua quæ mediocriter in glaciem sit concreta.—*Ibid.* 96.

The excrements of the braine are eyther thicke or thin: The thin are teares bursting from the braine by the angles of the eyes. The greater the flesh of those angles be, so much more plentifull be teares, chiefly if the complexion be colde and moyst, as of women. Teares be caused by heate which openeth, or colde which presseth the flesh, and causeth teares.—Widdowes *Nat. Phil.* (1621) 57.

Tears—*continued*

The second vse [of glandulous flesh] is, to couer the little corner conduit in the corner of the eye, by the which the excrements and naturall superfluities are conueyed into the nose. This excrement is a thinne liquid humour, which floweth out in weeping, or laughing, and whensoeuer the braine doth dis-burthen it selfe of these superfluities.—Banister *Guillemeau* (1622) I₁₁-I₁₂.

Qui lacrymarum materiam à parcius allabente humore distinguentes diversam utrique originem assignarunt: sic è venis oculorum hunc exsudare, illas à cerebro provenire Platerus statuit. Nec, qui è cerebro lacrymas derivant, inter se consentiunt: alii solô cerebrô contenti de viis dissentiunt, dum hi anteriores Choanæ canales, illi nervos, isti venas, &, nescis quas non alias, vias excogitarunt: quidam verò, præter cerebrum, alias in auxilium vocarunt partes; sic eas partim à cerebro per secundum ossis cuneiformis foramen, partim à vertice capitis & lateribus ad punctorum lacrymalium ductum confluere Veslingius putat. Qui cerebrô exclusô alia putarunt afferenda, nec hi inter se consentiunt, quidam enim ab oculorum nutrimento, alii à crystallini humoris, vitreique excrementis deducunt.—Steno *Obser. Anat.* (1662) 90-1.

As for the Fountain therefore, whence all our Tears flow, and the Matter whereof they consist; the successfull industry of Modern Anatomists hath discovered, that in the Glandules, placed at each corner of the Eyes, there is either from the blood brought thither by the arteries (as the vulgar doctrine is) or (as I, upon good reasons elsewhere delivered, conceive) from the Nutritive juice brought by nerves, separated, and kept in store a certain thin, clear and watery humor, partly saline, partly subacid in tast; the use whereof is aswell to keep the globes of the eyes moist and slippery, for their more easy motion; as to serve for Tears when we have occasion to shed them.—Charleton *Nat. Hist. Passions* (1674) 154.

Tears—*continued*

[According to Empedocles] Les Sueurs & les Larmes viennent du sang atténué & fondu. — Leclerc *Hist. Med.* (1696) 202.

JODELLE.—cristal ondoyant, 241.

DU BARTAS.—crystalline humeur, *Furies* 336. perles humides, *Magnif.* 248.

JAMES I.—Christall shining humour, *Furies* 690.

MARLOWE.—liquid pearle, *Hero and Leander* I. 297.

SHAKESPEARE.—brinish pearl, *Lucrece* 1213.

SPENSER.—Christalline humour, *F. Q.* II. xii. 65.

CHALKHILL.—briny showers, *Thea. and Clear.* 45.

E. FAIRFAX.—brinish flood, *Tasso* III. viii.

MURE.—cristall flood, I. 97.

DRAYTON.—liquid pearle, *Poly-Olb.* VI. 165.

DRUMMOND.—christall Brine, II. 51. liquid Chrystall, II. 141.

WHITING.—eye-lid rain, *CP* III. 505. sorrow's brine, III. 506.

CAREW.—briny dew, 29. pearly moisture, 108.

KYNASTON.—pearly showers, *Leo. and Syd.* 2332.

MILTON.—liquentis imbre salis, *In Obit. Præs. Eli.* 3.

DRYDEN.—wat'ry store, *Sig. and Guis.* 683.

GARTH.—briny Torrent, *Dispensary* 3.

Telescope

DAVENANT.—Optick Tubes, *Gond.* II. v. 16.

MILTON.—Optic Glass, *P. L.* I. 288. Optic Tube, III. 590.

THOMSON.—optic tube, *Autumn* 1093.

Telescope—*continued*

DESAGULIERS.—Galilaeo's new-invented Eyes, *Newt. Syst.* 15.

Volcano

NOTE.—*Burning mountain* was an established term for a volcano. A few occurrences of the phrase in scientific prose may be noted: Hooke *Spring*, in Gunther *Early Science in Oxford* VIII. 380; Lister, in *Phil. Trans.* XIV. 514; Ray *Physio-Theol.* 282; Dampier *New Voyage* 88; J. Chamberlayne *Nieuwentyt* II. 416. The phrase in French is *ardente montaigne* (see Chanoine *Columella* 433), and the phrase *ignivomous Mountains* occurs in *Phil. Trans.* I. 110.

———

SYLVESTER.—burning　　Mountaine, *1605* 373.

W. CHAMBERLAYNE.—burning mountains, *Phar.* III. iv. 194.

Water

NOTE.—It is sometimes difficult to distinguish between periphrases for *water* and those for *sea* or *ocean*, and it is quite probable that I have not always classified these phrases properly. Under *sea* I mean to place periphrases which signify sea or ocean, and under *water* periphrases which signify the liquid that makes up the larger bodies; the doubtful phrases are generally placed under *water*, rather than under *sea*.

———

VIRGIL.—caeruleum gremium, *Aen.* VIII. 713.

PRUDENTIUS.—uitreis liquoribus, *Cath.* V. 67.

DU BELLAY.—element liquide, I. 74. liqueur cristaline, I. 92.

CAMOENS.—humido elemento, *Lus.* 166b.

Water—*continued*

DU BARTAS.—du plus froid element, *I Sem.* III. 212. element humide, III. 348. ondeux element, IV. 167. marine humeur, VI. 484. crystal doux-coulant, *Eden* 76. moitte element, *Bab.* 420. vageux tombeau, *Colon.* 732. verre flottant, *Yvry* 325.

DU MONIN.—vagueus Element, *Urano.* 10b. glaceuse plaine, *Manip. Poet.* 49.

TASSO.—liquidi cristalli, *Mondo Creato* III. 131. liquido elemento, III. 429.

SPENSER.—watry bowres, *S. C.: Apr.* 39. christall flood, *F. Q.* I. xii. 7.

SHAKESPEARE.—wat'ry nest, *Lucrece* 1611. wat'ry glass, *M. N. D.* I. i. 210.

E. FAIRFAX.—watery store, *Tasso* XV. viii.

SYLVESTER.—liquid Christal, *1605* 350. liquid Glasse, 486. fibrous siluer, *1606* 9. crystall humor, *1611* 523. liquid Ice, 543. liquid Treasures, *1633* 492. liquid Elements, 519. liquid Silver, 606.

MARINO.—liquido mondo, *Rime* II. 47.

GÓNGORA.—liquido elemento, I. 25. crystal liquido, II. 61.

W. BROWNE.—wat'ry zone, *Brit. Past.* II. i. 984.

MURE.—liquid stoir, I. 40.

MURTOLA.—cristallino humore, *Creat. Mondo* V. xii. 4.

DRAYTON.—watry tribute, *Poly-Olb.* II. 173. liquid store, X. 6. watry Realme, XV. 296. Christall face, XXI. 56. watry walks, XXII. 382. liquid glasse, XXVI. 236. silver road, XXVII. 24. silver load, XXVII. 63. watry prease, XXVIII. 180. watry store, XXX. 101. liquid Pearle, *Nimph.* VI. 163.

Water—*continued*

DRUMMOND.—christall Plaine, I. 35. watrie Tribute, I. 47.

P. FLETCHER.—watry glasse, *Locusts* II. xxv. liquid walls, IV. iii. liquid plaine, V. xxiv. watry herse, *Purple Isl.* I. xxx.

WHITING.—juice of clouds, *CP* III. 495.

SANDYS.—liquid mirror, *Ovid's Met.* 68.

E. WALLER.—watery element, *Lady's Fishing* 20.

STANLEY.—floating Mirrours, *Sylvia's Park* 169. liquid treasure, *Ps. cxlviii* 6.

DAVENANT.—fleeting Element, *Gond.* I. ii. 47. Oisel's juice, III. iv. 24.

SHERBURNE.—Wat'ry Tribute, *Seneca's Ans.* 2. liquid Pearl, *Salmacis* 2. watery glasse, 13.

FANSHAWE.—liquid Element, *Lus.* II. lxvii. Sea's cleer Glass, II. xci. wavy Element, V. xx. humid Element, V. xlii. watry Element, V. lxxxvi. Crystal Element, VI. xx. Silver Tribute, X. cxx.

CHAPELAIN.—liquide crystal, *Pucelle* 135.

EVELYN.—liquid way, *Lucretius* 35.

W. CHAMBERLAYNE.—liquid element, *Phar.* I. iv. 418. liquid wealth, II. iv. 187.

MILTON.—Sea-paths, *Ps. viii* 22. watry bear, *Lyc.* 12. watrie Labyrinth, *P. L.* II. 584. watry gleam, IV. 461. crystal Wall, VII. 293. humid traine, VII. 306. watrie Glass, XI. 844. clear milkie juice, *S. A.* 550.

COWLEY.—liquid glass, 259.

K. PHILIPS.—liquid crystal, *CP* I. 606.

DRYDEN.—watery store, *Alb. and Alban.* I. i, in *Works* VII. 254. wat'ry road, *Geo.* II. 274. liquid

Water—*continued*

crystal, IV. 515. briny floods, *Aen.* III. 18. liquid way, V. 274. wat'ry pastures, VII. 967. liquid glass, VIII. 128. wat'ry track, X. 325. wat'ry course, X. 348. wat'ry way, *Cock and Fox* 314.

POPE.—wat'ry glass, *Summer* 28.

THOMSON.—limpid plain, *Summer* 484.

Waves

DU BARTAS.—vagueuses montaignes, *I Sem.* III. 57.

SHAKESPEARE.—liquid mountains, *Tro. and Cres.* I. iii. 40. liquid surge, *Timon* IV. iii. 442.

SYLVESTER.—waterie Mountaines, *1605* 419. foamy Mount, *1611* 615. salt surge, *1633* 225.

DRAYTON.—liquid Mountaines, *Poly-Olb.* II. 456.

HANNAY.—wat'ry hills, *Philo.* 1127.

DRUMMOND.—cristall mountaines, II. 58.

MARMION.—wat'ry regiment, *Cup. and Psy.* I. iv. 170.

FANSHAWE.—Sea's rolling Tow'rs, *Lus.* VII. lxxix.

MILTON.—watrie throng, *P. L.* VII. 297.

COWLEY.—watry War, 230.

DRYDEN.—wat'ry ranks, *Geo.* IV. 606. liquid mountains, *Aen.* I. 125. wat'ry war, II. 414.

Winds

VALERIUS FLACCUS.—volucrum gens turbida fratrum, *Argon.* VIII. 323.

RONSARD.—troupe naufragiere, VI. 421.

DU BARTAS.—esprits souffleurs, *I Sem.* II. 567. bande æolide, III. 157.

SYLVESTER.—Ayrie violence, *1605* 364. Earths sweeping Broomes, 398. Aeolian crowd, 399.

Winds—*continued*

BEAUMONT AND FLETCHER.—windy brood, *Philaster* IV. iii, in *B. and F.* I. 162.

SANDYS.—ayery motion, *Ovid's Met.* 111. ayery race, 111.

CHAPELAIN.—venteux Element, *Pucelle* 255.

Wine

OVID.—liquido Baccho, *Met.* XIII. 639.

VALERIUS FLACCUS.—Bacchi latices, *Argon.* IV. 533. dona Bacchi, V. 215.

NONNOS.—πορφυρέης ἐέρσης [purple juice], *Dionys.* XX. 294.

PONTANO.—bacchum fluentem, *Urania* II. 532.

DU BARTAS.—doux jus de la vigne, *I Sem.* IV. 640.

SYLVESTER.—Iuice of Bacchus clusters, *1605* 138. teares of pressed Grapes, 273.

DRAYTON.—liquid purple, *Elizium* 71.

Wine—*continued*

WHITING.—Bacchus water, *CP* III. 496.

FLATMAN.—generous juice, *CP* III. 399.

MILTON.—turbulent liquor, *S. A.* 552.

DRYDEN.—juicy vintage, *Ecl.* VII. 80. liquid harvest, *Geo.* II. 753.

Women

EURIPIDES.—θῆλυν σποράν [the female seed], *Hec.* 659.

SCÈVE.—lascif flambeau, 199.

JONSON.—female race, VII. 125.

SYLVESTER.—tender Female-kinde, *1633* 481.

GÓNGORA.—femenil tropa, II. 70.

WHITING.—female kind, *CP* III. 442. full-flanked train, III. 498.

MILTON.—fair femal Troop, *P. L.* XI. 614.

DRYDEN.—leaky kind, *Lucretius* IV. 20. female nation, *Epilogue to The Princess of Cleves* 21.

Epithets with the Suffix -*y* in English Scientific Literature

THE practice of writing scientific treatises in English involved the establishment of terminologies as accurate as those that had been developed in Latin and Greek. And since the writing of antiquity was still of consequence in the seventeenth and eighteenth centuries, it was also necessary that the English terms manifestly correspond with terms already developed in these other languages. It was not always easy to satisfy the two demands. Some equivalents were at hand: *water* could be used for *aqua* with complete confidence in its synonymous value and with no violence to English usage. But it was much more difficult to get equally satisfactory terms descriptive of appearance without introducing some inaccuracy or confusion of meaning. For example, *downy* gives a clear enough description of the appearance of certain twigs or fruits covered with a light down. Yet, though this word is conceivably precise, for the native speaker of English it has many other associations that work against its use in a single, limited application. It might mean fuzzy or feathery or merely soft, and its limitation to any one of these meanings would seem arbitrary and be confusing. As a scientific word, then, such a term suffers from its wide employment in a living language. On the other hand, *pappous* in its English orthography fully serves any demand for scientific accuracy and is free from the troublesome associations of daily use. But its meaning would not be known at first sight to anyone not trained in Latin, and it does in fact belong to a Latin rather than an English terminology. The advantage of its use in an English context is merely that the reader need not have mastered Latin syntax.

Throughout the seventeenth and eighteenth centuries scientists of all countries made increasing use of their native languages in recording their investigations. Such experiments in terminology as they undertook may be said to have come finally to one result: The basic language of science in any country is that country's language, but the terminology is predominantly Latin or Greek, although usually in the orthography and grammatical form it would take in the essay. The English experiments in search of a vernacular terminology ended in this way, as did those of other languages. This is perhaps fortunate, since the universal acceptance of Latin and Greek forms means that most scientific terms will be recognizably the same in the context of different vernaculars. What is important here, however, is that for many years many writers devoted themselves to the establishment of vernacular terminologies in the different fields of science, and though their efforts were for the most part finally defeated, for a considerable period they met with many successes. At times, in one field or another, the vernacular appeared to have won out, and though the great victories were transient, smaller ones have prevailed till now in some sciences, where the vernacular term survives along with the classic, though it does not replace it.

It is important in studying the language of poetry in this period to know the extent of the success of such experiments in the prose of the time. For not merely did the popular acceptance of scientific work give general currency to many special terms, but it is likely that the usefulness of certain methods of forming words and phrases became known through the wide circulation of scientific essays in which these methods were extensively developed. I should think a reader of that time, finding in the *Philosophical Transactions*, say, any number of epithets formed with the suffix -*y*, some of them unusual, would be impressed by them. I should think a group of these words might find a place in his vocabulary, as a fad or in some more constant use. That such a reader might, furthermore, adopt these terms, or terms like them, in writing poetry, is also to be supposed, though the supposition needs to be buttressed by more specific considerations. But the general proposition is reasonable that through the study of the use of epithets with this suffix in scientific prose we may arrive at conclusions that will be of immediate applicability in the study of the use of such terms in verse.

The wide employment of this form in poetry is common

knowledge; the following list of occurrences in prose shows that it was employed quite as widely and ingeniously in scientific investigation. Observing several of the prose passages, the reader may conclude that the verse use of the period was in no way more extreme or, according to modern taste, more absurd.

It may also be observed from such a list that it early became the custom in scientific writing to translate many Latin epithets by English adjectives having the suffix -*y*. The Latin suffixes -*osus*, -*us*, -*eus*, -*ius*, and some other forms, though often enough brought over into English in what is essentially their original form, were probably more frequently translated by -*y*. There is, for example, as we see in the following phrase from the *Philosophical Transactions* of 1667, the self-conscious habit of using the Latin and the English words to explain each other: "A Farinaceous or Mealy Tree."[1] John Evelyn at about the same time was making such entries as this in his gardener's notebook: "Lignous, such whose Rootes are woody."[2] The practice of using epithets with -*y* to take the place of the Latin form was perhaps most extensively developed by Thomas Martyn in the late eighteenth century. Here, for example, is a fairly typical entry in his botanical lexicon: "TOMENTOSUS (*Tomentum*, down, nap, cotton, or flocks . . .) Tomentose; or, if we must translate the term—Downy, Nappy, Cottony, or Flocky."[3]

A compilation of prose uses showing the extent to which this form was employed to translate Latin adjectival suffixes might lead to the supposition that many comparable terms in verse were derived from similar Latin originals, themselves in prose or verse. Though conclusions of this sort are obviously

---

[1] II. 485.   [2] *Gardiner* 19.

[3] *Language of Botany* (under *Tomentosus*). Martyn's practice, in fact, seems to represent the fullest development of the effort to translate Latin terms of a certain kind into native English forms. Because he is so patient and exhaustive in his efforts, I think I am justified in quoting him frequently in the following list, even though his date is rather later than that of any of the other writers I cite. The lateness of his work (the first edition was printed in 1793) may in itself have a special value, however, attesting that the practice he followed was vital to scientific writing at the very time Erasmus Darwin was bringing final notoriety to the elaborate stock diction of verse and using this particular form excessively. The reader may be reminded, however, that Sylvester and Chapman, among earlier poets, were perhaps equally extravagant in the use of this form (see J. M. Robertson, *Shakespeare and Chapman* [London, 1917] 54, and John Arthos, "Studies in the Diction of Neo-Classic Poetry" [MS thesis (1937) in the Harvard College Library] 148–53).

best based on the study of individual poets, the force of the analogy is inescapable.

The list that follows will show, moreover, that terms with the -*y* suffix were supposed to have dignity. Nowadays the suffix carries so many associations of the diminutive or the contemptuous that we find it difficult to grant a proper seriousness to many of the epithets in neoclassic verse. A list of prose uses, however, should make us take the form more seriously, and from this we may learn to admit a dignity in the practice of verse we have hitherto been disposed to deny.

There is still another consideration to cause us to compare the uses of verse and prose. Adjectives with the suffix -*y* are well adapted to describe the appearance of material things— "*glassy* stream," "*downy* twig," "*woody* stalk." Performing this function, they are also describing an aspect of the nature or composition of the object that accounts for its appearance. Such capacities are obviously of importance to the writers of scientific description, and this fact would in itself sufficiently explain the repeated use of this serviceable form in serious descriptive prose. It is consequently to be expected that poets with similar interests in the description of the nature of things would employ similar language forms. That such interests were important to many of the poets of the seventeenth and eighteenth centuries is, of course, the thesis of the present study.

For an explanation of the system of abbreviations, see page xiv. The quotations from the lexicons of Martyn and Berkenhout are to be found in those volumes under the key words.

Airy

Rain-Water is not only exhaled by the Beams of Heaven from the most clear and subtel Fountains, and impregnated with Cœlestial Influences, but also is, as it were, strained with Airy Motions and Winds, which fill it with a Saline and Balsamick Vertue.—Tryon *Way to Health* (1683) 146.

Benty

We see diverse benty grasses to thrive, especially on barren places, where scarce any thing else wil grow.—Hartlib *Husbandry* (1652) 40.

Bladdery

PABULOSUM *folium*. (*Pabula*, a pimple.) A pimply, bladdery or blistered leaf.—Martyn *Lang. Bot.* (1796).

Bloomy

With good reason did our Auncestors build their houses towards the South and the North, because through the northerne windowes, the north winde might in the summer passe in, to coole the bloomie aire in them.—Venner *Via Recta* (1620) 5.

Blushy

A Swan . . . whose leggs are . . . of a blushy red like those of a tame Goose.—Plot *Stafford.* (1686) 228.

Bony

Testaceous and bony substances belonging to Fish.—Plot *Oxford.* (1677) 114.

Branchy

I have a piece of branchy spar, which I found at a Mine on these Hills.—*Phil. Trans.* XI (1676), 731.

Branny

It must be confessed that the Nutrimentive Quality is contained in the fine Flour, and yet in the branny part is contained the opening and digestive Quality.—Tryon *Way to Health* (1683) 197.

Brawny

Elos is, when *vuea* being so farre thrust out of the eye-lids, becommeth hard, and the horny coat round about, being brawny, presseth it downe, as if it were the head of a nayle.—Banister *Guillemeau* (1622) H₂.

Briny

There may be such a Sand under the briny Bog near Church-hill-mill.—Plot *Oxford.* (1677) 40.

Broomy

This heathy, broomy, gorsy, barren sort of Soile.—Plot *Stafford.* (1686) 110.

Brushy

The brushy parts [of the comet] were fainter and paler towards the sides.—Hooke *Cometa* (1678), in Gunther *Early Science in Oxford* VIII. 219.

Chaffy

NETTLE. Seed-vessel; bearing chaffy tufts.—Wilkins *Real Character* (1668) 83.

Glumosi. Glumose, or chaffy.—Rose *Linnaeus* (1775) 37.

Chalky

Chalky or Calcarious Matter.—Morton *Northampton.* (1712) 413.

Clammy

That is called Εμπλασικὶν, that is clammy, which applyed to any place sticks tenaciously, and obstructs the pores of the skin, and fils them with much stuffe, as Rosin or Gum.—Tomlinson *Renodaeus* (1657) 30.

Viscous, clammy, like bird-lime.—Evelyn *Gardiner* (*c.* 1687) 15.

Clayey

As for your Claiy Land, make Channels to draw the water from it.—S. Gilbert *Flor. Vade-Mecum* (1682) 2.

Cliffy

[In the moon] there are also many craggy, solitary, steep and cliffy rocks.—Salusbury *Math. Coll.* (1661) 49.

Cloudy

If those Planets which rule the principal places of a Celestial Figure at the Suns Entrance into the Vernal Æquinox be combust, they portend a dark and cloudy air.—Dariott *Redivivus* (1653) 288.

Coaly

The Portugals scorch their ships, insomuch that in the quick works there is made a coaly crust of about an Inch thick.—*Phil. Trans.* I (1666) 190.

Cottony

Oaks bear also a knur, full of a Cottony matter, of which they Antiently made Wick for their Lamps and Candles.—Evelyn *Sylva* (1664) 16.

Cruddy

The cruddie part of the milke is of an heauy, grosse, and phlegmaticke substance.—Venner *Via Recta* (1620) 91.

Crusty

The Contents of these [petrifying] Waters being dropt and left behind in their Chanels, . . . they form a Crusty Covering upon the Bodies occurring in their Passage.—Morton *Northampton*. (1712) 271.

Dewy

The Rainbow is an Halo opposite to the sun or moon, in a dewy cloud, representing a bow of divers colours.—Comenius *Nat. Phil. Ref.* (1651) 136.

Downy

A pappous and downy Seed, having no milky Juice.—Morton *Northampton*. (1712) 369.

Dreggy

That water is esteemed to bee the best and wholsomest, which is most cleare and thin, pure in taste and smell, altogether clean from any impure, terrene, or other dreggy mixture.—Venner *Via Recta* (1620) 8.

Dusky

Their natural Colour is changed into a dull Green, mixed with a dusky Black.—Tryon *Way to Health* (1683) 127.

Earthy

To make tryal of the growth of Plants, in all kinds of simple Soils; either Earthy or Mineral.—Grew *Phil. Hist. Plants* (1682) 22.

Fatty

There are many Vessels, which may be call'd Adipous or Fatty, which issue out of this Membrane, and spreading themselves all over the Body, conveigh Fat to it, just as the Arteries carry the Blood all over the same.—*Phil. Trans.* II (1667), 553.

Feathery

PLUMOSUS *Pappus*. Plumose, feathered or compound Down. *Pilis pennatis constans*—s. *villosus compositus.*—A flying crown to some seeds, composed of compound or feathery hairs.—Martyn *Lang. Bot.* (1796).

Fenny

The very Towns in that which is vulgarly called the Fenny Part of the County, them I mean that border on the Fenland.—Morton *Northampton*. (1712) 265.

Ferny

[A certain region] is Heathy, Ferny and Furzy.—*Phil. Trans.* II (1667), 525.

Finny

The rest of this tribe [of fish], having a more oblong body, and a very rough skin, with finny substances, standing out from each side like wings.—Wilkins *Real Character* (1668) 133.

Fishy

I have been told that Soy is made partly with a fishy Composition, and it seems most likely by the Taste.—Dampier *Discov.* (1699) 26.

Flaggy

The Grass in these Savannahs at John Fernando's is not a long flaggy

Grass . . . but a sort of kindly Grass, thick and flourishing the biggest part of the Year.—Dampier *New Voyage* (1697) 68.

Fleshy

FLESHY leaf. *Folium carnosum.* Full of pulp within.—Martyn *Lang. Bot.* (1796).

Flinty

The Sand, Sparry and Flinty Matter being then soft, or in a state of solution.—J. Woodward *Nat. Hist. Earth* (1695) 21.

Floaty

[Gar-fish] are a sort of floaty or flying fish.—Dampier *Discov.* (1699) 176.

Flocky

(See page 395.)

Furzy

(See FERNY.)

Gemmy

Gravelly and arenous Earths of several sorts, before they were washed, appeared to consist mostly of rough crystals, of which some were very transparent and gemmy. —Evelyn *Terra* (1675) 14.

Glassy

The Vitrious or Glassie Humour, bigger than any of the rest, fills the backward Cavity of the Eye.— Harris *Lex. Tech.* (1704) (under *Humours*).

Glossy

NITIDUM *Folium;* bright, shining, glossy. — Berkenhout *Bot. Lex.* (1764).

Gorsy

(See BROOMY.)

Gouty

From the Swellings and Bunchings occasioned by these gleeting Springs, and the Wetness of this Sort of Land, it is, in some other Counties, called Gouty, and Weeping Land. —Morton *Northampton.* (1712) 39.

Gravelly

The inward parts of the present Earth are very irregular and confused. One region is chiefly Stony, another Sandy, a third Gravelly.— Whiston *New Theory* (1696) 205.

Grazy

When Corne is so sowne after the ordinary manner, much is buried in the furrowes; especially if the ground be grazy.—Hartlib *Husbandry* (1652) 8.

Gristly

Tendons . . . being of a nervy and half gristly substance.—Comenius *Nat. Phil. Ref.* (1651) 194.

Grovy

The Houses lie scattering up and down in the Grove . . . . In the dry Season these Grovy dwellings are very pleasant.—Dampier *Discov.* (1699) 36.

Gummy

The Age of Timber-trees, especially of such as be of a compact, resinous, or balsamical nature . . . are capable of very long duration and continuance: those of largest Roots, longer liv'd then the shorter; the dry, then the wet; and the gummy, then the watry.—Evelyn *Sylva* (1664) 80.

Hairy

Tamarinds and Dates macerated in vineger or other liquor, are after the same manner put into a hairy sieve for many definite uses, and so

pulped through with a Manipulus.
—Tomlinson *Renodaeus* (1657) 81.

HAIRY leaf. *Folium pilosum.* Covered with hairs—applied also to the style, and to seeds. *Hairy receptacle.* Having hairs between the florets.—Martyn *Lang. Bot.* (1796).

Hazy

First, As concerning the matter or substance of the Nucleus Star or body, of the hazy shining part encompassing it, and of the Tail or Blaze.—Hooke *Cometa* (1678), in Gunther *Early Science in Oxford* VIII. 224.

Heathy

(See BROOMY.)

Herby

The rest of the Seed consisted of two Lobes of a dark herby Colour made up of Globules.—*Phil. Trans.* XVII (1694), 706.

Horny

The second membrane or parchment skinne is named *Cornea*, that is, hornie, which is more strong and hard, resembling horne that is made thin and bright.—Banister *Guillemeau* (1622) A₅.

Husky

The branny and husky part is good in any Grain.—Tryon *Way to Health* (1683) 201.

Icy

The Chrystaline, or Icy Humour, which is contained in the *Tunica Uvea*, and is thicker than the rest.—Harris *Lex. Tech.* (1704) (under *Humours*).

Juicy

From whence have all those Juicy Fruits, as Grapes, Cherries, Gooseberries, Currants, and a thousand others, their agreeable Liquors, if it were not from Water?—J. Chamberlayne *Nieuwentyt* (1718) II. 464.

Kernelly

The cause of Moles in the womb, and of many kernelly and fleshy substances in other parts of the body.—*Phil. Trans.* II (1667), 507–8.

Knotty

Ganglium, is a concretion, or knottie growing upon some sinew, or tendon.—Banester *Tumors* (1633) 51.

Leady

There hapneth to this tumor . . . evill dispositions, worthy carefull fore-sight: to wit, corruption: which is signified by blacke or leadie colour, stinking savour, &c.—Banester *Tumors* (1633) 4.

Leafy

There seem'd to be a Leafy Matter, if I may so call it, intermixt with that of the Fruit.—Morton *Northampton.* (1712) 394.

FOLIOSUM *Capitulum [folium]* leafy, covered or intermixed with leaves, opposed to *nudum.*—Berkenhout *Bot. Lex.* (1764).

Leathery

Leathery or leather-like. See *Coriaceous.* [CORIACEOUS. Stiff like leather or parchment. Applied to the leaf, calyx, and capsule.]—Martyn *Lang. Bot.* (1796).

Limy

I having once ranged the Juice of *Angelica sativa Park.* amongst those, and yet I found it altered after a Years keeping, and grown very Limy.—*Phil. Trans.* XIX (1698), 378.

Loamy

In Transplanting the Orange, Lemmon & all other case & Tubb Trees, place them in rich mould taken from under the first Turfe of a pasture field a little loamy.—Evelyn *Gardiner* (*c.* 1687) 68.

Lousy

I call him the Lousie Beetle, because when taken, he is generally found to be infested with small Vermin, like Lice.—*Phil. Trans.* XIX (1698), 394.

Marbly

Salt Gem, is a white kinde of Euensalt, shining like Christall: It is also called Stonie, marbly, salt Sarmaticke, or Dacian.—Widdowes *Nat. Phil.* (1621) 29.

Marly

A Marly Earth, . . . an Earth that slaked like Marle.—Morton *Northampton.* (1712) 62.

Massy

Leaf Gold is yellow by reflected, and blue by transmitted Light, and massy Gold is yellow in all Positions of the Eye.—Newton *Opt.* (1730) 184.

Mattery

All Ulcers are cured by incarnating Mercury; All mattery gluish sores by Salt.—Pinnell *Croll* (1657) 123.

Mealy

(See page 395.)

Milky

The root is small hairie, full of milkie iuyce, as is also the whole plant.—Goodyer (1621), in Gunther *Early Brit. Bot.* 149.

Miry

Now, that stagnant Water, if the Earth be not naturally black, will impart that Tincture to it, is seen in the Mud of Pools, and old Ditches, and in the miry Earth of Bogs.—Morton *Northampton.* (1712) 38.

Morassy

These Trees commonly grow here . . . in a Champion dry Ground, such at least as is not drowned or morassy.—Dampier *Discov.* (1699) 87.

Mossy

Medlers are mossie [*lanuginosa*], Prunes (or Plums) are stonie.—Comenius *Gate of Tongues* (1637) 19.

Mouldy

Preserve [hazelnuts] therefore moist, not mouldy.—Evelyn *Sylva* (1664) 35.

Nappy

(See page 395.)

Nervy

The skin of the body is most glutinous, and altogether nervie.—Comenius *Nat. Phil. Ref.* (1651) 184.

Oily

Distillation is an eduction of a watry or oily humour out of any thing by heat.—Tomlinson *Renodaeus* (1657) 88.

Oozy

At Night we anchored in six Fathom Water, near a League from the Main, in good oazy Ground.—Dampier *New Voyage* (1697) 182.

Peaty

Boggy, peaty, and cold-black-lands.—Plot *Stafford.* (1686) 356.

Pebbly

The *Striæ* appear to be constituted of a Sparry and Pebly Matter intermixed.—Morton *Northampton.* (1712) 160.

Phlegmy

The super-abounding phlegmy matter, which suffocates the Spirits and stops the Passages, weakening the natural Heat and Action of the Stomach.—Tryon *Way to Health* (1683) 102.

Pimply

(See BLADDERY.)

Pitchy

Ampelite is a pitchie Earth, cleauing and blacke.—Widdowes *Nat. Phil.* (1621) 31.

Pithy

Upon the Anatomical Analysis of all the Parts of a Plant, I had certainly found, (and shall hereafter shew) That in all Plants, there are Two, and only Two Organical Parts essentially distinct, viz. The Pithy Part, and the Lignous Part, or such others as are analogous to either of these.—Grew *Phil. Hist. Plants* (1682) 19.

Pory

It seemed to be a disease, called in Greeke, *Symptosis*, in Latine, *Concidentia:* this came of drynesse of the brain, whereby the sinewes were withered and gathered together, and wrinkled, the holes or pory passages thereof were stopped.— Banister *Guillemeau* (1622) d₁₂–e₁.

Prickly

The Caper is a prickly shrub sending forth divers long weak trailing wooddy stalkes.—Coles *Adam in Eden* (1657) Fff₁b.

Puddly

Many sometimes are so unwilling that they had rather dye then drink such a deale of those muddy and pudly potions, which spoyl the complexion of a mans body, and which

the Physitian himselfe that prescribed it, and the Apothecary that mingled, would abhor and altogether refuse to drink in the like case.—Pinnell *Croll* (1657) 99.

Pulpy

PULPOSUM *folium.* A pulpy leaf, filled with a tenacious substance between the two surfaces.—Martyn *Lang. Bot.* (1796).

Rooty

A rare Plant . . . growing a considerable heigth, divideing its self into divers branches, from the naked parts of which . . . it drops down new rooty matter.—*Phil. Trans.* XIII (1683), 105.

Rushy

Rushy-lands.   Blith telleth us, good Remedies for these Inconveniences, (viz.) making deep trenches, oft mowings, Chalking, Liming, Dunging and Ploughing.—Hartlib *Husbandry* (1652) 44.

Sappy

If you view [a part of a bean] in a Microscope, or with a very good Spectacle-Glass, it hath some similitude to the Pith, while sappy in the Roots and Trunks of Plants.— Grew *Anat. Plants* (1682) 4.

Scaly

At the tops of the branches, stand such like scalie heads as Marjerom hath.—Coles *Adam in Eden* (1657) Ddd₃b.

(See also pages 297–9.)

Scurfy

SQUARROSUS . . . . Squarrose, by some translated Ragged; by others, Scurfy.—Martyn *Lang. Bot.* (1796).

Sedgy

The Mould of the Savannahs is generally black and deep, produc-

ing a coarse sort of sedgy Grass.—
Dampier *Discov.* (1699) 167.

Shaggy

HIRSUTUS.   Hirsute, rough with
hair, shaggy.—Martyn *Lang. Bot.*
(1796).

Shelly

The Tail of a Glow-Worm is made
of seven Shelly Rings.—Pointer
Weather (1738) 76.

Shrubby

Shrubby.   *Fruticōsus.*   Perennial,
with several woody stems.—Martyn
Lang. Bot. (1796).

Sinewy

It is a musculous membrane, which
in the middle of it hath a sinnewy
circle.—Digby *Two Treat.* (1644)
302.

Skinny

The maw and bellies of beasts are
of an hard, skinnie, and tough substance.—Venner *Via Recta* (1620)
71.

SCARIOSUM *folium.*   A Scariose leaf.
Called Skinny by Dr. Withering.—
Martyn *Lang. Bot.* (1796).

Slatty

Stony, slatty sorts of Marles.—Plot
Stafford. (1686) 120.

Slimy

The common Daffodill hath long,
fat, and thick leaves, full of a slimy
juyce.—Coles *Adam in Eden* (1657)
Oo₃.

Smoky

The privative damp or want of Air,
is best cured the same way the
smoaky damp is, by setting down
a shaft to the adit.—Plot *Stafford.*
(1686) 139.

Smutty

I account Smutty Corn an imperfect
or sick Graine, and suppose that by
a Microscope the imperfection may
be discerned.—Hartlib *Husbandry*
(1652) 11.

Sooty

Sooty, and friable Earth.—Morton
Northampton. (1712) 81.

Sparry

Coralloid Bodies of the Sparry Kind.
—Morton *Northampton.* (1712) 184.

Spiky

It is called in Latine *Lunaria Minor,*
. . . the divisions of the Leafe being
much like unto an half Moon, as
also, *Botrytis sive ramosa, aut racemosa,*
à capitibus in modum racemi formatis,
from the spiky head thereof, which
somewhat resembles a bunch of
Grapes.—Coles *Adam in Eden* (1657)
Bbbbb₁b.

Spiny

Spinosus.   Spiny or Thorny.—Martyn *Lang. Bot.* (1796).

Spiry

A thin spiry grass.—Plot *Oxford.*
(1677) 154.

Spoky

From amongst the said Leaves rise
up divers crested stalkes of a Cubit
high,   having   thereupon   divers
smaller stalkes of winged Leaves
also finely cut, but somwhat harsh
to the feeling and bearing at the
top spoky rundells or umbells beset
with white flowers.—Coles *Adam in*
Eden (1657) Iii₂b.

Spongy

For as the Elm does not thrive in
too dry, sandy or hot grounds, no
more will it abide the cold and
spungy.—Evelyn *Sylva* (1664) 19.

The Organ of [taste] is the Tongue and Palat, and it is done by the help of Spongy Flesh, and of Nerves which terminate in the Tongue.—Midgley *Nat. Phil.* (1687) 303.

Spriggy

The Flowers which are small, and of a dark yellow colour, do grow in a spiked fashion upon the tops of the spriggy branches, after which come very small long Pods.—Coles *Adam in Eden* (1657) Dddd₁b.

Springy

Such standing-Waters as are in a kind of springy Grounds are the best, but still much inferior to running-Waters.—Tryon *Way to Health* (1683) 152.

Stony

Now the cause of this Petrifying property, is a stony-juice; for the water which contains the Seeds of so many things, that of stones doth especially coagulate therein.—Evelyn *Lucretius* (1656) 130.

(See also under SLATTY.)

Strawy

Maudlin Tansy . . . having a yellowish flower, of a dry strawy consistence.—Wilkins *Real Character* (1668) 84.

Stringy

Stringy bituminous earths.—Plot *Stafford.* (1686) 114.

Sulphury

When sulphury exhalations are mixt with nitrous . . . they endure one another so long, as till the sulphur takes fire.—Comenius *Nat. Phil. Ref.* (1651) 133.

Thorny

THORNY. *Spinosus.* Set with thorns: as the stem of many shrubs.—Martyn *Lang. Bot.* (1796).

(See also under SPINY.)

Thready

The greatest double Marigold hath many large, fat, broad Leaves, springing immediately from a fibrous or threddy Root.—Coles *Adam in Eden* (1657) 182.

Twiggy

The English Cherrie tree groweth in time to be of a reasonable bignesse and height, spreading great armes, and also small twiggy branches plentifully. — Parkinson *Paradisus Terr.* (1629) 571.

Warty

The greater Verrucose or warty Water-Newt. — Morton *Northampton.* (1712) 440.

Watery

The unctious or oily sapour is sweet, and nourisheth, as Galen saith, (*cap.* 9. *lib.* 4. *simpl.*) that whatsoever nourisheth is sweet, or of a kinde of sweet sapour: yet they are distinct; for watry humidity is of sweet things, aery of fat things.—Tomlinson *Renodaeus* (1657) 39.

Wheyey

In milk, the cream . . . separates it self by little and little, from the wheyie parts, and gathers it self to the top.—Comenius *Nat. Phil. Ref.* (1651) 43.

Windy

Spittle is a windie foame cast out of the brest, and his parts.—Widdowes *Nat. Phil.* (1621) 59.

Woody

LIGNOSUS *Caulis* [*Lignum*, wood] woody, opposed to *herbaceus.*—Berkenhout *Bot. Lex.* (1764).

Woolly

Woolly. *Lanatus.* Clothed with a pubescence resembling wool: as the leaves of Horehound.—Martyn *Lang. Bot.* (1796).

Bibliography

NOTE.—For the sake of easy reference the Bibliography is assembled in a single alphabetical list, but in order to distinguish works of scientific interest an asterisk has been placed before each entry of that nature.

Works that in the text are cited for the language of the translation are listed in the Bibliography under the name of the translator.

LCL stands for "Loeb Classical Library."

CP stands for Saintsbury's collection, *Minor Poets of the Caroline Period.*

ABBOT, WILLIAM RICHARDSON, *Studies in the Influence of Du Bartas in England, 1584–1641.* MS thesis (1931) in the library of the University of North Carolina.

*ABERCROMBY, D., *Academia Scientiarum: Or The Academy of Sciences. Being a Short and Easie Introduction to the Knowledge of the Liberal Arts and Sciences.* London, 1687.

Académie des Jeux-Floraux: Actes et Délibérations du Collège de Rhétorique (1513– 1641), Vol. I, ed. F. de Gélis and J. Anglade. Toulouse: Édouard Privat, 1933.

ACCIUS. See Warmington, E. H.

*ACOSTA, JOSEPH DE. See Grimestone, Edward.

*ADANSON, MICHEL, *Famille des Plantes,* 2 vols. Paris, 1763.

ADDISON, JOSEPH, *The Campaign, A Poem, To His Grace the Duke of Marlborough.* London, 1705.

—— *The Works of Joseph Addison,* Vol. I, ed. George W. Greene. Philadelphia, 1880.

*AELIAN, *De Natura Animalium Libri XVII,* 2 vols., ed. Abraham Gronovius. Basel, 1774.

AESCHYLUS, 2 vols., with an English translation by Herbert Weir Smyth. LCL, 1930.

AIKIN, JOHN, *An Essay on the Application of Natural History to Poetry.* Warrington, England, 1777.

—— "An Essay on the Plan and Character of the Poem," prefixed to *The Seasons by James Thomson.* London, 1778.

AKENSIDE, MARK, *The Poetical Works of Mark Akenside,* ed. Rev. Alexander Dyce. Boston, 1865.

ALBERTI, FRANCESCO d'E., ed., *Nuovo Dizionario Italiano-Francese,* 2d ed. [Venice], 1796.

405

*Aldrovandus, Ulisses, *De Piscibus Libri V et De Cetis Liber I.* Frankfurt, 1623.

Allen, Katherine, *The Treatment of Nature in the Poetry of the Roman Republic.* Madison, 1899. Reprinted from the *Bulletin of the University of Wisconsin* ("Philology and Literature Series," I. 89–219).

*Alsted, Johannes-Henricus, *Encyclopædia septem tomis distincta.* Hessen-Nassau, 1630.

*—— *Systema Physicæ Harmonicæ; Quatuor libellis methodicè propositum.* Hessen-Nassau, 1612.

*—— *Theologia Naturalis Exhibens Augustissimam Naturæ Scholam; In qua Creaturæ Dei Communi sermone ad omnes pariter docendos vtuntur.* Hessen-Nassau, 1623.

Ambrose, St., *Sancti Ambrosii Opera,* Vol. I, ed. Karl Schenkel (*Corpus Scriptorum Ecclesiasticorum Latinorum,* XXXII). Vienna, 1896.

Anacreon. See Stanley, Thomas, *Anacreon, etc.*

Anonymous, "Augustan Poetic Diction; Nature, Art and Man's 'Imperium,'" *Times Literary Supplement,* January 4, 1936.

Apollonius Rhodius, *The Argonautica,* with an English translation by R. C. Seaton. LCL, 1912.

Aratus. See Callimachus and Lycophron; Cicero.

*Arber, Agnes, *Herbals, Their Origin and Evolution, A Chapter in the History of Botany, 1470–1670.* Cambridge, England, 1912.

*Arbuthnot, John, *An Examination of Dr. Woodward's Account of the Deluge, &c. With a Comparison between Steno's Philosophy and the Doctor's, in the Case of Marine Bodies dug out of the Earth.* London, 1697.

Argyropolus, Johannes. See Basil, St., *Hexameron, etc.*

Aristophanes, 3 vols., with an English translation by Benjamin Bickley Rogers. LCL, 1924.

*Aristotle, *On the Heavens,* with an English translation by W. K. Guthrie. LCL, 1939.

*—— *On the Parts of Animals,* ed. W. Ogle. London, 1882.

*—— *On the Soul, Parva Naturalia, On Breath,* with an English translation by W. S. Hett, 2 vols. LCL, 1935.

*—— *Opera Omnia, Graece et Latine,* 5 vols., ed. U. C. Bussemaker, Fred Dübner, and Emil Heitz. Paris, 1848–74.

Armstrong, John, *The Art of Preserving Health: A Poem.* London, 1744.

*Arnoldus de Villanova, *Regimen Sanitatis Salerni: or the Schoole of Salernes Regiment of Health . . . . Reviewed, Corrected and Inlarged.* London, 1634.

Arthos, John, "Studies in the Diction of Neo-Classic Poetry," MS thesis (1937) in the Harvard College Library.

*ASHMOLE, ELIAS, ed., *Theatrum Chemicum Britannicum. Containing Severall Poeticall Pieces of our Famous English Philosophers, who have written the Hermetique Mysteries in their owne Ancient Language.* London, 1652.

ASHTON, H., *Du Bartas en Angleterre.* Paris, 1908.

AUSONIUS. See *Poetæ Latini Minores;* Stanley, Thomas, *Anacreon, etc.*

AVITUS, ST. ALCIMUS, *De Origine Mundi. De Peccato Originali. De Sententia Dei. De Diluvio. De Transitu Maris Rubri*, ed. Menradus Moltherus. Basel, 1545.

—— *Œuvres Complètes de Saint Avit,* ed. Le Chanoine Ulysse Chevalier. Lyon, 1890. (Contains *De Initio Mundi.*)

AYRES, PHILIP. See Saintsbury, *CP* II.

BACON, SIR FRANCIS, *The Essays, or Counsels, Civil and Moral,* ed. Samuel H. Reynolds. Oxford, 1890.

*—— *The Works of Francis Bacon,* 15 vols., ed. James Spedding, Robert L. Ellis, and Douglas D. Heath. New York, 1869.

BAEHRENS, EMIL, ed., *Fragmenta Poetarum Romanorum.* Leipzig, 1886. (Contains Livius Andronicus.)

*BAKER, GEORGE, *The newe Iewell of Health, wherein is contayned the most excellent Secretes of Phisicke and Philosophie, deuided into fower Bookes . . . Gathered out of the best and most approued Authors, by that excellent Doctor Gesnerus . . . .* London, 1576.

BALDENSPERGER, FERNAND, "Pour une 'Revaluation' Littéraire du XVIIe Siècle Classique," *Revue d'Histoire littéraire de la France,* XLIV (1937), 1–15.

*BANESTER, JOHN, *The Workes of that famous Chyrurgian: Of Tumors; An Antidotary Chyrurgicall; A Storehouse of Physicall and Philosophicall Secrets; A Treatise of Chirurgerie.* London, 1633.

*BANISTER, RICHARD, tr., *A Treatise of One Hundred and Thirteene Diseases of the Eyes, and Eye-Liddes, by Jacques Guillemeau,* 2d ed. London, 1622.

BARFIELD, OWEN, *Poetic Diction, A Study in Meaning.* London: Faber and Gwyer, 1928.

BARLAEUS, CASPAR, *Casparis Barlæi Antverpiani Poemata,* 2 vols., 4th ed. Amsterdam, 1645–6.

*BARLOWE, WILLIAM, *Magneticall Aduertisements: Or Divers Pertinent obseruations, and approued experiments concerning the nature and properties of the Load-stone.* London, 1616.

*BARROW, ISAAC, *Lectiones Opticæ & Geometricæ.* London, 1674.

BARSTOW, MARJORIE L., *Wordsworth's Theory of Poetic Diction* ("Yale Studies in English," LVII). New Haven, 1917.

*BARTHOLOMEUS ANGLICUS, *De Proprietatib' rerum.* Nüremberg, 1492.

BASIL, ST., *Hexameron Magni Basilii per Joannem Argyropolum e greco in latinuz conuersum.* Rome, 1515.

—— *Opera,* in Migne, *Patrologia Graeca,* XXIX (1857).

—— *Opera Omnia Quae Exstant,* Vol. I, ed. Julian Garnier. Paris, 1721.

See also Daneau, Lambert, *Physique Francoise, etc.*

BATESON, F. W., *English Poetry and the English Language, An Experiment in Literary History.* Oxford: Clarendon Press, 1934.

BAUR, ALBERT, *Maurice Scève et la Renaissance Lyonnaise.* Paris, 1906.

BEACH, JOSEPH WARREN, *The Concept of Nature in Nineteenth-Century English Poetry.* New York: Macmillan, 1936.

*BEARE, JOHN I., *Greek Theories of Elementary Cognition from Alcmaeon to Aristotle.* Oxford, 1906.

BEAUMONT, FRANCIS, AND FLETCHER, JOHN, *Beaumont & Fletcher,* 2 vols., ed. J. St. Loe Strachey. London, 1887–93.

*BEIERLYNCK, LAURENS, *Magnum Theatrum Vitae Humanae.* Cologne, 1631.

BELL, ANDREW J., *The Latin Dual & Poetic Diction, Studies in Numbers and Figures.* London: Oxford University Press, 1923.

*BELON DU MANS, PIERRE, *L'Histoire de la Nature des Oyseaux, Avec leurs descriptions, & naïfs portraicts Retirez du Naturel: Escrite en sept livres.* Paris, 1555.

*—— *Portraits D'Oyseaux, Animaux, Serpens, Herbes, Arbres, Hommes et femmes, d'Arabie & Egypte.* Paris, 1557.

BENEDICT, SAMUEL, *Domini Guillelmi Salustii Bartasii, Poëtarum nostri seculi facilè Principis, Hebdomas II. À Samuele Benedicto M. D. Latinitate donata.* Leyden, 1609.

BENLOWES, EDWARD, *Theophila.* See Saintsbury, *CP* I.

*BERKELEY, GEORGE, *An Essay Towards a New Theory of Vision.* Dublin, 1709.

*BERKENHOUT, JOHN, *Clavis Anglica Linguæ Botanicæ; Or, A Botanical Lexicon; In Which The Terms of Botany, particularly those occurring in the Works of Linnæus, and other modern Writers, Are Applied, Derived, Explained, Contrasted, and Exemplified.* London, 1764.

BERTAUT, JEAN, *Les Œuvres Poétiques de M. Bertaut, Publiées D'Après l'Édition de 1620,* ed. Adolphe Chenevière. Paris, 1891.

*BESLER, MICHAEL RUPERT, *Gazophylacium Rerum Naturalium E Regno Vegetabili, Animali et Minerali Depromptarum, Nunquam Hactenus in Lucem Editarum.* [No pl.], 1642.

BION. See Stanley, Thomas, *Anacreon, etc.*

BLACKMORE, SIR RICHARD, *Creation. A Philosophical Poem. In Seven Books.* London, 1712.

BLACKWALL, ANTHONY, *An Introduction to the Classics; Containing, A Short Discourse on their Excellencies; And Directions how to Study them to Advantage.* London, 1718.

*BLANCANUS, JOSEPHUS, *Sphaera Mundi, seu Cosmographia, Demonstratiua, ac facili Methodo tradita: In Qua Totius Mundi Fabrica, Una cum Novis, Tychonis, Kepleri, Galilæi, aliorumque Astronomorum continetur adiuuentis.* Bologna, 1620.

*BLOME, RICHARD, tr., *An Entire Body of Philosophy, According to the Principles Of the Famous Renate Des Cartes . . . Written Originally in Latin by the Learned Anthony Le Grand,* 2 vols. London, 1694.

*BLUNDEVILLE, THOMAS, *The Theoriques of the seuen Planets.* London, 1602.

BOCCACCIO, GIOVANNI, *Il Filostrato e Il Ninfale Fiesolano,* ed. Vincenzo Pernicone. Bari: Laterza, 1937.

*BOCCONE, PAOLO, *Icones & Descriptiones Rariorum Plantarum Siciliæ, Melitæ, Galliæ, & Italiæ.* Oxford, 1674.

*BOCHART, SAMUEL, *Hierozoicon Sive bipertitum opus de Animalibus Sacræ Scripturæ.* London, 1663.

*BODAEUS, IOANNES. See Theophrastus, *De Historia Plantarum, etc.*

Bodenham's Belvedére, or The Garden of the Muses. Reprinted from the original edition of 1600 for the Spenser Society, 1875.

*BODIN, JEAN, *Universæ Naturæ Theatrum. In quo rerum omnium effectrices causæ, & fines quinque libris discutiuntur.* Lyon, 1596.

See also Knolles, Richard; Oppian, *Oppiani De Venatione, etc.*

*BOODT, ANSELM BOETHIUS DE, *Gemmarum et Lapidum Historia.* Hessen-Nassau, 1609.

BOSSUETUS, FRANCISCUS, *De Natura Aquatilium Carmen.* Leyden, 1558.

BOSWORTH, WILLIAM, *Arcadius and Sepha; To Mr. Emely.* See Saintsbury, *CP* II.

*BOYLE, ROBERT, *A Continuation of New Experiments Physico-Mechanical, Touching the Spring and Weight of the Air, and their Effects,* Part I. Oxford, 1669.

*—— *An Essay of the Great Effects of Even Languid and Unheeded Motion. Whereunto is Annexed An Experimental Discourse of some little observed Causes of the Insalubrity and Salubrity of the Air and its Effects.* London, 1690. (The *Discourse* has separate pagination.)

*—— *An Examen of Mr. T. Hobbes his Dialogus Physicus De Naturâ Aëris.* London, 1662.

*—— *Experiments and Considerations about the Porosity of Bodies, In Two Essays.* London, 1684.

*—— *Experiments and Considerations Touching Colours. First occasionally Written, among some other Essays, to a Friend; and now suffer'd to come abroad as The Beginning of An Experimental History of Colours.* London, 1664.

*—— *Experiments and Notes About the Mechanical Origine or Production of Electricity.* London, 1675. (*Old Ashmolean Reprints,* VII. Oxford, 1927.)

*BOYLE, ROBERT, *Experiments and Notes About the Mechanical Production of Magnetism.* London, 1676. (*Old Ashmolean Reprints*, VII. Oxford, 1927.)

*—— *A Free Enquiry Into the Vulgarly Receiv'd Notion of Nature.* London, 1686.

*—— *The General History of the Air, Designed and Begun.* London, 1692.

*—— *New Experiments and Observations Touching Cold, or, An Experimental History of Cold, begun.* London, 1683.

*—— *New Experiments Physico-Mechanical, Touching The Spring Of the Air, And its Effects.* Oxford, 1662.

*—— *Nova Experimenta Physico-Mechanica De Vi Aeris Elastica, & ejusdem Effectibus.* Oxford, 1661.

*—— *The Sceptical Chymist.* Oxford, 1680. (First edition 1661.)

*—— *Some Considerations Touching the Usefulnesse of Experimental Natural Philosophy,* 2 vols. Oxford, 1664–71.

*BRADLEY, RICHARD, *A Philosophical Account of the Works of Nature.* London, 1726.

BRADSTREET, ANNE, *The Poems of Mrs. Anne Bradstreet,* ed. Charles Eliot Norton. "The Duodecimos," 1897.

*BRAHE, TYCHO, *Astronomiae Instauratae Mechanica (1598),* ed. B. Hasselberg. Stockholm, 1901.

*—— *De Mundi Ætherei Recentioribus Phænomenis Liber Secundus.* Uranienborg, 1588.

BRASSE, JOHN, *Greek Gradus; or, Greek, Latin, and English Prosodial Lexicon.* London [n.d.].

BREDE, ALEXANDER, "Theories of Poetic Diction in Wordsworth and Others and in Contemporary Poetry," *Papers of the Michigan Academy of Science, Arts, and Letters,* XIV (1930), 537–65.

*BREDVOLD, LOUIS I., "Dryden, Hobbes, and the Royal Society," *Modern Philology,* XXV (1927–8), 417–38.

*—— *The Intellectual Milieu of John Dryden, Studies in Some Aspects of Seventeenth-Century Thought.* Ann Arbor: University of Michigan Press, 1934.

*—— "The Sources Used by Davies in *Nosce Teipsum,*" *Publications of the Modern Language Association,* XXXVIII (1923), 745–69.

*BREWSTER, SIR DAVID, *Memoirs of the Life, Writings, and Discoveries of Sir Isaac Newton,* 2 vols. Edinburgh, 1855.

*BREWSTER, EDWIN TENNEY, *Creation, A History of Non-Evolutionary Theories.* Indianapolis: Bobbs-Merrill, 1927.

*BRIGGS, WILLIAM, *Nova Visionis Theoria,* 2d ed. London, 1685.

*—— *Ophthalmo-graphia, sive Oculi ejusq; partium descriptio Anatomica,* 2d ed. London, 1685.

BROWER, REUBEN ARTHUR, "Dryden's Poetic Diction and Virgil," *Philological Quarterly*, XVIII (1939), 211–17.

*BROWN, HARCOURT, *Scientific Organizations in Seventeenth Century France (1620–1680)*. Baltimore: Williams and Wilkins, 1934.

*BROWNE, SIR THOMAS, *The Works of Sir Thomas Browne*, Vols. II–III, ed. Geoffrey Keynes. London: Faber and Gwyer, 1928.

BROWNE, WILLIAM, *Poems of William Browne of Tavistock*, 2 vols., ed. Gordon Goodwin. London [1893].

*BRUNFELS, OTHO, *Onomastikon Medicinæ. Continens Omnia nomina Herbarum, Fruticum, Suffruticum, Arborum.* Strasbourg, 1534.

BRUNOT, FERDINAND, *Histoire de la Langue Française des Origines à 1900. Tome III: La Formation de la Langue classique (1600–1660)*, Parts I and II. Paris, 1909–11. *Tome IV: La Langue classique (1660–1715)*, Part I. Paris, 1913.

BUCHANAN, GEORGE, *George Buchanan: A Memorial: 1506–1906*, ed. D. A. Millar. St. Andrews, Scotland, 1907.

BUCHLER, JOHANN, *Flores sive Phrasium Poeticarum Thesaurus Absolutissimus.* Cologne, 1631.

*BURNET, JOHN, *Early Greek Philosophy*, 2d ed. London, 1908.

*BURNET, THOMAS, *The Sacred Theory of the Earth*, 2 vols. London, 1719.

*—— *Telluris Theoria Sacra: Orbis Nostri Originem & Mutationes Generales, quas Aut jam subiit, aut olim subiturus est, Complectens*, 2 vols. London, 1681–9.

*BURTT, EDWIN ARTHUR, *The Metaphysical Foundations of Modern Physical Science.* New York: Harcourt, Brace, 1927.

BUSH, DOUGLAS, *Mythology and the Renaissance Tradition in English Poetry.* Minneapolis: University of Minnesota Press, 1932.

BUTLER, SAMUEL, *Hudibras, Written in the Time of the Late Wars*, ed. A. R. Waller. Cambridge, England, 1905.

*C., G., *A Treatise of Mathematicall Physick, Or a briefe Introduction to Physick, by Judiciall Astrologie.* London, 1653.

CALLIMACHUS AND LYCOPHRON, with an English translation by A. W. Mair; ARATUS, with an English translation by G. R. Mair. LCL, 1921.

CALPURNIUS SICULUS, T. See *Poetæ Latini Minores*.

*CAMENZIND, CLARA, *Die antike und moderne Auffassung vom Naturgeschehen mit besonderer Berücksichtigung der mittelalterlichen Impetustheorie.* Langensalza: Hermann Beyer, 1926.

CAMERON, MARGARET M., *L'Influence des Saisons de Thomson sur la Poésie Descriptive en France (1759–1810)*. Paris: Librairie Ancienne Honoré Champion, 1927.

CAMOENS, LUIZ DE, *Os Lusiadas de Luís de Camões*, reprint of 1572 edition, ed. José Maria Rodrigues. Lisbon: Tip. da Biblioteca Nacional, 1921.

CAMOENS, LUIZ DE.   See also Fanshawe, Sir Richard, *The Lusiad, etc.*

*CANEPARIUS, PETRUS MARIA, *De Atramentis Cuiuscunque Generis.*   Venice, 1619.

*CARDANUS, HIERONYMUS, *De Rerum Varietate Libri XVII.*   Basel, 1553.

CAREW, THOMAS, *The Poems and Masque of Thomas Carew*, ed. Joseph W. Ebsworth.   London, 1893.

*CARLEER, LÉON-HENRI-MARIE, *Examen des Principales Classifications Adoptées par les Zoologistes.*   Brussels, 1861.

*CARPENTER, NATHANAEL, *Philosophia Libera, Triplici Exercitationum Decade proposita.*   Oxford, 1622.

*CARUS, JULIUS VICTOR, *Geschichte der Zoologie bis auf Joh. Müller und Charl. Darwin.*   Munich, 1872.

*CASTELLI, Benoist.   See Saporta.

CATULLUS, *The Poems*, with an English translation by F. W. Cornish; TIBULLUS, translated by J. P. Postgate; *Pervigilium Veneris*, translated by J. W. Mackail.   LCL, 1935.

*CELSUS, *De Medicina*, 3 vols., with an English translation by W. G. Spencer.   LCL, 1935–8.

CHALKHILL, JOHN, *Thealma and Clearchus.*   See Saintsbury, *CP* II.

*CHAMBERLAYNE, JOHN, tr., *The Religious Philosopher: Or, the Right Use of the Contemplation of the World* [by Bernard Nieuwentyt], 3 vols.   London, 1718–19.

CHAMBERLAYNE, WILLIAM, *Pharonnida.*   See Saintsbury, *CP* I.

*CHANDLER, JOHN, tr., *Oriatrike, or Physick refined* [by Jean Baptiste van Helmont].   London, 1662.

*CHANOINE, CLAUDE COUTEREAU, *Columella, Les Douze Livres Des choses rustiques.*   Paris, 1556.

CHAPELAIN, JEAN, *La Pucelle ou La France Delivree, Poëme Heroïque.*   Paris, 1656.

CHAPMAN, GEORGE, *Homer's Odysses.*   London [1614].

—— *The Iliads of Homer, Prince of Poets.*   London [1611].

—— *The Poems of George Chapman*, ed. Phyllis Brooks Bartlett.   New York: Modern Language Association of America, 1941.

*CHARLETON, WALTER, *Natural History of the Passions.*   London, 1674.

*—— *Œconomia Animalis, Novis in Medicina Hypothesibus superstructa & Mechanicè explicata. Accessère ejusdem Dissertatio Epistolica, de Ortu Animæ Humanæ; & Consilium Hygiasticum.*   London, 1666.

*—— *Onomasticon Zoicon Plerorumque Animalium Differentias & Nomina Propria pluribus Linguis exponens.*   London, 1668.

*—— Tr., *A Ternary of Paradoxes: The Magnetick Cure of Wounds; The Nativity of Tartar in Wine; The Image of God in Man* [by Jean Baptiste van Helmont].   London, 1650.

*Chastel, Sieur de Marly le, tr., *Histoire Generalle des Indes Occidentales & Terres neuues, qui iusques à present ont esté descouuertes* [by Lopez de Gomara]. Paris, 1569.

*Châtres, Pierre-Julien-Brodeau de Moncharville de, *Preuves des Existences, Et Nouveau Système de l'Univers, ou Idée d'une Nouvelle Philosophie.* Paris, 1702.

Chaucer, Geoffrey, *The Complete Works of Geoffrey Chaucer,* ed. F. N. Robinson. Boston: Houghton, Mifflin, 1933.

*Cicero, M. *Tullii Ciceronis Scripta Quae Manserunt Omnia,* ed. C. F. W. Mueller: Part IV, Vol. II. Leipzig, 1905. (Contains *De Natura Deorum.*) Part IV, Vol. III. Leipzig, 1910. (Contains the translations of Aratus.)

*Clarke, John, tr., *Rohault's System of Natural Philosophy, Illustrated with Dr. Samuel Clarke's Notes Taken mostly out of Sir Isaac Newton's Philosophy,* 2 vols., 2d ed. London, 1728–9.

Claudian, 2 vols., with an English translation by Maurice Platnauer. LCL, 1922.

Cléric, Le P. Pierre, *Pieces de Poesie Presentées A L'Academie des Jeux-Floraux, De Toulouse. Pour les Prix de l'Année M.DCC.III.* Toulouse, 1703.

Cleveland, John. See Saintsbury, *CP* III.

*Coffin, Charles Monroe, *John Donne and the New Philosophy.* New York: Columbia University Press, 1937.

*Cogan, Thomas, *The Haven of Health, Chiefly made for the comfort of Students.* London, 1612. (First published 1589?)

*Cole, Abdiah, tr., *The Compleat Practise of Physick, in Eighteen Several Books . . . By N. Culpeper, Abdiah Cole, and William Rowland . . . . Being chiefly a Translation of The Works of . . . Lazarus Riverius.* London, 1655.

Coleridge, S. T., *Biographia Literaria,* 2 vols., ed. J. Shawcross. Oxford, 1907.

*Coles, William, *Adam in Eden: Or, Natures Paradise. The History of Plants, Fruits, Herbs and Flowers.* London, 1657.

*Collier, Katharine B., *Cosmogonies of Our Fathers, Some Theories of the Seventeenth and Eighteenth Centuries.* New York: Columbia University Press, 1934.

Colluthus. See Oppian, Colluthus, Tryphiodorus; Sherburne, Edward, *Salmacis, etc.*

*Columella, L. *Iuni Moderati Columellae Rei Rusticae Libri VI–VII,* ed. Vilelmus Lundström (*Collectio Scriptorum Veterum Vpsaliensis*). Gotoburgi: Eranos' Förlag, 1940.

See also Chanoine, Claude Coutereau.

Combs, Homer Carroll, and Sullens, Zay Rusk, *A Concordance to the English Poems of John Donne.* Chicago: Packard and Company, 1940.

*COMENIUS, JOHANN AMOS, *The Gate of Tongves unlocked and opened. Or else, A Seminarie or seed-plot of all Tongues and Sciences*, ed. John Anchoran, 3d ed. London, 1637.

*—— *Naturall Philosophie Reformed by Divine Light: or, A Synopsis of Physicks.* London, 1651. (The translator is unknown to me.)

*—— *The Orbis Pictus*, ed. C. W. Bardeen. Syracuse, 1887. (The accompanying translation, by Charles Hoole, is reprinted from the English edition of 1727.)

CONGREVE, WILLIAM, *The Works: Comedies, Incognita, Poems*, ed. F. W. Bateson. London: P. Davies, 1930.

COOK, A. S., "Four Notes," *Studies in Philology*, XVI (1919), 177–86.

*COOKE, JAMES, *Mellificium Chirurgiæ: Or, The Marrow of Chirurgery. Much Enlarged. To which is now added Anatomy, Illustrated with twelve Brass Cuts, And also the Marrow of Physick: Both in the newest way.* London, 1676.

COOPER, LANE, *A Concordance of the Latin, Greek, and Italian Poems of John Milton.* Halle: Max Niemeyer, 1923.

—— Ed., *The Greek Genius and Its Influence.* New Haven, 1917.

*COPERNICUS, *De Revolutionibus Orbium cœlestium, Libri VI.* Nüremberg, 1543.

CORDIER, ANDRÉ, *Études sur le Vocabulaire Épique dans l'"Énéide."* Paris: Société d'Édition "Les Belles Lettres," 1939.

*CORNFORD, FRANCIS M., *Plato's Cosmology, The Timaeus of Plato translated with a running commentary.* New York: Harcourt, Brace, 1937.

COUAT, AUGUSTE, *Alexandrian Poetry under the First Three Ptolemies, 324–222 B.C.*, translated by James Loeb. London: Heinemann, 1931.

COULTER, CORNELIA C., "Compound Adjectives in Early Latin Poetry," *Transactions and Proceedings of the American Philological Association*, XLVII (1916), 153–72.

COWLEY, ABRAHAM, *Poems*, ed. A. R. Waller. Cambridge, England, 1905.

CRASHAW, RICHARD, *The Poems, English, Latin and Greek of Richard Crashaw*, ed. L. C. Martin. Oxford: Clarendon Press, 1927.

CREECH, THOMAS, tr., *The Five Books of M. Manilius, Containing a System of the Ancient Astronomy and Astrology . . . Done into English Verse*, London, 1697. (The fifth book has separate pagination.)

—— *The Idylliums of Theocritus.* Oxford, 1684.

—— *Lucretius, His Six Books of Epicurean Philosophy.* London, 1683.

CREORE, A. E., "Du Bartas: A Reinterpretation," *Modern Language Quarterly*, I (1940), 503–26.

CROISET, ALFRED AND MAURICE, *Histoire de la Littérature Grecque*, 5 vols. Paris, 1887–99.

*CROLL, OSWALD, *Basilica Chymica: in fine libri additus est tractatus novus de signaturis rerum internis.* Frankfurt, 1609.

See also Pinnell, Henry.

*CROOKE, HELKIAH, *A Description of the Body of Man. Together with the Controversies Thereto Belonging. Collected and Translated out of all the Best Authors of Anatomy, Especially out of Gasper Bauhinus and Andreas Laurentius.* London, 1615.

*CRUM, RALPH B., *Scientific Thought in Poetry.* New York: Columbia University Press, 1931.

*CULPEPER, NICHOLAS, tr., *The Compleat Practise of Physick, in Eighteen Several Books . . . By N. Culpeper, Abdiah Cole, and William Rowland . . . . Being chiefly a Translation of The Works of . . . Lazarus Riverius.* London, 1655.

*—— *Mr. Culpepper's Treatise of Aurum Potabile, Being a Description of the Threefold World, Viz: Elimentary, Celestiall, Intellectuall.* London, 1656.

*—— *The English Physitian: Or An Astrologo-Physical Discourse of the Vulgar Herbs of this Nation.* London, 1652.

*CURRY, WALTER CLYDE, *Chaucer and the Mediaeval Sciences.* New York: Oxford University Press, 1926.

CYPRIANUS GALLUS, *Cypriani Galli Poetae Heptateuchos accedunt incertorum . . . carmina,* ed. Rudolph Peiper. Vienna [1891]. (Contains *Iona* and *Sodoma* by "Incertus.")

*DAMPIER, WILLIAM, *A New Voyage Round the World,* ed. Sir Albert Gray. London: Argonaut Press, 1927.

*—— *Voyages and Discoveries,* ed. Clennell Wilkinson. London: Argonaut Press, 1931.

*DAMPIER-WHETHAM, W. C. D., *A History of Science and Its Relations with Philosophy and Religion.* New York: Macmillan, 1931.

*DANEAU, LAMBERT, *Physice Christiana, Sive, Christiana de Rerum Creatarum Origine, & vsu disputatio,* 4th ed. Geneva, 1602.

*—— *Physices Christianæ Pars Altera; Sive De Rervm Creatarvm Natvra,* 4th ed. Geneva, 1606.

*—— *Physique Francoise, Comprenant en Treize liures ou traittez, assauoir l'un d'Aristote, onze de Basile, & un de Iehan Damascene, le discours des choses Naturelles tant Celestes, que Terrestres, selon que les Philosophes les ont descrites, & les plus anciens Peres ou Docteurs Chrestiens, les ont puis apres considerees, & mieux rapportees à leur vrai but. Le tout nouuellement traduit de Grec en François.* Geneva, 1581.

DANTE, *Le Opere di Dante, Testo Critico della Società Dantesca Italiana.* Florence, 1921.

*DARIOTT, CLAUDIUS, *Dariotus Redivivus: Or a briefe Introduction Conducing to the Judgement of the Stars, enlarged by N. S.* [Nathaniel Spark]. London, 1653.

*DAUDIN, HENRI, *Les Méthodes de la Classification et L'Idée de Série en Botanique et en Zoologie de Linné à Lamarck (1740–1790)*. Paris: Librairie Félix Alcan, 1926.

DAVENANT, SIR WILLIAM, *Gondibert: An Heroick Poem.* London, 1651.

—— *Love and Honour and The Siege of Rhodes*, ed. James W. Tupper. Boston, 1909.

DAVIES, CICELY, "Ut Pictura Poesis," *Modern Language Review*, XXX (1935), 159–69.

DAVIES, SIR JOHN, *Nosce teipsum. This Oracle expounded in two Elegies. 1. Of Humane knowledge. 2. Of the Soule of Man, and the immortalitie thereof.* London, 1599.

—— *Orchestra, Or A Poeme of Dauncing.* London, 1596.

DAVIES OF HEREFORD, JOHN, *Microcosmos. The Discovery of the Little World, with the government thereof.* Oxford, 1603.

—— *Wittes Pilgrimage, (by Poeticall Essaies) Through a World of amorous Sonnets, Soule-passions, and other Passages, Diuine, Philosophicall, Morall, Poeticall, and Politicall.* London [1605?].

DAVIS, B. E. C., *Edmund Spenser, A Critical Study.* Cambridge: Cambridge University Press, 1933.

DAWSON, JOHN CHARLES, *Toulouse in the Renaissance.* New York: Columbia University Press, 1923.

DEANE, C. V., *Aspects of Eighteenth Century Nature Poetry.* Oxford: Blackwell, 1935.

DEFERRARI, ROY J., AND CAMPBELL, JAMES M., *A Concordance of Prudentius.* Cambridge: Mediaeval Academy of America, 1932.

—— FANNING, SISTER MARIA W.; AND SULLIVAN, SISTER ANNE S., *A Concordance of Lucan.* Washington: Catholic University of America Press, 1940.

DELARUELLE, L., "Recherches sur les sources de Du Bartas dans la 'Première Semaine,'" *Revue d'Histoire littéraire de la France*, XL (1933), 321–54.

DEMETRIUS, *On Style*, with an English translation by W. Rhys Robert. LCL, 1927.

DENHAM, SIR JOHN, *The Poetical Works of Sir John Denham*, ed. Theodore H. Banks, Jr. New Haven: Yale University Press, 1928.

DENNYS, JOHN, *The Secrets of Angling: Teaching, The choisest Tooles Baytes and seasons, for the taking of any Fish, in Pond or Riuer: practised and familiarly opened in three Bookes.* London, 1613.

*DERHAM, WILLIAM, *Physico-Theology: or, A Demonstration of the Being and Attributes of God, from his Works of Creation*, 3d ed. London, 1714.

*DESAGULIERS, J. T., tr., *The Motion of Water, and other Fluids, Being a Treatise of Hydrostaticks* [by Edmé Mariotte]. London, 1718.

DESAGULIERS, J. T., *The Newtonian System of the World, The Best Model of Government: An Allegorical Poem*. Westminster, 1728.

*DESCARTES, RENÉ, *Discours de la Methode, Pour bien conduire sa raison, & chercher la verité dans les sciences*. Leyden, 1637.

*—— *A Discourse of a Method for the well guiding of Reason, and the Discovery of Truth in the Sciences*. London, 1649.

*—— *Le Monde de Mr Descartes, ou Le Traité de la Lumiere et des Autres Principaux objets des Sens*. Paris, 1664.

*—— *Œuvres de Descartes*, 11 vols., ed. Charles Adam and Paul Tannery. Paris, 1897–1909.

DES-MARESTS, Le Sieur, *La Comparaison de la Langue et de la Poësie Françoise, Avec la Grecque & la Latine, Et des Poëtes Grecs, Latins & François*. Paris, 1670.

DIAPER, WILLIAM, *Dryades; Or, The Nymphs Prophecy. A Poem*. London, 1713.

—— AND JONES, JOHN, *Oppian's Halieuticks, Of the Nature of Fishes and Fishing of the Ancients*. Oxford, 1722.

*DIELS, HERMANN, *Elementum, Eine Vorarbeit zum Griechischen und Lateinischen Thesaurus*. Leipzig, 1899.

*—— Ed., *Die Fragmente der Vorsokratiker*, Vol. I, 2d ed. Berlin, 1906. (Contains the fragments of Empedocles and Parmenides.)

*—— Ed., *Poetarum Philosophorum Fragmenta*. Berlin, 1901.

*DIGBY, KENELM, *Two Treatises. In the one of which, The Nature of Bodies; In the Other, The Nature of Mans Soule; Is Looked Into: In Way of Discovery, of the Immortality of Reasonable Soules*. Paris, 1644.

*DIODORUS OF SICILY, 3 vols., with an English translation by C. H. Oldfather. LCL, 1933–9.

*DIOSCORIDES. See Goodyer, John; Matthiolus.

DONNE, JOHN, *The Poems of John Donne*, ed. H. J. C. Grierson. New York: Oxford University Press [1912].

DRACONTIUS, BLOSSIUS AEMILIUS, *Blosii Aemilii Dracontii Carmina*, ed. Friedrich Vollmer (*Monumenta Germaniae Historica*, XIV). Berlin, 1905.

DRAYTON, MICHAEL, *The Works of Michael Drayton*, 4 vols., ed. J. William Hebel. Oxford: Shakespeare Head Press, 1931–3.

DRUMMOND, WILLIAM, *The Poetical Works of William Drummond of Hawthornden*, 2 vols., ed. L. E. Kastner. Manchester, 1913.

DRYDEN, JOHN, *Essays of John Dryden*, 2 vols., selected and edited by W. P. Ker. Oxford: Clarendon Press, 1926.

—— *The Poems of John Dryden*, ed. John Sargeaunt. London: Oxford University Press, 1929.

—— *The Poetical Works of John Dryden*, ed. George R. Noyes. Boston, 1909.

DRYDEN, JOHN, *The Works of John Dryden*, 18 vols., ed. Sir Walter Scott, revised by George Saintsbury.   Edinburgh, 1882–93.

DU BARTAS, GUILLAUME DE SALUSTE, *The Works of Guillaume De Salluste Sieur Du Bartas*, 3 vols., ed. Urban T. Holmes, Jr., John C. Lyons, and Robert W. Linker.   Chapel Hill: University of North Carolina Press, 1935–40.

See also Benedict, Samuel; Du Monin, Jean-Édouard; Guisone, Ferrante; James I of England; Sylvester, Josuah.

DU BELLAY, JOACHIM, *Œuvres Poétiques*, 6 vols., ed. Henri Chamard.   Paris: Société des Textes Français Modernes, 1908–31.

DUBOUL, AXEL, *Les Deux Siècles de l'Académie des Jeux Floraux*, 2 vols.   Toulouse, 1901.

*DU HAMEL, JEAN-BAPTISTE, *Astronomia Physica, seu De Luce, Natura, et Motibus Corporum Cælestium Libri Duo*.   Paris, 1660.

*—— *De Meteoris et Fossilibus Libri Duo*.   Paris, 1660.

*—— *Philosophia Vetus et Nova Ad Vsum Scholæ Accommodata, In Regia Burgundia Olim Pertracta*, 2 vols., 3d ed.   Paris, 1684.

*DUHEM, PIERRE, *Le Système du Monde, Histoire des doctrines cosmologiques de Platon à Copernic*, Vol. I.   Paris, 1913.

DU MONIN, JEAN-ÉDOUARD, *Burgundionis Gyani Beresithias, sive mundi creatio, Ex Gallico G. Salustij du Bartas Heptamero expressa.   Eiusdem Edoardi manipulus poëticus non insulsus*.   Paris, 1579.   (The *Manipulus Poëticus* has separate pagination.)

*DU MOULIN, MONSIEUR, *Physique ou Science Naturelle*.   Paris, 1644.

*DUNCAN, CARSON S., *The New Science and English Literature in the Classical Period*.   Menasha, Wisconsin, 1913.

DUNSTER, CHARLES, *Considerations on Milton's Early Reading, and the Prima Stamina of his Paradise Lost*.   London, 1800.

DURLING, DWIGHT L., *Georgic Tradition in English Poetry*.   New York: Columbia University Press, 1935.

DYER, JOHN, *The Poetical Works of Armstrong, Dyer, and Green*, ed. Charles Cowden Clarke.   Edinburgh, 1868.

*DYGGES, LEONARD, *A Prognostication (1555)* (*Old Ashmolean Reprints*, III.   Oxford, 1926).

ELIOT, SIR THOMAS, *The Dictionary*.   London, 1538.

ELTON, OLIVER, "The Poet's Dictionary," *Essays and Studies by Members of the English Association*, XIV (1929), 7–19.

*EMERY, CLARK, "Optics and Beauty," *Modern Language Quarterly*, III (1942), 45–50.

*EMPEDOCLES, *The Fragments of Empedocles, translated into English Verse by William Ellery Leonard*.   Chicago, 1908.

See also Diels, Hermann, *Die Fragmente der Vorsokratiker*.

England's Helicon 1600, 1614, 2 vols., ed. Hyder Edward Rollins. Cambridge: Harvard University Press, 1935.

Englands Parnassus, Compiled by Robert Allot, 1600, ed. Charles Crawford. Oxford, 1913.

ENNIUS, *Ennianae Poesis Reliquiae*, ed. Ioannes Vahlen. Leipzig: Teubner, 1928.

ENNODIUS, MAGNUS FELIX, *Opera Omnia*, ed. Wilhelm Hartel (*Corpus Scriptorum Ecclesiasticorum Latinorum*, VI). Vienna, 1882.

ESTIENNE, HENRI, *Thesaurus Graecae Linguae*, 4 vols. London, 1816–18.

EUGENIUS TOLETANUS, *Eugenii Toletani Episcopi Carmina et Epistulae*, ed. Friedrich Vollmer (*Monumenta Germaniae Historica*, XIV). Berlin, 1905.

EUPHRO. See Kock, Theodore.

EURIPIDES, 4 vols., with an English translation by Arthur S. Way. LCL, 1912–29.

—— *Euripidis Tragoediae*, Vol. III, ed. August Nauck. Leipzig, 1885. (Contains the Fragments.)

*EVELYN, JOHN, *Directions for the Gardiner at Says-Court*, ed. Geoffrey Keynes. London: Nonesuch Press, 1932.

—— *An Essay on the First Book of T. Lucretius Carus De Rerum Natura. Interpreted and Made English Verse by J. Evelyn*. London, 1656.

*—— *Sylva, or A Discourse of Forrest-Trees, And the Propagation of Timber in His Majesties Dominions*. London, 1664.

*—— *Terra: A Philosophical Discourse of Earth*, ed. A. Hunter. York, 1786.

Examen Poeticum: Being the Third Part of Miscellany Poems. Containing Variety of New Translations of the Ancient Poets. Together with many Original Copies, By the Most Eminent Hands. London, 1693.

*FABRICIUS, JOANNES, *Differentiæ Animalium Quadrupedum Secundum Locos Communes, Opus ad animalium cognitionem apprimè conducibile*. Zurich, 1555.

*FABRICIUS AB AQUAPENDENTE, HIERONYMUS, *De Locutione et eius Instrumentis*, ed. Johannes Ursinus. Venice, 1601.

*—— *De Respiratione et Eius Instrumentis, Libri duo*. Batavia, 1615.

*—— *De Visione, Voce, Auditu*. Venice, 1600. (In three parts, each with separate pagination.)

FAIRFAX, EDWARD, tr., *Jerusalem Delivered, A Poem, by Torquato Tasso*, ed. Henry Morley. London, 1890.

*FAIRFAX, NATHANIEL, *A Treatise of the Bulk and Selvedge of the World. Wherein The Greatness, Littleness and Lastingness of Bodies are freely Handled*. London, 1674.

*FANIANUS, IOANNES CHRYSIPPUS, *De Arte Metallicæ Metamorphoseos Liber singularis*. Paris, 1560.

FANSHAWE, SIR RICHARD, *The Fourth Book of Virgil's Aeneid*, ed. A. L. Irvine. Oxford: Blackwell, 1924.

—— *The Lusiad by Luis de Camoens, Translated by Sir Richard Fanshawe*, ed. Jeremiah D. M. Ford. Cambridge: Harvard University Press, 1940.

FIALON, EUGÈNE, *Étude Historique et Littéraire sur Saint Basile Suivie de l'Hexaméron Traduit en Français*. Paris, 1869.

*FISCHARTUS, JOANNES, *Onomastica II. I. Philosophicum Medicum, Synonymum ex varijs vulgaribusque linguis. II. Theophrasti Paracelsi: hoc est, earum vocum, quarum in scriptis eius solet usus esse, explicatio*. Strassbourg, 1574.

FLATMAN, THOMAS. See Saintsbury, *CP* III.

FLETCHER, GILES AND PHINEAS, *Poetical Works*, 2 vols., ed. Frederick S. Boas. Cambridge, England, 1908–9.

*FLUDD, ROBERT, *De Fluctibus Philosophia sacra & vere Christiana Seu Meteorologia Cosmica*. Frankfurt, 1626.

*FONTENELLE, BERNARD DE. See Glanvill, Joseph, *A Plurality, etc.*

*FORTESCUE, THOMAS, tr., *The Forest, or Collection of Historyes no lesse profitable, then pleasant and necessary* [by Pedro Mexia]. London, 1576.

*FOXIUS MORZILLUS, SEBASTIANUS, *De aquarum generibus*. Basel, 1558.

FRACASTORO, GIROLAMO. See Tate, Nahum.

*FRANZIUS, WOLFGANG, *Historia Animalium Sacra in qua Plerorumque Animalium Praecipuae Proprietates ingratiam Studiosorum Theologiae & Ministrorum Verbi ad usum . . . accommodantur*. Leyden, 1624.

*FREIND, JOHN, *The History of Physick; From the Time of Galen, To the Beginning of the Sixteenth Century. Chiefly with Regard to Practice*, 2 vols. London, 1725–6.

*FRENCH, JOHN, tr., *A New Light of Alchymie: Taken out of the fountaine of Nature, and Manuall Experience. To which is added a Treatise of Sulphur: Written by Micheel Sandivogius*. London, 1650.

*—— *Of the Nature of Things, Nine Books* [by Paracelsus]. London, 1650.

*FULKE, WILLIAM, *A goodly Gallery with a most pleasaunt Prospect, into the garden of naturall contemplation, to beholde the naturall causes of all kind of Meteors*. London, 1571.

*FUSIL, C.-A., *La Poésie Scientifique de 1750 à nos jours*. Paris, 1917.

*GADROYS, CLAUDE, *Le Systeme du Monde, Selon Les Trois Hypotheses, Où conformement aux loix de la Mechanique l'on explique dans la supposition du mouvement de la Terre Les Apparences des Astres, La Fabrique du Monde, La Formation des Planetes, La Lumiere, la Pesânteur, &c*. Paris, 1675.

*GALATEUS, ANTONIUS, *Liber De Situ Elementorum*. Basel, 1558.

*GALEN, ed. O. Hartlich (*Corpus Medicorum Graecorum*, ed. Academiae Berolinensis Havniensis Lipsiensis, V4, 2). Leipzig and Berlin: Teubner, 1923.

*GALILEO, *Dialogo.* Florence, 1632.

See also Salusbury, Thomas, *The System of the World, etc.*

GAMBER, L'ABBÉ STANISLAS, *Le Livre de la "Genèse" dans la Poésie Latine au Vme Siècle.* Paris, 1899.

GARTH, SAMUEL, *The Dispensary, A Poem in Six Canto's.* London, 1700.

*GASSENDI, PIERRE, *The Vanity of Judiciary Astrology. Or Divination By the Stars. Lately written in Latin . . . . Translated into English by a Person of Quality.* London, 1659.

GAY, JOHN, *Rural Sports. A Poem.* London, 1713.

*GEBER. See Russell, Richard.

*GEMINUS, *Gemini Elementa Astronomiae,* ed. Karl Manitius. Leipzig, 1898.

GENEST, M. L'ABBÉ CHARLES-CLAUDE, *Principes de Philosophie, ou Preuves Naturelles de l'Existence de Dieu et de l'Immortalité de l'Ame.* Paris, 1716.

*GESNER, CONRAD, *Icones Animalium Quadrupedum Viviparorum et Oviparorum, Quæ in Historia Animalium Conradi Gesneri Describuntur, Cum Nomenclaturis Singulorum Latinis, Italicis, Gallicis et Germanicis Plerunque, Per Certos Ordines Digestæ.* Zurich, 1553. Second edition, Zurich, 1560.

See also Baker, George; Topsell, Edward.

*GILBERT, ALLAN H., "Milton and Galileo," *Studies in Philology,* XIX (1922), 152–85.

*GILBERT, SAMUEL, *The Florists Vade-Mecum. Being a Choice Compendium of whatever worthy Notice hath been Extant for the Propagation, Raising, Planting, Encreasing and Preserving the rarest Flowers and Plants.* London, 1682.

*GILBERT, WILLIAM, *De Magnete, Magneticisque Corporibus, et de Magno magnete tellure.* London, 1600. Facsimile published by Mayer and Müller. Berlin, 1892.

*—— *De Mundo nostro Sublunari Philosophia Nova, Opus posthumum,* ed. William Boswell. Amsterdam, 1651.

*GLANVILL, JOSEPH, *A Plurality of Worlds. Written in French by the Author of the Dialogues of the Dead* [Bernarde de Fontenelle]. London, 1688.

*—— *Plus Ultra: or, The Progress and Advancement of Knowledge Since the Days of Aristotle.* London, 1668.

*—— *The Vanity of Dogmatizing* (1661), ed. Moody E. Prior. New York: Columbia University Press, 1931. (Published for the Facsimile Text Society.)

*GLASER, CHRISTOPHER, *The Compleat Chymist, Or, A New Treatise of Chymistry. Written in French by Christopher Glaser, Apothecary in Ordinary to the French King,* 4th ed. London, 1677.

GODOLPHIN, SIDNEY. See Saintsbury, *CP* II.

GOELZER, HENRI, AND MEY, ALFRED, *Le Latin de Saint Avit.* Paris, 1909.

GOLDING, ARTHUR, *Shakespeare's Ovid, Being Arthur Golding's Translation of the Metamorphoses*, ed. W. H. D. Rouse (*The King's Library*). London, 1904.

*GOLDSMITH, OLIVER, *A History of the Earth, and Animated Nature*, 8 vols. London, 1774.

GOMARA, LOPEZ DE. See Chastel, Sieur de Marly le.

GÓNGORA Y ARGOTE, LUIS DE, *Obras Poeticas de D. Luis de Góngora*, 3 vols., ed. R. Foulché-Delbosc. New York: Hispanic Society of America, 1921.

See also Stanley, Thomas, *Sylvia's Park, etc.*

*GOODYER, JOHN, tr., *The Greek Herbal of Dioscorides (1655)*, ed. R. T. Gunther. Oxford: Oxford University Press, 1934.

GOOGE, BARNABE, *Eglogs, Epytaphes, & Sonettes (1563)*, ed. Edward Arber. London, 1871.

GOULART, SIMON. See Lodge, Thomas, *A Learned Summarie, etc.*

Gradus ad Parnassum, with the English Meanings, edited by the late Dr. Carey, recently revised, corrected, and augmented by a Member of the University of Cambridge. London, 1876.

GRATIUS FALISCUS. See *Poetæ Latini Minores;* Wase, Christopher.

The Greek Anthology, 5 vols., with an English translation by W. R. Paton. LCL, 1916–18.

The Greek Bucolic Poets, with an English translation by J. M. Edmonds. LCL, 1912. (Contains Theocritus.)

GREENE, ROBERT, *Groats-Worth of Witte, bought with a million of Repentance; The Repentance of Robert Greene*, 1592 (Bodley Head Quartos). London: Bodley Head, 1923.

*GREENLAW, EDWIN, "The New Science and English Literature in the Seventeenth Century," *Johns Hopkins Alumni Magazine*, XIII (1925), 331–59.

—— "Spenser and Lucretius," *Studies in Philology*, XVII (1920), 439–64.

GREGORY, JAMES, *Optica Promota.* See *Scriptores Optici.*

*GREW, NEHEMIAH, *The Anatomy of Plants, Begun. With a General Account of Vegetation, Grounded thereupon, The First Book*, 2d ed. London, 1682.

*—— *The Anatomy of Plants. With an Idea of a Philosophical History of Plants.* London, 1682.

*—— *An Idea of a Philosophical History of Plants. Read before the Royal Society, January 8. and January 15. 1672*, 2d ed. London, 1682.

*—— *Musæum Regalis Societatis. Or A Catalogue & Description Of the Natural and Artificial Rarities Belonging to the Royal Society and preserved at Gresham Colledge.* London, 1681.

*GRIMESTONE, EDWARD, tr., *The Naturall and Morall Historie of the East and West Indies* [by Joseph de Acosta]. London, 1604.

GROOM, BERNARD, *The Formation and Use of Compound Epithets in English Poetry from 1579* (S. P. E. Tract No. XLIX). Oxford: Clarendon Press, 1937.

—— "Some Kinds of Poetic Diction," *Essays and Studies by Members of the English Association*, XV (1929), 139–60.

*GUILLEMEAU, JACQUES, *Traité Des Maladies De L'Oeil, Qui Sont En Nombre de Cent treize, ausquelles il est suiect.* Paris, 1585.

See also Banister, Richard.

GUISONE, FERRANTE, *La Divina Settimana; Cioè, I Sette Giorni della Creatione del Mondo, Del Signor Guglielmo Di Salusto Signor Di Bartas; Tradotta di rima Francese in verso sciolto Italiano.* Venice, 1593.

*GUNTHER, R. T., *Early British Botanists and Their Gardens, Based on Unpublished Writings of Goodyer, Tradescant, and Others.* Oxford: Oxford University Press, 1922.

*—— *Early Science in Oxford*, 10 vols. London and Oxford, 1920–35. (Privately printed.)

HABINGTON, WILLIAM, *Castara*, ed. Edward Arber (*English Reprints*). Westminster, 1895.

HALL, JOHN. See Saintsbury, *CP* II.

*HALLER, PAUL, *Comenius und der naturwissenschaftliche Unterricht.* Leisnig, 1906.

*HALLIWELL, JAMES ORCHARD, ed., *A Collection of Letters Illustrative of the Progress of Science in England from the Reign of Queen Elizabeth to that of Charles the Second.* London, 1841.

HAMMOND, WILLIAM. See Saintsbury, *CP* II.

HANNAY, PATRICK, *Philomela; Sheretine and Mariana; Elegies; Sonnets.* See Saintsbury, *CP* I.

*HARRIS, JOHN, *Lexicon Technicum: Or, An Universal English Dictionary of Arts and Sciences: Explaining not only The Terms of Art, But the Arts Themselves*, Vol. I. London, 1704.

*HARTLIB, SAMUEL, *Samuel Hartlib his Legacie: Or An Enlargement of the Discourse of Husbandry Used in Brabant & Flaunders*, 2d ed. London, 1652.

*HARVEY, GIDEON, *Archelogia Philosophica Nova, Or New Principles of Philosophy.* London, 1663. (In two parts, each with separate pagination.)

HARVEY, THOMAS, *The Bucolicks of Baptist Mantuan in Ten Eclogues, Translated out of Latine into English.* London, 1656.

*HARVEY, WILLIAM, *The Anatomical Exercises—De Motu Cordis 1628: De Circulatione Sanguinis 1649: The first English text of 1653 now newly edited by Geoffrey Keynes.* London: Nonesuch Press, 1928.

*—— *Exercitatio Anatomica de Motu Cordis et Sanguinis in Animalibus* (1628), facsimile in *Monumenta Medica*, Vol. V, ed. Henry Sigerist. Florence, 1928.

*—— *Exercitationes de Generatione Animalium. Quibus accedunt quædam De Partu: de Membranis ac humoribus Uteri: & de Conceptione.* London, 1651.

HAVENS, RAYMOND DEXTER, *The Influence of Milton on English Poetry.* Cambridge, Massachusetts, 1922.

HEATH, JOHN, *Two Centuries of Epigrammes.* London, 1610.

*HERACLEITUS, *On the Universe*, with an English translation by W. H. S. Jones. LCL, 1931.

HERBERT OF CHERBURY, EDWARD, *The Poems English & Latin of Edward Lord Herbert of Cherbury*, ed. G. C. Moore Smith. Oxford: Clarendon Press, 1923.

*HERESBACHIUS, CONRAD, *Rei Rusticæ Libri Quatuor, Vniversam Rusticam Disciplinam Complectentes, vnâ cum appendice oraculorum rusticorum Coronidis vice adiecta.* Cologne, 1571.

HERRICK, ROBERT, *The Poetical Works of Robert Herrick*, ed. F. W. Moorman. Oxford, 1915.

Hesiod, The Homeric Hymns and Homerica, with an English translation by Hugh G. Evelyn-White. LCL, 1914.

HESTEAU, CLOVIS, LE SIEUR DE NUISEMENT, *Poème Philosophic de la Verité de la Phisique Mineralle.* Paris, 1620.

*HESTER, JOHN, *A hundred and fourtene experiments and cures of the famous Phisition Philippus Aureolus Theophrastus Paracelsus, Translated out of the Germane tongue into the Latine. Whereunto is added certaine excellent and profitable workes by B. G. A. Portu Aquitano. Also certaine secretes of Isack Hollandus concerning the Vegetall and Animall worke. Also the Spagerick Antidotarie for Gunshot of Iosephus Quirsitanus.* [No pl., n.d.]

HISCOCK, W. G., "A Poem Attributed to Dryden," *Times Literary Supplement*, April 18, 1936, p. 340.

*HOBBES, THOMAS, *Thomæ Hobbes Malmesburiensis Opera Philosophica Quæ Latine Scripsit Omnia*, ed. William Molesworth, Vol. I. London, 1839.

*HOFFMANN, FRIEDRICH, *Opuscula Physico-Medica*, 2 vols. Ulm, 1725–6.

*HOLDER, WILLIAM, *Elements of Speech: An Essay of Inquiry into the Natural Production of Letters.* London, 1669.

*HOLLAND, PHILEMON, tr., *The Historie of the World. Commonly called, The Naturall Historie of C. Plinius Secundus, Translated into English*, 2 parts. London, 1601.

HOMER, *The Iliad*, 2 vols., with an English translation by A. T. Murray. LCL, 1929–30.

—— *The Odyssey*, 2 vols., with an English translation by A. T. Murray. LCL, 1927–8.

See also Chapman, George.

HOOKE, ROBERT. (Lithoprint copies of the works listed below appear in R. T. Gunther, *Early Science in Oxford*, VIII.)

*—— *Animadversions On the first part of the Machina Coelestis.* London, 1674.

*HOOKE, ROBERT, *An Attempt to prove the Motion of the Earth from Observations.* London, 1674.

*—— *A Description of Helioscopes.* London, 1676.

*—— *Lampas: or, Descriptions of some Mechanical Improvements of Lamps & Waterpoises.* London, 1677.

*—— *Lectures and Collections: Cometa and Microscopium.* London, 1678.

*—— *Lectures De Potentia Restitutiva, or of Spring, Explaining the Power of Springing Bodies.* London, 1678.

*HOOLE, CHARLES. See Comenius, Johann Amos, *The Orbis Pictus.*

HORACE, *The Odes and Epodes*, with an English translation by C. E. Bennett. LCL, 1934.

—— *Satires, Epistles, and Ars Poetica*, with an English translation by H. Rushton Fairclough. LCL, 1936.

*HORTOLANUS JUNIOR, *The Golden Age: Or, the Reign of Saturn Review'd.* London, 1698.

*HOWELL, JAMES, *Dodona's Grove, Or, The Vocall Forrest.* London, 1640.

HUGHES, JOHN, *An Ode to the Creator of the World. Occasion'd by the Fragments of Orpheus.* London, 1713.

HUGHES, MERRITT Y., *Virgil and Spenser.* Berkeley: University of California Press, 1929.

*HUMPHREYS, SAMUEL, tr., *Spectacle de la Nature: Or, Nature Display'd* [by Noël Antoine Pluche]. London, 1733.

*HUYGHENS, CHRISTIAAN, *Œuvres Complètes de Christaan Huygens.* The Hague: Société Hollandaise des Sciences, 1913 (Vol. XIII), 1937 (Vol. XIX).

INCERTUS, *Iona* and *Sodoma.* See Cyprianus Gallus.

JACKS, LEO V., *St. Basil and Greek Literature* ("The Catholic University of America Patristic Studies," I). Washington, D.C.: Catholic University of America Press, 1922.

JAGO, RICHARD, *Edge-Hill, Or, The Rural Prospect Delineated and Moralized.* London, 1767.

JAMES I OF ENGLAND, *His Maiesties Poeticall Exercises, At Vacant Houres* [1591]. Edinburgh, 1818. (Contains the translation of Du Bartas's *Furies.*)

*JENNISON, GEORGE, *Noah's Cargo, Some Curious Chapters of Natural History.* London: A. and C. Black, 1928.

JODELLE, ÉTIENNE, *Les Amours et autres poésies d'Estienne Jodelle*, ed. Ad. van Bever. Paris, 1907.

*JOHNSON, FRANCIS R., *Astronomical Thought in Renaissance England, A Study of the English Scientific Writings from 1500 to 1645.* Baltimore: Johns Hopkins Press, 1937.

*JOHNSON, THOMAS, *The Workes of that Famous Chirurgeon Ambrose Parey translated out of Latine and compared with the French.* London, 1634.

*JOHNSON, WILLIAM, *Lexicon Chymicum. Cùm Obscuriorum verborum, Et Rerum Hermeticarum, Tum Phrasium Paracelsicarum, In Scriptis ejus: Et aliorum Chymicorum, passim occurrentium, planam explicationem continens.* London, 1657.

JONES, JOHN.   See Diaper, William, and Jones, John.

JONES, RICHARD F., *Ancients and Moderns, A Study of the Background of the Battle of the Books* ("Washington University Studies, New Series, Language and Literature," No. 6). St. Louis, 1936.

*—— "Science and English Prose Style in the Third Quarter of the Seventeenth Century," *Publications of the Modern Language Association,* XLV (1930), 977–1009.

*—— "Science and Language in England of the Mid-Seventeenth Century," *Journal of English and Germanic Philology,* XXXI (1932), 315–31.

*JONES, WILLIAM, *Physiological Disquisitions; or Discourses on the Natural Philosophy of the Elements.* London, 1781.

JONSON, BEN, *Ben Jonson,* ed. C. H. Herford, Percy Simson, and Evelyn Simson, 7 vols. Oxford: Clarendon Press, 1925–41.

*JONSTON, JOHN, *Notitia Regni Mineralis, Seu Subterraneorum Catalogus.* Leipzig, 1661.

JUVENCUS, C. VETTIUS AQUILINUS, *Gai Vetti Aqvilini Ivvenci Evangeliorvm libri qvattvor,* ed. Johann Huemer (*Corpus Scriptorum Ecclesiasticorum Latinorum,* XXIV). Vienna, 1891.

*KEPLER, JOHANN, *Ioh. Keppleri Mathematici Olim Imperatorii Somnium, Seu Opus Posthumum De Astronomia Lunari. Divulgatum à M. Ludovico Kepplero Filio.* Frankfurt, 1634. (Contains Kepler's translation of Plutarch's *Libellus De Facie, Quæ in Orbe Lunæ Apparet.*)

*KEYDELL, RUDOLF, "Oppian's Gedicht von der Fischerei und Aelians Tiergeschichte," *Hermes,* LXXII (1937), 411–34.

KING, HENRY.   See Saintsbury, *CP* III.

*KIRCHER, ATHANASIUS, *Mundus Subterraneus,* 2 vols. Amsterdam, 1664–5.

*—— *Physiologia Kircheriana Experimentalis.* Amsterdam, 1680.

*KNOLLES, RICHARD, *The Six Bookes of a Common-Weale, Out of the French and Latine Copies* [of Jean Bodin], *done into English.* London, 1606.

KOBER, ALICE E., *The Use of Color Terms in the Greek Poets.* Geneva, N. Y.: W. F. Humphrey Press, 1932.

KOCK, THEODORE, ed., *Comicorum Atticorum Fragmenta,* Vol. III. Leipzig, 1888. (Contains Euphro.)

*Krantz, Émile, *Essai sur l'Esthétique de Descartes, Étudiée dans les Rapports de la Doctrine Cartésienne avec la Littérature Classique Française au XVIIe Siècle*. Paris, 1882.

Kynaston, Sir Francis, *Leoline and Sydanis*. See Saintsbury, *CP* II.

Labriolle, Pierre de, *History and Literature of Christianity from Tertullian to Boethius*, tr. Herbert Wilson. London: Kegan Paul, 1924.

*La Chambre, Marin Cureau de, *Nouvelles Pensees, Sur les Causes de la Lumiere, Du Desbordement du Nil, et De l'Amour d'Inclination*. Paris, 1634.

Lactantius, L. *Caeli Firmiani Lactanti Opera Omnia*, Part II, Fasc. I, ed. Samuel Brandt and Georgius Laubmann (*Corpus Scriptorum Ecclesiasticorum Latinorum*, XXVII). Vienna, 1887.

La Fontaine, Jean de, *Poëme Du Quinquina, Et Autres Ouvrages en Vers*. Paris, 1682.

La Motte, Houdar de, *Odes de M. D***, Avec un Discours sur la Poésie en général, & sur l'Ode en particulier*. Paris, 1707.

*Lanson, Gustave, "L'Influence de la Philosophie Cartésienne sur la Littérature Française," *Revue de Métaphysique et de Morale*, IV (1896), 517-50.

*Lasswitz, Kurd, *Geschichte der Atomistik vom Mittelalter bis Newton*, 2 vols. Hamburg and Leipzig, 1890.

*Lauthier, Honoré Maria, *Lettre à Monsieur Begon . . . Contenant, Un Abregé de la Vie de M. De Tournefort*. Paris, 1717.

Lavarenne, Maurice, *Étude sur la Langue du Poète Prudence*. Paris: Société Française d'Imprimerie et de Librairie, 1933.

*Leclerc, Daniel, *Histoire de la Medecine ou L'on void l'origine & le progrès de cet Art, de Siécle en Siécle, depuis le commencement du Monde*. Geneva, 1696.

*Le Febure, Nicasius, *A Compleat Body of Chymistry: translated by P. D. C. Esq.*, 2 parts. London, 1664.

*Le Grand, Antoine. See Blome, Richard.

Lemmi, Charles W., *The Classic Deities in Bacon, A Study in Mythological Symbolism*. Baltimore: Johns Hopkins Press, 1933.

Lilly, Marie Loretto, *The Georgic, A Contribution to the Study of the Vergilian Type of Didactic Poetry* ("Hesperia: Studies in Philology," No. 6). Baltimore, 1919.

*Lilly, William, *Annus Tenebrosus, or The Dark Year (1652)*. London, 1652.

*—— Tr., *The Book of Knowledge: Treating of the Wisdom of the Ancients* [by Erra Pater]. Worcester, England [n.d.].

*—— *The Starry Messenger; or, An Interpretation of that strange Apparition of three Suns seene in London, 19 Novemb. 1644 being the Birth Day of King Charles*. London, 1645.

*LINNAEUS, CAROLUS, *Animalium Specierum In Classes, Ordines, Genera, Species Methodica Dispositio.* Leyden, 1759.

*—— *Critica Botanica In qua Nomina Plantarum Generica, Specifica, Variantia Examini Subjiciuntur, Selectiora Confirmantur, Indigna Rejiciuntur.* Leyden, 1737.

*—— *Systema Naturæ per Regna Tria Naturæ.* Leyden, 1735.

See also Milne, Colin; Rose, Hugh.

LIPPIUS, LAURENTIUS, *Oppiani Anazarbei De piscatu libri V. Laurentio Lippio interprete. De venatione libri IIII. ita conuersi, vt singula verbis singulis respondeant.* Paris, 1555.

*LIPSIUS, JUSTUS, *Manuductionis Ad Stoicam Philosophiam Libri Tres: L. Annæo Senecæ, aliisque scriptoribus illustrandis.* Antwerp, 1604.

*—— *Physiologiæ Stoicorum Libri Tres: L. Annæo Senecæ, aliisque scriptoribus illustrandis.* Antwerp, 1604.

LIVIUS ANDRONICUS. See Baehrens, Emil; Warmington, E. H.

LOCKWOOD, LAURA E., *Lexicon to the English Poetical Works of John Milton.* New York, 1907.

*LODGE, THOMAS, tr., *A Learned Summarie upon the Famous Poeme of William of Salust, Lord of Bartas* [by Simon Goulart]. London, 1637.

*—— *The Works of Lucius Annæus Seneca, Both Morrall and Natural.* London, 1614.

LOGAN, JAMES VENABLE, *The Poetry and Aesthetics of Erasmus Darwin.* Princeton: Princeton University Press, 1936.

LONDON, WILLIAM, *A Catalogue of the most vendible Books in England, Orderly and Alphabetically Digested.* London, 1657.

*LOVEJOY, ARTHUR O., *The Great Chain of Being, A Study of the History of an Idea.* Cambridge: Harvard University Press, 1936.

*LOVELL, ROBERT, *Enchiridion Botanicum. Or A Compleat Herball Containing the Summe of what hath hitherto been published either by Ancient or Moderne Authors both Galenicall and Chymicall, touching Trees, Shrubs, Plants, Fruits, Flowers, &c.* Oxford, 1659.

*—— *Pammineralogicon. Or An Universal History of Mineralls.* Oxford, 1661.

*—— *Panzoologicomineralogia. Or a Compleat History of Animals and Minerals, Containing the Summe of all Authors, both Ancient and Modern.* Oxford, 1661.

*LOWER, RICHARD, *Tractatus de Corde. Item De Motu & Colore Sanguinis et Chyli in eum Transitu.* London, 1669.

LUCAN, *M. Annaei Lucani Belli Civilis Libri Decem,* ed. A. E. Housman. Oxford: Blackwell, 1926.

See also May, Thomas.

LUCRETIUS, *De Rerum Natura,* with an English translation by W. H. D. Rouse. LCL, 1924.

LUCRETIUS. See also Creech, Thomas, *Lucretius, etc.;* Evelyn, John, *An Essay, etc.*

LYCOPHRON. See Callimachus and Lycophron.

MACAULAY, THOMAS BABINGTON, *Critical, Historical and Miscellaneous Essays,* Vol. I. New York, 1860.

MACKAIL, J. W., *Lectures on Greek Poetry,* 2d ed. London, 1911.

—— *The Springs of Helicon.* London, 1909.

*MACKAILE, MATTHEW, *The Diversitie of Salts and Spirits Maintained.* Aberdeen, 1683.

MacLEOD, MALCOLM, *A Concordance to the Poems of Robert Herrick.* New York: Oxford University Press, 1936.

*MAGINUS, JOHANNES ANTONIUS, *Novæ Coelestium Orbium Theoricæ congruentes cum obseruationibus N. Copernici.* Venice, 1589.

MAISIÈRES, MAURY THIBAUT DE, *Les Poèmes Inspirés du Début de la Genèse à l'Époque de la Renaissance.* Louvain: Librairie Universitaire, 1931.

MANETHON. See *Poetæ Bucolici et Didactici.*

MANILIUS, *M. Manilii Astronomicon,* 5 vols., ed. A. E. Housman. Cambridge: Cambridge University Press, 1937.

See also Creech, Thomas, *The Five Books, etc.;* Sherburne, Edward, *The Sphere, etc.*

MANN, ELIZABETH L., "The Problem of Originality in English Literary Criticism, 1750–1800," *Philological Quarterly,* XVIII (1939), 97–118.

MANTUAN. See Harvey, Thomas.

*MAPLET, JOHN, *A Greene Forest, or a naturall Historie.* Reprinted from the edition of 1567 with an introduction by W. H. Davies. London: Hesperides Press, 1930.

MARINO, GIOVANNI BATTISTA, *Rime,* 2 parts. Venice, 1608. (The parts have separate pagination and separate title pages.)

See also Stanley, Thomas, *Sylvia's Park, etc.;* Sherburne, Edward, *Salmacis, etc.*

*MARIOTTE, EDMÉ, *Traité du Mouvement des Eaux et des Autres Corps Fluides.* Paris, 1686.

*—— *Traité de la Percussion ou Chocq des Corps.* Paris, 1673.

See also Desaguliers, J. T., *The Motion, etc.*

MARLOWE, CHRISTOPHER, *The Works of Christopher Marlowe,* ed. C. F. Tucker Brooke. Oxford, 1910.

MARMION, SHAKERLEY, *Cupid and Psyche.* See Saintsbury, *CP* II.

*MARTIN, BENJAMIN, *The Philosophical Grammar, Being a View of the Present State of Experimental Physiology, or Natural Philosophy.* London, 1735.

MARTIN, JEAN, tr., *L'Arcadie de Messire Iaques Sannazar, gentil homme Napolitan, excellent Poete entre les modernes, mise d'Italien en Francoys.* Paris, 1544.

*MARTYN, THOMAS, *The Language of Botany: Being a Dictionary of the Terms Made Use of in that Science, Principally by Linneus: With Familiar Explanations, and an Attempt to Establish Significant English Terms,* 2d ed. London, 1796.

MARVELL, ANDREW, *The Poems and Letters of Andrew Marvell,* 2 vols., ed. H. M. Margoliouth. Oxford: Clarendon Press, 1927.

*MASSON, JOHN, *The Atomic Theory of Lucretius.* London, 1884.

*MATTHIOLUS, PETRUS ANDREAS, *Commentarii, In Libros Sex Pedacii Dioscoridis Anazarbei, De Medica Materia.* Venice, 1554.

MAY, THOMAS, tr., *Lucan's Pharsalia: Or The Civill Warres of Rome, betweene Pompey the great, and Iulius Cæsar. The whole ten Bookes. Englished, by Thomas May.* London, 1627.

MAYNARD, FRANÇOIS DE, *Œuvres Poétiques de François de Maynard,* 3 vols., ed. Gaston Garrisson. Paris, 1885–8.

*MAYOW, JOHN, *Tractatus Quinque Medico-Physici.* Oxford, 1674.

*McCOLLEY, GRANT, "Milton's Dialogue on Astronomy: The Principal Immediate Sources," *Publications of the Modern Language Association,* LII (1937), 728–62.

*MEAGER, LEONARD, *The New Art of Gardening, With the Gardener's Almanack.* London, 1697.

MELLERIO, L., *Lexique de Ronsard, Précédé d'une Étude sur son vocabulaire, son orthographe et sa syntaxe.* Paris, 1895.

*MERRETT, CHRISTOPHER, tr., *The Art of Glass, Wherein Are shown the wayes to make and colour Glass, Pastes, Enamels, Lakes, and other Curiosities* [by Antonio Neri]. London, 1662.

*—— *The Character of a Compleat Physician, Or Naturalist.* London [1680?].

MERRICK, JAMES, tr., *Tryphiodorus, The Destruction of Troy, Being the Sequel of the Iliad.* Oxford, 1739.

*MERSENNE, MARIN, *Harmonie Universelle, Contenant la Theorie et la Pratique de la Musique.* Paris, 1636.

MEUNIER, LOUIS-FRANCIS, *Les Composés qui Contiennent un Verbe à un Mode Personnel en Latin, en Français, en Italien et en Espagnol.* Paris, 1875.

*MEXIA, PEDRO. See Fortescue, Thomas.

MIDDLETON, THOMAS, *The Works of Thomas Middleton,* 5 vols., ed. Rev. Alexander Dyce. London, 1840.

*MIDGLEY, ROBERT, *A New Treatise of Natural Philosophy, Free'd from the Intricacies of the Schools.* London, 1687.

*MILIUS, ABRAHAM, *De Origine Animalium, et Migratione Populorum.* Geneva, 1667.

*MILNE, COLIN, tr., *Institutes of Botany; Containing Accurate, compleat and easy Descriptions of all the known Genera of Plants: Translated from the Latin of the celebrated Charles von Linné.* London, 1771.

MILTON, JOHN, *The Student's Milton*, ed. Frank A. Patterson. New York: F. S. Crofts, 1934.

The Mirror for Magistrates, ed. Lily B. Campbell. Cambridge: Cambridge University Press, 1938.

*MIZALDUS, ANTONIUS, *Meteorologia, siue aeriarum commentariolus.* Paris, 1547.

MOORE, C. A., "The Return to Nature in English Poetry of the Eighteenth Century," *Studies in Philology*, XIV (1927), 243–91.

MORE, HENRY, *Philosophical Poems of Henry More, Comprising Psychozoia and Minor Poems*, ed. Geoffrey Bullough. Manchester: Manchester University Press, 1931.

MORELLUS, FEDERICUS, tr., *Hexaemeron . . . . Opus Sex Dierum, Seu; Mundi Opificium: Georgii Pisidæ Diaconi & Referendarij Constantinopolitanæ Ecclesiæ, Poëma. Omnia nunc primùm Græcè in lucem edita, & Latinis versibus eiusdem generis expressa, per Fed. Morellum.* Paris, 1585.

*MORGAN, BETTY TREBELLE, *Histoire du Journal des Sçavans Depuis 1665 Jusqu'en 1701.* Paris: Les Presses Universitaires de France, 1928.

*MORISON, ROBERT, *Plantarum Historiæ Universalis Oxoniensis Pars Secunda Seu Herbarum Distributio Nova.* Oxford, 1680.

*MORNET, DANIEL, *Les Sciences de la Nature en France, au XVIIIe Siècle.* Paris, 1911.

*MORTON, JOHN, *The Natural History of Northampton-shire.* London, 1712.

MOSCHUS. See Stanley, Thomas, *Anacreon, etc.*

*MOUFET, THOMAS, *Insectorum sive Minimorum Animalium Theatrum: Olim ab Edoardo Wottono. Conrado Gesnero. Thomaque Pennio inchoatum: Tandem Tho. Moufeti Londinâtis operâ sumptibusque, maximis concinnatum, auctum, perfectum.* London, 1634.

*MOXON, JOSEPH, *A Discourse of the Antiquity, Progress, and Augmentation of Astronomie.* (This work is appended to *A Tutor to Astronomie and Geographie*, with separate pagination.)

*—— *A Tutor to Astronomie and Geographie: Or an Easie and speedy way to know the Use of both the Globes, Cœlestial and Terrestrial.* London, 1659.

*MUIR, M. M. PATTISON, *A History of Chemical Theories and Laws.* New York, 1907.

MURE, SIR WILLIAM, *The Works of Sir William Mure of Rowallan*, 2 vols., ed. William Tough. Edinburgh, 1898.

MURTOLA, GASPARO, *Della Creatione del Mondo, Poema Sacro.* Venice, 1608. Another edition, Macerata, 1618.

—— *Rime del Sig. Gasparo Murtola*, 2d ed. Venice, 1604.

Musæ Anglicanæ, 2 vols., 5th ed. London, 1741.

Musarum Anglicanarum Analecta, Vol. I, 3d ed., Vol. II, 2d ed. London, 1714.

Musarum Anglicanarum Analecta: Sive, Poemata quædam melioris notæ, seu hactenus Inedita, seu sparsim Edita, 2 vols. Oxford, 1692–9.

NAEVIUS. See Warmington, E. H.

NEMESIANUS. See *Poetæ Latini Minores*.

*NERI, ANTONIO. See Merrett, Christopher, *The Art of Glass, etc.*

*NEWTON, SIR ISAAC, *Opticks: Or, A Treatise of the Reflexions, Refractions, Inflexions and Colours of Light*. London, 1704. (First book has separate pagination).

*—— *Opticks, or A Treatise of the Reflections, Refractions, Inflections & Colours of Light*. Reprinted from the 4th edition (1730), with an introduction by E. T. Whittaker. London: G. Bell, 1931.

*—— *Philosophiæ Naturalis Principia Mathematica*. London, 1686 [1687].

*—— *Principia*, 3d ed. (1726). Reprinted for Sir William Thomson and Hugh Blackburn. Glasgow, 1871.

*—— *Sir Isaac Newton's Mathematical Principles of Natural Philosophy and His System of the World, Translated into English by Andrew Motte in 1729*, ed. Florian Cajori. Berkeley: University of California Press, 1934.

NICANDER, *Theriaca et Alexipharmaca*, ed. Otto Schneider. Leipzig, 1866.

*NICERON, IOANNIS FRANCISCUS, *Thaumaturgus Opticus*. Paris, 1646.

*NICOLSON, MARJORIE, "Milton and the Telescope," *English Literary History*, II (1935), 1–32.

*—— *Newton Demands the Muse, Newton's Opticks and the Eighteenth Century Poets*. Princeton: Princeton University Press, 1946.

*—— AND MOHLER, NORA M., "The Scientific Background of Swift's *Voyage to Laputa*," *Annals of Science*, II (1937), 299–334; 405–30.

*NIEUWENTYT, BERNARD. See Chamberlayne, John.

NONNOS, *Dionysiaca*, 3 vols., with an English translation by W. H. D. Rouse. LCL, 1940–2.

NORRIS, JOHN, *A Collection of Miscellanies: Consisting of Poems, Essays, Discourses & Letters*, 2d ed. London, 1692. (First published 1687.)

*OLSCHKI, LEONARDO, *Geschichte der neusprachlichen wissenschaftlichen Literatur*, 2 vols. Heidelberg, 1919, and Leipzig, 1922.

OPPIAN, *Oppiani Anazarbei De piscatu libri V. Laurentio Lippio interprete. De venatione libri IIII. ita conuersi, vt singula verbis singulis respondeant*. Paris, 1555.

—— *Oppiani De Venatione Libri. IIII. Ioan. Bodino . . . interprete*. Paris, 1555.

See also Diaper, William, and Jones, John.

OPPIAN, COLLUTHUS, TRYPHIODORUS, with an English translation by A. W. Mair. LCL, 1928. (All citations of Oppian's *Cynegeticon* and *Halieuticon* are to this edition.)

ORAS, ANTS, *Milton's Editors and Commentators from Patrick Hume to Henry John Todd (1695–1801).* London: Oxford University Press, 1931.

*ORNSTEIN, MARTHA, *The Rôle of Scientific Societies in the Seventeenth Century.* Chicago: University of Chicago Press, 1928.

Orphica, ed. Eugen Abel. Leipzig, 1885.

*OSLER, SIR WILLIAM, *The Evolution of Modern Medicine.* New Haven, 1921.

OTWAY, THOMAS, *The Works of Thomas Otway,* 2 vols., ed. J. C. Ghosh. Oxford, 1932.

OVID, *The Art of Love, and other poems,* with an English translation by J. H. Mozley. LCL, 1939.

—— *Fasti,* with an English translation by Sir James G. Frazer. LCL, 1931.

—— *Heroides and Amores,* with an English translation by Grant Showerman. LCL, 1925.

—— *Metamorphoseon Libri XV. Interpretatione et Notis Illustravit Daniel Crispinus,* ed. John Freind. Oxford, 1696.

—— *Metamorphoses,* 2 vols., with an English translation by Frank Justus Miller. LCL, 1929–33.

—— *Tristia, Ex Ponto,* with an English translation by Arthur L. Wheeler. LCL, 1924.

See also Sandys, George.

PACUVIUS. See Warmington, E. H.

*PARACELSUS. See Fischartus, Joannes; French, John, *Of the Nature of Things;* Hester, John; Pinnell, Henry.

PARÉ, AMBROSE. See Johnson, Thomas.

*PARKINSON, JOHN, *Paradisi in Sole Paradisus Terrestris. A Garden of all sorts of pleasant flowers.* London, 1629.

PARMENIDES. See Diels, Hermann, *Die Fragmente der Vorsokratiker.*

PARRY, MILMAN, *L'Épithète Traditionnelle dans Homère.* Paris: Société d'Édition "Les Belles-Lettres," 1928.

—— "The Traditional Metaphor in Homer," *Classical Philology,* XXVIII (1933), 30–43.

PEACHAM, HENRY, *The Period of Mourning. Disposed into six Visions. In Memorie of the late Prince.* London, 1613.

PELLISSIER, GEORGES, *La Vie et les Œuvres de Du Bartas.* Paris, 1883.

PERSIUS FLACCUS, *Satires,* ed. Augustin Cartault. Paris: Société d'Édition "Les Belles-Lettres," 1920.

*PHAYER, THOMAS, *The Regiment of life, whereunto is added a treatyse of the Pestilence, with the booke of children newly corrected and enlarged.* London, 1546.

PHILIPS, JOHN, *The Poems of John Philips*, ed. M. G. Lloyd Thomas. Oxford: Blackwell, 1927.

PHILIPS, KATHARINE. See Saintsbury, *CP* I.

PHILLIPS, EDWARD, *A New World of Words, or a General Dictionary.* London, 1658.

Philosophical Transactions of the Royal Society. London, 1665–1710.

The Phœnix Nest, 1593, ed. Hyder Edward Rollins. Cambridge: Harvard University Press, 1931.

*PICTORIUS, GEORGE, *Medicinæ tam simplices quàm compositæ, ad omnes fermè corporis humani præter naturam affectus, ex Hippocrate, Galeno, Auicenna, Aegineta, & alijs.* Basel, 1560.

PINDAR, *The Odes*, with an English translation by Sir John Sandys. LCL, 1930.

*PINNELL, HENRY, tr., *Philosophy Reformed & Improved in Four Profound Tractates. The I. Discovering the Great and Deep Mysteries of Nature: By that Learned Chymist & Physitian Osw. Crollius. The other III. Discovering the Wonderfull Mysteries of the Creation, By Paracelsus: Being His Philosophy to the Athenians.* London, 1657.

PISIDAS, GEORGE, *Hexaemeron . . . . Opus Sex Dierum, Seu, Mundi Opificium . . . . Omnia nunc primùm Græcè in lucem edita, & Latinis versibus eiusdem generis expressa, per Fed. Morellum.* Paris, 1585.

—— *Opera*, in Migne, *Patrologia Graeca*, XCII (1865).

*PITFIELD, ALEXANDER, *The Natural History of Animals Containing the Anatomical Description of Several Creatures Dissected by the Royal Academy of Sciences at Paris.* London, 1702.

*PITTET, ARMAND, *Vocabulaire Philosophique de Sénèque*, 1re Livraison. Paris: Société d'Édition "Les Belles Lettres," 1937.

*PLAT, HUGH, *Diuers Chimicall Conclusions concerning the Art of Distillation. With many rare practises and vses thereof, according to the Authors own experience.* London, 1594.

*—— *The Jewell House of Art and Nature, Conteining diuers rare and profitable Inuentions, together with sundry new experimentes in the Art of Husbandry, Distillation, and Moulding.* London, 1594.

PLATO, Vol. VII (*Timaeus*), with an English translation by Rev. R. G. Bury. LCL, 1929.

See also Cornford, Francis M.

*PLATTES, GABRIEL, *A Discovery of Infinite Treasure, Hidden since the Worlds Beginning.* London, 1639.

PLAUTUS, 5 vols., with an English translation by Paul Nixon. LCL, 1917–38.

*PLINY, *Natural History*, Vols. I and III, with an English translation by H. Rackham. LCL, 1938–40.

*—— *Naturalis Historiae Libri XXXVII*, Vol. II, ed. Karl Mayhoff. Leipzig, 1919.

See also Holland, Philemon.

*PLOT, ROBERT, *The Natural History of Oxford-shire, Being an Essay toward the Natural History of England.* Oxford, 1677.

*—— *The Natural History of Stafford-shire.* Oxford, 1686.

*PLUCHE, NOËL ANTOINE. See Humphreys, Samuel.

*PLUTARCH, *Moralia*, Vol. V, ed. Gregorius N. Bernardakis. Leipzig, 1893. (Contains *De Placitis Philosophorum*.)

*—— *Scripta Moralia*, Vol. II, ed. Fredericus Dübner. Paris, 1890.

See also Kepler, Johann.

Poetæ Bucolici et Didactici, ed. Ameis, Lehrs, Dübner, Bussemaker, and Kœchly. Paris, 1862. (Contains Manethon.)

Poetæ Christiani Minores, Part I (*Corpus Scriptorum Ecclesiasticorum Latinorum*, XVI). Vienna, 1888. (Contains Proba, Victor.)

Poetæ Latini Minores, Vol. I, ed. N. E. Lemaire. Paris, 1824. (Contains Ausonius, Calpurnius Siculus, Gratius Faliscus, Nemesianus.)

Poetae Latini Rei Venaticae Scriptores et Bucolici Antiqui, ed. Caspar Barthin, Jan van Vliet, etc. Leyden, 1728.

A Poetical Rhapsody, 1602–1621, 2 vols., ed. Hyder Edward Rollins. Cambridge: Harvard University Press, 1931–2.

*POGGENDORFF, J. C., *Geschichte der Physik.* Leipzig, 1879.

*POINTER, JOHN, *A Rational Account of the Weather*, 2d ed. London, 1738.

*POLLUX, *Historia Physica seu Chronicon ab Origine Mundi, usque ad Valentis Tempora*, ed. Ignatius Hardt. Leipzig, 1792.

*—— *Onomasticon*, Fasc. I, ed. Eric Bethe (*Lexicographi Graeci*, Vol. IX). Leipzig, 1900.

*POMEY, FRANÇOIS-ANTOINE, *Indiculus Vniversalis, Rerum ferè omnium, quæ in Mundo sunt, Scientiarum item, Artiúmque Nomina, Aptè, breuitérque colligens. L'Vnivers en Abregé.* Lyon, 1667.

PONTANO, GIOVANNI, *Ioannis Ioviani Pontani Carmina*, Vol. I, ed. Benedetto Soldati. Florence, 1902.

POOLE, JOSUA, *The English Parnassus: Or, A Helpe to English Poesie.* London, 1657.

POPE, ALEXANDER, *The Complete Poetical Works of Alexander Pope*, ed. Henry W. Boynton. Boston and New York, 1903.

POPE, ALEXANDER, *Imitations of Horace, with An Epistle to Dr. Arbuthnot, and The Epilogue to the Satires,* ed. John Butt (Twickenham Edition, Vol. IV). London: Methuen, 1939. (Poems cited: *Horace's Epistles, Odes,* and *Satires.*)

—— *The Rape of the Lock, and Other Poems,* ed. Geoffrey Tillotson (Twickenham Edition, Vol. II). London: Methuen, 1940. (Poems cited: *The Rape of the Lock, The Temple of Fame, Eloisa to Abelard.*)

POPE, EMMA FIELD, "Renaissance Criticism and the Diction of the *Faerie Queene,*" *Publications of the Modern Language Association,* XLI (1926), 575–619.

*POWER, HENRY, *Experimental Philosophy.* London, 1664.

PRAZ, MARIO, "Stanley, Sherburne and Ayres as Translators and Imitators of Italian, Spanish and French Poets," *Modern Language Review,* XX (1925), 280–94; 419–31.

—— *Studi sul Concettismo.* Milan: Soc. Editrice "La Cultura," 1934.

PRETI, GIROLAMO. See Sherburne, Edward, *Salmacis, etc.;* Stanley, Thomas, *Oronta, etc.,* and *Sylvia's Park, etc.*

*PRISCIAN, *Prisciani Lydi Quae Extant, Metaphrasis in Theophrastum et Solutionum ad Chosroem Liber,* ed. I. Bywater. Berlin, 1886.

PROBA FALCONIA. See *Poetæ Christiani Minores.*

PRUDENTIUS, *Aurelii Prudentii Clementis Carmina,* ed. Johann Bergman (*Corpus Scriptorum Ecclesiasticorum Latinorum,* LXI). Vienna and Leipzig, 1926.

*PTOLEMY, *L'Ottica,* ed. Gilberto Govi. Turin, 1885.

*PURCHAS, SAMUEL, *A Theatre of Politicall Flying-Insects.* London, 1657.

*—— [*A Theatre of Politicall Flying-Insects*] *The Second Part, Being Meditations and Observations, Theologicall, and Morall, Upon the Nature of Bees.* London, 1657.

QUAYLE, THOMAS, *Poetic Diction, A Study of Eighteenth Century Verse.* London: Methuen, 1924.

QUILLET, CLAUDIUS. See Rowe, Nicholas.

RALEIGH, SIR WALTER, *The Works of Sir Walter Raleigh,* 8 vols., ed. William Oldys and Thomas Birch. Oxford, 1829.

RANDOLPH, THOMAS, *The Muses Looking Glasse.* Oxford, 1640.

—— *Poems, With the Muses Looking-Glasse, and Amyntas, The second Edition Enlarged.* Oxford, 1640.

RANNIE, DAVID WATSON, "Keats's Epithets," *Essays and Studies by Members of the English Association,* III (1912), 92–113.

RAPIN, RENÉ, *Hortorum Libri IV. Cum Disputatione De Cultura Hortensi.* Paris, 1665.

*RAY, JOHN, *A Collection of English Words . . . With Catalogues of English Birds and Fishes*. London, 1674.

*—— *Synopsis Methodica Animalium Quadrupedum et Serpentini Generis*. London, 1693.

*—— *Three Physico-Theological Discourses*, 4th ed. London, 1721.

*—— *The Wisdom of God Manifested in the Works of the Creation*. London, 1691.

RAYMOND, MARCEL, *L'Influence de Ronsard sur la Poésie Française (1550–1585)*, 2 vols. Paris: Librairie Ancienne Honoré Champion, 1927.

*READ, JOHN, *Prelude to Chemistry, An Outline of Alchemy, Its Literature and Relationships*. London: G. Bell, 1936.

*REILEY, KATHARINE C., *Studies in the Philosophical Terminology of Lucretius and Cicero*. New York, 1909.

*REISCH, GREGORIUS, *Margarita Philosophica*. [No pl.], 1504.

*RENODAEUS, JOANNES. See Tomlinson, Richard.

*REY, JEAN, *Essais de Jean Rey*, ed. Maurice Petit. Paris, 1907.

*REYMOND, ARNOLD, *History of the Sciences in Greco-Roman Antiquity*, translated by Ruth Gheury de Bray. New York: E. P. Dutton [n.d.].

REYNOLDS, MYRA, *The Treatment of Nature in English Poetry between Pope and Wordsworth*. Chicago, 1909.

RIBBECK, OTTO, ed., *Scenicae Romanorum Poesis Fragmenta (Tragicorum Latinorum Reliquiae, I)*. Leipzig, 1852.

*RICCIOLUS, JOHANNES BAPTISTA, *Almagestum Novum, Astronomiam Veterem Novamque Complectens*, 2 vols. Bologna, 1651.

*RIGAUD, STEPHEN JORDAN, ed., *Correspondence of Scientific Men of the Seventeenth Century, in the Collection of the Right Honourable the Earl of Macclesfield*, 2 vols. Oxford, 1841.

*RIPLEY, GEORGE, *The Compound of Alchymy. Or The ancient hidden Art of Archemie: Conteining the right & perfectest meanes to make the Philosophers Stone, Aurum potabile, with other excellent Experiments*. London, 1591.

*RIVERIUS, LAZARUS, *Medicina Practica in succinctum Compendium redacta, Studio & Sumptibus Bernhardi Verzaschæ*. Basel, 1663.

See also Cole, Abdiah; Culpeper, Nicholas, *The Compleat Practise, etc.*

ROBBINS, FRANK E., *The Hexaemeral Literature, A Study of the Greek and Latin Commentaries on Genesis*. Chicago, 1912.

ROBERTSON, J. M., *Shakespeare and Chapman*. London, 1917.

ROBERTSON, WILLIAM, *Phraseologia Generalis; . . . A Full, Large, and General Phrase Book; Comprehending, Whatsoever is Necessary and most Usefull, in all other Phraseological Books, (hitherto, here, Published;) and Methodically Digested; for the more speedy, and Prosperous Progress of Students, in their Humanity Studies* Cambridge, England, 1681.

*ROBIN, P. ANSELL, *Animal Lore in English Literature*. London: John Murray, 1932.

*—— *The Old Physiology in English Literature*. London, 1911.

ROCHESTER, JOHN WILMOT EARL OF, *The Collected Works of John Wilmot, Earl of Rochester*, ed. John Hayward. London: Nonesuch Press, 1926.

*ROHAULT, JAQUES, *Traité de Physique*, Vol. II. Amsterdam, 1672.

See also Clarke, John.

RONSARD, PIERRE DE, *Œuvres Complètes de Ronsard, Texte de 1578*, 7 vols., ed. Hugues Vaganay. Paris: Librairie Garnier, 1923–4.

ROSCOMMON, EARL OF, *Miscellaneous Works*. London, 1709.

*ROSE, HUGH, tr., *The Elements of Botany: Containing The History of the Science: . . . Being a Translation of the Philosophia Botanica* [by Linnaeus]. London, 1775.

*ROSSE, ALEXANDER, *The New Planet no Planet: or, The Earth no wandring Star; Except in the wandring heads of Galileans*. London, 1646.

*ROUBAIS DE TOURCOIN, JAQUES DE, *Dissertation Physique Concernant la Cause de la Variation du Barometre*, ed. S. Dury De Champdoré. Leyden, 1719.

ROUSSEAU, JEAN BAPTISTE, *Œuvres Poétiques, Avec un Commentaire par M. Amar*, 2 vols. Paris, 1824.

ROWE, NICHOLAS, *Callipædia. A Poem. In Four Books. With Some Other Pieces* [translated from the Latin of Claudius Quillet]. London, 1712.

ROY, PIERRE-CHARLES, *Les Elemens, Troisiéme Ballet Dansé par le Roy, Dans son Palais des Tuilleries, Le Mercredy trente-uniéme jour de Decembre 1721*. [Paris], 1721.

RUBEL, VERÉ L., *Poetic Diction in the English Renaissance, From Skelton through Spenser*. New York: Modern Language Association of America, 1941.

*RUSSELL, RICHARD, tr., *The Works of Geber, The Most Famous Arabian Prince and Philosopher*. London, 1686.

RUTILIUS, *Rutilii Claudii Namatiani De Reditu Suo Libri Duo*, ed. Charles H. Keene, tr. George F. Savage-Armstrong. London, 1907.

RYLANDS, GEORGE, "English Poets and the Abstract Word," *Essays and Studies by Members of the English Association*, XVI (1931), 53–84.

—— *Words and Poetry*. London: Hogarth Press, 1928.

SAINT-LAMBERT, JEAN FRANÇOIS, *Les Saisons, Poëme*, ed. le Comte de Boissy-D'Anglas. Paris, 1828.

SAINTE-BEUVE, *Les Grands Écrivains Français du XVIᵉ Siècle: Les Poètes*, ed. Maurice Allem. Paris: Librairie Garnier, 1926.

SAINTSBURY, GEORGE, *A History of Elizabethan Literature*. New York, 1912.

—— Ed., *Minor Poets of the Caroline Period*, 3 vols. Oxford, 1905–21.

*Salusbury, Thomas, *Mathematical Collections and Translations*, Vol. I. London, 1661.

*—— Tr., *The System of the World in Four Dialogues. Wherein the Two Grand Systemes of Ptolomy and Copernicus are largely discoursed of: by Galileus Galileus Linceus, Englished from the Original Italian Copy*. London, 1661.

*Sandivogius. See French, John, *A New Light of Alchymie, etc.*

Sandys, George, *Ovid's Metamorphosis Englished, Mythologiz'd, And Represented in Figures* [by G. S.]. London, 1640. (First edition 1626.)

Sannazaro, Giacomo, *Arcadia, Di Nuovo Ristampata, Et Ritornata alla sua Vera Lettione. Da M. Lodvico Dolce*. Venice, 1556.

See also Martin, Jean.

*Saporta, tr., *Traicté de la Mesure des Eaux Courantes de Benoist Castelli*. Castres, France, 1664.

*Sauveur, Joseph, *Principes d'Acoustique et de Musique, ou Systême General des Intervalles des Sons, & de son application à tous les Systêmes & à tous les Instrumens de Musique*. [No pl., n.d.]

Scarron, Paul, *Les Œuvres de Monsieur Scarron, Reveuës, corrigées, & augmentées de nouveau*, 2 vols. Paris, 1695.

Scève, Maurice, *Œuvres Poétiques Complètes de Maurice Scève*, ed. Bertrand Guégan. Paris: Librairie Garnier, 1927.

*Schmidt, Albert-Marie, *La Poésie Scientifique en France au Seizième Siècle*. Paris: Albin Michel, 1939.

Scopa, Giuseppe, "Le fonti del 'Mondo creato' di Torquato Tasso," *Rivista Abruzzese di Scienze, Lettere ed Arti*, XXIII (1908), 171–86; 308–19; 427–43; 549–59.

*Scribonius. See Widdowes, Daniel.

**Scriptores Optici; or, A Collection of Tracts Relating to Optics*, ed. Charles Babbage. London, 1823. (Contains the *Optica Promota* of Gregory.)

**Scriptores Rei Rusticae*, 5 vols., ed. Gottlob Schneider. Tours, 1828–30.

*Seager, H. W., *Natural History in Shakespeare's Time*. London, 1896.

*Sedgwick, W. T., and Tyler, H. W., *A Short History of Science*. New York: Macmillan, 1921.

Sellar, W. Y., *The Roman Poets of the Augustan Age: Virgil*. Oxford, 1877.

*Seneca, *Naturalium Quæstionum ad Lucilium libri septem, à Matthæo Fortunato, Erasmo Roterodamo, & Lodoico Strebæo diligentissime recogniti*. Paris, 1540.

*—— *Naturalium Quaestionum Libros VIII*, ed. Alfred Gercke. Leipzig, 1907.

*—— *Physical Science in the Time of Nero, Being a Translation of the Quaestiones Naturales*, by John Clarke. London, 1910.

—— *Tragedies*, 2 vols., with an English translation by Frank Justus Miller. LCL, 1927–9.

SENECA. See also Lipsius, Justus; Lodge, Thomas, *The Works . . . of Seneca, etc.;* Sherburne, Edward, *Medea, etc.,* and *Seneca's Answer, etc.*

SHADWELL, THOMAS, *The Complete Works of Thomas Shadwell,* 5 vols., ed. Montague Summers. London: Fortune Press, 1927.

SHAKESPEARE, WILLIAM, *The Complete Plays and Poems of William Shakespeare,* ed. W. A. Neilson and C. S. Hill. Cambridge, 1942.

SHERBURNE, EDWARD, tr., *Medea: A Tragedie. Written in Latine by Lucius Annæus Seneca. Englished by E. S. Esq.* London, 1648.

—— *Salmacis, Lyrian & Sylvia, Forsaken Lydia, The Rape of Helen, A Comment thereon, With Severall other Poems and Translations* [from Girolamo Preti, St. Amant, Marino, Colluthus, and Theocritus]. London, 1651.

—— *Seneca's Answer, To Lucilius His Quære; Why Good Men suffer misfortunes seeing there is a Divine Providence? Written Originally in Latine Prose, And Now Translated into English Verse.* London, 1648.

—— *The Sphere of Marcus Manilius Made An English Poem: With Annotations And An Astronomical Appendix.* London, 1675.

SIDNEY, SIR PHILIP, *The Complete Works of Sir Philip Sidney,* 3 vols., ed. Albert Feuillerat. Cambridge: Cambridge University Press, 1922–6.

*SIMONETA, PETER PAUL, *Compendium Totius Medicinæ.* Venice, 1594.

*SINGER, CHARLES, *From Magic to Science.* London: E. Benn, 1928.

*—— *A Short History of Medicine.* New York: Oxford University Press, 1928.

SOPHOCLES, 2 vols., with an English translation by F. Storr. LCL, 1912–13.

—— *The Fragments of Sophocles,* 3 vols., ed. A. C. Pearson. Cambridge, England, 1917.

*SPARK, NATHANIEL. See Dariott, Claudius.

SPENCE, JOSEPH, *Polymetis,* ed. Nicholas Tindal. London, 1802.

SPENSER, EDMUND, *The Poetical Works of Edmund Spenser,* ed. J. C. Smith and E. de Selincourt. London: Oxford University Press, 1926.

*SPIGEL, ADRIAN, *De Humani Corporis Fabrica Libri Decem.* Frankfurt, 1632.

*SPRAT, THOMAS, *The History of the Royal-Society of London,* 2d ed. London, 1702.

—— *The Plague of Athens, Which Hapned in the Second Year of the Peloponnesian Warre. First Describ'd in Greek by Thucydides; Then in Latin by Lucretius; Now attempted in English, after incomparabl[e] Dr. Cowley's Pindarick way.* London, 1659.

SQUIRES, VERNON PURINTON, "Milton's Treatment of Nature," *Modern Language Notes,* IX (1894), 454–74.

STANLEY, THOMAS, tr., *Anacreon. Bion. Moschus. Kisses, by Secundus. Cupid Crucified, by Ausonius. Venus Vigils, Incerto Authore.* [London], 1651.

—— Tr., *Aurora, Ismenia* [by Don Juan Perez de Montalvan]. [London], 1648.

*STANLEY, THOMAS, *The History of Philosophy, Containing those on whom the Attribute of Wise was conferred*, 2 vols. London, 1655–6. (In eight parts, each individually dated and with separate pagination.)

*—— *The History of Philosophy. The Third and Last Volume, In Five Parts*. London, 1660. (The parts are numbered from one to five; each is individually dated and has separate pagination.)

—— Tr., *Oronta, The Cyprian Virgin: By Sigr. Girolamo Preti*. London, 1647.

—— *A Paraphrase upon Psalm CXLVIII. And Part of Psalm CXXXIX. Out of French*, in *Poems and Translations*. (The *Paraphrase* has separate pagination.)

—— *Poems*. London, 1652.

—— *Poems and Translations*. [London], 1647. (*Poems* and *Translations* are in separate sections, each with separate pagination.)

—— Tr., *Sylvia's Park, by Theophile. Acanthus Complaint, by Tristan. Oronta, by Preti. Echo, by Marino. Loves Embassy, by Boscan. The Solitude. by Gongora*. [London], 1651.

STATIUS, 2 vols., with an English translation by J. H. Mozley. LCL, 1928.

*STENO, NICHOLAS, *Observationes Anatomicæ, Quibus Varia Oris, Oculorum, & Narium Vasa describuntur, novique salivæ, lacrymarum & muci fontes deteguntur*. Leyden, 1662.

*STEPHANUS, CAROLUS, *Prædium Rusticum*. Paris, 1629.

*STIMSON, DOROTHY, *The Gradual Acceptance of the Copernican Theory of the Universe*. New York, 1917.

STORER, WALTER HENRY, *Virgil and Ronsard*. Paris: Librairie Ancienne Édouard Champion, 1923.

SUSEMIHL., FRANZ, *Geschichte der griechischen Litteratur in der Alexandrinerzeit*, 2 vols. Leipzig, 1891–2.

*SWAN, JOHN, *Speculum Mundi. Or A Glasse Representing the Face of the World . . . Whereunto is Joyned an Hexameron*, 2d ed. London, 1643.

SYLVESTER, JOSUAH, *Bartas, His Deuine Weekes & Workes Translated*. [London, 1605.]

—— *Du Bartas, His Deuine Weekes and Workes Translated*. London [1611].

—— *Du Bartas, His Diuine Weekes and Workes with A Compleate Collection of all the other most delight-full Workes Translated and written by y*[t] *famous Philomusus*. London, 1633.

—— *Posthumus Bartas. The Third Day of his Seconde Weeke*. [London], 1606.

*TACHENIUS, OTTO, *Otto Tachenius. his Hippocrates Chymicus*. [Translated by J. W.] London, 1696.

TASSO, TORQUATO, *Poemi Minori di Torquato Tasso*, Vol. II, ed. Angelo Solerti. Bologna, 1891.

See also Fairfax, Edward.

Tate, Nahum, tr., *Syphilis*. *Written (In Latin) By that Famous Poet and Physician Fracastorius*, appended to *Examen Poeticum: Being The Third Part of Miscellany Poems*. London, 1693.

Taylor, George Coffin, *Milton's Use of Du Bartas*. Cambridge: Harvard University Press, 1934.

*Temple, William, The Archbishop of York, "Poetry and Science," *Essays and Studies by Members of the English Association*, XVII (1932), 7–24.

Theocritus. See Creech, Thomas, *The Idylliums, etc.; The Greek Bucolic Poets;* Sherburne, Edward, *Salmacis, etc.*

*Theophrastus, *Enquiry into Plants, and Minor Works on Odours and Weather Signs*, 2 vols., with an English translation by Sir Arthur Hort. LCL, 1916.

*—— *Theophrasti Eresii Opera, Quæ Supersunt, Omnia*, ed. Frederick Wimmer. Paris: Firmin-Didot, 1931.

*—— *Theophrastii Eresii De Historia Plantarum Libri Decem, Græcè & Latinè . . . illustravit Ioannes Bodæus*. Amsterdam, 1644.

See also Turnebus, Adrian.

Thomson, James, *The Complete Poetical Works of James Thomson*, ed. J. Logie Robertson. London, 1908.

Tibullus. See Catullus.

Tillotson, Geoffrey, "Eighteenth-Century Poetic Diction," *Essays and Studies by Members of the English Association*, XXV (1939), 59–80.

—— *On the Poetry of Pope*. Oxford: Clarendon Press, 1938.

*Tilyard, E. M. W., *The Elizabethan World Picture*. New York: Macmillan, 1944.

Timotheus of Miletus, *Die Perser*, ed. Ulrich von Wilamowitz-Möllendorff. Leipzig, 1903.

*Tomlinson, Richard, tr., *A Medicinal Dispensatory, Containing The whole Body of Physick* [by Joannes Renodaeus]. London, 1657.

*Topsell, Edward, *The Historie of Foure-Footed Beastes, Collected out of all the Volumes of Conradus Gesner, and all other Writers to this present day*. London, 1607.

Tottel's Miscellany, (*1557–1587*), 2 vols., ed. Hyder Edward Rollins. Cambridge: Harvard University Press, 1928–9.

*Tournefort, Joseph Pitton, *Elemens de Botanique, Ou Methode Pour Connoître Les Plantes*, 3 vols. Paris, 1694.

Traherne, Thomas, *The Poetical Works of Thomas Traherne*, ed. Gladys I. Wade. London: P. J. and A. E. Dobell, 1932.

Trapp, Joseph, *Lectures on Poetry Read in the Schools of Natural Philosophy At Oxford, . . . Translated from the Latin, With additional Notes, by William Clarke and William Bowyer*. London, 1742.

TRAPP, JOSEPH, *Prælectiones Poeticæ: In Schola Naturalis Philosphiæ Oxon. Habitæ*, Vol. I. Oxford, 1711. Third edition, 2 vols., London, 1736.

*TRYON, THOMAS, *The Way to Health, Long Life and Happiness*. London, 1683.

TRYPHIODORUS. See Merrick, James; Oppian, Colluthus, Tryphiodorus.

*TURNEBUS, ADRIAN, *Theophrastus De Igne Libellus, Ab Adriano Turnebo . . . illustratus.* Harderwijck, 1656.

UPHAM, A. H., *The French Influence in English Literature*. New York, 1908.

VALERIUS FLACCUS, with an English translation by J. H. Mozley. LCL,1934.

VALVASONE, ERASMO DI, *Angeleida*. Venice, 1590.

—— *La Caccia, con le annotationi di M. Olimpio Marcucci.* Bergamo, 1593.

—— *La Caccia dell' Ill. Sig. Erasmo di Valvasone, Ricoretta & di molte stanze ampliata. Con le Annotationi di M. Olimpio Marcucci.* Venice [1602].

VAN DOREN, MARK, *The Poetry of John Dryden*. New York, 1920.

*VAN HELMONT, JEAN BAPTISTE. See Chandler, John; Charleton, Walter, *A Ternary of Paradoxes, etc.*

VAUGHAN, HENRY, *The Works of Henry Vaughan*, 2 vols., ed. Leonard C. Martin. Oxford, 1914. (Consecutive pagination.)

*VAUGHAN, THOMAS, *Euphrates, Or the Waters of the East; Being a short Discourse of that Secret Fountain, whose Water flows from Fire; and carries in it the Beams of the Sun and Moon.* London, 1655.

*VENNER, TOBIAS, *Via Recta ad Vitam longam, Or a Plaine Philosophical Discourse of the Nature, faculties, and effects, of all such things, as by way of nourishments, and Dieteticall obseruations, make for the preseruation of Health.* London, 1620.

*VESALIUS, *De Humani Corporis Fabrica*. Basel, 1543.

VICTOR, MARIUS. See *Poetæ Christiani Minores*.

VIRGIL, *The Minor Poems*, in *Virgil*, with an English translation by H. Rushton Fairclough, Vol. II. LCL, 1934.

—— *P. Vergili Maronis Opera*, ed. Frederick A. Hirtzel. Oxford, 1900.

See also Fanshawe, Sir Richard, *The Fourth Book of Virgil's Aeneid;* Warton, Joseph.

WALLER, EDMUND, *The Poems of Edmund Waller*, 2 vols., ed. G. Thorn Drury. London [1904].

*WALLER, RICHARD, tr., *Essayes of Natural Experiments Made in the Academie del Cimento, . . . Written in Italian by the Secretary of that Academy.* London, 1684.

WARMINGTON, E. H., ed., *Remains of Old Latin*, Vol. II. LCL, 1936. (Contains Livius Andronicus, Naevius, Pacuvius, and Accius.)

WARTON, JOSEPH, "Prefatory Dedication," to *The Works of Virgil, in Latin and English*, Vol. I, ed. Christopher Pitt and Joseph Warton, 3d ed. London, 1778.

WASE, CHRISTOPHER, *Grati Falisci Cynegeticon. Or, A Poem of Hunting by Gratius the Faliscan. Englished and Illustrated.* London, 1654.

WATSON, FOSTER, *The Beginnings of the Teaching of Modern Subjects in England.* London, 1909.

*WEDEL, GEORGE WOLFFGANG, *De Sale Volatile Plantarum.* Frankfurt, 1672.

*WELLMANN, M., "Leonidas von Byzanz und Demostratos," *Hermes,* XXX (1895), 161–76.

WHEELER, ARTHUR L., "Remarks on Roman Poetic Diction," *Classical Weekly,* XII (1919), 179–82, 188–92.

*WHEWELL, WILLIAM, *History of the Inductive Sciences,* 2 vols. New York, 1866.

*—— *The Philosophy of the Inductive Sciences,* 2 vols. London, 1840.

*WHISTON, WILLIAM, *A New Theory of the Earth, From its Original, to the Consummation of all Things.* London, 1696.

WHITAKER, VIRGIL K., "Du Bartas' Use of Lucretius," *Studies in Philology,* XXXIII (1936), 134–46.

WHITEHEAD, PAUL, *The State Dunces. Inscribed to Mr. Pope.* London, 1733.

WHITING, NATHANIEL, *Albino and Bellama.* See Saintsbury, *CP* III.

*WHITTAKER, E. T., *A History of the Theories of Aether and Electricity.* London, 1910.

*WIDDOWES, DANIEL, *Naturall Philosophy: Or A Description of the World, Namely, Of Angels, of Man, of the Heauens, of the Ayre, of the Earth, of the Water: and of the Creatures in the whole World.* [Translated from Scribonius.] London, 1621. Second edition, London, 1631.

*WILKINS, JOHN, *A Discourse concerning A New world & Another Planet In 2 Bookes.* London, 1640.

*—— *The Discovery of a World in the Moone.* London, 1638.

*—— *An Essay Towards a Real Character, And a Philosophical Language.* London, 1668.

*—— *The First Book. The Discovery of a New World. Or, A Discourse tending to prove, that 'tis probable there may be another habitable World in the Moone. With a Discourse concerning the possibility of a Passage thither,* 3d impression. London, 1640.

WILLEY, BASIL, *The Seventeenth Century Background.* London: Chatto and Windus, 1934.

*WILLIS, THOMAS, *Cerebri Anatome: Cui Accessit Nervorum Descriptio et Usus.* London, 1664.

WILLOUGHBY, HENRY, *Willobie His Avisa (1594),* ed. G. B. Harrison. London: Bodley Head, 1926.

WINSLOW, ANN, "Re-evaluation of Pope's Treatment of Nature," *University of Wyoming Publications,* IV (1938), 21–43.

WITHALS, JOHN, *A Dictionarie in English and Latine for Children.* London, 1602.

WITHER, GEORGE, *Britain's Remembrancer, Containing A Narration of the Plagve lately past.* London, 1628.

*WOLF, A., *A History of Science, Technology, and Philosophy in the 16th & 17th Centuries.* London: Allen and Unwin, 1935.

*WOODWARD, HEZEKIAH, *A Gate to Sciences, Opened By a Natural Key: Or, A Practicall Lecture upon the great Book of Nature, whereby the childe is enabled to reade the Creatures there.* London, 1641.

*WOODWARD, JOHN, *An Essay toward a Natural History of the Earth: And Terrestrial Bodies, Especially Minerals: As also of the Sea, Rivers, and Springs. With an Account of the Universal Deluge: And of the Effects that it had upon the Earth.* London, 1695.

WORDSWORTH, WILLIAM, *The Poetical Works of Wordsworth,* ed. Thomas Hutchinson, revised by Ernest de Selincourt. London: Oxford University Press, 1939.

*WOTTON, EDWARD, *De Differentiis Animalium Libri Decem.* Paris, 1552.

*WREN, CHRISTOPHER AND STEPHEN, eds., *Parentalia: Or, Memoirs of the Family of the Wrens.* London, 1750.

WYLD, HENRY CECIL, "Diction and Imagery in Anglo-Saxon Poetry," *Essays and Studies by Members of the English Association,* XI (1925), 49–91.

YOUNG, EDWARD, *The Poetical Works of Edward Young,* 2 vols. Boston, 1866.

Index

Abbot, W. R.: on Swan's obligations to Du Bartas, 46 n.; on Du Bartas's influence, 80 n.

Abercromby, David: quoted, 277, 290, 294, 330, 355

Accius: quoted, 227, 363, 380, 386

Acevedo, A. M. de: 75

Adanson, Michel: his classification terminology, 43 and n.

Addison, Joseph: quoted, 193, 204, 258, 267

Aelian: 43 n., 73, 74, 79; quoted, 43 n.

Aeschylus: quoted, 110, 222–3, 224, 244, 302, 358, 367, 370, 373, 375

Aikin, John: 8, 22, 23, 27; his criticism of stock poetic language and mythology, 9; his doctrine of accuracy in description, 10; his criticism of Thomson as a poet of nature, 10, 12; on the value of natural philosophy for poetry, 10; limitations of his criticism, 11; application of his standards to Virgil, 20

Akenside, Mark: quoted, 30

Alberti, F. d'E.: quoted, 30–1 n.

Alcmaeon: 286

Aler, Paul: 15 n.

Alexander, William: quoted, 119

Alexander the Great: 70, 81

Alexandrian poetry: its didactic elements, 69–71; its influence on writers of the early Christian period, 75

Alhazen: 126; quoted, 31

Alsted, J.-H.: 55 n.; quoted, 103–4, 141, 154, 160, 163, 234, 246, 250, 260, 293, 304, 314, 322

Ambrose, St.: 56, 74

Anaxagoras: 51, 57, 67; on sensitive plants, 63–4 n.; on the four elements, 300

Anaximenes: 52

Anglo-Saxon translation of the Psalms: 131

Apollonius Rhodius: quoted, 372

Aratus: 24, 46 n.; as a didactic poet, 69, 70; quoted, 94, 220, 222, 287

Arbuthnot, John: quoted, 192

Archaisms: 2, 12 n.; in Dryden, 6 and n.

Archimedes: 73

Argyropolus, Johannes: 130 n.; quoted, 97, 135, 153, 163, 191, 228, 239, 264, 292, 327, 339, 346

Aristophanes: quoted, 93–4, 134, 186, 220, 221, 224, 359, 375, 381, 386

Aristotle: 57, 59 and n., 63, 71, 72, 73, 74, 81, 87 n., 130 n., 310, 343 n., 364; his terminology for schemes of classification, 42, 297, 298 n.; the adequacy of his terminology, 44; on the four elements, 52; on the soul, 62; on theories of vision, 287; on the nature of vocal sound, 310; quoted, 32, 42, 55, 96, 97, 146, 153, 228, 329, 338, 364, 371

Armstrong, John: quoted, 92, 362

Arnoldus de Villanova: quoted, 104

Arthos, John: 75 n., 395 n.

Ashmole, Elias: quoted, 159

Astrological beliefs: 61

Astronomicon (Manilius): 16, 23, 71

Augustan diction: in Latin phrase books, 15, 15–16 n.

447

Ausonius: 74; quoted, 14, 186, 227, 244, 368, 376

Authorized Version of the Bible: quoted, 185

Avitus, St.: 16, 73, 75, 311; quoted, 13, 94, 132, 134, 195, 202, 212, 237, 261, 274, 294, 311, 344, 358, 362, 376

Ayres, Philip: quoted, 152, 160, 199, 209, 213, 219, 231, 270, 296, 334, 340, 342, 361, 369

Bacon, Francis: 38; quoted, 30, 32, 92, 108, 118, 122, 124, 135, 139, 166, 179, 184, 192, 197, 203, 235, 240, 284, 327, 330, 332–3, 335, 339, 347, 352, 355

Baker, George: quoted, 321

Banester, John: quoted, 139, 210, 352, 400

Banister, Richard: quoted, 104, 120, 160, 200, 214, 267, 289, 309–10, 310, 389, 397, 400, 402

Barlaeus, Caspar: quoted, 233, 380

Barrow, Isaac: quoted, 284–5

Barstow, M. L.: 12 n.

Bartholomeus Anglicus: quoted, 56

Basil, St.: 74, 75; as a model for writers of hexaemeral literature, 73; quoted, 58–9 n., 239

Bateson, F. W.: 47 n.; on poetic diction, 12 n.; on poetic diction and scientific language, 28–9 n.

Beare, J. I.: on ancient theories of vision, 126, 286–7; on ancient theories of vocal sound, 310–11

Beaumont, Francis, and Fletcher, John: quoted, 392

Beierlynck, Laurens: quoted, 298

Belon du Mans, Pierre: quoted, 159, 196

Benlowes, Edward: quoted, 105, 119, 136, 194, 204, 236, 256, 270, 300, 309, 313, 357, 361, 362, 369, 371, 379, 383, 384, 386, 388

Berkeley, George: quoted, 204, 265

Berkenhout, John: 396; quoted, 324, 399, 400, 404

Bertaut, Jean: quoted, 145, 159, 249, 337, 360, 362, 378, 385, 387

Besler, M. R.: quoted, 234

Binary terms: in Linnaeus, 41

Blackmore, Sir Richard: 16; quoted, 13, 81, 96, 105, 121, 141, 160, 162, 175, 191, 219, 235, 238, 260, 276, 292, 304, 309, 326, 332, 367, 370

Blancanus, Josephus: quoted, 169, 243

Blome, Richard: quoted, 164, 184, 240, 253, 324, 348–9

Blundeville, Thomas: quoted, 260

Boccaccio: quoted, 261

Bodaeus, Ioannes: 278; quoted, 214, 246, 279, 327

Bodin, Jean: 130 n.; quoted, 32, 121, 154, 163, 168, 228–9, 229, 245, 284, 289, 298, 314, 370

Boethius: 311

Boodt, A. B. de: quoted, 118, 154

Bosworth, William: quoted, 361

Boyle, Robert: 39, 45, 51, 67, 143, 185; quoted, 30, 31, 32–3, 35, 98, 101, 108, 118, 128, 137, 148, 164, 169, 176, 180, 185, 205, 211, 264, 322, 353, 366

Bradley, Richard: quoted, 297 n., 298 n., 299

Brahe, Tycho: 87 n.; quoted, 97, 243, 254, 293

Briggs, William: quoted, 31, 128

Brooke, Henry: 16

Browne, Sir Thomas: quoted, 122, 130, 197, 267

Browne, William: 302 n.; quoted, 95, 103, 111, 112, 114, 123, 126, 162, 181, 190, 193, 206, 210, 211, 236, 245, 295, 299, 300, 313, 320, 324, 331, 335, 351, 354, 358, 360, 366, 369, 378, 380, 381, 383, 385, 390

Brunfels, Otto: 130 n.

Brunot, Ferdinand: on style in scientific writing, 39 and n.

Buchanan, George: 15, 16, 24, 79 n.; quoted, 21, 202 n., 357

Buchler, Johann: 15–16 n., 24 n.

Burnet, John: his paraphrase of Empedocles, 153

Burtt, E. A.: 58 n.; on Newtonian teleology, 82

Butler, Samuel: quoted, 157, 218, 357

Callimachus: 68 n.; quoted, 221, 256, 358

Camenzind, Clara: on ancient teleological views, 54 n.

Camoens, Luiz de: quoted, 94, 110, 113, 128, 144, 157, 182, 189, 195, 198, 248, 251, 262, 274, 277, 294, 312, 320, 337, 344, 354, 357, 360, 363, 368, 373, 377, 380, 385, 387, 390

Cardanus, Hieronymus: quoted, 139

care: as a stock poetic term, 20 n.

Carew, Thomas: quoted, 99, 109, 129, 361, 362, 363, 369, 373, 378, 380, 383, 387, 389

Carleer, L.-H.-M.: 46 n., 297 n.

Catullus: quoted, 197–8, 366, 376, 380, 381, 384

Celsus: quoted, 31, 127, 326

Chalkhill, John: quoted, 340, 360, 362, 363, 369, 389

Chamberlayne, John: quoted, 102, 136, 201, 241, 255, 265, 268, 269, 281, 310, 355, 374, 390, 400

Chamberlayne, William: quoted, 95, 121, 127, 157, 173, 193, 207, 260, 263, 275, 278, 283, 286, 288, 299, 307, 318, 325, 326, 329, 350, 361, 362, 363, 365, 370, 383, 384, 386, 390, 391

Chandler, John: quoted, 239, 250, 347

Chanoine, C. C.: quoted, 390

Chapelain, Jean: 79 n.; quoted, 13, 103, 106, 115, 133, 145, 157, 158, 165, 170, 172, 188, 196, 238, 249, 272, 295, 334, 357, 359, 365, 369, 373, 379, 380, 383, 386, 388, 391, 392

Chapman, George: his use of epithets with the suffix -y, 395 n.; quoted, 99, 119, 134, 136, 159, 182, 206, 213, 217, 257, 273, 281, 288, 303, 313, 337, 340, 360, 362, 367, 378

Charleton, Walter: on the style of scientific writing, 45; on theories of the soul, 62–3; his classification terminology, 297; quoted, 45, 62–3, 120, 137, 184, 203, 211, 253, 281, 297, 348, 364–5, 389

Chastel, Sieur de Marly le: quoted, 147, 355

Chastillon, Nicolas: 15 n.

Châtres, P.-J.-B. de M. de: quoted, 388

Chaucer: quoted, 303, 311, 374, 387

Chênedollé, C.-J. L. de: 87

Cicero: 74; on the composition of the human body, 60, 143; quoted, 60, 140, 143, 167, 181, 259, 338, 375, 381, 384, 386

Cinna: quoted, 384

Clarke, John: quoted, 161, 285

Classification: its principles in relation to the forms of scientific terminology, 36–7, 41; in Aristotle, 42, 44, 297; in the sixteenth century, 42; in Comenius, 42–3 n.; in Adanson, 43 and n.; as the characteristic activity of Alexandrian science, 70–1; as an interest of sixteenth- and seventeenth-century science, 81–2; in Charleton, 297

Claudian: 73, 74; quoted, 130, 226, 359, 360

Clemens Alexandrinus: 61

Cléric, P.: quoted, 273, 361, 379

Cleveland, John: quoted, 359, 361

Cogan, Thomas: quoted, 118, 355

Coleridge, S. T.: 27; on poetic diction, 11–12; his criticism of the Gradus, 22 n.; his doctrine concerning truth and pleasure in the formation of poetic language, 24 and n.

Coles, William: quoted, 34, 35, 92, 209, 229, 280, 293, 318, 335, 402, 403, 404

Columella: 46 n.; quoted, 228

Comenius, J. A.: 42 n., 364 n.; on the relationship of spirit to matter, 59 n.; on the source of vital heat, 62; quoted, 32, 43 n., 55, 59 n., 92, 98, 104, 108, 116, 122, 124, 128, 135, 137, 139, 148, 154, 160, 164, 166, 192, 197, 200, 203, 207, 209, 235, 243, 254, 267, 293, 305, 314, 330, 333, 339, 347, 366, 398, 399, 401, 404

Compound epithets: 2; various types, 4; used in schemes of classification, 19; in Greek and Latin, 20 n., 34; in scientific prose, 34; in Greek and Latin verse, 68 n.

Congreve, William: quoted, 175, 210, 384

Cook, A. S.: 308 n.

Cooke, James: quoted, 201

Copernicus: 73, 85; quoted, 191, 260

Cordier, André: 25 n.

Corneille: 16

Couat, Auguste: on Alexandrian didactic poetry, 69–70; on the status of Alexandrian science, 70

Coulter, C. C.: on Greek and Latin compounds, 68 n.

Coverdale translation of the Bible: 131; quoted, 185

Cowley, Abraham: 301; quoted, 17, 107, 120, 125, 133, 135, 146, 152, 158, 160, 168, 174, 178, 183, 187, 190, 199, 202, 207, 208, 218, 235, 236, 238, 242, 243, 249–50, 263, 266, 278, 282, 296, 301, 304, 308, 318, 319, 321, 323, 338, 346, 352, 354, 358, 359, 361, 367, 375, 379, 384, 386, 391

Crashaw, Richard: quoted, 129, 240, 326

Creation, The (Blackmore): 16, 23

Creech, Thomas: 297; quoted, 14, 105, 124, 135, 170, 219, 243, 275, 297, 304, 346, 369, 370, 380

Croiset, A. and M.: on Theocritus' style, 70 n.

Croll, Oswald: quoted, 55, 61, 207, 346

Crooke, Helkiah: quoted, 101–2, 124, 128, 139, 166, 252, 350

Culpeper, Nicholas: quoted, 148, 214, 305

Cyprianus Gallus: 75; quoted, 244, 384

Dampier, William: quoted, 32, 34, 119, 122, 125, 140, 161, 230, 232, 390, 398, 398–9, 399, 401, 402–3

Dampier-Whetham, W. C. D.: 81 n.

Daneau, Lambert: 59 n.; quoted, 55–6, 97, 100, 116, 128, 130, 136, 154, 163, 175, 191, 196, 200, 205, 207, 239, 298, 304, 322, 323, 327, 355, 371

Dante: quoted, 113

Dariott, Claudius: quoted, 33, 108, 166, 200, 277, 374, 397

Darwin, Erasmus: 24 n., 395 n.

Davenant, Sir William: 302 n.; quoted, 114, 124, 151, 165, 190, 202, 210, 218, 247, 249, 266, 282, 292, 331, 345, 354, 359, 361, 362, 369, 379, 381, 383, 386, 387, 389, 391

Davies, Sir John: quoted, 107, 119, 206, 217, 351

Davies of Hereford, John: quoted, 112, 129, 195, 217, 308, 313, 345, 360

Dawson, J. C.: 78 n.

Decorum: as a factor in the formation of Latin poetic diction, 25; in the diction of neoclassic poetry, 26–7

Definition: as a principle in the formation of stock phrases, 17–19; in Descartes and French classicism, 18 n.; in scientific terminology, 41–2

Delaruelle, L.: 79 n.

Democritus: 71, 143, 300; on the nature of the soul, 62, 343, 364; his theory of sound, 311

Denham, Sir John: quoted, 124, 292, 366

Dennys, John: quoted, 133, 138, 278, 378

Derham, William: 90, 311; quoted, 32, 149, 156, 176, 209, 322, 333, 341

Desaguliers, J. T.: quoted, 19, 141, 340, 388, 390

Descartes: 38, 49, 50, 51, 67, 287; his emphasis on definition, 18 n.; quoted, 31, 128, 161, 163–4, 169, 175, 179, 200, 203, 239, 241, 250, 254, 264, 268, 284, 322, 324

Des-Marests, Le Sieur (Nicolas): 68 n.

Diaper, William: quoted, 110, 124, 165, 184, 214, 219, 237, 246, 270, 278, 283–4, 296, 307, 318, 321, 332, 338, 359, 361, 362, 363, 370, 373, 379

Didactic poetry: as a vehicle for the description of nature, 16, 23; in Greek, 68, 69; as criticized by Warton, 69; as written by Lucretius, Virgil, and Oppian, 69, 71; in the early Christian period, 73–4; in Du Bartas, 75

Digby, Kenelm: quoted, 98, 104, 135, 148, 239, 241, 314, 322, 324, 333, 353, 403

Digges, T.: quoted, 179

Diodorus of Sicily: quoted, 57–8

Diogenes Laertius: quoted, 163

Dioscorides: quoted, 279

Divine Comedy, The: 16

Donne, John: 140 n., 286; quoted, 107, 117, 119, 136, 145, 178, 187, 188, 202, 208, 218, 257, 286, 291–2, 320, 329, 345, 354, 361, 378

Dracontius: 74, 75; quoted, 94, 174, 226, 271, 360, 382

Drayton, Michael: quoted, 14, 95, 103, 111, 112, 113, 115, 117, 121, 123, 133, 134, 138, 140, 158, 165, 167, 170, 180, 187, 190, 193, 194, 217, 230, 233, 247, 258, 262, 270, 273, 275, 281, 300, 307, 316, 319, 325, 329, 331, 340, 341, 345, 349, 351, 359, 360, 363, 366, 367, 369, 372, 375, 378, 380, 383, 385, 389, 390, 391, 392

Drummond, William: quoted, 14, 105, 106, 111, 114–15, 117, 125, 127, 133, 138, 145, 158, 165, 171, 172, 187, 194, 195, 217, 259, 263, 269, 272, 275, 276, 303, 318, 323, 326, 331, 334, 357, 359, 361, 362, 367, 369, 373, 378, 380, 383, 385, 387, 389, 391

Dryden, John: 16, 67, 90, 301, 356, 365; application of Quayle's analysis of the elements of stock diction to Dryden's verse, 2–6; use of stock diction in his plays, 17; Macaulay's criticism of his diction, 27 n.; on the combining of elements, 83, 84; his personifications, 83, 84; on Lucretius' use of *image*, 201 n.; quoted, 2, 3, 4, 5, 6, 13, 14, 17–18, 31, 92, 96, 99, 100, 103, 105, 106, 107, 109, 111, 112, 113, 114, 115, 116, 118, 120, 121, 123, 124, 126, 127, 130, 133, 135, 136, 138, 146, 152, 160, 162, 165, 167, 168, 172, 173, 178, 182, 183, 188, 189, 191, 193, 194, 196, 199, 201 n., 203, 204, 207, 209, 210, 212, 213–14, 214, 218, 219, 231, 233, 235, 238, 240, 243, 245, 247, 250, 252, 256, 257, 258, 260, 263, 267, 270, 272, 273, 275, 276, 278, 280, 282, 283, 288, 292, 295, 296, 300, 302, 304, 307, 308, 309, 313, 317, 318, 319, 320, 321, 325, 326, 332, 335, 338, 341, 342, 346, 350, 352, 354, 357, 358, 359, 361, 362, 363, 365, 365–6, 366, 367, 369, 370, 371, 372, 373, 374, 379, 380, 381, 384, 386, 388, 389, 391, 392

Du Bartas: 16, 68 n., 83, 176 n.; in school curricula, 46 n.; his relation to earlier hexaemeral writers, 75; his importance in the Renaissance, 75–6; an analysis of his poetry, 76–80; as influenced by the Pléiade and poets of the Jeux floraux, 78; his obligations to classical Latin poets, 78–9; his obligations to scientific writers, 79; his influence on English poetry, 75 and n., 80; his imagery,

84; quoted, 13, 76, 77, 78, 79–80,
  95, 104, 108, 110, 113, 114, 115,
  117, 119, 126, 129, 132, 134, 138,
  144, 150, 156, 158, 159, 161, 164,
  170, 171, 174, 177 n., 186, 190, 193,
  195, 198, 202, 217, 232, 238, 245,
  248, 253, 257, 262, 269, 272, 274,
  279, 281, 282, 291, 296, 303, 312,
  316, 317, 320, 323, 334, 337, 344,
  356, 357, 358, 359, 360, 362, 363,
  365, 366–7, 368–9, 370, 371, 373,
  374, 375, 377, 379, 380, 381, 382,
  384, 385, 387, 389, 390, 391, 392
Du Bellay, Joachim: quoted, 13, 106,
  126, 144, 195, 202, 237, 274, 282,
  303, 317, 320, 357, 366, 368, 370,
  373, 374, 375, 377, 380, 382, 385,
  387, 390
Du Hamel, J.-B.: quoted, 98, 197,
  201, 244, 246, 253, 339
Duhem, Pierre: on Eudoxus, 315
Du Monin, J.-É.: quoted, 14, 161, 186,
  217, 363, 367, 368, 384, 385, 390
Du Moulin, Monsieur: quoted, 139,
  293
Dyer, John: quoted, 175, 332, 346,
  367, 373, 380
Dygges, Leonard: quoted, 107, 116,
  121, 147, 163, 200, 293, 339

Egyptian theories of nature: 52, 57–8
Elegantiæ Poeticæ: 22
Elemental composition: 52; teleologi-
  cally controlled, 54, 300–1
Eliot, Sir Thomas: quoted, 228
Empedocles: 26, 63, 68, 69, 128 n.,
  274 n., 389; on the attraction and
  repulsion of elements, 54; his theory
  of vision, 286–7; quoted, 13, 93, 146,
  149, 153, 221, 222, 224, 237, 258,
  316, 328, 367
England's Helicon: quoted, 300
Englands Parnassus: quoted, 132
Ennius: 25, 68 n., 140 n., 274 n., 357
  n.; quoted, 110, 197, 216, 225, 242,
  360, 375, 380, 381, 384, 386
Ennodius: 74; quoted, 227, 382

Epicurus: 49, 71, 143, 300, 301;
  quoted, 55
Erasmus: 75
Eratosthenes: 73
Estienne, Henri: 16 n.; quoted, 244 n.
Euclid: 70, 73
Eudoxus: 70, 315
Eugenius Toletanus: quoted, 227, 368
Euphro: quoted, 367
Euripides: quoted, 99, 113, 223, 274,
  358, 359, 372, 374, 381, 386, 392
Evelyn, John: 185 n., 395; quoted,
  103, 111, 117, 135, 138, 160, 162,
  178, 183, 188, 199, 205, 208, 213,
  214, 218, 229, 231, 246, 250, 253,
  270, 276, 277, 316, 335–6, 336, 352,
  379, 383, 391, 395, 397, 398, 399,
  401, 403, 404

Fabricius, Joannes: quoted, 135, 153
Fabricius ab Aquapendente, Hieronymus: quoted, 31, 127, 168, 203, 252,
  309, 346–7, 388
Fairfax, Edward: quoted, 112, 117,
  121, 158, 187, 188, 213, 236, 238,
  269, 281, 294, 299, 307, 313, 319,
  323, 324, 341, 345, 351, 357, 360,
  362, 375, 378, 383, 389, 390
Fairfax, Nathaniel: 47 n.
Fanshawe, Sir Richard: quoted, 91,
  109, 110, 112, 116, 129, 133, 145,
  167, 172, 181, 182, 233, 245, 273,
  280, 288, 332, 338, 357, 359, 361,
  362, 363, 367, 370, 379, 381, 383,
  386, 388, 391
Fell, John: quoted, 146, 280
Flamsteed, John: quoted, 265
Flatman, Thomas: quoted, 114, 165,
  168, 181, 203, 237, 263, 272, 276,
  278, 308, 321, 358, 361, 362, 369,
  381, 386, 392
Fletcher, Giles: quoted, 106, 178, 249,
  255, 283
Fletcher, Phineas: 16; quoted, 13, 105,
  106, 109, 125, 158, 162, 187, 195,
  206, 218, 231, 236, 238, 243, 245,
  247, 249, 256, 266, 270, 273, 281,

283, 303, 307, 313, 323, 329, 337, 340, 361, 362, 365, 369, 375, 391

Flores Poetarum: 22

Fludd, Robert: quoted, 141, 284, 371–2

Ford, Simon: quoted, 233, 245, 273, 369

Fortescue, Thomas: 60 n.

Foxius Morzillus, Sebastianus: quoted, 92

Fracastoro, Girolamo: on life as atomic activity, 301

Franzius, Wolfgang: quoted, 42

Freind, John: quoted, 171 n., 244, 330, 341, 355

French, John: quoted, 234, 239, 250, 276, 304, 341, 347

French classicism: 18 n.

Fulke, William: quoted, 160, 163, 203, 293

Furetière, Antoine: 47

Fusil, C.-A.: 87 n.; on Latin models of eighteenth-century French scientific poetry, 79 n.

Gadroys, Claude: quoted, 192, 322

Galen: 46, 73, 364; on the soul, 62; the spiritual basis of his physiology, 342–3

Galileo: 39, 45, 81, 82, 87 n., 177 n.; quoted, 100, 137, 141, 179, 192, 252, 260, 284, 289, 366, 374

Gamber, Stanislas: on early Christian hexaemeral poets, 73, 74

Garth, Samuel: quoted, 235, 309, 389

Gassendi, Pierre: 311; quoted, 211

Gay, John: quoted, 136, 231, 260, 300, 329, 372, 386

Genesis, Book of: 58 and n., 73

Genest, C.-C.: 79 n.; quoted, 96, 116, 118, 120, 159, 168, 175, 196, 214, 239, 246, 254, 264, 267, 283, 292, 321, 323, 375, 379, 384, 386, 388

genus: as a name, 41; as a conception, remarked on by Adanson and Whewell, 43 n.; as a conception important in the formation of poetic diction, 215–16

Georgics (Virgil): 71

Gesner, Conrad: 79, 81; quoted, 100, 147, 153

Gilbert, A. H.: 177 n.

Gilbert, Samuel: quoted, 281, 397

Gilbert, William: 38, 49, 81, 130–1 n.; quoted, 30, 56, 100, 141, 147, 175, 179, 191, 200, 276, 284, 293, 322, 374

Glanvill, Joseph: quoted, 98, 148, 179, 184, 205, 246, 255, 261, 268, 293, 330, 339, 350, 353

Glaser, Christopher: quoted, 122, 166, 324

Godolphin, Sidney: quoted, 105, 278, 362

Golding, Arthur: quoted, 102, 104, 216, 247, 281, 312, 320

Goldsmith, Oliver: 131 n.

Góngora: quoted, 91, 113, 115, 117, 132, 138, 145, 158, 159, 165, 171, 182, 183, 198, 217, 233, 251, 255, 259, 262, 269, 272, 279, 283, 291, 294, 313, 316, 317, 320, 334, 345, 354, 356, 359, 360, 362, 369, 372, 378, 381, 383, 390, 392

Goodyer, John: quoted, 254, 327, 401

Googe, Barnabe: quoted, 106, 117, 177, 189, 316, 331, 344, 377, 387

Gradus ad Parnassum: 24; poetical dictionaries criticized by Aikin, 9; its importance, 15 and n.; criticized by Trapp, 22; criticized by Coleridge, 22 n.; its equivalent in Pliny, 47

Gratius Faliscus: 74; quoted, 248

Gray, Thomas: on poetic diction, 12 n.

Greek: compound epithets, 20 n., 68 n.; generic terms, 219–25; terminology in English scientific writing, 394

Greek Anthology: quoted, 116, 382

Greene, Robert: quoted, 326

Greenough, C. N.: xi, 356

Gregory, James: quoted, 203

Gresham College: 44–5

Grew, Nehemiah: quoted, 33, 232, 324, 336, 398, 402

Grimestone, Edward: quoted, 191

Groom, Bernard: on compound epithets, 4 n.

Grovius (Grove, Robert): quoted, 346, 362

Guillemeau, Jacques: quoted, 120, 214

Habington, William: quoted, 123, 272

Hackneyed words: 2; criticized by Warton, 9; criticized by Aikin, 9, 10; not made so by inaccurate use, 11; as related to mythological subjects, 86–7

Hall, John: quoted, 121, 127, 151, 158, 236, 253, 361, 362, 383

Halley, Edmund: quoted, 30

Hammond, William: quoted, 127, 141, 362

Hannay, Patrick: quoted, 105, 127, 129, 172, 206, 257, 266, 279, 308, 313, 361, 391

Harris, John: quoted, 31, 128, 140, 285, 349, 399, 400

Hartlib, Samuel: quoted, 396, 399, 402, 403

Harvey, Gideon: quoted, 289, 327, 355

Harvey, Thomas: quoted, 91, 125, 196, 210, 292, 296, 335, 342, 373, 380

Harvey, William: 81; on scientific writing as literature, 45; relates aether to vital heat, 62; quoted, 30, 45, 120, 160, 169, 179, 200, 229, 241, 250, 268, 347

Heath, John: quoted, 180

Heracleitus: 52, 61, 63, 84; his idea of the flux, 53; quoted, 163

Herbert of Cherbury, Edward: quoted, 213, 266

Herrick, Robert: quoted, 119, 199, 233, 270, 300, 307, 309

Hesiod: 70; quoted, 221, 224, 375, 381

Hesteau, Clovis: quoted, 198, 291

Hexaemeral literature: as developed by Basil, 73; in early Christian Latin poetry, 74; its culmination in the Renaissance, 75; Renaissance editions of earlier hexaemeral writings, 75; Renaissance hexaemeral poems, 75–6; the relationship of early and late hexaemeral writing, 75; its use of scientific knowledge, 73–5

Hilary of Poitiers: 75

Hippocrates: 143, 343

Hiscock, W. G.: 233 n.

Hobbes, Thomas: quoted, 98, 102, 176, 197, 201, 314, 324

Hoffmann, Friedrich: quoted, 176

Holder, William: quoted, 289, 315, 351

Holland, Philemon: quoted, 32, 53, 121, 139, 160, 200, 229, 231, 246, 267, 298, 346, 364, 371

Homer: 49, 68 n., 69, 70, 274 n.; his use of stock epithets, 25–6; quoted, 93, 220, 222, 244, 279, 302, 312, 375, 380, 381

Hooke, Robert: quoted, 30, 38, 98, 101, 139, 141, 164, 169, 176, 205 n., 250, 261, 366, 390, 397, 400

Hoole, Charles: quoted, 43 n., 139, 209

Horace: 22 n., 308 n.; quoted, 227, 308 n., 351, 370, 374

Hortolanus Junior: quoted, 99, 185, 251, 322

Howell, James: quoted, 92, 124, 147–8, 366

Hughes, John: quoted, 105, 112, 118, 123, 191, 361, 374

Humphreys, Samuel: quoted, 136

Huyghens, Christiaan: 38; quoted, 99, 240, 241, 255, 285, 290

Incertus: quoted, 271, 368

Jacks, L. V.: 73 n.

Jago, Richard: quoted, 127, 364, 366

James I of England: quoted, 106, 172, 195, 319, 360, 367, 377, 389

Jerome, St.: on the creation, 58–9 n.

Jeux floraux: Du Bartas's obligations to the poets of the Toulouse school, 78

Jodelle, Étienne: quoted, 138, 171, 272, 317, 368, 385, 389

Johnson, F. R.: on scientific books in English, 38 n.

Johnson, Thomas: quoted, 267, 335

Johnson, William: 131 n.

Jones, John: on the mutual obligations of epic poets and naturalists, 86; quoted, 135, 136, 146, 152, 204, 256, 329, 362, 370, 379

Jonson, Ben: quoted, 140, 392

Jonston, John: quoted, 234, 241

Justinus: 75

Juvencus: 75; quoted, 244

Keats, John: 12 n.

Kepler, Johann: 58, 67, 81, 87 n.; quoted, 97, 192, 252, 261, 264, 289

King, Henry: quoted, 174, 361

Kircher, Athanasius: quoted, 101, 137, 264, 366

Knolles, Richard: quoted, 168-9

Kober, A. E.: 279 n.

Krantz, Émile: on Descartes and classicism, 18 n.

Kynaston, Sir Francis: 131; quoted, 131, 247, 283, 308, 354, 374, 379, 387, 389

Labriolle, Pierre de: 74 n.

La Chambre, M. C. de: quoted, 122

Lactantius: 73; quoted, 216, 360, 382

La Fontaine, Jean de: 79 n.; quoted, 103, 175, 199

La Motte, Houdar de: quoted, 146, 334, 380

Latin: its importance in scientific terminology, 37-40, 393-4; used for scientific writing, 38 and n.; compound epithets as periphrases, 20 n., 68 n.; generic terms, 216, 225-8; suffixes translated into English, 395-6

Latinisms: 2; used by Dryden, 5

Lauthier, H. M.: 302 n.

Leclerc, Daniel: quoted, 389

Le Febure, Nicasius: quoted, 215

Lemery, Nicolas: 39

Lemmi, C. W.: 58 n.

Lilly, William: quoted, 61, 148, 315

Linnaeus: 38, 44; principles of his terminology, 40, 41, 42; quoted, 149, 234

Lippius, Laurentius: quoted, 271, 368

Lipsius, Justus: quoted, 191-2, 239, 304

Lister, Martin: quoted, 390

Livius Andronicus: quoted, 375

Lodge, Thomas: quoted, 54, 97, 147, 207, 293, 330, 339

Lovejoy, A. O.: 86

Lovell, Robert: quoted, 35, 299

Lower, Richard: quoted, 280-1

Lucan: 140 n., 161 n.; quoted, 91, 132, 137, 143, 170, 173, 177, 181, 194, 198, 201, 204, 206, 209, 212, 232, 248, 251, 253, 265, 322, 336, 351, 353, 362, 376, 382, 384, 386-7

Lucretius: 24, 49, 58, 67, 69, 71, 74, 79 n., 83, 140 n., 161 n., 201 n., 322 n., 343, 364, 365 n.; in the development of poetic diction, 15, 75; as a didactic poet, 16; on the world as an organism, 71; his use of scientific terminology, 72; as a source for Du Bartas, 78-9; his use of the word *elementa*, 142-3; on the four elements, 300-1; quoted, 14, 55, 94, 110, 137, 143, 164, 171, 173, 176, 188, 201, 209, 216, 227, 237, 240, 241, 242, 244, 251, 253, 256, 259, 261, 265, 271, 274, 290, 302, 320, 328, 336, 343, 351, 358, 360, 362, 363, 364, 367, 370, 373, 375, 380, 381, 384, 386

Lycophron: quoted, 223, 259, 302, 375, 380

Macaulay, T. B.: 86; his criticism of Dryden's language, 27 n.

Mackail, J. W.: on Alexandrian art, 69; on Alexandrian poetry, 71

Mackaile, Matthew: quoted, 333
Maginus, J. A.: quoted, 141
Mair, A. W.: 43 n.
Maisières, M. T. de: 59 n., 75 and n.
Manethon: 74; quoted, 374
Manilius: 24, 74, 87 n., 301; as a
   didactic poet, 71–2; his use of scien-
   tific terminology, 72; quoted, 94,
   170, 173, 177, 189, 225, 226, 227,
   228, 237, 261, 271, 274, 282, 290,
   302, 344, 360, 368, 374, 376, 381,
   384, 386
Mann, E. L.: 9 n.
Maplet, John: quoted, 63–4 n., 118,
   160, 200, 264, 327, 341
Marino, G. B.: quoted, 390
Mariotte, Edmé: quoted, 131, 176,
   197, 255
Marlowe, Christopher: quoted, 132,
   161, 259, 269, 291, 374, 389
Marmion, Shakerley: quoted, 109,
   115, 123, 208, 210, 275, 331, 334,
   391
Martin, Benjamin: quoted, 333
Martin, Jean: quoted, 296
Martyn, Thomas: 395, 396; on form-
   ing scientific terminology, 39–40;
   on translating Latin terms, 395 n.;
   quoted, 34, 40, 230, 395, 396, 398,
   399, 400, 402, 403, 404
Marvell, Andrew: quoted, 146, 152,
   157, 159, 309
Matthiolus, P. A.: quoted, 327
May, Thomas: 302 n.; quoted, 95,
   121, 145, 178, 188, 210, 275, 363,
   378
Mayow, John: quoted, 197, 238, 306
Meager, Leonard: quoted, 232
Merrett, Christopher: quoted, 185 n.,
   186, 333
Merrick, James: quoted, 288
Mersenne, Marin: quoted, 175
Mexia, Pedro: 60 n.
Microcosm and macrocosm: 60–3,
   66, 67, 143
Middleton, Thomas: quoted, 233,
   356, 360

Midgley, Robert: quoted, 180, 268,
   322, 404
Milius, Abraham: quoted, 155–6,
   184, 230, 299
Milton: 128, 149, 176–7 n., 185, 286,
   308 n., 311, 322 n.; works in the
   curriculum at his school, 46 n.; on
   the bird of God, 59; his use of
   mythology, 83–4; his use of personification, 83; quoted, 13, 14, 19–20,
   83, 91, 95, 99, 101, 103, 106, 107,
   111, 112, 114, 115, 117, 121, 123,
   125, 129, 133, 136, 138, 141, 145,
   146, 149, 151, 151–2, 152, 157, 158,
   162, 165, 167, 168, 170, 171, 173,
   174, 177 n., 181, 182, 185, 187, 189,
   190, 193, 194, 196, 199, 202, 204,
   207, 212, 213, 218, 231, 236, 238,
   240, 242, 245, 247, 249, 252, 254,
   257, 258, 260, 263, 266–7, 270, 275,
   276, 278, 280, 282, 283, 286, 288,
   292, 295, 296, 299, 304, 307, 308,
   308 n., 309, 311, 313, 316, 319, 325,
   329, 332, 334, 335, 338, 340, 342,
   346, 349, 350, 354, 357–8, 359, 361,
   363, 365, 366, 367, 369, 370, 371,
   372, 374, 375, 379, 380, 383, 383 n.,
   386, 388, 389, 391, 392
Minucius Felix: 301
Mirror for Magistrates, The: quoted, 230
Mizaldus, Antonius: quoted, 160, 163,
   293
More, Henry: 16; quoted, 95, 218,
   231, 238, 323, 329
Morellus, Federicus: quoted, 91, 95,
   190, 195, 204, 225, 251, 287, 337,
   344
Morton, John: quoted, 32, 33, 34, 102,
   122, 125, 206, 230, 232, 234, 235,
   255, 299, 333, 336, 366, 372, 397,
   398, 399, 400, 401, 403, 404
Moufet, Thomas: quoted, 372
Moxon, Joseph: quoted, 108, 118, 122,
   192, 261, 355, 374
Muir, M. M. P.: on seventeenth-century ideas about the elements, 143
Mure, Sir William: quoted, 107, 114,
   122, 129, 151, 157, 167, 168, 172,

188, 190, 202, 238, 259, 266, 275, 307, 316, 318, 319, 357, 357 n., 358, 362, 369, 373, 378, 383, 385, 387, 389, 390

Murtola, Gasparo de: 75; quoted, 91, 150, 167, 273, 369, 378, 390

Musæ Anglicanæ (5th ed.): quoted, 175, 205, 242, 273, 311, 370

Musarum Anglicanarum Analecta (1st ed.): quoted, 146, 233, 245, 273, 280, 346, 362, 369

Mythological figures: criticized by Warton, 9; criticized by Aikin, 9; as a means of definition, 19; interpreted by natural philosophy, 57–9, 62; in Du Bartas, 76–7, 84; in Milton, 83; in Lucretius, 84; in conflict with the mathematical view of nature, 85; as ornament, 86; become hackneyed, 87

Natural description: by means of stock diction in poetry, 7; in language used by poetry and science, 28 and n.; effected through a stable vocabulary in many periods, 80

Natural philosophy: Aikin's view of its value for poetry, 10; as truth, 11; Trapp's view of its relation to the language of poetry, 23; its language, 28 and n.; its control over scientific language, 50–2; explained by means of personification and mythology, 57–9, 62; its stable conceptions represented in an epitome, 64–6; its state in the Alexandrian period, 69; and didacticism, 69–70; as an instrument for the didacticism of Lucretius, Virgil, and Manilius, 71–2; in the literature of the early Christian period, 73–4; fundamentally changed by 1700, 81–6; effect of fundamental changes upon its language, 88

Nature, philosophies of: governing the use of scientific writing, 50–2; their stability, 52, 64, 80–4; including notions of elemental harmony and flux, 53; dependent upon preliminary observations, 70–1; in the literature of the early Christian period, 73; in Du Bartas, 76; in the seventeenth and eighteenth centuries, 83–5

Naude, Gabriel: on Du Bartas's method of composing, 78

Nemesianus: 74

Neoclassic poetry: 2

Neologisms: 39

New English Dictionary: xi, 131

Newton, Sir Isaac: 38, 67, 81, 85, 205 n.; his teleology, 82; his description of the compensatory principle, 84; quoted, 35, 84, 99, 101, 108, 125, 131, 142, 166, 176, 180, 192, 203–4, 205, 206, 208, 253, 261, 265, 268, 277, 285, 315, 331, 339, 340, 348, 401

Nicander: 69, 70

Niceron, I. F.: quoted, 264

Nicias: 70

Nonnos: 73, 74; quoted, 116, 137, 212, 221, 223, 225, 241–2, 256, 259, 322–3, 328, 336, 353, 358, 359, 362, 363, 368, 372, 372–3, 373, 376, 382, 384, 392

Norris, John: quoted, 152, 183, 252, 309, 350

Oldenburg, Henry: 45

Oppian: 43 n., 69, 73, 74; quoted, 113, 134, 150, 173, 194–5, 220, 221, 222, 223–4, 224, 358, 366, 368, 370, 373, 376

Original perception: Warton's doctrine, 9; discussed by E. L. Mann, 9 n.; Wordsworth's doctrine, 9 n.

Orpheus: 61

Orphica: quoted, 144, 358, 376, 382, 384, 387

Osler, Sir William: 37 n.

Otway, Thomas: quoted, 219, 258, 361, 374

Ovid: 21, 22 n., 78–9, 308 n.; quoted, 60, 91, 94, 99, 120, 122, 140, 143, 171, 198, 216, 256, 279, 290, 302,

308 n., 325, 336, 349, 353, 365 n.,
373, 374, 376, 380, 382, 384, 386,
392

Pacuvius: quoted, 164, 194, 225, 336,
358, 363, 367, 370
Palladius: 74
Paracelsus: 61; quoted, 55
Paradise Lost: 59
Parkinson, John: quoted, 35, 229,
231, 333, 404
Parmenides: quoted, 312
Parry, Milman: on the traditional
epithet in Homer, 25–6
Passero, Felice: 75
Pastoral poetry: its use of stock diction,
17
Pellissier, Georges: 79 n.
Periphrasis: characteristic of stock
diction, 3; in the poetry of various
periods, 13–14; as a form of defini-
tion, 17–18, 20 n.; in French clas-
sicism, 18 n.; in scientific prose, 32–
3; binary terms in Linnaeus, 41; as
expressed in Greek and Latin com-
pound words, 68; in the two-word
form, 356
Persius: quoted, 248
Personification of abstract ideas: 2; in
Dryden, 5–6, 83, 84; as definition,
18–19; in explanation of the universe, 57–8; in the Stoics, 58; in
Kepler, 58; in Du Bartas, 76–8; in
Milton, 83; as ornament, 85–6; in
Pope, 85; in conflict with mathematical philosophies, 85–6
Personification of material things: in
Dryden, 6; as a means of definition,
18–19
Phayer, Thomas: quoted, 147
Philips, John: quoted, 234, 338, 363,
379, 384
Philips, Katharine: quoted, 270, 297,
342, 361, 391
Phillips, Edward: quoted, 101
Philosophical Transactions: 394, 395; the
form of its contributions, 44–5;
quoted, 33, 34, 35, 98, 101, 102,

104, 116, 124, 128, 135, 140, 141,
142, 148–9, 164, 166, 169, 184, 197,
201, 208, 209, 215, 231, 234, 240,
241, 244, 247, 250, 253, 254, 255,
264, 268, 271, 277, 281, 285, 289–
90, 290, 294, 306, 324, 330, 333, 339,
341, 347–8, 348, 351, 353, 355, 366,
372, 390, 395, 397, 398, 400, 401,
402
Phœnix Nest, The: quoted, 320
Phrase books: their importance for
versifiers, 15 n.
Pictorius, George: quoted, 92
Pindar: quoted, 279, 375, 381, 386
Pinnell, Henry: quoted, 55, 148, 154–
5, 208, 229, 322, 324, 366, 401, 402
Pisidas, George: 73; quoted, 174, 208,
222, 223, 328, 373
Pittet, Armand: 72 n.
Plat, Hugh: quoted, 92, 147
Plato: 61, 63, 67, 287, 310; on the
humors and the elements, 60, 143;
quoted, 60, 96, 131, 143, 175, 287
Plattes, Gabriel: quoted, 339
Plautus: quoted, 14, 367, 375
Pléiade, the: 78
Pliny: 46, 47, 62 n., 72, 74, 79, 130 n.;
as the *Janua linguæ Latinæ,* 47; on
elemental combination, 53; on the
vital spirit, 364; quoted, 32, 92,
100, 101, 228, 298, 326, 350, 371
Plot, Robert: 205 n., 297, 366; on the
style of scientific writing, 45–6;
quoted, 35, 46, 92–3, 102, 119, 135,
140, 148, 156, 161, 205, 209, 230,
234, 241, 251, 271, 297, 299, 341,
366, 397, 401, 403, 404
Plutarch: 128 n.; quoted, 118, 261,
289, 304, 354
"Poetic diction": requiring a store of
terms, 1; includes phrase forms, 6–7;
criticized by Wordsworth, 9 n., 11–
12; studied by Coleridge, 11; in
Gray's conception, 12 n.; used by
Wordsworth, Keats, and Shelley,
12 and n.; in relation to philosophic
truth, 23; and decorum, 25, 26–7;
depends on complex sources, 67; as

dependent on scientific terminology in Latin poetry, 72; in Du Bartas, 79; its stability affirmed through the emulation of scientific practice, 81, 86–8; properly studied in individual poems, 86; as the common creation of poets and scientists, 87. *See also* Stock poetic diction

Poetical dictionary: see *Gradus ad Parnassum*

Poetical Rhapsody, A: quoted, 295

Pointer, John: quoted, 34, 156, 161, 166, 184, 230, 324, 349, 403

Pollux: quoted, 31, 135, 168

Pomey, F.-A.: quoted, 164, 235, 250

Pontano, Giovanni: 16, 79 n.; quoted, 13, 14, 110, 132, 134, 137, 156, 170, 171, 174, 177, 181, 182, 189, 216, 232, 237, 245, 262, 274, 290–1, 323, 360, 363, 368, 372, 374, 376–7, 382, 384–5, 387, 392

Poole, Josua: 15–16 n.

Pope, Alexander: 22, 26, 27, 68 n., 90, 140 n., 302 n.; criticized by Aikin, 10 n.; his idea of nature, 84–5; quoted, 14, 85, 92, 96, 100, 103, 110, 114, 116, 124, 126, 130, 133, 139, 157, 159, 167, 172, 173, 178, 182, 183–4, 188, 194, 203, 212, 231, 243, 250, 252, 256, 258, 263, 270, 275, 276, 278, 280, 282, 295, 314, 317, 320, 323, 325, 332, 335, 342, 346, 350, 357, 359, 361, 363, 367, 370, 372, 373, 374, 379, 380, 381, 384, 386, 388, 391

Power, Henry: quoted, 55, 305–6

Powle, Stephen: quoted, 288–9

Present participle: characteristic of stock diction, 3; an eighteenth-century use, 3; its use as an epithet in scientific prose, 35

Principia (Newton's): 38

Priscian: quoted, 100

Proba Falconia: quoted, 271

Prudentius: 15, 73; quoted, 94, 137, 144, 164, 167, 174, 177, 181, 182, 186, 189, 194, 206, 226, 227, 248, 251, 255, 261, 265, 274, 282, 290, 303, 312, 326, 328, 336, 344, 357, 358, 360, 362, 366, 368, 372, 373, 376, 382, 387, 390

Ptolomy: 73, 126, 287; quoted, 321

Purchas, Samuel: quoted, 246, 372

Pythagoras: 52, 83, 310

Quayle, Thomas: on the elements of eighteenth-century poetic diction, 2–7

Raleigh, Sir Walter: on the microcosm and macrocosm, 60–1; quoted, 254, 320

Randolph, Thomas: quoted, 114, 122, 145, 181, 332, 361

Rapin, René: quoted, 174

Ray, John: 44, 297; quoted, 56, 156, 299, 306, 366, 390

Raymond, Marcel: on Du Bartas's method, 77 n.

Reiley, K. C.: 55 n.; on the ancient terminology for elements, 142–3, 300 n.

Reisch, Gregorius: quoted, 92, 178, 288, 338

Renan, Ernest: 58 n.

Rey, Jean: quoted, 100, 139, 207, 239, 254, 276, 293

Reymond, Arnold: on the Heracleitan flux, 53

Ricciolus, J. B.: 374; quoted, 118, 289, 355, 366, 374

Robertson, J. M.: 395 n.

Robin, P. A.: 342 n.; on the relation of the humors to the elements, 143

Robin Hood: quoted, 363

Robbins, F. E.: 73 n.

Rohault, Jaques: 39; quoted, 118, 141, 240

Rondelet: 79

Ronsard, Pierre de: 23, 68 n.; his criticism of Virgil's epithets, 22 and n.; his importance for Du Bartas, 78; quoted, 14, 95, 103, 106, 108, 110, 114, 115, 132, 138, 157, 181, 182–3, 189, 193, 195, 198, 232, 235, 245, 248, 262, 272, 291, 295, 296, 303,

317, 331, 334, 335, 344, 357, 360, 362, 366, 368, 370, 373, 374, 375, 377, 379, 380, 382, 385, 391
Roscommon, Earl of: quoted, 219
Rose, Hugh: quoted, 397
Rosse, Alexander: quoted, 35, 141, 192, 252
Roubais de Tourcoin, Jaques de: quoted, 247, 294
Royal Society: 44, 47 n., 48
Russell, Richard: quoted, 93
Rutilius: quoted, 344

Sainte-Beuve: on Du Bartas's method of composition, 78
Saint-Lambert, J. F.: 87
Saintsbury, George: on Sylvester's importance in the poetry of natural description, 75 n.
Salusbury, Thomas: quoted, 252, 277, 397
Sandys, George: 90; quoted, 13, 103, 109, 112, 125, 133, 135, 136, 138, 157, 158, 160, 162, 165, 167, 168, 170, 178, 182, 187, 188, 193, 196, 206–7, 210, 212, 213, 233, 243, 249, 257, 266, 276, 282, 292, 295, 296, 299, 303, 313, 321, 325, 326, 329, 334, 335, 340, 345, 349, 352, 356, 361, 365, 370, 371, 374, 375, 379, 383, 387, 391, 392
Saporta: quoted, 104
Sauveur, Joseph: quoted, 315
Scarron, Paul: quoted, 162
Scève, Maurice: quoted, 108, 174, 189, 216, 269, 275, 291, 357, 362, 366, 377, 382, 385, 387, 392
Scientific language: its relation to poetic diction as discussed by F. W. Bateson, 28–9 n.; having terms in common with poetry, 30–5, 67, 394; the principles and conditions governing its formation, 36–47, 393–4; the problem of style, 40; its stability, 48, 64, 67; the value of a fixed terminology, 49–51, 394; changes in the meaning of its terms, 49–50; its dependence upon theory,

50; its dependence upon philosophy, 51–2; as a resource for the establishment of Latin poetic diction, 72; as used by hexaemeral writers, 74, 79; as the equivalent of poetic diction, 86, 87; conditions under which it comes to be misunderstood, 88; involving the translation of Latin forms, 393–4, 395
Senault: 63 n.
Seneca: 45, 130 n., 298 n.; on the four elements, 54; his terms for the Creator, 72; quoted, 101, 196, 199, 205, 228, 252, 254, 298 n., 314, 350, 374, 379, 386
Shadwell, Thomas: his mockery of scientific language, 39 n., 286
Shakespeare: 16, 285; quoted, 104, 109, 119, 140, 144, 150, 157, 158, 165, 167, 177, 208, 210, 211, 240, 249, 253, 258, 266, 269, 275, 279, 285, 308, 318, 335, 340, 351, 354, 359, 362, 363, 365, 366, 367, 374, 375, 378, 383, 385, 387, 389, 390, 391
Shelley, P. B.: 12 n.; quoted, 381
Sherburne, Edward: 87 n., 298 n., 301; his analysis of Manilius' didacticism, 71–2; quoted, 14, 72, 87 n., 91–2, 95–6, 96, 99, 105, 108, 109, 117, 119, 123, 136, 140, 167, 170, 178, 183, 183 n., 187, 189, 191, 196, 207, 210, 213, 236, 236 n., 245, 252, 254, 257, 260, 263, 270, 272, 282, 293, 298 n., 300, 301, 316, 317, 329, 331, 338, 340, 349, 352, 356, 369, 379, 380, 384, 386, 388, 391
Sidney, Sir Philip: quoted, 91
Simoneta, P. P.: quoted, 388
Singer, Charles: 301 n.; on Galen's physiology, 62, 343
Solinus: 79
Sophocles: quoted, 93, 219, 220, 220–1, 222, 225, 277, 358, 359, 363, 366, 367, 373, 380, 386
Spence, Joseph: 278
Spenser, Edmund: 6, 15, 140 n., 322 n.; quoted, 13, 95, 103, 109, 111,

112, 113, 115, 120, 123, 125, 126, 129, 132, 134, 136, 138, 144, 150, 156, 159, 166, 170, 171, 172, 177, 180, 183, 186, 190, 192, 194, 195, 198, 202, 209, 211, 213, 217, 230, 233, 236, 238, 243, 245, 247, 249, 251, 255, 257, 262, 266, 269, 272, 277, 281, 283, 291, 294, 295, 296, 299, 303, 306, 307, 312, 316, 317, 318, 319, 320, 324, 326, 328, 331, 334, 337, 341, 344, 356, 358, 362, 365, 366, 369, 370, 373, 378, 380, 383, 385, 389, 390

Spigel, Adrian: quoted, 310

Spontaneous generation: 56

Sprat, Thomas: 38 n., 46, 86, 90; quoted, 212, 266, 319, 331, 345

Stanley, Thomas: quoted, 98, 99, 101, 111, 129, 139, 161, 174, 187, 229, 239, 252, 257, 263, 295, 301, 305, 308, 314–15, 318, 319, 321, 342, 350, 352, 359, 361, 363, 373, 379, 380, 386, 391

Statius: quoted, 14, 177, 186, 226, 259, 349, 360, 382

Steno, Nicholas: quoted, 389

Stephanus, Carolus: quoted, 327

Stock poetic diction: its elements, 2; its faults, 7; descended from antiquity, 9; criticized by Aikin, 9; the importance of its individual terms, 12–13, 27–9; used by Dryden in his plays, 17; its importance for Virgil, 20 and n.; criticized for irrelevance by Trapp and Ronsard, 22; as used by Virgil, 24–5; as used by Homer, 25–6; its differing functions in oral and written literature, 26; giving the effect of irrelevance, 27–8; its emphatic use of generic terms, 215–16. *See also* "Poetic diction"

Stock words: common to verse and scientific prose, 89–90; a numerical estimate, 89

Stoics: 58, 63, 343

Strabo: 73

Strebaeus, J. L.: 45 n.

Style in scientific prose: 40–7

Sublimity: 10

Suffixes: the variety of their use in scientific epithets, 34–5; translated from Latin into English, 395–6

Swan, John: 46 n., 131 n.; quoted, 239, 352

sylvan scene: 20 n.

Sylvester, Josuah: 79 n., 81, 185; his importance for later English poetry, 75 and n., 80; compared with Du Bartas, 80; his use of epithets with the -*y* suffix, 395 n.; quoted, 14, 95, 103, 105, 106, 107, 109, 111, 113, 114, 115, 117, 121, 123, 125, 126, 129, 132, 134, 138, 145, 151, 158, 159, 161, 165, 170, 171, 172, 178, 180, 185, 187, 188, 190, 193, 194, 198, 202, 212, 217, 230, 233, 236, 245, 247, 253, 255, 257, 258, 259, 260, 262, 266, 269, 272, 275, 278, 281, 283, 291, 296, 299, 300, 303, 306, 307, 308, 316, 317, 319, 323, 326, 328, 331, 334, 335, 337, 345, 354, 356, 357, 358, 359, 360, 362, 363, 366, 367, 369, 370, 371, 372, 373, 374, 375, 378, 380, 381, 383, 384, 385, 387, 390, 391, 392

Tachenius, Otto: quoted, 324

Tasso: 16; quoted, 14, 110, 114, 117, 129, 132, 144, 171, 198, 202, 208, 233, 251, 257, 262, 272, 277, 279, 283, 312, 316, 317, 345, 357, 360, 362, 367, 369, 370, 372, 373, 377–8, 380, 383, 387, 390

Technical terms: 2, 12 n.; in Dryden, 6; in scientific prose, 40–1; approved by Ronsard, 78

Teleology: in ancient thought, 54 n.; governing the four elements, 55, 63; in Lucretius and Virgil, 71; in early Christian literature, 73–4; in Newton, 82; its defeat in the eighteenth century, 82, 85

Terms of art: *see* Technical terms

Testament of Cressid, The: 16

Thales: 51, 52, 63

Theocritus: 17, 20, 78; as criticized by Warton, 8, 16 n.; his method of description, 70 and n.

Theophrastus: 42, 278; quoted, 100, 239, 330

Thomson, James: 6, 29 n., 85, 87, 90, 302 n.; the source of his images, 8; criticized by Aikin, 10, 12; quoted, 18–19, 31, 85, 96, 107, 111, 121, 133, 146, 163, 181, 184, 188, 193, 196, 203, 205, 207, 219, 234, 235, 242, 242 n., 252, 256, 273, 282, 332, 334, 342, 358, 359, 361, 363, 364, 367, 370, 372, 373, 375, 379, 380, 384, 386, 388, 389, 391

Tibullus: quoted, 349

Tillotson, Geoffrey: 20 n.

Timaeus: 60

Timotheus of Miletus: quoted, 375

Tindall, Nicholas: quoted, 278

Tomlinson, Richard: quoted, 34, 102, 104, 141, 201, 215, 327, 397, 399–400, 401, 404

Tottel's Miscellany: quoted, 216

Tournefort, J. P.: 302; quoted, 215, 230

Traherne, Thomas: quoted, 208, 250, 307, 321, 323

Trapp, Joseph: 8, 27; his criticism of Virgil, 21–2; on the subordination of language to the purpose of the poem, 22; on poetic diction and philosophic truth, 23; in opposition to the views of Coleridge, 24; the limitations of his criticism, 25

Trevisa, J.: quoted, 56

Tryon, Thomas: quoted, 108, 156, 293, 396, 397, 398, 400, 402, 404

Tryphiodorus: quoted, 344

Turnebus, Adrian: quoted, 102, 184

Valerius Flaccus: quoted, 226, 232, 256, 374, 376, 382, 384, 387, 391, 392

Valvasone, Erasmo di: quoted, 122, 140, 249, 357

van Vliet, Jan (Vlitius): quoted, 248 n.

Vaughan, Henry: quoted, 157, 173, 181, 242, 349, 369

Vaughan, Thomas: quoted, 305

Vaumorière, P. d'O. de: quoted, 39 n.

Venner, Tobias: quoted, 92, 100, 276, 396–7, 398, 403

Vesalius: quoted, 168

Victor, Marius: 73, 74, 75; quoted, 368

Vincent of Beauvais: 311

Virgil: 26, 27, 74, 75, 79 n., 82, 140 n., 149, 161 n., 322 n., 365; his importance in the development of poetic diction, 15, 20 and n.; as a didactic poet, 16; his language criticized by Trapp, 21–2; his epithets criticized by Ronsard, 22 and n.; his use of stock diction, 24–5; his relation to the Alexandrians, 69; on the world as an organism, 71; his influence on writers of the early Christian period, 73; as a source for Du Bartas, 78–9; quoted, 13, 24, 25, 71, 94, 110, 122, 134, 150, 156, 164, 171, 173, 182, 182 n., 186, 189, 194, 198, 201, 204, 206, 212, 216, 225, 226, 227, 232, 234, 237, 240, 242, 244, 248, 248 n., 251, 261, 271, 273, 274, 279, 290, 294, 302, 312, 321 n., 325, 328, 344, 353, 358, 359, 360, 365, 365 n., 367–8, 370, 372, 373, 374, 376, 380, 381, 384, 386, 390

Waller, Edmund: quoted, 115, 208, 352, 362, 379, 381, 391

Waller, Richard: quoted, 122, 166, 230, 315

Warton, Joseph: 22, 69; his criticism of Thomson, 8, 12; on the importance of Theocritus, 8; his attitude toward original perception, 9 and n.

Wase, Christopher: on Pliny as a dictionary, 47; quoted, 47, 321

Watson, Foster: on seventeenth-century curricula, 46 n.; on scientific gardens, 82

Wedel, G. W.: quoted, 230

Whewell, William: on the formation of scientific language, 41; on Adanson's terminology, 43 n.; his coinage of *scientist*, 45 n.; on ancient optics, 126; on the significance of the idea of elements, 142

Whiston, William: quoted, 104, 176, 180, 331, 399

Whitehead, Paul; quoted, 282

Whiting, Nathaniel: quoted, 91, 121, 122, 127, 167, 181, 183, 190, 206, 213, 218, 236, 280, 288, 294, 303, 316, 318, 329, 335, 351, 359, 361, 362, 363, 367, 374, 380, 383, 386, 389, 391, 392

Widdowes, Daniel: quoted, 97, 116, 163, 214, 229, 260, 298, 322, 330, 341, 371, 388, 401, 402, 404

Wilkins, John: quoted, 32, 33, 97, 166, 169, 179, 230, 333, 366, 372, 397, 398, 404

Willis, Thomas: 62; quoted, 229, 280

Willoughby, Henry: quoted, 274, 380

Winslow, Ann: 12 n.

Withals, John: quoted, 147, 179

Wither, George: quoted, 354

Wolf, Abraham: 311

Woodward, Hezekiah: quoted, 169

Woodward, John: quoted, 120, 209, 211, 234, 261, 268, 277, 399

Wordsworth, William: 8, 27; on poetic diction, 11–12; his use of poetic diction, 12 and n.

Wotton, Edward: quoted, 32, 182 n., 228, 298, 350

Wren, Christopher: quoted, 91, 169

Xenophanes: 301

-y suffix: in Dryden's epithets, 2–3; in scientific prose, 33, 393–404; as a translation of Latin suffixes, 395–6; in sixteenth- and seventeenth-century English poetry, 395 n.

Young, Edward: quoted, 191

UNIVERSITY OF MICHIGAN PUBLICATIONS

*Orders and requests for detailed book lists should be directed
to the University of Michigan Press*

SERIES IN LANGUAGE AND LITERATURE

Vol. I. STUDIES IN SHAKESPEARE, MILTON AND DONNE. By Members of the English Department. Pp. v + 232. $2.50.

Vol. II. ELIZABETHAN PROVERB LORE IN LYLY'S 'EUPHUES' AND IN PETTIE'S 'PETITE PALLACE,' WITH PARALLELS FROM SHAKESPEARE. By Morris P. Tilley. Pp. x + 461. $3.50.

Vol. III. THE SOCIAL MODE OF RESTORATION COMEDY. By Kathleen M. Lynch. Pp. xi + 242. $2.50.

Vol. IV. STUART POLITICS IN CHAPMAN'S 'TRAGEDY OF CHABOT.' By Norma D. Solve. Pp. x + 176. $2.50.

Vols. V–VI. EL LIBRO DEL CAUALLERO ZIFAR. By C. P. Wagner.
Vol. V. PART I. TEXT. Pp. xviii + 532. With 9 plates. $5.00.
Vol. VI. PART II. COMMENTARY. (*In preparation.*)

Vol. VII. STRINDBERG'S DRAMATIC EXPRESSIONISM. By C. E. W. L. Dahlström. Pp. xi + 242. $2.50.

Vol. VIII. ESSAYS AND STUDIES IN ENGLISH AND COMPARATIVE LITERATURE. By Members of the English Department. Pp. vii + 231. $2.50.

Vol. IX. TOWARD THE UNDERSTANDING OF SHELLEY. By Bennett Weaver. Pp. xii + 258. $2.50.

Vol. X. ESSAYS AND STUDIES IN ENGLISH AND COMPARATIVE LITERATURE. By Members of the English Department. Pp. v + 278. $2.50.

Vol. XI. FRENCH MODAL SYNTAX IN THE SIXTEENTH CENTURY. By Newton S. Bement. Pp. xviii + 168. $2.50.

Vol. XII. THE INTELLECTUAL MILIEU OF JOHN DRYDEN. By Louis I. Bredvold. Pp. viii + 189. $2.50.

Vol. XIII. ESSAYS AND STUDIES IN ENGLISH AND COMPARATIVE LITERATURE. By Members of the English Department. Pp. vii + 328. $3.00.

Vols. XIV–XV. THREE CENTURIES OF FRENCH POETIC THEORY (1328–1630). By W. F. Patterson.
Vol. XIV. PARTS I–II. Pp. xx + 978. $5.00.
Vol. XV. PARTS III–IV. Pp. v + 523. $3.50.

Vol. XVI. THE SOURCES OF JOHN DRYDEN'S COMEDIES. By N. B. Allen. Pp. xviii + 298. $3.00.

Vol. XVII. ELIZABETHAN COMIC CHARACTER CONVENTIONS AS REVEALED IN THE COMEDIES OF GEORGE CHAPMAN. By P. V. Kreider. Pp. xi + 206. $2.50.

Vol. XVIII. THE AESTHETIC THEORY OF THOMAS HOBBES, WITH SPECIAL REFERENCE TO THE PSYCHOLOGICAL APPROACH IN ENGLISH LITERARY CRITICISM. By Clarence DeWitt Thorpe. (Out of print.)

VOL. XIX.   THOMAS DE QUINCEY'S THEORY OF LITERATURE.   By Sigmund
K. Proctor.   Pp. viii + 313. $3.50.
VOL. XX.   WORDSWORTH'S FORMATIVE YEARS.   By George W. Meyer.   Pp.
viii + 265. $3.50.
VOL. XXI.   PHONETICS: A CRITICAL ANALYSIS OF PHONETIC THEORY AND A
TECHNIC FOR THE PRACTICAL DESCRIPTION OF SOUNDS.   By Kenneth L.
Pike.   Pp. x + 182. $2.50.
VOL. XXII.   TEXTUAL CRITICISM AND JEHAN LE VENELAIS.   By Edward B.
Ham.   Pp. v + 109. $2.00.
VOL. XXIII.   FLORIANT ET FLORETE.   By Harry F. Williams.   Pp. xvi +
316. $4.00.
VOL. XXIV.   THE LANGUAGE OF NATURAL DESCRIPTION IN EIGHTEENTH-
CENTURY POETRY.   By John Arthos.   Pp. xiv + 463. $6.00.